Macmillan/McGraw-Hill READING

Mc Graw Hill **Macmillan McGraw-Hill**

Contributors

The Princeton Review, Time Magazine, Accelerated Reader

The Princeton Review is not
affiliated with Princeton
University or ETS.

learning through listening

Students with print disabilities may be eligible to obtain an accessible, audio version
of the pupil edition of this textbook. Please call Recording for the Blind & Dyslexic at
1-800-221-4792 for complete information.

The McGraw·Hill Companies

**Macmillan
McGraw-Hill**

Published by Macmillan/McGraw-Hill, of McGraw-Hill Education, a division of The McGraw-Hill Companies, Inc.,
Two Penn Plaza, New York, New York 10121.

Copyright © 2005 by Macmillan/McGraw-Hill. All rights reserved. The contents, or parts thereof, may be reproduced in
print form for non-profit educational use with Macmillan/McGraw-Hill Reading, provided such reproductions bear copyright
notice, but may not be reproduced in any form for any other purpose without the prior written consent of The McGraw-Hill
Companies, Inc., including, but not limited to, network storage or transmission, or broadcast for distance learning.

Printed in the United States of America

6 7 8 9 073/043 09 08 07 06 05

Macmillan/McGraw-Hill READING

Authors

James Flood

Jan E. Hasbrouck

James V. Hoffman

Diane Lapp

Donna Lubcker

Angela Shelf Medearis

Scott Paris

Steven Stahl

Josefina Villamil Tinajero

Karen D. Wood

Managing the

Computer Center

Working with Words Station

Writing Station

Reading and Listening Station

Word Box

Welcome!

Classroom

Social Studies Station

TEACHING TIP

MANAGEMENT
Provide children in each group with their own list of centers they will go to. Children can check off each center after finishing their work. Early finishers can read a book from the Reading Center.

Teacher Directed Small Group Instruction

Sample Management Plan

Group 1	Group 2	Group 3	Group 4
With Teacher	Reading or Writing Workstation	Working with Words Station	Cross-Curricular or Computer Station
Reading or Writing Workstation	**With Teacher**	Cross-Curricular or Computer Station	Working with Words Station
Working with Words Station	Cross-Curricular or Computer Station	**With Teacher**	Reading or Writing Workstation
Cross-Curricular or Computer Station	Working with Words Station	Reading or Writing Workstation	**With Teacher**

Creating WORKSTATIONS

Establishing independent workstations and other independent activities is a key to helping you manage the classroom as you meet with small groups.

Reading

Set up a classroom library including the Leveled Books and other independent reading titles that have been previously read during small-group instruction. See the Theme Bibliography on pages T88–T89 for suggestions. Include titles based on discussions of students' fiction and nonfiction preferences.

- Self-Selected Reading
- Paired Reading
- Student Anthology selection from the Listening Library

Writing

Focus the unit's writing projects on explanatory writing. Weekly writing assignments are found at the end of each selection. The unit writing process project, Explanatory Writing, can also be the focus of the Writing Station. Equip the Writing Station with the following materials:

- Samples of published explanatory writing
- Explanatory Writing samples, available in the **Teacher's Writing Resource Handbook**, pages 22–23

Computer

Students can access the Internet to complete the Research and Inquiry activities suggested throughout the unit. Look for Internet connections in the following Research and Inquiry projects:

- Find Out More project at the end of each selection
- Cooperative Theme Project: Presenting a Report About Clouds
- Cross-Curricular Activities
- Bringing Groups Together project

Working with Words

Selection Vocabulary
Have students create a word search by writing the selection vocabulary words on graph paper, then filling in the remaining boxes with random letters. They should also write sentences with context clues so their partner knows which vocabulary words are included.

High-Frequency Words
Create word cards for the following high-frequency words: *both, school, call, green, don't,* and *cold.* Also, create numerous cards for the same word but with different letters omitted. Have students match the incomplete word cards with the original word cards.

TEACHING TIP

MANAGEMENT
If the classroom space is limited, incorporate workstation suggestions into a class assignment chart.

Shelve materials for each project in the classroom and distribute them as you assign an activity.

Have students work in groups, in pairs, or independently at their desks.

Cross-Curricular
STATIONS

Set up a Cross-Curricular Station to help extend selection concepts and ideas. Cross-Curricular activities can be found throughout the unit.

Science

- Mammals, 270
- Animal Talk, 302
- Evolution of the Horse, 326
- Endangered Animals, 360

Math
3 + 2

- Time, 272
- Addition, 306
- Timing the Riders, 328
- How Many in All?, 362

Social Studies

- Community Business, 276
- Antarctica, 296
- Food of the Future, 334
- Tigers, 352

Art

- Round-Robin Picture, 278
- Comic Strip, 332

Additional Independent Activities

The following independent activities offer students practice exercises to help reinforce the concepts and skills taught within the unit.

PUPIL EDITION: READER RESPONSE

Story Questions to monitor student comprehension of the selection. The questions are leveled, progressing from literal to critical thinking.

Story Activities related to the selection. Four activities are always provided: one writing activity, two cross-curricular activities, and a research and inquiry activity in the Find Out More project that encourages students to use the Internet for research.

LEVELED PRACTICE

Each week, Reteach, Practice, and Extend pages are offered to address the individual needs of students as they learn and review skills.

McGraw-Hill Reading

Theme Chart

MULTI-AGE Classroom

Using the same global themes at each grade level facilitates the use of materials in multi-age classrooms.

GRADE LEVEL	Experience — Experiences can tell us about ourselves and our world.	Connections — Making connections develops new understandings.
Kindergarten	**My World** — We learn a lot from all the things we see and do at home and in school.	**All Kinds of Friends** — When we work and play together, we learn more about ourselves.
Subtheme 1	At Home	Working Together
Subtheme 2	School Days	Playing Together
1	**Day by Day** — Each day brings new experiences.	**Together Is Better** — We like to share ideas and experiences with others.
2	**What's New?** — With each day, we learn something new.	**Just Between Us** — Family and friends help us see the world in new ways.
3	**Great Adventures** — Life is made up of big and small experiences.	**Nature Links** — Nature can give us new ideas.
4	**Reflections** — Stories let us share the experiences of others.	**Something in Common** — Sharing ideas can lead to meaningful cooperation.
5	**Time of My Life** — We sometimes find memorable experiences in unexpected places.	**Building Bridges** — Knowing what we have in common helps us appreciate our differences.
6	**Pathways** — Reflecting on life's experiences can lead to new understandings.	**A Common Thread** — A look beneath the surface may uncover hidden connections.

Themes: Kindergarten – Grade 6

Six Units IN EVERY GRADE

Expression	Inquiry	Problem Solving	Making Decisions
There are many styles and forms for expressing ourselves.	By exploring and asking questions, we make discoveries.	Analyzing information can help us solve problems.	Using what we know helps us evaluate situations.
Time to Shine We can use our ideas and our imagination to do many wonderful things.	**I Wonder** We can make discoveries about the wonders of nature in our own backyard.	**Let's Work It Out** Working as part of a team can help me find a way to solve problems.	**Choices** We can make many good choices and decisions every day.
Great Ideas	In My Backyard	Try and Try Again	Good Choices
Let's Pretend	Wonders of Nature	Teamwork	Let's Decide
Stories to Tell Each one of us has a different story to tell.	**Let's Find Out!** Looking for answers is an adventure.	**Think About It!** It takes time to solve problems.	**Many Paths** Each decision opens the door to a new path.
Express Yourself We share our ideas in many ways.	**Look Around** There are surprises all around us.	**Figure It Out** We can solve problems by working together.	**Starting Now** Unexpected events can lead to new decisions.
Be Creative! We can all express ourselves in creative, wonderful ways.	**Tell Me More** Looking and listening closely will help us find out the facts.	**Think It Through** Solutions come in many shapes and sizes.	**Turning Points** We make new judgments based on our experiences.
Our Voices We can each use our talents to communicate ideas.	**Just Curious** We can find answers in surprising places.	**Make a Plan** Often we have to think carefully about a problem in order to solve it.	**Sorting It Out** We make decisions that can lead to new ideas and discoveries.
Imagine That The way we express our thoughts and feelings can take different forms.	**Investigate!** We never know where the search for answers might lead us.	**Bright Ideas** Some problems require unusual approaches.	**Crossroads** Decisions cause changes that can enrich our lives.
With Flying Colors Creative people help us see the world from different perspectives.	**Seek and Discover** To make new discoveries, we must observe and explore.	**Brainstorms** We can meet any challenge with determination and ingenuity.	**All Things Considered** Encountering new places and people can help us make decisions.

Express Yourself

We share our ideas in many ways.

ARTHUR WRITES A STORY.....258A

written and illustrated by
Marc Brown

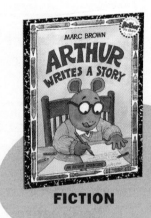

FICTION

SKILLS			
Phonics	**Comprehension**	**Vocabulary**	**Study Skill**
• **Introduce** Silent Letters	• **Introduce** Fantasy and Reality	• **Review** Context Clues	• Reference Sources: Use a Dictionary
• **Review** Silent Letters			

BEST WISHES, ED 290A

written and illustrated by
James Stevenson

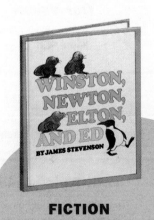

FICTION

SKILLS			
Phonics	**Comprehension**	**Vocabulary**	**Study Skill**
• **Introduce** /ər/er	• **Introduce** Cause and Effect	• **Review** Context Clues	• Reference Sources: Read an Encyclopedia
• **Review** /ər/, /ən/, /əl/; Silent Letters			

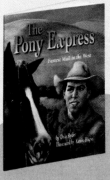

INFORMATIONAL TEXT

 Leveled Books

WEEK 1 — Arthur Writes a Story	WEEK 2 — Best Wishes, Ed
Easy: *Don't Float in Blue Jam*	**Easy:** *How Animals Use Color*
Independent: *My Own Team: The Bill Reidy Story*	**Independent:** *Ready Set Go!*
Challenge: *Harry the Troll and the Three Billy Goats Gruff*	**Challenge:** *Rin Tin Tin: Top Dog in the Movies*

✔ Tested Skills

☑ **Phonics** Introduce Silent Letters, 258G–258H Review Silent Letters, 289E–289F Review Silent Letters, 289G–289H	☑ **Phonics** Introduce /ər/er, 290G–290H Review /ər/er, 319E–319F Review /ər/, /ən/, /əl/; Silent Letters, 319G–319H
☑ **Comprehension** Introduce Fantasy and Reality, 289I–289J	☑ **Comprehension** Introduce Cause and Effect, 319I–319J
☑ **Vocabulary** Review Context Clues, 289K–289L	☑ **Vocabulary** Review Context Clues, 319K–319L
☑ **Study Skills** Reference Sources, 288	☑ **Study Skills** Reference Sources, 318

Minilessons

Context Clues, 265	**Summarize,** 297
Setting, 267	**Reference Materials,** 301
Main Idea, 269	**Phonics and Decoding:** Long *a*, 313
Make Inferences, 271	**Analyze Character,** 305
Phonics and Decoding: Digraph *th*, 283	**Context Clues,** 311

Language Arts

Writing: Explanatory Writing, 289M	**Writing:** Explanatory Writing, 319M
Grammar: Action Verbs, 289O	**Grammar:** Present-Tense Verbs, 319O
Spelling: Words with Silent Letters, 289Q	**Spelling:** Words with /ər/er, 319Q

Activities

Curriculum Connections

Read Aloud: "The Tall Tales," 258E	Read Aloud: "Penguins," 290E
Phonics Rhyme: "Chalk Drawings," 258	Phonics Rhyme: "The Visit," 290
Science: Mammals, 270	Social Studies: Antarctica, 296
Math: Time, 272	Science: Animal Talk, 302
Social Studies: Community Business, 276	Math: Addition, 306
Art: Round-Robin Picture, 278	

CULTURAL PERSPECTIVES

Fairy Tales, 280	The Inuit, 308

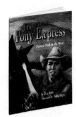   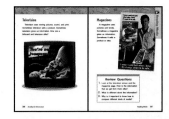

WEEK 3 The Pony Express	**WEEK 4** Nine-In-One, Grr! Grr!	**WEEK 5** Change for the Quarter	**WEEK 6** Review, Writing, Reading Information Assessment
Easy: *The Ghost on the Train* **Independent:** *Messengers from the Sky* **Challenge:** *Sending a Message with Dots and Dashes*	**Easy:** *First Food: A South American Folktale* **Independent:** *Hare and Tortoise* **Challenge:** *How Frog Lost His Tail*	*Self-Selected Reading of Leveled Books*	*Self-Selected Reading*

☑ **Phonics** Introduce Short *e: ea*, 320G–320H Review Short *e*, 341E–341F Review Short *e*; /ər/, /ən/, /əl/; Silent Letters, 341G–341H	☑ **Phonics** Introduce Long *e: y, ey*, 342G–342H Review Long *e*, 369E–369F Review Long *e*; Short *e*; /ər/, /ən/, /əl/, 369G–369H	☑ **Phonics** Review Long *e*; Short *e*; /ər/, /ən/, /əl/; Silent Letters, 370G–370H	☑ **Assess Skills** Silent Letters /ər/er, /ən/en, /əl/le Short *e: ea* Long *e: y, ey* Fantasy and Reality Cause and Effect Context Clues Synonyms
☑ **Comprehension** Review Fantasy and Reality, 341I–341J	☑ **Comprehension** Review Cause and Effect, 369I–369J	☑ **Comprehension** Review Cause and Effect, 379E–379F Review Fantasy and Reality, 379G–379H	☑ **Assess Grammar and Spelling** Review Verbs, 381I Review Spelling Patterns, 381J
☑ **Vocabulary** Introduce Synonyms, 341K–341L	☑ **Vocabulary** Review Synonyms, 369K–369L	☑ **Vocabulary** Review Synonyms, 379I–379J Review Context Clues, 379K–379L	☑ **Unit Progress Assessment**
☑ **Study Skills** Reference Sources, 340	☑ **Study Skills** Reference Sources, 368	☑ **Study Skills** Reference Sources, 378	☑ **Standardized Test Preparation**
Using Text Features, 325 **Context Clues,** 327 **Main Idea,** 329 **Phonics and Decoding:** *Long a,* 333	**Setting,** 347 **Short *e*,** 349 **Summarize,** 351 **Make Inferences,** 355		📰 **Reading Media** 381A

🖊 **Writing:** Explanatory Writing, 341M **Grammar:** Past-Tense Verbs, 341O **Spelling:** Words with Short *e: ea*, 341Q	🖊 **Writing:** Explanatory Writing, 369M **Grammar:** The Verb *Have*, 369O **Spelling:** Words with Long *e: y, ey*, 369Q	🖊 **Writing:** Explanatory Writing, 379M **Grammar:** Sentence Combining, 379O **Spelling:** Words from Math, 379Q	🖊 **Unit Writing Process:** Explanatory Writing, 381C

Read Aloud: "Crazy Horse Keeps a Promise," 320E	**Read Aloud:** "The Tiger Story," 342E	**Read Aloud:** "The Golden Touch," 370E	👥 **GROUP** **Cooperative Theme Project Research and Inquiry:** Presenting a Report About Clouds, 256J
Phonics Rhyme: "The Pony Express," 320	**Phonics Rhyme:** "Tiger's Friends," 342	**Phonics Rhyme:** "Fifty Cents," 370	
Science: Evolution of the Horse, 326	**Social Studies:** Tigers, 352		
Math: Timing the Riders, 328	**Music:** Make Up a Song, 354		
Art: Comic Strip, 332	**Science:** Endangered Animals, 360		
Social Studies: Food of the Future, 334	**Math:** How Many in All?, 362		
The Horse in Different Cultures, 330	Laotian Story Cloths, 358		

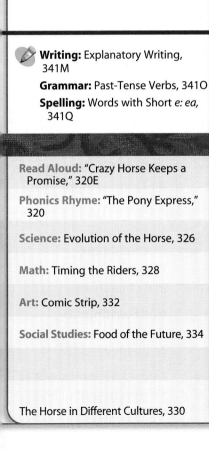
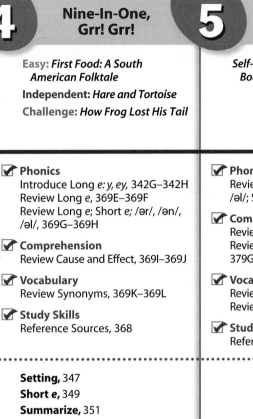
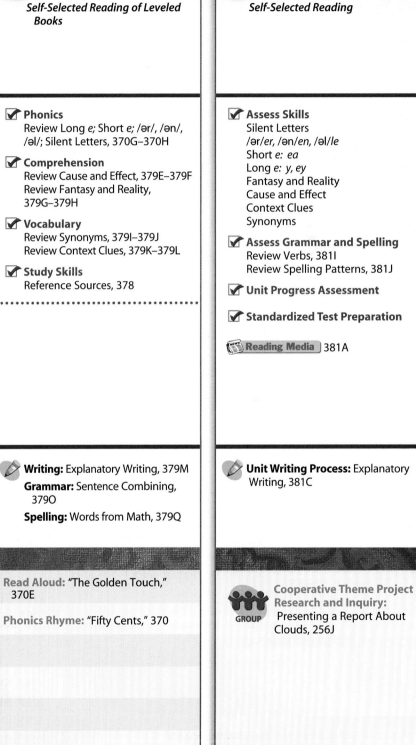

Unit Resources

LITERATURE

LEVELED BOOKS

 Easy:
- *Don't Float in Blue Jam*
- *How Animals Use Color*
- *The Ghost on the Train*
- *First Food: A South American Folktale*

Independent:
- *My Own Team: The Bill Reidy Story*
- *Ready Set Go!*
- *Messengers from the Sky*
- *Hare and Tortoise*

Challenge:
- *Harry the Troll and the Three Billy Goats Gruff*
- *Rin Tin Tin: Top Dog in the Movies*
- *Sending a Message with Dots and Dashes*
- *How Frog Lost His Tail*

THEME BIG BOOK
Share *Dear Rebecca . . .* to set the unit theme and make content-area connections.

LISTENING LIBRARY Children can listen to audio recordings of selections and poetry.

Macmillan/McGraw-Hill

 **Intervention**
Easy Leveled Books
Skills Intervention Guide
Phonics Intervention Guide

SKILLS

LEVELED PRACTICE

Practice: Student practice for phonics, comprehension, vocabulary and study skills; plus practice for instructional vocabulary and story comprehension. Take-Home Story included for each lesson.

Reteach: Reteaching opportunities for students who need more help with each assessed skill.

Extend: Extension activities for vocabulary, comprehension, story and study skills.

TEACHING CHARTS Instructional charts for modeling vocabulary and tested skills. Also available as **transparencies**.

WORD BUILDING MANIPULATIVE CARDS
Letter and word cards to utilize phonics and build instructional vocabulary.

LANGUAGE SUPPORT BOOK
ESL Parallel lessons and practice for students needing language support.

PHONICS/PHONEMIC AWARENESS PRACTICE BOOK
Additional practice focusing on key phonetic elements.

FLUENCY ASSESSMENT
Evaluation and practice for building reading fluency.

LANGUAGE ARTS

GRAMMAR PRACTICE BOOK
Provides practice for grammar and mechanics lessons.

SPELLING PRACTICE BOOK
Provides practice with the word list and spelling patterns. Includes home involvement activities.

DAILY LANGUAGE ACTIVITIES
Sentence activities that provide brief practice and reinforcement of grammar, mechanics, and usage skills. Available as **blackline masters and transparencies.**

WRITING PROCESS TRANSPARENCIES
Model each stage of the writing process.

HANDWRITING HANDBOOKS
Available for instruction and practice.

McGraw-Hill School
TECHNOLOGY

 CD-ROM
Provides phonics support.

 Extend lesson activities through research and inquiry ideas. Visit **www.mhschool.com/reading.**

Vocabulary PuzzleMaker Provides practice with instructional vocabulary.

Handwriting CD-ROM Provides practice activities.

Mind Jogger Videos Review grammar and writing skills.

	EASY	ON-LEVEL	CHALLENGE	LANGUAGE SUPPORT

UNIT 3

Arthur Writes a Story

EASY

Leveled Book:
Don't Float in Blue Jam

Reteach, 85–92

Alternate Teaching Strategies, T64–T76

 **Writing:** Picture and Caption, 289M–289N

 **Phonics CD-ROM**

 **Intervention**

ON-LEVEL

Leveled Book:
My Own Team: The Bill Reidy Story

Practice, 85–92

Alternate Teaching Strategies, T64–T76

Writing: Homework Assignment, 289M–289N

Phonics CD-ROM

CHALLENGE

Leveled Book:
Harry the Troll and the Three Billy Goats Gruff

Extend, 85–92

Writing: Song, 289M–289N

Phonics CD-ROM

LANGUAGE SUPPORT

Teaching Strategies, 260A, 260C, 261, 262, 264, 273, 289N

Language Support, 91–99

Alternate Teaching Strategies, T64–T76

Writing: Write a Library Guide, 289M–289N

Phonics CD-ROM

Best Wishes, Ed

Leveled Book:
How Animals Use Color

Reteach, 93–100

Alternate Teaching Strategies, T64–T76

Writing: Postcard, 319M–319N

Phonics CD-ROM

Intervention

Leveled Book:
Ready Set Go!

Practice, 93–100

Alternate Teaching Strategies, T64–T76

Writing: Journal, 319M–319N

Phonics CD-ROM

Leveled Book:
Rin Tin Tin: Top Dog in the Movies

Extend, 93–100

Writing: Instructions, 319M–319N

Phonics CD-ROM

Teaching Strategies, 292A, 292C, 293, 294, 301, 307, 313, 319N

Language Support, 100–108

Alternate Teaching Strategies, T64–T76

Writing: Write a Guide, 319M–319N

Phonics CD-ROM

The Pony Express

Leveled Book:
The Ghost on the Train

Reteach, 101–108

Alternate Teaching Strategies, T64–T76

Writing: Mail a Note, 341M–341N

Phonics CD-ROM

Intervention

Leveled Book:
Messengers from the Sky

Practice, 101–108

Alternate Teaching Strategies, T64–T76

Writing: Write Directions, 341M–341N

Phonics CD-ROM

Leveled Book:
Sending a Message with Dots and Dashes

Extend, 101–108

Writing: Letter of Explanation, 341M–341N

Phonics CD-ROM

Teaching Strategies, 322A, 322C, 323, 325, 329, 333, 341N

Language Support, 109–117

AlternateTeaching Strategies, T64–T76

Writing: Write Directions, 341M–341N

Phonics CD-ROM

Nine-in-One, Grr! Grr!

Leveled Book:
First Food: A South American Folktale

Reteach, 109–116

Alternate Teaching Strategies, T64–T76

Writing: Write a Caption, 369M–369N

Phonics CD-ROM

Intervention

Leveled Book:
Hare and Tortoise

Practice, 109–116

Alternate Teaching Strategies, T64–T76

Writing: Write a Report, 369M–369N

Phonics CD-ROM

Leveled Book:
How Frog Lost His Tail

Extend, 109–116

Writing: Write a Folktale, 369M–369N

Phonics CD-ROM

Teaching Strategies, 344A, 344C, 345, 353, 357, 369N

Language Support, 118–126

Alternate Teaching Strategies, T64–T76

Writing: Write a Report, 369M–369N

Phonics CD-ROM

Change for the Quarter

Review

Reteach, 117–124

Alternate Teaching Strategies, T64–T76

Writing: Draw Collectibles, 379M–379N

Phonics CD-ROM

Intervention

Review

Practice, 117–124

Alternate Teaching Strategies, T64–T76

Writing: Interview, 379M–379N

Phonics CD-ROM

Review

Extend, 117–124

Writing: Another Point of View, 379M–379N

Phonics CD-ROM

Teaching Strategies, 372A, 372C, 373, 379N

Language Support, 127–135

Alternate Teaching Strategies, T64–T76

Writing: Write a How-To Article, 379M–379N

Phonics CD-ROM

319F, 319H; 320H, 337, 341F, 341H; 342H, 365, 369F, 369H; 370H, 375, 379F, 379H

- Comprehension, 284, 285, 289J; 314, 315, 319J; 336, 337, 341J; 364, 365, 369J; 374, 375, 379J

- Vocabulary, 289L, 319L, 341L, 369L, 379L

Performance Assessment

- Scoring Rubrics, 289N, 319N, 341N, 369N, 379N

- Research and Inquiry, 256J, 381

- Listening, Speaking, Viewing Activities, 258E, 258/259, 260C, 260–285, 289D, 289M–N; 290E, 290/291, 292C, 292–315, 319D, 319M–N; 320E, 320/321, 322C, 322–337, 341D, 341M–N; 342E, 342/343, 344C, 344–365, 369D, 369M–N; 370E, 370/371, 372C, 372–375, 379D, 379M–N

- Portfolio, 289N, 319N, 341N, 369N, 379N

- Writing, 289M–N, 319M–N, 341M–N, 369M–N, 379M–N, 381C–H

- Fluency, 284, 314, 336, 364, 374

Leveled Practice

Practice, Reteach, Extend

- **Phonics and Decoding**
  Silent Letters, 85, 89, 90, 98, 106
  /ər/er, 93, 97, 98, 106, 114
  Short e: ea, 101, 105, 106, 114
  Long e: y, ey, 109, 113, 114

- **Comprehension**
  Fantasy and Reality, 91, 107, 122
  Cause and Effect, 99, 115, 121

- **Vocabulary Strategies**
  Context Clues, 92, 100, 124
  Synonyms, 108, 116, 123

- **Study Skills**
  Reference Sources, 88, 96, 104, 112, 120

Arthur Writes a Story, 41–44
Best Wishes, Ed, 45–48
The Pony Express, 49–52
Nine-in-One, Grr! Grr! 53–56
Change for the Quarter, 57–58

Unit 3 Tests

- **Phonics and Decoding**
  Silent Letters
  /ər/er
  Short e: ea
  Long e: y, ey

- **Comprehension**
  Fantasy and Reality
  Cause and Effect

- **Vocabulary Strategies**
  Context Clues
  Synonyms

Grammar and Spelling Assessment

- **Grammar**
  Verbs, 69, 75, 81, 87, 93, 95–96

- **Spelling**
  Unit 3 Assessment, 95–96

Fluency Assessment

- Fluency Passages, 38–41

Diagnostic/Placement Evaluation

- Informal Reading Inventories

- Running Record

- Phonemic Awareness Assessment

- Placement Tests

Test Preparation

- Test Power, 289, 319, 341, 369, 379

- Additional standardized test preparation materials available

💿 **Reading Test Generator**

- Assessment Software

Assessment Checklist

Student .... Grade ....

Teacher ....

	Arthur Writes a Story	Best Wishes, Ed	The Pony Express	Nine-in-One, Grr! Grr!	Change for the Quarter	Assessment Summary
LISTENING/SPEAKING						
Participates in oral language experiences						
Listens and speaks to gain knowledge of culture						
Speaks appropriately to audiences for different purposes						
Communicates clearly						
READING						
Uses phonological awareness strategies, including						
• blending, segmenting, deleting, substituting sounds						
Uses a variety of word identification strategies:						
• Phonics and decoding: silent letters						
• Phonics and decoding: /ər/er						
• Phonics and decoding: short e: ea						
• Phonics and decoding: long e: y, ey						
• Context Clues						
• Synonyms						
Reads with fluency and understanding						
Reads widely for different purposes in varied sources						
Develops an extensive vocabulary						
Uses a variety of strategies to comprehend selections:						
• Fantasy and Reality						
• Cause and Effect						
Responds to various texts						
Analyzes the characteristics of various types of texts						
Conducts research using various sources:						
• Reference Sources						
Reads to increase knowledge						
WRITING						
Writes for a variety of audiences and purposes						
Composes original texts using the conventions of written language such as capitalization and penmanship						
Spells proficiently						
Composes texts applying knowledge of grammar and usage						
Uses writing processes						
Evaluates own writing and writing of others						

+ Observed   − Not Observed

Introduce the Theme

Express Yourself

We share our ideas in many ways.

DISCUSS THE THEME Read the theme statement to children. Tell them that people share their ideas in many ways.

- What are some of the ways in which people share ideas?

- Do you share ideas with your friends through conversation? Can people express themselves through stories, poems, plays, essays, art, music, television, and movies? How?

- What are your favorite ways of sharing ideas? Why?

SHARE A STORY Use the Big Book *Dear Rebecca, Winter is Here* to establish the unit theme. Have children discuss how this writer's description of winter relates to Express Yourself.

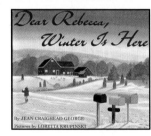

PREVIEW UNIT SELECTIONS Have children preview the unit by reading the titles, paging through the selections, and looking at the illustrations.

- How might these stories relate to the theme Express Yourself?

- Compare and contrast how the characters might express themselves in the selected stories.

- Which illustrations are your favorite? Why?

As children read the literature, encourage them to compare the characters, settings, and events that develop the unit theme Express Yourself.

THEME CONNECTIONS

Each of the five selections relates to the unit theme Express Yourself as well as to the global theme Experience.

Arthur Writes a Story A boy learns to express his own ideas in his writing.

Best Wishes, Ed A letter unexpectedly brings a penguin and a whale together.

The Pony Express A whole country expresses itself in letters.

Nine-in-One Grr! Grr! A bird tricks a tiger with a clever play on words.

Change for the Quarter Each state's history will be expressed in a new design for the quarter.

Research and Inquiry

 Theme Project: Presenting a Report About Clouds Have children work in teams to brainstorm what they know about clouds.

Make a Resource Chart Have children list all the facts they know about clouds as well as things they would like to learn. Then have them create a three-column chart. In the first column have them list questions they need to answer in order to prepare their presentations. In the second column have them list resources that will help them answer their questions. After they finish their research, they can write the answers in the third column. Remind children to identify and record their sources properly.

Design a Display After they have completed their research, children will present their plan for their cloud study. Encourage children to be thorough. They can use pictures from books and/or pictures they have drawn; they can also present their information on posters and in oral and written reports.

QUESTIONS	POSSIBLE RESOURCES	ANSWERS
• What are the different kinds of clouds? • What does each kind look like? • What kind of weather does each kind of cloud bring?	• Reference book/encyclopedia • Science book • Internet	

See **Wrap Up the Theme,** page 380.

Research Strategies

Share these tips for using the encyclopedia to find information on clouds:

• Select the volume with the first letter of the word.

• Look up the word alphabetically by using the first, second, and third letters. (CLO; cloud)

• Use the boldface words in the upper left and right hand corners as alphabetical guides.

• Take good notes. Remember to fill in important details and to identify your resources.

 interNET CONNECTION Children can learn more about using an encyclopedia by visiting **www.mhschool.com/reading.**

Poetry

Read the Poem

READ ALOUD Read "Cloud Dragons" by Pat Mora aloud to children and pose the following questions to lead a class discussion:

- How does this poem relate to the unit theme Express Yourself?
- Have you ever looked at clouds? What shapes did you see?
- What do you like *most* and *least* about the poem?

Listening Library Children can listen to an audio recording of the poem.

CHORAL READING Organize the class into two groups. Have one group read the stanzas that begin with a question, and direct the other group to read the stanzas that begin with a response. Discuss the similarities and differences between how the groups read their assigned stanzas, focusing on the volume and intonation of their voices.

Learn About Poetry

WORD CHOICE Explain that writers pick their words very carefully because words help shape ideas and feelings. Write the word *caballitos* (cah bah YEE tos) on the chalkboard and tell children it means "little horses." Ask:

- What does this word tell you about the poet?
- How does the author's choice of words affect the overall feeling and flow of the poem?
- What do you think of first when you hear the title "Cloud Dragons"?

Identify and discuss examples of words chosen for rhyme.

256

MEET THE POET

ABOUT PAT MORA Pat Mora was born on January 9, 1942, in El Paso, Texas, but grew up speaking mostly Spanish at home. Pat Mora has received critical acclaim for her works that portray cultural diversity and visual beauty of the Southwest as well as the theme of identity, especially that of woman and her connection with the various forms of the "earth mother."

Express Yourself

Cloud Dragons

What do you see
in the clouds so high?
What do you see in the sky?

Oh, I see dragons
that curl their tails
as they go slithering by.

What do you see
in the clouds so high?
What do you see? Tell me, do.

Oh, I see *caballitos*
that race the wind
high in the shimmering blue.

by Pat Mora

257

Poetry

RHYTHM Explain that in poetry, *rhythm* is similar to the beat in music. It creates recognizable patterns by accenting certain sounds and words.

- Help children identify examples of rhythmic patterns in the poem, "Cloud Dragons."

- How does rhythm affect the way the message is expressed in this poem? Identify and discuss other elements that contribute to the rhythm of the poem, such as punctuation and the "question and answer" structure.

Oral Response

SMALL-GROUP DISCUSSIONS Have 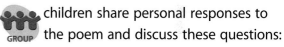 children share personal responses to the poem and discuss these questions:

- What are Cloud Dragons? Are they real or imagined by the writer? How do you know?

- What do you notice about the second and last stanzas? How do the answers to these questions relate to the unit theme Express Yourself?

- What does the poem "Cloud Dragons" mean to you?

- Do you usually prefer reading about real-life people and events or about imaginary people and events? Why?

WRITE A POEM

Poetry Activity Invite children to write a poem about creativity. They may use the same format as *Cloud Dragons,* or you may choose to model another poem for them to follow. First, discuss the meaning and brainstorm examples of *creativity*. Next, brainstorm words associated with creativity and fill them in on a word web together on the chalkboard. Suggest that children use these word lists to write their poems.

Make a Creativity Work Station Ask children to help you assemble a creativity work station. Decorate the station with children's poems about creativity. Provide a creativity project involving different subjects each week. Include a suggestion box where children can submit other ideas for creativity projects.

Concept
- Pleasing Others/
  Be Yourself

Phonics
- Silent Letters

Vocabulary
- decided
- float
- important
- library
- planet
- proud

Anthology

Arthur Writes a Story

Selection Summary Arthur doesn't think he'll have trouble writing a story for Mr. Ratburn's class—until his friends start giving him advice.

Rhyme applies to phonics

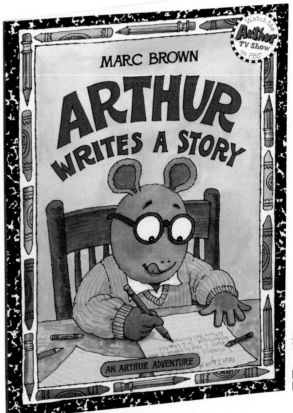

Listening Library

INSTRUCTIONAL pages 260–289

About the Author/Illustrator When Marc Brown was a boy, he spent most of his time drawing. His first book was *Arthur's Nose,* the first in a series of stories about a young aardvark with glasses. Mr. Brown says, "The art work is … easier for me than the writing."

Same Concept, Skills and Vocabulary!

Leveled Books

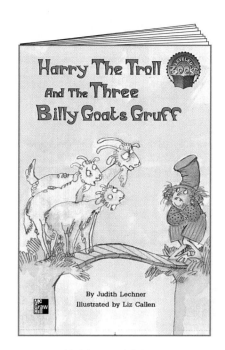

EASY
Lesson on pages 289A and 289D
`DECODABLE`

INDEPENDENT
Lesson on pages 289B and 289D

🏠 *Take-Home version available*

CHALLENGE
Lesson on pages 289C and 289D

Leveled Practice

EASY

Reteach, 85–92 Blackline masters with reteaching opportunities for each assessed skill

INDEPENDENT/ON-LEVEL

Practice, 85–92 Workbook with Take-Home stories and practice opportunities for each assessed skill and story comprehension

CHALLENGE

Extend, 85–92 Blackline masters that offer challenge activities for each assessed skill

Quizzes Prepared by Accelerated Reader®

WORKSTATION Activities

Social Studies ... **Community Business,** *276*

Science .... **Mammals,** *270*

Math .... **Time,** *272*

Art .... **Round-Robin Picture,** *278*

Language Arts .. **Read Aloud,** *258E*

Cultural
Perspectives ..... **Fairy Tales,** *280*

Writing .... **Writing a Library Guide,** *286*

Research
and Inquiry ...... **Find Out More,** *287*

 Internet
Activities .... **www.mhschool.com/reading**

READING AND LANGUAGE ARTS

DAY 1 — *Focus on Reading and Skills*

DAY 2 — *Read the Literature*

READING AND LANGUAGE ARTS	DAY 1 Focus on Reading and Skills	DAY 2 Read the Literature
● **Phonics Daily Routines**	Daily **Phonics** Routine: **Segmenting,** 258H **Phonics** CD-ROM	Daily **Phonics** Routine: **Blending,** 260A **Phonics** CD-ROM
● **Phonological Awareness** ● **Phonics** *Silent Letters* ● **Comprehension** ● **Vocabulary** ● **Study Skills** ● **Listening, Speaking, Viewing, Representing**	**Read Aloud: Tall Tale,** 258E "The Tall Tales" ☑ **Develop Phonological Awareness,** 258F Silent Letters ☑ **Introduce Silent Letters,** 258G–258H **Teaching Chart 71** Reteach, Practice, Extend, 85 Phonics/Phonemic Awareness Practice Book, 69–72 **Read** **Apply Silent Letters,** 258/259 "Chalk Drawings" **ⓘ** Intervention Program	**Build Background,** 260A Develop Oral Language **Vocabulary,** 260B–260C *decided important planet* *float library proud* **Word Building Manipulative Cards** **Teaching Chart 72** Reteach, Practice, Extend, 86 **Read** **Read the Selection,** 260–285 Comprehension ☑ Silent Letters ☑ Fantasy and Reality **Genre:** Fantasy, 261 **Writer's Craft:** Formal/Informal Language, 268 **Cultural Perspectives,** 280 **ⓘ** Intervention Program
● **Curriculum Connections**	**Link** Language Arts, 258E	**Activity** Science, 270
● **Writing**	**Writing Prompt:** Do you like to share your writing with your friends? Tell why or why not.	**Writing Prompt:** Your friend just told you your writing is not very good. How do you feel about your friend? How do you feel about your writing? **Journal Writing,** Quick-Write, 285
● **Grammar**	**Introduce the Concept: Action Verbs,** 289O Daily Language Activity: Write the correct action verb. **Grammar Practice Book,** 65	**Teach the Concept: Action Verbs,** 289O Daily Language Activity: Write the correct action verb. **Grammar Practice Book,** 66
● **Spelling** *Silent Letters*	**Pretest: Words with Silent Letters,** 289Q **Spelling Practice Book,** 65, 66	**Teach the Pattern: Words with Silent Letters,** 289Q **Spelling Practice Book,** 67

Meeting Individual Needs

 = **Skill Assessed in Unit Test**

 Intervention Program Available

 **Read EVERY DAY**

| **DAY 3** — *Read the Literature* | **DAY 4** — *Build Skills* | **DAY 5** — *Build Skills* |

DAY 3

Daily  **Phonics Routine:**
Fluency, 287

 Phonics CD-ROM

Rereading for Fluency, 284

Story Questions and Activities, 286–287
Reteach, Practice, Extend, 87

Study Skill, 288
☑ Reference Sources
Teaching Chart 73
Reteach, Practice, Extend, 88

Test Power, 289

Read the Leveled Books, 289A–289D
Guided Reading
☑ Silent Letters
☑ Fantasy and Reality
☑ Instructional Vocabulary

ⓘ **Intervention Program**

Activity Math, 272

✏ **Writing Prompt:** Your friend just told you your writing is terrific. How do you feel about your writing? How do you feel about your friend?

Explanatory Writing, 289M
Prewrite, Draft

Practice and Write: Action Verbs, 289P
Daily Language Activity: Write the correct action verb.

Grammar Practice Book, 67

Practice and Extend: Words with Silent Letters, 289R

Spelling Practice Book, 68

DAY 4

Daily **Phonics Routine:**
Writing, 289F

 Phonics CD-ROM

 Read the Leveled Books and the Self-Selected Books

☑ **Review Silent Letters,** 289E–289F
Teaching Chart 74
Reteach, Practice, Extend, 89
Language Support, 96
Phonics/Phonemic Awareness Practice Book, 69–72

☑ **Cumulative Review,** 289G–289H
Teaching Chart 75
Reteach, Practice, Extend, 90
Language Support, 97
Phonics/Phonemic Awareness Practice Book, 69–72

Minilessons, 265, 267, 269, 271, 283

ⓘ **Intervention Program**

Activity Social Studies, 276

✏ **Writing Prompt:** You want to talk to your teacher about your writing. Write a short note asking for a meeting next Monday. Use abbreviations in your note.

Explanatory Writing, 289M
Revise
Meeting Individual Needs for Writing, 289N

Practice and Write: Abbreviations, 289P
Daily Language Activity: Write the correct action verb.

Grammar Practice Book, 68

Practice and Write: Words with Silent Letters, 289R

Spelling Practice Book, 69

DAY 5

Daily **Phonics Routine:**
Discriminating, 289H

Phonics CD-ROM

Read Self-Selected Books

☑ **Introduce Fantasy and Reality,** 289I–289J
Teaching Chart 76
Reteach, Practice, Extend, 91
Language Support, 98

☑ **Review Context Clues,** 289K–289L
Teaching Chart 77
Reteach, Practice, Extend, 92
Language Support, 99

Listening, Speaking, Viewing, Representing, 289N
Share the Library Guides
Multimedia

Minilessons, 265, 267, 269, 271, 283

ⓘ **Intervention Program**

Activity Arts, 278

✏ **Writing Prompt:** You are a famous writer. Some people like your work. Some do not. Whose opinion do you think is the most important, other people's or your own? Why?

Explanatory Writing, 289M
Edit/Proofread, Publish

Assess and Reteach: Action Verbs, 289P
Daily Language Activity: Write the correct action verb.

Grammar Practice Book, 69, 70

Assess and Reteach: Words with Silent Letters, 289R

Spelling Practice Book, 70

 **Link**
Language Arts

Read Aloud

The Tall Tales
a tall tale by Tanya Lee

There once lived three brothers who were known throughout the land for the tall tales they told. They would travel from place to place telling their strange stories to whomever would listen. No one ever believed their tales and all who heard them would cry out with exclamations of disbelief.

One day while traveling very far from home, the three brothers came upon a wealthy prince. The prince was dressed very elegantly and bedecked in jewels such as the three men had never seen in their lives. They thought how wonderful it would be to have such possessions, so they devised a plan whereby they could use their storytelling ability to trick the prince out of his belongings.

They said to the prince: "Let's tell each other stories of past adventures and if anyone should doubt the truth of what the other is saying, then that person must become a slave to the others."

Continued on pages T2–T3

Oral Comprehension

LISTENING AND SPEAKING Read aloud this story about three brothers who like telling tall tales. When you have finished reading, ask, "Did you enjoy listening to these tall tales? What types of stories do you enjoy listening to most? Can you tell me why?"

GENRE STUDY: TALL TALE Discuss some of the characteristics of tall tales.

• Explain that in tall tales characters do things that ordinary people could never do. Ask children to recall events in the story that seem exaggerated.

• Tall tales are often humorous. Ask children, "What do you think is funny about this story? Why do you think it's funny?"

• Have children tell their own tall tales. Remind them to include larger-than-life heroes who solve big problems.

Activity Encourage children to illustrate one of the tall tales told by the brothers. Have them write a sentence or two under the illustration to describe the scene. Display their work around the room. ▶ **Visual/Linguistic**

Develop Phonological Awareness

Blend Sounds

MATERIALS
- Phonics Picture Cards

Teach Place the Phonics Picture Card for nest behind your back so that children cannot see it. Say the sounds /n/-/e/-/s/-/t/. Tell children you will say the sounds together to name the picture card. Say *nest* and then show the card.

Practice Have children blend sounds together for the following words. Tell them to listen carefully to the sounds they hear in each word: *knot, write, sight, half, thumb, crumb.*

Segment Sounds

MATERIALS
- Word Building Boxes from *Word Building Cards*
- Red paper dots

Teach Display a Word Building Box with 5 sections. Tell children you will count the number of sounds you hear in the word *crumb*. Place a counter in each box as you say each sound: /k/-/r/-/u/-/m/. Tell children the word crumb has 4 sounds. Have them say the sounds with you as you point to each box.

Practice

knot: /n/-/o/-/t/	wrap: /r/-/a/-/p/
nest: /n/-/e/-/s/-/t/	thumb: /th/-/u/-/m/
sweat: /s/-/w/-/e/-/t/	knit: /n/-/i/-/t/

Delete Sounds

MATERIALS
- Colored blocks

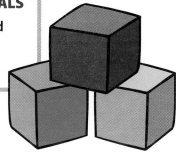

Teach Slowly say /b/-/a/-/n/-/d/ and place four blocks side by side with some space between each block. Push the blocks together and say *band.* Then take the first block away. Tell children that without the /b/ sound, the word *band* becomes *and.*

Practice Repeat the activity with these words:
stop—without the *s, tray*—without the *t, ramp*—without the *p, start*—without the final *t, small*—without the *s, trace*—without the *t, flake*—without the *f, train*—without the *t*

INFORMAL ASSESSMENT Observe children as they blend, segment, and delete sounds. If children have difficulty, see Alternate Teaching Strategies on p. T64.

TESTED **OBJECTIVES**

Children will:

• recognize when letters *l*, *b*, *k*, *w*, *g*, *h*, and *gh* are silent in a word.

• read words that include silent letters *l*, *b*, *k*, *w*, *g*, *h*, and *gh*.

MATERIALS

• **Teaching Chart 71**

• letter cards and word building boxes from the **Word Building Manipulative Cards**

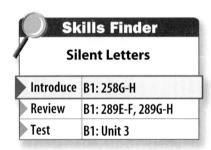

Skills Finder

Silent Letters

Introduce	B1: 258G-H
Review	B1: 289E-F, 289G-H
Test	B1: Unit 3

SPELLING/PHONICS
CONNECTIONS

Words with silent letters: *l*, *b*, *k*, *w*, *g*, *h*, *gh*
See 5-Day Spelling Plan, pages 289Q–289R.

Introduce Silent Letters

▐ **TEACH** ▌

Identify Silent Letters   Let children know they will learn to read words with the silent letters *l*, *b*, *k*, *w*, *g*, *h*, and *gh*.

• Display the letter cards for *l*, *b*, *k*, *w*, *g*, *h*, and *gh*.

• Explain that in some words these letters do not make their sound.

BLENDING Model and Guide Practice with Silent Letters

• Display **Teaching Chart 71**. Run your hand under the word *lamb* as you say it slowly. Have children repeat the word slowly and listen to each sound as they say it aloud.

• Ask a volunteer to identify the silent letter (*b*) and circle it.

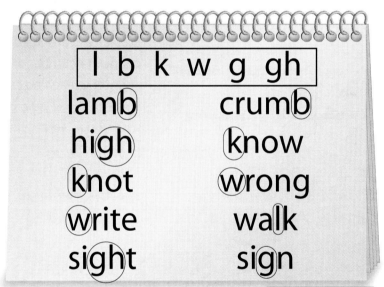

Teaching Chart 71

Use the Words in Context   • Use each word in context to reinforce its meaning. Example: *Sam sang the song, "Mary Had a Little Lamb."*

Repeat the Procedure   • Repeat with each word listed on the chart.

PRACTICE

SEGMENTING
Build Words with Silent Letters

PARTNERS

Have partners use letter cards and word building boxes to build words with silent letters *b, k, w, l, g, h,* or *gh.* Children might start with the words on **Teaching Chart 71.** Have partners take turns saying the word aloud while the other identifies the silent letter(s) in it.

▶ **Auditory/Linguistic**

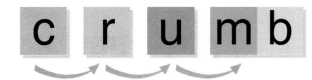

ASSESS/CLOSE

Read Words with Silent Letters and Use Words in Context

To assess children's ability to identify silent letters in words, observe children as they identify the silent letter or letters in each word they build with their letter cards in the Practice activity. Then encourage them to use their words in sentences.

ADDITIONAL PHONICS RESOURCES

Phonics/Phonemic Awareness Practice Book, pages 69–72

McGraw-Hill School
TECHNOLOGY

Phonics CD-ROM

activities for practice with Decoding and Building

Meeting Individual Needs for Phonics

EASY	ON-LEVEL	CHALLENGE
Name ___ Date ___ **Reteach 85**	Name ___ Date ___ **Practice 85**	Name ___ Date ___ **Extend 85**
Silent Letters	**Silent Letters**	**Silent Letters**

EASY — Reteach 85

Say the word h**igh**. Note that the letters **gh** are silent.

Circle the word that names each picture. Underline the letters that are silent.

1. hand (thumb)
2. (knee) finger
3. (write) right
4. road (sign)
5. (walk) drive
6. day (night)

Book 2.1/Unit 3
Arthur Writes a Story
At Home: Read with children a few pages from a familiar book. Ask them to identify ten words with silent letters.
85

ON-LEVEL — Practice 85

Write the words. Then say each word. Circle the silent letter or letters in each word.

| l | b | k | w | g | h | gh |

1. could — cou**l**d
2. knee — **k**nee
3. sign — si**g**n
4. thumb — thum**b**
5. high — hi**gh**
6. tow — to**w**
7. white — **w**hite
8. lamb — lam**b**
9. know — **k**now
10. light — li**gh**t
11. which — w**h**ich
12. should — shou**l**d

Book 2.1/Unit 3
Arthur Writes a Story
At Home: Have children think of a word that rhymes with each of the words above.
85

CHALLENGE — Extend 85

| chalk | wrong | walk | fright | wreck | high |
| fight | talk | write | sign | might | half |

Choose eight words from the box. Write a sentence for each word.

1. ___ Sentences will vary.
2. ___
3. ___
4. ___
5. ___
6. ___
7. ___
8. ___

Book 2.1/Unit 3
Arthur Writes a Story
At Home: Have children look at the words in the box. Ask them to cross out the letters that you do **not** say.
85

Reteach, 85   **Practice, 85**   **Extend, 85**

Daily Routines

DAY 1 **Segmenting** List the following words on the chalkboard: *sign, knit, thumb.* Read each word aloud and have children identify the silent letters, and circle the silent letter in each word.

DAY 2 **Blending** Write the words *kneel, fight,* and *wrap* on the chalkboard. Have children identify the letters they did not sound out. Ask children to blend the sounds to read each word.

DAY 3 **Fluency** Write the following sentence on the chalkboard and ask children to silently blend the sounds in each word together and then read the sentences aloud. *I know which letters to write in the word night.*

DAY 4 **Writing** Have children write two words with silent letters in a sentence. You may suggest that their sentence be related to a story they have already read.

DAY 5 **Discriminating** Write the following pairs of words on the chalkboard: *comb, cube; keep, knob; wrist, word; wiggle, sign.* Ask children to read each pair of words and say which letter is silent.

OBJECTIVES

Children will read words that include silent letters *l, b, k, w, g, h,* and *gh.*

Apply Silent Letters

Chalk Drawings

Larry the Lamb brought out his chalk,
And drew a white sun on the sidewalk.
Betsy the Calf shook her head,
"Don't you know the sun should be red?"
Nate the Gnat buzzed up to see.
"Larry, I think it needs a tree."
Larry the Lamb thought for a while.
Then he gave his friends some chalk
And they all drew together on the sidewalk!

258

259

Anthology pages 258–259

Read and Build Fluency

READ THE POEM Invite children to listen and follow along in the text as you read aloud "Chalk Drawings." Model how the voice changes when reading narration and dialog. Then point to each word as you reread and have children raise their hands each time you read a word with a silent letter.

REREAD FOR FLUENCY Write the following **PARTNERS** words on the chalkboard: *lamb, chalk, gnat, thought.* Point to the words and ask children to blend the sounds to make each word. Ask a volunteer to read each word aloud and to name the silent letter or letters. Have partners reread the story as they take turns acting out the parts of Larry, Betsy, and Nate.

Dictate and Spell

DICTATE WORDS Say the word *lamb* aloud.
JOURNAL Segment it into its three individual sounds. Repeat the word and say it in a sentence, such as, "The lamb stayed close to its mother." After children repeat the word aloud, have them write the word. Have them circle the silent letter. Then repeat the process using the words *bought, chalk,* and *gnat.* Ask children if they can suggest other words with silent letters that are not from the poem, such as, *high, knot,* and *write.*

Intervention Skills Intervention Guide, for direct instruction and extra practice of silent letters

Build Background

Concept: Pleasing Others/Be Yourself

Evaluate Prior Knowledge

CONCEPT: PLEASING OTHERS/BE YOURSELF Ask children to suggest what they think the words *Be Yourself* mean. Use the following activities to help children focus on their own personalities and interests.

MAKE A WORD WEB FOR PERSONALITY TRAITS Work with children to create a word web to record different kinds of traits or qualities people can have. For example, have children think about whether they are outgoing or shy.

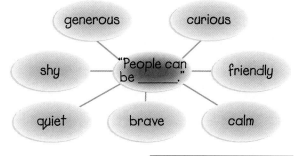

generous   curious

shy   "People can be _____."   friendly

quiet   brave   calm

> Graphic Organizer 13

MAKE A SELF-PORTRAIT Have children draw pictures of themselves doing things they enjoy. Have them write sentences about themselves using personality traits from the web or other traits they may have.

Develop Oral Language

CONNECT WORDS AND ACTIONS

ESL Assign opposing personality traits to partners and have them role-play a scenario. For example:

- Partner 1: shy
- Partner 2: friendly
- Situation: a birthday party

Encourage children to use actions and facial expressions to demonstrate how someone who is shy (or sociable) might act in the specific situation. Ask children to describe how they were feeling as they did the role plays.

▶ **Kinesthetic/Linguistic**

DAILY Phonics ROUTINES

DAY 2 **Blending** Write the words *kneel*, *fight*, and *wrap* on the chalkboard. Have children identify the letters they did not sound out. Ask children to blend the sounds to read each word.

 **Phonics CD-ROM**

LANGUAGE SUPPORT

Use the **Language Support Book**, pages 91–94 to help with Build Background concepts. Ask children to describe how they were feeling as they did the role plays.

TESTED
OBJECTIVES

Children will use context and structural clues to determine the meanings of vocabulary words.

Definitions

important (p. 262) having great value or meaning

decided (p. 276) made up one's mind

library (p. 271) collection of reading materials

float (p. 268) drift on top of water or in the air

planet (p. 273) heavenly body that circles the sun

proud (p. 282) very pleased or satisfied

Story Words

These words from the selection may be unfamiliar. Before children read, have them check the meanings and pronunciations of the words in the Glossary, beginning on page 398, or in a dictionary.

- stegosaurus, p. 269
- Jurassic Period, p. 269
- country-western song, p. 274

important
decided
library
float
planet
proud

Teach Vocabulary in Context

Identify Vocabulary Words Display **Teaching Chart 72** and read the passage with children. Have volunteers circle each vocabulary word and underline other words that are clues to its meaning.

Arthur's Report

1. Arthur had an (important) report to do for school. **2.** He needed to choose a topic, so he (decided) to do his report about Earth's water supply. **3.** He went to the (library) to get books about seas and oceans. **4.** Arthur learned why boats can (float) on water. **5.** Arthur wrote a great report about water on our (planet) Earth. **6.** He felt very (proud) of his hard work.

Teaching Chart 72

Discuss Meanings Ask questions like these to help clarify word meanings:

- Do you think school is important? Why or why not?
- What is the base word in *decided*? What does it mean?
- What can you do at a library?
- What is something that can float on water?
- If you could travel in space, what planet would you go to?
- Would you feel proud if you passed a test? Why or why not?

Practice

Draw the Word Meaning **GROUP** Organize the class into groups. Have each child pull a card from the vocabulary card pile and draw a picture of its meaning. Children take turns presenting their pictures to the group and asking others to identify their words. ▶ **Visual/Linguistic**

 **proud**    **planet**   **float**

> **Word Building Manipulative Cards**

Write Questions **PARTNERS** **WRITING** Have partners write questions that use each vocabulary word. Then have them exchange questions and write answers to the other's questions. ▶ **Linguistic**

Assess Vocabulary

Identify Word Meaning in Context **PARTNERS** **WRITING** Invite children to write a context sentence for each vocabulary word. Ask them to leave a blank for the actual vocabulary word. Children should then exchange papers with a partner and fill in the missing words. Ask them to circle the context clues that helped them guess the missing word.

SPELLING/VOCABULARY CONNECTIONS

See Spelling Challenge Words, pages 289Q–289R.

LANGUAGE SUPPORT

See the **Language Support Book**, pages 91–94, for teaching suggestions for Vocabulary.

Vocabulary PuzzleMaker

Provides vocabulary activities.

Meeting Individual Needs for Vocabulary

EASY	ON-LEVEL	ON-LEVEL	CHALLENGE

EASY — Reteach, 86

Name _____ Date _____ **Reteach 86**

Vocabulary

| decided | float | important | library | planet | proud |

Choose a word from the box to match each clue. Write the word on the line.

1. what Earth is — planet
2. made up your mind — decided
3. building with many books in it — library
4. to feel very good about what you have done — proud
5. when something means a lot, it is — important
6. to move along slowly in the air or on water — float

At Home: Ask children to think of words that rhyme with two of the vocabulary words.

86   Book 2.1/Unit 3 Arthur Writes a Story

ON-LEVEL — Practice, 86

Name _____ Date _____ **Practice 86**

Vocabulary

Choose a word from the box to complete each sentence. Write the word on the line.

| decided | float | important | library | planet | proud |

1. Jenny went to the ___ to find some books.
   library
2. Paul's and Carol's kites ___ in the wind.
   float
3. Lily ___ to help clean up the park.
   decided
4. Baseball is very ___ to Lou.
   important
5. Jade's parents were very ___ when she won.
   proud
6. Earth might be the only ___ with life on it.
   planet

At Home: Ask children to illustrate four sentences and write another sentence to go with them.

86   Book 2.1/Unit 3 Arthur Writes a Story

ON-LEVEL — Practice, 86a — Take-Home Story

The Important Planet

I should just throw out all my books and grow food, it thought. Then it had a better idea. The planet decided to call the food planet. "I have some books for you!" the library planet told the food planet. The food planet checked out every cookbook ever written. And, thanks to two important planets, everyone ate well that day!

At Home: Discuss with children why it is important to be yourself. How can you help others be yourself?

86a

CHALLENGE — Extend, 86

Name _____ Date _____ **Extend 86**

Vocabulary

Use each word in the box to write a story about the picture.

| library | proud | planet |
| decided | important | float |

Stories will vary.

At Home: Write each vocabulary word on a card. Have children state each word's definition. Write the definitions on other cards. Use the cards to play a memory game. Store the words in a shoe box and add new words regularly.

86   Book 2.1/Unit 3 Arthur Writes a Story

Reteach, 86   Practice, 86   Practice, 86a Take-Home Story   Extend, 86

Comprehension

Prereading Strategies

PREVIEW AND PREDICT Have children preview the story by reading the title and taking a **picture walk** through the illustrations. Ask questions such as:

- Where do you think this story takes place?

- Do you think this is a realistic story or a make-believe story? Why? (Make-believe: Characters are animals behaving like humans.) *Genre*

- What do you think this story will be about?

Have children record their predictions about the story:

PREDICTIONS	WHAT HAPPENED
The story takes place in school.	
Arthur writes a story for school and everyone likes it.	

SET PURPOSES What do children want to find out by reading this story? For example:

- What does Arthur write about?

- Does the teacher like Arthur's story?

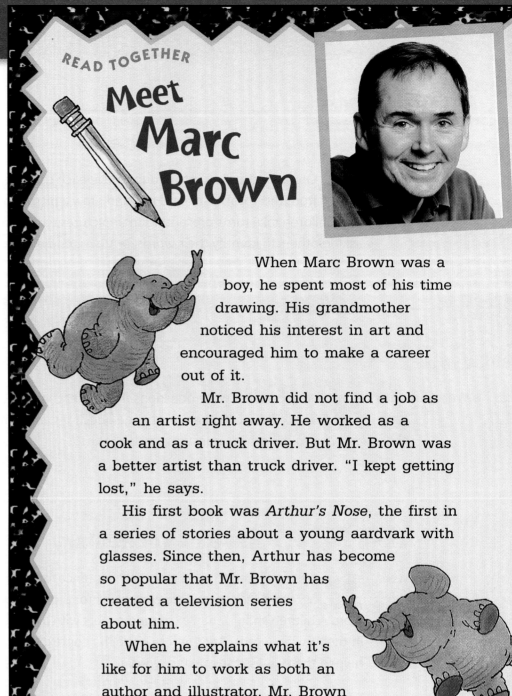

READ TOGETHER

Meet Marc Brown

When Marc Brown was a boy, he spent most of his time drawing. His grandmother noticed his interest in art and encouraged him to make a career out of it.

Mr. Brown did not find a job as an artist right away. He worked as a cook and as a truck driver. But Mr. Brown was a better artist than truck driver. "I kept getting lost," he says.

His first book was *Arthur's Nose*, the first in a series of stories about a young aardvark with glasses. Since then, Arthur has become so popular that Mr. Brown has created a television series about him.

When he explains what it's like for him to work as both an author and illustrator, Mr. Brown says, "The artwork is easier for me than the writing."

260

Meeting Individual Needs • Grouping Suggestions for Strategic Reading

EASY	ON-LEVEL	CHALLENGE
Read Together Read the story aloud and track main events. Invite children to reread in chorus simple sentences throughout the story. As you read with children, model strategies to summarize the story.	**Guided Instruction** Read the selection with children, using the Comprehension prompts. You may want to have the children read the story first on their own. Monitor any comprehension difficulties children may have and focus on appropriate Comprehension questions.	**Read Independently** Remind children that retelling the main events to themselves in their own words as they read can help them summarize.

Written and Illustrated by **MARC BROWN**

ARTHUR WRITES A STORY ①

261

LANGUAGE SUPPORT

A blackline master of the story map can be found in the **Language Support Book**.

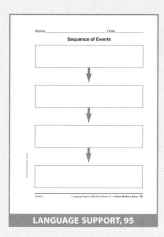

Name_____ Date_____
Sequence of Events

LANGUAGE SUPPORT, 95

Comprehension

✓  **Apply Silent Letters**

STRATEGIC READING Paying attention to the important events on each page in the story will help you understand and summarize the story. Let's make a story map to keep track of the main events.

MAIN EVENTS

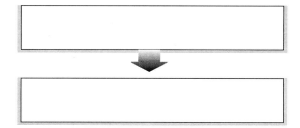

① **Phonics SILENT LETTERS** Let's read the title aloud together. What is the first sound you hear in the word *writes*? (*r*) What letter is silent in the word *writes*? (*w*) *Blending*

Genre

Fantasy

Explain that fantasies:

- include characters or settings that don't actually exist.
- tell about events that could not happen in real life.
- may be mostly realistic stories, with animals as the main characters.

Activity After reading *Arthur Writes A Story,* invite volunteers to give examples of **fantastic,** or unreal, characteristics from the story. Have them pay close attention to the illustrations. Then, encourage children to compare Arthur to a real person. Ask, "In what ways are you and Arthur alike?

261

Comprehension

2 The picture and the words on this page have important information. What do they tell us about the kind of student Arthur seems to be? Is he interested in his homework? (Arthur seems interested in the homework. He asks the teacher for more information.) *Make Inferences*

3 **Phonics** **SILENT LETTERS** Let's read the last sentence on page 263 aloud. Which two words in that sentence contain silent letters? *Graphophonic Cues*

MODEL I'll reread the last sentence to myself and pay close attention to each word. When I come to the word *knew*, I hear a /n/ sound at the beginning of the word. But I can see that the word begins with the letter *k*. So *k* must be silent. As I read on, I see that *write* sounds like it begins with an /r/ sound. So the *w* must be silent.

Write a story.
1. Have a beginning, a middle, and an end.
2. Use details.
3. Be creative.

Arthur's teacher, Mr. Ratburn, explained the homework.

"What should the story be about?" Arthur asked.

 "Anything," Mr. Ratburn said. "Write about something that is important to you."

262

LANGUAGE SUPPORT

ESL There are several compound words on page 262 that children may not be able to read. List the words and show them how each is made up of two smaller words: *homework, anything, something.*

Write each word part on an index card, then have children match the index cards to form the compound words. Have children choose two of the compound words and write sentences using the words.

Arthur started his story the minute he got home. He knew exactly what he wanted to write about. **3** **4**

Comprehension

4 Look at the words and picture on this page. How does Arthur feel about writing this story? (excited) How do you know? (smiling face, started immediately, knew what he wanted to write about) *Make Inferences*

LONG VOWELS Look at the last word in the first sentence on page 263. Let's say the word. (*home*) What vowel sound do you hear? (ō)

PREVENTION/INTERVENTION

LONG VOWELS Write the word *home* on the chalkboard. Remind children that the long *o* sound is spelled *o-e* in the word *home*.

• What sound does the *o* make? (ō)

• How do you know? (The letters *o-e* make the long *o* sound.)

Repeat this exercise with the word *write*. Have children brainstorm a list of other words with long vowels spelled with a silent *e*. Have them use the words in sentences orally. *Graphophonic Cues*

263

Comprehension

5 What is the first main event in the story? Let's write the first main event in our story map. *Sequence of Events*

MODEL I'll think about what I have read so far. . . . The first main event is that Arthur writes a story for his homework about how he got his pet dog.

MAIN EVENTS

Arthur writes a story about his pet dog.

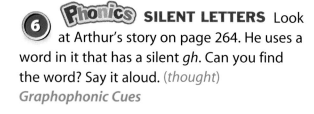

6 **Phonics** **SILENT LETTERS** Look at Arthur's story on page 264. He uses a word in it that has a silent *gh*. Can you find the word? Say it aloud. (*thought*) *Graphophonic Cues*

How I Got My Puppy Pal

I always wanted a dog, but first I had to prove I was responsible. So I started Arthur's Pet Business. My mom made me keep all the animals in the basement. It was a lot of work, but it was fun until I thought I lost Perky. But then I found her, and she had three puppies! And I got to keep one of them. That's how I got my dog Pal.

The End

264

LANGUAGE SUPPORT

ESL Some children may have difficulty keeping track of who is talking on page 265. Point out how the quotation marks surround the words each character says, and how the word *said* shows who is talking.

Have partners tell each other what color they like. Have children write the sentences on paper with the color they chose in crayon. Tell them to use quotes and the word *said*.

Arthur read his story to D.W.

"That's a boring story," D.W. said. **(7)**
"Does it have to be real life? Because **(8)**
your life is so dull."

"I don't want to write a boring
story," said Arthur.

"If it were me," D.W. suggested,
"I'd make the story about
getting an elephant."

265

Comprehension

(7) D.W. doesn't seem to like Arthur's story.
What kind of sister do you think D.W. is
to Arthur? Why? (honest, blunt, doesn't seem
to mind hurting Arthur's feelings) *Make
Inferences*

(8) Do you agree with D. W. that Arthur's
story is boring? Why or why not?
(Possible response: Yes, an elephant is more
interesting than a dog.) *Judgments and
Decisions*

Minilesson

REVIEW/MAINTAIN
Context Clues

Remind children that they can figure out the
meaning of an unfamiliar word by reading
other words or sentences that surround it
and by looking for picture clues.

- Have children reread D. W.'s words in the
  second paragraph on page 265.

- Ask what clues, or other words, help
  children figure out the meaning of the
  word *dull*. (*boring*)

Activity Have children reread the first
sentence in Arthur's story on page 264. Have
children draw a picture and write a sentence
that helps the reader understand the meaning of the word *responsible*.

265

Comprehension

9 Did Arthur change his story? How do you know? (Yes, he's now writing about elephant puppies.) *Make Inferences*

10 Compare Buster's opinion of Arthur's story to D.W.'s opinion. How are they different? How are they the same? (Neither D.W. nor Buster really seems to like Arthur's story. D.W. told Arthur what he should write about. Buster told him about his story idea.) *Compare and Contrast*

The next day, Arthur read his new story to Buster.

9 "Did you like the part about the elephant puppies?" he asked.

10 "It's okay, I guess," said Buster. "I'm writing a cool story about outer space."

266

Maybe my story should take place on the **11** moon, thought Arthur. **12**

267

Comprehension

11 **Phonics** **SILENT LETTERS** Look at the sentence on page 267. Which letter is silent in *should*? (*l*) What words have silent *l* in them and rhyme with *should*? (*could, would*) *Graphophonic Cues*

12 Does Arthur seem sure of himself and sure about what he is writing? (no) Do his friends' opinions make him change his mind? (yes) Find examples from the story to support your answer. *Character*

Minilesson

REVIEW

Setting

Review the meaning of setting: where and when the story takes place.

- Ask children to give the setting of Arthur's original story. (at Arthur's house and in his basement)
- On page 267, Arthur is considering a new setting for his story. Where would this story take place? (on the moon) When would this story take place?

Activity Have children write a paragraph about Arthur on the moon. Ask children to use details that describe the setting.

Comprehension

CONTRACTIONS Read the word *wouldn't* in the last sentence on this page. *Wouldn't* means *would not*. Which two words are combined to form *wouldn't*? (*would not*)

13 **Phonics** **SILENT LETTERS** Look at the second paragraph on page 268. Which letters are silent in the words *weigh* and *high?* (*gh*) *Graphophonic Cues*

On Wednesday, Arthur read his newest story to the Brain.

13 "Scientifically speaking, elephants would weigh less on the moon, but wouldn't float that high," said the Brain.

268

Writer's Craft

FORMAL OR INFORMAL LANGUAGE

Explain: Informal language is casual, like language spoken between friends. Formal language is spoken in school and used in writing books. It follows the rules of grammar and the words are more precise.

Example: When the Brain explains the scientific information about elephants on the moon, the author is using formal language. When Arthur is writing his original story, he is using informal language.

PARTNERS Have partners use formal language orally. Ask children to explain an idea from science using formal language. Then have them use informal language to tell a friend about science class.

PREVENTION/INTERVENTION

CONTRACTIONS Explain to children that sometimes two words are combined to form one word. This is called a *contraction*. Tell them that one way to recognize a contraction is that they will see two words joined together by an apostrophe. The apostrophe replaces a letter in one of the words.

Have children identify which letter the apostrophe replaces in the contractions *couldn't* and *don't*. (*o*) *Syntactic Cues*

Comprehension

14 What did the Brain do for his story that Arthur has not done yet? (research) What do you think Arthur will do next? Why? (Research for his story. Arthur changes his story to meet each friend's suggestions.) *Make Inferences*

TEACHING TIP

BACKGROUND INFORMATION Show a picture of a stegosaurus to the children and point out the bony plates along its back. Tell children that the stegosaurus was a plant-eater that lived during the Jurassic Period, nearly 200 million years ago.

"So you don't like it?" asked Arthur.

"A good story should be well researched," said **14** the Brain. "Like mine: 'If I Had a Pet Stegosaurus in the Jurassic Period.'"

269

Minilesson

REVIEW/MAINTAIN

Main Idea

Review that the main idea tells what is most important about a story.

• Ask children to state the main idea of *Arthur Writes a Story* from what they have read thus far. (The main idea so far is that Arthur keeps changing his story because of other people's opinions.)

Activity Have children write paragraphs on any topic they choose and exchange them with their partners. Have partners identify the main idea of each other's paragraphs.

Comprehension

 Let's look at our story map. What main event can we add to it? *Sequence of Events*

MAIN EVENTS

Arthur writes a story about his pet dog.

Arthur changed his story and put his friends' ideas into it.

270

Cross Curricular: Science

MAMMALS Point out that Arthur is researching a mammal. Explain that scientists classify animals in different categories: mammals, reptiles, amphibians, birds, fish.

RESEARCH AND INQUIRY Have groups choose a category and brainstorm lists of as many animals as they can in their category. Have them use an encyclopedia to add more animals to their lists.

▶ **Logical/Interpersonal**

interNET CONNECTION For more information on animals, have children visit **www.mhschool.com/reading**.

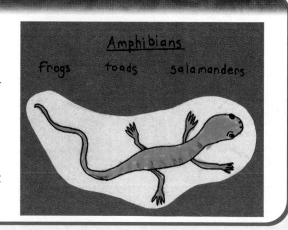

Arthur hurried to the library.

"What are all those books for?" asked Francine.

"Research," said Arthur. "I'm writing about my pet five-toed mammal of the genus *Loxodonta*."

"Your *what?*" asked Francine.

"My elephant!" Arthur explained.

"Oh," said Francine. "I'm putting jokes **15** in my story."

16

271

Comprehension

16 Now Francine is talking to Arthur. What does she tell him? What do you think Arthur will do? Why? (She says that she is putting jokes in her story. Arthur will probably put jokes in his, because he keeps adding other people's ideas to his story.) *Make Predictions*

Minilesson

REVIEW/MAINTAIN

Make Inferences

Remind children that they can tell what a character is like by using picture clues, and the character's words and actions.

• Ask children to think about how Francine feels about Arthur's story idea. (not very enthusiastic) Have children look at the picture on page 270 and reread page 271. Discuss how Arthur probably feels and why. (Arthur is enthusiastic about his story. He wants people to enjoy his story.)

Activity Ask children to act out a scene from the story. Have others make inferences about the thoughts and feelings of the characters in the scene.

Comprehension

17 Arthur is worried about his story. What do you think he is worried about? (He is worried that there are no jokes in his story.)
Make Inferences

18 **Phonics** SILENT LETTERS
Which word in the first sentence has silent letters? (*through*) What are the silent letters? (*gh*) *Graphophonic Cues*

17 All through dinner, Arthur worried about his story.

18 "Please pass the corn," asked Father.

272

Activity

Cross Curricular: Math

TIME Discuss what Arthur is doing in the picture. Ask children whether they think it is morning or night.

Have children work in pairs. Help each pair make a clock out of a paper plate and show a time for dinner. Have them write the time on an index card that they show

on their clocks and identify whether it is A.M. or P.M. Then have children show a time on the clock for breakfast, write the time on another index card, and identify it as A.M. or P.M. ▶ **Mathematical/Kinesthetic**

Comprehension

19 Arthur seems very excited. Why is he so pleased? (He thought of a joke for his story.) *Cause and Effect*

TEACHING TIP

MANAGEMENT You may wish to wait and do the Language Support features during a rereading of the story. Other children can continue to read independently while you work with children that may need extra support.

"Corn! That's it!" said Arthur. "Purple corn **19** and blue elephants! On Planet Shmellafint! Now *that's* funny."

"Arthur is acting weirder than usual," said D.W.

273

LANGUAGE SUPPORT

ESL Children may need help understanding the word *worried* on page 272. Read aloud the first sentence on page 272. Ask children to make a face that shows what a person who is feeling worried might look like. Then read aloud the rest of the text on pages 272–273. Ask children to make a face that shows how Arthur feels now. Invite them to look at the picture on page 272. Ask them if Arthur looks worried or happy in the picture.

Have volunteers act out the parts of Arthur, Father, and D. W. on pages 272–273.

Comprehension

 What are Arthur and Prunella talking about? (the country-western song Prunella wrote) **What do you think Arthur will do? Why?** (write a song for his story, because he always tries to do what his friends have done) *Make Predictions*

Ⓢ ELF-MONITORING STRATEGY

REREADING Rereading part of the story can help readers understand events.

MODEL I'm not sure who wrote the song. When I reread this page I see that it was Prunella who said, "That kid was me."

Fluency

READ DIALOGUE Have children focus on the words that are surrounded by quotation marks. Ask them to identify the speaker for each quote. Then have volunteers play the roles of Prunella and Arthur by speaking the words that they each say on these pages. Emphasize that they must only read the words within the quotation marks as they play their roles.

On Thursday, everyone at the Sugar Bowl was talking about their stories.

"Last year, a kid wrote a country-western song for her story," said Prunella. "And she got an A+."

274

Comprehension

21 Let's look at the picture. Where do you think this part of the story takes place? At what time of the day? How can you tell? (In an ice cream parlor or candy store in the afternoon. They are having soft drinks, and probably wouldn't be out on their own at night.) *Setting*

"How do you know?" asked Arthur.

"That kid was me," explained Prunella. "Mr. Ratburn said I should send it to a record company. It was *that* good."

"Wow!" said Arthur.

275

Comprehension

22 Where do you think Arthur is now? What time of day is it? How can you tell? (He's probably in his room. I can see that he is at his desk from the picture. It is at night. I know this from the words and the picture.) **Setting**

23 **Phonics** **SILENT LETTERS** Which word in the first sentence has silent letters? (*night*) What are the letters that you do not sound out? (*gh*) What are some words that rhyme with this word? Let's list them on the chalkboard to see if they have the same silent letters. (Answers will vary. Possible answers: *might, fight, tight, sight, white, kite*) **Graphophonic Cues**

22

23 That night, Arthur's imagination went wild. He decided to turn his story into a song. He even made up a dance

24 to go with it.

Activity

Cross Curricular: Social Studies

COMMUNITY BUSINESS Remind children that Arthur and his friends gathered at a local soda shop. Brainstorm a list of other community businesses in your own neighborhood.

RESEARCH AND INQUIRY Have groups choose a community business from the neighborhood to find out about. Then have them give a short presentation about what they learned.

▶ **Linguistic/Interpersonal**

Comprehension

24 Arthur is adding more to his story, so we can add more to our story map. What can we add now? *Sequence of Events*

MAIN EVENTS

Arthur writes a story about his pet dog.

⬇

Arthur changed his story and put his friends' ideas into it.

⬇

Arthur made up a song and dance to go with his story.

 CONTEXT CLUES Read the first sentence on page 276. What does the word *imagination* mean?

 PREVENTION/INTERVENTION

CONTEXT CLUES Remind children that clues to the meaning of an unfamiliar word can be found in the surrounding sentences.

• Have children read the paragraph on page 276.

• Write a list of clues on the chalkboard that help define imagination. (*went wild, made up*)

Ask children what else give them clues about the word's meaning. (the illustration) *Semantic Cues*

Comprehension

25 Arthur is performing his story for his family. How do you think he might sound? Try role-playing Arthur in this scene. Act out how he might sound and look. *Role-Play*

Later, he tried it out on his family.

"... Now this little boy

Can go home and enjoy

His own personal striped elephant.

And you will see

How happy he will be

Here on Planet . . . Shmellafint!"

"Well," said Arthur. "What do you think?"

25 Mother and Father smiled.

278

Susan had a birthday party.

Activity

Cross Curricular: Art

ROUND-ROBIN PICTURE Point out how each of Arthur's friends added an idea to his story. Tell children that they will make an add-on picture.

- Take a large piece of paper. Ask a volunteer to start off the picture by drawing a person or an animal.

- Have children continue the picture, each adding a new idea. Continue passing the picture around until each child has added to it.

- Display the finished drawing. Invite children to work together to come up with a title for the picture.
  ▶ **Linguistic/Spatial**

26 Look at Arthur's family and reread their words. How do you think they feel about Arthur's story? (They seem confused by his story.) *Make Inferences*

27 What do you think will happen in school when Arthur reads his story? *Make Predictions*

MODEL I know that when Arthur read his story to his family, they did not seem to understand it. Arthur's grandmother thought it was confusing. When I look at the picture, I can see that his parents look confused too. I think that when Arthur reads his story at school, the kids may not understand the story either.

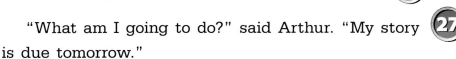

"It's nice," said Grandma Thora. "But a little confusing."

"Too bad you can't dance," said D.W. **26**

"What am I going to do?" said Arthur. "My story **27** is due tomorrow."

That night Arthur didn't sleep very well.

The next day, Arthur worried until Mr. Ratburn finally called on him.

279

Comprehension

28 Read the text on page 281 and look at the picture on page 280. How do you think Binky felt about Arthur's story? How can you tell? (Possible response: He felt confused. He is trying to figure out if the story is true.) *Make Inferences*

280

CULTURAL PERSPECTIVES

FAIRY TALES Point out that each of Arthur's friends gave him ideas for telling his story in a different way. Explain that many familiar fairy tales are told in different ways in other cultures. For example, in the Korean version of *Cinderella*, a black ox instead of a fairy godmother helps the Cinderella character.

RESEARCH AND INQUIRY Have children find versions of fairy tales from other cultures and share them with the class.

When Arthur's song and dance was over, **29** the classroom was so quiet, it was almost spooky. Binky raised his hand. "Did that really happen?"

"Sort of," said Arthur. "It started as the story of how I got my dog."

"I'd like to hear that story," said Mr. Ratburn.

281

Comprehension

29 Arthur is going to tell the class the first version of the story he wrote. Do you think they will like this story better than the one he just read them? (Possible answer: They will like the story about Arthur's dog because it is interesting and easy to understand.) *Make Predictions*

Comprehension

30 What was Arthur's main problem in writing his story? (He was trying to please everyone with his story.) **How was his problem solved?** (The teacher helped him see that his own story was really the best.)
Problem and Solution

Visual Literacy

VIEWING AND REPRESENTING

Ask children to look closely at the illustration on page 282. Point out the "thought balloon" next to Arthur. Explain that a "balloon" is placed next to a character in an illustration to show what a character is thinking. What is Arthur thinking about in the picture as he tells his story? (He is thinking about his dog.) What clue in the picture tells the reader how Arthur feels about this story? (The expression on his face; he is smiling as he tells the story; he is happy.)

"The title was 'How I Got My Puppy Pal,'" said Arthur.

Arthur told how proud he was of his pet business and how scared he was when Perky disappeared. And he told how happy he was to find her under his bed and how surprised he was to see her three puppies.

30 "And the best part is," said Arthur, "I got to keep one!"

282

Buster said, "I like that story better than your other one."

"Great story!" said Binky.

"I think Arthur's story was the best!" said Francine.

31

283

Comprehension

31 How did the class like Arthur's new story? Why? (Possible response: They liked this one much better because it really happened. Everything in the story made sense, unlike the first story.) *Confirm Predictions*

Minilesson

REVIEW/MAINTAIN

Digraph: *th*

Remind children that when the letters *t* and *h* are spelled together they form a new sound: /th/. Ask children to suggest words that begin with the /th/ sound.

- Have children look at page 283 and identify and read words that contain the /th/ sound: (*than, the, that*)

Activity Read a list of words, some with and some without the /th/ sound. Have children stand when they hear a word with the /th/ and sit when they do not.

Phonics CD-ROM Have children use the Interactive Phonics activities on the CD-ROM for more reinforcement.

Comprehension

 Let's complete our story maps.
Sequence of Events

MAIN EVENTS

> Arthur writes a story about his pet dog.

↓

> Arthur changed his story and put his friends' ideas in it.

↓

> Arthur made up a song and dance to go with his story.

↓

> Mr. Ratburn and the class preferred Arthur's story about his dog.

RETELL THE STORY Have partners use their story map to retell the story. One partner can retell the first half of the story, referring to the story map when needed, and the other can tell the second half. *Summarize*

SELF-ASSESSMENT

- How did I use the main events in my story map to help me keep track of this story?
- How did I use the pictures to help me understand the events and characters in this story?

TRANSFERRING THE STRATEGIES

- How can I use these strategies to help me read other stories?

 "Good work," said Mr. Ratburn. "Of course, I expect you to write it all down by Monday."

Then Mr. Ratburn gave Arthur a gold sticker. "Oh, and one more thing," he said.

284

REREADING FOR *Fluency*

PARTNERS Children who need fluency practice can work in pairs. Have partners choose a page from the story to read aloud to each other. Have them each practice their pages several times, then record their improved readings on audiocassette.

READING RATE When you evaluate reading rate, have children read aloud from the story for one minute. Place a stick-on note after the last word read.

Count words read. To evaluate children's performance, see the Running Record in the **Fluency Assessment** book.

i Intervention For leveled fluency passages, lessons, and norm charts, see **Skills Intervention Guide**, Part 5, Fluency.

"Leave out the dancing!"

285

Comprehension

Return to Predictions and Purposes

Review with children their story predictions and reasons for reading the story. Were their predictions correct? Did they find out what they wanted to know?

PREDICTIONS	WHAT HAPPENED
The story takes place in school.	The story took place in school and in other places in Arthur's neighborhood.
Arthur writes a story for school, and everyone likes it.	At first everyone does not like Arthur's story. Then, he tells his original story, and they like that one.

INFORMAL ASSESSMENT

HOW TO ASSESS

 SILENT LETTERS Write the following words on the chalkboard: *through, lamb, know, write, talk.* Have children read each word and circle the silent letters.

SUMMARIZE Have children write a summary of *Arthur Writes a Story* in their own words. They may refer to their story map for help.

FOLLOW UP

SILENT LETTERS Have children who have difficulty with silent letters keep a list of these words as they come across them in their reading.

SUMMARIZE Children who have difficulty summarizing the story can use rereading strategies to help them understand the events.

LITERARY RESPONSE

QUICK-WRITE Have children complete the following sentence in their journals: I did (or did not) like the first story Arthur read because _____.

ORAL RESPONSE Have students share and compare their journal entries and discuss similarities and differences in each other's opinions. Which story did they like best?

Story Questions

Arthur Writes a Story

Have children discuss or write answers to the questions on page 286.

Answers:

1. Arthur writes his first story about how he got his dog. *Literal/Plot*

2. Arthur thinks his friends' ideas are better than his own. *Inferential/ Character*

3. Arthur's class likes the story about the puppy better because it is his own. *Inferential/Character*

4. The story is mostly about the process Arthur goes through to write a story. *Summarize*

5. Arthur reads his original story to the class, and Peter invites a girl to his "all boys" birthday party. *Reading Across Texts*

Write a Library Guide For a full writing process lesson, see the explanatory writing lesson on pages 289M–289N.

Story Questions & Activities
READ TOGETHER

1 What does Arthur write his first story about?

2 Why does Arthur keep changing his story?

3 Why do you think Arthur's class likes the story about the puppy better than the one about the elephant?

4 What is this story mostly about?

5 How do both Arthur and Peter from "A Letter to Amy" show that they can think for themselves?

Write a Library Guide

Arthur had to go to the library to find books about elephants. Write a guide that tells how to find a book in your school library. Include any helpful hints you have learned from your librarians. Make sure all the steps are in the right order.

Meeting Individual Needs

EASY	ON-LEVEL	CHALLENGE
Name_____ Date_____ **Reteach** 87	Name_____ Date_____ **Practice** 87	Name_____ Date_____ **Extend** 87
Story Comprehension	**Story Comprehension**	**Story Comprehension**
Put an **X** by the sentence that tells about "Arthur Writes a Story."	Think about "Arthur Writes a Story." Write **T** if the statement is true about the story. Write **F** if the statement is not true about the story.	Choose something that is important to you. Write a story about it.
___ I. Arthur had no homework.	_T_ I. Arthur is a student.	Stories will vary.
X 2. Arthur writes about a dog.	_F_ 2. D.W. is Arthur's mother.	
X 3. Arthur writes about the moon.	_F_ 3. Arthur is working on a music project.	
___ 4. Arthur writes about D.W.	_T_ 4. Arthur has to write a story for class.	
X 5. The Brain writes about dinosaurs.	_T_ 5. At first, Arthur writes about his puppy.	
___ 6. D.W. plays with eggs.	_T_ 6. Arthur writes several different stories.	
X 7. Arthur does research in the library.	_F_ 7. The Brain is Arthur's teacher.	Read each question. Circle your answer.
___ 8. Francine has no jokes in her story.	_F_ 8. Penelope is Arthur's friend.	Does your story have a beginning, a middle, and an end? Yes No
X 9. Arthur's family did not like his story.	_T_ 9. Arthur's class likes his story about the puppy.	Did you use details? Yes No
X 10. Everyone likes Arthur's story about his puppy.	_T_ 10. Arthur's class does not like his song and dance story.	Were you creative? Yes No
	_T_ 11. Arthur got a gold sticker for his story.	What do you think Arthur would tell you about your story?
	_F_ 12. Francine wrote a song for her story.	
Book 2.1/Unit 3 Arthur Writes a Story **At Home:** Tell children a simple, familiar story. Ask them to summarize the story in one sentence. 87	Book 2.1/Unit 3 Arthur Writes a Story **At Home:** Have children draw a picture to go along with one of the statements they marked **true**. 87	Write your story over on another piece of paper. Make any changes you like.
		Book 2.1/Unit 3 Arthur Writes a Story **At Home:** Ask children to think of advice they would give Arthur the next time he has to write a story. 87
Reteach, 87	**Practice, 87**	**Extend, 87**

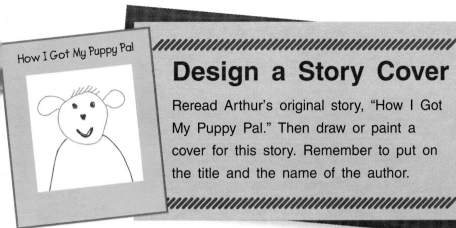

How I Got My Puppy Pal

Design a Story Cover

Reread Arthur's original story, "How I Got My Puppy Pal." Then draw or paint a cover for this story. Remember to put on the title and the name of the author.

Write a Poem

Write a poem about something that is important to you. Use colorful words that describe what you're writing about. Be creative.

Find Out More

Arthur is told that his story about elephants should be well researched. If you were writing a story about elephants, what important facts would you need to know?

287

Story Activities

Design a Story Cover

Materials: paper, pencils, paints, paintbrushes, felt-tipped markers, tape

GROUP Reread Arthur's original story, "How I Got My Puppy Pal." Then have students draw or paint a cover for this story. Remember to put the title and name of the author on the cover. Hang a clothesline at the bottom of a bulletin board and clip the covers to it with clothespins.

Write a Poem

Materials: paper, pencils, pens

ONE Brainstorm with students ideas for their poems. Have students make a list of description words about their ideas and develop their poems from their description word lists.

Find Out More

Have children list their questions about elephants. After they finish their list have them use the library and the Internet to find the answers.

 Review with students how to log on to ***www.mhschool.com/reading*** so that they can find out more about elephants.

After page 287, see Selection Assessment.

DAILY Phonics ROUTINES

DAY 3 **Fluency** Write the following sentence on the chalkboard, and ask children to silently blend the sounds in each word and read the sentence aloud. *I know which letters to write in the word night.*

 **Phonics CD-ROM**

Study Skills

REFERENCE SOURCES

OBJECTIVES

Students will use a dictionary to find out spelling, pronunciation, and meaning of unfamiliar words.

PREPARE Read the passage with the students. Display **Teaching Chart 73**.

TEACH Explain that a dictionary can help find the pronunciation, spelling, and meaning of unfamiliar words. Demonstrate how to look up a word in the dictionary.

PRACTICE Have students answer questions 1–4. Review the answers with them. **1.** three entries **2.** piano/plum **3.** a fruit with smooth, purple skin **4.** A dictionary can help you find out the meaning and spelling of unfamiliar words.

ASSESS/CLOSE Have students find and make a list of words that they can't pronounce or don't understand in *Arthur Writes a Story*. Have them use a real dictionary to look up these words.

Study Skills

Use a Dictionary

piano • plum

piano A large musical instrument with black and white keys. Jeff practices the *piano* every day.
  pi•an•o (pee AN oh) *noun, plural* **pianos**.

planet A large body that moves around the sun in a circle. There are nine *planets* that revolve around the sun.
  plan•et (PLAN it) *noun, plural* **planets**.

plum A fruit with smooth, purple skin. I like to have a *plum* with my lunch.
  plum (PLUM) *noun, plural* **plums**.

Use the part of a dictionary page to answer the questions.

1 Each word in a dictionary is called an **entry**. How many entries are on this part of a dictionary page?

2 What are the guide words on this page?

3 What is the meaning of the word *plum*?

4 How can a dictionary be helpful when you are reading or writing?

Meeting Individual Needs

EASY	ON-LEVEL	CHALLENGE
Reteach, 88	Practice, 88	Extend, 88

DIRECTIONS:
Read the story. Then read each question about the story.

SAMPLE

The Island

Linda Lizard lived on an island. Her friends were Tom Turtle and Sandy Seagull.

Linda wanted to see if there were other islands. But she did not know how to swim. Tom offered to take Linda on his back so they could look. Sandy did not think it was safe. In fact, she thought it sounded <u>dangerous</u>.

Linda and Tom went into the water. The ocean was rough. Linda couldn't hold on. She began to slide into the sea. Sandy flew into the air from the beach. She picked Linda out of the water and took her back to shore. Linda was wet but not hurt.

"Thanks for saving me," Linda said to Sandy. Tom and Linda both said they would be more careful.

1 You know this story is make-believe because—
   ○ seagulls don't fly
   ● animals don't talk
   ○ there are no islands

2 In this passage, <u>dangerous</u> means—
   ○ that it is not fun
   ● that it is not safe
   ○ that it is not special

289

Test Power

THE PRINCETON REVIEW

Read the Page

Explain to children that you will be reading this story as a group. You will read the story, and they will follow along in their books.

Request that children put pens, pencils, and markers away, since they will not be writing in their books.

Discuss the Questions

QUESTION 1: Remind children about the difference between fact and fiction. Have them look at the choices and choose the one that is true in the real world.

QUESTION 2: Instruct children to look for other words in the story to help establish the meaning of "dangerous." The clues here can be found in the immediately preceding sentence, "Sandy did not think that it was safe to swim."

Leveled Books

EASY

Don't Float in Blue Jam

☑ **Phonics** Silent Letters

☑ **Instructional Vocabulary:**
decided, float, important, library, planet, proud

Written by Dan Feury
Illustrated by Heather Maione

ⓘ **Intervention** ▶ **Skills**
Intervention Guide, for direct instruction and extra practice of phonics and vocabulary.

Answers to Story Questions

1. He is new to the school.
2. because he wants Bill and Tim to like him
3. because he said how he really felt
4. a boy who finds that people will still like him even if he doesn't always agree with them
5. Answers will vary.

The Story Questions and Activity below appear in the Easy Book.

Story Questions and Writing Activity

1. Why is Jason standing by himself at the beginning of the book?
2. Why does Jason say he likes TV better than the movies?
3. Why do you think Jason feels proud of himself on page 14?
4. What is this story mostly about?
5. What are some ways that Jason is like Arthur? What makes him different?

What Do You Like the Best?

Do you like playing football? Baseball? Going to the movies? What is your favorite activity? Draw a picture of yourself doing your favorite activity. Share your picture with the class.

from Don't Float in Blue Jam

Guided Reading

PREVIEW AND PREDICT Take a **picture walk** through page 6 of the story with children. As children look at the illustrations, have them predict what the story is about. Chart their ideas.

SET PURPOSES Have children discuss why they want to read *Don't Float in Blue Jam.* For example, children may want to know what blue jam is!

READ THE BOOK Use questions like the following to guide children's reading or after they have read the story independently.

Page 5: Read aloud the word *might.* What sound do the letters *gh* make? (The letters are silent.) Say the words *tight, light.* Do you hear the *gh*? (no) *Phonics and Decoding*

Page 8: Do you think people could really float in blue jam? (no) If people can't really float in blue jam, where can they float? *Fantasy and Reality/Instructional Vocabulary*

Pages 12–14: What is Jason's problem? (He wants to go to the library, but he's afraid of what Bill and Tim might say.) How does he solve his problem? (He tells his

friends that he wants to go.) *Problem and Solution*

Page 16: What do you think Jason will do the next time his friends ask him to do something he doesn't want to do? Why do you think so? *Make Predictions*

RETURN TO PREDICTIONS AND PURPOSES Discuss children's predictions. Ask which were close to the story and why. Have children review their purposes for reading. Did they find out what they wanted to know?

LITERARY RESPONSE Discuss these questions:

• What was your favorite part of the story?

• Would you do what Jason did? Why or why not?

Also see the story questions and activity in *Don't Float in Blue Jam.*

See the **Phonics** CD-ROM for practice using words with silent letters.

Leveled Books

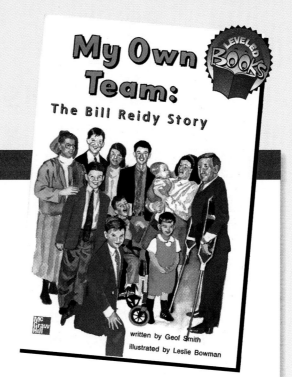

My Own Team: The Bill Reidy Story

written by Geof Smith
illustrated by Leslie Bowman

INDEPENDENT

My Own Team: The Bill Reidy Story

☑ **Silent Letters**

☑ **Instructional Vocabulary:** *decided, float, important, library, planet, proud*

Guided Reading

PREVIEW AND PREDICT Take a **picture walk** through page 5 of the story. Have children predict what the story is about.

SET PURPOSES Have children record what they want to find out by reading the story. For example, they may want to know what kind of team Bill Reidy joins.

READ THE BOOK Use the following questions to guide children's reading or after they have read the story independently.

Pages 2–3: Read aloud the last word in the second line on page 2. *(sign)* Which letter is silent? *(g) Phonics and Decoding*

Pages 8–9: What kind of person was Bill Reidy when he was a boy? How can you tell? (He wasn't a quitter. The things he had to do weren't easy, but he kept trying.) *Character/Make Inferences*

Page 13: How do you know that *My Own Team: The Bill Reidy Story* is a true story? (The story was in newspapers and magazines: he owns an actual restaurant.) *Fantasy and Reality*

Pages 14–16: Do you think any of Bill Reidy's children will grow up to play baseball? Why or why not? *Make Predictions*

Page 16: Find the word *important*. What is important to Bill Reidy? (family, friends, and work) What things are important to you? *Instructional Vocabulary*

RETURN TO PREDICTIONS AND PURPOSES Review children's predictions and purposes for reading.

LITERARY RESPONSE Discuss these questions:

• Do you admire Bill Reidy? Why?

• Can you think of other people who have overcome odds to achieve a goal?

Also see the story questions and activity in *My Own Team: The Bill Reidy Story*.

See the **Phonics CD-ROM** for practice using words with silent letters.

Answers to Story Questions

1. Because he can't walk by himself. As a child, he had an illness that hurt his legs badly.
2. He has nine children and a baseball team has nine players. They all work together to help each other.
3. Chapter 3; Bill's Own Team
4. With hard work and help, a person can deal with a terrible problem and succeed.
5. Answers will vary.

The Story Questions and Activity below appear in the Independent Book.

Story Questions and Writing Activity

1. Why does Bill need crutches?
2. Reread pages 14 and 15 of this book. What does Bill mean when he says that he has a baseball team of his own?
3. In which section of the story would you find information about Bill's baseball team?
4. What is the main idea of the book?
5. Although Bill has a handicap, he has been able to do many things his own way. How is this like Arthur in *Arthur Writes a Story*?

Your Own Way

Think of something you like to do your own special way. Draw a picture of yourself doing this and write a sentence or two describing what you are doing.

from *My Own Team: The Bill Reidy Story*

Leveled Books

Harry The Troll
And The Three
Billy Goats Gruff

By Judith Lechner
Illustrated by Liz Callen

CHALLENGE

Harry the Troll and the Three Billy Goats Gruff

☑ **Phonics** Silent Letters

☑ **Instructional Vocabulary:** *decided, float, important, library, planet, proud*

Answers to Story Questions

1. to eat grass
2. He's much bigger and stronger than Harry.
3. Because he realizes that Harry wants to play with friends and learn new things, and he wants what's best for Harry.
4. a troll who is different, and whose family comes to accept his difference
5. Answers will vary.

The Story Questions and Activity below appear in the Challenge Book.

Story Questions and Writing Activity

1. Why are the goats going up the mountain?
2. Why is Big Billy Goat Gruff not afraid of Harry?
3. Why do you think Harry's father lets him go with the goats?
4. What is this story mostly about?
5. If Harry the Troll had talked to Arthur about writing a story, what do you think he would say?

Brothers and Sisters

There are two children in Harry's family. The Billy Goats Gruff are brothers, so there are three children in their family. The chart shows the numbers in each family.

Number of Children

	1	2	3	4	5	6	7	8	9
Troll	X								
Gruff			X						

Find out how many children are in the families of the kids in your class. Then make a chart to show how many families have 1 child, 2 children, 3 children, and so on.

from Harry the Troll and the Three Billy Goats Gruff

Guided Reading

PREVIEW AND PREDICT As you take the **picture walk**, have children predict what the story is about. Chart their ideas.

SET PURPOSES Have children write why they want to read the story. For example, they may want to hear another version of the *Three Billy Goats Gruff*.

READ THE BOOK Use the following questions to guide children's reading or after they have read the story independently.

Page 2: Is this story real or make-believe? How can you tell? (make-believe; animals don't talk.) *Fantasy and Reality*

Page 4: Find the word *climb*. Which letter in the word *climb* is silent? (*b*) *Phonics and Decoding*

Page 6: Does Ma want Harry to do something that will make her happy or angry when she says "Make us proud"? *Instructional Vocabulary*

Pages 13–15: What kind of troll do you think Harry is? (friendly; stands up for what he believes) What makes you think so? *Character*

Page 16: What kinds of things do you think Harry found out about the world after he joined his friends, the three billy goats? *Make Predictions*

RETURN TO PREDICTIONS AND PURPOSES Have children review their predictions and purposes for reading.

LITERARY RESPONSE Discuss these questions:

- Do you think Harry made a good decision to be friends with the three billy goats? Why?

- Did you like this version of the story or the original story more? Explain.

Also see the story questions and activity in *Harry the Troll and The Three Billy Goats Gruff*.

See the **Phonics** CD-ROM for practice using words with silent letters.

Bringing Groups Together

Anthology and Leveled Books

Connecting Texts

CHARACTER CHARTS
Write the story titles on a chart titled *Be Yourself*. Discuss with children the problem the main character in each story had and how these characters solved their problems by doing things their own way. Call on volunteers from each reading level and write their suggestions on the chart.

Use the chart to talk about why it's important to be yourself.

Arthur Writes a Story	Don't Float in Blue Jam	My Own Team: The Bill Reidy Story	Harry the Troll and the Three Billy Goats Gruff
• Arthur was afraid his story wasn't good enough. • Arthur finally told the story he wanted to tell in the beginning.	• Jason was afraid he wouldn't have friends if he didn't agree with them. • Jason did what he wanted to do and found he had friends anyway.	• Bill Reidy couldn't walk without crutches, and lost the chance to play baseball. • He opened a restaurant. He had lots of children and made his own baseball team.	• Harry didn't want to be mean like the other trolls. • He made friends with the billy goats and was on his way to learning more about the world.

Viewing/Representing

GROUP PRESENTATIONS Divide the class into four groups, one for each of the four books read in the lesson. Have each group draw pictures of the main events and orally summarize the story. Have each group present its pictures and summary.

AUDIENCE RESPONSE
Ask children to watch and listen carefully to the presentations. Allow time for questions after each group presents.

Research and Inquiry

MORE ABOUT LIBRARIES Encourage children to find out more about their school or local library. They can:

• invite a librarian to talk with the class about different library features.

• take a tour of their local library.

• use the internet to find information about famous libraries, such as the Library of Congress.

 interNET CONNECTION Log on to *www.mhschool.com/reading* for more information about libraries.

OBJECTIVES

Children will:

- recognize silent letters *b, k, l, w, g, h,* and *gh* in words.
- read words with silent letters *b, k, l, w, g, h,* and *gh.*

MATERIALS
- **Teaching Chart 74**

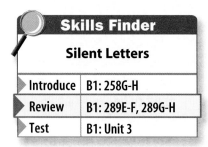

Skills Finder

Silent Letters

Introduce	B1: 258G–H
Review	B1: 289E-F, 289G–H
Test	B1: Unit 3

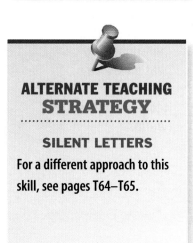

ALTERNATE TEACHING STRATEGY

SILENT LETTERS

For a different approach to this skill, see pages T64–T65.

Review Silent Letters

PREPARE

Identify Silent Letters *b, k, l, w, g, h,* and *gh* in Words

- Write the following on the chalkboard: *Jen made a fingerprint with her thumb high on the wall.* Read the sentence aloud. Ask children to identify the silent letters *b, k, l, w, g, h* or *gh* in the words in the sentence. (*b* in *thumb, gh* in *high*)

- Tell children they will review reading words with silent letters *b, k, l, w, g, h,* and *gh.* Remind children that silent letters mean letters that have no sound in a word.

TEACH

BLENDING Model and Guide Practice with Words with Silent Letters *b, k, l, w, g, h,* and *gh*

- Display **Teaching Chart 74.** Tell children to say the first word slowly and listen to each sound as they say it aloud.

- Ask volunteers to cover the silent letter in this word and say the word again. Ask: Did the sound of word change when we covered the silent letter? (no) Why not? (because you do not say the sound /l/ when you say the word *talk*)

- Encourage children to identify a word in the second column that also contains a silent *l* and draw a line from *talk* to that word. (*walk*)

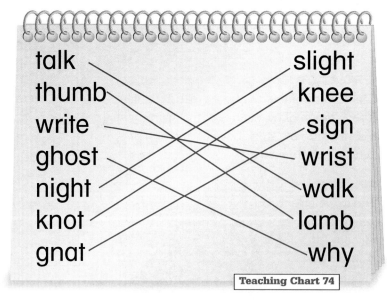

talk   slight
thumb   knee
write   sign
ghost   wrist
night   walk
knot   lamb
gnat   why

Teaching Chart 74

Use the Word in Context

- Have volunteers use each word in a sentence. Example: *I like to talk on the phone.*

Repeat the Procedure

- Repeat the procedure telling children to identify a word in column 2 with the same silent letter as a word in column 1.

BLENDING
Categorizing Words with Silent Letters

PARTNERS

Write the following letter headings on the chalkboard:

Silent *b*	Silent *k*	Silent *w*
Silent *g*	Silent *h*	Silent *gh*

Have children work in pairs. Give children a time limit to brainstorm and list as many words with the silent letter(s) as they can on their own category sheets. When time is up, have pairs share and compare lists. Help students categorize words into word families. ▶ **Linguistic**

ASSESS/CLOSE

Read Silent-Letter Words

To assess children's ability to read silent-letter words, check their word lists from the Practice activity. Have each partner read three words from the list and identify the silent letter in each.

ADDITIONAL PHONICS RESOURCES

Phonics/Phonemic Awareness Practice Book, pages 69–72

McGraw-Hill School
TECHNOLOGY

 Phonics CD-ROM

activities for practice with Blending and Segmenting

DAILY Phonics ROUTINES

DAY 4
Writing Have children write two words with silent letters in a sentence. You may suggest that their sentence be related to a story they have already read.

Phonics CD-ROM

SPELLING/PHONICS CONNECTIONS

Words with silent letters: See the 5-Day Spelling Plan, pages 289Q–289R.

i Intervention ▶ Skills
Intervention Guide, for direct instruction and extra practice of silent letters

Meeting Individual Needs for Phonics

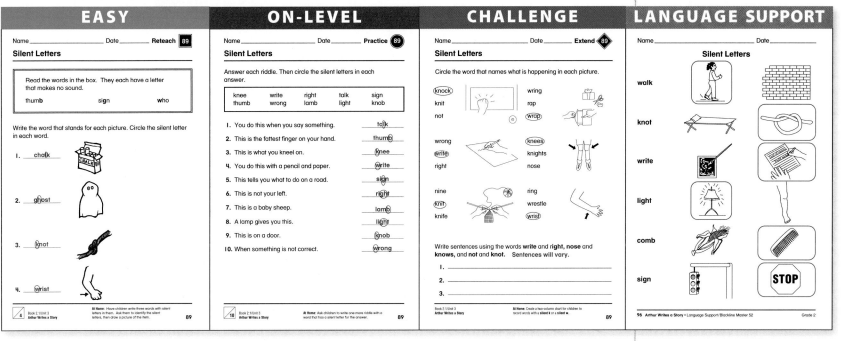

Reteach, 89   Practice, 89   Extend, 89   Language Support, 96

TESTED OBJECTIVES

Children will:

- recognize silent letters *k, w, gh*.
- read words with silent letters.

MATERIALS

- **Teaching Chart 75**
- letter cards from **Word Building Manipulative Cards**
- index cards

Skills Finder

Silent Letters

Introduce	B1: 258G–H
Review	B1: 289E–F, 289G–H
Test	B1: Unit 3

LANGUAGE SUPPORT

You may want to suggest that second-language learners work with fluent English speakers on blending and decoding words with silent letters, since in Spanish and Italian, silent letters are not common.

Review Silent Letters

PREPARE

Identify Words with Silent *k, w, gh*

- Write the following words on the chalkboard:

  knew   **written**   **tight**

- Have volunteers come to the chalkboard to read the words, identify the silent letters, and circle them.

TEACH

BLENDING
Model and Guide Practice with Silent Letters

Dear Skippy,

We are going camping at (High) Point tomorrow (night.) Would you like to come? (I know) it would be a lot of fun. We can sit around the campfire and tell stories all (night.) Please let me know if you can come. I will (write) a list of what you will need to bring.

Your friend,

Stanley

Teaching Chart 75

- Display **Teaching Chart 75.** Tell children there are many words in this passage with the silent letters *k, w, gh.*
- Run your finger under the first sentence, reading it aloud.
- Have children repeat the sentence slowly. Tell them to identify the silent letters in each word as they read.
- Ask volunteers to circle the words in the sentence with silent letters. Then ask other volunteers to underline the silent letters.

Use the Words in Context

Have volunteers use the words with silent letters from the **Teaching Chart** in their own sentences to reinforce their meanings. Example: *I can throw the ball very high.*

Repeat the Procedure

Continue with each sentence in **Teaching Chart 75.** Have children read, circle words, and underline silent letters and reread. Finally, have a volunteer read the whole passage aloud.

289G *Arthur Writes a Story*

PRACTICE

WORD BUILDING
Build Words with Silent Letters

GROUP

Have children work in small groups and use letter cards from the **Word Building Manipulative Cards** to build as many words with the silent letters reviewed as possible. Write words on index cards and underline the silent letters in them with a red marker. Create a silent-letter word wall on the bulletin board. Encourage children to classify the words into sets based on similar silent letters. ▶ **Linguistic/Spatial**

ASSESS/CLOSE

Identify Silent-Letter Words Orally

Use your observations from the Practice activity to determine if children need more reinforcement with silent letters *k, w,* and *gh*. Ask children to read some of the words they formed aloud.

ADDITIONAL PHONICS RESOURCES

Phonics/Phonemic Awareness
Practice Book,
pages 69–72

McGraw-Hill School
TECHNOLOGY

Phonics CD-ROM

activities for practice with
Blending and Segmenting

DAY 5 **Discriminating** Write the following pairs of words on the chalkboard: *comb, cube; keep, knob; wrist, word; wriggle, sign.* Ask children to read each pair of words and say which letter is silent.

Phonics CD-ROM

ALTERNATE TEACHING STRATEGY

SILENT LETTERS

For a different approach to teaching this skill, see pages T64–T65.

i **Intervention** Skills **Intervention Guide,** for direct instruction and extra practice of silent letters

Meeting Individual Needs for Phonics

EASY

Name_____ Date_____ Reteach **90**
Silent Letters

Read the following sentence.
The stop sign was red.
The letter **g** in **sign** is silent.

Choose the word that completes the sentence.
Write the word on the line.

| knock | talked | why | write | lambs | high |

1. I will ___knock___ on the door.

2. The kite flew very ___high___ .

3. Did you ___write___ down his phone number?

4. I ___talked___ to him on the phone.

5. We have two ___lambs___ on our farm.

6. Pat knows ___why___ Sid is laughing.

At Home: Have children circle the silent letter or letters in each of the words they wrote.
90 — Book 2.1/Unit 3 — Arthur Writes a Story — 6

ON-LEVEL

Name_____ Date_____ Practice **90**
Silent Letters

Finish each sentence below. Circle the word that completes the sentence. Then write the answer.

1. Most people sleep at ___night___ .
   (night) knew written

2. Do you ___know___ her name?
   high bright (know)

3. I ___walk___ to school, but he takes the bus.
   weigh (walk) knock

4. I ___wrote___ him a letter.
   high (wrote) talking

5. I could not untie the ___knot___ .
   (knot) flight knee

6. Baby sheep are called ___lambs___ .
   limbs rams (lambs)

7. My ___knee___ is part of my leg.
   knock arm (knee)

8. I ___talk___ on the telephone.
   (talk) walk wink

At Home: Have children illustrate one of the sentences above.
90 — Book 2.1/Unit 3 — Arthur Writes a Story — 8

CHALLENGE

Name_____ Date_____ Extend **90**
Silent Letters

Cut out the picture cards and word cards.
Mix them up. Put them face down and try to make pairs.
Write a short story using some of the words from the cards.

At Home: Take turns telling a story about the picture each time a match is made. Use the word with the silent letter.
90 — Book 2.1/Unit 3 — Arthur Writes a Story

LANGUAGE SUPPORT

Name_____ Date_____
Picture-Word Match

| knee | thumb | calf |
| wrote | night | sign |

Grade 2 — Language Support/Blackline Master 53 • Arthur Writes a Story — 97

^{TESTED} **OBJECTIVES**

Children will distinguish between fantasy and reality.

MATERIALS

- **Teaching Chart 76**

Skills Finder

Fantasy and Reality

Introduce	B1: 289I-J
Review	B1: 341I-J, 379G-H
Test	B1: Unit 3

TEACHING TIP

MAIN IDEA As a class, determine the main idea of the teaching chart. Determine if the main idea is based on reality or fantasy. Have children locate details that are based on reality and others that are based on fantasy. Ask if it is possible to have a main idea based on reality and details based on fantasy.

SELF-SELECTED Reading

Children may choose from the following titles:

ANTHOLOGY

- *Arthur Writes a Story*

LEVELED BOOKS

- *Don't Float in Blue Jam*
- *My Own Team: The Bill Reidy Story*
- *Harry the Troll and the Three Billy Goats Gruff*

Bibliography, pages T88–T89

Introduce Fantasy and Reality

PREPARE

Fantasy/Reality Explain that some stories are *fantasies*. They contain events that could never happen in real life. Other stories are about events that could happen in real life. Ask students whether *Jamaica Tag-Along* tells about events that could happen in real life. Ask if Arthur acts like a real aardvark.

TEACH

Read the Passage

Arthur the Aardvark

Our class read a very good story about an aardvark named Arthur. The story was written by Marc Brown. Everyone in the class enjoyed the story, and now some of the children are reading other stories about Arthur.

Arthur lives in a house with his mom, dad, and sister. He goes to school with his friends, who are also animals. Arthur writes a story about things he does not know about—elephants in outer space!

Teaching Chart 76

Discuss Fantasy and Reality

- Have volunteers circle the passage that can be classified as reality and underline the passage that is not. (Children should realize that the first passage could actually happen in real life, while the second—which says that an aardvark wrote a story—could not.)

- Then discuss why one passage could happen and why one could not.

PRACTICE

Find Examples

PARTNERS

Have children work in pairs to find examples of events in *Arthur Writes a Story* that are fantasy. Remind them to include events in the story Arthur writes. Then have them change each event so that it can be classified as reality. ▶ **Linguistic**

ASSESS/CLOSE

Reality and Fantasy Pictures

Have children make two pictures: one that is an example of reality and one that is an example of fantasy.

ALTERNATE TEACHING STRATEGY

....

FANTASY AND REALITY

For a different approach to teaching this skill, see page T67.

 **Intervention** **Skills**

Intervention Guide, for direct instruction and extra practice of fantasy and reality

---

Meeting Individual Needs for Comprehension

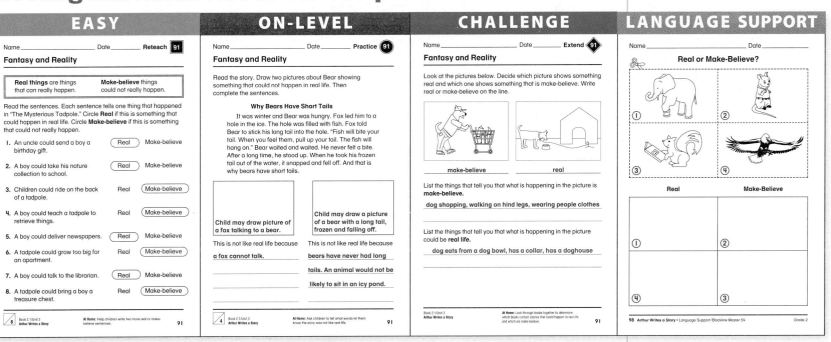

Reateach, 91   Practice, 91   Extend, 91   Language Support, 98

 **OBJECTIVES**

Children will use syntax (word order) and other context clues to figure out the meaning of unfamiliar words.

MATERIALS
• Teaching Chart 77

Skills Finder

Context Clues

Introduce	B1: 91K-L
Review	B1: 113K-L, 123I-J, 289K-L, B2: 179K-L
Test	B1: Unit 1
Maintain	B1: 311, 327; B2: 51, 83

TEACHING TIP

CONTEXT CLUES Help children use context clues. Read: Arthur is very *conscientious*. He gives Pal food and water. He takes Pal for a walk everyday. Arthur pays attention to Pal's needs.

Discuss the context clues that help children determine the meaning of *conscientious*. Then have children generate sentences that describe a person who is conscientious.

Review Context Clues

PREPARE

Discuss the Order of Words in a Sentence

Write the following sentences on the chalkboard:

Arthur wrote a silly story.
Wrote Arthur a silly story.

Ask children which sentence makes sense and why. (sentence 1, because of the word order) Point out that in English we often write the noun (or what the sentence is about) first, followed by the action word—what the noun does.

TEACH

Read the Passage and Model the Skill

Display and read **Teaching Chart 77** aloud with children. Suggest children look for clues that can help them figure out the meaning of the italicized words. Model how to use syntax and familiar words to figure out the meaning of new words.

Arthur's Friends Have Ideas

Arthur wrote about his puppy. He told how he proved that he was *responsible* enough to be trusted with a pet. D.W. thought that was boring. She *suggested* that he write about elephants. The Brain told Arthur to *research*, or look up information, about his story topic. Every time he heard a new idea, Arthur *decided* to choose a new topic.

Teaching Chart 77

MODEL I'm not sure what the word *responsible* means. It comes after the words "he was" so I know it will tell me something about Arthur. The next part of the sentence is "enough to be trusted." This tells me that *responsible* must mean *being trusted*.

PRACTICE

Identify Context Clues

GROUP

Have volunteers underline the context clues that help them figure out the meaning of *suggested*, *research*, and *decided* on **Teaching Chart 77**. Then have them explain what they think each word means.

▶ **Interpersonal/Visual**

ASSESS/CLOSE

Use Context Clues and Syntax to Complete Sentences

Ask children to write sentences for *researched, decided, suggested,* and *responsible*. Remind them to use context clues and word order to show the meaning of the word.

ALTERNATE TEACHING STRATEGY

CONTEXT CLUES

For a different approach to teaching this skill, see page T68.

ⓘ Intervention ▶ **Skills Intervention Guide,** for direct instruction and extra practice of context clues

Meeting Individual Needs for Vocabulary

EASY	ON-LEVEL	CHALLENGE	LANGUAGE SUPPORT

EASY

Name_____ Date_____ **Reteach** 92

Context Clues

> A **context clue** is a word or words that help you figure out the meaning of an unknown word.

Look for the context clue that can help you figure out the meaning of the underlined word. Then answer the questions.

1. In the story the king was important because he was a great man.
   a. What is the context clue? _____ **great**
   b. Is the context clue before or after? _____ **after**

2. The boring story was not very interesting to read.
   a. What is the context clue? _____ **not very interesting**
   b. Is the context clue before or after? _____ **after**

3. The boy wrote about the moon and the sun because he liked outer space.
   a. What is the context clue? _____ **the moon and the sun**
   b. Is the context clue before or after? _____ **before**

4. Because the toy airplane was so light, it floated in the air.
   a. What is the context clue? _____ **so light**
   b. Is the context clue before or after? _____ **before**

At Home: Have children write a sentence using a new word and adding a context clue to explain the new word.

92

Book 2.1/Unit 3
Arthur Writes a Story 8

ON-LEVEL

Name_____ Date_____ **Practice** 92

Context Clues

You can use **context clues** to help you figure out the meaning of an unknown word.

Write the clue words that help you figure out the meaning of the word in dark print. Then write **before** or **after** to show if the clue words come before or after the word.

1. At night I like to look at the stars in the sky through my **telescope**. The telescope makes things that are far away seem closer.

   makes things that are far away seem closer; after

   look at the stars in the sky through; before

2. I saw a bright ball of gas through my telescope. It had a tail. I think this is called a **comet**.

   a bright ball of gas that has a tail

   before

3. I like books about the stars. Someday I hope to be an **astronaut**. An astronaut is a person who is trained to travel in space.

   a person who is trained to travel in space

   after

4. We saw the largest planet in the sky. This planet is one of the brightest objects in the sky. It is called **Jupiter**.

   the largest planet in the sky

   before

At Home: Encourage children to identify two new words in a favorite story or book and to figure out the meanings of the words using context clues.

92

Book 2.1/Unit 3
Arthur Writes a Story 8

CHALLENGE

Name_____ Date_____ **Extend** 92

Context Clues

Circle the words that help you tell what the underlined words mean.

1. The story about dinosaurs should be well researched. I will find lots of information about dinosaurs before I write it.
   find lots of information

2. Did you find out about elephants scientifically?
   No. I could not do tests and experiments to learn about them.
   do tests and experiments to learn about them

3. Were you sad when the dog disappeared?
   Yes. I could not see him, and I did not know where to find him.
   could not see him; did not know where to find him

Write a word from the box to finish the sentences.

mammal	imagination	business

4. Arthur started a pet _____ **business** _____ so he could work and earn money.

5. D.W. did not think a _____ **mammal** _____ like an elephant could live in outer space.

6. The more Arthur used his _____ **imagination** _____, the wilder his story became.

At Home: Ask children to identify clues in pictures and words in sentences that help them figure out the meanings of words they don't know.

92

Book 2.1/Unit 3
Arthur Writes a Story

LANGUAGE SUPPORT

Name_____ Date_____

What Kind of Word Is It?

1. The bell rings. Sam hurries to the door.

   boy   (runs)   fast

2. The little elephant was just a baby. The gigantic elephant was its mother.

   (big)   animal   cared

3. Did he create the story without help?

   reader   (make up)   alone

4. Several children liked the story.

   (many)   clapped   loudly

5. Can't you find your shoes? Did you look beneath the bed?

   hunt   lost   (under)

Grade 2

Language Support/Blackline Master 55 • **Arthur Writes a Story** 99

Reteach, 92   **Practice, 92**   **Extend, 92**   **Language Support, 99**

**GRAMMAR/SPELLING
CONNECTIONS**

See the 5-Day Grammar and Usage Plan on action verbs, pages 289O–289P.

See the 5- Day Spelling Plan on words with silent letters, pages 289Q–289R.

TEACHING TIP

Technology
Encourage children to save their writing periodically as they write on a computer. Remind them always to save their work before shutting off the computer.

Transition Words
Encourage children to use transition words to link their sentences together. Explain that transition words help show what happened first, next, and last. Ask children to explain how to make a sandwich using transition words. As they explain the process, list the transition words used on the board.

**Handwriting
CD-ROM**

Explanatory Writing

Prewrite

WRITE A LIBRARY GUIDE Present this writing assignment: Write a guide that tells how to find a book in your school library. Include any helpful hints you have learned from your librarians.

STEPS-IN-A-PROCESS FLOWCHART Ask students to think of everything they need to do when they look for a book in the library. Have students organize this information by filling in their steps-in-a-process flowcharts about how to use a library.

Draft

USE THE FLOWCHART Students can use their flowcharts to help organize their *How to Use a Library* guides.

Tell students that visualizing themselves going through the process of using the library will help them keep all the steps in order. Encourage them to elaborate with physical details that will help the reader "see" the library.

Revise

SELF-QUESTIONING Ask children to assess their drafts.

• Are my steps clear and in a logical order?

• Will a reader be able to use my guide to find a book at the library?

• What details would improve my *How to Use a Library* guide?

Edit/Proofread

CHECK FOR ERRORS Students should reread their guides for organization, spelling, grammar, and punctuation.

Publish

SHARE GUIDES Invite students to design and produce covers for their guides. Have them make copies to distribute to first-grade classrooms.

How to Use a Library

Tell the librarian the name and the author of the book you are trying to find. The librarian will help you look up a number in a place called the card catalog that shows where the book is. You can look up the book by the title or sometimes you can look up where the book is found by the name of the author.

When you find the number on the card, write it on paper. The librarian will take you to the place where you will see the same number on the book shelf. Sometimes you have to look for the book by finding the author's name on the shelf. When that happens, the librarian will show you where books by your author are. Then you look for the book with the title you want.

Presentation Ideas

SHARE THE LIBRARY GUIDES Have students take turns showing and reading their guides to the class. Invite students to ask questions and make positive commentary or suggestions.

▶ **Speaking/Linguistic**

MULTIMEDIA Discuss with students examples of different ways to present this information and why it would be useful. For example: a student could make an audiocassette recording of the instructions. Have students implement one or more of their examples for use in the school library.

▶ **Viewing/Representing**

Consider students' creative efforts, possibly adding a plus (+) for originality, wit, and imagination.

Scoring Rubric

Excellent	Good	Fair	Unsatisfactory
4: The writer	**3:** The writer	**2:** The writer	**1:** The writer
• presents a clear, organized guide.	• presents a guide in an organized manner.	• presents the steps-in-a-process, but not in logical sequence.	• presents random, unrelated information in a disorganized manner
• provides supporting information and vivid details.	• provides some supporting information and details.	• provides few or vague supporting details.	• presents no supporting details.
• uses advanced vocabulary, language mechanics, stylistic devices.	• uses appropriate vocabulary, language mechanics, and stylistic devices.	• makes some errors in use of vocabulary, language mechanics, and stylistic devices.	• makes errors in use of vocabulary, language mechanics, and stylistic devices.

Incomplete 0: The writer leaves the page blank or fails to respond to the writing task. The student does not address the topic or simply paraphrases the prompt. The response is illegible or incoherent.

Meeting Individual Needs for Writing

EASY	ON-LEVEL	CHALLENGE
Picture and Caption Ask students to draw their favorite scene from *Arthur Writes a Story* and write a sentence about it.	**Homework Assignment** Direct students to pretend that they are Arthur's teacher, Mr. Ratburn. Have them write Arthur's homework assignment.	**Song** Have students write a song about Arthur the aardvark from *Arthur Writes a Story*. Ask students to explain how Arthur wrote his story. Invite students to perform their songs for the class.

Listening and Speaking

LISTENING Have children
- listen for details that will help in finding books.
- determine if there is an order to the process.
- maintain eye contact.

SPEAKING Have children
- speak clearly and at a volume that others can hear from across the room.
- pause, and include eye contact when reading the report.
- make the report more exciting by varying the intonation in the voice.

LANGUAGE SUPPORT

 Ask ESL students to work with English-fluent partners at the drafting stage. Have them read and comment on each other's drafts. The ESL student can make content suggestions and the English-fluent student can help provide language support as needed.

 Invite students to include their stories or another writing project in their portfolios.

PORTFOLIO

5 Day Grammar and Usage Plan

LANGUAGE SUPPORT

ESL Assign an action verb to each child and have the child act it out. Others have to try to identify the action verb. Model it first.

DAILY LANGUAGE ACTIVITIES

Write each day's activities on the board, or use **Transparency 11.** For each sentence, have children fill in an action verb. Sample answers are given.

Day 1

1. Arthur _____ his bike to school. rode
2. Mr. Ratburn _____ to the class. talked
3. Arthur _____ a question. asked

Day 2

1. Later, Arthur _____ his story. wrote
2. Arthur _____ the lost puppy. found
3. Buster _____ his story to Arthur. showed

Day 3

1. Arthur _____ his story to D.W. read
2. D.W. _____ to Arthur's story. listened
3. Brian _____ down the street. lived

Day 4

1. Arthur _____ for library books. looked
2. The children _____ about their stories. talked
3. Arthur _____ his story into a song. turned

Day 5

1. Arthur _____ to his song. danced
2. Mother _____ Arthur's song. liked
3. Arthur _____ his friends about his pet business. told

Daily Language Transparency 11

DAY 1 Introduce the Concept

Oral Warm-Up Read this sentence aloud: *Arthur writes a story.* Ask children, "What does Arthur do?" Have a child identify the action word in his or her answer.

Introduce Action Verbs Explain that an action word often tells what someone or something is doing. Give other examples of action words and present:

> **Action Verbs**
>
> An **action verb** is a word that shows action.

Present the Daily Language Activity. Then have children write the three sentences below and underline the action verb in each sentence.

- Josh <u>reads</u> the story.
- Jan <u>sings</u> a song.
- The class <u>dances</u> to the music.

WRITING Assign the daily Writing Prompt on page 258C.

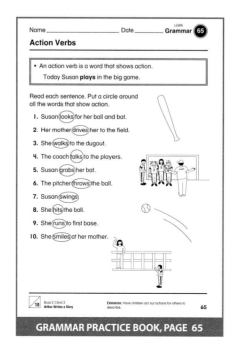

GRAMMAR PRACTICE BOOK, PAGE 65

DAY 2 Teach the Concept

Review Action Verbs Ask a child to explain how to recognize an action verb.

More Action Verbs Write the following examples on the board: *Tim likes cake. Jan thinks about the story.* Point out that *likes* and *thinks* are action verbs. Explain that verbs can express both actions that you can see and those you can't. Present:

> **Action Verbs**
>
> Some action verbs tell about actions that are hard to see.

Present the Daily Language Activity. Then have children write the following sentences and underline the action verbs in each sentence.

- Dawn <u>hears</u> the song.
- Ben <u>knows</u> the story.
- David <u>likes</u> the puppy.

 WRITING Assign the daily Writing Prompt on page 258C.

GRAMMAR PRACTICE BOOK, PAGE 66

Action Verbs

DAY 3 Review and Practice

Learn from the Literature Review action verbs. Read the sentence on page 274 of *Arthur Writes a Story:*

> **Arthur hurried to the library.**

Ask children to identify the action verb in the sentence and to explain their answer.

Identify Action Verbs Present the Daily Language Activity. Then have children find other examples of action verbs in *Arthur Writes a Story*. List and discuss their findings on the chalkboard. Have children use these examples in their own sentences.

 Assign the daily Writing Prompt on page 258D.

DAY 4 Review and Practice

Review Action Verbs Help children write a class story and have them underline the action verbs in the story. Present the Daily Language Activity and have children supply an action verb in each sentence.

Mechanics and Usage Before children begin the daily Writing Prompt, review the following:

Abbreviations

- An **abbreviation** is a short form of a word.
- Most titles of people are abbreviations.
- An abbreviation begins with a capital letter and ends with a period.

Write the following sentence on the board and ask children to identify the abbreviation.

- Mr. Ratburn is Arthur's teacher.

Assign the daily Writing Prompt on page 258D.

DAY 5 Assess and Reteach

Assess Use the Daily Language Activity and page 69 of the **Grammar Practice Book** for assessment.

Reteach Write the following poem on the board and have children pantomime as you read it.

- Stretch tall, bend low
- Grab an ankle, touch a toe
- Clap hands, hop twice
- Run in place
- And say, "How nice."

Reread the poem and have children identify the action verbs. Display the words on the word wall.

Use page 70 of the **Grammar Practice Book** for additional reteaching.

Assign the daily Writing Prompt on page 258D.

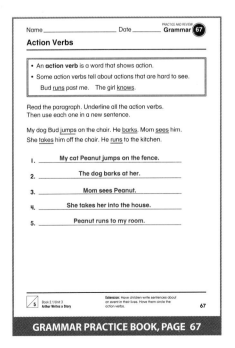

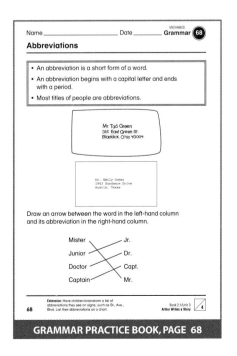

Read each sentence. Write the verb in each sentence on the line.

1. Jason runs to the ball park. — runs
2. He throws the first ball. — throws
3. Claire hits it hard. — hits
4. Claire reaches first base. — reaches
5. Claire looks at home plate. — looks
6. She tries to go home. — tries
7. Jason tags Claire. — tags
8. Jason and Claire play well. — play

GRAMMAR PRACTICE BOOK, PAGE 67

GRAMMAR PRACTICE BOOK, PAGE 68

GRAMMAR PRACTICE BOOK, PAGE 69

GRAMMAR PRACTICE BOOK, PAGE 70

5 Day Spelling Plan

LANGUAGE SUPPORT

Make letter cards for the letters *l*, *b*, *k*, *w*, and *gh*. Have students take turns saying a Spelling Word and placing a letter card against the identical silent letter in the word.

DICTATION SENTENCES

Spelling Words

1. He can jump high.
2. I know a cute baby.
3. She used half of the clay.
4. He wrote to me.
5. My thumb is red.
6. You can pet the lamb.
7. I hurt my knee.
8. I hurt my right arm.
9. He made a knot.
10. We can write to her.

Challenge Words

11. I decided to go.
12. The book is important.
13. We went to the library.
14. He saw a planet.
15. She is proud of me.

Assess Prior Knowledge

Use the Dictation Sentences at left and **Spelling Practice Book** page 65 for the pretest. Allow students to correct their own papers. If students have trouble, have partners give each other a midweek test on Day 3. Students who require a modified list may be tested on the first five words.

Spelling Words		Challenge Words
1. **high**	6. lamb	11. **decided**
2. **know**	7. knee	12. **important**
3. half	8. right	13. **library**
4. **wrote**	9. knot	14. **planet**
5. thumb	10. write	15. **proud**

*Note: Words in **dark type** are from the story.*

Word Study

On page 66 of the **Spelling Practice Book** are word study steps and an at-home activity.

Sort and Spell Words

Write the words *lamb*, *thumb*, *knot*, *wrote*, and *right* on the chalkboard. Have students read the words and identify the silent letter or letters in each word.

Ask students to read aloud the ten spelling words before sorting them according to the spelling pattern.

Silent *l*	Silent *k*	Silent *gh*
walk	know	high
	knee	right
Silent *b*	knot	
thumb	**Silent *w***	
lamb	wrote	
	write	

Word Wall

Have students look through newspaper articles for new words containing the silent *l*, *b*, *k*, *w*, and *gh* and add them to the classroom word wall, underlining the spelling pattern in each word.

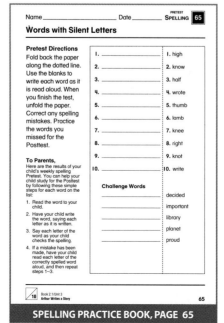

SPELLING PRACTICE BOOK, PAGE 65

WORD STUDY STEPS AND ACTIVITY, PAGE 66

SPELLING PRACTICE BOOK, PAGE 67

Words with Silent Letters

DAY 3 — Practice and Extend

Word Meaning: Endings Remind students that the past tense of a verb (action word) is usually formed by adding *-ed*. Tell them that when the base word ends with a single consonant, they must double the consonant before adding *-ed*—for example, *stop/stopped*. Have students form the past tense of *knot, tap, clip, pop,* and *slam*.

Glossary Review the pronunciation key in the Glossary. Have partners:

- write each Challenge Word.

- look up the pronunciation for each word in the Glossary. (Remind students that words with endings, such as *decided*, are listed in their base-word form.)

- use the pronunciation key to say the words aloud.

DAY 4 — Proofread and Write

Proofread Sentences Write these sentences on the chalkboard, including the misspelled words. Ask students to proofread, circling incorrect spellings and writing the correct spellings. There are two spelling errors in each sentence.

> I ⟨rote⟩ it the ⟨rite⟩ way. **(wrote, right)**
>
> I hurt my ⟨nee⟩ and my ⟨thum⟩. **(knee, thumb)**

Have students create additional sentences with errors for partners to correct.

 Writing Have students use as many spelling words as possible in the daily Writing Prompt on page 258D. Remind students to proofread their writing for errors in spelling, grammar, and punctuation.

DAY 5 — Assess and Reteach

Assess Students' Knowledge Use page 70 of the **Spelling Practice Book** or the Dictation Sentences on page 289Q for the posttest.

Personal Word List If students have trouble with any words in the lesson, have them create a personal list of troublesome words in their journals. Have students write a definition for each word.

Students should refer to their word lists during later writing activities.

Worksheet — Page 68

Name_____ Date_____ PRACTICE AND EXTEND SPELLING **68**

Words with Silent Letters

| high | half | thumb | knee | knot |
| know | wrote | lamb | right | write |

Write a spelling word to complete each sentence.

1. Help me untie the ___knot___
2. I will give you ___half___ of my apple.
3. A baby sheep is called a ___lamb___.
4. Do you ___know___ the answer?
5. Your ___thumb___ is on your hand.
6. You can bend your leg at the ___knee___
7. The opposite of **left** is ___right___
8. The opposite of **low** is ___high___
9. I will ___write___ a letter to my mom.
10. I ___wrote___ a letter to my brother.

Word Builder
Be a word builder. Add the ending *-ed* to the word. First, double the final consonant.
knot + t + ed = ___knotted___

Challenge Extension: Have children complete this sentence: I think the library is important because

68 | Book 2.1/Unit 3 — Arthur Writes a Story | 10

SPELLING PRACTICE BOOK, PAGE 68

Worksheet — Page 69

Name_____ Date_____ PROOFREAD AND WRITE SPELLING **69**

Words with Silent Letters

Proofreading Activity
There are six spelling mistakes in the story below. Circle each misspelled word. Write the words correctly on the lines below.

One day a first grader in my school had a ⟨kot⟩ in his shoelace. He was ⟨haf⟩ my size. He asked me to help him. I didn't ⟨noe⟩ the ⟨rit⟩ way to get the knot out. I tried pulling it, but that didn't work. I took his shoe off and set it on my ⟨nee⟩. Then I could hold the shoe with my ⟨thum⟩ and undo the knot with my fingers. Afterwards, his mother wrote my mother a note saying that I was a great kid.

1. ___knot___   2. ___half___   3. ___know___
4. ___right___   5. ___knee___   6. ___thumb___

Writing Activity
Write about a time when someone helped you. Use four of your spelling words. Circle the spelling words you use.

_____
_____
_____
_____
_____

10 | Book 2.1/Unit 3 — Arthur Writes a Story | 69

SPELLING PRACTICE BOOK, PAGE 69

Worksheet — Page 70

Name_____ Date_____ POSTTEST SPELLING **70**

Words with Silent Letters

Look at the words in each set. One word in each set is spelled right. Use a pencil to color in the circle in front of that word. Before you begin, look at the sample sets of words. Sample A has been done for you. Do Sample B by yourself. When you are sure you know what to do, you may go on with the rest of the page.

Sample A
- (A) sihg
- (B) siep
- ● sigh
- (D) sighe

Sample B
- (E) curri
- ● curl
- (G) kurl
- (H) curlo

1.
- (A) hih
- (B) hihg
- ● high
- (D) hihgt

2.
- (E) kno
- ● know
- (G) khow
- (H) noo

3.
- (A) haf
- ● half
- (C) haff
- (D) havf

4.
- (E) wote
- (F) roate
- (G) whote
- ● wrote

5.
- ● thumb
- (B) thum
- (C) tfum
- (D) thumgh

6.
- ● lamb
- (F) lamm
- (G) lamme
- (H) labm

7.
- (A) kne
- (B) nea
- (C) nei
- ● knee

8.
- (E) kot
- (F) knoght
- ● knot
- (H) khot

9.
- (A) riyte
- ● right
- (C) riht
- (D) ritgh

10.
- (E) wite
- ● write
- (G) rwite
- (H) wrrite

70 | Book 2.1/Unit 3 — Arthur Writes a Story | 10

SPELLING PRACTICE BOOK, PAGE 70

Concept
- Special Abilities

Comprehension
- Fantasy and Reality

Phonics
- /ər/er

Vocabulary
- climbed
- couple
- drifted
- half
- message
- notice

Anthology

Best Wishes, Ed

Selection Summary A penguin learns how to use his special ability to help others. They, in turn, help him find the friends he has lost.

Rhyme applies to phonics

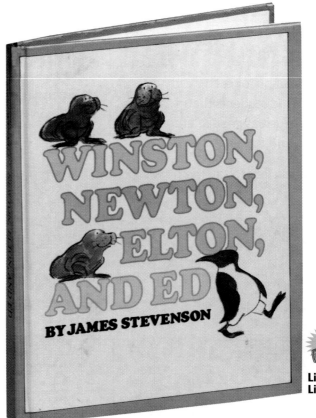

Listening Library

INSTRUCTIONAL pages 292–319

About the Author/Illustrator Award-winning author/illustrator James Stevenson began writing and drawing as a child. He believes that movies and comic books have helped him learn to tell stories with more than just words.

Same Concept, Skills and Vocabulary!

Leveled Books

EASY
Lesson on pages 319A and 319D
DECODABLE

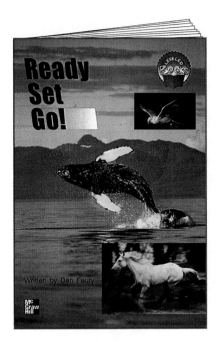

INDEPENDENT
Lesson on pages 319B and 319D
🏠 *Take-Home version available*

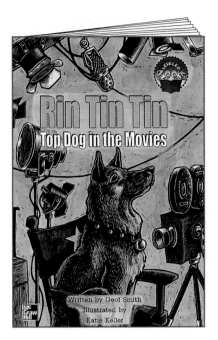

CHALLENGE
Lesson on pages 319C and 319D

Leveled Practice

EASY
Reteach, 93–100 Blackline masters with reteaching opportunities for each assessed skill

INDEPENDENT/ON-LEVEL
Practice, 93–100 Workbook with Take-Home stories and practice opportunities for each assessed skill and story comprehension

CHALLENGE
Extend, 93–100 Blackline masters that offer challenge activities for each assessed skill

Quizzes Prepared by 📖 **Accelerated Reader**

WORKSTATION Activities

Social Studies ... Antarctica, *296*

Science............ Animal Talk, *302*

Math............... Addition, *306*

Language Arts .. Read Aloud, *290E*

Writing........... Write a Guide, *316*

Cultural
Perspectives ..... The Inuit, *308*

Research
and Inquiry ...... Find Out More, *317*

 Internet
Activities........ www.mhschool.com/reading

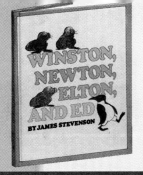

Suggested Lesson Planner

READING AND LANGUAGE ARTS	DAY **1** *Focus on Reading and Skills*	DAY **2** *Read the Literature*
● **Phonics Daily Routines**	Daily Routine: **Segmenting,** 290H **CD-ROM**	Daily Phonics Routine: **Blending,** 292A Phonics **CD-ROM**

● **Phonological Awareness**
 	
 ● **Phonics /ər/er**
 	
 ● **Comprehension**
 	
 ● **Vocabulary**
 	
 ● **Study Skills**
 	
 ● **Listening, Speaking, Viewing, Representing**
	Read Aloud: Poem, 290E
	 "Penguins"
	
	 ☑ **Develop Phonological Awareness,** 290F
	
	 ☑ **Introduce /ər/er,** 290G–290H
	 Teaching Chart 78
	 Reteach, Practice, Extend, 93
	 Phonics/Phonemic Awareness Practice Book, 73–76
	
	 Apply /ər/ er, 290/291
	 "The Visit"
	
	  Intervention Program
		Build Background, 292A
		 Develop Oral Language
		
		 Vocabulary, 292B–292C
		 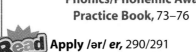
		 climbed drifted message
		 couple half notice
		 Word Building Manipulative Cards
		 Teaching Chart 79
		 Reteach, Practice, Extend, 94
		
		 Read the Selection, 292–315
		 Comprehension
		 ☑ /ər/er
		 ☑ Fantasy and Reality
		
		 Genre: Fantasy, 293
		
		 Cultural Perspectives, 308
		
		  Intervention Program

● **Curriculum Connections**	**Link** Science, 290E	**Link** Social Studies, 292A
● **Writing**	**Writing Prompt:** This story is about talking animals. What kind of voice do you think Ed the penguin has? Describe it.	**Writing Prompt:** Imagine how storybook animals learn to read and write. What kind of school do penguins have? What does it look like? Who is the teacher? Write about it. **Journal Writing,** Quick-Write, 315
● **Grammar**	**Introduce the Concept: Present-Tense Verbs,** 319O Daily Language Activity: Change past-tense verbs to present tense. **Grammar Practice Book,** 71	**Teach the Concept: Present-Tense Verbs,** 319O Daily Language Activity: Write present tense verbs correctly. **Grammar Practice Book,** 72
● **Spelling /ər/er**	**Pretest: Words with /ər/er,** 319Q **Spelling Practice Book,** 71, 72	**Teach the Pattern: Words with /ər/er,** 319Q **Spelling Practice Book,** 73

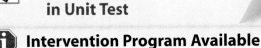
DAY 3 — Read the Literature

Daily Phonics **Routine:**
Word Building, 317

Phonics **CD-ROM**

Rereading for Fluency, 314

Story Questions and Activities, 316–317
Reteach, Practice, Extend, 95

Study Skill, 318
☑ Reference Sources
Teaching Chart 80
Reteach, Practice, Extend, 96

Test Power, 319

 Read the Leveled Books, 319A–319D
Guided Reading
☑ /ər/*er*
☑ Fantasy and Reality
☑ Instructional Vocabulary

 Intervention Program

Activity Social Studies, 296; Science, 302

Writing Prompt: What is it like to live in a very cold place? Describe a day on a frozen island.

Explanatory Writing, 319M
Prewrite, Draft

Practice and Write: Present-Tense Verbs, 319P
Daily Language Activity: Write present tense verbs correctly.
Grammar Practice Book, 73

Practice and Extend: Words with /ər/*er*, 319R

Spelling Practice Book, 74

DAY 4 — Build Skills

Daily Phonics **Routine:**
Fluency, 319F

Phonics **CD-ROM**

 Read the Leveled Books and the Self-Selected Books

☑ **Review /ər/*er*,** 319E–319F
Teaching Chart 81
Reteach, Practice, Extend, 97
Language Support, 105
Phonics/Phonemic Awareness
Practice Book, 73–76

☑ **Cumulative Review,** 319G–319H
Teaching Chart 82
Reteach, Practice, Extend, 98
Language Support, 106
Phonics/Phonemic Awareness
Practice Book, 73–76

Minilessons, 297, 301, 305, 311, 313

 Intervention Program

---

Activity Math, 306

Writing Prompt: Think about the different animals you are familiar with. Which ones are friendly with other animals? Explain.

Explanatory Writing, 319M
Revise

Meeting Individual Needs for Writing, 319N

Practice and Write: Present-Tense Verbs, 319P
Daily Language Activity: Write present tense verbs correctly.
Grammar Practice Book, 74

Practice and Write: Words with /ər/*er*, 319R

Spelling Practice Book, 75

DAY 5 — Build Skills

Daily Phonics **Routine:**
Writing, 319H

Phonics **CD-ROM**

Read Self-Selected Books

☑ **Introduce Cause and Effect,** 319I–319J
Teaching Chart 83
Reteach, Practice, Extend, 99
Language Support, 107

☑ **Review Context Clues,** 319K–319L
Teaching Chart 84
Reteach, Practice, Extend, 100
Language Support, 108

Listening, Speaking, Viewing, Representing, 319N
Design a Cover
Give a Lecture

Minilessons, 297, 301, 305, 311, 313

Intervention Program

Writing Prompt: How do different animals get around? Do they fly, walk, swim, or hop? Describe two animals and how they get around.

Explanatory Writing, 319M
Edit/Proofread, Publish

Assess and Reteach: Present-Tense Verbs, 319P
Daily Language Activity: Write present tense verbs correctly.
Grammar Practice Book, 75, 76

Assess and Reteach: Words with /ər/*er*, 319R

Spelling Practice Book, 76

Language Arts

Read Aloud

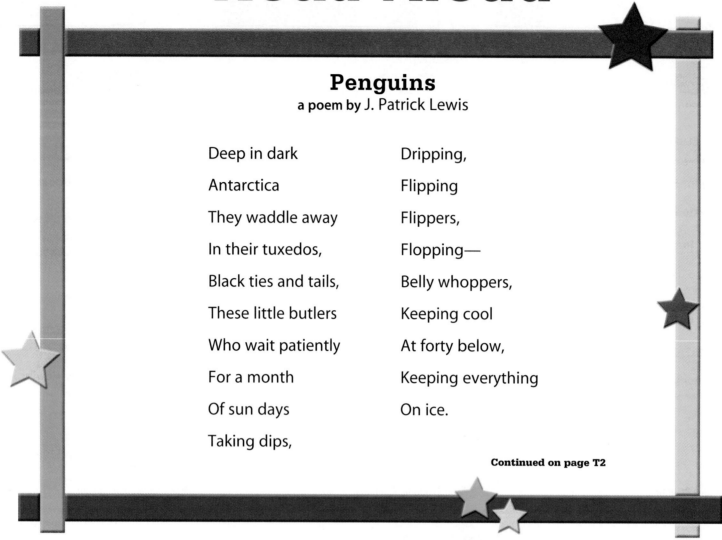

Penguins
a poem by J. Patrick Lewis

Deep in dark

Antarctica

They waddle away

In their tuxedos,

Black ties and tails,

These little butlers

Who wait patiently

For a month

Of sun days

Taking dips,

Dripping,

Flipping

Flippers,

Flopping—

Belly whoppers,

Keeping cool

At forty below,

Keeping everything

On ice.

Continued on page T2

Oral Comprehension

LISTENING AND SPEAKING Encourage children to think about comparing and contrasting by reading aloud this poem about penguins. When you have finished, ask students: What did the poet compare penguins to in this poem? Then ask students: In what ways are penguins like butlers? How are penguins and butlers different?

GENRE STUDY: POETRY Discuss the literary devices and techniques used in *Penguins*.

- Discuss how the poet uses assonance, the repetition of vowel sounds, in the poem. Have children identify sections of the poem that incorporate assonance.

- Have children locate Antarctica in an atlas or on the globe. Discuss the climate in Antarctica. Ask, "What does the poem tell you about Antarctica?"

- Have children picture the penguins in their minds. Ask children to describe what the penguins are doing. Ask, "Which words from the poem help you picture the penguins in your mind?"

Activity Encourage children to create a funny character based on the movements of a penguin. Help them visualize such a character by asking them to walk as a penguin walks, or to move their heads and arms as a penguin might. Have children perform their characters by role-playing a short improvisational scene. ▶ **Kinesthetic**

Develop Phonological Awareness

Blend Sounds

MATERIALS
- Phonics Picture Posters

Teach Tell children they are going to play a sound game. You will say the sounds of a word and they will put the sounds together to tell you the word. Demonstrate by saying: /ō/-/v/-/ər/. *If I put the sounds together, what word do I get?* (over)

Practice Have children continue blending the sounds to say the word. Use the following list of words: *corner, star, never, bird, fork, winter,* and *bread.* You may wish to use the Phonics Picture posters (picture side only) with the lesson.

Segment Sounds

MATERIALS
- Toy hammer, or a picture of a hammer

Teach Tell children they are going to listen for the /ər/ sound in words. You will say a word and they will repeat it. Then they are to say the word again, sound by sound. Demonstrate by holding up a toy hammer and saying: *Hammer,* /h/-/a/-/m/-/ər/. Have children repeat the sounds.

Practice If available, hold up pictures or objects for the words below. Have children listen for the /ər/ sound as they say the word, then say each sound in the word: *water, river, tiger, feather, runner, paper, camper,* and *hiker.*

Delete Sounds

crack-rack

Teach Tell children you are going to say a word, and they should listen carefully. Say: *crack. Now I'll say some of the sounds in the word . . .* /r/-/a/-/k/. *What sound did I leave off?* (/k/) *If I leave off the /k/ sound in crack, the new sound is* rack.

Practice Have children delete the sounds in parentheses from the words below.

hand (h)	dresser (ər)	driver (ər)
pail (l)	planter (ər)	sneaker (ər)

INFORMAL ASSESSMENT Observe children as they blend, segment, and delete sounds. If children have difficulty, see Alternate Teaching Strategies on p. T69.

 **OBJECTIVES**

Children will:

- identify /ər/er.
- blend and read /ər/er words.

....

MATERIALS
- **Teaching Chart 78**
- letter and variant vowel cards from the **Word Building Manipulative Cards**

Skills Finder	
/ər/ er	
Introduce	B1: 290G-H
Review	B1: 319E-F, 319G-H; B2: 180G-H, 211E-F
Test	B1: Unit 3
Maintain	B2: 55, 257

SPELLING/PHONICS CONNECTIONS

Words with /ər/er: See 5-Day Spelling Plan, pages 319Q–319R.

TEACHING TIP

SEGMENTING Review that the sounds /ər/, /ən/, and /əl/ are formed with the letters *er, en,* and *le.* Write *brother, happen,* and *giggle* on the chalkboard. Invite children to circle the letters in each word that form the /ər/, /ən/, and /əl/ sounds and to read each word aloud.

Introduce /ər/er

TEACH

Identify /ər/er Introduce the /ər/er sound. Tell children they will learn to read words with the letters *er* which stand for the /ər/ sound.

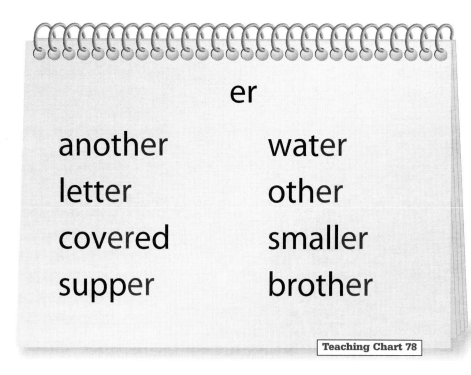

er

another   water

letter   other

covered   smaller

supper   brother

Teaching Chart 78

BLENDING
Model and Guide Practice with Words

- Display **Teaching Chart 78** for /ər/er words and model the sound. Have children repeat the /ər/er sound as you point to the letters at the top.

- Have children blend the sounds with you as you run your finger under the word *another.* a n o th er

- Have a volunteer fill in the letters that make the /ər/ sound in the word *letter.* Have children blend the word.

Use the Word in Context
- Have volunteers create sentences using the word. Example: *I need another ten minutes to study.*

Repeat the Procedure
- Follow the same procedure asking volunteers to fill in the rest of the missing letters and blend the words on the chart.

Identify /ən/ and /əl/
- Introduce the /ən/, and /əl/ sounds. Write these words on the board and read them aloud: *eleven, oven, candle* and *apple.* Point to the letters *en* and explain that these make the /ən/ sound in *eleven.* Repeat the process with the word *candle.* Ask a volunteer to underline the letters that form the /ən/ sound in *oven* and the /əl/ sound in *apple.*

 **PRACTICE**

WORD BUILDING
Build /ər/ Words

ONE

Have children use letter cards to add *er* to words. Build the word *high*, asking children to repeat after you. Add the letters *er* and ask children what the new word means. Ask them to change the following verbs into nouns: *walk, play, work,* and *jump.*

▶ **Kinesthetic/Linguistic**

h i g h e r

ASSESS/CLOSE

Read and Build a Word Wall of /ər/ Words

To assess children's ability to build and read /ər/ words, observe them as they work on the Practice activity. Ask each child to read and spell aloud two words from the practice list. Have the class build a Word Wall of /ər/ words. Have children read the rhyme on pages 290–291.

ADDITIONAL PHONICS RESOURCES

Phonics/Phonemic Awareness Practice Book,
pages 73–76

McGraw-Hill School
TECHNOLOGY

Phonics **CD-ROM**

activities for Practice with Blending and Segmenting

Meeting Individual Needs for Phonics

EASY	ON-LEVEL	CHALLENGE

Reteach, 93

Practice, 93

Extend, 93

Daily Routines

DAY 1 **Segmenting** Write a list of /ər/ words on the chalkboard. Ask children to copy the list and circle the letters that stand for the /ər/ sound.

DAY 2 **Blending** Write the spelling of each sound in *other* as you say it. Have children blend the sounds together to read the word. Repeat with *river*.

DAY 3 **Word Building** Have children work with partners. One child says the first syllable of a word that contains the /ər/ sound. The other child completes the word with the letters *er*. Then the partners switch roles.

DAY 4 **Fluency** Write the following words on the board: *weather, bother, feather, sweater*. Point to each word and ask children to blend the sounds silently. Ask a volunteer to read aloud each word.

DAY 5 **Writing** Have children work in small groups to write about *Best Wishes, Ed* using *er* words.

**OBJECTIVES**

Children will blend and
read /ər/er words.

Apply **/ər/er**

> **The Visit**
>
> A penguin went to visit my brother,
> Then he asked to meet my mother.
> He stayed with me and read my letters,
> Ate my fish and wore my sweaters.
> He only left when he discovered
> That I had another brother.

Anthology pages 290–291

Read and Build Fluency

READ THE POEM Children should listen closely for
the /ər/ sound as they follow along as you read "The
Visit." Model fluent reading by expressively reading the
poem aloud. Then, for auditory modeling, ask them to
read the poem aloud in unison.

REREAD FOR FLUENCY Encourage fluent
reading by engaging in a choral reading with the
children. As you read the poem aloud together, gradu-
ally fade your voice back as children become more fluent. Increase your volume if needed to keep the children
on track. Remind children to read the lines as if they
were telling the story to a friend.

Dictate and Spell

DICTATE WORDS Say the word *brother*.
Segment it into its individual sounds. Say *brother*
again and use it in a sentence, for example, "My brother
baked brownies." Encourage children to pronounce the
word *brother*. Have them write the letter or letter patterns for each sound until the word is complete. Repeat
the process with *mother, letter, sweater, discover*.
Continue the process using words other than those in
the poem, such as, *water, another,* and *supper*.

 **Intervention** **Skills Intervention Guide,**
for direct instruction and extra practice of /ər/er

Build Background

Social Studies

Concept: Special Abilities

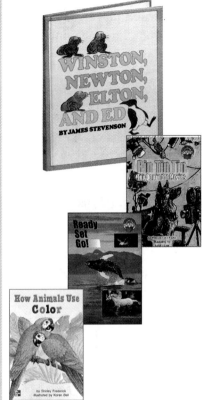

Evaluate Prior Knowledge

CONCEPT: SPECIAL ABILITIES Ask children to share what they know about special abilities. Have them list some people, such as athletes, artists, or actors whose skill they admire.

  MAKE A WORD WEB Help children create a word web to record the different kinds of special abilities that people have.

▶ **Linguistic/Spatial**

baking pies

playing the violin

writing poetry

special abilities

painting pictures

hitting home runs

being funny

> **Graphic Organizer 29**

  WRITE A FAN LETTER Have children write a letter to someone they admire. The person may be famous or a friend. Encourage children to tell the person why they admire him or her.

Develop Oral Language

MAKE A PUPPET Have children make

ESL hand puppets by drawing faces on socks with laundry markers. Children can use their puppets to act out a special ability, such as playing ball or painting a picture. Ask children what activities their puppets are doing and how they learned to do them.

▶ **Kinesthetic/Linguistic**

DAILY Phonics **ROUTINES**

DAY 2 **Blending** Write the spelling of each sound in *other* as you say it. Have children blend the sounds together to read the word. Repeat with *river*.

Phonics **CD-ROM**

LANGUAGE SUPPORT

Additional support for building background may be found in the **Language Support Book** on pages 100–103.

Children will use context and structural clues to determine the meanings of vocabulary words.

Definitions

climbed (p. 313) moved upward or over, across, or through something

couple (p. 313) two things that are the same or go together in some way

half (p. 297) either of two equal parts

message (p. 302) information sent to someone

drifted (p. 298) floated

notice (p. 295) pay attention to

Story Words

These words from the selection may be unfamiliar. Before children read, have them check the meanings and pronunciations of the words in the Glossary, beginning on page 398, or in a dictionary.

• penguin, p. 294

• tern, p. 301

• iceberg, p. 302

climbed
couple
half
message
drifted
notice

Vocabulary

Teach Vocabulary in Context

Identify Vocabulary Words   Display **Teaching Chart 79** and read the passage with children. Have volunteers circle each vocabulary word and underline other words that are clues to its meaning.

Penny's Note

1. Penny the penguin (climbed) over a big pile of snow to get to the water. 2. She caught a (couple) of fish for lunch. 3. Penny divided the fish into two equal parts so she could give (half) to her friend Harry. 4. She wrote a (message) to Harry, telling him to swim over for lunch. 5. Then she put it in a bottle and watched as it (drifted) across the water. 6. Penny hoped that Harry was paying attention and would (notice) the bottle.

Teaching Chart 79

Discuss Meanings   Ask questions like these to help clarify word meanings:

• When you're at the top of something, have you climbed or fallen to get there?

• If you take a couple of apples, how many do you take?

• If you have drifted across the lake, have you rowed or floated?

• If I give you half my cookie, is my piece as big as yours?

• What are some ways you send a message?

• What animals did you notice at the zoo?

Practice

Create Riddles  Partners can take turns choosing vocabulary cards from a pile. The one who has chosen a card can make up a riddle using the word on his or her card. The other child must try to solve it. ▶ **Oral/Linguistic**

Word Building Manipulative Cards

Write a Note Have students use the vocabulary words to write a note describing a day spent at a mountain lake. Have children refer to the Glossary as needed. ▶ **Linguistic/Intrapersonal**

Assess Vocabulary

Identify Word Meaning in Context Ask each child to write a context sentence for one of the vocabulary words. Then have them exchange papers and draw a picture that represents their partner's sentence. Ask each child to write and illustrate at least three sentences.

SPELLING/VOCABULARY CONNECTIONS
See Spelling Challenge Words, pages 319Q.

LANGUAGE SUPPORT

See the **Language Support Book**, pages 100–103, for teaching suggestions for Vocabulary.

Vocabulary PuzzleMaker

Provides vocabulary activities.

Meeting Individual Needs for Vocabulary

EASY	ON-LEVEL	ON-LEVEL	CHALLENGE

EASY

Name _____ Date _____ **Reteach** 94

Vocabulary

Choose a word from the box to complete each sentence. Write the word on the line.

climbed   couple   drifted   half   message   notice

1. My brother gave me ___half___ of his orange.

2. Bruce and Will ___climbed___ up the hill.

3. The sailboat ___drifted___ away in the wind.

4. Kelly read the ___message___ from the teacher out loud.

5. Will she ___notice___ that a storm is coming?

6. We have a ___couple___ of hours to play before dark.

At Home: Ask children to write a new sentence for each word in the box.

Book 2.1/Unit 3
Best Wishes, Ed

94

ON-LEVEL

Name _____ Date _____ **Practice** 94

Vocabulary

Choose words from the box to finish the letter. Write the words on the lines.

climbed   couple   drifted   half   message   notice

Dear Louis,

Thanks for sending me the ___message___ about the camping trip. I have been to Mountain Park. I ___climbed___ to the top of the mountain with my mother. It took us a ___couple___ of hours. We were very high up. A cloud ___drifted___ by right next to us. Coming down was easy. It took us only ___half___ as long as going up. My legs got very tired. But I didn't even ___notice___ it until we stopped. I hope we can climb again next summer.

Your friend,
Pete

At Home: Ask children to write the message that Louis might have written to Pete about the camping trip.

Book 2.1/Unit 3
Best Wishes, Ed

94

ON-LEVEL

A Message from the Sun

That night I slept under a big tree. In the morning, I felt someone tap my fingers. It was the sun!

"Good morning," the sun said.

"Do you see now why I set early in winter? It is so people like you will get the sleep they need!"

"Thank you!" I said. I happily walked home. The sun kept me warm the whole way.

At Home: Talk with children about times of the year and when the sun sets during those times. How does the sun affect our days?

94a

CHALLENGE

Name _____ Date _____ **Extend** 94

Vocabulary

Write a sentence to tell what each word means. Sample answers are shown.

1. climbed ___Climbed means moved up.___

2. couple ___Couple means a pair of people, animals, or objects.___

3. drifted ___Drifted means to float away.___

4. half ___Half means one of two equal parts.___

5. message ___Message means information that should be sent to someone.___

6. notice ___Notice means to see something.___

Choose one of the words. Draw a picture to show what it means.

At Home: Create a board for children to write and pin messages to.

Book 2.1/Unit 3
Best Wishes, Ed

94

Comprehension

Prereading Strategies

PREVIEW AND PREDICT Have children read the title. Then take a **picture walk** through the selection and ask children these questions:

- Where does this story take place?
- What will the story be about?
- Do you think this story is about real penguins? Why or why not? (No. They act like people.) *Genre*

Have children record their predictions about the story and the main character.

PREDICTIONS	WHAT HAPPENED
One penguin gets separated from his friends.	
He meets a bird and a whale.	

SET PURPOSES Have children ask themselves questions about the selection. For example:

- Why does the penguin write things in the snow?
- What will happen to him?

READ TOGETHER

☀ Meet James Stevenson

James Stevenson began writing and drawing as a child. He loved to watch movies and read comic books. He says that both activities influenced the books he writes for children.

He says, "I think that my experience and creative mind have been formed by movies and comic books. I like to write. I like to draw. I like to paint. And in writing picture books I found a way to tell a story without using just words."

When asked if he prefers drawing to writing, he said, "I think that drawing is the more childlike and natural. When you're a little kid, you grab crayons, you don't grab the typewriter. I think drawing is a little more fun than writing, but whether it's more satisfying by the time you're old, I don't know."

292

Meeting Individual Needs • Grouping Suggestions for Strategic Reading

EASY	ON-LEVEL	CHALLENGE
Read Together Read the story with children and then have them use the **Listening Library.** Help children make and use a Fantasy and Reality chart. Comprehension and Intervention prompts offer additional help with decoding and comprehension.	**Guided Instruction** Preview the story words on page 293. Read the story with children, using the Comprehension questions. Have them make and use Fantasy and Reality charts to record the events of the story. You may wish to have children use the **Listening Library,** when they reread the story.	**Read Independently** Have children set purposes before they read. Remind children that distinguishing between fantasy and reality can help them understand the story. Have them complete a Fantasy and Reality chart. After reading, have children use the chart to retell the events.

BEST WISHES, ED

by JAMES STEVENSON

293

Comprehension

☑ **Phonics** Apply /ər/*er* Words

☑ **Apply Fantasy and Reality**

STRATEGIC READING Before reading the story, let's make a Fantasy and Reality chart. This chart will help us figure out which events could happen in real life and which could not.

FANTASY	REALITY

1 Look at the picture on page 293. What can you tell about where the story takes place? (There is a lot of ice and snow. It must be a very cold place.) *Setting*

Genre

Fantasy

Tell children that in fantasies:

• the events probably could not really happen in real life.

• the setting may take place in an imaginary world.

• the main characters may be animals that act like real people.

Activity After reading *Best Wishes, Ed*, place children in teams of three or four. Provide each group with a two-column chart labeled *Same/Different*. Ask children to compare *Best Wishes, Ed* to *Arthur Writes a Story*. Allow groups to share their findings with the class.

293

LANGUAGE SUPPORT

This chart is available as a blackline master in the **Language Support Book**.

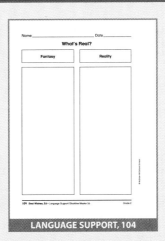

LANGUAGE SUPPORT, 104

Comprehension

② **FANTASY AND REALITY** What are some things the author tells us on this page that are make-believe, or fantasy?

MODEL The author tells us that the penguins in this story live on a big island of ice. Since the ones I saw at the zoo also live on pieces of ice, I believe that this could be true. The author also tells us that these penguins call each other by name and do things people do. I think these penguins are more like people than animals, so I would say this story is fantasy.

Ed lived on a big island of ice
with Betty, Freddy, Al,
and a lot of other penguins.
② Every day they had fun
throwing snowballs
and sliding on the ice.

294

Fluency

READ WITH EXPRESSION Have partners take turns reading aloud pages 294 and 295. Point out that the word *splat* on page 295 is in capital letters and has an exclamation point after it.

Remind children to:

- change the pace of their reading to suit the action being described.
- pause at commas, ellipses, and periods.
- express what the characters are feeling when they read dialogue.

LANGUAGE SUPPORT

ESL To help children understand what a "big island of ice" is, ask them to look at the picture on page 296. Have children point out a big island of ice and a small island of ice.

Use gestures and sound effects to explain the word *SPLAT* on page 295.

Ask children to describe situations in which they heard the sound *splat*. Then ask children to guess what *got soaked* means. (covered with water)

Comprehension

3 What causes the penguins to get soaked? (A whale named Ernest swims by and splashes them.) *Cause and Effect*

4 Why might the whale have done this? Do you think the whale is a bully? (Ed says that Ernest doesn't notice penguins. Maybe he doesn't pay attention to the penguins because he's so much bigger than they are.) *Make Inferences*

But they always watched out
for Ernest, the big whale.
Every time he went by . . .
SPLAT!
Ed and everybody got soaked.

"Watch what you are doing!"
Betty would yell.

But Ernest swam right by.
"Ernest doesn't even notice penguins,"
said Ed.

295

Comprehension

⑤ FANTASY AND REALITY Ed, the penguin, thinks he dreamed that the ice cracked. But, in the story, the ice really did break. Do you think it could have done so in reality as well?

MODEL To decide whether the event of the ice breaking could have really happened, I will look at my own experience. I have seen the ice on a river break up into big chunks like islands. So I know that ice can really break up into big pieces.

Let's begin our Fantasy and Reality chart.

FANTASY	REALITY
Penguins act like people.	Penguins do not act like people.
Ed dreams that the ice breaks.	Ice can break.

One night when Ed was asleep, there was a loud cracking noise. It sounded like ice breaking. **⑤** Ed thought it was a dream.

Activity

Cross Curricular: Social Studies

ANTARCTICA Tell children that most penguins live on Antarctica, a cold and icy continent. Have children use a map to answer these questions.

- Is Antarctica divided into countries?
- Which ocean surrounds Antarctica?

RESEARCH AND INQUIRY Have children find out what kind of animals and plants live in Antarctica. Encourage children to use the information they gained through research to locate factual information from the story. ▶ **Visual/Spatial**

Antarctica

When Ed woke up in the morning,
he found that the island of ice
had broken in half.
He was all alone
on an island of his own.

6

7

297

Comprehension

6 Why do you think the ice broke up? (Ice melts and breaks apart when it gets warmer. Maybe it got warm where Ed lives.) *Make Inferences*

7 Look at the picture that stretches across pages 296 and 297. Who do you think the tiny figures shown on page 296 are? Explain your answer. (They're probably Ed's playmates, because he's looking toward them as though he wishes he were with them.) *Draw Conclusions*

Minilesson
REVIEW/MAINTAIN
Summarize

Tell children that summarizing the story at this point can help them pay better attention to the next event. This is because the events of a story usually involve a problem. Having a clear idea of what that problem is will help them see how it was solved.

Activity Have children list the story events up to page 297 when Ed gets separated from his friends. Then ask them to try to predict how he will rejoin them.

Comprehension

8 The story says that Ed's friends grew smaller as his island drifted away. Did his friends really grow smaller? What do you think was happening? (As the island drifted farther away, his friends looked like they were getting smaller and smaller.) *Draw Conclusions*

9 Why do you think Ed walks around his island? (He was probably looking for some of his friends.) *Make Inferences*

TEACHING TIP

MANAGEMENT As children read the story for the first time, you may wish to use the Comprehension questions and the Language Support features. You may wish to wait until the second reading to do the activities and Minilessons.

8 Ed's friends got smaller and smaller as his island drifted away. Ed watched until he couldn't see them anymore.

298

Then he walked
around his island.
There was nobody on it at all.
At last he came to his
own footprints again.

299

Comprehension

10 Pretend our classroom is Ed's ice island. Show me how you think Ed walks around the island. Is he looking around or walking with his head down? *Pantomime*

11 Ed is now by himself on an ice island. What do you think he will do next? (Maybe he will shout for help.) *Make Predictions*

Comprehension

12 When Ed waves to the birds, why do you think they don't wave back? (Maybe they couldn't wave because they needed their wings to fly. Maybe they were too far away to see Ed.) *Make Inferences*

13 **Phonics** **/ər/** Read the first line on page 300. Which word ends with the sound /ər/? (*over*) How is the sound spelled? (*er*) Now let's all read aloud the last two lines on page 300. Which word has the sound /ər/? (*letters*) Let's read the word, blending the sounds of the letters together. *Graphophonic Cues*

p/i **PHONICS AND DECODING** What sound is the same in the words *wave* and *day* on page 300? (/ā/)

12 Some birds flew over.
Ed waved,
13 but they did not wave back.
"I guess I will be here
the rest of my life," Ed said.
At the end of the day,
he wrote "I GIVE UP"
in big letters in the snow.
Then he went to sleep.

300

---

p/i **PREVENTION/INTERVENTION**

PHONICS AND DECODING Say the words *wave* and *day* aloud. Ask children to repeat the words with you. Have children say the vowel sound that they hear in both words. (/ā/) Ask them to find the words on page 300.

How is long *a* spelled in the word *wave*? (*a_e*) How is it spelled in the word *day*? (*ay*) Have children name other words with /ā/ and these spellings. *Graphophonic Cues*

In the morning a tern woke him up.
"Hey," said the tern,
"did you write that thing in the snow?"

"Yes," said Ed.

"Could you write something
for me?" asked the tern.

"I guess so," said Ed.
"What do you want?"

301

Comprehension

14 What caused the tern to become interested in Ed? (He wanted to know if Ed wrote the message.) Why was the tern interested in Ed's message? (He wanted Ed to write a message for him.) *Cause and Effect*

15 What does Ed say when the tern asks him to write something? (Ed says, "*I guess so.*") Now look at Ed in the illustration on page 301. Does he look excited? Why do you think he doesn't look more interested? (Maybe he feels he will never get off the ice island.) *Make Inferences*

Minilesson

REVIEW/MAINTAIN

Using Reference Materials

Help children use reference materials to obtain additional information about terns. Brainstorm a list of reference materials that children could use to research terns.

Activity Ask children to work in small groups to research terns. Have children locate examples from the story where information about terns is based on reality and where the information is fantasy. Ask groups to create a Reality/Fantasy chart about terns. Encourage children to share their information with classmates.

LANGUAGE SUPPORT

ESL For children who may be having difficulty following the story, have them create a flow-chart. Suggest that children draw four large rectangles, one on top of the other. Then have them draw a picture of the first main event in the top rectangle. They can draw the second event in the second rectangle and continue adding to the chart as they read. You may wish to have them label each picture with a simple sentence.

Comprehension

16 Ed writes a message for the tern in the snow. What does this tell you about Ed?

(He is a nice penguin who helps others.)
Character

ⓢELF-MONITORING STRATEGY

ASK FOR HELP Ask your teacher or a partner if you are not sure why characters act in a certain way. You may find that some of your classmates are having the same problem.

MODEL I couldn't figure out why Ed didn't ask the tern to help him off the island. Other kids said that they didn't understand it either. We all talked about it and decided that maybe Ed needed a ride back to his friends. The tern looks too small to carry Ed.

"Tell my friends to meet me at the blue iceberg," said the tern. "And sign it 'Talbot.' That is my name."

16 Talbot flew away, and Ed wrote the message.

MEET TALBOT AT THE BLUE ICEBERG

302

Activity

Cross Curricular: Science

ANIMAL TALK Tell children that animals communicate in these ways:

- Rabbits thump the ground to warn others of danger.
- Dolphins whistle through their blow holes to send each other messages.

▶ **Linguistic/Logical**

RESEARCH AND INQUIRY Have children find other facts about animal communication to share with the class.

inter NET CONNECTION For more information about animal communication, visit **www.mhschool.com/reading.**

1. Cats hiss when they are about to fight.

2. Birds act like they are hurt to fool hunters.

Pretty soon, Talbot's friends flew over and read the message. They waved to Ed, and Ed waved back. **17**

303

Comprehension

17 Something Ed did has caused some new events. What did Ed do that was different? How did this change things? *(Ed wrote the message for Talbot, the tern. Talbot's friends flew over, read it, and waved to Ed.)* ***Cause and Effect***

PHONICS AND DECODING Find the word on page 302 that has the same vowel sound as blue. *(flew)* Read the word. What vowel sound do you hear? *(/ü/)*

PREVENTION/INTERVENTION

PHONICS AND DECODING Have children say the words *blue* and *flew*. Ask them what vowel sound they hear. *(/ü/)* Have them find *blue* and *flew* on page 302. Ask them how the /ü/ sound is spelled in *blue*. *(ue)* Ask them how the /ü/ sound is spelled in *flew*. *(ew)* Encourage children to name other words which contain the /ü/ sound spelled *ue* and *ew*. *Graphophonic Cues*

Comprehension

18 How do you think Talbot feels about the favors Ed has done for the birds? What makes you think so? (Talbot was probably grateful because he brought Ed a fish and praised him.) *Make Inferences*

19 **FANTASY AND REALITY** The birds are stopping and asking Ed to write messages. Do you think this could happen in real life? How do animals communicate with each other? (through sounds and motions)

It's time to add to our Fantasy and Reality chart.

FANTASY	REALITY
Penguins act like people.	Penguins don't act like people.
Ed dreams that the ice breaks.	Ice can break.
Ed talks to the birds.	Animals communicate using sounds and motions.

All day long, birds stopped and asked Ed to write messages for them.
By the end of the day, the whole island was covered with messages.
Ed was very tired.

304

Talbot landed and gave Ed a fish.
"You are doing a great job,"
said Talbot.
"How come you look so gloomy?"

"I miss my friends
on my old island," said Ed.

"Where is your old island?"
asked Talbot.

305

Comprehension

 CONTEXT CLUES   Read the fourth line on page 305. What do you think the word *gloomy* means?

 PREVENTION/INTERVENTION

CONTEXT CLUES Some children may not understand the word *gloomy*. Have them look for clues to its meaning in the next sentence: *"I miss my friends on my old island," said Ed.* Have children show on their faces how they think Ed feels when he says this. Then ask them what they think the word *gloomy* might mean. Help them to see that *gloomy* means sad. Have children write a sentence of their own using the word *gloomy*. *Semantic Cues*

Minilesson
REVIEW/MAINTAIN
Analyze Character

Tell children that they can understand story characters by noticing how they act and what they say. Help children analyze Ed's character by asking them these questions:

• How does Ed feel about his friends?

• What does Ed do for the terns?

Activity Have children work with a partner to come up with a list of words that describe Ed.

Comprehension

20 Why can't Ed go look for the island where his friends are? *(He can't fly.)* Does Talbot understand why Ed cannot look for his friends? Explain. *(Not really. Talbot thinks flying is easy.)* **Character Analysis**

21 How does Ed feel when Talbot flies away? What makes you think so? *(He feels even more discouraged. He thinks that he'll have to spend the rest of his life writing messages. In the picture, he looks sadder than ever.)* **Make Inferences**

> ## TEACHING TIP
>
> **MANAGEMENT** You may wish to give interested children some enrichment activities.
> - Have them write their own ending to the story.
> - Have them write a parallel story about Ed's penguin friends and their plans to help him.

"Way over there someplace," said Ed.

20 "Too bad you can't fly," said Talbot. "You could spot it from the air."

"Well, I can't fly," said Ed.

"It's not very hard," said Talbot.

"It is for penguins," said Ed.

Talbot flew away.
21 "I guess I will spend the rest of my life writing messages," Ed said to himself.

306

Activity

Cross Curricular: Math

ADDITION Point out to children that Ed has spent two days on the ice island. Tell children that each day the ice island has floated two miles farther from Ed's old home. Ask children how far the island will have floated in four days if it continues to travel two miles each day.

Activity Have children make up their own word problem such as, "How far will Ed have floated in five days?" Have them exchange problems with a partner.

▶ **Mathematical/Linguistic**

When Ed got up the next morning, he found a surprise.

307

Comprehension

22 What surprise did Ed get in the morning? (a message) Who do you think wrote it and why? (Talbot, he's the other main character in the story.) *Draw Conclusions*

23 How do you suppose Ed feels as he reads the message in the snow? (surprised and pleased) *Make Inferences*

LANGUAGE SUPPORT

ESL Draw a picture on the board of Ed sitting in the middle of an ice island. Make an arrow pointing to the ground in front of him and label it *here*. Read the first sentence on page 306 aloud. Ask a child to point to where *way over there* would be. (somewhere on the board a long distance from Ed on his island) Make an arrow pointing to this distant point and label it *way over there*.

Point to the arrows under Ed's feet on page 307. Make walking motions with your fingers and say: *He's following the arrows.*

307

Comprehension

24 What has happened so far in the story? (Ed has been separated from his friends. He has written messages for other animals and now has finally received a message meant for him.) *Sequence of Events*

25 **Phonics** /ər/ Let's read aloud the sentence on page 308. Is there a word in that sentence that has the same /ər/ sound as *brother*? (*another*) Let's read the word, blending the sounds of the letters together. How is the /ər/ sound spelled? (*er*) *Graphophonic Cues*

SIT HERE AND WAIT →

24
25 He followed the arrows until he came to another message.

308

CULTURAL PERSPECTIVES

THE INUIT Tell children that, like Antarctica, the Arctic region is cold and has few plants and animals. No one lives in Antarctica besides scientists who study local geography. In the Arctic, however, a people called the Inuit have adapted to the cold climate.

RESEARCH AND INQUIRY Ask children to write a report on Inuit shelter, clothing, or food.

▶ **Linguistic**

The Inuit live in houses made of stone that are grouped together in small villages.

He sat down on the X and waited.

Comprehension

26 Why do you think the author doesn't tell us why Ed is supposed to wait?
(Maybe he wants the reader to feel surprised.)
Make Inferences

27 Who would like to pretend to be Ed and tell us what it feels like to wait for a surprise? Perhaps Ed will tell us what he thinks the surprise might be. *Role-Play*

Comprehension

28 Why did Ed get soaked? (Ernest, the whale, has come to Ed's island and has caused the water to splash over him.) *Cause and Effect*

29 **FANTASY AND REALITY** Look at pages 310 and 311. What events could happen in real life? (Whales splash water. Whales swim near places where penguins live.) What events could never happen? (Penguins and whales talk. Whales give penguins rides.)

Let's add these ideas to our Fantasy and Reality chart.

FANTASY	REALITY
Penguins act like people.	Penguins don't act like people.
Ed dreams that the ice breaks.	Ice can break.
Ed talks to the birds.	Animals communicate using sounds and motions.
Whales talk to penguins and give them rides.	Whales swim near places where penguins live.

Suddenly there was a great SPLAT!
Ed was soaked.

28 It was Ernest.
"I understand you are looking
for a ride to that island
29 with all the penguins on it,"
said Ernest.

310

310 *Best Wishes, Ed*

"How did you know?" asked Ed.

"Talbot told me," said Ernest.
"Hop aboard."

311

Comprehension

30 What caused Talbot to ask Ernest to give Ed a ride back to his island? (Talbot liked Ed and wanted to help him.) **Make Inferences**

Minilesson
REVIEW/MAINTAIN
Context Clues

Have children look at the word *splat* on page 310. Ask them to find clues to the word's meaning. Children should recognize that the picture and the statement *Ed was soaked* suggest that *splat* is something a big wave might do. Point out that the sound of the word also expresses its meaning.

Activity Have children think of other words that imitate a sound such as *chirp*, *thump*, *ting-a-ling*. Then ask them to draw cartoons showing things that make these sounds.

Comprehension

31 Why do you think Ed stopped to write a message? (He wants to tell Talbot that he knows it was Talbot that helped him.) What does this tell you about Ed? (He is grateful and polite.) **Make Inferences**

32 Look at Ernest's remark "*Well, make it snappy. I have other things to do besides give rides to penguins.*" What does this tell us about Ernest's character? (Ernest is helpful but a little grumpy. He feels that he is more important than penguins.) **Character**

31 "Wait one second," said Ed. "I have to leave a message."

"Well, make it snappy," said Ernest. **32** "I have other things to do besides give rides to penguins."

Ed quickly wrote the message in the snow.

33 THANK YOU, TALBOT. BEST WISHES, Ed

312

Then he climbed
on top of Ernest's back.
Ernest gave a couple of (34)
big splashes with his tail,
and then they were racing
across the water.

313

Comprehension

(33) Why do you think Ed ends his message
by writing "Best wishes"? ("Best wishes"
is a polite way to end a message.)
Draw Conclusions

(34) Can you explain how Ernest helped to
solve Ed's problem? (He gave Ed a ride
back to the island where Ed's friends are.)
Problem and Solution

Minilesson
REVIEW/MAINTAIN
Long *a*

Have children read aloud the second sentence on page 313. Point out that both *gave* and *tail* have the long *a* sound.

Make a chart on the chalkboard with the two spellings, *a-e* and *ai*, as column headings. Ask volunteers to name words that rhyme with *tail* and add them to the chart.

Activity Have children brainstorm other words with long *a* spelled *a-e* and *ai*. Create a wall chart and list the words.

LANGUAGE SUPPORT

ESL Some children may not understand the word *climbed*. Have children demonstrate how they think Ed moves when he climbs on top of Ernest's back. Then read the word *climbed* in the first sentence on page 313. Have children make drawings of children climbing something, such as a mountain or a tree. Ask them to write a sentence under the picture telling what the children did. For example, *He climbed a tree.*

Comprehension

35 **FANTASY AND REALITY** The events on this page are similar to the ones on page 310. What are they? (Whales talk to penguins and give them rides. Penguins talk to each other. Whales splash water.) Let's review our Fantasy and Reality chart and add to it or change it if necessary.

FANTASY	REALITY
Penguins act like people.	Penguins don't act like people.
Ed dreams that the ice breaks.	Ice can break.
Ed talks to the birds.	Animals communicate using sounds and motions.
Whales talk to penguins and give them rides. Penguins also talk to each other.	Whales swim near places where penguins live.

RETELL THE STORY Ask children to use their charts to help them retell the main events of the selection. *Summarize*

SELF-ASSESSMENT

Have children ask themselves the following questions to assess how they are reading:

- How did the Fantasy and Reality chart help me understand this story?
- How did I use the pictures and letters and sounds I know to help me read the words in the story?

TRANSFERRING THE STRATEGIES

- How can I use these strategies to help me read other stories?

"Ed is back!" yelled Betty.

"Hooray!" shouted Freddy and Al.

Ed slid off Ernest's back.
"Thanks a lot, Ernest," called Ed.

"That's O.K.," said Ernest.
"Just don't expect a ride every day."

"We're so glad you are back, Ed," said Betty.

"We missed you a lot," said Freddy and Al.

35 "I missed you," said Ed.

314

REREADING FOR *Fluency*

ONE Children who need fluency practice can read along silently or aloud as they listen to the story on audiocassette.

READING RATE When you evaluate reading rate, have children read aloud from the story for one minute. Place a stick-on note after the last word read. Count words read. To evaluate chil-

dren's performance, see the Running Record in the **Fluency Assessment** book.

Intervention For leveled fluency passages, lessons, and norm charts, see **Skills Intervention Guide**, Part 5, Fluency.

SPLAT! They were all soaked, as Ernest swam away.

"Hey," said Betty, "he did it again!"

"Ernest doesn't notice penguins," said Freddy.

"Sometimes he does," said Ed.

315

Comprehension

Return to Predictions and Purposes

Reread children's predictions about the story. Discuss the predictions, noting which needed to be revised. Then ask children if the story answered the questions they had before they read it.

PREDICTIONS	WHAT HAPPENED
One penguin gets separated from his friends.	Ed, the penguin, ends up on a floating ice island.
He meets a bird and a whale.	The tern asks Ernest, the whale, to bring Ed back to his friends.

HOW TO ASSESS

Phonics WORDS WITH /ər/ er Have children turn to page 300. Have them point to and read the word *letters*. Next, have children point to and read the word *over* on the same page.

FANTASY AND REALITY Have children describe two fantastic events and two realistic events in the story. Encourage them to explain why the events could or could not have happened.

FOLLOW UP

Phonics WORDS WITH /ər/ er Continue to model the blending of sounds in words with /ər/ *er* for children who are having difficulty pronouncing and recognizing the words.

FANTASY AND REALITY Children who are having difficulty with this concept can review their Fantasy and Reality charts.

LITERARY RESPONSE

QUICK-WRITE Have children write an entry in their journals that Ed might have written when he was separated from his friends.

JOURNAL

ORAL RESPONSE Have children use their journal entries to discuss these questions:

- If you were a character in the story, how would you have helped Ed to get off his island?
- Do you think that Ed's ability to write messages for his friends made him special?

Story Questions

Best Wishes, Ed

Have students discuss or write answers to the questions on page 316.

Answers:

1. The island of ice broke in half.
   Literal/Cause and Effect

2. Talbot asks Ernest, the whale, to carry Ed back to his friends. *Problem and Solution*

3. The penguins complain when Ernest splashes them. This is funny because the penguins are acting like people. *Fantasy and Reality*

4. The story is about Ed and his new friends who help him. *Summarize*

5. Talbot and Ernest; The rules would be: Members must help one another.
   Critical/Reading Across Texts

Write a Guide For a full writing-process lesson related to this suggestion, see the lesson on explanatory writing on page 319M.

Story Questions & Activities

1. How does Ed wind up alone?

2. How does Talbot help Ed?

3. What are some funny things that happen in the story? Why are they funny?

4. What is this story mostly about?

5. Imagine that Ed is forming a "Best Friends Club." Who would be in it and what kinds of rules might it have?

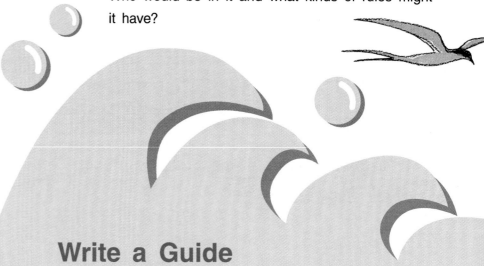

Write a Guide

Choose something you like to do and make a guide of "helpful hints" for someone who is learning to do the same thing. You can include both things that people have taught you and ideas of your own.

Meeting Individual Needs

EASY	ON-LEVEL	CHALLENGE
Name _____ Date _____ Reteach 95 **Story Comprehension** Fill in the chart about "Best Wishes, Ed." CHARACTERS: Ed, Talbot, Ernest, the other birds and penguins. BEGINNING OF THE STORY: Ed lives on an ice island with his friends. One night the ice breaks apart and Ed floats away. MIDDLE OF THE STORY: Ed meets Talbot the tern. He begins to write messages for the birds on the surface of the ice. Then someone writes a message for him. END OF THE STORY: Ernest the whale rescues Ed and brings him back to his friends. Book 2.1/Unit 3 Best Wishes, Ed At Home: Have children illustrate one of their answers. 95	Name _____ Date _____ Practice 95 **Story Comprehension** Think about "Best Wishes, Ed." Who said each sentence? Color the answer. 1. Ernest does not even notice penguins. color 2. I will be here all my life. color 3. Will you write a letter for me? color 4. I do not know how to fly. color 5. I have lots of things to do besides helping penguins. color Book 2.1/Unit 3 Best Wishes, Ed At Home: Have children tell at least one other thing Ed said during the story. 95	Name _____ Date _____ Extend 95 **Story Comprehension** These parts of the story "Best Wishes, Ed" are out of order. Number the steps in the order they happened. 5 Ed found a surprise message. 2 Ed was asleep, and there was a loud cracking noise. 3 Ed was alone on an island of his own. 6 Ernest gave Ed a ride home. 1 Ed and his friends had fun throwing snowballs and sliding on the ice. 4 Talbot asked Ed to write something for him in the snow. Write a thank you message for Ed to leave for Ernest. Answers will vary. Book 2.1/Unit 3 Best Wishes, Ed At Home: Invite children to retell the story of "Best Wishes, Ed." Ask them to brainstorm other ways Ed could have solved his problem. 95
Reteach, 95	Practice, 95	Extend, 95

Create a Secret Message

Write a secret message. Dip a paintbrush in lemon juice. Then write on a piece of paper. After the paper dries, hold it near a light bulb. When the paper gets warm, the secret message will appear.

Where in the World?

Penguins live in only five places. With your class, find these places on a map or globe: Antarctica, Australia, New Zealand, South Africa, and the Galápagos Islands.

Find Out More

There is more than just one kind of penguin. Use an encyclopedia to find the names of at least three different types. Where is each penguin found? What is the average size of each kind?

317

Story Activities

Create a Secret Message

Materials: lemon juice, paper, paintbrushes

PARTNERS Have pairs of children write messages to each other using lemon juice. When they have finished writing, they can exchange papers and hold them up to a light bulb until the writing becomes visible.

Where in the World?

Materials: world map or globe

GROUP Have children work together to locate the natural habitats of penguins. Have them choose penguins from two different places and compare and contrast their environments.

Find Out More

GROUP **RESEARCH AND INQUIRY** Have children draw pictures of one of the kinds of penguins they have researched. They can show the penguin nesting or finding food in its habitat.

interNET CONNECTION Go to *www.mhschool.com/reading* for more information or activities on the topic.

FORMAL ASSESSMENT

After page 317, see Selection Assessment.

DAILY **Phonics** ROUTINES

DAY 3 **Word Building** Have children work with partners. One child says the first syllable of a word with /ər/*er*. The other child completes the word with the letters *er*. Then the partners switch roles.

Phonics CD-ROM

317

Study Skills

REFERENCE SOURCES

OBJECTIVES   Children will look up entries in an encyclopedia.

PREPARE   Examine the passage with children. Display **Teaching Chart 80.**

TEACH   Discuss how to use the guide words.

PRACTICE   Have children answer questions 1–4. Review the answers with them.

1. islands near cold water in the southern part of Earth **2.** Penguins cannot fly. **3.** by using their wings and feet **4.** Alike—both have guide words and entries in alphabetical order. Different—encyclopedias have more information and cross references.

ASSESS/CLOSE   Have children look up Antarctica in an encyclopedia. Have them list two things that they learned about Antarctica by reading the entry.

STUDY SKILLS

Read an Encyclopedia

pen   **Pennsylvania**

Penguins

Penguins are birds that are not able to fly. But penguins can swim underwater. Their wings look like flippers, and their bodies are covered with short feathers. All penguins have black and white feathers. Some have stripes across their chests.

Penguins hatch their young from eggs

Penguins eat mostly fish. Penguins dive into the water to catch their food. They use their wings and their webbed feet to swim. Penguins live on islands near cold water in the southern part of the Earth.

Use the encyclopedia entry to answer the questions.

1 Where do penguins live?

2 What is the most surprising fact about penguins?

3 How do penguins swim?

4 How are encyclopedias and dictionaries alike? How are they different?

Meeting Individual Needs

EASY

Name_____ Date_____ Reteach 96
Read an Encyclopedia

An **encyclopedia** is good place to get general information on a subject.

Encyclopedias are organized into books called **volumes.** If there are many entries that start with one letter, there may be two volumes for that letter. Like a dictionary page, a typical encyclopedia page has guide words at the top.

Decide if an entry would be found on a page with the guide words mentioned. Answer **Yes** or **No.**

1. Would the entry word **plow** be found between **plant** and **plywood**? ___yes___

2. Would the entry word **king** be found between **knee** and **Korea**? ___no___

3. Would the entry word **Montana** be found between **money** and **month**? ___yes___

4. Would the entry word **fig** be found between **figure skating** and **film**? ___no___

5. Would the entry word **railroad** be found between **red blood cell** and **rink**? ___no___

96   At Home: Ask children to think of an encyclopedia entry that could go between each of the five sets of guide words in the questions.   Book 2.1/Unit 3 **Best Wishes, Ed** 5

Reteach, 96

ON-LEVEL

Name_____ Date_____ Practice 96
Use an Encyclopedia

Study the sample **encyclopedia** page shown below. Some encyclopedia entries have **cross references.** These point you to related entries you might like to read.

Poland — Police

Poland is a country in central Europe. It borders on the Baltic Sea. Its name comes from a tribe of people called the Polane. They lived over a thousand years ago in that area. Poland has rich natural resources and is famous for its industry.

Polar bear is a large white bear found near the Arctic Ocean. A full-grown bear can be over nine feet tall and weigh close to 1,000 pounds. Polar bears are great hunters and strong swimmers. (See also *Bears*)

Police are government workers who make sure people obey the law. Police control traffic and try to find out who committed crimes. They also help out during natural disasters like floods or tornadoes. There are city police and state police. Each group enforces the laws, but state police serve cities that don't have their own police force. Police officers are sometimes called cops. It is thought the word comes from their copper badges.

Use the entries above to answer the following questions.

1. How much does a polar bear weigh? __close to 1,000 pounds__

2. The word for Poland comes from what tribe of people? __the Polane__

3. What kind of cities do state police serve? __cities without their own police force__

4. Where is the country of Poland found? __in central Europe__

5. What other entry does the entry under *Polar bear* tell you to read? __Bears__

96   At Home: Ask children to draw a picture of a polar bear.   Book 2.1/Unit 3 **Best Wishes, Ed** 5

Practice, 96

CHALLENGE

Name_____ Date_____ Extend 96
Read an Encyclopedia

Read the encyclopedia entry to learn about whales. Then answer the questions.

Whales
Whales are mammals who live their whole lives in the water. Whales have a layer of blubber on their bodies to keep them warm and floating. They breathe air through holes on the top of their heads.

Whales use their hearing to help them find their way in the water. Some whales swim alone in the sea. Other whales swim with their families or in groups with hundreds of other whales. People think the blue whale may be the largest animal ever to have lived.   Sample answers are given.

1. Make a list of ways Ernest in "Best Wishes, Ed" is like a real whale.

     __He lives in the water.__
     __He breathes.__
     __He swims alone in the sea.__

2. What does Ernest do that a real whale could not?
     __He can speak.__
     __He can give a penguin a ride.__

96   At Home: Help children use an encyclopedia to learn more about their favorite animal.   Book 2.1/Unit 3 **Best Wishes, Ed**

Extend, 96

TEST POWER

Read the story again if the questions seem too hard.

DIRECTIONS:
Read the story. Then read each question about the story.

SAMPLE

Never Too Old

In 1962, John Glenn was the first man from the United States to go into space. He went in a spaceship called *Friendship 7.*

He went around the Earth in *Friendship 7* three times. The trip took five hours. *Friendship 7* landed safely on the same day that it left. John Glenn was a hero.

In 1998, John Glenn went into space again. He was seventy-seven years old. He was the oldest man ever to go into space. He went in a spaceship called *Discovery.*

Discovery landed after nine days in space.

John Glenn was a hero again in 1998. He proved you are never too old to be a hero.

1 How old was John Glenn when he went into space in 1998?
- ○ Sixty-seven years old
- ● Seventy-seven years old
- ○ Twenty-eight years old

2 John Glenn was a hero in 1962 because he —
- ● went into space
- ○ walked on the moon
- ○ made friends in space

319

Test Power

THE PRINCETON REVIEW

Read the Page

Explain to children that you will be reading this story as a group. You will read the story, and they will follow along in their books.

Request that children put pens, pencils, and markers away, since they will not be writing in their books.

Discuss the Questions

QUESTION 1: Instruct children to look back to the passage and find some mention of Glenn's flight in 1998. The answer can be found in the eighth sentence, which states that Glenn was 77 years old.

QUESTION 2: Remind children to reread the lines about becoming a hero. Ask: What does the story say? Answer: He went around Earth in Friendship 7.

Leveled Books

How Animals Use Color

by Shirley Frederick
illustrated by Karen Bell

Intervention ▶ **Skills**

Intervention Guide, for direct instruction and extra practice of vocabulary and comprehension

EASY

How Animals Use Color

☑ **Phonics** /ər/ *er*
☑ **Fantasy and Reality**
☑ **Instructional Vocabulary:** *climbed, couple, drifted, half, message, notice*

Guided Reading

PREVIEW AND PREDICT Take a **picture walk** through page 7. Have children predict what the story is about by looking at the illustrations.

SET PURPOSES Have children discuss why they want to read the story. Children may want to learn more about how animals use color to survive.

READ THE BOOK Use the following questions to guide children's reading or after they have read the story independently.

Pages 2–4: Do you think this story will be about make-believe animals or real life animals? (Real life; the story tells facts about animals that are true in real life.) *Fantasy and Reality*

Page 5: Find the word *notice*. Do the seals *notice* the bear? (No.) If you *notice* something, do you see it or not? (You see it.) *Instructional Vocabulary*

Page 7: Find the word *water*. What sound do the letters *er* make in the word? (/ər/) *Phonics and Decoding*

Page 9: What might happen if a fox tried to eat a bright-colored animal?

(The rabbit might get bitten and hurt.) *Make Predictions*

Page 14: How do deer warn each other of danger? (They put up their tails.) What will the deer do once they have their tails up? (They will run to a safe place.) *Cause and Effect*

RETURN TO PREDICTIONS AND PURPOSES Have children review their predictions and purposes for reading. Did they find out what they wanted to know?

LITERARY RESPONSE Discuss these questions:

- Which animal do you think was the best at hiding? Explain.

- Can you think of an animal you would like to be? What colors would you have, and how could your colors help you?

Also see the story questions and activity in *How Animals Use Colors*.

See the **Phonics** CD-ROM for practice with /ər/ *er*.

Answers to Story Questions

1. Animals hide so other animals won't find them and eat them.
2. A mountain lion was chasing them.
3. Nests that look like piles of grass and sticks are hard to find.
4. Animals use color in many ways.
5. If Ed went swimming in the water, he would be hard to see. His dark back would be dark like the water.

The Story Questions and Activity below appear in the Easy Book.

Story Questions and Writing Activity

1. Why do animals hide?
2. Why did the deer run away?
3. Why do birds make their nests out of grass and sticks?
4. What is the book mainly about?
5. How could Ed the penguin use his colors to help him hide?

Hide the Bugs

On a piece of white paper, draw ten bugs. Make five of them white. Make the others the same color as the floor. Put the bugs in different places on the floor. Ask a friend to find the bugs. Did color help the bugs hide?

from How Animals Use Color

Leveled Books

INDEPENDENT

Ready Set Go!

☑  /ər/ *er*

☑ **Fantasy and Reality**

☑ **Instructional Vocabulary:** *climbed, couple, drifted, half, message, notice*

Guided Reading

PREVIEW AND PREDICT Take a **picture walk** through page 6. As children study the illustrations, have them predict what the story is about.

SET PURPOSES Have children write or draw why they want to read *Ready Set Go!* Children may want to learn about how fast different animals can go.

READ THE BOOK Use the following questions to guide children's reading after they have read the story independently.

Pages 2–5: Compare the animals pictured on pages 2–3 with those on pages 4–5. Which are make-believe? Which are real? How can you tell? (The animals on pages 2–3 are make-believe because they are running a race. The animals on the next two pages are real because they are in actual photographs.) *Fantasy and Reality*

Page 7: Read the first sentence. What word has the /ər/ sound? (*water*) Which letters make the /ər/ sound? (*er*) *Phonics and Decoding*

Page 11: Find the word *couple*. How many fins would a "couple of fins" be? *Instructional Vocabulary*

Page 12: What kind of wings does the falcon have? (long pointed) What do the falcon's wings help it to do? (fly fast and catch its prey) *Cause and Effect*

RETURN TO PREDICTIONS AND PURPOSES Have children review their predictions and purposes for reading.

LITERARY RESPONSE Discuss these questions:

- What surprised you about the movement of the animals you read about?

- Which of these animals interested you the most?

Also see the story questions and activity in *Ready Set Go!*

See the **Phonics** CD-ROM for practice using words with the /ər/ sound.

Answers to Story Questions

1. Because some live on land, some live in water, and some move through the sky.
2. Fish can't breathe on land. A tortoise can't hold a flag, etc.
3. It has a big fin on its back that looks like the sail of a boat.
4. Different animals travel at different speeds, depending on where they live and what they have to do.
5. Penguins can walk on land and swim in the water, but they can not fly. Penguins would travel fastest in the water because they have flippers and webbed feet.

The Story Questions and Activity below appear in the Independent Book.

Story Questions and Writing Activity

1. Why do some animals run, some swim, and some fly?
2. Compare the pictures on pages 2–3 and pages 8–9. What are the differences between the two types of pictures?
3. How do you think the sailfish got its name?
4. What is the main idea of the book?
5. What different ways is Ed, as a penguin, able to travel? How would Ed travel fastest—by land, air or water?

Ready? Set. Guess!

Look at the picture on pages 14 and 15. Estimate how many inches apart the falcon and the duck are. Now measure that distance with a ruler. Write your answers on a piece of paper. How close were you? Try it again with other animals in this book.

from *Ready Set Go!*

Leveled Books

CHALLENGE

Rin Tin Tin: Top Dog In The Movies

☑  /ər/ *er*
☑ **Fantasy and Reality**
☑ **Instructional Vocabulary:** *climbed, couple, drifted, half, message, notice*

Guided Reading

PREVIEW AND PREDICT Take a **picture walk** through page 7. Have children predict what the story is about by studying the illustrations.

SET PURPOSES Have children write one or two sentences describing why they want to read *Rin Tin Tin: Top Dog in the Movies*. For example, children may want to know how a dog can become a movie star.

READ THE BOOK Use the following questions to guide children's reading or after they have read the story independently.

Pages 2–4: Do you think this story will be about a real-life dog or a make-believe one? How can you tell? (real-life; it tells about real events and the illustrations look real.) *Fantasy and Reality*

Page 5: How could you describe Rin Tin Tin? (strong, fast, quick learner) What did Lee begin to think that Rin Tin Tin might be able to do? (star in movies) *Cause and Effect*

Page 7: Find the word *letters*. What sound do the letters *er* make in the word *letter*? (/ər/) *Phonics and Decoding*

Page 8: Find the word *messages*. What is the purpose of a message? *Instructional Vocabulary*

Page 11: How is a movie like real life? What makes a movie make-believe? *Fantasy and Reality*

Page 15: What do you think Rin Tin Tin's puppies were like? What special things might they be able to do? Why? *Make Predictions*

RETURN TO PREDICTIONS AND PURPOSES Have children review their predictions and purposes for reading.

LITERARY RESPONSE Discuss these questions:

• What did you like best about Rin Tin Tin?

• Do you think dogs ought to be trained to do tricks in the movies? Why or why not?

Also see the story questions and activity in *Rin Tin Tin: Top Dog in the Movies*.

See the  **CD-ROM** for practice using words with the /ər/ sound.

Answers to Story Questions

1. He finds a mother dog and her puppies in Europe after World War I. He takes his favorite puppy back home with him and names it Rin Tin Tin.

2. Today movies are in color.

3. At the beginning because that is real life. When he meets the snake, it is only a movie.

4. Rin Tin Tin was a wonderful animal performer who could make the pretend world of the movies look very real.

5. Answers will vary.

The Story Questions and Activity below appear in the Challenge Book.

Story Questions and Writing Activity

1. How does Lee first meet Rin Tin Tin?

2. How were movies in Rin Tin Tin's day different from movies today?

3. Is Rin Tin Tin in more danger at the beginning of the book when his mother has no food, or when he meets the snake on page 9? Why?

4. What is the main idea of this book?

5. If Ed were to star in his own movie, what do you think it would be about?

Lights! Camera! Action!

Draw a picture of Rin Tin Tin in a scene from a movie. Write a paragraph that describes what is happening.

from *Rin Tin Tin: Top Dog in the Movies*

Bringing Groups Together

Anthology and Leveled Books

Connecting Texts

ANIMAL BEHAVIOR CHARTS
Write the story titles on a chart. Discuss with children the special abilities and physical characteristics the animals in each story have. Call on volunteers from each reading level to write their contributions on the chart. For *Best Wishes, Ed*, encourage children to list only the real-life characteristics of the animals in the story.

Use the chart to discuss special abilities and physical characteristics of animals.

Best Wishes, Ed	How Animals Use Color	Ready Set Go!	Rin Tin Tin: Top Dog in the Movies
• Penguins are black and white. • Penguins live on the ice. • Penguins can't fly. • Whales are good swimmers.	• Polar bears have white fur to help them hide in snow and hunt. • Birds use their colorful feathers to find each other. • Animals with bright colors warn other animals that they bite.	• Cheetah can run faster than any other animal on land. • Sailfish is the fastest fish in the ocean. • Falcon's long, pointed wings help make it a fast flyer.	• Rin Tin Tin is a quick learner. • He is very smart and knows a lot of tricks. • He enjoys acting in movies.

Viewing/Representing

GROUP PRESENTATIONS Divide the class into four groups, one for each of the four books read in the lesson. Have each group draw pictures of the kinds of animals highlighted in the book and show a special behavior or physical characteristic of each of those animals. Have each group present its pictures to the class.

AUDIENCE RESPONSE
Ask children to look carefully at the drawings of each group. Have them identify the animals illustrated, and discuss the different kinds of things the animals can do.

Research and Inquiry

MORE ABOUT ANIMALS Have children think about other kinds of animals they would like to learn more about. Invite them to

• look through classroom and school library books to learn more about animals.

• visit a local zoo or pet shop where children can see different kinds of animals firsthand.

• invite a veterinarian to come to the classroom to talk about animals and different ways to care for them.

 interNET CONNECTION Go to *www.mhschool.com/reading* for more information about animals.

OBJECTIVES

Children will:

• blend and identify /ər/*er* words.

....

MATERIALS:

• **Teaching Chart 81**

Skills Finder

	/ər/ **er**
Introduce	B1: 290G-H
Review	B1: 319E-F, 319G-H; B2: 180G-H, 211E-F
Test	B1: Unit 3
Maintain	B2: 55, 257

ALTERNATE TEACHING STRATEGY

....

/ər/**er**

For a different approach to teaching this skill, see pages T69–T70.

- -

TEACHING TIP

SPELLING PATTERNS

Help children use spelling patterns to decode words. Write the following words on the board: *sister, oven, candle.* Read the words aloud, pointing to each syllable as you say it. Have children underline the letters that make the /ər/, /ən/, /əl/ sounds in each word.

- -

Review /ər/er

PREPARE

Listen for /ər/*er* Words

Read this sentence aloud. Have volunteers repeat the words with the /ər/ sound.

• The famous *writer* sent *letters* to his *father, mother, sister,* and *brother.*

TEACH

BLENDING Model and Guide Practice with /ər/*er* Words

• Display **Teaching Chart 81.** Tell children that they will review words with /ər/*er*. Have volunteers underline all the words in the passage with the /ər/*er* sound.

• Blend the sounds of *teacher* with children.

> Max told the <u>teacher</u> that he had to write <u>another</u> <u>paper</u>. His dog had chewed a <u>corner</u> off the first one. Then his little <u>sister</u> had spilled <u>water</u> on it. The ink had smeared, and all the <u>letters</u> had run <u>together</u>.
>
> Teaching Chart 81

Use the Word in Context

• Have children write sentences that show the meaning of *teacher.* Ask volunteers to read their sentences. Example: *My teacher is teaching me to read.*

Repeat the Procedure

• Follow the same procedure for the words *another, paper, corner, sister, water, letters,* and *together.*

Identify /ən/, /əl/ Words

• Write the words *apple, candle, oven* and *seven* on the board and read them aloud. Ask children to listen for the /ən/ and /əl/ sounds. Have a volunteer underline the letters that stand for the /ən/ and /əl/ sounds.

PRACTICE

BUILDING/ BLENDING
Build *er* Words

GROUP

Write the following words on the chalkboard: *read, burn, work, sing,* and *play.* Ask volunteers to write new words by adding the letters *er* to each word. Ask the class to blend in unison each new word. Have children categorize the list into words with the /ər/ sound and words without the /ər/ sound. Use words with and without *er* in sentences. Then have children determine the meaning of the words based on the context of the sentences. Discuss how the *er* ending changes the meaning of the words. ▶ **Linguistic/Interpersonal**

ASSESS/CLOSE

Read and Use /ər/ *er* Words in Context

To assess children's ability to blend and identify /ər/*er* words, observe children as they do the Practice activity. Ask children if they had difficulty recognizing the sound that *er* represents. Have the class blend the words again and use them in sentences.

ADDITIONAL PHONICS RESOURCES

Phonics/Phonemic Awareness Practice Book, pages 73–76

McGraw-Hill School
TECHNOLOGY
Phonics CD-ROM
activities for practice with **Blending and Discriminating**

DAILY Phonics ROUTINES

DAY 4 **Fluency** Write the following words on the board: *weather, bother, feather, sweater.* Point to each word, asking children to blend the sounds silently. Ask a volunteer to read aloud each word.

Phonics CD-ROM

SPELLING/PHONICS CONNECTIONS
Words with /ər/*er*: See 5-Day Spelling Plan, pages 319Q–319R.

i Intervention ▶ **Skills**
Intervention Guide, for direct instruction and extra practice of /ər/ *er*

Meeting Individual Needs for Phonics

| EASY | ON-LEVEL | CHALLENGE | LANGUAGE SUPPORT |

EASY

Name_____ Date_____ Reteach **97**
/ ər/ er, / ən/, / əl/

Say the following words.
sing**er**   giv**en**   hand**le**

Circle the word that has the same ending sound as the underlined word.

1. baker   (listen)   widen
2. (button)   candle   ribbon
3. farmer   mantle   (helper)
4. (flower)   hotter   gentle
5. (bagel)   novel   raven
6. (handle)   swimmer   able

Book 2.1/Unit 3
Best Wishes, Ed
At Home: With children, walk around your house and identify five things that end in the *er* sound.   **97**

ON-LEVEL

Name_____ Date_____ Practice **97**
/ər/ er, /ən/ en, /əl/ le

Write the word that answers each riddle.

| apple | open | letters | flower | seven | table |

1. You can eat on it. You can put things on it. What is it?
   table
2. This pretty thing can be many different colors. It can grow in a garden or in a pot. What is it?
   flower
3. You can eat this fruit or bake it in a pie. What is it?
   apple
4. This number comes before eight. It is one more than six. What number is it?
   seven
5. A, B, and C are three of these. You write them every day. What are they?
   letters
6. When the door is not closed, what is it?
   open

Book 2.1/Unit 3
Best Wishes, Ed
At Home: Help children make up a riddle that has an answer that rhymes with **flower**.   **97**

CHALLENGE

Name_____ Date_____ Extend **97**
/ ər/er, / ən/, / əl/

Look at the picture. Unscramble the word that tells about the picture.

1. ouplec
   couple
2. veen
   even
3. vercoed
   covered
4. tterles
   letters
5. allersm
   smaller

Create your own scrambled word with a picture clue. Use the word **water.**

Book 2.1/Unit 3
Best Wishes, Ed
At Home: Have children look for words that rhyme with the words above.   **97**

LANGUAGE SUPPORT

Name_____ Date_____
Word Slide

camp	sing
fish	talk
mark	teach
paint	wait

er

Grade 2   Language Support/Blackline Master 57 • **Best Wishes, Ed** 105

Reteach, 97   Practice, 97   Extend, 97   Language Support, 105

319F

OBJECTIVES

Children will:

• review /ər/er; /ən/en; /əl/le.

• review silent letters: l, b, w, g, gh.

MATERIALS:

• Teaching Chart 82

Skills Finder

/ər/ er	
Introduce	B1: 290G-H
Review	B1: 319E-F, 319G-H; B2: 180G-H, 211E-F
Test	B1: Unit 3
Maintain	B2: 55,257

Review /ər/er; /ən/en; /əl/le, and Silent Letters

PREPARE

Identify /ər/er; /ən/en; /əl/le, and Silent l, b, w, g, gh

Write the words *another, other, covered, letters, water, smaller, even, couple, walked, half, climbed, whole, sign, right, night, write,* and *wrote* on the chalkboard. Underline the letters that stand for the following sounds: /ər/, /ən/, /əl/ as well as the silent letters *l, b, w, g, gh.* Tell children that they are going to review these sounds and silent letters.

TEACH

Blend Words with /ər/, /ən/, and /əl/ and Words with Silent Consonants

• Display **Teaching Chart 82**. Use the first words under each heading to model making words with the sound or sounds shown in the heading.

• Have children fill in the blanks in the second word under each heading and blend the sounds of each word.

ə Words
(/ər/, /ən/,/əl/)

le<u>tter</u>
eve<u>n</u>*
coup<u>le</u>
smal<u>ler</u>
ov<u>er</u>*
bubb<u>le</u>

Silent Consonants
(l, b, w, g, gh)

ca<u>l</u>f
lim<u>b</u>
<u>w</u>rap
<u>g</u>naw
hei<u>gh</u>t

ha<u>l</u>f
clim<u>b</u>ed
<u>w</u>hole
si<u>g</u>n
ri<u>gh</u>t

Other possible answers: ever, oven

Teaching Chart 82

Use the Words in Context

Have children use the words in sentences to reinforce their meanings. Example: *I wrote a letter to my friend who just moved away.*

Repeat the Procedure

Continue with **Teaching Chart 82**. Have children repeat the procedure for the rest of the words on the chart.

PRACTICE

WORD MEANING
Use Words in Context

ONE

Continue to display **Teaching Chart 82.** Invite children to use the words on the chart to create context sentences. Encourage children to illustrate their sentences. ▶ **Kinesthetic/Linguistic**

ASSESS/CLOSE

Build Fluency in Words with the /ər/, /ən/and /əl/ Sounds and with Silent Letters

To assess children's ability to blend and write words with the /ər/, /ən/, /əl/ sounds and words with the silent letters *l, b, w, g, gh,* observe children as they do the Practice activity. Encourage children to read their sentences aloud.

ADDITIONAL PHONICS RESOURCES

Phonics/Phonemic Awareness Practice Book
pages 73–76

McGraw-Hill School
TECHNOLOGY

Phonics **CD-ROM**

activities for practice with Blending

DAY 5 **Writing** Have children work in small groups to write about *Best Wishes, Ed* using *er* words.

Phonics **CD-ROM**

ALTERNATE TEACHING
STRATEGY
....

WORDS WITH /ər/ OR WITH SILENT LETTERS

For a different approach to teaching this skill, see pages T64–T65, T69, and T70.

ⓘ **Intervention** ▶ **Skills Intervention Guide,** for direct instruction and extra practice of /ər/, /ən/, /əl/, and silent letters

---

Meeting Individual Needs for Phonics

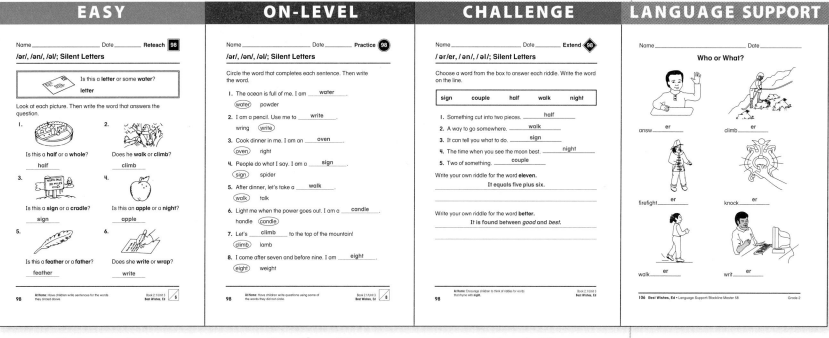

EASY	**ON-LEVEL**	**CHALLENGE**	**LANGUAGE SUPPORT**
Reteach, 98	Practice, 98	Extend, 98	Language Support, 106

OBJECTIVES

Children will understand cause-and-effect relationships.

....

MATERIALS:
• **Teaching Chart 83**

....

Skills Finder

Cause and Effect

Introduce	B1: 319I-J
Review	B1: 369I-J, 379E-F
Test	B1: Unit 3
Maintain	B1: 201

TEACHING TIP

CAUSE-EFFECT Have children explore why it is important to know the causes of events. Ask them to think of things that might change their behavior, such as the weather.

SELF-SELECTED Reading

....

Students may choose from the following titles.

ANTHOLOGY

• *Best Wishes, Ed*

LEVELED BOOKS

• *How Animals Use Color*
• *Ready Set Go!*
• *Rin Tin Tin: Top Dog in the Movies*

Bibliography, page T88–T89

Introduce Cause and Effect

PREPARE

Introduce the Concept Tell children that the cause is the reason something happens and the effect is the thing that happens.

TEACH

Model Cause and Effect Review "The Sunny Day" with children. Ask them to think about how or why things happen as you read the passage.

The Sunny Day

Ed and Betty decided to take a ride in the sunshine. A small piece of ice had broken off from their island. It was big enough for two penguins to ride on. They packed a lunch, and set off. Soon, Betty noticed that their little ice boat was getting smaller. Before too long, (Betty and Ed were in the water, completely wet.) Their boat was gone! "What happened?" cried Ed. Betty pointed at the sky. "The sun was so warm, it melted our boat away," answered Betty. "From now on we'll only go for rides on cold, cloudy days."

Teaching Chart 83

Have children identify and underline the cause in the story. Then have them identify and circle the effect.

MODEL This is what happens: Ed and Betty wind up in the water. That's the effect. The hot sun melted the ice they were sitting on. That's what made the effect happen, so the sun is the cause.

Identify an Implied Cause

Explain: Sometimes the reader is not given the cause of an effect. The cause is not stated directly. Write on the board: *The rain had stopped, and the sun was shining. The puddles of water were gone.* Ask: *What caused the puddles to disappear? How do you know?* Point out that the answer is not stated, but it is implied.

PRACTICE

Infer Cause and Effect

GROUP

Ask children why Betty and Ed decided to go for a ride. (because it was a sunny day) Ask them what would have happened if Betty and Ed went for a ride on a cold or cloudy day. (The ice wouldn't have melted, and they would have stayed dry.) ▶ **Logical/Linguistic**

ASSESS/CLOSE

Write a Story

Have children write a brief story that tells about something happening because of weather.

ALTERNATE TEACHING STRATEGY
....

CAUSE AND EFFECT

For a different approach to teaching this skill, see page T71.

Intervention ▶ **Skills Intervention Guide,** for direct instruction and extra practice of Cause and Effect

Meeting Individual Needs for Comprehension

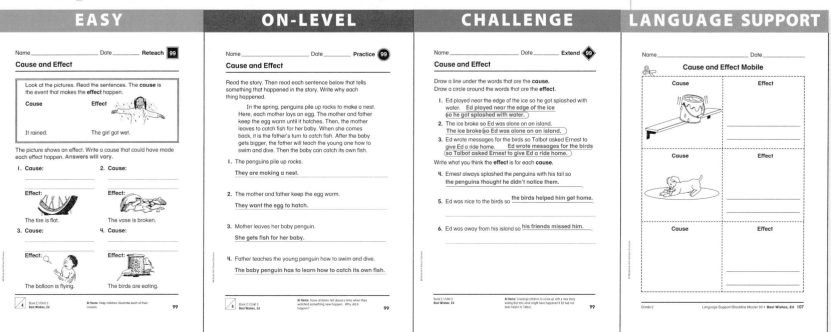

| EASY | ON-LEVEL | CHALLENGE | LANGUAGE SUPPORT |

Reteach, 99   Practice, 99   Extend, 99   Language Support, 107

TESTED
✔ OBJECTIVES

Children will use context clues, including word order, to understand unfamiliar words.

MATERIALS
• Teaching Chart 84

Skills Finder

Context Clues

Introduce	B1: 91K-L
Review	B1: 113K-L, 123I-J, 289K-L, B2: 179K-L
Test	B1: Unit 1
Maintain	B1: 311, 327; B2: 51,83

TEACHING TIP

WORD ORDER Have children brainstorm one list of nouns and one list of verbs. Write the lists on the chalkboard, and ask volunteers to create sentences from the lists. Have students listen to each other's sentences and identify correct word order.

Review **Context Clues**

PREPARE

Understanding Word Order
Remind children that most sentences tell *who* (noun) *is doing* (verb) something. Explain that understanding where words belong in a sentence can help them figure out unfamiliar words.

TEACH

Recognizing Word Order
Display **Teaching Chart 84.** Have children use word order in the passage below to help them figure out the underlined words.

A Cold Day

The penguins <u>slide</u> on the ice. They have fun all day. Talbot the <u>tern</u> flew over the island. He <u>skids</u> onto the ice. The penguins <u>waddle</u> slowly across the ice. "Hello, Talbot!" they cry. Then Ernest swims by and makes a big wave. Water <u>splashes</u> on to the iceberg. But everyone is ready. They put up their umbrellas and stay nice and dry.

Teaching Chart 84

MODEL I'm not sure what *slide* means. The sentence begins with "The penguins," so I know it is about penguins. *Slide* comes next, so it must mean something that the penguins are doing. "On the ice" comes after *slide*. I know that ice is slippery, so I think that *slide* means the same as *slip*.

PRACTICE

Using Clues and Word Order

Have children use context clues and word order to figure out the meaning of the other underlined words in the passage on **Teaching Chart 84.** ▶ **Spatial/Linguistic**

ASSESS/CLOSE

Write Sentences Using Clues

To assess children's understanding of the words from the **Teaching Chart,** have them write new sentences that correctly use *tern, skids, waddle,* and *splashes*.

ALTERNATE TEACHING STRATEGY
....

CONTEXT CLUES

For a different approach to teaching this skill, see page T68.

---

i **Intervention** ▶ **Skills Intervention Guide,** for direct instruction and extra practice of context clues

---

Meeting Individual Needs for Vocabulary

EASY	ON-LEVEL	CHALLENGE	LANGUAGE SUPPORT

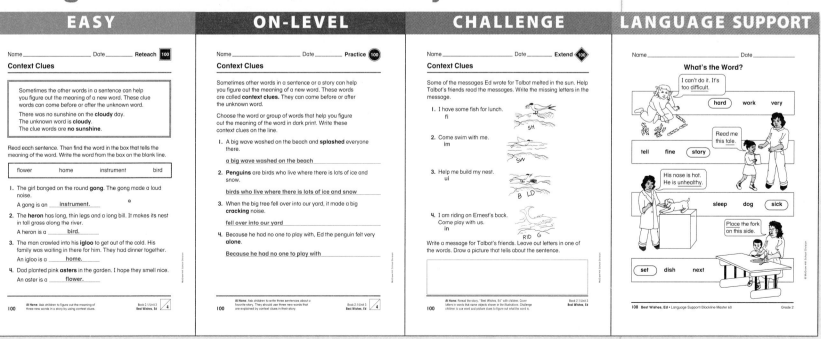

Reteach, 100   **Practice, 100**   **Extend, 100**   Language Support, 108

319L

Explanatory Writing

GRAMMAR/SPELLING
CONNECTIONS

See the 5-Day Grammar and Usage Plan on pages 319O–319P.

See the 5-Day Spelling Plan pages 319Q–319R.

TEACHING TIP

Technology Ask a volunteer to show the class how to create a header. Children should learn how to include their name, class, and date. Tell them that once the header is created it will appear on every page.

Handwriting Remind children to take their time to write neatly. All capital letters should be the same size, and all small letters should be the same size.

Handwriting CD-ROM

Prewrite

WRITE A GUIDE Present this writing assignment: Choose an activity that you enjoy, and make a guide for beginners. Include "helpful hints" that you have learned from others, and tips that you have discovered through your own experience.

MAKE A SCHEDULE Have children make a list of their favorite activities.

Strategy: Make an Outline Once children have chosen an activity, have them make an outline that covers the following topics:

- Steps needed to do the activity
- Hints from other people and your own tips about how to do the activity
- Stories from your own learning experience

Draft

USE THE OUTLINE Encourage children to write freely, using the information from their outline. Tell them they can add details and personal anecdotes. Remind them that they are writing for someone who is completely new to this activity.

Revise

SELF-QUESTIONING Ask children to assess their drafts.

- Did I clearly list the steps for doing this activity?
- Have I answered the kinds of questions a beginner might ask?
- Have I provided "helpful hints" from my own experience?

Have children trade guides with a peer to get feedback on the clarity of their explanatory writing.

Edit/Proofread

CHECK FOR ERRORS Children should check their guides for errors in spelling, grammar, and punctuation.

Publish

"HOW-TO" LIBRARY Children can create a "How-To" reference section in their classroom library. Help them make their guides into pamphlets. Encourage children to read other pamphlets, and try out new activities.

HOW TO RIDE A BIKE WITHOUT TRAINING WHEELS

Do you know how to ride your bicycle without the training wheels yet? If you do not, I have some helpful hints for you. First, have your mom or dad make the wheels higher for you. Practice riding that way for a few days. This helps you find your balance.

Next ask someone to take the training wheels off the bike. Try getting on the bike with it leaning against something strong like the side of a building. That helps you get your balance too. When you push off, keep the handle bars nice and straight.

Be sure to take short rides at first and go slow. Then you won't crash into something or fall. I rode along the sidewalk near my front lawn. So when I fell, I fell on soft grass. I hope you can use these helpful hints.

Presentation Ideas

DESIGN A COVER Have children design a cover for their pamphlets. Photocopy their designs and create a display for your classroom "reference" section.

▶ **Viewing/Representing**

GIVE A LECTURE Have children use their pamphlets to give an informal talk on their topic. Encourage the audience to comment and ask questions about the new activity.

▶ **Speaking/Listening**

How to Ride a Bike Without Training Wheels

Listening and Speaking

LISTENING Have children
- determine if the sequence of events is critical to the activity.
- listen for detailed tips.
- note any questions about the process of doing the activity.

SPEAKING Have children
- use the pamphlets as a guide; do not read them word for word.
- maintain eye contact in various areas of the room.
- use simple gestures and movements that enhance the presentation.

LANGUAGE SUPPORT

ESL When children read each other's guides, ask them to notice words that are unfamiliar. Have them ask the writer to explain the meaning by making a sketch or diagram.

 PORTFOLIO Invite children to include their guides or another writing project in their portfolios.

Consider children's creative efforts, possibly adding a plus (+) for originality, wit, and imagination.

Scoring Rubric

Excellent	Good	Fair	Unsatisfactory
4: The writer • clearly presents topic and necessary steps in detail. • anticipates questions a beginner might ask. • elaborates on hints with personal experiences.	**3:** The writer • presents basic steps needed to perform the activity. • attempts to anticipate questions from beginners. • provides some helpful hints for activity.	**2:** The writer • gives basic steps but presentation may not be clear. • understands that guide is for beginners, but does not anticipate questions. • presents few details and examples.	**1:** The writer • fails to present basic steps for activity. • has not included details or examples. • has little grasp of purpose and audience of the writing.

Incomplete 0: The writer leaves the page blank or fails to respond to the writing task. The writer does not address the topic or simply paraphrases the prompt. The response is illegible or incoherent.

Meeting Individual Needs for Writing

EASY	ON-LEVEL	CHALLENGE
Postcard Have children write a postcard from Ed to his penguin friends. Remind children of Ed's problem in the story and encourage them to write and draw a suitable picture for their cards.	**Journal** Have children imagine that they are Ed. They can write at least three journal entries describing his time alone on the island.	**Instructions** Have children write instructions for Ed telling him how to get off the island. Instructions may include details from the story or be original.

5 Day Grammar and Usage Plan

LANGUAGE SUPPORT

Write action verbs such as *jump, clap, wave, shake, hop,* on slips of paper and let one child or two or more children pantomime the action for the others. Ask children to say the appropriate sentence after observing the action. For example: *One child jumps. Three children jump.*

DAILY LANGUAGE ACTIVITIES

Write the Daily Language Activities on the chalkboard each day or use **Transparency 12**. Have children correct the sentences orally, using the present tense of the verb.

Day 1

1. They walked around the island. walk
2. They played every day. play
3. We yelled, "Walk carefully!" yell

Day 2

1. Every day Ernest splash. splashes
2. Ed always wait for her. waits
3. Ed and Betty walks on the ice. walk

Day 3

1. The noise sound like music. sounds
2. Ed wave to the birds. waves
3. The ice break. breaks

Day 4

1. Ed write messages. writes
2. Ed look for his friends. looks
3. Ernest swim. swims

Day 5

1. Ed ride with Ernest. rides
2. Talbot give Ed a fish. gives
3. Ed and Talbot races. race

Daily Language Transparency 12

DAY 1 — Introduce the Concept

Oral Warm-Up Read this sentence aloud. *The boy talks to his bird.* Ask children whether it tells what is happening now or what happened in the past. Point out the verb ending *s*.

Introduce Present-Tense Verbs The tense of a verb tells when the action takes place. Discuss:

Present-Tense Verbs

• Some verbs tell about actions that happen now.

• These verbs are in the **present tense**.

Present the Daily Language Activity and have children correct orally. Then have children write a sentence that includes a present-tense verb and underline it.

 WRITING Assign the daily Writing Prompt on page 290C.

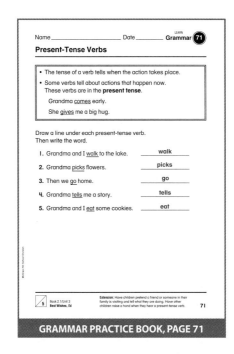

GRAMMAR PRACTICE BOOK, PAGE 71

DAY 2 — Teach the Concept

Review Present-Tense Verbs Ask children what a present-tense verb tells about.

Introduce Subject-Verb Agreement Present the following and discuss:

Present-Tense Verbs

• A present-tense verb must **agree** with its subject.

• Add *-s* to most verbs if the subject is a singular noun.

• Add *-es* to verbs that end with *s, ch, sh, x,* or *z*.

• Do not add *-s* or *-es* if the subject is a plural noun.

Present the Daily Language Activity. Then have children complete the following sentence using the present tense of the verb *reach: Meg _____ higher than Sara.* (reaches)

 WRITING Assign the daily Writing Prompt on page 290C.

GRAMMAR PRACTICE BOOK, PAGE 72

Present-Tense Verbs

Learn from the Literature Review present-tense verbs. Read the seventh line of *Best Wishes, Ed,* on page 300.

> **At the end of the day he wrote, "I GIVE UP!"**

Write the sentence *I give up!* on the chalkboard. Ask children to identify the present-tense verb. Change the subject to *Ed, the penguins,* and other singular and plural noun subjects. Ask children to tell how the verb changes.

Form Present-Tense Verbs Present the Daily Language Activity and have children correct the sentences orally.

Point out the sentence *"I guess so," said Ed* on page 301. Ask children to identify the present-tense verb. Change the subject to *Ed* and *the penguins.* Ask children to tell what happens to the verb. (must add -es) Do the same with the second paragraph on page 305.

Assign the daily Writing Prompt WRITING on page 290D.

Review Present-Tense Verbs Ask children to find the present-tense verbs from the Daily Language Activities for Days 2–3, and to use them in new sentences. Introduce the Daily Language Activity for Day 4.

Mechanics and Usage Before students begin the daily Writing Prompt on page 290D, review the use of commas. Display and discuss:

> **Commas**
>
> Use commas to separate three or more words in a series.

Write the following sentence on the board and ask children to put commas in the correct places. *Ed dances sings and plays the piano.* (dances, sings,)

Assign the daily Writing Prompt WRITING on page 290D.

Assess Use the Daily Language Activity and page 75 of the **Grammar Practice Book** for assessment.

Reteach Have students review making a verb agree with its subject by adding *-s* or *-es.*

Write the following verbs on the board: *dance, dances; tap, taps; brush, brushes; drive, drives; eat, eats.* Have children use the verbs in sentences. Write the sentences on the board. Identify the *-s* or *-es* added to verbs that tell what only one person or thing does in the present.

Have children write sentences with present-tense verbs for the word wall. Sentences may reflect activities the children do each day.

Use page 76 of the **Grammar Practice Book** for additional reteaching.

Assign the daily Writing Prompt WRITING on page 290D.

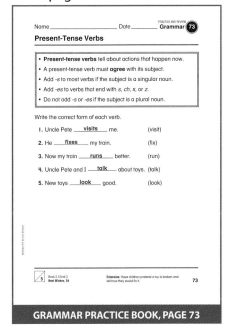

GRAMMAR PRACTICE BOOK, PAGE 73

GRAMMAR PRACTICE BOOK, PAGE 74

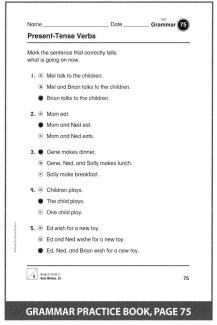

GRAMMAR PRACTICE BOOK, PAGE 75

GRAMMAR PRACTICE BOOK, PAGE 76

5 Day Spelling Plan

LANGUAGE SUPPORT

ESL Have children illustrate the meaning of each spelling word through doing pantomimes, making simple blackboard drawings, or using the word in a sentence. After a child illustrates each word, ask the others to guess what it is.

DICTATION SENTENCES

Spelling Words

1. The water is cold.
2. The other boy is gone.
3. She is over there.
4. The girl is at the corner.
5. The letter came too.
6. Our driver is good.
7. The winter is cold.
8. I never fall.
9. The farmer is away.
10. Her father has a new house.

Challenge Words

11. I climbed to the top.
12. That couple was there.
13. It drifted into town.
14. The message is late.
15. I saw the notice.

DAY 1 Pretest

Assess Prior Knowledge Use the Dictation Sentences at left and **Spelling Practice Book** page 71 for the pretest. Allow students to correct their own papers. If students have trouble, have partners give each other a midweek test on Day 3. Students who require a modified list may be tested on the first five words.

	Spelling Words		Challenge Words
1. **water**	6. driver	1. **climbed**
2. **other**	7. winter	2. **couple**
3. **over**	8. never	3. **drifted**
4. corner	9. farmer	4. **message**
5. letter	10. father	5. **notice**

*Note: Words in **dark type** are from the story.*

Word Study On page 72 of the **Spelling Practice Book** are word study steps and an at-home activity.

DAY 2 Explore the Pattern

Sort and Spell Words Say the words *other, water, over.* Ask students how the endings of the words sound the same. Tell students that these words end with a vowel sound called a *schwa* followed by *r*.

Ask students to read aloud the ten Spelling Words before sorting them according to the spelling pattern.

/ər/ spelled *er* in words ending with:

ther	ter	ner
other	water	corner
father	letter	
ver	winter	**mer**
over		farmer
driver		
never		

Word Wall As students read other stories and texts, have them look for new words with /ər/ spelled *er* and add them to a classroom word wall, underlining the spelling pattern.

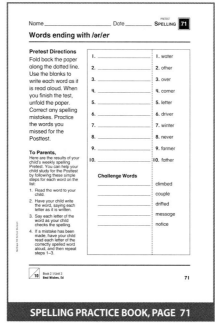

SPELLING PRACTICE BOOK, PAGE 71

WORD STUDY STEPS AND ACTIVITY, PAGE 72

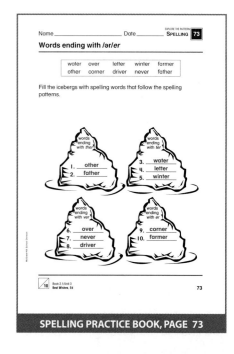

SPELLING PRACTICE BOOK, PAGE 73

Words with /ər/ er

DAY 3 Practice and Extend

Word Meaning: Words in Context
Use one sentence to describe each word. For example: *This is something I put in a mailbox.* Each time, see if students can identify the word you are describing. Then have students use the word in a sentence.

Glossary Have students:

- write each Challenge word.
- look up the definition of each word.
- write one definition for each word.

DAY 4 Proofread and Write

Proofread Sentences Write these sentences on the chalkboard, including the misspelled words. Ask students to proofread, circling incorrect spellings and writing the correct spellings. There are two spelling errors in each sentence.

> Her fathir was nevar home. (father, never)
>
> The farmur has the leter. (farmer, letter)

Have students create additional sentences with errors for partners to correct.

WRITING **Writing** Have students use as many spelling words as possible in the daily Writing Prompt on page 290D. Remind students to proofread their writing for errors in spelling, grammar, and punctuation.

DAY 5 Assess and Reteach

Assess Students' Knowledge Use page 76 of the **Spelling Practice Book** or the Dictation Sentences on page 319Q for the posttest.

Personal Word List If students have
JOURNAL trouble with any words in the lesson, have them create a personal list of troublesome words in their journals. Have partners challenge each other with a spelling quiz from their personal word lists.

Students should refer to their word lists during later writing activities.

Spelling Practice Book, Page 74

Name _____ Date _____ PRACTICE AND EXTEND SPELLING **74**

Words ending with /ər/ er

| water | over | letter | winter | farmer |
| other | corner | driver | never | father |

Use spelling words to complete each sentence.

1. The opposite of **always** is ____never____.
2. ____Winter____ is my favorite season because I like to ice skate.
3. Another word for **dad** is ____father____.
4. The opposite of **under** is ____over____.
5. I wrote a ____letter____ to my friend.
6. Meet me at the ____corner____ of Main Street and Oak Avenue.
7. Do you want this one or the ____other____ one?
8. Do you want a drink of ____water____?
9. A ____farmer____ grows food.
10. The bus ____driver____ takes my money.

Challenge Extension: Have children pretend they are shipwrecked. They may use challenge words to write a message to put in a bottle.

74   Book 2.1/Unit 3 Best Wishes, Ed

SPELLING PRACTICE BOOK, PAGE 74

Spelling Practice Book, Page 75

Name _____ Date _____ PROOFREAD AND WRITE SPELLING **75**

Words ending with /ər/ er

Read the sentences. There is one spelling mistake in each sentence. Circle the mistake. Write the correct word on the line.

1. Tom, please send me a leter.
2. Matt, why don't you swim ovir here today?
3. Who wants to go fishing with Sue and her fathir?
4. There will be a wintor party for all of the penguins on Saturday night.
5. Mike is looking for othur penguins to help build a snowman.
6. Please meet me at the cornir.

1. ____letter____ 2. ____over____ 3. ____father____
4. ____winter____ 5. ____other____ 6. ____corner____

Writing Activity
Pretend that you are a farmer. Write a letter to your city friend and invite him to visit you. Tell him what he will see at your farm. Use four of your spelling words. Circle the spelling words you use.

_____
_____
_____
_____

10 Book 2.1/Unit 3 Best Wishes, Ed   75

SPELLING PRACTICE BOOK, PAGE 75

Spelling Practice Book, Page 76

Name _____ Date _____ POSTTEST SPELLING **76**

Words ending with /ər/ er

Look at the words in each set. One word in each set is spelled right. Use a pencil to color in the circle in front of that word. Before you begin, look at the sample sets of words. Sample A has been done for you. Do Sample B by yourself. When you are sure you know what to do, you may go on with the rest of the page.

Sample A
- Ⓐ paeper
- Ⓑ parper
- ● paper
- Ⓓ peper

Sample B
- ● half
- Ⓕ haf
- Ⓖ halfe
- Ⓗ haffe

1.
- Ⓐ watir
- Ⓑ wator
- ● water
- Ⓓ watar

6.
- Ⓔ drivor
- Ⓕ drivur
- ● driver
- Ⓗ drivar

2.
- ● other
- Ⓕ othir
- Ⓖ othar
- Ⓗ othur

7.
- ● winter
- Ⓑ wintor
- Ⓒ wintere
- Ⓓ wintur

3.
- Ⓐ ovir
- Ⓑ ovar
- ● over
- Ⓓ ovur

8.
- Ⓔ nevur
- Ⓕ nevir
- ● never
- Ⓗ nevar

4.
- ● corner
- Ⓕ cornir
- Ⓖ cornor
- Ⓗ cornure

9.
- Ⓐ farmir
- ● farmer
- Ⓒ farmor
- Ⓓ farmar

5.
- Ⓐ leter
- Ⓑ lettir
- Ⓒ lettor
- ● letter

10.
- Ⓔ fathur
- Ⓕ fathre
- Ⓖ fathir
- ● father

76   Book 2.1/Unit 3 Best Wishes, Ed   10

SPELLING PRACTICE BOOK, PAGE 76

319R

Concept
- Types of Communication

Comprehension
- Cause and Effect

Phonics
- Short *e*

Vocabulary
- arrive
- early
- finished
- record
- rushed
- success

Reaching All Learners

Anthology

The Pony Express

Selection Summary Children will read about the daring young riders of mail on the Pony Express, the fastest delivery service 19th century America had yet known.

Rhyme applies to phonics

Listening Library

INSTRUCTIONAL pages 322–341

About the Author Dale Ryder loves history and has always been interested in the story of the Pony Express. Ryder does not have a pony, but does live with a dog who is not at all interested in delivering mail.

About the Illustrator Kunio Hagio always knew he wanted to be an artist. But when he was 16, his right hand was hurt in an accident and the doctors thought he'd never draw again. Today he says, "There's nothing you can't overcome if you don't believe any reasons to quit."

Same Concept, Skills and Vocabulary!

Leveled Books

EASY
Lesson on pages 341A and 341D

INDEPENDENT
Lesson on pages 341B and 341D

 Take-Home version available

CHALLENGE
Lesson on pages 341C and 341D

Leveled Practice

EASY
Reteach, 101–108 Blackline masters with reteaching opportunities for each assessed skill

INDEPENDENT/ON-LEVEL
Practice, 101–108 Workbook with Take-Home stories and practice opportunities for each assessed skill and story comprehension

CHALLENGE
Extend, 101–108 Blackline masters that offer challenge activities for each assessed skill

Quizzes Prepared by ⬛ **Accelerated Reader**

WORKSTATION Activities

Social Studies . . .	Food of the Future, *334*
Science	Evolution of the Horse, *326*
Math	Timing the Riders, *328*
Art	Comic Strip, *332*
Language Arts . .	Read Aloud, *320E*
Writing	Write Directions, *338*
Cultural Perspectives	The Horse in Different Cultures, *330*
Research and Inquiry	Find Out More, *339*
Internet Activities	www.mhschool.com/reading

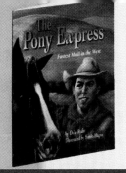

READING AND LANGUAGE ARTS	**DAY 1** *Focus on Reading and Skills*	**DAY 2** *Read the Literature*
● **Phonics Daily Routines**	Daily **Phonics** Routine: **Segmenting,** 320H **Phonics** CD-ROM	Daily **Phonics** Routine: **Discriminating,** 322A **Phonics** CD-ROM
● **Phonological Awareness** ● **Phonics** *Short e* ● **Comprehension** ● **Vocabulary** ● **Study Skills** ● **Listening, Speaking, Viewing, Representing**	**Read Aloud: Legend,** 320E "Crazy Horse Keeps a Promise" ☑ **Develop Phonological Awareness,** 320F Short *e* ☑ **Introduce Short *e: ea,** 320G–320H **Teaching Chart 85** **Reteach, Practice, Extend,** 101 **Phonics/Phonemic Awareness** **Practice Book,** 77–80 **Read Apply Short *e: ea,** 320/321 "The Pony Express" ⓘ Intervention Program	**Build Background,** 322A Develop Oral Language **Vocabulary,** 322B–322C *arrive finished rushed* *early record success* **Teaching Chart 86** **Word Building Manipulative Cards** **Reteach, Practice, Extend,** 102 **Read the Selection,** 322–337 Comprehension ☑ Short *e* ☑ Cause and Effect **Genre:** Informational Story, 323 **Writer's Craft:** Transitions, 331 **Cultural Perspectives,** 330 ⓘ Intervention Program
● **Curriculum Connections**	**Link** Language Arts, 320E	**Link** Social Studies, 322A
● **Writing**	**Writing Prompt:** When was the last time you sent someone a postcard, letter, or greeting card? Describe what you did.	**Writing Prompt:** Imagine you were once a Pony Express rider. Write about what you did and what happened. **Journal Writing,** Quick-Write, 337
● **Grammar**	**Introduce the Concept: Past-Tense Verbs,** 341O Daily Language Activity: Change present tense verbs to past tense. **Grammar Practice Book,** 77	**Teach the Concept: Past-Tense Verbs,** 341O Daily Language Activity: Change present tense verbs to past tense. **Grammar Practice Book,** 78
● **Spelling** *Short e*	**Pretest: Words with Short *e,** 341Q **Spelling Practice Book,** 77, 78	**Teach the Pattern: Words with Short *e,** 341Q **Spelling Practice Book,** 79

Meeting Individual Needs

 ✓ = **Skill Assessed in Unit Test**

ⓘ **Intervention Program Available**

 **Read EVERY DAY**

 **DAY 3** **Read the Literature**

 **DAY 4** **Build Skills**

 DAY 5 **Build Skills**

Daily  **Phonics** Routine:
Letter Substitution, 339

 Phonics CD-ROM

Daily  **Phonics** Routine:
Writing, 341F

Phonics CD-ROM

Daily  **Phonics** Routine:
Fluency, 341H

Phonics CD-ROM

Rereading for Fluency, 336

Story Questions and Activities,
338–339
  Reteach, Practice, Extend, 103
Story Activities, 339

Study Skill, 340
  ✓ Reference Sources
  Teaching Chart 87
  Reteach, Practice, Extend, 104

Test Power, 341

 Read the Leveled Books, 339A–339D
  Guided Reading
  ✓ Short *e*
  ✓ Cause and Effect
  ✓ Instructional Vocabulary

ⓘ Intervention Program

Read **Read the Leveled Books and the Self-Selected Books**

  ✓ **Review Short *e*,** 341E–341F
    Teaching Chart 88
    Reteach, Practice, Extend, 105
    Language Support, 114
    Phonics/Phonemic Awareness
    Practice Book, 77–80

  ✓ **Cumulative Review,** 341G–341H
    Teaching Chart 89
    Reteach, Practice, Extend, 106
    Language Support, 115
    Phonics/Phonemic Awareness
    Practice Book, 77–80

  Minilessons, 325, 327, 329, 333

ⓘ Intervention Program

Read **Read Self-Selected Books**

  ✓ **Review Fantasy and Reality,** 341I–341J
    Teaching Chart 90
    Reteach, Practice, Extend, 107
    Language Support, 116

  ✓ **Introduce Synonyms,** 341K–341L
    Teaching Chart 91
    Reteach, Practice, Extend, 108
    Language Support, 117

  Listening, Speaking, Viewing, Representing, 341N
    Design a Poster
    Give a Demonstration

  Minilessons, 325, 327, 329, 333

ⓘ Intervention Program

Activity Science, 326; **Math,** 328

Activity Art, 332

Activity Social Studies, 334

 **Writing Prompt:** You once were a mailperson. You delivered happy mail and sad mail. Tell what you thought about and how you felt.

Explanatory Writing, 341M
  Prewrite, Draft

Writing Prompt: Write a letter telling a friend why you liked being a mailperson.

Explanatory Writing, 341M
  Revise

Meeting Individual Needs for Writing, 341N

Writing Prompt: Write a story about a storm that was so heavy the mail could not be delivered.

Explanatory Writing, 341M
  Edit/Proofread, Publish

Practice and Write: Past-Tense Verbs, 341P
  Daily Language Activity: Change present tense verbs to past tense.

Grammar Practice Book, 79

Practice and Write: Past-Tense Verbs, 341P
  Daily Language Activity: Change present tense verbs to past tense.

Grammar Practice Book, 80

Assess and Reteach: Past-Tense Verbs, 341P
  Daily Language Activity: Change present tense verbs to past tense.

Grammar Practice Book, 81, 82

Practice and Extend: Words with Short *e*, 341R

Spelling Practice Book, 80

Practice and Write: Words with Short *e*, 341R

Spelling Practice Book, 81

Assess and Reteach: Words with Short *e*, 341R

Spelling Practice Book, 82

Link

Language Arts

Read Aloud

Crazy Horse Keeps a Promise
a Sioux legend

On the day Crazy Horse was born, a horse dashed through the Sioux camp in the Black Hills of South Dakota. People said, "This is a sign from the Great Spirit! After all, wasn't our first horse a gift from the Great Spirit? It is because of the horse that our hunters could provide us with plenty to eat. This baby will be a great hunter, warrior, and leader. We should name him Crazy Horse."

Even as a young boy, Crazy Horse was a legendary hunter and warrior. Before he turned thirteen, he was able to capture horses from the enemy. He led his first war party before turning twenty. He dazzled his own people and his enemies by his skill and daring as he fought to preserve his people's way of life.

Throughout his life, Crazy Horse never signed a treaty, never agreed to move to a reservation, and never surrendered to the white man's ways. One of the few contacts he had with a white man was with a news photographer.

Continued on page T4

Oral Comprehension

LISTENING AND SPEAKING As you read this legend aloud, encourage children to listen for details that make Crazy Horse a hero to his people. When you have finished reading, ask:

• "Could an ordinary person do the things Crazy Horse did as a young boy? What things did Crazy Horse do that are heroic?"

GENRE STUDY: LEGEND Discuss common characteristics of legends. Explain that a legend is a story about people, or a person, who actually lived. Some parts of the story are true and some parts are made up.

• Discuss the setting of "Crazy Horse Keeps a Promise." What clues can children find about time and place? Explain that most legends have a historical setting.

• Point out that this legend tells about a real person. Ask children to give examples from the story of things that Crazy Horse actually did.

• Explain how this legend tells about Crazy Horse's heroism. Ask children what heroic qualities Crazy Horse had.

Activity Guide children in looking for a biography of Crazy Horse in an encyclopedia. Ask them to verify which details of Crazy Horse's life are true.

▶ **Linguistic/Logical**

Develop Phonological Awareness

Blend Sounds

MATERIALS
- Phonics Pictures from *Word Building Cards*

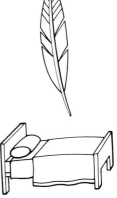

Teach Tell children they are going to put some sounds together to make words. Hold up the Phonics Picture for *bed*. Say the sounds for the word and have children blend the sounds with you to say the whole word. Invite children to listen as you say some more sounds. Say, /b/-/r/-/e/-/d/. *If you put the sounds together what is the word?* (bread) Ask children to say the middle sound they hear in both *bed* and *bread*. Repeat using the picture of *feather* and the word *fed*.

Practice Have children blend the sounds for the following words: *head, lead, weather, read, dead,* and *sweat*.

Segment Sounds

MATERIALS
- Word Building Boxes from *Word Building Cards*
- counters

Teach Display a Word Building Box with four sections. Say: *ready . . . /r/-/e/-/d/-/ē/.* Place a counter in the second box. Then say: *The /ē/ sound is the second sound in* ready.

Practice Distribute Word Building Boxes and counters to each child. Using the following words, have them place counters in the box where the short *e* sound is heard: *head, end, tread, dread, read,* and *envy*. Then ask them to repeat the sound /e/.

Substitute Sounds

MATERIALS
- colored blocks

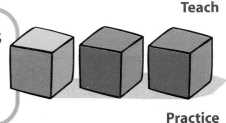

Teach Give each child a set of blue- and orange-colored blocks. Demonstrate what you expect children to do. Say: *bed . . . /b/-/e/-/d/* as you place three blue blocks in front of you. Then say: *Now I'll change a sound in the word to make it* lead *. . . /l/-/e/-/d/.* Replace the first blue block with an orange block.

Practice Have children substitute sounds using the colored blocks as you say the following sets of words: *tread/dread; park/part; read/road; sock/sick.*

  **ASSESSMENT** Observe children as they blend, segment, and substitute sounds. If children have difficulty, see Alternate Teaching Strategies on p. T72.

OBJECTIVES

Children will:

• identify short *e*: *ea*.

• decode and read short *e*: *ea* words.

. . . .

MATERIALS:

• **Teaching Chart 85**

• letter cards from the **Word Building Manipulative Cards**

Skills Finder

Short *e*: *ea*

Introduce	B1: 320G-H
Review	B1: 341E-F, 341G-H
Test	B1: Unit 3
Maintain	B1: 349

SPELLING/PHONICS CONNECTIONS

Words with short *e*: *ea*: See 5-Day Spelling Plan, pages 341Q–341R.

TEACHING TIP

HOMOGRAPHS Explain that words can look alike, but sound different and have different meanings. Write the word "lead" on the board. Invite children to read the word aloud and use it in a sentence. Encourage children to use both meanings: lead pencil, and lead a horse. Explain that children can use context clues to determine which pronunciation and meaning make sense.

Introduce Short *e*: *ea*

TEACH

Identify the Letters *ea* as the Symbol for the Sound /e/

Tell children they will learn to read words with the letters *ea*, which stand for the short *e* sound.

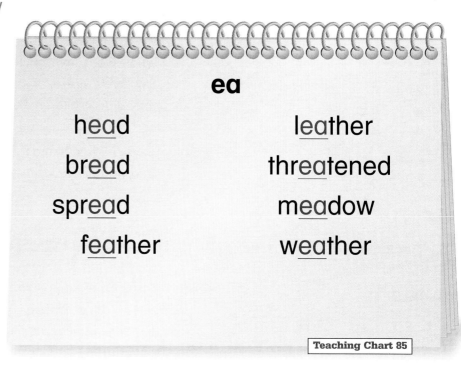

ea

head	leather
bread	threatened
spread	meadow
feather	weather

Teaching Chart 85

BLENDING
Model and Guide Practice with Short *ea* words

• Display **Teaching Chart 85**. Point to the letters *ea* at the top and explain that this is a spelling pattern for the short *e* sound. Have children repeat the short *e* sound as you point to the letters.

• Write the letters *ea* on the blank space in the first example. Have children blend the sounds with you as you run your finger under the word *head*.   *h   ea   d*   *head*

• Write *ea* on the blank of the incomplete word *br__d*. Have children blend the sounds together and read the word.

• Repeat the process using the remaining incomplete words in column 1.

Use the Words in Context

• Have volunteers use the completed words from column 1 on the **Teaching Chart** in sentences to reinforce their meanings. Example: *I like to spread peanut butter on bread.*

Repeat the Procedure

• Follow the same procedure to complete column 2 on the chart.

PRACTICE

LETTER SUBSTITUTION
Build Short e: ea Words with Letter Cards

ONE

Have children use letter cards to build and read the word *leather*. Then tell them to change the word to *feather* by substituting *f* for *l*. Have children build the word *weather* by substituting *w* for *f*. Have children build other word groups such as *bread, head, spread*. ▶ **Visual/Linguistic**

ASSESS/CLOSE

Read Short e: ea Words

To assess children's ability to build and read short *e: ea* words, observe them as they work on the Practice activity. Then have children read the phonics rhyme on pages 320–321 in their books.

ADDITIONAL PHONICS RESOURCES

Phonics/Phonemic Awareness Practice Book, pages 77–80

McGraw-Hill School **TECHNOLOGY**

Phonics CD-ROM activities for practice with **Blending and Segmenting**

Meeting Individual Needs for Phonics

EASY	ON-LEVEL	CHALLENGE

EASY

Name _____ Date _____ Reteach 101

Short e: ea

Say the following words. Listen to the sound the letters ea make in each word.

lea**d**   brea**d**   he**alth**

Circle the word that completes each sentence. Then write the word.

1. You eat ____breakfast____ in the morning.
   head   (breakfast)   milk

2. Joe put a hat on his ____head____.
   lead   foot   (head)

3. It was so cold, Kim could see her ____breath____.
   coat   (breath)   read

4. My father ____read____ me the book.
   (read)   showed   red

5. Shari likes the hot ____weather____.
   health   (weather)   day

6. The saddle was made of ____leather____.
   (leather)   wool   head

Book 2.1/Unit 3
The Pony Express   **At Home:** Help children think of other words with the short e sound spelled ea.   101

Reteach, 101

ON-LEVEL

Name _____ Date _____ Practice 101

Short e: ea

Say the words. What sound do both words have in common?

ready   feather

The sound made by the letters **ea**.

| bread | ready | breath | leather |
| weather | steady | breakfast | head |

Read the story below. Then choose a word from the box to write on each line.

The ____weather____ was very cold that morning. Johnnie had a hot ____breakfast____. He had a piece of ____bread____ with jam and some eggs. He put a warm hat on his ____head____. Then he went outside and put the ____leather____ saddle on his horse. It was so cold, he could see his ____breath____.

Finally, he was ____ready____. But the ice and snow were slippery. Johnnie shouted, "____Steady____" to his horse. It would be a day of hard work!

Book 2.1/Unit 3
The Pony Express   **At Home:** Have children pronounce each of the words they wrote. Then have them underline the letters that make the sound of short e in each word.   101

Practice, 101

CHALLENGE

Name _____ Date _____ Extend 101

Short e: ea

Look at each picture clue. Write a word clue for each one. Write the picture name in the puzzle.

| feather | sweater | thread | head | bread |

S W E A T E R
          H
          R
F E A T H E R
B R E A D   A
          D

Across
1. ![shirt] You wear it to keep warm.
3. ![feather] Birds have these.
5. ![bread] You eat it with butter.

Down
2. ![spool] You can sew with it.
4. ![head] It is at the end of your neck.

Book 2.1/Unit 3
The Pony Express   **At Home:** Challenge children to create their own crossword puzzles. Use either pictures or riddles to give the clues.   101

Extend, 101

Daily Routines

DAY 1
Segmenting Write a list of short *e: ea* words on the chalkboard. Ask children to copy down the list, and then to circle the letters that make the short *e: ea* sound in the words on the list.

DAY 2
Discriminating Write a variety of short *e: ea* words and long *e: ea* words on the chalkboard. Read the list and ask children to clap when they hear words with the short *e: ea* sound.

DAY 3
Letter Substitution Using the CVVC flipchart, have pairs of children build *head*. Taking turns, tell one child to change one or more letters to build a new word and ask the partner to read it.

DAY 4
Writing Have children write two sentences about *The Pony Express* using words with the short *e: ea* sound. Then have them read the sentences, blending the sounds of the *e: ea* words.

DAY 5
Fluency Ask children to circle the short *e: ea* words on page 332 of *The Pony Express* and to blend the words silently. Then ask children to read the page aloud in unison.

Apply Short *e: ea*

The Pony Express

Have you read the news?
Hurry! Spread the news!
The Pony Express is ahead!
A truck can send a letter
But a pony is much better.
The Pony Express is ahead!
Do you want to send your mail
But a truck is sure to fail?
Try a pony, instead!

320

321

Anthology pages 320–321

Read and Build Fluency

READ THE POEM Have children listen to the recording of "The Pony Express" as they track the print. Point out the short *e: ea* words. Encourage them to hear how the recorded voice changes when reading statements, questions, and exclamations.

RERED FOR FLUENCY Encourage partners PARTNERS to take turns reading the poem aloud to one another. Ask children to focus on punctuation and expression of emotion as they read. Remind them to pause after commas, to add emphasis to sentences that end in exclamation points, and to vary the ending tone for questions.

Dictate and Spell

DICTATE WORDS Say the short *e: ea* word *read* JOURNAL aloud. Then segment it into its three individual sounds. Repeat the word and use it in a sentence, such as, "Sasha read three poems this week." Have children repeat the word and write the letters for each sound to make the whole word. Then repeat these steps with the words *spread, ahead,* and *instead.* Continue the exercise with other short *e: ea* words not found in the poem, such as *bread* and *weather.*

Intervention **Skills Intervention Guide,** for direct instruction and extra practice of short *e: ea*

Build Background

Social Studies

Concept: Types of Communication

Evaluate Prior Knowledge

CONCEPT: TYPES OF COMMUNICATION These selections are concerned with types of communication. Have children list types of communication, such as the regular mail, telephone, or e-mail, that they or their parents use.

DEVELOP METHODS OF COMMUNICATION Have children brainstorm ways that they and their friends might communicate if there were no telephones or mail delivery. For example, they might take turns delivering and picking up messages for each other. Ask children to make a chart showing each method of communication, its advantages and its disadvantages.

▶ **Linguistic/Visual**

Method	Advantages	Disadvantages
Message runner	The message runner gets to visit all of his or her friends.	The message runner would have to do a lot of running around.

Graphic Organizer 30

MAKE A LIST Have children list the different reasons that they and their family use the telephone.

ONE WRITING

Develop Oral Language

PEN PALS Have non-English-speaking children sit with English-speaking partners. Have all class members write letters to friends in another class describing their day at school. Tell them to use cartoon pictures with short explanatory captions and balloons for dialogue. Partners can read each other's letters and then ask each other questions when they are unable to understand something in the letters. Encourage them to address and mail their letters.

ESL

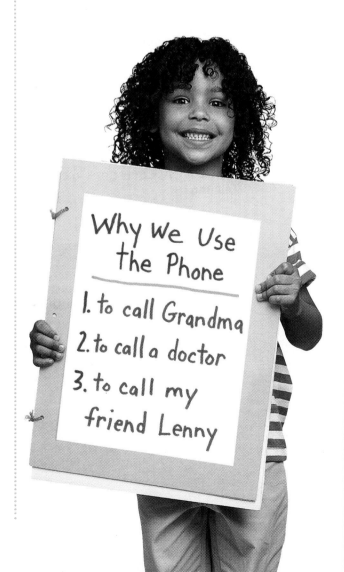

Why We Use
the Phone

1. to call Grandma
2. to call a doctor
3. to call my
   friend Lenny

DAILY Phonics ROUTINES

DAY 2 **Discriminating** Write a variety of short *e*: *ea* words and long *e*: *ea* words on the chalkboard. Read the list and ask children to clap when they hear *e* words with the short *e*: *ea* sound.

 Phonics CD-ROM

LANGUAGE SUPPORT

Additional support for building background may be found in the **Language Support Book**, pages 109–112.

Children will use context and structural clues to determine the meanings of vocabulary words.

rushed

arrive

early

record

finished

success

Definitions

rushed (p. 326) hurried

arrive (p. 324) to reach a destination

early (p. 329) before the usual or expected time

record (p. 336) a best performance

finished (p. 336) ended, completed

success (p. 336) a thing that goes well

Story Words

These words from the selection may be unfamiliar. Before children read, have them check the meanings and pronunciations of the words in the Glossary, beginning on page 398, or in a dictionary.

• express, p. 324

• *mochila,* p. 325

• stagecoach, p. 330

• buffalo, p. 335

• stampede, p. 335

• telegraph, p. 336

Vocabulary

Teach Vocabulary in Context

Identify Vocabulary Words Display **Teaching Chart 86** and read the passage with children. Have volunteers circle each vocabulary word and underline other words that are clues to its meaning.

Jack Gets the Job

1. When he read the want ad, Jack (rushed) to the Pony Express office as fast as he could. **2.** He wanted to (arrive) before anyone else got there. **3.** In fact, he was so (early) that he had to wait a long time before he could get in the office. **4.** The manager of the Pony Express told Jack that he was looking for the fastest horseback rider in town and asked him what his (record) time for riding 75 miles was. **5.** Jack said that he had once (finished) such a ride in seven hours. **6.** The talk was a complete (success), and Jack got the job.

Teaching Chart 86

Discuss Meanings Ask questions like these to help clarify word meanings:

• Do you have to rush when you have plenty of time to get to school?

• When you arrive someplace, do you say "hello" or "good-bye"?

• When you get to the movies early, do you have to hurry in?

• When you're finished with dinner, do you wash dishes or set the table?

• What is the record in your school for running the fastest race?

• What is something you did that was a success?

 **Activities**

Practice

Using Context Clues
 PARTNERS

 WRITING

Partners can take turns choosing vocabulary cards from a pile. The partner who has chosen a card writes a sentence using the word on the card. He or she can then read the sentence aloud leaving out the vocabulary word for the partner to identify.

▶ **Kinesthetic/Linguistic**

rushed   arrive   finished

Word Building Manipulative Cards

Write a Poem
GROUP

 WRITING

Have the class use the vocabulary words to write a poem. Help them brainstorm rhymes. Have children refer to the Glossary as needed. ▶ **Linguistic/Oral**

SPELLING/VOCABULARY CONNECTIONS
See Spelling Challenge Words, pages 341Q–341R.

LANGUAGE SUPPORT

See the **Language Support Book**, pages 109–112, for teaching suggestions for Vocabulary.

Vocabulary PuzzleMaker

Provides vocabulary activities.

Assess Vocabulary

Identify Word Meaning in Context
PARTNERS

WRITING

Have each child write five questions, using a different vocabulary word in each question. Then have partners exchange questions. Partners should write answers to each question, using the vocabulary words in their answers whenever possible.

Meeting Individual Needs for Vocabulary

EASY	ON-LEVEL	ON-LEVEL	CHALLENGE

EASY

Name _____ Date _____ Reteach 102
Vocabulary

Choose a word from the box to complete each sentence. Write the word in the empty boxes.

| arrive | early | finished | record | rushed | success |

1. The girls ___ to the store.
   r u s h e d

2. The train will ___ at three o'clock.
   a r r i v e

3. Our class had great ___ at spelling.
   s u c c e s s

4. Patty set the ___ in the swim race.
   r e c o r d

5. My dad gets up ___ in the morning.
   e a r l y

6. I ___ my homework then went out to play.
   f i n i s h e d

At Home: Ask children to write a sentence for three of the vocabulary words.
102   Book 2.1/Unit 3 The Pony Express

ON-LEVEL

Name _____ Date _____ Practice 102
Vocabulary

Choose a word from the box that has the opposite or the same meaning as the underlined word. Write the word on the line.

| arrive | early | finish | record | rush | success |

1. If you start a game, be sure to __finish__ it.

2. There's no hurry to get there, so don't __rush__!

3. Please don't be late. Try to be __early__.

4. When you __arrive__, call and let me know you have gotten there.

5. Karla set a world __record__ because she was the first and only woman to climb the mountain.

6. Our team is not a failure. It is a __success__.

At Home: Ask children to make up a short story using the words in the box.
102   Book 2.1/Unit 3 The Pony Express

ON-LEVEL

Waiting for Beth

Soon Freddy and his father were running out the door. "We must rush!" said Freddy's father.
At the train station, they ran all the way to Beth's train. She watched them come.
"I think you two just broke my record!" laughed Beth. And together they all walked slowly back home.

At Home: Talk with children about a time someone they loved came to visit. What did they do together?

102a

CHALLENGE

Name _____ Date _____ Extend 102
Vocabulary

Would you like to learn horseback riding? Write a letter about it to a friend. Use some of the words in the box.

| record | rush | success | early | arrive | finish |

Dear _____,

_____
_____
_____
_____
_____
_____
_____

Sincerely,

At Home: Have children define each word in the box.
102   Book 2.1/Unit 3 The Pony Express

Reteach, 102

Practice, 102

Practice, 102a
Take-Home Story

Extend, 102

322C

Comprehension

Prereading Strategies

PREVIEW AND PREDICT Have children look at page 322. Read the names of the author and illustrator aloud. Then take a **picture walk** through the selection. Talk about the details of the illustrations.

- When did the events in the article happen?
- Will there be one main character or many?
- What will the selection be about?
- Is this selection about events that really happened or make-believe events? How can you tell? (It has real names and dates.) *Genre*

Next, have children record their predictions about the story.

PREDICTIONS	WHAT HAPPENED
Young men delivered mail by horseback.	
The Pony Express was the fastest way to send mail for one year.	

SET PURPOSES Have children ask themselves questions about the selection. For example:

- Why was the mail delivered by horseback?

READ TOGETHER

Meet Dale Ryder

Dale Ryder is a writer who lives in New York City. Ryder has always been interested in the Pony Express. This is Ryder's first story for children.

Meet Kunio Hagio

When Kunio Hagio was growing up in Chicago, he knew he wanted to be an artist. But when he was 16, his right hand was so badly hurt in an accident that the doctors thought he'd never be able to draw again. Today he says, "There's nothing you can't overcome if you don't believe any reasons to quit." Kunio Hagio lives and works in Sedona, Arizona.

322

Meeting Individual Needs · Grouping Suggestions for Strategic Reading

EASY

Read Together Read the selection together with children or have them use the **Listening Library**. Help children chart the cause-and-effect relationships in the selection. Comprehension and Intervention prompts offer additional help with decoding and comprehension.

ON-LEVEL

Guided Instruction Read the selection with children. You may wish to have the children read the selection first on their own. Monitor any difficulties in reading that children may have in order to determine which parts of the Comprehension to emphasize. After reading the story with children, have children reread it.

CHALLENGE

Independent Reading Have children set purposes before they read. Remind children that identifying cause-and-effect relationships between events can help them understand the selection. After reading, have children retell the events. Children can use the cause-and-effect relationships they identify for group discussions.

The Pony Express

Fastest Mail in the West

by Dale Ryder
Illustrated by Kunio Hagio

323

This chart is available as a blackline master in the **Language Support Book**.

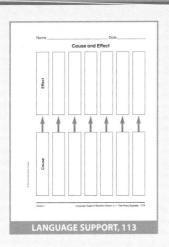

LANGUAGE SUPPORT, 113

Comprehension

 Apply Short *e*: *ea*

☑ Apply Cause and Effect

STRATEGIC READING This selection describes the way mail was delivered in the United States over one hundred years ago. Seeing how one event or action causes another can help us understand why things happened the way they did. Let's make a chart to record the causes and effects in this article.

CAUSE	EFFECT

 Where did the Pony Express deliver mail? (in the West) *Draw Conclusions*

Genre

Informational Story

Explain that an informational story:

- tells a story, although the plot may be very simple.
- presents information in an easy-to-understand way.
- has characters and settings that are usually realistic.

Activity After children read *The Pony Express*, ask them to look on page 325, where the author describes a *mochila*. Ask, "What is a mochila? (a knapsack) Does the author describe it in a way that is easy to understand?" As children reread the story, encourage them to record the main events on a simple time line.

323

Comprehension

② **CAUSE AND EFFECT** Why did Johnnie Frye decide to become a rider for the Pony Express?

MODEL Johnnie read the ad. He thought he fit the description in the ad. That must be why he joined the Pony Express. I'll add that to the Cause-and-Effect chart.

CAUSE	EFFECT
Johnnie saw an interesting ad.	He became a Pony Express rider.

③ Do you think other young men will join the Pony Express too? Why or why not? (Yes; other men will want the adventure.) *Make Predictions*

Fluency

GROUP READING

Have the class reread to achieve fluency.

• Have a volunteer read the text from the "Wanted" poster aloud.

• Have the class read page 324 aloud.

• Point out to children that sometimes there is information in the art that will help them understand the text.

• Remind children to think about what is happening in the story and read with the appropriate expression.

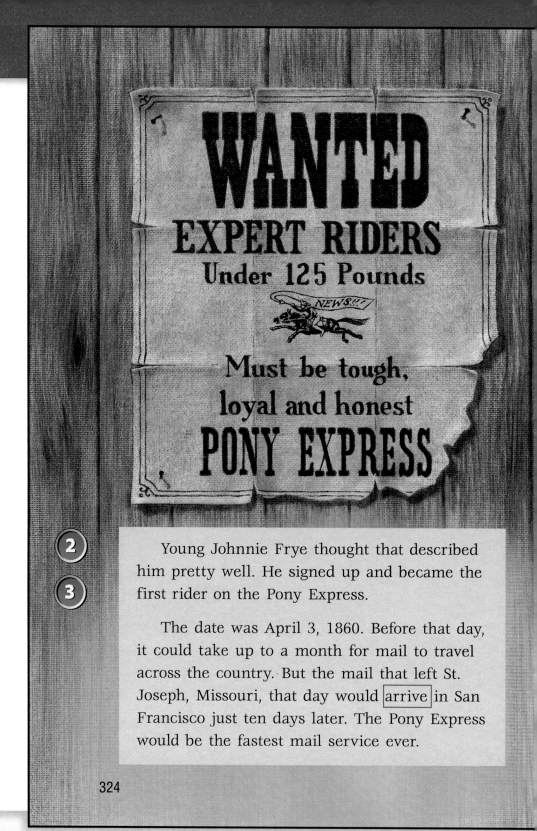

WANTED
EXPERT RIDERS
Under 125 Pounds

NEWS!!!

Must be tough,
loyal and honest
PONY EXPRESS

②
③

Young Johnnie Frye thought that described him pretty well. He signed up and became the first rider on the Pony Express.

The date was April 3, 1860. Before that day, it could take up to a month for mail to travel across the country. But the mail that left St. Joseph, Missouri, that day would arrive in San Francisco just ten days later. The Pony Express would be the fastest mail service ever.

324

An excited crowd gathered and watched as Johnnie put the special, very light saddle on his pony. Over the saddle lay a thin piece of leather called a *mochila*. *Mochila* is the Spanish word for knapsack. It had pockets in its four corners. The pockets, called *cantinas*, held the newspapers, letters, and telegrams that the Pony Express riders would take to California.

④

325

Comprehension

④ **CAUSE AND EFFECT** Why did an excited crowd gather? (They wanted to watch Johnnie take off on his first trip.) Why was this trip so important? (It was the first trip of the Pony Express, the fastest mail service ever.)

TEACHING TIP

BACKGROUND INFORMATION Remind children that there were no automobiles or planes during the time of the Pony Express, and that there were many places trains did not travel to. You may want to use TV programs or movies about the Old West as references. Remind children of movies they might have seen in which people traveled in stage-coaches and covered wagons.

Minilesson

REVIEW/MAINTAIN

Using Text Features

Help children use features of the text to increase their level of understanding. Show children the word *mochila* from page 325. Tell children that this word is written in italics. Explain that italics are often used to emphasize foreign words. In this case, the author is emphasizing the Spanish words *mochila* and *cantinas*.

Activity Have children work in pairs to develop sentences that contain Spanish words. Encourage children to locate other Spanish words that relate to the story by asking those fluent in Spanish or by using an English/Spanish dictionary. Ask children to use the intonation of their voice to emphasize the Spanish words when they say their sentences. Have children give enough information about the words for others to guess their meaning.

LANGUAGE SUPPORT

ESL Write the phrasal verbs *pulled into* and *kept its promise* on the board and ask children to explain in their own words what they mean. (*pulled into* = arrived; *kept its promise* = did what it said it would do)

Make up original sentences that can be restated using these verbs. Ask children to restate each sentence using the correct phrasal verb. Say: *The school bus <u>arrived at</u> the parking lot at 8:00. The school <u>did what it said it would do</u> and gave a party on the last day of school.*

325

Comprehension

5 Why did Johnny leave at 7:00 P.M. instead of in the morning? (The Pony Express was trying to get to San Francisco as soon as possible.) Did the Pony Express riders ride through the night? Why? (Yes, to save time getting across the country.) *Draw Conclusions*

6 **CAUSE AND EFFECT** Why did Johnnie need to change horses every 10 or 12 miles? (The horses got tired. A fresh horse could run faster.) Let's add to our chart.

CAUSE	EFFECT
Johnnie saw an interesting ad.	He became a Pony Express rider.
The ponies got tired.	The riders switched horses every 10 or 12 miles.

7 What do you think Johnnie did after he finished his ride? (rested) *Draw Conclusions*

---

5 At 7:00 p.m. Johnnie set off. Everybody waved and cheered as he rushed away from them.

6 Johnnie rode on through the Missouri night. Every 10 to 12 miles he pulled up to a station to change horses. In less than two minutes, he threw the mochila onto the fresh horse and dashed off again.

7 Johnnie and his pony took a ferry across the Missouri River into Kansas. They sped across the flat prairie. Then, after 60 miles and eight hours of riding, Johnnie passed the mochila on to another rider.

8 New riders took over every 60 to 75 miles. They rode over the dusty plains, waded through rivers, and climbed over the rugged Rocky Mountains. They rode all day, west with the sun, and they rode all night, under dark, lonely skies.

326

Activity

Cross Curricular: Science

EVOLUTION OF THE HORSE Horses weren't always big, strong animals. The ancestor of the horse was no bigger than a medium-sized dog. Instead of a single hoof on all four feet, it had four toes on its front feet and three toes on its back feet.

RESEARCH AND INQUIRY Have children find illustrations of the prehistoric horse. Ask them to draw a picture comparing a modern horse with its ancestor.
▶ **Logical/Visual**

Comprehension

WORD STRUCTURE Let's read the second sentence of the last paragrah. What does the fifth word mean?

CAUSE AND EFFECT The author describes the land the riders rode over. What effect did the land have on the ponies and the riders? (It made the riding difficult.) Let's add to our Cause-and-Effect chart.

CAUSE	EFFECT
Johnnie saw an interesting ad.	He became a Pony Express rider.
The ponies got tired.	The riders switched horses every 10 or 12 miles.
The route covered plains, rivers, and mountains.	Riding was difficult.

Minilesson

REVIEW/MAINTAIN

Context Clues

Point out the word *rugged* in the last paragraph on page 326. Ask children to find context clues that will help them understand this word. Call their attention to the verb "climbed over." Ask children if they have to climb over things when the ground is smooth and flat. Then have them describe what the ground is like when they do have to climb over things. (rough, steep, rocky)

Activity Invite children to write a sentence that gives context clues for the word *rugged*.

PREVENTION/INTERVENTION

WORD STRUCTURE Write the word *dust* on the board. Ask volunteers to describe dust. (dry, powdery dirt) Explain that the letter *y* gives the meaning "having" or "full of" and turns a noun into a word that can describe another noun. Ask children what the plains were like. (They were full of dust.) Have children add the letter *y* to the end of the words *chalk*, *sugar*, and *curl*. Then ask children to use the words in sentences. *Syntactic Cues*

327

Comprehension

9 What happened before the steamer ship left Sacramento? (William Hamilton arrived in Sacramento and put the mail in the ship.) *Sequence of Events*

10 **CAUSE AND EFFECT** Why was there a celebration in St. Joseph when the Pony Express rider came back ten days after leaving California? (It meant that the first mail delivery by Pony Express had been made on time.)

328

Activity

Cross Curricular: Math

TIMING THE RIDERS Remind children that each Pony Express rider rode about 60 to 75 miles of the way. We read on page 326 that Johnnie started his ride at 7 P.M. on April 3rd and ended it eight hours later. Ask children at what time on April 4th Johnnie gave his *mochila* to another rider. (3 A.M.) Ask students to draw two clocks—one showing 7 P.M. and dated April 3rd, the other showing 3 A.M. and dated April 4th. Let children count the hours from 7 to midnight on the 3rd, then from midnight to 3 on the 4th.

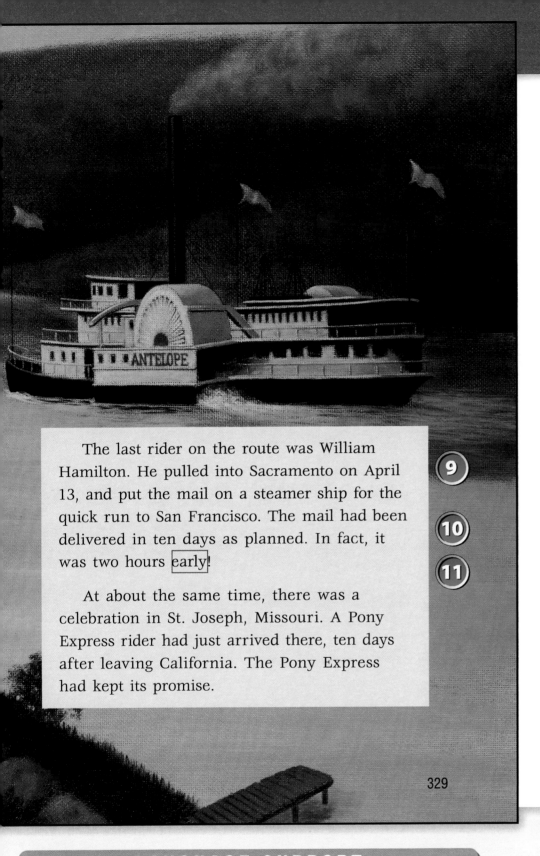

The last rider on the route was William Hamilton. He pulled into Sacramento on April 13, and put the mail on a steamer ship for the quick run to San Francisco. The mail had been delivered in ten days as planned. In fact, it was two hours early!

At about the same time, there was a celebration in St. Joseph, Missouri. A Pony Express rider had just arrived there, ten days after leaving California. The Pony Express had kept its promise.

9

10

11

329

Comprehension

11 Why might William Hamilton have arrived in Sacramento two hours early? (Since this was the first test of the Pony Express, all the riders might have been excited and ridden as fast as they could. Nice weather might also have helped them make good time.) *Draw Conclusions*

Minilesson

REVIEW/MAINTAIN

Main Idea

Remind children that the main idea:

• tells what an article is about.

• includes only important information.

Ask children to name the main idea of the article. (The Pony Express succeeded in its attempt to deliver mail faster than any other method could.)

Activity Write the main idea on the chalkboard. Help children to brainstorm several details that support the main idea.

LANGUAGE SUPPORT

Point out the proper names on page 329, such as *William Hamilton*, *Sacramento*, and *San Francisco*. Explain to children that proper names are always capitalized. Write a list of nouns, including proper nouns and common nouns. Read the words aloud and have children raise their hands when they hear one that should be capitalized.

For additional practice, encourage children to write their own lists of proper and common nouns, being sure to capitalize the proper nouns.

Comprehension

12 What do you think is the main idea on page 330? (William Russell wanted to create a faster way to carry mail to California.) What is a detail that supports this idea? (People didn't want to wait a month for news from home.) *Main Idea*

SELF-MONITORING STRATEGY

VERIFYING FACTUAL INFORMATION
Knowing and using strategies to discover whether information in a story is true can help you better understand the story. You can check another source to obtain additional information.

MODEL I read in my book that in 1860 horses were the fastest way to deliver mail. I used an encyclopedia to find out that most horses could run about 10 mph. Since the stations were about 10 miles apart, it must have taken the riders one hour to reach the next station.

The Fastest Mail Ever

William H. Russell knew that many people had moved out west to California. There were no telegraph lines or railroad tracks that went all the way across the country at that time. But no one wanted to wait a month to get news from back home. Russell believed that horseback riders would be the fastest way to deliver mail to the West. Riders were much faster than stagecoaches.

12

330

CULTURAL PERSPECTIVES

THE HORSE IN DIFFERENT CULTURES
Ask groups of children to research the role of the horse in different cultures, such as: the Arabian stallion, the thoroughbred, the quarter horse, the horse in Native American culture, and the horse in ancient Greek myth.

RESEARCH AND INQUIRY Have each group draw illustrations and write one or two paragraphs about their subject.
▶ **Visual/Linguistic**

inter NET CONNECTION Children can learn more about horses by visiting **www.mhschool.com/reading.**

The thoroughbred horse is a racing horse.

Russell set to work. He built stations for switching horses all the way from St. Joseph to Sacramento. The stations were 10 to 12 miles apart. That was short enough for the horses to run between them at top speed.

Twenty-five of the 190 stations were called home stations. There the riders could rest at the end of their route. The 165 smaller "swing" stations were relay posts where the riders changed horses.

(13)

331

Comprehension

(13) Why were the stations William Russell built 10 to 12 miles apart? (Ten to 12 miles was a short enough distance for the horses to run at top speed.) *Draw Conclusions*

(p/i) **CONTEXT CLUES** Look at the seventh word in the first line on page 331. What does it mean?

Writer's Craft

TRANSITIONS

Explain: An author uses transitions to connect one idea to another. Transitions move the story forward in time. Examples of transitions include: *first, next, finally, afterwards.*

Example: Direct children's attention back to the second paragraph on page 329. *At about the same time, there was a celebration in St. Joseph, Missouri.* The transition tells us that the actions in the story were taking place at the same time.

PARTNERS Have partners use transitions as they describe the process of getting ready for school. Ask the person listening to make a list of the transitions used. Switch roles.

(p/i) **PREVENTION/INTERVENTION**

CONTEXT CLUES Tell children to use prior knowledge and context clues to figure out what *station* means. Ask them to identify the place where trains stop to let people on or off. Ask them what the riders in this selection do when they come to a home station. (get off their horses and rest) Using these two clues, define *station*. (A station is a stopping place for travelers.) *Semantic Cues*

Comprehension

(14) **Phonics** **SHORT** *e: ea* Point to the last word in the third paragraph on page 333. Blend the sounds as you run your finger under the word. What is the sound made by the letters *ea*? Let's say the word together. Who can make a sentence with *weather*? *Graphophonic Cues*

(15) **CAUSE AND EFFECT** Why were the Sierra Nevada Mountains the most dangerous part of the Pony Express route?

MODEL Let's see … It says here that many times snow would fall and cover the trails. It sounds like it was very difficult for the riders to see sometimes. That's what made the Sierra Nevada mountains so dangerous.

332

Activity

Cross Curricular: Art

COMIC STRIP Tell children that they are going to make a comic strip of a Pony Express rider.

• Have children illustrate a different scene on each of four pieces of paper. Children can mix them up and invite a partner to place them in order.

• The first page will show the rider leaving town, the second will show him riding on a plain, the third will show him riding up a mountain path, and the fourth will show him passing the *mochila* to a fresh rider.

Russell now needed 400 horses. He bought fast, long-legged horses for going over flat land, and smaller, tough horses for the mountains. The horses of the Pony Express needed to be faster than most other horses, to keep the riders and the mail safe.

The regular Pony Express route was about 2000 miles. The riders started in Missouri, then went through Kansas. Finally, they rode along the Oregon Trail, passing through what is now Nebraska and Wyoming.

The most dangerous part of the Pony Express route was the Sierra Nevada Mountains. Mountain storms often covered the trail with snow. When the wind blew the snow into piles 10 feet high or more, a rider could go over a cliff. The rider had to know the trails well enough to find his way in any weather.

Those Daring Young Men

All the riders were a lot like Johnnie Frye—small, young men who had grown up riding over the mountains and the prairies. About 180 riders rode for the Express. Most were 19 or 20 years old, but at least one was as young as 11!

14

15

16

333

Comprehension

16 On page 333, we read about all the dangers and hardships that the Pony Express riders had to face. What word could you use to describe these young men we have read about? (*brave*) Make a generalization about the riders. (Pony Express riders were brave.) **Make Generalizations**

Minilesson

REVIEW/MAINTAIN

Long *a*

Point out the following words on page 333: *trails* and *mail*. Ask children to:

- point to the letters *ai*.
- say the sound that *ai* stands for here. (/ā/)
- blend each word as you run your hand underneath it.

Encourage children to think of other words they know in which *ai* stands for the long *a* sound.

Activity Have children use their words to create rhymes.

Phonics CD-ROM Have children use the interactive phonics activities on the CD-ROM for more reinforcement.

LANGUAGE SUPPORT

ESL Some children may not be familiar with the term *prairie*. Have them turn back to page 330. Ask volunteers to describe the landscape shown in the illustration. (big, flat area) Explain that this kind of area is called a *prairie*. Invite ESL children to tell the class the word in their language that names a large, flat area. Ask if anyone knows another English word that means the same as *prairie*. (*plain*)

Comprehension

17 The author says that the Pony Express helped keep the East and West together. How do you think it did that? (The author says that the riders kept East and West together by bringing letters and newspapers. Keeping in touch with distant friends and relatives helps you feel connected to them. Having the same information about what is happening in a country helps to make the people of that country feel united.) *Draw Conclusions*

18 **CAUSE AND EFFECT** Why did the young riders on the Pony Express become famous? (People told stories and newspapers wrote articles about them.)

19 Invite two volunteers to role-play Johnnie and the woman who invented doughnuts. Have Johnnie "gallop" by the woman as she hands him an object shaped like a piece of bread. Ask children: What would Johnnie look like catching a doughnut on his finger as he gallops by? Make believe your chair is a pony. Show how you would catch the doughnut. *Pantomime*

334

Activity

Cross Curricular: Social Studies

FOOD OF THE FUTURE Tell children that some common foods were invented for a reason. Have them look in the encyclopedia to learn the origin of such foods as the sandwich.

Children can then draw food items that might be invented for the future.

Encourage them to use their imaginations in creating foods for space travel, or different ways of living.
▶ **Logical/Kinesthetic**

Mix with water for a yummy dinner!

Word of the brave deeds of the Pony Express riders spread. They rode through storms and over flooded rivers. They were threatened by bandit attacks and buffalo stampedes. But the motto of the Pony Express was "The mail must go through!"—and it always did.

The Pony Express's work was very important. The letters and newspapers delivered by the riders helped keep the East and the West together. One rider, Bill Campbell, carried President Abraham Lincoln's Inaugural Address to the people of California.

Newspapers printed thrilling stories about the Pony Express riders. The young men became famous. Johnnie Frye, the first rider out of St. Joseph, was a real favorite. Many came out to watch him ride by. One story says that a woman invented the doughnut hole so that Johnnie could catch her cakes on his finger as he rode by!

The most famous rider was Bill Cody, later known as Buffalo Bill. He began riding for the Pony Express when he was only 15 years old.

Legend has it that on one trip there was no one to take over after Bill's ride. He had to ride another 76 miles to the next home station.

335

Comprehension

 How would the riders' experiences have been different if they had had highways to ride on? (faster, easier, less dangerous) *Setting*

 Phonics **SHORT** *e: ea* Look at the third sentence in the first paragraph. Point to the third word. *Graphophonic Cues*

MODEL I know *ed* is an ending, so I won't worry about those letters yet. I'll frame the rest of the word with my fingers. The word starts with /thr/. The letters *ea* spell /e/ here. I know the rest. Now I can blend the sounds in the smaller word. /thr/ /e/ /t/ /ən/

P/i **Phonics** Find the third word in the third line on page 335. Say it aloud. (rivers)

TEACHING TIP

CULTURAL UNDERSTANDING Help children use their knowledge of the culture of the Early American frontier to assist in understanding the story. Ask children to compare and contrast the lives of people living in 1860 with those living today. Encourage children to list advances in communication devices and transportation on their charts.

LIFE TODAY	LIFE IN 1860

P/i **PREVENTION/INTERVENTION**

Phonics Write the following words on a large sheet of paper: *river, rider, later.* Cover the first syllable of each word with a self-stick note, so that only the *er* shows. Have children read the *er* and identify the vowel. Then, have a volunteer pull off the self-stick note covering the first syllable of *rider* and blend the sounds together. Have another volunteer repeat the procedure with the word *later.* Then have the whole class read the words aloud with you. *Graphophonic Cues*

Comprehension

22 **CAUSE AND EFFECT** Why did the Pony Express end? (It was replaced by the telegraph.) What was the advantage of the telegraph? (It was faster.) Let's put this final item in our Cause-and-Effect chart.

CAUSE	EFFECT
Johnnie saw an interesting ad.	He became a Pony Express rider.
The ponies got tired.	The riders switched horses every 10 or 12 miles.
The route covered plains, rivers, and mountains.	Riding was difficult.
The cross-country telegraph wires were completed.	The Pony Express ended.

RETELL THE STORY Encourage children to use their charts to help them retell the selection. Then challenge them to write one sentence that summarizes the story. *Summarize*

STUDENT SELF-ASSESSMENT

- How did filling in the Cause and Effect chart help me understand the selection?
- How did using what I know about letter sounds and word meanings help me read unfamiliar words?

TRANSFERRING THE STRATEGY

- How can I use these strategies to help me read other stories?

Before he could rest, the eastbound mail arrived. Bill took that mail and went back over his route. The entire trip, back and forth, was 384 miles. If this is true, Buffalo Bill holds the record for the longest Pony Express ride.

The Last Ride

22 But even though it was a success, the Pony Express would not last long. On October 24, 1861, the cross-country telegraph line was finished. Now a message could be sent across the country in minutes.

The last Pony Express rider handed over his mail pouch on November 21, 1861.

Although the Pony Express lasted only a year and a half, the riders became part of American legend. They had shown great daring and skill.

And it all started with Johnnie Frye, racing alone through that April night in 1860. He was proud to be part of the Pony Express. He knew that it was up to him to make sure that the mail went through. And it did.

336

REREADING FOR *Fluency*

 PARTNERS Children who need fluency practice can work in pairs rereading a page of the selection.

READING RATE When you evaluate reading rate, have children read aloud from the story for one minute. Place a stick-on note after the last word read. Count words read. To evaluate chil-dren's performance, see the Running Record in the **Fluency Assessment** book.

i Intervention For leveled fluency passages, lessons, and norm charts, see **Skills Intervention Guide**, Part 5, Fluency.

337

Comprehension

Return to Predictions and Purposes

Review with children their predictions. Were they correct?

PREDICTIONS	WHAT HAPPENED
Young men delivered mail by horseback.	They had to ride a long way and face bad weather.
The Pony Express was the fastest way to send mail for one year.	It ended when the telegraph, which could send messages in seconds, was invented.

INFORMAL ASSESSMENT

HOW TO ASSESS

SHORT *e* Have children turn to page 333. Ask them to find and read a word on this page that rhymes with *feather*.

CAUSE AND EFFECT Have children explain why the Pony Express was started and why it ended.

FOLLOW UP

SHORT *e* Continue to model the blending of sound in short *e: ea* words for children who are having difficulty pronouncing and recognizing the words.

CAUSE AND EFFECT Encourage children who have difficulty with the concept of cause and effect to review their charts.

LITERARY RESPONSE

QUICK-WRITE Have children write their thoughts about the story in their journals. They can get started with these questions:

- Would you have liked to ride for the Pony Express?

- How might it feel to ride alone all night?

- How do you think mail will be delivered in the future?

- What jobs are there today that call for working with horses? Which would you most like to do? Why?

ORAL RESPONSE Have children discuss their journal responses in small groups.

Story Questions

The Pony Express

Have children discuss or write answers to the questions on page 338.

Answers:

1. a mail service from St. Joseph, Missouri, to San Francisco, California, that operated in 1860 and 1861. *Literal/Main Idea*

2. They needed to be light so that the horses could run faster and longer. *Inferential/ Cause and Effect*

3. They probably liked the excitement and admiration. *Inferential/Character*

4. The Pony Express succeeded in being faster than previous mail-delivery services. *Main Idea/Summarize*

5. Yes, José was responsible and skilled with animals. *Critical/Reading Across Texts*

Write Directions For a full lesson related to this writing suggestion, see the lesson on explanatory writing on pages 341M–341N.

Story Questions & Activities

1. What was the Pony Express?

2. Why did the riders for the Pony Express have to be under 125 pounds?

3. What did the Pony Express riders like about their work?

4. What is the main idea of this selection?

5. Would José from "Roundup at Rio Ranch" be a good rider for the Pony Express? Why or why not?

Write Directions

Explain how to mail a letter. Make sure to include important information. Tell the steps in the right order, starting with putting the letter in an envelope.

Meeting Individual Needs

EASY	ON-LEVEL	CHALLENGE
Name_____ Date_____ Reteach 103	Name_____ Date_____ Practice 103	Name_____ Date_____ Extend 103
Story Comprehension	**Story Comprehension**	**Story Comprehension**

EASY — Reteach, 103

Write an **X** next to the sentences that describe facts from "The Pony Express."

- X 1. Pony Express riders carried their papers in a "mochila," or knapsack.
- X 2. Johnnie and his pony crossed the Missouri River on a ferry.
- X 3. William Russell built stations for the Pony Express riders.
- ___ 4. The Pony Express route was one million miles long.
- X 5. Buffalo Bill was a famous Pony Express rider.
- X 6. Newspapers and letters traveled on the Pony Express.
- ___ 7. The telephone ended the Pony Express.
- X 8. The motto of the Pony Express was "The mail must go through."
- X 9. Pony Express riders were faster than a stagecoach.
- ___ 10. The Pony Express is still in use today.

ON-LEVEL — Practice, 103

Answer the following questions about "The Pony Express."

1. What was the Pony Express?
   The Pony Express was a way to carry mail from Missouri to California in record time.

2. Why did William Russell start the Pony Express?
   Many people had moved out West, and they needed mail and news delivered as fast as possible.

3. What did the riders of the Pony Express carry?
   newspapers and letters

4. What were the riders on the Pony Express like?
   Most were young and small; they were good horseback riders.

5. What was the motto of the Pony Express?
   The mail must go through!

6. Why did the Pony Express stop after just a short time?
   The telegraph line across the country was completed.

CHALLENGE — Extend, 103

A San Francisco newspaper wants you to write two stories about the Pony Express. Tell the story of how it started and how it ended. Read the headlines and write the story.
Answers will vary. Sample answers shown.

The Fastest Mail Ever — April 3, 1860
William H. Russell believes that the fastest way to deliver mail in California is to send it out by horse. He is hiring young men to ride their horses from station to station. All together, Russell will hire about 180 men to ride 2,000 miles!

Telegragh Takes Over — November 21, 1861
Pony Express riders will be out of a job. The daring riders can carry mail across the country faster than by stagecoach. But the new telegraph will get messages from the East to California in just seconds.

Reteach, 103   Practice, 103   Extend, 103

Make a Map of the Pony Express

Trace the outline of a map of the United States. Then find, mark, and label one of the places mentioned in "The Pony Express." You might look for St. Joseph, Missouri, or the Rocky Mountains, or San Francisco, California.

Make a Collage

The Pony Express helped news travel quickly between East and West. How do people get mail and news now? Draw or cut out pictures of things people use to get mail. Make a collage that shows these inventions.

Find Out More

The cross-country telegraph caused the end of the Pony Express. What is the telegraph? Who invented it? How long did it take to get messages?

339

Story Activities

Make a Map of the Pony Express

Materials: tracing paper, pencils, map of the United States

ONE Provide a map of the United States. Help children to locate both the beginning and end of the Pony Express route and have them work out the best route for the riders to follow.

Make a Collage

Materials: magazines and newspapers, scissors, large sheet of paper, paste

ONE Have children brainstorm ways that people get mail and news now. Help them find magazines that show computers, televisions, and fax machines.

Find Out More

RESEARCH AND INQUIRY Have children work in groups to collect information about the telegraph. Encourage them to use encyclopedias and history books as well as the Internet to research the topic.

*inter***NET** CONNECTION Go to **www.mhschool.com /reading** for more information or activities on the topic.

DAILY Phonics ROUTINES

DAY 3 **Letter Substitution**
Using the CVVC flipchart, have pairs of children build *head*. Taking turns, tell one child to change one or more letters to build a new word and ask the partner to read it.

Phonics CD-ROM

339

Study Skills

Use a Telephone Directory

The white pages list the phone numbers of people.

96 Jagoda–Jenson

Jagoda Nadine F 13 West 25th St	.878-1315
Jaime Raul 20 Christopher St	.715-2596
Jamison Andrew 16 East 16th St	.878-6945
Jamison Andrew 40 Maidstone Ln	.605-7344

The yellow pages list the phone numbers of businesses.

30 Coin Dealers–Computer Dealers
Coin Dealers

Murray's Rare Coins 1 University Pl	.949-9142
Stone's Coin Co. 40 Bedford St	.654-6087

Comic Books

Comic Vault 424 East 3rd St	.805-3984
Quick Comics 60 Brook Rd	.716-4747

Computer Dealers

The Computer Cave 222 2nd Ave	.493-2180

1 What is the phone number of Quick Comics?

2 What is the address of Stone's Coin Co.?

3 Why do you think phone directories include addresses?

4 How are the white pages and the yellow pages of a phone book different?

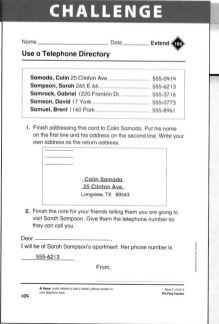

REFERENCE SOURCES

 **OBJECTIVES**

Children will:

- find telephone numbers and addresses.
- differentiate between the yellow pages and the white pages.

PREPARE Display **Teaching Chart 87**.

TEACH Explain that the words on the upper left corner of the samples show the alphabetical range of the names on that page.

PRACTICE Have children answer questions 1–4. Review the answers with them. **1.** 716-4747 **2.** 40 Bedford St. **3.** to differentiate between people with the same name. **4.** The white pages show the names of people, the yellow pages show the names of businesses.

ASSESS/CLOSE Have children use the yellow pages to find and list comic book stores.

Meeting Individual Needs

EASY	ON-LEVEL	CHALLENGE
Name___ Date___ Reteach 104 **Use a Telephone Directory**	Name___ Date___ Practice 104 **Use a Telephone Directory**	Name___ Date___ Extend 104 **Use a Telephone Directory**

EASY

Name_____ Date_____ Reteach **104**

Use a Telephone Directory

A **telephone directory** has the phone number and address of most people and businesses who own a telephone in your area.

The White Pages lists the phone numbers of people and businesses in alphabetical order by name. The Yellow Pages lists phone numbers and addresses of businesses in the area. It is organized by the type of business.

Decide if the White or the Yellow pages would best help you to answer these questions.

1. Where should I look for the phone number of my cousin, Jimmy Kerso? _____White_____

2. Where should I look for bicycle repair shops? _____Yellow_____

3. Where could I find the address of Raul Nickelson?
_____White_____

4. Where could I find the home number of Dr. Paula Edwards?
_____White_____

5. Where would I find a gardening store in the neighborhood?
_____Yellow_____

At Home: Have children look in a real Yellow Pages for bicycle repair shops and gardening stores.

104   Book 2 1/Unit 3 **5**
The Pony Express

ON-LEVEL

Name_____ Date_____ Practice **104**

Use a Telephone Directory

A **telephone directory** lists people and businesses in alphabetical order.

Study the sample page below. Use it to answer the questions that follow.

192   Hodges — Holmes

HODGES Catherine Near Rd Red Bank 555-9863
    Kenneth 1692 West Walnut Martiesville 555-2347
    P.C. 1324 Weston Rd Riverton 555-4376
HOFFMAN Nelson 45 Brushy Hill Rd Lambert 555-9898
    Michelle M 373 South St Remertown 555-3245
HOFFMANN SEE ALSO HOFFMAN, HOFMAN, HOFMANN

1. What is the phone number of P.C. Hodges? 555-4376

2. What other spellings of Hoffmann are suggested? Hoffman, Hofman, and Hofmann

3. Pretend you're looking for someone named Hoffman. You don't know the first name. But you know the person lives in Lambert. Which Hoffman would you pick? _____Nelson_____

4. Suppose you're looking for someone named Holton. Would you find that person on this page? Why or why not? No, Holton would come after the guide word Holmes.

At Home: Ask children how many different people listed on this page have the last name Hodges

104   Book 2 1/Unit 3 **4**
The Pony Express

CHALLENGE

Name_____ Date_____ Extend **104**

Use a Telephone Directory

Samada, Colin 25 Clinton Ave 555-0414
Sampson, Sarah 265 E 66 555-6213
Samrock, Gabriel 1220 Franklin Dr 555-3716
Samson, David 17 York 555-0773
Samuel, Brent 1160 Park 555-8961

1. Finish addressing this card to Colin Samada. Put his name on the first line and his address on the second line. Write your own address as the return address.

Colin Samada
25 Clinton Ave.
Longview, TX 89543

2. Finish the note for your friends telling them you are going to visit Sarah Sampson. Give them the telephone number so they can call you.

Dear _____,
I will be at Sarah Sampson's apartment. Her phone number is
_____555-6213_____

From, _____

At Home: Invite children to find a friend's phone number in your telephone book.

104   Book 2 1/Unit 3
The Pony Express

Reteach, 104   Practice, 104   Extend, 104

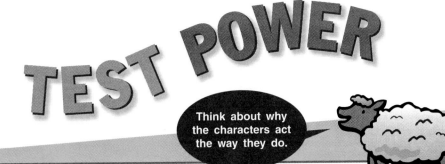

TEST POWER

Think about why the characters act the way they do.

DIRECTIONS:

Read the story. Then read each question about the story.

SAMPLE

The Boy Who Cried Wolf

Long ago, a boy lived on a sheep farm. His job was to keep the sheep safe. The farmers told him to yell if he saw a wolf. Wolves would eat the sheep.

One day, the boy was bored. He wanted to have some fun. He yelled, "Help! I see a wolf."

The farmers heard him. They ran to help. When they got to the boy, he laughed, "There is no wolf. I was playing a joke." The farmers were angry.

The next day a wolf crept out of the woods. "Help!" yelled the boy. "A wolf is eating the sheep." The farmers heard the boy but did not go to him. They all thought that he was playing another joke.

1 Why didn't the farmers run to help the boy?
- ● They did not believe him.
- ○ They did not hear him.
- ○ They were sleeping.

2 Which is a FACT from this story?
- ● The boy played a joke.
- ○ The farmers played a joke.
- ○ The sheep played a joke.

341

Test Power

THE PRINCETON REVIEW

Read the Page

Explain to children that you will be reading this story as a group. You will read the story, and they will follow along in their books.

Request that children put pens, pencils, and markers away, since they will not be writing in their books.

Discuss the Questions

QUESTION 1: Instruct children to look back to the passage and reread the lines where the farmers do not run to help the boy. The story says that the farmers didn't believe the boy.

QUESTION 2: This question asks the reader to find something stated as a fact in the passage. Instruct children to look back to the passage and find the choice that is stated in the story. The tenth sentence states that the boy was playing a joke.

Leveled Books

Intervention ▶ **Skills**
Intervention Guide, for direct
instruction and extra practice of
vocabulary and comprehension

EASY

The Ghost on the Train

☑ **Phonics** Short *e*

☑ Cause and Effect

☑ Instructional Vocabulary:
*arrive, early, finished, record,
rushed, success*

written by Emily North
illustrated by Monica Passicot

Answers to Story Questions

1. on the Denver-to-Kansas City
train

2. They saw something small and
white rushing by them. But they
couldn't figure out what it was.

3. She ends up finding the thief,
who's actually a little, lost boy.

4. how a girl solves the mystery of
the train ghost

5. No. There wouldn't have been
anywhere for a little boy to
hide.

**The Story Questions and Activity
below appear in the Easy Book.**

Story Questions and Activity

1. Where does Grace's father work?

2. Why do people think that they've
seen a ghost?

3. What happened when Grace went
looking for the ghost?

4. What is this story mostly about?

5. Do you think this story could have
taken place on a Pony Express
ride? Why or why not?

Which Is Closest?

The train that Grace's father works on
goes from Denver, Colorado, to
Kansas City, Missouri. Look at a map
of the United States. Find Denver and
Kansas City on the map. Then find
where you live. Which of the two
cities is closer to your town or city?
Draw a picture to show how you
might travel to that city. Label two
other cities you would pass through
on your way there.

from The Ghost on the Train

Guided Reading

PREVIEW AND PREDICT Take a **picture walk** with children through page 4 of
the story. Encourage them to study the
illustrations and predict what the story is
about. Chart their ideas.

SET PURPOSES Have children write sentences describing why they want to read
The Ghost on the Train. For example: *I want
to see if the ghost in the story is real.*

READ THE BOOK Use questions like the
following to guide children's reading or after
they have read the story independently.

Page 3: Find the word *arrived.* Can you
think of a word that means the opposite of
arrived? (left) *Vocabulary*

Page 4: What did Grace's mother say
about ghosts? (There are no such things.)
What could the passenger actually have
seen on the train? *Fantasy and Reality*

Page 6: Why might the train to Denver be
unsuccessful? (If people are afraid of the
ghost, they'll be afraid to ride on the train
and there will be no passengers.) *Cause
and Effect*

Page 10: Find the word *head.* What sound
do the letters *ea* make in the word *head*?
What other words can you think of that use
the letters *ea* to make the short *e* sound?
(bread, spread, instead) **Phonics and Decoding**

Page 12: What did Grace find in the mail
car besides mail? (a small boy) Was the
small boy the ghost everyone thought they
saw? How can you tell? *Make Inferences*

**RETURN TO PREDICTIONS AND
PURPOSES** Discuss children's predictions.
Ask which were close to the story and why.
Have children review their purposes for
reading. Did they find out what they want-
ed to know?

LITERARY RESPONSE Discuss these
questions:

• Why do you think people like to read
ghost stories?

• What was your favorite part of the story?

Also see the story questions and activity in
The Ghost on the Train.

See the **Phonics** CD-ROM for practice
using words with short *e: ea.*

Leveled Books

INDEPENDENT

Messengers from the Sky

☑ **Short** *e*

☑ **Cause and Effect**

☑ **Instructional Vocabulary:**
arrive, early, finished, record, rushed, success

Guided Reading

PREVIEW AND PREDICT Take a **picture walk** with children through page 5 of the story. Encourage them to determine what the story is about by studying the illustrations. Chart children's ideas.

SET PURPOSES Have children jot down a purpose for reading. For example, who are the messengers?

READ THE BOOK Use questions like the following to guide children's reading or after they have read the story independently.

Page 6: What are some possible causes for the ability that homing pigeons have to find their way home? (They can use the sun, tiny magnets, or their sense of smell.) *Cause and Effect*

Page 10: Why were pigeons used by armies? (carry messages) What effect could these pigeons have on the army? (They could carry secret information, deliver food, carry messages asking for more soldiers.) *Cause and Effect*

Page 15: Find the word *arrive*. What words in another sentence mean almost the same thing? *(come back)* *Vocabulary*

Page 16: Find the word *weather*. What sound do the letters *ea* make in the word *weather*? What other words can you think of that have the short *e* sound spelled *ea*? *(breath, bread, leather)* *Phonics and Decoding*

RETURN TO PREDICTIONS AND PURPOSES: Discuss children's predictions. Ask which were close to the story and why. Have children review their purposes for reading. Did they find out what they wanted to know?

LITERARY RESPONSE Discuss these questions:

- What other uses can you think of for carrier pigeons?

- What was your favorite part of the story?

Also see the story questions and activity in *Messengers from the Sky*.

See the  **CD-ROM** for practice using words with short *e*.

Answers to Story Questions

1. two thousand miles
2. They are able to find their way back home from great distances. They can fly quickly from one place to another.
3. Electronic messages are carried faster and more safely.
4. The story is about carrier pigeons and how they have been useful to people.
5. Answers will vary, but students should glean that by sending a message via carrier pigeon, it will arrive much more quickly.

The Story Questions and Activity below appear in the Independent Book.

Story Questions and Activity

1. How many miles did the homing pigeon fly from South America to New York?
2. Why do carrier pigeons make good messengers?
3. Why do you think carrier pigeons are no longer important messengers during wartime?
4. What is the story about?
5. Imagine that you lived in New York and had to send a message quickly to someone who lived in California. You only could use a Pony Express rider or a carrier pigeon. Which one would you use to carry the message and why?

A Good Life for the Birds?

Homing pigeons like "Big Tom," "The Mocker," and "President Wilson" were often hurt while doing jobs for people. Write one or two sentences telling whether or not it was fair for people to use birds in this way.

from Messengers from the Sky

Leveled Books

Sending a Message
with Dots ... and Dashes...

written by Emily North
illustrated by Krysten Brooker

CHALLENGE

Sending a Message with Dots ... and Dashes ...

☑ **Short** *e*
☑ **Cause and Effect**
☑ **Instructional Vocabulary:** *arrive, early, finished, record, rushed, success*

Guided Reading

PREVIEW AND PREDICT Discuss each illustration through page 7. As you take the **picture walk** with children, encourage them to predict what the story is about. Chart their ideas.

SET PURPOSES Have children write or draw why they want to read *Sending a Message with Dots ... and Dashes __ __.* For example: *I want to learn about Morse code.*

READ THE BOOK Use questions like the following to guide children's reading or after they have read the story independently.

Page 14: Find the word *rush*. Were things moving quickly or slowly? *(quickly)* *Vocabulary*

Page 15: Find the word *weather*. What sound do the letters *ea* make in the word *weather*? Can you find other words on this page that contain the short *e* spelled with an *e* instead of an *ea*? *(telegraph, send, best, record)* *Phonics and Decoding*

Page 16: What other kinds of communication tools did the telegraph lead to? (telephone, faxes, e-mail) Would these machines have come along without the invention of the telegraph? Why? Why not? *Cause and Effect*

RETURN TO PREDICTIONS AND PURPOSES Discuss children's predictions. Ask which were close to the story and why. Have children review their purposes for reading. Did they find out what they wanted to know?

LITERARY RESPONSE Discuss these questions:

- Why do you think Samuel Morse's invention was useful?

- How do you think inventors like Samuel Morse are different from other people?

Also see the story questions and activity in *Sending a Message with Dots ... and Dashes __ __.*

See the **Phonics CD-ROM** for practice using words with short *e: ea*.

Answers to Story Questions

1. Samuel Morse
2. The telegraph works by electricity and electricity is carried in the wires.
3. Unless others saw that it worked and wanted to use it, his invention would be useless.
4. The invention of the telegraph by Samuel Morse changed the way we communicate.
5. At one time, both of them were new inventions and were the fastest way to send messages.

The Story Questions and Activity below appear in the Challenge Book.

Story Questions and Writing Activity

1. Who invented the telegraph?
2. Why were wires necessary for the telegraph to work?
3. After Morse invented the telegraph, he had to prove to other people that it worked. Why was this important?
4. What is the main idea of the book?
5. How were the inventions of the Pony Express riders and the telegraph alike?

Activity

Write a simple message using the Morse Code key on page 16. Trade with other class members and decode the message. And don't forget to sign your name!

from Sending a Message with Dots ...

Bringing Groups Together

Anthology and Leveled Books

Connecting Texts

WORD WEB
Write the story titles on the upper and lower right- and left-hand corners of a chart. Draw a circle with the word *Communication* in the middle of the chart. Have children identify the means of communication featured in each book. Then draw a line from the word *communication* in the center of the chart to the words children contribute for each title.

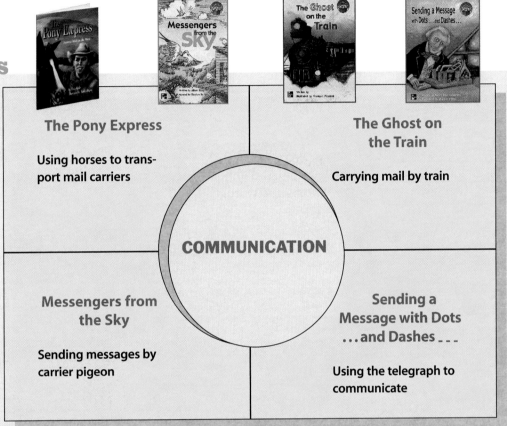

The Pony Express

Using horses to transport mail carriers

The Ghost on the Train

Carrying mail by train

COMMUNICATION

Messengers from the Sky

Sending messages by carrier pigeon

Sending a Message with Dots ...and Dashes _ _ _

Using the telegraph to communicate

Viewing/Representing

GROUP PRESENTATIONS Divide the class into four groups. Have each group work together to pantomime one form of communication for the rest of the group.

AUDIENCE RESPONSE Ask children to watch each presentation carefully to determine what type of communication is being represented.

Research and Inquiry

MORE ABOUT COMMUNICATION Have children investigate other types of communication by doing the following:

- Look at picture books, reference books, and other sources of information about communication.

- Invite someone to come and demonstrate sign language to children.

- Plan a field trip to an area store specializing in communication technology.

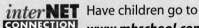 Have children go to **www.mhschool.com/reading** for more information or activities about communication.

 Children can write what they learned about various forms of communication in their journals.

341D

OBJECTIVES

Children will:

- blend and identify short *e: ea* words.

- review blends.

MATERIALS

- **Teaching Chart 88**

Skills Finder

Short *e: ea*

Introduce	B1: 320G–H
Review	B1: 341E–F, 341G–H
Test	B1: Unit 3
Maintain	B1: 349

ALTERNATE TEACHING STRATEGY

SHORT *e: ea*

For a different approach to teaching this skill, see pages T72–T73.

TEACHING TIP

SHORT *e: ea* When decoding unfamiliar words containing the letters *ea*, encourage children to try pronouncing the letters with a short *e* sound and a long *e* sound, so they may listen for which sounds more correct. Tell children to also use context clues.

Review Short *e: ea*

PREPARE

Review Short *e: ea*

Read this sentence aloud and have volunteers repeat the words with the short *e* sound.

To be <u>healthy</u>, <u>spread</u> apple butter <u>instead</u> of real butter on <u>bread</u>.

TEACH

BLENDING Model and Guide Practice with Short *e : ea* Words

- Display **Teaching Chart 88**. Have volunteers underline all the words in the passage with the short *e* sound.
- Blend the sounds of *weather* with children. w ea th er weather

> It was bad <u>weather</u> outside. The rain was <u>heavy</u>. But, Johnnie was inside <u>spreading</u> jam on the warm <u>bread</u> his mother made. He was planning on spending a <u>pleasant</u> day inside. First he would begin by enjoying a good <u>breakfast</u>.

Teaching Chart 88

Use the Word in Context

- Have children write sentences that show the meaning of *heavy*. Ask volunteers to read their sentences. Example: *There was flooding due to the heavy rains.*

Repeat the Procedure

- Follow the same procedure for the words *weather, spreading,* and *bread.*

PRACTICE

DISCRIMINATING
Identifying Words
with Short _e: ea_

GROUP

Have children work in small groups to make a set of cards with the following words: _treat, spread, threaten, meat, leather, feather, pleat, sweat,_ and _please._ Ask the children to take turns drawing a card, saying the word, and placing the word into a pile based on its word family. After all words have been placed into word families, ask children to identify the vowel sound as long _e_ or short _e_ for each word family.

▶ **Auditory/Linguistic**

ASSESS/CLOSE

Read and Use
Words with Short
_e: ea_ in Context

To assess children's ability to blend and identify short _e: ea_ words, observe them as they engage in the Practice activity. Ask children if they had difficulty deciding which words belonged in either pile. Collect the cards with the words that children found difficult and have the entire class discuss whether they go into the long _e_ or short _e_ pile. Encourage children to use each word in context.

ADDITIONAL PHONICS RESOURCES

Phonics/Phonemic Awareness
Practice Book,
pages 77–80

McGraw-Hill School
TECHNOLOGY

 CD-ROM
activities for practice with
Blending and Segmenting

DAY 4 **Writing** Have children write two sentences about _The Pony Express_ using words with the short _e: ea_ sound. Then have them read the sentences, blending the sounds of the _e: ea_ words.

Phonics CD-ROM

SPELLING/PHONICS CONNECTIONS
Words with short _e: ea:_ See 5-Day Spelling Plan, pages 341Q–341R.

i **Intervention** ➤ **Skills**
Intervention Guide, for direct instruction and extra practice of short _e: ea_

Meeting Individual Needs for Phonics

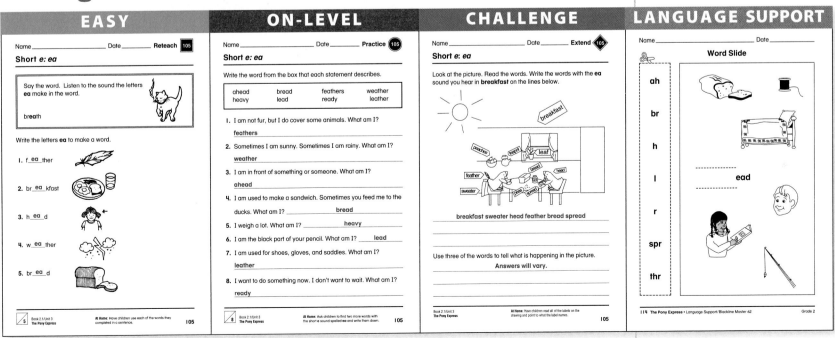

EASY	ON-LEVEL	CHALLENGE	LANGUAGE SUPPORT
Reteach, 105	Practice, 105	Extend, 105	Language Support, 114

TESTED
OBJECTIVES

Children will:
- review short *e*: *e, ea.*
- review /ər/*er*; /ən/*en*; /əl/*le.*
- review silent consonants: *l, b, k, g, gh.*

MATERIALS:
- **Teaching Chart 89**

Skills Finder

Short e: ea

Introduce	B1: 320G-H
▶ Review	B1: 341E-F, 341G-H
Test	B1: Unit 3
▶ Maintain	B1: 349

Review Short e; /ər/, /ən/, /əl/; Silent Letters

PREPARE

Review Short e; /ər/, /ən/, /əl/; Silent Letters

Write the words *leather, rider, even, saddle, half, climbed, knapsack, signed,* and *doughnut* on the chalkboard. Underline the letters that stand for the following sounds: short *e,* /ər/, /ən/, /əl/, as well as the silent letters *l, b, k, g, gh.* Tell children that they are going to review these sounds and silent letters.

TEACH

BLENDING
Model and Guide Practice with Short e; /ər/, /ən/, /əl/; and Silent Letters

- Display **Teaching Chart 89**. Use the first words in each column to model making words with the letters shown in the heading of each column.
- Have children fill in the blanks in the second word in each column and blend the sounds of each word.

ea	(er en le)	Silent Consonants (l b k g gh)
weather	better, soften, bottle	walk, knee, climb, sign, through
feather	letter	half
sweat	even	comb
breath	trouble	knife
		sign
		high

Teaching Chart 89

Use the Words in Context

Have children write sentences and use each word in context. Example: *The weather has been very sunny and pleasant lately.*

Repeat the Procedure

Continue with **Teaching Chart 89**. Have children repeat the procedure for the rest of the words on the chart.

PRACTICE

WORD MEANING
Use Words in Context

Continue to display **Teaching Chart 89**. Invite children to use the words on the chart to create context sentences. Encourage children to illustrate their sentences. ▶ **Linguistic/Intrapersonal**

ONE

ASSESS/CLOSE

Build Fluency in Words with Short e; /ər/, /ən/, /əl/ Sounds; and Silent Letters

To assess children's ability to blend and write short e words, words having the /ə/ sound and the silent consonants l, b, k, g, gh, observe children as they continue their Practice activity. Encourage children to read their sentences aloud.

ADDITIONAL PHONICS RESOURCES

Phonics/Phonemic Awareness Practice Book, pages 77–80

McGraw-Hill School
TECHNOLOGY

Phonics **CD-ROM**
activities for practice with **Blending and Segmenting**

DAILY Phonics ROUTINES

DAY 5
Fluency Ask children to circle the short e: ea words on page 332 of *The Pony Express* and to blend the words silently. Then ask children to read the page aloud in unison.

Phonics **CD-ROM**

ALTERNATE TEACHING STRATEGY

SHORT e: /ən/, /ər/, AND SILENT LETTERS
See Alternate Teaching Strategy, pages T65, T70, T73.

i **Intervention** **Skills**
Intervention Guide, for direct instruction and extra practice of short e; /ər/; /ən/; /əl/ sounds and silent letters

Meeting Individual Needs for Phonics

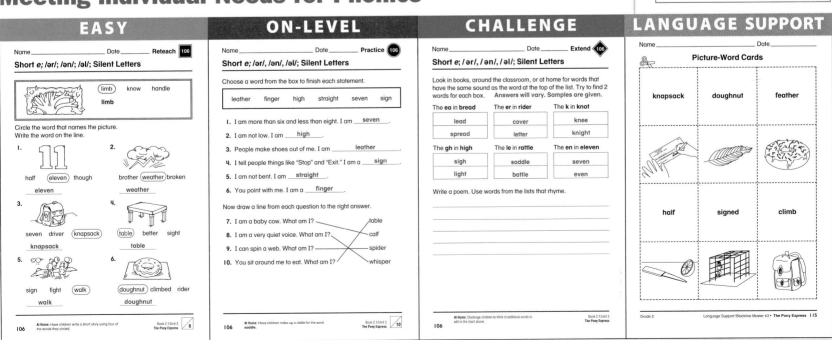

EASY	ON-LEVEL	CHALLENGE	LANGUAGE SUPPORT
Reteach, 106	Practice, 106	Extend, 106	Language Support, 115

341H

OBJECTIVES

Children will distinguish between fantasy and reality.

MATERIALS:
- **Teaching Chart 90**

Skills Finder

Fantasy and Reality

Introduce	B1: 289I-J
Review	B1: 341I-J, 379G-H
Test	B1: Unit 3

TEACHING TIP

BACKGROUND KNOWLEDGE To open a discussion with children about the concept of fantasy, tell children that they can use their knowledge of real life to determine reality or fantasy. If something cannot really happen, it is fantasy. Fantasy stories include events or characters that cannot occur in real life.

SELF-SELECTED Reading

Children may choose from the following titles.

ANTHOLOGY

- *The Pony Express*

LEVELED BOOKS

- *The Ghost on the Train*
- *Messengers from the Sky*
- *Sending a Message with Dots and Dashes*

Bibliography, pages T88–T89

Review Fantasy and Reality

PREPARE

Review Fantasy and Reality   Encourage children to compare the events in "The Three Bears" with the events in *The Pony Express*. Ask volunteers to tell which piece of writing is about events that can't happen.

TEACH

Read "Johnnie's Flying Horse" and Model the Skill   Review "Johnnie's Flying Horse" with children. Ask them if all the events in the story could really happen.

Johnnie's Flying Horse

Johnnie begged his horse to go faster. Because the other rider had been late, he was behind with the mail. Now he had to finish an eight-hour ride in only four hours.

"Come on, fella," Johnnie said to his horse. "You're just as proud of working for the Pony Express as I am."

Suddenly Johnnie felt the horse rising from the ground. To his amazement, he saw great wings spreading from the horse's sides. "Yeehaw!" he yelled, as they soared into the sky. They were going to make the mail boat after all.

Teaching Chart 90

Ask a volunteer if this is a realistic story or a fantasy. Have the child explain his or her answer.

MODEL Two things tell me that this story is a fantasy—the title and the last event in which the horse grew wings and took off. I know that horses can't fly.

PRACTICE

Write a Skit

GROUP

Have groups of children write fantasy skits about a familiar event, such as a birthday party or a first day at school. ▶ **Interpersonal/Kinesthetic**

ASSESS/CLOSE

Perform a Skit Have each group perform their skit for the class. After each scene, ask the class to identify which event in the skit made it a fantasy.

ALTERNATE TEACHING STRATEGY
....

FANTASY AND REALITY
For a different approach to teaching this skill, see page T67.

Intervention ▶ **Skills**
Intervention Guide, for direct instruction and extra practice of fantasy and reality

Meeting Individual Needs for Comprehension

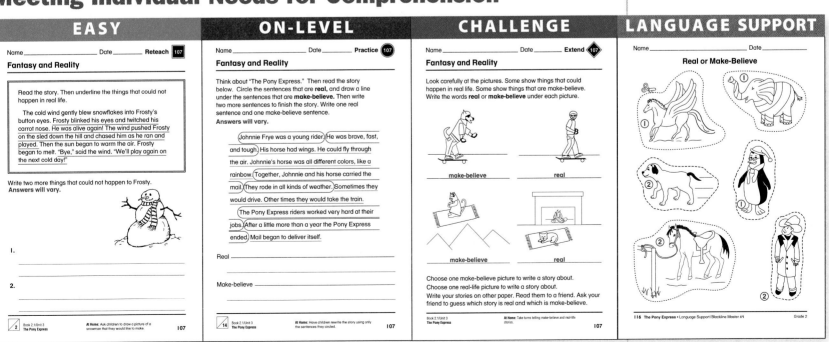

| EASY | ON-LEVEL | CHALLENGE | LANGUAGE SUPPORT |

Reteach, 107   Practice, 107   Extend, 107   Language Support, 116

OBJECTIVES

Children will identify and create synonym pairs.

MATERIALS
- **Teaching Chart 91**
- blank cards

Skills Finder

Synonyms

Introduce	B1: 341K-L
Review	B1: 369K-L, 379I-J
Test	B1: Unit 3

TEACHING TIP

SYNONYMS Have children choose five items in the classroom. Ask them to list the words and their synonyms on a bulletin-board display. Suggest that they illustrate their synonym pairs with drawings. Ask children to describe their synonym pairs to a partner.

Introduce Synonyms

PREPARE

Defining Synonyms

Explain: A synonym is a word with the same or almost the same meaning as another word. For example, *large* is a synonym for *big*. Ask children if they can think of another word that means almost the same as *pony*. (horse)

TEACH

Read "Riders Wanted" and Model the Skill

Have children read the passage on **Teaching Chart 91**.

Riders Wanted

Tom was a good horseback rider. When he saw the want ad for a Pony Express rider, he knew he would get the job. He told the man in charge of hiring, "I'm just the person you want. I'm loyal, and dependable. But most of all, I'm brave. I'm the most courageous person you've ever met."

Teaching Chart 91

Help children determine what *courageous* means.

MODEL I know that the word *courage* is probably the base word for *courageous*. Because the writer used *courageous* and *brave* to mean the same thing, these words are probably synonyms.

PRACTICE

Synonym Game

GROUP

Divide the class into two teams. Tell children that you are going to call out some words. The members of each team will list on paper the synonyms for as many words as they can. The team that lists the most correct synonyms will win. Some words with simple synonyms are *pretty, thin, mean, hurry, penny, shiny, cold, warm.* ▶ **Linguistic/Interpersonal**

Synonym Card Game

PARTNERS

Have children work in pairs to play a synonym card game. Have pairs generate a list of synonyms for the words in the previous activity and write them on index cards. Ask one person to draw a card and use the word in a sentence. Then ask the partner to think of a synonym for the word and use it in a sentence. Switch roles.

ASSESS/CLOSE

Make a Pair   To assess children's understanding of synonyms, observe them as they continue their game. Pass out blank cards to the children and encourage them to create their own synonym pairs.

ALTERNATE TEACHING STRATEGY

SYNONYMS

For another approach to teaching this skill, see page T74.

**Intervention** ▶ **Skills**

Intervention Guide, for direct instruction and extra practice of synonyms

Meeting Individual Needs for Vocabulary

EASY	ON-LEVEL	CHALLENGE	LANGUAGE SUPPORT

EASY

Name_____ Date_____ **Reteach** 108

Synonyms

A **synonym** is a word that means the same or nearly the same as another word.
The puppy is very **little**.
The puppy is very **small**.
Little and **small** are synonyms.

Read each sentence. Then circle the word that means the same or nearly the same as the word in dark print.

1. Timmy was the **fastest** runner and won first prize.
   a. happiest
   b. tallest
   c. (quickest)

2. When the team won the game, everyone **cheered**.
   a. (yelled)
   b. watched
   c. started

3. The children played games at the party and had a **joyous** time.
   a. unfriendly
   b. (happy)
   c. mean

4. Juan **dashed** down the street with a letter to give to the mailman.
   a. talked
   b. fell
   c. (ran)

5. The train **arrived** on time at the Main Street station.
   a. (came)
   b. left
   c. washed

6. The **tiny** clown laughed.
   a. happy
   b. (small)
   c. silly

At Home: Have children think of a word and its synonym. Then have them write a sentence using both words.

108   Book 2.1/Unit 3 The Pony Express   6

ON-LEVEL

Name_____ Date_____ **Practice** 108

Synonyms

Synonyms are two words that have the same or nearly the same meaning.

The **angry** bears ran toward each other in the forest.
The **mad** bears ran toward each other in the forest.
Angry and **mad** are synonyms.

Read each sentence. Write a synonym for the word in dark print.

1. The mouse was too **small** to jump on the table and eat the cheese.
   tiny or short

2. Meg was **sad** because she hurt her arm when she fell down.
   unhappy

3. My friend Ed and his family live in the log **cabin** in the woods.
   house

4. Tom thought the picture of the pig riding a horse was **silly**.
   funny

5. Lisa picked the **tulips** from the garden and put them in a basket.
   flowers

At Home: Encourage children to identify six words that describe objects in their home or school. Then ask them to substitute a synonym for each describing word.

108   Book 2.1/Unit 3 The Pony Express   5

CHALLENGE

Name_____ Date_____ **Extend** 108

Synonyms

Cut out the playing cards below. Place the cards face down. Play with a friend. Turn a card over. Match it to its synonym. Keep the cards if they match. Turn both cards back over if they do not match. Keep playing until all of the cards are gone.

one	single	two
double	three	triple
little	small	close
near	take	grab
shut	close	funny
silly	go	leave

At Home: Play the game with children. Challenge them to come up with new playing cards to add to the level of difficulty.

108   Book 2.1/Unit 3 The Pony Express

LANGUAGE SUPPORT

Name_____ Date_____

Tic-Tac-Word

carry	change	cheer
fast	letters	rushed
see	ship	start

mail	watch	take
shout	dashed	boat
quick	trade	begin

Grade 2   Language Support/Blackline Master 65 • The Pony Express   117

Reteach, 108   **Practice, 108**   **Extend, 108**   **Language Support, 117**

Explanatory Writing

GRAMMAR/SPELLING
CONNECTIONS

See the 5-Day Grammar and Usage Plan on past-tense verbs, pages 341O–341P.

See the 5-Day Spelling Plan on pages 341Q–341R.

TEACHING **TIP**

Technology
Many children may need practice using the keyboard. Have them practice typing this sentence: *The quick brown fox jumped over the lazy dog.* It uses every letter in the alphabet.

Addressing Envelopes Model the proper way to address an envelope. Point out the placement of the return address, the recipient's address, and the stamp. Help children proofread for capitalization of names, street names, and state abbreviations.

Handwriting CD-ROM

Prewrite

WRITE DIRECTIONS Present this writing assignment: Explain how to mail a letter. Make sure to include important information. Tell the steps in the right order, starting with putting the letter in an envelope.

VISUALIZE Have children imagine themselves mailing a letter. Ask them what is the very first thing that they do after writing the letter.

Strategy: Make a Flowchart After children have visualized the process, have them make a flowchart illustrating the steps in mailing a letter.

Draft

USE THE FLOWCHART Children can build their drafts on the steps outlined in their flowcharts. To expand the lesson, have children write explanations of how to mail postcards and how to buy stamps.

Revise

SELF-QUESTIONING Guide children to assess their drafts.

- Was my explanation of how to mail a letter clear?
- Did I give the steps in the correct order?

 Have children trade explanations with a partner to get feedback and another point of view.

Edit/Proofread

CHECK FOR ERRORS Children should check their explanations for errors in spelling, grammar, and punctuation.

Publish

MAKE A POSTER Children can combine their explanations and their flowcharts to make a poster.

HOW TO MAIL A LETTER

After you have written your letter, follow these steps:

1. Fold the letter neatly, put it in an envelope, and seal the envelope.

2. Write the address of the person to whom you are sending the letter on the front of the envelope. If he or she lives in an apartment, be sure to include the apartment number. Don't forget to write the zip code.

3. Write your own name and address in the upper left corner of the envelope.

4. Put a stamp on the upper right corner of the envelope. Make sure that you have paid the correct amount of postage.

5. Place the letter in the mail box. If you want it to get to the person quickly, you might want to mail the letter in the post office.

Presentation Ideas

DESIGN A POSTER Have children make drawings to illustrate their posters.
▶ **Viewing/Representing**

GIVE A DEMONSTRATION Have children demonstrate how to mail a letter by acting out all the steps as they give their explanations. ▶ **Speaking/Listening**

Consider children's creative efforts, possibly adding a plus (+) for originality, wit, and imagination.

Scoring Rubric

Excellent	Good	Fair	Unsatisfactory
4: The writer	**3:** The writer	**2:** The writer	**1:** The writer
• clearly presents an explanation of how to mail a letter.	• gives a basic explanation of the steps needed to mail a letter.	• attempts to explain how to mail a letter.	• fails to present a basic explanation of how to mail a letter.
• gives steps in proper sequence.	• presents the steps in proper sequence.	• includes all the steps, but sequence is confused.	• has not included all the steps.
• shows a good sense of the audience.	• has a sense of the audience.	• shows some sense of audience.	• has not listed steps in proper sequence.
			• has no sense of audience.

Incomplete 0: The writer leaves the page blank or fails to respond to the writing task. The writer does not address the topic or simply paraphrases the prompt. The response is illegible or incoherent.

Meeting Individual Needs for Writing

EASY	ON-LEVEL	CHALLENGE
Mail a Note Have children write a brief note about some incident in the school day. Then have them mail it to a friend or relative.	**Write Directions** Have students write directions to the town library. Have them illustrate their directions with a simple map.	**Letter of Explanation** Have children pretend they are Pony Express riders. Have them write a letter to a friend explaining what their duties are.

Viewing and Speaking

VIEWING Have children
- look for the logical sequence of mailing a letter.
- look for common details in the posters.
- note the variety of ways that the same message can be communicated.

SPEAKING Have children
- use transitional words to help the audience follow along.
- keep their heads held high to project their voices across the room.
- hold up the envelopes so that others can see them.

LANGUAGE SUPPORT

ESL Explain that posters do not always use complete sentences. Give examples of the kind of captions that appear on posters: *Put letter in envelope. Close envelope.*

PORTFOLIO Invite children to include their explanations or another writing project in their portfolios.

5 Day Grammar and Usage Plan

ESL Have pairs draw two picture cards. One partner will draw a picture that can be labeled "Now." The other partner draws a picture that can be labeled "Yesterday." Have them say a sentence for each picture, using the correct tense.

DAILY LANGUAGE ACTIVITIES

Write the Daily Language Activities on the chalkboard each day or use **Transparency 13**. For each sentence, have children correct the verb orally.

Day 1
1. People watch yesterday. watched
2. The riders show up last week. showed
3. Horses rush away last night. rushed

Day 2
1. Boys sign up last month. signed
2. Girls wave good-bye yesterday. waved
3. They tap on the glass. tapped

Day 3
1. Bill ship boxes last week. shipped
2. John and Bill work yesterday. worked
3. Riders move out last May. moved

Day 4
1. Long ago, riders drop off letters. dropped
2. They stop many years ago. stopped
3. Mail arrive late last month. arrived

Day 5
1. We paste a stamp on the letter yesterday. pasted
2. We plan to mail it then. planned
3. Who invent the stamp? invented

Daily Language Transparency 13

DAY 1 — Introduce the Concept

Oral Warm-Up Write this sentence on the chalkboard: *Yesterday I walked five miles.* Ask children whether it tells what is happening now or what already happened. Point out the *-ed* ending.

Introduce Past-Tense Verbs Review verb tenses with children. Present:

Past-Tense Verbs

- Verbs can tell about actions that already happened.
- These verbs are in the **past tense**.
- Add *-ed* to most verbs to tell about an action in the past.

Present the Daily Language Activity and have children correct orally. Then ask them to write their own sentences using the past-tense forms.

 Assign the daily Writing Prompt on page 320C.

DAY 2 — Teach the Concept

Review Past-Tense Verbs Write *help*, *walk*, and *look* on the board. Have children orally use these verbs in sentences that start with the word *yesterday*. Point out how *-ed* must be added to each verb.

Introduce Spelling Changes Explain that some verbs have to be spelled differently in the past tense. Present the following:

Past-Tense Verbs

- If a verb ends with one consonant, double the consonant and add *-ed*.
- If a verb ends with *e*, drop the *e* and add *-ed*.

Present the Daily Language Activity. Then have children write the words *drop*, *slice*, and *brush* in the past tense. Discuss any spelling changes that had to be made.

 Assign the daily Writing Prompt on page 320C.

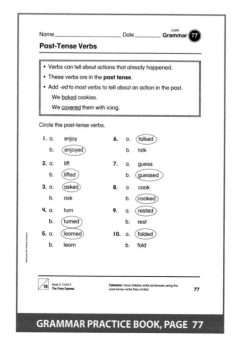

GRAMMAR PRACTICE BOOK, PAGE 77

GRAMMAR PRACTICE BOOK, PAGE 78

3410 *The Pony Express*

Past-Tense Verbs

Learn from the Literature Review past-tense verbs. Read the sentence on page 328 of *The Pony Express*.

> Everybody waved and cheered as he rushed away from them.

Have children identify the past-tense verbs in this sentence.

Use Past Tense in Sentences Present the Daily Language Activity. Then have children write three sentences using the present tense of the verbs *work, move,* and *stop.* Then tell them to end their sentences with the words *long ago.* Have them change the verbs to show that actions happened in the past. Have volunteers explain how each verb should be changed. (*work:* add *-ed; move:* drop the *e* and add *-ed; stop:* double the final *p* and add *-ed.*)

 Assign the daily Writing Prompt on page 320D.

Review Past-Tense Verbs Write on the board the sentences from the Daily Language Activities for Days 2 and 3. Have children use the verbs in their own past-tense sentences.

Mechanics and Usage Before children begin the Daily Writing Prompt on page 320D, review letter punctuation. Display and discuss:

Letter Punctuation

- Begin the greeting and closing in a letter with a capital letter.
- Use a comma after the greeting in a letter.
- Use a comma after the closing in a letter.
- Use a comma between the day and year in a date.
- Use a comma between the names of a city and a state.

 Assign the daily Writing Prompt on page 320D.

Assess Use the Daily Language Activity and page 81 of the **Grammar Practice Book** for assessment.

Reteach Divide children into teams. Write a list of the present tense of the shorter verbs used in the Daily Language Activity in a scrambled form. For example, write *shaw* for *wash.* You may want to use these words in sentences that provide clues as to their correct form. Give the members of each team different colored pieces of chalk. Have team members take turns unscrambling the verbs and writing their past-tense forms on the board. Give extra points for writing the correct past tense of verbs with spelling changes.

Use page 82 of the **Grammar Practice Book** for additional reteaching.

 Assign the daily Writing Prompt on page 320D.

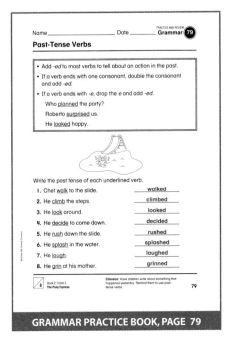

GRAMMAR PRACTICE BOOK, PAGE 79

GRAMMAR PRACTICE BOOK, PAGE 80

GRAMMAR PRACTICE BOOK, PAGE 81

5 Day Spelling Plan

To help students find the number of syllables in a word, have them tap out the number of vowel sounds they hear. Point out the difference between vowels, which may be silent, and vowel sounds, which correlate with the number of syllables.

DICTATION SENTENCES

Spelling Words

1. The sack is made of leather.
2. My bread is hot.
3. The weather is bad.
4. I spread out the leaf.
5. Her breakfast is cold.
6. She is ready to stay.
7. I meant to write to you.
8. My feather is brown.
9. She went instead of me.
10. The meadow is green.

Challenge Words

11. He can arrive there.
12. I went there early.
13. She can finish the work.
14. Her record is new.
15. I had success before.

DAY 1 — Pretest

Assess Prior Knowledge Use the Dictation Sentences at left and **Spelling Practice Book** page 77 for the pretest. Allow students to correct their own papers. If students have trouble, have partners give each other a midweek test on Day 3. Students who require a modified list may be tested on the first five words.

	Spelling Words			Challenge Words
1.	**leather**	6.	ready	11. **arrive**
2.	bread	7.	meant	12. **early**
3.	**weather**	8.	feather	13. **finish**
4.	spread	9.	instead	14. **record**
5.	breakfast	10.	meadow	15. **success**

*Note: Words in **dark type** are from the story.*

Word Study On page 78 of the **Spelling Practice Book** are word study steps and an at-home activity.

SPELLING PRACTICE BOOK, PAGE 77

WORD STUDY STEPS AND ACTIVITY, PAGE 78

DAY 2 — Explore the Pattern

Sort and Spell Words Say *bread, breakfast,* and *meadow.* Ask students to identify the first vowel sound in each word. Write the words so that students can see the short *e* sound spelled *ea.* Then have them listen for other vowel sounds in *breakfast* and *meadow* and identify the number of syllables.

Have students read aloud the ten spelling words before sorting them according to number of syllables.

Words with One Syllable	Words with Two Syllables	
bread	leather	feather
spread	weather	instead
meant	breakfast	meadow
	ready	

Word Wall Have students look through stories or poems for new words with the short *e* sound spelled *ea* and add them to the classroom word wall, underlining the spelling pattern in each word.

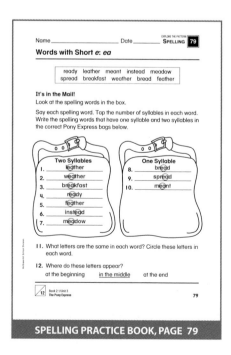

SPELLING PRACTICE BOOK, PAGE 79

Words with Short *e*: *ea*

DAY 3 Practice and Extend	**DAY 4** Proofread and Write	**DAY 5** Assess and Reteach

DAY 3 — Practice and Extend

Word Meaning: Fill-Ins Write sentences on the chalkboard and ask students to fill in the missing spelling word. For example: *I eat _____ in the morning.* Then see if students can write their own sentences to be filled in by a partner.

Glossary Tell students that some entries in the Glossary provide additional verb forms. Have students:

- write the Challenge Words *arrive*, *finish*, and *record*.

- look up other verb forms of these words found in the Glossary.

- write a sentence for each of these words using a verb form.

DAY 4 — Proofread and Write

Proofread Sentences Write these sentences on the chalkboard, including the misspelled words. Ask students to proofread, circling incorrect spellings and writing the correct spellings. There are two spelling errors in each sentence.

> I had ⟨bred⟩ for ⟨brekfast.⟩ (bread, breakfast)

> They were not ⟨redy⟩ for the bad ⟨wether.⟩ (ready, weather)

Have students create additional sentences with errors for partners to correct.

Writing Have students use as many spelling words as possible in the daily Writing Prompt on page 320D. Remind students to proofread their writing for errors in spelling, grammar, and punctuation.

DAY 5 — Assess and Reteach

Assess Students' Knowledge Use page 82 of the **Spelling Practice Book** or the Dictation Sentences on page 341Q for the posttest.

Personal Word List If students have trouble with any words in the lesson, have them create a personal list of troublesome words in their journals. Have students try to think of rhyming words for each word on their personal word list.

Students should refer to their word lists during later writing activities.

SPELLING PRACTICE BOOK, PAGE 80

Name _____ Date _____ SPELLING 80
Words with Short *e*: *ea*

| ready | leather | meant | instead | meadow |
| spread | breakfast | weather | bread | feather |

Write a spelling word to complete each sentence.

1. Shoes and belts are made of ___leather___.
2. The ___weather___ can be hot or cold, rainy or clear.
3. A bird's ___feather___ is very light in weight.
4. Another name for a field of grass is a ___meadow___.
5. What do you think he ___meant___ by that?
6. In the morning I get ___ready___ for school.
7. Put the ___bread___ in the toaster.
8. Jeffrey likes to ___spread___ jam on his toast.
9. I think I'll wear my red gloves ___instead___ of my brown ones.

Word Builder

10. Be a word builder. Build a spelling word from the shorter words.

break + fast = ___breakfast___

SPELLING PRACTICE BOOK, PAGE 81

Name _____ Date _____ SPELLING 81
Words with Short *e*: *ea*

Proofreading Activity
There are six spelling mistakes in the journal below. Circle each misspelled word. Write the words correctly on the lines below.

Today was my first day as a Pony Express rider. In the morning the ⟨wether⟩ was beautiful. I had some ⟨bred⟩ for ⟨brekfst.⟩ I was too excited to eat anything else. I was ⟨reddy⟩ when the other rider got to my station. I put my ⟨lether⟩ bags across the saddle. Then, I jumped on my horse and was off! At first I rode along a river. After that I rode through a ⟨medow⟩ full of pretty wildflowers. Being a Pony Express rider is the best job I ever had!

1. ___weather___ 2. ___bread___ 3. ___breakfast___
4. ___ready___ 5. ___leather___ 6. ___meadow___

Writing Activity
Pretend you are the Pony Express rider. Write about an exciting day you had. Use four of your spelling words. Circle the words you use.

SPELLING PRACTICE BOOK, PAGE 82

Name _____ Date _____ SPELLING 82
Words with Short *e*: *ea*

Look at the words in each set. One word in each set is spelled correctly. Use a pencil to color in the circle in front of that word. Before you begin, look at the sample sets of words. Sample A has been done for you. Do Sample B by yourself. When you are sure you know what to do, you may go on with the rest of the page.

Sample A
- Ⓐ watur
- ● water
- Ⓒ watir
- Ⓓ wator

Sample B
- ● yellow
- Ⓕ yello
- Ⓖ yellar
- Ⓗ yellur

1.
- Ⓐ leather
- Ⓑ laether
- ● leather
- Ⓓ layther

2.
- Ⓔ brede
- Ⓕ braed
- ● bread
- Ⓗ brid

3.
- ● weather
- Ⓑ wuther
- Ⓒ wather
- Ⓓ wether

4.
- Ⓔ spraed
- Ⓕ sprede
- Ⓖ spreed
- ● spread

5.
- Ⓐ bredfast
- ● breakfast
- Ⓒ brakfast
- Ⓓ brefast

6.
- Ⓔ rady
- ● ready
- Ⓖ redy
- Ⓗ reddy

7.
- Ⓐ ment
- Ⓑ mante
- Ⓒ mente
- ● meant

8.
- Ⓔ feather
- Ⓕ faether
- Ⓖ fether
- Ⓗ feither

9.
- Ⓐ instaed
- ● instead
- Ⓒ instede
- Ⓓ instade

10.
- Ⓔ medow
- Ⓕ maedow
- ● meadow
- Ⓗ medou

Concept
• Animals in Folktales

Comprehension
• Fantasy and Reality

Phonics
• Long *e*: *y, ey*

Vocabulary
• Earth
• forget
• lonely
• memory
• mountain
• wonderful

Reaching All Learners

Anthology

Nine-in-One, Grr! Grr!

Selection Summary A lonely tiger tries to remember the magic words for having many cubs, but a clever bird will do anything to stop her.

Told by Blia Xiong
Adapted by Cathy Spagnoli
Illustrated by Nancy Hom

Listening Library

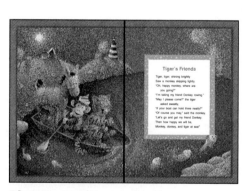

Rhyme applies to phonics

INSTRUCTIONAL pages 344–369

About the Author Blia Xiong (BLEE-AH SHONG) first heard *Nine-in-One, Grr! Grr!* when she was three. When asked how she remembers a story, she explains, "When I listen to a story, I listen very closely. I make pictures in my mind. Then I can remember what I hear."

About the Illustrator Nancy Hom was born in southern China and grew up in New York City. In addition to *Nine-in-One, Grr! Grr!* she has illustrated the Cambodian folktale *Judge Rabbit and the Tree Spirit*.

Leveled Books

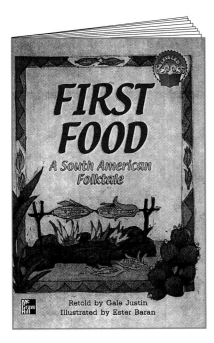

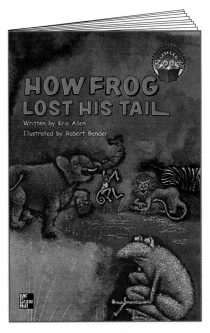

EASY
Lesson on pages 369A and 369D

DECODABLE

INDEPENDENT
Lesson on pages 369B and 369D

🏠 *Take-Home version available*

CHALLENGE
Lesson on pages 369C and 369D

Leveled Practice

EASY

Reteach, 109–116 Blackline masters with reteaching opportunities for each assessed skill

INDEPENDENT/ON-LEVEL

Practice, 109–116 Workbook with Take-Home stories and practice opportunities for each assessed skill and story comprehension

CHALLENGE

Extend, 109–116 Blackline masters that offer challenge activities for each assessed skill

Quizzes Prepared by **Accelerated Reader**

WORKSTATION Activities

Suggested Lesson Planner

READING AND LANGUAGE ARTS	**DAY 1** *Focus on Reading and Skills*	**DAY 2** *Read the Literature*
● **Phonics Daily Routines**	Daily **Phonics** Routine: **Segmenting**, 342H **Phonics CD-ROM**	Daily **Phonics** Routine: **Blending**, 344A **Phonics CD-ROM**
● **Phonological Awareness** ● **Phonics** *Long e* ● **Comprehension** ● **Vocabulary** ● **Study Skills** ● **Listening, Speaking, Viewing, Representing**	**Read Aloud: Myth,** 342E "The Tiger Story" ☑ **Develop Phonological Awareness,** 342F Long *e* ☑ **Introduce Long** *e***,** 342G–342H **Teaching Chart 92** Reteach, Practice, Extend, 109 **Phonics/Phonemic Awareness Practice Book,** 81–84 **Apply Long** *e***,** 342–343 "Tiger's Friends" Intervention Program	**Build Background,** 344A Develop Oral Language **Vocabulary,** 344B–344C  <table><tr><td>Earth</td><td>lonely</td><td>mountain</td></tr><tr><td>forget</td><td>memory</td><td>wonderful</td></tr></table> **Word Building Manipulative Cards** **Teaching Chart 93** Reteach, Practice, Extend, 110 **Read the Selection,** 344–365 Comprehension ☑ Long *e* ☑ Fantasy and Reality **Genre:** Folktale, 345 **Cultural Perspectives,** 358  Intervention Program
● **Curriculum Connections**	**Link** Language Arts, 342E	**Link** Social Studies, 344A
● **Writing**	**Writing Prompt:** Describe a tiger or other wild animal. Remember to tell about the different body parts it has.	**Writing Prompt:** Tell about the items you have in your desk, backpack, or pockets. **Journal Writing,** Quick-Write, 365
● **Grammar**	**Introduce the Concept: The Verb** *Have,* 369O Daily Language Activity: Write the correct form of *have.* **Grammar Practice Book,** 83	**Teach the Concept: The Verb** *Have,* 369O Daily Language Activity: Write the correct form of *have.* **Grammar Practice Book,** 84
● **Spelling** *Long e*	**Pretest: Words with Long** *e***,** 369Q **Spelling Practice Book,** 83, 84	**Teach the Pattern: Words with Long** *e***,** 369Q **Spelling Practice Book,** 85

 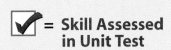
 **DAY 3** *Read the Literature*	 **DAY 4** *Build Skills*	 **DAY 5** *Build Skills*
Daily  Routine: **Fluency,** 367  **CD-ROM**	Daily  Routine: **Writing,** 369F **CD-ROM**	Daily **Phonics** Routine: **Letter Substitution,** 369H **Phonics CD-ROM**

Rereading for Fluency, 364
 	
Story Questions and Activities, 366–367
   Reteach, Practice, Extend, 111
 	
Study Skill, 368
   ✔ Reference Sources
   Teaching Chart 94
   Reteach, Practice, Extend, 112
 	
Test Power, 369
 	
 Read the Leveled Books, 369A–369D
   Guided Reading
   ✔ Long *e*
   ✔ Fantasy and Reality
   ✔ Instructional Vocabulary
 	
 Intervention Program
	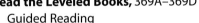 **Read the Leveled Books and the Self-Selected Books**
	
	   ✔ **Review Long *e*,** 369E–369F
	      Teaching Chart 95
	      Reteach, Practice, Extend, 113
	      Language Support, 123
	      Phonics/Phonemic Awareness
	         Practice Book, 81–84
	
	   ✔ **Cumulative Review,** 369G–369H
	      Teaching Chart 96
	      Reteach, Practice, Extend, 114
	      Language Support, 124
	      Phonics/Phonemic Awareness
	         Practice Book, 81–84
	
	   Minilessons, 347, 349, 351, 355
	
	 Intervention Program
		Read Self-Selected Books
		
		   ✔ **Review Cause and Effect,** 369I–369J
		      Teaching Chart 97
		      Reteach, Practice, Extend, 115
		      Language Support, 125
		
		   ✔ **Review Synonyms,** 369K–369L
		      Teaching Chart 98
		      Reteach, Practice, Extend, 116
		      Language Support, 126
		
		   Listening, Speaking, Viewing, Representing, 369N
		      Illustrate the Report
		      Guide a Tour
		
		   Minilessons, 347, 349, 351, 355

Activity Social Studies, 352; Music, 354	 Science, 360	**Activity** Math, 362

Writing Prompt: Remember the last time you visited the doctor or dentist? What did he or she have in his or her office? Write about it.
 	
Explanatory Writing, 369M
   Prewrite, Draft
	Writing Prompt: You are going to write a book about the tiger and the bird. Write the title.
	
	Explanatory Writing, 369M
	   Revise
	
	Meeting Individual Needs for Writing, 369N
		Writing Prompt: Did you ever use a song or rhyme to remember something? Tell what you wanted to remember and how you remembered it.
		
		Explanatory Writing, 369M
		   Edit/Proofread, Publish

Practice and Write: The Verb *Have*, 369P
   Daily Language Activity: Write the correct form of *have*.
Grammar Practice Book, 85
	Practice and Write: The Verb *Have*, 369P
	   Daily Language Activity: Write the correct form of *have*.
	Grammar Practice Book, 86
		Assess and Reteach: The Verb *Have*, 369P
		   Daily Language Activity: Write the correct form of *have*.
		Grammar Practice Book, 87, 88

Practice and Extend: Words with Long *e*, 369R **Spelling Practice Book,** 86	**Practice and Write: Words with Long *e*,** 369R **Spelling Practice Book,** 87	**Assess and Reteach: Words with Long *e*,** 369R **Spelling Practice Book,** 88

Read Aloud

The Tiger Story
a myth from Vietnam

Long ago when the world was new and animals and men spoke the same language, the tiger looked quite different. His skin was the color of bright shining gold, and was without stripes. Although he was very beautiful, he was also a vicious hunter and was feared throughout the land.

One day a farmer, who had been plowing his field at the edge of the jungle, left his water buffalo to drink at the stream while he himself slept in the shade. The day was very hot and he slept for a long time.

The tiger, who had been watching from the jungle, pounced before the water buffalo. Before the beast had a chance to react in fear, the tiger spoke to him in a gentle reassuring voice, "Don't worry, poor helpless beast of burden, for I have not come to harm you, but only to ask you some questions. Why is that you who are so strong allow that man who is so small and weak to work you all day in the hot sun?"

Continued on pages T4–T5

Oral Comprehension

LISTENING AND SPEAKING Read the myth aloud. Suggest that children think about the storyteller's purpose as they listen. After you've finished reading, ask, "According to this myth, how did the tiger get its stripes?" Reread the myth. Then ask, "What do you like most about this myth? Why? What do you like least? Why?"

GENRE STUDY: MYTH Discuss some of the characteristics of myths. Explain that myths helped ancient people understand the natural world around them.

• Have children discuss the setting of "The Tiger Story." Point out that most myths are set in ancient times.

• Talk about the tiger and water buffalo. Ask, "How were these animals different from real animals?" *(they could talk)*

• Finish your discussion by asking children to name other things or events in nature that ancient people might have tried to explain in stories.

Activity Encourage children to make a cartoon strip that illustrates an original myth. Remind them that their cartoons should explain an event in nature.
▶ **Visual/Linguistic**

Develop Phonological Awareness

Blend Sounds

MATERIALS

- Phonics Pictures from *Word Building Cards*

Teach Tell children they are going to say the sounds of a word with you and then put the sounds together to say the whole word. Hold up the Phonics Picture *key*. Say: /k/-/ē/ . . . *Let's put the sounds together. Key. What sound do you hear at the end of the word?"* (/ē/) Repeat with the Phonics Picture *baby*. Then say: /k/-/ē/; /b/-/ā/-/b/-/ē/; *what sound do you hear in both words?* (/ē/)

Practice Have children blend the sounds for these words: *happy, turkey, valley, penny, lady, tiny, many, every,* and *money.* Then say the words *happy, valley,* and *penny,* and ask where the /ē/ sound is. (at the end)

Segment Sounds

MATERIALS

- colored blocks

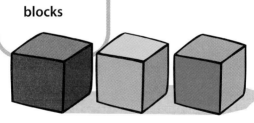

Teach Tell children they are going to play a name game. To demonstrate the game, say the name *Penny*, then say the sounds /p/-/e/-/n/-/ē/, placing one block in front of you for each sound. Then count the blocks and tell children the name *Penny* has four sounds.

Practice Distribute five blocks to each child. Have children segment and count the number of sounds in these names: *Benny, Judy, Bob, Kitty, Amy, Rusty, Jeff, Debra,* and *Ira.*

Substitute Sounds

MATERIALS

- Phonics Picture Posters

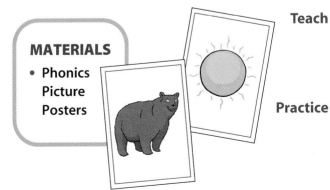

Teach Display the Phonics Picture Poster of the *sun.* Have children say the word *sun* with you. Then tell children if you change the beginning sound of *sun* to /f/, you make the word *fun.* Have children repeat both words with you: *sun/fun.* Repeat with words *bear/hair.*

Practice Have children substitute the beginning sounds for the following words: *valley/Sally; penny/Lenny; money/ honey; candy/dandy; puppy/guppy; city/pity;* and *silly/Willy.*

 ASSESSMENT Observe children as they blend, segment, and substitute sounds. If children have difficulty, see Alternate Teaching Strategies on p. T72.

OBJECTIVES

Children will:

- identify /ē/ *y, ey.*
- blend and read long *e: y, ey* words.

MATERIALS

- **Teaching Chart 92**
- **Word Building Manipulative Cards**
- index cards

Skills Finder	
Long *e: y, ey*	
Introduce	B1: 342G-H
Review	B1: 369E-F, 369G-H, 370G-H
Test	B1: Unit 3
Maintain	B1: 227; B2: 347

SPELLING/PHONICS CONNECTIONS

Words with long *e:* See the 5-Day Spelling Plan, pages 369Q–369R.

TEACHING TIP

SUFFIXES Point out that *y* and *ey* spellings for long *e* usually come at the end of a word.

Write words ending with *y* and *ey* on the board. Classify the words into *y* or *ey* endings. Have children stress the long *e* sound as they say the word aloud.

Introduce Long *e: y, ey*

TEACH

Identify *y* and *ey* as Symbols for the Sound /ē/

Tell children they will learn to read words in which the letters *y* and *ey* stand for the /ē/ sound.

- Write the letters *y* and *ey* on the chalkboard and have children say /ē/ as you point to them.

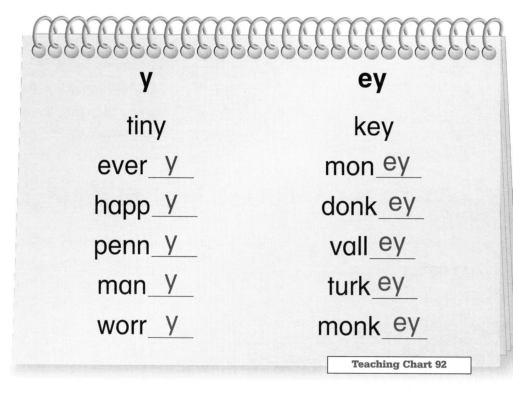

y	ey
tiny	key
ever_y_	mon_ey_
happ_y_	donk_ey_
penn_y_	vall_ey_
man_y_	turk_ey_
worr_y_	monk_ey_

Teaching Chart 92

BLENDING
Model and Guide Practice with Long *e: y, ey* Words

- Display **Teaching Chart 92**. Point to *y* at the top of the first column. Tell children that this letter sometimes stands for the long *e* sound.
- Run your finger under *tiny*, blending letters to read the word. Have children repeat after you.
- Ask children to identify which letter in *tiny* stands for the long *e* sound.
- Have volunteers add *y* to the other words in the first column of the chart, blending and reading each aloud. Ask children to blend and read all the words in the completed column.

Use the Words in Context

- Have children use the words in sentences to reinforce their meanings. Example: *It's important to smile and be happy.*

Repeat the Procedure

- Follow the same procedure to complete the second column on the chart.

PRACTICE

BLENDING
Build Long *e: y, ey*
Words with
Letter Cards

PARTNERS

Have partners use letter cards to build words from the teaching chart. Then encourage them to think of and build other words in which *y* or *ey* stand for the long *e* sound. Have children blend and read each word aloud as they build them. ▶ **Auditory/Linguistic**

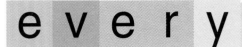 
e v e r y   k e y

ASSESS/CLOSE

Identify and Read
Words with
Long *e: y, ey*

To assess children's ability to build and read words with long *e* spelled *y* and *ey*, observe their work on the Practice activity. Ask each child to read and spell aloud two words from the **Teaching Chart**. Then have children turn to page 342 in their books and read "Tiger's Friends" aloud with them. Ask volunteers to identify long *e: y, ey* words in the poem.

ADDITIONAL PHONICS RESOURCES

Phonics/Phonemic Awareness
Practice Book,
pages 81–84

McGraw-Hill School
TECHNOLOGY

Phonics CD-ROM
activities for Practice with
Blending and Segmenting

Meeting Individual Needs for Phonics

EASY	ON-LEVEL	CHALLENGE

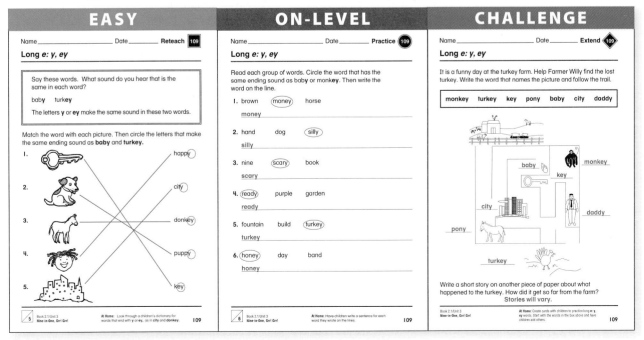

Reteach, 109   Practice, 109   Extend, 109

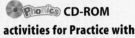

Daily Routines

DAY 1
Segmenting Write *y* and *ey* on the board. Invite children to create words using the long *e* sound these letters make. Have them use different colored chalk to write *y* and *ey*.

DAY 2
Blending Write the spelling of each sound in *every* as you say it. Have children blend the sounds together to read the word. Repeat with *turkey*.

DAY 3
Fluency Hold up index cards with words containing the long *e* sound spelled *y* and *ey*. Ask volunteers to blend the sounds in each word silently and then read each word aloud.

DAY 4
Writing Have children write short rhymes using words with long *e* spelled *y* or *ey*. Have children read aloud their rhymes as listeners raise their hands when they hear words with the sound /ē/.

DAY 5
Letter Substitution Have partners work together to build words ending with the long *e* sound spelled *y* or *ey*. Invite children to take turns changing letters to build new words.

Apply **Long** *e: y, ey*

Tiger's Friends

Tiger, tiger, shining brightly
Saw a monkey skipping lightly.
"Oh, happy monkey, where are
   you going?"
"I'm taking my friend Donkey rowing."
"May I please come?" the tiger
   asked sweetly,
"If your boat can hold three neatly?"
"Of course you may," said the monkey.
"Let's go and get my friend Donkey.
Then how happy we will be,
Monkey, donkey, and tiger at sea!"

Anthology pages 342–343

Read and Build Fluency

READ THE POEM Tell children they will now read a poem called "Tiger's Friends." As students track their text, model voice and facial expression when reading aloud the dialogue of the different characters. Then, for auditory modeling, engage in a choral reading of the poem.

REREAD FOR FLUENCY Ask children to
GROUP reread the poem in groups of three. Have them take the roles of Tiger, Monkey, and narrator. Remind children who are reading a character's part to say the words the way the character might speak. Encourage them to pause after commas, add emphasis to sentences that end in exclamation points, and to vary their tone for questions.

Dictate and Spell

DICTATE WORDS Say the long *e* word *monkey.*
JOURNAL Then segment the word into its individual parts. Say *monkey* again and use it in a sentence, such as, "The monkey sat on the man's shoulder." Have children repeat the word. Then direct them to write down the letter or letter patterns for each sound until they make the entire word. Continue the exercise with other long *e* words from the poem, such as, *happy* and *donkey.* Then use words outside the poem, such as, *every* and *key.*

i **Intervention** **Skills Intervention Guide,**
for direct instruction and extra practice of long *e, y, ey*

Build Background

Social Studies

Concept: Animals in Folktales

Evaluate Prior Knowledge

CONCEPT: ANIMALS IN FOLKTALES
Ask children if they have ever read a folktale such as *Goldilocks*, *Puss-in-Boots*, or *Little Red Riding Hood*. Discuss how animal characters act in those stories. Ask children to compare these animal characters to real animals.

MAKE A CHART Work with children to record their responses on a chart. For example:

Animal	Folktale Character	Real Animal
bear	lives in a house sleeps in a bed	lives in a cave sleeps on the ground
cat	wears clothes talks	does not wear clothes meows

Graphic Organizer 30

DRAW A PICTURE Invite children to draw

an animal character from a folktale, and a real-life version of the same kind of animal. Have children write two or three sentences describing differences between the two.

Develop Oral Language

DESCRIBING ANIMALS IN FOLKTALES
Ask children to tell about animals that appear in folktales from their cultures. Encourage them to name the animal, draw a picture of it on the board, and give a brief summary of the folktale. ▶ **Visual/Kinesthetic**

DAILY Phonics ROUTINES

DAY 2 **Blending** Write the spelling of each sound in *every* as you say it. Have children blend the sounds together to read the word. Repeat with *turkey*.

 **Phonics CD-ROM**

LANGUAGE SUPPORT

Use the **Language Support Book**, pages 118–121, to help build background.

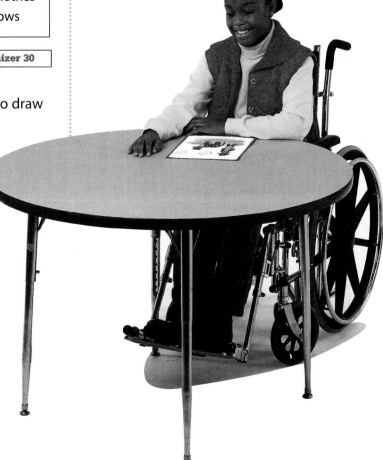

OBJECTIVES

Children will use context and structural clues to determine the meanings of vocabulary words.

Earth
lonely
wonderful
forget
mountain
memory

Vocabulary

Teach Vocabulary in Context

Definitions

Earth (p. 344) planet on which we live

lonely (p. 344) having a sad feeling because one is by oneself

wonderful (p. 351) very good

forget (p. 351) not remember something

mountain (p. 353) piece of land that rises high above the surrounding area

memory (p. 352) ability to remember things

Identify Vocabulary Words Display **Teaching Chart 93** and read the passage with children. Have volunteers circle each vocabulary word and underline other words that are clues to its meaning.

Good News
1. A long time ago Tiger and her mate lived together with other animals on the planet Earth. **2.** They had no children and often felt lonely. **3.** Then great Shao gave Tiger wonderful news that made her very happy. She would have many tiger cubs. **4.** "Remember what I tell you!" said Shao. "Don't forget my words!" **5.** It was a long way down the high mountain to Tiger's home. **6.** "I have such a poor memory," said Tiger. "How will I make sure that I will always remember what he said?"

Teaching Chart 93

Story Words

These words from the selection may be unfamiliar. Before children read, have them check the meanings and pronunciations of the words in the Glossary, beginning on page 398, or in a dictionary.

• bamboo, p. 346
• Shao, p. 346
• pheasant, p. 355
• quail, p. 355
• Hmong, p. 364

Discuss Meanings Ask questions like these to help clarify word meanings:

• What shape is Earth?
• Tell about a time when you felt lonely.
• Have you ever heard any wonderful news? How did it make you feel?
• Which is taller, your school or a mountain?
• What happens when you forget to water a plant?
• When you meet a new person, what about him or her sticks in your memory most—the person's name or the person's face?

Practice

Demonstrate Word Meaning

GROUP

Read **Teaching Chart 93** substituting *Grr! Grr!* for each vocabulary word. Direct children to hold up the correct vocabulary card to replace *Grr! Grr!* in each sentence. ▶ **Linguistic**

earth   lonely   mountain

| **Word Building Manipulative Cards** |

Write Captions
PARTNERS
WRITING

Have children work in pairs. Each child can draw a picture based on a vocabulary word. Have partners exchange drawings and write captions for each other's picture using the vocabulary words. ▶ **Linguistic/Spatial**

Assess Vocabulary

Identify Word Meaning in Context

GROUP
WRITING

Have children form small groups. Assign each group three vocabulary words and ask them to write a riddle for each word. Suggest that they use synonyms, antonyms, and definitions as clues for their riddles. Have different groups exchange riddles for members to solve.

SPELLING/VOCABULARY CONNECTIONS

See Spelling Challenge Words, pages 369Q–369R.

LANGUAGE SUPPORT

See the **Language Support Book**, pages 118–121, for teaching suggestions for Vocabulary.

Vocabulary PuzzleMaker

Provides vocabulary activities.

Meeting Individual Needs for Vocabulary

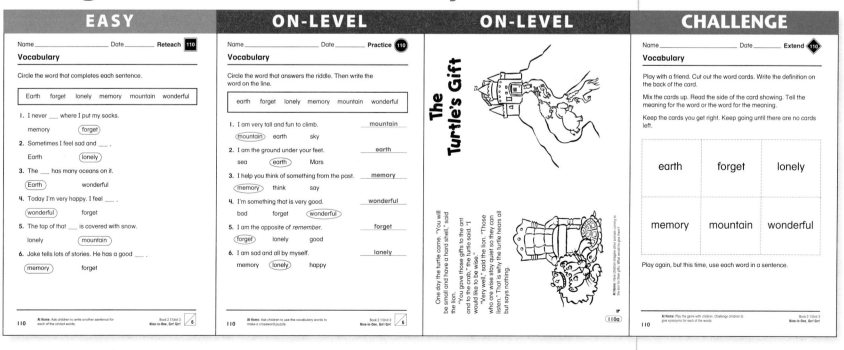

EASY	ON-LEVEL	ON-LEVEL	CHALLENGE
Reteach, 110	Practice, 110	Practice, 110a Take-Home Story	Extend, 110

Comprehension

Prereading Strategies

PREVIEW AND PREDICT Have children read the title and then take a **picture walk** through the story.

- What clues do the pictures give about the characters in this story?

- Will the story tell about real events or made-up events? How do you know? (Made-up events. Animals don't really speak.) *Genre*

- What will this story probably be about?

Have children make predictions about the story and the main character.

PREDICTIONS	WHAT HAPPENED
The tiger will go on a journey.	
The man will tell the tiger something.	

SET PURPOSES What do children want to find out by reading the story? For example:

- Where does the tiger go?

- Who is the man in the story?

- What does Nine-in-One mean?

A FOLK TALE FROM THE HMONG PEOPLE OF LAOS
TOLD BY BLIA XIONG

NINE▸IN▸ONE, GRR! GRR!

ADAPTED BY CATHY SPAGNOLI
ILLUSTRATED BY NANCY HOM

Many years ago when the earth was nearer the sky than it is today, there lived the first tiger. She and her mate had no babies and so the lonely tiger often thought about the future, wondering ①how many cubs she would have.

344

Meeting Individual Needs • Grouping Suggestions for Strategic Reading

EASY	ON-LEVEL	CHALLENGE
Reading Together Invite children to join in as you read the story aloud and then have them listen to the **Listening Library.** While reading or listening, model the strategy of paying attention to which events and details in the story could happen in real life, and which could not.	**Guided Instruction** You may want to have children read the story first on their own. As the class reads together, focus on prompts concerning the key Comprehension skill to help children to distinguish fantasy from reality.	**Read Independently** Encourage children to set purposes before they read. After reading, have children retell the story, stopping to point out and discuss details and events that could not happen in real life. Have students set up a Fantasy and Reality chart as on page 345. After reading, they can use the chart to help them summarize the story.

345

Comprehension

 Phonics Apply Long *e* Words

 Apply Fantasy and Reality

STRATEGIC READING Some things in this story are fantasy and couldn't really happen. Other things are realistic and could happen in real life. Let's prepare Reality and Fantasy charts to help keep track of which story events could happen in real life, and which could not.

REALITY	FANTASY

1 **FANTASY AND REALITY** The story says Tiger is thinking about the future. Do you think real tigers think about the future or wonder how many cubs they will have? Why? (No, real tigers do not act like people.)

Genre

Folktale

Explain that a folktale:

- generally features a simple plot with events that repeat.
- has stereotyped characters that may be *all* good or *all* bad.
- usually has a rural setting and events take place in the distant past.

Activity After children read *Nine-in-One, Grr! Grr!*, briefly discuss how the characters, setting, and events make this story a folktale. Challenge them to compare and contrast this folktale with the realistic fiction selection *Ann's First Day*. Encourage them to discuss the author's purpose of writing each selection.

LANGUAGE SUPPORT

A blackline master of the Reality and Fantasy chart is available in the **Language Support Book**.

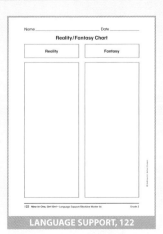

LANGUAGE SUPPORT, 122

Comprehension

2 Why does Tiger decide to visit Shao? (She wants to ask how many cubs she will have.) What do you predict she will find out? *Cause and Effect*

3 Tiger is going to visit Shao. Describe the character Shao. (He lives in the sky. He is kind, gentle, and wise.) *Character*

TEACHING TIP

BACKGROUND INFORMATION Explain that *Nine-in-One, Grr! Grr!* is a Laotian tale that was passed down from generation to generation through storytelling. Have children locate Laos on the globe. Discuss the climate, animals, and natural features of Laos. Have children predict the types of animals that will be in the story. Encourage children from Southeast Asia to share their knowledge of Laos with classmates.

Tiger decided to visit the great god Shao, who lived in the sky, who was kind and gentle and knew everything. Surely Shao could tell her how many cubs she would have.

Tiger set out on the road that led to the sky. She climbed through forests of striped bamboo and wild banana trees, past plants curved like rooster tail feathers, and over rocks shaped like sleeping dragons.

346

At last Tiger came to a stone wall. Beyond the wall was a garden where children played happily under a plum tree. A large house stood nearby, its colorful decorations shining in the sun. This was the land of the great Shao, a peaceful land without sickness or death.

347

Comprehension

4 **FANTASY AND REALITY** The story tells about children playing in a garden. Then the text says that this is a place without sickness or death. Could this happen in real life?

MODEL I think that some of these things could happen in real life. Children playing in a garden is an event that could happen in real life. But a land without sickness or death is not. So the first part of this text is realistic and the second part is fantasy.

Minilesson

REVIEW/MAINTAIN

Setting

Reread pages 344–346 with children. Have them tell which parts of the story and the illustrations gave them clues about the setting, or when the story takes place. Ask children:

- Where does the story take place?
- What details in the text and the pictures give you clues about the setting?

Activity Have children use the text and picture on page 347 to describe where Shao lives.

Comprehension

5 Point to the word in the story that tells how Tiger is feeling. (*lonely*) Look at the drawing of the tiger. How does her face help you understand what she is feeling? *Character*

6 **Phonics** **LONG e: *y*** Let's read page 348 aloud. Can you find four words on this page that end with the long *e* sound spelled with a *y*? (*softly, gently, respect-fully, lonely*) Let's blend each of these words. *Graphophonic Cues*

Shao himself came out to greet Tiger. The silver coins dangling from his belt sounded softly as he walked.

5 "Why did you come here, Tiger?" he asked gently.

6 "O great Shao," answered Tiger **7** respectfully, "I am lonely and want to know how many cubs I will have."

348

Fluency

PARTNERS **READ DIALOGUE** Model using expression to read dialogue.

- Read page 348 aloud, modeling how a voice changes when reading narration and dialogue.

- Model the difference between reading a question and reading a statement. Guide children to hear how your voice goes up at the end of a question.

- Model how to "gently" ask a question and how to answer a question with respect.

- Invite partners to take the parts of Tiger and Shao and read pages 348 and 351. Encourage children to make their voices and facial expressions fit the characters.

349

Comprehension

7 **FANTASY AND REALITY** What does Tiger do when Shao asks her why she has come here? (She answers him.) Can a real tiger answer a question? (no) Would a real tiger ask how many cubs she will have? (no) In real life, do tigers have cubs? (yes) Let's fill in our chart.

REALITY	FANTASY
Tigers have cubs.	Tigers do not ask how many cubs they will have.

Minilesson

REVIEW/MAINTAIN

Short *e*

Remind children that the letter *e* stands for different sounds. Read aloud page 348. Ask:

- Which word, *greet* or *belt*, has the short *e* sound? (belt)
- Does the *e* in *gently* stand for the short or long *e* sound? (short *e*)
- Does the first *e* or the second *e* in the word **respectfully** stand for the short *e* sound? (second *e*)

Activity Have children write a sentence using *gently* and another short *e* word.

Phonics CD-ROM Have children use the activities on the CD-ROM for reinforcement.

Comprehension

8 How does Tiger feel when Shao tells her she will have nine cubs each year? How can you tell? *Make Inferences*

MODEL I think that Tiger feels happy because she purrs and says, *How wonderful*. When I look at the picture, I see that Tiger is smiling. The text and the picture help me to make the inference that Tiger is happy with Shao's answer to her question.

350

Visual Literacy

VIEWING AND REPRESENTING

Ask children why nine small tigers are sitting over Tiger in the illustration on this page. Explain that the bubble around the cubs shows that Tiger is thinking about them; they are not really there. Ask children if they can think of other visual elements that appear in illustrations, but are never seen in real life. (word balloons, movement lines.)

Shao was silent for a moment. Then he replied, "Nine each year."

"How wonderful," purred Tiger. "Thank you so much, great Shao." And she turned to leave with her good news.

"One moment, Tiger," said Shao. "You must remember carefully what I said. The words alone tell you how many cubs you will have. Do not forget them, for if you do, I cannot help you."

At first Tiger was happy as she followed the road back to earth. But soon, she began to worry.

(8)

(9)

(10)

351

Comprehension

(9) What was Shao's warning to Tiger? (He warned her to remember what he said.) Why did he give her this warning? (He cannot help her if she forgets the words.) Why was Tiger worried? (She was afraid she would forget the information.) *Plot*

(10) **Phonics** LONG *e* Let's read the first sentence in the last paragraph. Can you find the word *happy*? What sound does the letter *y* make in *happy*? (long *e*) *Graphophonic Cues*

P/i **PHONICS AND DECODING** Have children read aloud the words *turned* and *her* in the second paragraph on page 351. Ask children what sound is the same in both words. (/ûr/)

Minilesson

REVIEW/MAINTAIN

Summarize

Remind children that summarizing a story:

- retells the events that have happened so far.
- focuses briefly on the main events.

Work with children to write a summary of the story so far. Have them look back through the story for key events.

Activity Draw on the chalkboard an outline of a tiger with stripes. Have children suggest the story's main events. List each event on one of the tiger's stripes.

 PREVENTION/INTERVENTION

PHONICS AND DECODING Say the words *turned* and *her* aloud. Ask children to say what sound they hear in both words. (/ûr/) Write the words on the board. Invite a volunteer to come up and circle the letters that spell the /ûr/ sound in each word. (*ur, er*)

Have children brainstorm a list of words that have the /ûr/ sound spelled *ur*. (*fur, curl, burn, hurt*) *Graphophonic Cues*

Comprehension

11 **FANTASY AND REALITY** Why did
Tiger make up a song? (to help her
remember Shao's words) Can real tigers make
up songs? (no)

TEACHING TIP

MEMORY SKILLS Ask children to share any
special tricks they use to help them to remember
things. Prompt them to mention writing lists,
tying a string around a finger, making up poems
and songs, and so on.

h dear," she said to herself. "My memory
is so bad. How will I ever remember those
important words of Shao?" She thought and
11 she thought. At last, she had an idea. "I'll
make up a little song to sing. Then I won't
forget." So Tiger began to sing:

Nine-in-one, Grr! Grr!
Nine-in-one, Grr! Grr!

352

Activity

Cross Curricular: Social Studies

TIGERS Ask children to share facts they
know about tigers. Prompt them to
describe what tigers look like.

RESEARCH AND INQUIRY Have children work in small groups. Ask them to
find out where tigers live, and help them
to find these locations, and mark them on
a world map. Have children compare and
contrast the facts about tigers to the Tiger
character in the story.

▶ **Linguistic/Interpersonal**

interNET
CONNECTION Children can learn more
about tigers by visiting
www.mhschool.com/reading.

12 Tiger is singing a song so that she will remember what Shao said. Do you think Tiger will forget what Shao said by the time she gets home? Why or why not? *Make Predictions*

Down the mountain went Tiger, past the rocks shaped like sleeping dragons, past the plants curved like rooster tail feathers, through the forests of striped bamboo and wild banana trees. Over and over she sang her song:

12

> **Nine-in-one, Grr! Grr!**
> **Nine-in-one, Grr! Grr!**

353

LANGUAGE SUPPORT

ESL Help children understand the word *curved* on page 353. Ask a volunteer to draw a curve on the chalkboard. Show children how objects in the room (for example: a plant, a feather) are curved. Have children trace the curves of the river in the illustration on page 353 and on classroom objects as they say *curve*.

Comprehension

13 Can you describe the land where Tiger lives? Is it a city or a wild place? What kinds of animals live there? Are there any trees? Any mountains? What else do you know about the place where Tiger lives? *Setting*

SELF-MONITORING STRATEGY

PARAPHRASE Paraphrasing, or retelling the story in your own words, can help you to understand the plot, or what is happening in a story, as you continue to read.

MODEL It's hard for me to remember everything that's happened so far. I will go back through the story and look at the pictures to remind myself of important events. Then I'll retell what has happened so far in my own words. That way I can be sure that I really know the plot of the story.

354

Activity

Cross Curricular: Music

MAKE UP A SONG Have children brainstorm names or dates they need to remember (birthdays, planets, holidays).

- Have children work in small groups to choose something they would like to remember. Have them write it down, adding rhymes where possible.

- Ask them to fit the words to the melody of a familiar song such as, "Happy Birthday."

- Invite each group to share its song with the class.

> Nine whole planets to you. Nine whole planets to you. Mercury, Venus, Earth, Mars, Jupiter, Saturn, Neptune, Uranus, Pluto, too.

(13) **(14)** **(15)** s Tiger came closer to her cave, she passed through clouds of tiny white butterflies. She heard monkeys and barking deer. She saw green-striped snakes, quails and pheasants. None of the animals listened to her song—except one big, clever, black bird, the Eu bird.

"Hmm," said Bird to herself. "I wonder why Tiger is coming down the mountain singing that song and grinning from ear to ear. I'd better find out." So Bird soared up the ladder which was a shortcut to Shao's home.

355

Comprehension

(14) What do you think the Eu bird will do when she gets to Shao's home? (ask Shao why Tiger is so happy) *Make Predictions*

(15) **Phonics** **LONG e: ey** Let's read aloud the second sentence on page 355. Which word has the long e sound spelled *ey*? *(monkey) Graphophonic Cues*

Minilesson

REVIEW/MAINTAIN

Make Inferences

Remind children that to make inferences, we use what we read and what we already know. Ask children to make an inference about how Tiger is feeling now.

- Ask children what they do when they are happy. (smile) Guide children to see if the illustration gives any clues about how Tiger is feeling. (Yes; she is smiling.)
- Reread together the second paragraph on page 355. Then ask children how Bird knew that Tiger was happy. (Tiger was singing and grinning from ear to ear.)

Activity Invite children to pantomime scenes from familiar stories. Have other children make inferences about the characters' feelings based on facial expressions and/or body language.

Comprehension

16 Why does Bird think it would be terrible if Tiger had nine cubs a year? (She thinks the tigers would eat all the other animals.) *Make Inferences*

17 **Phonics** **LONG *e*: *y*** Let's read the last paragraph on page 356. Can you find the word with the long *e* sound spelled *y*? (*every*) *Graphophonic Cues*

p/i **CONCEPTS OF PRINT** What punctuation clues in the text tell you that the bird has strong feelings about what she is saying? (exclamation points) *Syntactic Cues*

TEACHING TIP

PUNCTUATION Write on the chalkboard sentences with no punctuation at the end. Ask volunteers to add a period, question mark, or exclamation mark, and to read the sentence aloud with the expression indicated by the punctuation mark. Children may have two or more choices for some sentences; if so, compare how the sentence would be read using each appropriate punctuation mark.

---

 wise Shao," asked Bird politely, "why is Tiger singing over and over:

Nine-in-one, Grr! Grr!
Nine-in-one, Grr! Grr!

And Shao explained that he had just told Tiger she would have nine cubs each year.

16 "That's terrible!" squawked Bird. "If Tiger has nine cubs each year, they will eat all of us. Soon there will be nothing but tigers in the land. You must change what you said, O Shao!"

17
18 "I cannot take back my words," sighed Shao. "I promised Tiger that she would have nine cubs every year as long as she remembered my words."

356

---

p/i **PREVENTION/INTERVENTION**

CONCEPTS OF PRINT
Understanding punctuation helps readers to understand a story. Some of Bird's dialogue ends with an exclamation point, which means that her feelings are strong. Ask children to find other sentences in the story that end with exclamation points. Invite volunteers to read them with the full feeling an exclamation point indicates. Ask other volunteers to read these sentences as they would if they ended with a period instead. *Syntactic Cues*

357

Comprehension

18 Do you think Shao cares about the Eu bird's problem? (yes) How can you tell? (His face looks sad; he sighs.) Why doesn't he do something to help the Eu bird? (He already made a promise to Tiger.) *Make Inferences*

LANGUAGE SUPPORT

ESL To make sure that English learners understand the events in the story so far, work with them to create a list of the main events. You may wish to list the events on the board as children name them, or else have them list the events themselves. Then have children work with a partner to role-play each event.

Comprehension

⑲ The story says that Bird has a plan. What do you think she will do next?
Make Predictions

MODEL Let's see if the text will give me clues about what Bird will do next. Bird now knows that in order for Tiger to have nine cubs, she must remember Shao's words. Then Bird goes in search of Tiger. I predict that Bird will try to make Tiger forget Shao's words.

"As long as she remembered your words," repeated Bird thoughtfully. "Then I know what I must do, O great Shao."

⑲ Bird now had a plan. She could hardly wait to try it out. **⑳** Quickly, she returned to earth in search of Tiger.

358

CULTURAL PERSPECTIVES

LAOTIAN STORY CLOTHS The illustrator made the pictures in *Nine-in-One, Grr! Grr!* look like a story cloth. Tell children that this style re-creates one way the Hmong people of Laos record their history and legends.

Activity Ask small groups to make story cloths about a favorite story. Children can draw and cut out the main characters. They can paste the figures onto black felt or construction paper.
▶ **Kinesthetic/Spatial**

Comprehension

20 What causes Bird to go back to earth and search for tiger? (She has a plan.) *Cause and Effect*

p/i **INFLECTIONAL ENDINGS** Let's reread the first sentence on page 358. Find the words *remembered* and *repeated*. What ending do both words have? (*-ed*) What kind of word usually has an *-ed* ending? (a verb)

---

p/i **PREVENTION/INTERVENTION**

INFLECTIONAL ENDINGS Explain that when *-ed* is added to a verb it shows that the action happened in the past.

Write *remembered* and *repeated* on the chalkboard. Underline the *-ed* endings. Guide children to see the base words *remember* and *repeat*. Explain that these verbs show actions that happen in the present.

Invite children to name verbs that happen in the present, such as *play*, *work*. Write their responses on the chalkboard. Have volunteers add *-ed* to each verb. Have children use the new words in sentences. *Semantic Cues*

359

Comprehension

21 Why was Tiger concentrating so hard on her song? (She didn't want to forget it.) *Draw Conclusions*

Bird reached her favorite tree as old grandmother sun was setting, just in time to hear Tiger coming closer and closer and still singing:

Nine-in-one, Grr! Grr!
Nine-in-one, Grr! Grr!

21 Tiger was concentrating so hard on her song that she didn't even see Bird landing in the tree above her.

360

Cross Curricular: Science

ENDANGERED ANIMALS Explain that tigers are endangered animals. Discuss what it means for an animal to be endangered.

RESEARCH AND INQUIRY Have pairs of children research an endangered animal and make a poster about it. Encourage chil-

dren to include illustrations, facts, and ways people can protect and save the animal.

▶ **Logical/Spatial**

Comprehension

22 Why did Tiger forget her song? (because Bird made noise by flapping her wings) *Cause and Effect*

23 **FANTASY AND REALITY** Bird flaps her wings. Could this happen in real life? (yes) Bird talks to Tiger. Could this happen in real life? (no) Let's add this information to our charts.

REALITY	FANTASY
Tigers have cubs.	Tigers do not ask how many cubs they will have.
Birds flap their wings.	Birds do not talk to tigers.

Suddenly, Bird began to flap her wings furiously. "Flap! Flap! Flap!" went Bird's big, black wings.

"Who's that?" cried Tiger.

"It's only me," answered Bird innocently.

Tiger looked up and growled at Bird:

"Grr! Grr! Bird. You made me forget my song with all your noise."

361

LANGUAGE SUPPORT

ESL Help children to understand the meaning of the word *furiously* in the phrase *flap her wings furiously*. (with great strength or force) Ask children to pantomime how Bird flapped her wings furiously. Elicit examples of other things that might be done *furiously*. (cleaning, running, jumping, knocking, and so on) Let children pantomime these activities.

361

Comprehension

24 Does Bird have Shao's song right? (no) Do you think she has changed the song by mistake, or on purpose? (on purpose) How can you tell? (She had a plan to make Tiger forget her song.) *Draw Conclusions*

25 Let's compare this illustration to the one on page 350. How have Tiger's thoughts changed? (She is thinking of one tiger cub now, instead of nine.) *Compare and Contrast*

362

Cross Curricular: Math

HOW MANY IN ALL? Ask children how many cubs Tiger would have in one year if Bird had not tricked her. (nine)

- Have partners figure out how many cubs Tiger would have in one, two, and three years if she had nine cubs each year. Children can keep track of their

counting using counters or tally marks.

- Have each pair record their results on a chart.

▶ **Logical/Mathematical/Spatial**

"h, I can help you," chirped **(24)** Bird sweetly. "I heard you **(25)** walking through the woods. You were singing:

One-in-nine, Grr! Grr!
One-in-nine, Grr! Grr! **(26)**

"Oh, thank you, thank you, Bird!" cried Tiger. "I will have one cub every nine years. **(27)** How wonderful! This time I won't forget!"

363

Comprehension

(26) Does Tiger know she has been tricked? (no) How can you tell? (She thanks Bird and seems very happy.) *Character*

(27) Bird was worried that if Tiger had nine cubs every year, the tigers would eat all the other animals. How did Bird solve her problem? (She changed the words of Tiger's song, so that Tiger will only have one cub every nine years.) *Problem and Solution*

Comprehension

28 **FANTASY AND REALITY** According to this story, there aren't many tigers because of the trick Bird played on Tiger. Do you think this really happened? (no) Why are there so few tigers? (People hunted them.) Let's add this information to our chart.

REALITY	FANTASY
Tigers have cubs.	Tigers do not ask how many cubs they will have.
Birds flap their wings.	Birds do not talk to tigers.
There are so few tigers because people hunted them.	There are so few tigers because Bird tricked Tiger.

RETELL THE STORY Ask children to work in groups of four to retell the story. One child can play Tiger, one can play Shao, one can play Bird, and one can act as the narrator. Encourage them to use their Reality/Fantasy charts to help them to remember events from the story. *Summarize*

 SELF-ASSESSMENT

Have children ask themselves the following questions to assess how they are reading:

- How did I use clues in the story and what I already knew to help me understand which story events could not occur in real life?

- How did I use the letters and sounds I know to help me read the words in the story?

TRANSFERRING THE STRATEGIES

- How can I use these strategies to help me read other stories?

So Tiger returned to her cave, singing happily:

One-in-nine, Grr! Grr!
One-in-nine, Grr! Grr!

And that is why, the Hmong **28** people say, we don't have too many tigers on the earth today!

364

 **REREADING FOR** *Fluency*

ONE Children who need fluency practice can read along silently or aloud as they listen to the recording of the story.

READING RATE When you evaluate reading rate, have children read aloud from the story for one minute. Place a stick-on note after the last word read. Count words read. To evaluate

children's performance, see the Running Record in the **Fluency Assessment** book.

i **Intervention** For leveled fluency passages, lessons, and norm charts, see **Skills Intervention Guide**, Part 5, Fluency.

AD TOGETHER MEET BLIA XIONG ◄

Blia Xiong (BLEE-AH SHONG) first heard *Nine-in-One, Grr! Grr!* when she was a little child. She says, "This story was carried in my family for a long time. I was three when I first heard it. I still remember my mother telling me this funny story with a tiger singing in Laotian, 'Nine-in-One, Grr! Grr!'"

In Laos, the tiger is a wild animal that is feared. Some people think the tiger is magical. She says, "The part I like most is when the bird hears the song and figures out how to trick the tiger. The clever bird does something about the powerful tiger."

Blia Xiong was told stories by her mother, her father, and her grandfather before them. Now she tells her children the stories she hears. When asked how she remembers a story, she says, "When I listen to a story, I listen very closely. I make pictures in my mind. Then I can remember what I hear."

MEET NANCY HOM ►

Nancy Hom was born in southern China and grew up in New York City. In addition to *Nine-in-One, Grr! Grr!* she has illustrated the Cambodian folk tale *Judge Rabbit and the Tree Spirit.*

365

LITERARY RESPONSE

QUICK-WRITE Invite children to record thoughts about the story in their journals. Have them describe the characters and tell how they felt about each one.

ORAL RESPONSE Have children discuss these questions:

• How did Tiger try to remember Shao's words? Did it work? Why or why not?

• If you were a character in the story, would you have tricked Tiger as Bird did? Why or why not?

• What other stories have you read that were fantasies?

Comprehension

Return to Predictions and Purposes

Have children reread and discuss their predictions about the story. Were their predictions correct?

PREDICTIONS	WHAT HAPPENED
The tiger will go on a journey.	Tiger went to see the great Shao.
The man will tell the tiger something.	Shao told Tiger how many cubs she would have.

INFORMAL ASSESSMENT

HOW TO ASSESS

LONG e: y, ey Have children turn to page 355 and find two words that end with the long *e* sound. *(tiny, monkeys)* Have them write each of these words and underline the letters that spell the long *e* sound.

FANTASY AND REALITY Review the strategy of looking for clues that tell whether a story is a realistic one or a fantasy. Then challenge each child to choose a story event or detail, and to identify whether or not it could happen in real life.

FOLLOW UP

LONG e Continue to point out words with the long *e* sound spelled *y* or *ey.*

FANTASY AND REALITY Children who have difficulty distinguishing between fantasy and reality can reread their Reality/Fantasy charts to help them identify events that could not happen in real life.

Story Questions

Nine-in-One, Grr! Grr!

Have children discuss or write answers to the questions on page 366.

Answers:

1. Tiger wants to ask Shao how many cubs she will have. *Literal/Cause and Effect*

2. Bird is afraid that if Tiger has nine cubs a year, there will be nothing but tigers in the land. *Inferential/Draw Conclusions*

3. Tiger talks and sings. *Literal/Fantasy and Reality*

4. The story is about a tiger who is tricked by a bird. *Critical/Summarize*

5. This story's illustrations look like a story cloth. The pictures in *Luka's Quilt* look like a quilt. Both stories have pictures that look like they are made from cloth. *Critical/Reading Across Texts*

Write a Report For a full lesson on explanatory writing, see pages 369M–369N.

Story Questions & Activities

1. Why does Tiger visit the great Shao?

2. Why does Bird want to make Tiger forget her song?

3. What are some things Tiger does in the story that real tigers do not do?

4. What is this story mostly about?

5. Compare the illustrations in this story to the illustrations in "Luka's Quilt." How are the pictures different? How are they alike?

Write a Report

The tiger in this story will teach her children how to be good tigers. Choose an animal you like. What do you know about that kind of animal? What do you like about it? What would it teach its children?

Meeting Individual Needs

EASY	ON-LEVEL	CHALLENGE
Name_____ Date_____ **Reteach** 111	Name_____ Date_____ **Practice** 111	Name_____ Date_____ **Extend** 111
Story Comprehension	**Story Comprehension**	**Story Comprehension**
Fill in the following chart with information from "Nine-in-One, Grr! Grr!"	Think about "Nine-in-One, Grr! Grr!" Put an X by each sentence that tells about something that happened in this story.	Fill in the chart to tell about "Nine-in-One, Grr! Grr!"
Main Characters: Tiger, great god Shao, Bird	___ Tiger lived in the sky.	1. Title: _____ Nine in One, Grr! Grr!
Setting: a long time ago where the Earth met the Sky	X The great god Shao knew everything.	2. Characters (who): _____ Tiger
Beginning of the Story: The tiger visits Shao, the god in the sky. She asks Shao how many cubs she will have. Shao says that she will have "nine each year."	X Tiger asks Shao how many cubs she will have.	_____ Shao
	___ Tiger is sad after she talks to Shao.	_____ Bird
	X Tiger makes up a song to help her remember what Shao told her.	3. Problem: _____ Bird thinks Tiger will have many babies who will then eat all the birds.
Middle of the Story: Tiger makes up a song to remember "nine each year." Bird does not want Tiger to have nine cubs each year.	___ Tiger forgets how to get home.	4. Solution: _____ Bird fools Tiger into wishing for one baby every nine years.
	X Bird doesn't want Tiger to have nine cubs every year.	
	___ Shao promises Bird he will change what he said to Tiger.	5. Favorite Part: _____ Answers will vary.
End of the Story: Bird flaps her wings to make Tiger forget her song. Then Bird tells Tiger that her song was really "one-in-nine . . ." Tiger believes Bird. That is why people say there are not many tigers today.	X Bird makes Tiger change her song.	6. A Picture:
	X Tiger will have one cub every nine years.	
Book 2.1/Unit 3 Nine-in-One, Grr! Grr! **5**	Book 2.1/Unit 3 Nine-in-One, Grr! Grr! **10**	Book 2.1/Unit 3 Nine-in-One, Grr! Grr!
At Home: Ask children to illustrate a scene from "Nine-in-One, Grr! Grr!" Then have them explain their illustration. 111	At Home: Ask children how they would change the false statements on this page to make them true statements. 111	At Home: Have children write a note to the tiger telling her about the bird's trick and giving her advice on what she should do next. 111
Reteach, 111	**Practice, 111**	**Extend, 111**

Multiplying Tigers

In the story, Tiger wonders how many cubs she will have. If Tiger has one cub every nine years, how many cubs will she have in 18 years?

The Biggest Cat in the World

The Siberian tiger can grow up to 4 feet tall and over 9 feet long. And that does not include its tail! Work together to make a life-size drawing of a Siberian tiger. Use a large piece of paper and a ruler.

Find Out More

Go to the library to find another story or folk tale about a tiger. What country does the story come from? Read it. Then write down your favorite part of the story.

367

Story ACTIVITIES

Multiplying Tigers

Materials: counters, paper, pencils

PARTNERS Have children work in pairs to figure out how many cubs Tiger will have in 18 years if she only has one cub every nine years. Have each pair draw a picture and write a number sentence to show their answer.

The Biggest Cat in the World

Materials: large sheet of paper (4 feet by 9 feet or larger), yardstick, felt-tipped markers

GROUP Have children measure themselves to help them understand how long and how tall this tiger can be. Tape paper to the chalkboard. Have children work together to draw a life-size model of a Siberian tiger.

Find Out More

RESEARCH AND INQUIRY Direct **PARTNERS** children to appropriate reference resources to look for stories and folk tales about tigers.

inter NET CONNECTION For more information about tigers go to **www.mhschool.com/reading**.

FORMAL ASSESSMENT

After page 367, see Selection Assessment.

DAILY Phonics ROUTINES

DAY 3 **Fluency** Hold up index cards with words containing the long *e* sound spelled *y* and *ey*. Ask volunteers to blend the sounds in each word silently and then read each word aloud.

Phonics CD-ROM

Study Skills

REFERENCE SOURCES

ⓣOBJECTIVES

Children will use a dictionary to find word meanings, parts of speech, pronunciation, and example sentences.

PREPARE Display **Teaching Chart 94.** Read the first paragraph with children and discuss using dictionaries.

TEACH Point out where to look in the sample dictionary page for word pronunciations, meanings, parts of speech, plural forms, example sentences, and illustrations.

PRACTICE Help children use the sample dictionary page to answer questions 1–4. Review answers with them. **1.** A tiger is a large powerful member of the cat family. **2.** Words in a dictionary are alphabetical. **3.** a noun **4.** It makes me laugh when someone tickles my feet.

ASSESS/CLOSE Have children look up words in a dictionary and report on the information they find.

Meeting Individual Needs

STUDY SKILLS

Use a Dictionary

ticket/tight

ticket   A card or piece of paper that gives the person who holds it the right to be admitted or to get a service. You need a *ticket* to ride the train.
     tick·et (TIHK it) *noun, plural* **tickets**.

tickle   To touch people in a way that makes them laugh. It makes me laugh when someone *tickles* my feet.
     tick·le (TIHK uhl) *verb*, **tickled, tickling**.

tiger   A large, powerful animal that is a member of the cat family. Most tigers have an orange or yellow coat with black or brown stripes. Tigers live in Asia. We saw *tigers* at the zoo.
     ti·ger (TĪ guhr) *noun, plural* **tigers**.

Use the part of a dictionary page to answer the questions.

① What is the meaning of the word *tiger?*

② Why does *tickle* come between *ticket* and *tiger?*

③ What part of speech is the word *ticket?*

④ What is the example sentence for *tickle?*

EASY	ON-LEVEL	CHALLENGE
Name_____ Date_____ **Reteach** 112	Name_____ Date_____ **Practice** 112	Name_____ Date_____ **Extend** 112
Use a Dictionary	**Use a Dictionary**	**Use a Dictionary**
Sometimes a word has two or more different meanings. A **dictionary** can use the word in sentences that illustrate different meanings of the word.	A **dictionary entry** contains many different parts. Study the entry shown below. See if you can pick out each different part.	Find each word in the dictionary. Write the definition. List the word that comes before and after the word. **Sample answers shown.**
Study the dictionary definitions below. Beneath each definition are two sentences. Each has a blank space beside it. Write the number of the meaning of the entry word that's being used in the sentence.	**pup 1.** a young dog; puppy. **2.** the young of some other animals, such as the fox, wolf, or seal. *The mother fox takes good care of her pup.* (pup) *noun, plural* **pups**	1. Word before: _____ tactless tadpole: _____ the larva of a frog or toad
pe·ri·od (pîr′ē əd) *noun* **1.** a portion of time. **2.** A punctuation mark (.) used at the end of a sentence. It is also used after an abbreviation. *plural* **periods**.		Word after: _____ tag
	Complete the exercise based on the dictionary definition above.	2. Word before: _____ practically practice: _____ to work at often so as to learn well
1. Karen used a pen to put a period at the end of her sentence. _____ 2	1. entry word _____ pup	Word after: _____ prairie
2. Our lunch hour came in the fourth period. _____ 1	2. definition #2 _____ 2. the young of some other animals, such as the fox, wolf, or seal	3. Word before: _____ hopper hopscotch: _____ a game in which a player tosses a stone into sections of a figure drawn on the ground and hops through the figure and back to pick up the stone
dunk (dungk) *verb* **1.** To dip something such as a doughnut in a liquid. **2.** To shove a basketball into the basket forcefully. **dunked, dunking**.	3. part of speech _____ noun	Word after: _____ horde
	4. plural form _____ pups	4. Word before: _____ wing wink: _____ to close and open the eyelids quickly
3. The whole class was allowed to dunk their crackers in the soup. _____ 1	5. pronunciation guide _____ (pup)	Word after: _____ winner
4. Lena jumped off Brenda's back and managed to dunk the ball. _____ 2	6. example sentence for definition #2 _____ The mother fox takes good care of her pup.	
112 At Home: Ask children to identify the part of speech of **period** and **dunk**. Book 2.1/Unit 3 Nine-in-One, Grr! Grr! 4	112 At Home: Ask children to make up a sentence using the first definition for "pup." Book 2.1/Unit 3 Nine-in-One, Grr! Grr! 6	112 At Home: Look up other words together in a children's dictionary. Talk about the language that the dictionary uses to explain words. Book 2.1/Unit 3 Nine-in-One, Grr! Grr!

Reteach, 112   Practice, 112   Extend, 112

TEST POWER

Think about the story as you read it.

DIRECTIONS:

Read the story. Then read each question about the story.

SAMPLE

The Garden

Each morning, the sun comes up. The birds in the garden start to sing. The wet grass starts to dry. The crickets and grasshoppers get to work. They wash the dishes. They sweep the floor. The ants put on their glasses to look closely at the flowers. The ladybugs polish the leaves with rags. All day the insects work to make the garden beautiful. At the end of the day, everyone but the crickets climbs into bed. The crickets have one more job. They will make music for the others in the garden.

1 Why does the grass start to dry?
- ● The sun shines on it.
- ○ The crickets and grasshoppers hop through it.
- ○ The ants look at it closely.

2 How do you know this story is make-believe?
- ○ Insects don't live in the garden.
- ○ There are no such things as ladybugs.
- ● Ants don't wear glasses.

369

Test Power

THE PRINCETON REVIEW

Read the Page

Explain to children that you will be reading this story as a group. You will read the story, and they will follow along in their books.

Request that children put pens, pencils, and markers away, since they will not be writing in their books.

Discuss the Questions

QUESTION 1: Direct children to read the first few sentences of the story, where the grass is mentioned. Since all the events of the story begin with "The sun comes up," the most reasonable inference is that the sun is the cause.

QUESTION 2: Remind children about the difference between fact and fiction. Children should find a choice that shows the story to be fictional.

Leveled Books

FIRST FOOD
A South American Folktale

Mc Graw Hill

retold by Gale Justin
illustrated by Ester Baran

i **Intervention** ▶ **Skills**

Intervention Guide, for direct instruction and extra practice of vocabulary and comprehension

EASY

First Food: A South American Folktale

☑ **Long *e*: *y, ey***

☑ **Fantasy and Reality**

☑ **Instructional Vocabulary:**
Earth, forget, lonely, memory, mountain, wonderful

Guided Reading

PREVIEW AND PREDICT Discuss the illustrations through page 7 of the story. As you take the **picture walk**, have children predict what the story will be about. Chart their ideas.

SET PURPOSES Have children decide why they want to read the story. For example, they may want to learn a new folktale, more about Lizard and Parrot, or about how people learned to plant corn.

READ THE BOOK Use questions like the following to guide children's reading or after they have read the story independently.

Page 3: Read aloud the last sentence. What word ends with the same sound as *suddenly?* (only) What is the sound? (long *e*) What letter spells the sound? *(y) Phonics and Decoding*

Page 4: How is the Sun in the story different from the real sun? (The Sun in the story thinks and acts like a person.) *Fantasy and Reality*

Page 6: Why are the animals so *lonely?* (They have no friends to do things with.)

What keeps you from feeling lonely? *Instructional Vocabulary*

Page 15: What problem did Lizard and Parrot solve? (how to get fire to cook the corn) How did they solve it? (They used a stick to take fire from the sun.) *Problem and Solution*

Page 16: What things make this story make-believe? (talking animals, animals fed by the sun) *Fantasy and Reality*

RETURN TO PREDICTIONS AND PURPOSES Discuss children's predictions. Ask which were close to the story. Did children find out what they wanted to know?

LITERARY RESPONSE Discuss these questions:

• What was your favorite part of this story?

• Do you think what the Sun did was right?

Also see the story questions and activity in *First Food.*

See the **Phonics** **CD-ROM** for practice using long *e* words.

Answers to Story Questions

1. yellow corn
2. The animals in the story can talk to each other and solve problems like real people.
3. because the Sun thought of the animals as children
4. Parrot and Lizard meeting and working together to feed themselves.
5. Answers will vary.

The Story Questions and Activity below appear in the Easy Book.

Story Questions and Activity

1. What do the animals eat?
2. What is different about the animals in the story and real animals?
3. Why did the Sun not want the animals to know how to plant corn?
4. What is this story mostly about?
5. If the lizard and the parrot in this story wanted to come up with a song like the one the tiger made up in *Nine-in-One, Grr! Grr!,* what might they sing?

Animal Friends

Draw a picture of Parrot and Lizard after the story. Use dialogue bubbles to have them talk to each other. What things would they do together? What would they say to each other?

from *First Food*

Leveled Books

INDEPENDENT

Hare and Tortoise

- ☑ **Long *e*: *y*, *ey***
- ☑ **Fantasy and Reality**
- ☑ **Instructional Vocabulary:** *Earth, forget, lonely, memory, mountain, wonderful*

Guided Reading

PREVIEW AND PREDICT Take a **picture walk** through page 7 of the story. See if children can predict what the story will be about.

SET PURPOSES Have children discuss and record why they want to read *Hare and Tortoise*.

READ THE BOOK Use the following questions to guide children's reading or after they have read independently.

Page 3: Read aloud the last word in the third sentence. *(memory)* What sound does the letter *y* make? (long *e*) What other words on the page have /ē/ sound spelled *y*? *(really, happy) Phonics and Decoding*

Page 4: What things in the story could happen only in make-believe? (animals talking, wearing clothes) What is realistic about the characters? (They talk, feel, and act like people in real life.) *Fantasy and Reality*

Page 7: What does Lemming mean when he says that Tortoise is the slowest animal on earth? (that tortoise is the slowest animal that exists) Can you think of other slow animals that live on earth? *Instructional Vocabulary*

Page 15: What did Hare discover when he woke up? (that Tortoise had won the race) Why did Tortoise win? (He kept trying to do his best.) *Cause and Effect*

Page 16: What kind of personality does Tortoise have? (determined, hard-working) What kind of personality does Hare have? (loves to brag, self-interested) *Make Inferences*

RETURN TO PREDICTIONS AND PURPOSES Discuss children's predictions. Ask which were close to the story and why. Have children review their purposes for reading. Did they find out what they wanted to know?

LITERARY RESPONSE Discuss these questions:

- Were you in favor of Tortoise winning the race?

- Do you think that Hare learned anything from losing?

Also see the story questions and activity in *Hare and Tortoise*.

See the **Phonics CD-ROM** for practice using long *e* words.

Answers to Story Questions

1. They draw straws, and the one with the shortest straw must race.
2. Because he is so sure he will win that he stops to take a nap.
3. Answers will vary.
4. A race between the fast hare and the slow tortoise, which because the hare naps, the tortoise wins.
5. Answers will vary.

The Story Questions and Activity below appear in the Independent Book.

Story Questions and Writing Activity

1. How do the animals decide who will race against Hare?
2. Why doesn't Hare win?
3. In real life, animals can't talk, and they don't act like the ones in this story. Do these animals remind you of anyone you know?
4. What is the story mostly about?
5. Do any of the animals in this story act like any of the animals in *Nine-in-One, Grr, Grr*?

An Animal's Home Is Its Castle

In some of the pictures in this book you can see a castle. Choose two of the animal characters in this book and draw a picture of the house you think they might have. Write a short paragraph about how the houses are alike and different.

from Hare and Tortoise

Leveled Books

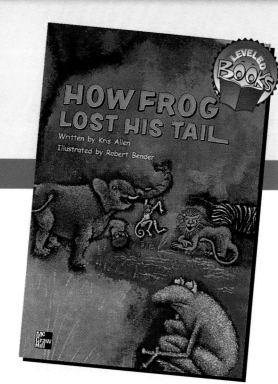

CHALLENGE

How Frog Lost His Tail

- ☑ **Long *e*: *y, ey***
- ☑ **Fantasy and Reality**
- ☑ **Instructional Vocabulary:**
  Earth, forget, lonely, memory, mountain, wonderful

Answers to Story Questions

1. He has no tail.
2. a long time ago
3. No, it's because he's mean to them.
4. It tells why frogs don't have tails.
5. No, she has a bad memory; Yes, she's much nicer than the Frog.

The Story Questions and Activity below appear in the Challenge Book.

Story Questions and Activity

1. Why do the other animals laugh at Frog in the beginning?
2. What does the phrase "when Earth was young" mean?
3. Do the animals really leave Frog alone just because he has no tail?
4. What is the main idea of this story?
5. Would the tiger in *Nine in One, Grr! Grr!* keep the promise to Water?

A New Tail

Think of another animal that doesn't have a tail. What kind of tail do you think would look nice on it? Draw a picture of this animal with your idea of its "perfect" tail.

from How Frog Lost His Tail

Guided Reading

PREVIEW AND PREDICT Read the title with children and take a **picture walk** through page 7. Have children predict what the story will be about.

SET PURPOSES Have children write several sentences describing why they want to read *How Frog Lost His Tale*. For example: I want to find out why frogs don't have tails.

READ THE BOOK Use the following prompts while children are reading or after they have read the story independently.

Page 3: Read aloud the word in line six. *(dizzy)* What vowel sound do you hear at the end of the word? (long *e*) Read aloud the next two lines. What word ends in the same sound? *(monkey)* How is the sound spelled in each word? (*y, ey*) *Phonics and Decoding*

Page 5: How did Frog treat the other animals? (He was unkind to them.) What did the animals decide to do? (leave Frog's water hole) *Cause and Effect*

Page 6–7: What is realistic about this story? (The characters look like real animals; their thoughts and feelings are believable.)

What could happen only in fantasy? (animals and water talking; water offering Frog a tail)

Page 9: How can a wonderful memory help Frog? (He won't forget his promise to Water.) How does your memory help you?

Page 16: Do you think this story tells us the actual reason why frogs don't have tails? What makes you think so? *Fantasy and Reality*

RETURN TO PREDICTIONS AND PURPOSES Discuss children's predictions. Ask which were close to the story and why. Have children review their purposes for reading. Did they find out what they wanted to know?

LITERARY RESPONSE Discuss these questions:

- What was your favorite part of the story?
- Do you think that Frog learned a lesson?

Also see the story questions and activity in *How Frog Lost His Tail.*

See the **Phonics** CD-ROM for practice using words with long *e*.

Bringing Groups Together

Anthology and Leveled Books

Connecting Texts

CHARACTER CHARTS
Write the story titles on a chart. Discuss the main characters in each story and their relationship to the other characters in the folktales. Have children write their contributions on the chart.

Use the chart to talk about the main characters in the stories and their relationships to one another.

Nine-in-One, GRR! GRR!	First Food Folktale	Hare and Tortoise	How Frog Lost His Tail
• Tiger • Great God Shao • Bird • Tiger asks Shao for help. • Bird tries to confuse Tiger for her own benefit.	• Parrot • Lizard • Sun • Parrot and Lizard want to grow their own corn. Sun does not want them to.	• Hare • Tortoise • Hare and Tortoise race. Tortoise wins. • Other animals support Tortoise.	• Frog • Water • Frog wants a tail. Water gives it to him and takes it away when Frog disobeys him.

Viewing/Representing

Divide the class into four groups, each group representing one of the stories in the lesson. Have members of each group take turns dramatizing the role of a main character in their story. Each group will perform its dramatizations for the rest of the class.

AUDIENCE RESPONSES
As children watch each dramatization, see if they can identify the personality of each character being represented.

How Frog Lost His Tail. A Play

Research and Inquiry

MORE ABOUT FOLKTALES Invite children to become acquainted with other folktales. They can:

• Look at classroom and school library books that feature folktales.

• Invite a storyteller to the classroom to share a folktale.

• Watch a folktale on videotape.

interNET CONNECTION Visit *www.mhschool.com/reading* for more information about folktales.

Children can write brief summaries of their favorite folktales in their journals.

JOURNAL

Children will:

• identify /ē/y, ey.

• blend and read words in which long e is spelled y or ey.

MATERIALS

• Teaching Chart 95

Skills Finder

Long e: y, ey

Introduce	B1: 342G–H
Review	B1: 369E–F, 369G–H, 370G–H
Test	B1: Unit 3
Maintain	B1: 227; B2: 347

TEACHING TIP

LONG e Remind children there are other ways to spell the long e sound. Ask what other letter combinations can spell this sound. (ea, ie, ee) Ask volunteers for words using these other spellings of /ē/.

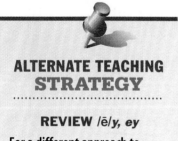

ALTERNATE TEACHING STRATEGY

REVIEW /ē/y, ey

For a different approach to teaching this skill, see pages T75–T76.

Review Long e: y, ey

PREPARE

Listen for Words with the Sound /ē/

Read aloud the following passage and have children raise their hands whenever they hear a word with the /ē/ sound: *My family got a tiny cat. It makes her happy to play with my house keys.*

TEACH

BLENDING Model and Guide Practice with Long e Words

• Display **Teaching Chart 95.** Tell children that they will review the long e sound spelled y and ey. Instruct children that these long e spellings often come at the end of a word.

• Point to y at the top of the first column. Say the sound /ē/. Have children repeat after you.

• Run your finger under *baby*, blending letters to read the word. Have children repeat after you. Ask a volunteer to underline the letter that makes the /ē/ sound in *baby*.

• Have volunteers write in letters to complete the words in the first column on the chart. Have each child blend the sounds together to read the words.

• Read aloud with children all the words in the completed column.

y	ey
bab<u>y</u>	mon<u>ey</u>
funn<u>y</u>	k<u>ey</u>
bod<u>y</u>	donk<u>ey</u>
softl<u>y</u>	vall<u>ey</u>

Teaching Chart 95

Use the Words in Context

Use the words in sentences to reinforce their meanings. Example: *The baby was playing with the rattle.*

Repeat the Procedure

• Follow the same procedure to complete the second column on the chart with words in which long e is spelled ey.

PRACTICE

DISCRIMINATING
Read Words
with /ē/ y, ey

PARTNERS

Give partners a list of 10 words, 7 of which contain the long e sound spelled with *y* or *ey*. Ask partners to take turns reading the list aloud to each other. The first child reads a random word from the list. The second child raises a hand when the word contains long e. Then the child should circle the letters in the word that make the long e sound and read a new one to the first child. Children should continue until all the long e words are read. Have students underline one word family in red and the other in blue. ▶ **Linguistic/Auditory**

ASSESS/CLOSE

**Read and Use
Long e Words
in Context**

To assess children's mastery of reading words with long e spelled *y* or *ey*, observe their work in the Practice activity. Ask each group member to read aloud three circled words from their list.

ADDITIONAL PHONICS RESOURCES

Phonics/Phonemic
Awareness Practice Book,
pages 81–84

McGraw-Hill School
TECHNOLOGY

 CD-ROM

activities for practice with
Building Words

 **CD-ROM**

**SPELLING/PHONICS
CONNECTIONS**
Words with long e: *y, ey*: See the
5-Day Spelling Plan, pages
369Q–369R.

i **Intervention** ▶ **Skills**
Intervention Guide, for direct instruction and extra practice of long e

Meeting Individual Needs for Phonics

EASY	ON-LEVEL	CHALLENGE	LANGUAGE SUPPORT

EASY

Name_____ Date_____ Reteach **113**
Long e: y, ey

The sound of long e can be spelled with a **y** as in **family**. The sound of long e can also be spelled with an **ey** as in **donkey**.

Choose the word from the box that best completes each sentence.

| funny | monkey | worry | Nancy |
| penny | many | key | family |

1. My friend ___Nancy___ loves to swim.
2. John tells ___funny___ jokes.
3. Sally lost her house ___key___.
4. There are three kids in my ___family___.
5. I saw a ___monkey___ with big ears at the circus.
6. Don't ___worry___ about that noise.
7. When I see a ___penny___, I pick it up.
8. There are ___many___ animals in the zoo.

Book 2.1/Unit 3
Nine-in-One, Grr! Grr!
At Home: Ask children to draw a picture with five things that end in y or ey. Have them list these items, then ask a friend or family member to identify the y or ey items in the picture.
113

ON-LEVEL

Name_____ Date_____ Practice **113**
Long e: y, ey

Read the sentence. Then circle the word that ends in y or ey and completes the sentence. Write the word and circle the y or ey ending.

1. The ___baby___ was in her carriage.
   bag   band   (baby)
2. Jean and Pat were very ___happy___.
   (happy)   crying   purple
3. Tawana saved her ___money___.
   apples   (money)   birds
4. Don't ___worry___; the rain will stop soon!
   eat   sleep   (worry)
5. The ___monkey___ loved to climb.
   truck   (monkey)   girl
6. There are four people in my ___family___.
   cave   (family)   foot

Book 2.1/Unit 3
Nine-in-One, Grr! Grr!
At Home: Have children list ten words that end with -y or -ey.
113

CHALLENGE

Name_____ Date_____ Extend **113**
Long e: y, ey

Play a game of "I Spy." Look around your classroom or in picture books. Write about something that you see that ends with the same sound as **furry** and **valley**. The first one is done for you.
Answers will vary; some samples are given.

1. I spy an animal that swings from the branches. It looks like an ape, but it is not one. It is a monkey.
2. I spy a green piece of paper. It can be used to buy things.
   It is money.
3. I spy ___a little horse. It is a pony.___
4. I spy ___an object that opens a door. It is a key.___
5. I spy ___a person who is a woman. She is a lady.___

Book 2.1/Unit 3
Nine-in-One, Grr! Grr!
At Home: Play a game of "I Spy." Take turns describing words that end with the ey or y that makes the long e sound, such as donkey and baby.
113

LANGUAGE SUPPORT

Name_____ Date_____
Word Maker

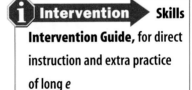

cit	donk
happ	hon
man	
tin	monk
mon	turk

y

ey

Grade 2
Language Support/Blackline Master 67 • Nine-in-One, Grr! Grr! 123

Reteach, 113   Practice, 113   Extend, 113   Language Support, 123

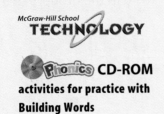

OBJECTIVES

Children will:

- review /ē/ y, ey; /e/ ea; /ər/ er, /ən/ en; and /əl/ le.

....

MATERIALS
- **Teaching Chart 96**
- **Word Building Manipulative Cards**

Skills Finder	
Long e: y, ey	
Introduce	B1: 342G-H
Review	B1: 369E-F, 369G-H, 370G-H
Test	B1: Unit 3
Maintain	B1: 227; B2: 347

Review Long e; Short e; /ər/, /ən/, /əl/

PREPARE

Discriminate Words with Long e, Short e, and er, en, le

Write *tiny, monkey, feathers, better, even,* and *puddle* on the chalkboard. Ask volunteers to read the words and underline the letters that spell the following sounds: /ē/, /e/, /ər/, /ən/, /əl/.

TEACH

BLENDING Model and Guide Practice With Long e, Short e, and er, en, le

Display **Teaching Chart 96**. Point to *er* at the top of the first group. Say the /ər/ sound, and have children repeat. Ask a volunteer to identify and underline the letters that stand for the /ər/ sound in the first word in the group, *better*.

er	**ea**	**en**
better	head	garden
closer	feathers	listen
answer	bread	children
y	**le**	**ey**
happy	little	key
many	people	monkey
worry	able	money

Teaching Chart 96

- Ask a volunteer to add the /ər/ sound to the next two words on the chart. Blend and read aloud both completed /ər/ words. Have children repeat them.

Use the Words in Context

Use the words in sentences to reinforce their meanings. Example: *You can see better if you sit closer to the chalkboard.*

Repeat the Procedure

Follow the same procedure to complete the rest of the chart.

PRACTICE

WORD BUILDING
Build and Sort Words with /ē/ y, ey; /e/ ea; /ər/ er, /ən/ en, /əl/ le

GROUP

Have groups of five sit in circles. The first child picks a sound from the chart, pronounces it, and uses letter cards to build a word containing that sound. The child then blends and reads the word, and the group repeats. Then the child calls on a classmate who repeats the procedure with a second sound. Continue until all sounds have been covered at least once. Then encourage children to suggest other words with any of the sounds, write the words and place in the appropriate category.

▶ **Linguistic/Auditory**

ASSESS/CLOSE

Write and Read Words with /ē/ y, ey; /e/ ea; /ər/ er, /ən/ en, /əl/ le

Use your observations from the Practice activity to determine if children need more reinforcement in any of the sounds. Have children write sentences using words with at least three sounds from the chart. Ask children to read their sentences aloud to the class.

ADDITIONAL PHONICS RESOURCES

McGraw-Hill School
TECHNOLOGY

Phonics/Phonemic Awareness Practice Book, pages 81–84

 **CD-ROM**
activities for practice with **Building and Sorting**

DAY **5** **Letter Substitution**
Have partners work together to build words ending with the long e sound spelled y or ey. Invite children to take turns changing letters to build new words.

 **CD-ROM**

ALTERNATE TEACHING STRATEGY
....
REVIEW LONG e, SHORT e, AND ə
For a different approach to teaching this skill, see pages T69–T70, T72–T73, T75–T76.

ℹ **Intervention** **Skills**
Intervention Guide, for direct instruction and extra practice of long e, short e, /ər/, /ən/, /əl/

Meeting Individual Needs for Phonics

EASY	ON-LEVEL	CHALLENGE	LANGUAGE SUPPORT

EASY — Reteach 114
Name_____ Date_____
Long e; Short e; /ər/, /ən/, /əl/

That bird has pretty ___.
(feathers) every better

Circle the word that completes the sentence. Then write it.

1. We saw a __monkey__ at the zoo.
   (monkey) many listened

2. The __garden__ was filled with flowers.
   (garden) listen worry

3. I __met__ the class president.
   children (met) tiny

4. The __mother__ bird feeds the baby birds.
   (mother) went even

5. The __people__ waited for the play to start.
   happy clever (people)

At Home: Have children draw a picture to go with one of the sentences above.
Book 2.1/Unit 3 Nine-in-One, Grrr! Grrr! 10
114

ON-LEVEL — Practice 114
Name_____ Date_____
Long e; Short e; /ər/, /ən/, /əl/

Choose the word that completes each sentence. Write the word on the line.

| shiny | children | bread | apple | key |
| sneakers | sell | freeze | lead | weather |

1. This gold ring is very __shiny__.
2. The __children__ wait for the school bus.
3. I pick an __apple__ from the tree.
4. I can't find one of my __sneakers__.
5. You need __bread__ to make a sandwich.
6. He opens the door with a __key__.
7. We will listen to the __weather__ report so we will know what to wear.
8. We will __freeze__ water to make ice.
9. If you __lead__, we will follow.
10. Stores don't give things away; they __sell__ them.

At Home: Have children write a rhyming poem using at least one of the words above.
Book 2.1/Unit 3 Nine-in-One, Grrr! Grrr! 10
114

CHALLENGE — Extend 114
Name_____ Date_____
Long e; Short e; /ər/, /ən/, /əl/

Look at the picture. List the items in the picture that match the sound of the word in the box. You will list one item in two boxes.

BULLETIN BOARD!

1. **ea** as in thread
   feather
   bread

2. **ey** as in money
   monkey
   donkey

3. **y** as in funny
   pony
   puppy

4. **le** as in couple
   saddle
   castle

5. **en** as in even
   eleven
   garden

6. **er** as in after
   fingers
   feather

Choose a word from the boxes. Use the word in a sentence.
_____

At Home: Help children find more words to add to each of the lists.
Book 2.1/Unit 3 Nine-in-One, Grrr! Grrr!
114

LANGUAGE SUPPORT
Name_____ Date_____
Read and Draw

Draw a garden at night.	Draw half a doughnut.
Draw eleven feathers.	Draw a climbing monkey.

124 Nine-in-One, Grrr! Grrr! • Language Support/Blackline Master 68   Grade 2

Reteach, 114   Practice, 114   Extend, 114   Language Support, 124

369H

OBJECTIVES

Children will review cause and effect.

MATERIALS
• Teaching Chart 97

Skills Finder

Cause and Effect

Introduce	B1: 319I-J
Review	B1: 369I-J, 379E-F
Test	B1: Unit 3
Maintain	B1: 201

LANGUAGE SUPPORT

ESL Ask each child to briefly describe a common activity, such as *I eat breakfast.* Ask *Why do you do this?* Have the speaker say a reason, or cause, for his or her activity, and then restate it to show cause/effect. Example: *I eat breakfast because I am hungry. I am hungry, so I eat breakfast.*

SELF-SELECTED Reading

Children may choose from the following titles.

ANTHOLOGY

• *Nine-in-One, Grr! Grr!*

LEVELED BOOKS

• *First Food: A South American Folktale*

• *Hare and Tortoise*

• *How Frog Lost His Tail*

Bibliography, page T88–T89

Review Cause and Effect

PREPARE

Review Cause and Effect — Remind children that things happen for a reason, both in real life and in stories. One event, or cause, leads to another event, or effect.

TEACH

Read "A Happy Dog" and Model the Skill — Display **Teaching Chart 97.** Read aloud with children the story, "A Happy Dog."

A Happy Dog

It is a hot day, so Dog is thirsty. She trots past Cat to find some water. Cat gets scared and runs up Bird's tree. Bird thinks Cat is chasing him. Bird flaps his wings furiously. He flies out of the tree, straight into the bird bath. Water splashes onto the ground, and Dog licks it up. Dog wags her tail because she has found some nice, cool water!

Teaching Chart 97

MODEL Bird got scared because Cat ran into the tree. That made Bird fly into the bird bath, and the water splashed out. Dog needed to find some water because he was thirsty. Cat is scared of Dog, so he ran up Bird's tree when Dog walked by. Cat scared Bird, so he flew out of his tree into the birdbath. This caused water to splash out of the birdbath onto the ground. Now Dog has something to drink, all because he walked by Cat! Every action in this story led to something else.

Make Cause-and-Effect Chart

GROUP

Have children work in small groups to prepare a two-column Cause-and-Effect chart. Children should provide entries from **Teaching Chart 97** for both columns. Have them add to the chart until they have included all the events from the story. Point out that some events can be both a cause and an effect. ▶ **Linguistic**

CAUSE	EFFECT
It is hot.	Dog needs something to drink.
Dog trots past Cat.	Cat gets scared.
	Cat runs up into a tree.
Bird gets scared.	
Water splashes out.	

ASSESS/CLOSE

Change a Cause

Discuss with children what would happen if one of the causes in the story were changed, such as beginning with a cold day instead of a hot day. Ask children to imagine and discuss how the story might change, even if the characters and setting stayed the same. Create with the class a new Cause-and-Effect chart for the new story.

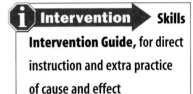

ALTERNATE TEACHING STRATEGY

For a different approach to teaching this skill, see page T71.

ℹ **Intervention** ▶ **Skills Intervention Guide,** for direct instruction and extra practice of cause and effect

Meeting Individual Needs for Comprehension

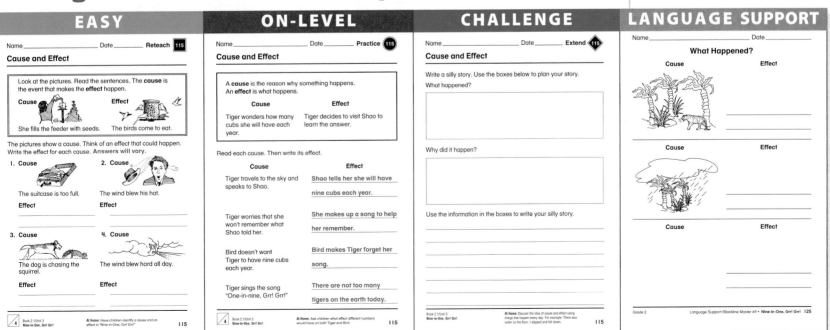

EASY	ON-LEVEL	CHALLENGE	LANGUAGE SUPPORT
Reteach, 115	Practice, 115	Extend, 115	Language Support, 125

OBJECTIVES

Children will identify and use synonyms.

....

MATERIALS

• **Teaching Chart 98**

Skills Finder

Synonyms

Introduce	B1: 341K–L
Review	B1: 369K–L, 379I–J
Test	B1: Unit 3

TEACHING TIP

SYNONYMS Have children think of synonyms for objects in their classroom, or have them look at pictures and think of synonyms that describe a part of the picture. Ask children to describe the pictures to a partner using their synonyms.

Review Synonyms

PREPARE

Define Synonym Write *jump* and *hop* on the chalkboard. Point out that these words mean just about the same thing. Tell children that words that mean the same thing are called synonyms. Ask children for other synonyms for *jump*. (Examples: *leap, spring*)

TEACH

Read "Lion's Problem" and Identify Synonyms Have children read aloud together the passage on **Teaching Chart 98**. Point to the word *big* and tell children the passage contains three synonyms for this word. Ask volunteers to find and underline them. *(large, giant, huge)* Have volunteers find another word that has two synonyms and underline them in a different color. *(crying, weeping, sobbing)*

Lion's Problem

Bird saw a <u>big</u> lion who was <u>crying</u>. She asked Tiger, "Why is the <u>large</u> lion <u>weeping</u>?"

"Lion is <u>sobbing</u> because he was walking through the bushes and got a <u>giant</u> thorn stuck in his <u>huge</u> paw," Tiger told her.

Teaching Chart 98

MODEL I know that synonyms are words that have the same meaning. In this story the words *big* and *large* are used to describe the lion. I know that *big* means almost the same thing as *large*. I am not sure what *huge* means, but I bet *huge* is a synonym for those other words, because a *big* lion would have a *big* paw. I know that a giant is a being of great size. That helps me to know that the thorn in lion's paw is large. *Giant* is a synonym for *large* and *huge*.

PRACTICE

Naming Synonyms

PARTNERS

Write on the board the words *child*, *tiny*, and *angry*. Challenge partners to brainstorm one or two synonyms for each of these words. (Examples: *child–tot, kid; tiny–little, small; angry–mad, upset*)

▶ **Linguistic**

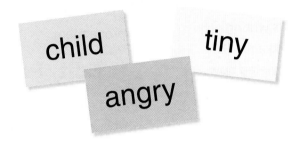

child

tiny

angry

ASSESS/CLOSE

Use Synonyms

Have each partner write three sentences, each using a synonym for *child*, *tiny*, and *angry*. Have partners substitute synonyms from lists into each others' sentences. Discuss with children whether the meaning of a sentence changes when one of the words is replaced by a synonym.

ALTERNATE TEACHING STRATEGY

SYNONYM

For a different approach to teaching this skill, see page T74.

Intervention **Skills Intervention Guide,** for direct instruction and extra practice of synonyms

Meeting Individual Needs for Vocabulary

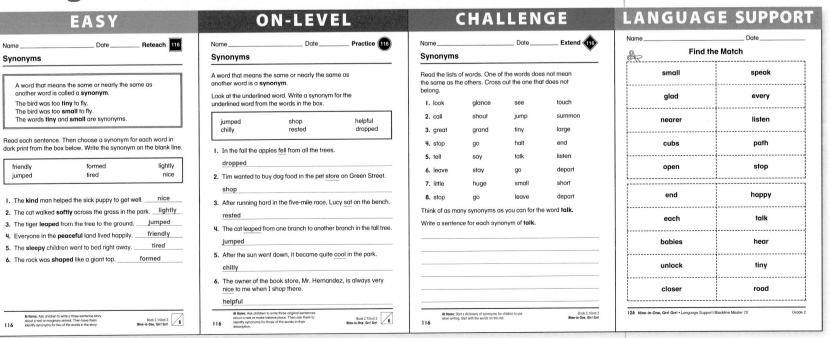

EASY	ON-LEVEL	CHALLENGE	LANGUAGE SUPPORT
Reteach, 116	Practice, 116	Extend, 116	Language Support, 126

GRAMMAR/SPELLING
CONNECTIONS

See the 5-Day Grammar and Usage Plan on *have* and *has*, Pages 369O–369P.

See the 5-Day Spelling Plan on words with long *e* spelled *y* and *ey*, pages 369Q–369R.

TEACHING TIP

Technology
Center a title in the middle of the page to make it easy to identify. Highlight the title and click on the Center function in the toolbar. This feature will automatically center any highlighted text. Remind children to check their title for capitalization of important words.

Handwriting
Remind children to print legibly. They should leave a little extra space between sentences and stay within the margins.

Handwriting
CD-ROM

Explanatory Writing

Prewrite

WRITE A REPORT Present this writing assignment: Choose a type of wild animal that interests you. Explain step-by-step how it raises its young.

EXPLORING TOPICS Once children have chosen their animals, have partners ask each other questions about their topic animals to help focus the reports.

Strategy: Make a Chart Children can use a graphic organizer to plan their research and writing. Guide them to fill in what they know, and their most important questions. Provide resources such as the encyclopedia and non-fiction books.

Draft

USE THE CHART Guide children to refer to their charts to organize information and include important details. Remind them to describe how their animal rears its young in a chronological, step-by-step sequence. Invite them to enrich their explanations with description and action words.

Revise

FOCUSING ON ELABORATION Remind children to add important details that may be missing from their drafts. They should also check to make sure their facts are presented in correct order. Have children consider if they need to:

- correct the time-order of their steps.
- make descriptions clearer.
- add specific details and lively verbs to enliven their facts.

 Children can trade reports and make **PARTNERS** suggestions to each other about how to improve them.

Edit/Proofread

CHECK FOR ERRORS Ask children to read over their reports, checking spelling, grammar, and punctuation.

Publish

SHARE THE REPORTS Post the reports in the classroom and allow time for children to read each other's work. Guide children to attach self-stick notes to the reports stating what facts they found most interesting.

Baby Birds

All birds hatch from eggs. The female lays her eggs in a nest built by herself or her mate or by both of them. Most birds have one mate at a time, with whom they raise one or two sets of babies a year.

Most baby birds remain in the nest for several weeks or months after hatching. Their parents feed and protect them until they can care for themselves. Most birds leave their parents when they are a few months old.

Presentation Ideas

ILLUSTRATE THE REPORT Have children draw pictures of their topic animals to illustrate their reports. They can add a caption or labels about interesting features of their animals.

▶ **Viewing/Representing**

GUIDE A TOUR Let children pretend they are tour guides in a zoo. Have them use their reports as notes for a "tour" given to zoo visitors.

▶ **Speaking/Listening**

Consider students' creative efforts, possibly adding a plus (+) for originality, wit, and imagination.

Scoring Rubric

Excellent	Good	Fair	Unsatisfactory
4: The writer • presents a well-constructed, accurate explanation. • provides facts in a step-by-step order. • enlivens material with vivid descriptive language.	**3:** The writer • presents solid, accurate report. • follows a step-by-step order. • provides sufficient supporting detail.	**2:** The writer • attempts to tell how an animal rears its young. • may not follow a complete step-by-step format. • may not provide accurate supporting detail.	**1:** The writer • may not explain a step-by-step factual process. • may list vague or irrelevant facts or details. • may have trouble with sequence or structure.

Incomplete   0: The writer leaves the page blank or fails to respond to the writing task. The student does not address the topic or simply paraphrases the prompt. The response is illegible or incoherent.

Meeting Individual Needs for Writing

EASY

Write a Caption Have each child draw a picture of his or her favorite animal in its natural habitat. Ask children to label each picture with a caption describing the animal, its natural habitat, and what the animal is doing.

ON-LEVEL

Write a Report Ask children to write a short news report about an experience they have had with an animal. Children may wish to illustrate their news reports.

CHALLENGE

Write a Folktale Invite children to write a short story or folktale about their favorite animal. Encourage them to use real facts about the animal in their story or folktale.

Viewing and Speaking

VIEWING Have children
• look for how the illustration relates to the spoken information.
• determine how the captions or labels add to the illustration.
• think about how to summarize each illustration.

SPEAKING Encourage children to
• use the voice to emphasize important details.
• use gestures to direct attention to the illustrations.
• maintain eye contact with various areas of the room.

ESL If children from other countries wish to write about animals not found in the United States, give them key vocabulary words in English. They may need to know the name of the animal as well as words to describe its young, its food, and how it nurtures its offspring.

PORTFOLIO Invite children to include their animal reports in their portfolios.

5 Day Grammar and Usage Plan

LANGUAGE SUPPORT

Make a chart like the one below, outlining the use of the verb forms *has* and *have*. Explain how to use the chart and display it for easy reference.

I or you	have
one person or thing	has
more than one person or thing	have

DAILY LANGUAGE ACTIVITES

Write the Daily Language Activities on the chalkboard each day or use **Transparency 14**. Have children correct the sentences orally to make the subject and the verb agree or to correct the tense. Some sentences may have two answers; ask children to explain their choice.

Day 1

1. Tiger have a question for Shao. has
2. The bird have black feathers. has
3. The tigers has many stripes. have

Day 2

1. He has a talk with her last week. had
2. Many years ago Shao has a song. had
3. One day the bird has a great idea. had

Day 3

1. The tiger have no cubs. has, had
2. Tiger has a long trip last night. had
3. The trees has many leaves. have, had

Day 4

1. The rooster have tail feathers. has, had
2. The bird have big wings. has, had
3. Tiger has two cubs last year. had

Day 5

1. The birds has homes in the trees. had, have
2. Eu have a good plan. has, had
3. Tiger have a cave. has, had

Daily Language Transparency 14

3690 *Nine-in-One, Grr! Grr!*

DAY 1 **Introduce the Concept**

Oral Warm-Up Read these three sentences aloud. *My friend has a coat. Do you have a coat? We all have coats.* Ask children to identify the verbs. (has, have)

Introduce the Verb *Have* Tell children the verb *have* has special forms in the present tense. Present and discuss:

The Verb *Have*

- The verb *have* has special forms in the present tense.
- Use *has* when the subject is singular.
- Use *have* when the subject is plural or *I* or *you*.

Present the Daily Language Activity and have children correct orally. Then have children write one sentence with *has* and one with *have*.

 Assign the daily Writing Prompt on page 342C.

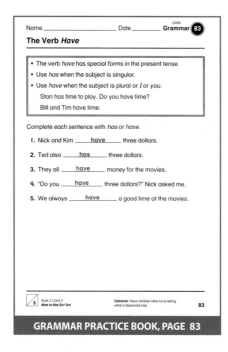

Name _____ Date _____ Grammar **83**

The Verb *Have*

- The verb *have* has special forms in the present tense.
- Use *has* when the subject is singular.
- Use *have* when the subject is plural or *I* or *you.*
  Stan has time to play. Do you have time?
  Bill and Tim have time.

Complete each sentence with *has* or *have*.

1. Nick and Kim ____**have**____ three dollars.
2. Ted also ____**has**____ three dollars.
3. They all ____**have**____ money for the movies.
4. "Do you ____**have**____ three dollars?" Nick asked me.
5. We always ____**have**____ a good time at the movies.

GRAMMAR PRACTICE BOOK, PAGE 83

DAY 2 **Teach the Concept**

Review Present Tense of *Have* Write *I, you, we* on the chalkboard and have children give you the past-tense of *have* that goes with each pronoun.

Introduce *Had* Remind children that the past-tense form of a verb tells what already happened. Explain that the verb *have* has a special form to tell about the past. Present:

Past Tense of *Have*

- The past tense form of the verb *have* is *had*.

Present the Daily Language Activity. Then have children write sentences beginning *I had, You had, We had*. You may want to provide a context for the sentences, such as *Let's think about what we had for lunch today.*

 Assign the daily Writing Prompt on page 342C.

Name _____ Date _____ Grammar **84**

The Verb *Have*

- The past-tense form of the verb *have* is *had*.
  Ted had a good time at the movies.
  Nick and Kim also had a good time.

Each sentence has the present-tense of *have*. Change the sentence to past tense. Write the new sentence.

1. Our family has many pets.
   _____**Our family had many pets.**_____
2. I have a rabbit.
   _____**I had a rabbit.**_____
3. Uncle Ned has a dog.
   _____**Uncle Ned had a dog.**_____
4. My two cousins have fish.
   _____**My two cousins had fish.**_____
5. We all have turtles.
   _____**We all had turtles.**_____

GRAMMAR PRACTICE BOOK, PAGE 84

The Verb *Have*

DAY 3 — Review and Practice

Learn from the Literature Review forms of *have*. Read line nine on page 356 of *Nine-in-One, Grr! Grr!*

> If Tiger <u>has</u> nine cubs each year, they will eat all of us.

Ask children to identify the present-tense form of the verb *have* in the sentence. Ask why *has* is used.

Use Forms of Have Present the Daily Language Activity and have children correct the sentences orally. Then have children look at pictures of people in a catalog and write sentences using *has* or *have*. For example, *She has red hair. They have long coats.*

 WRITING Assign the daily Writing Prompt on page 342D.

DAY 4 — Review and Practice

Review the Verb *Have* Write this sentence on the board: *I have a dog.* Then change the subject to *The man, The children, We,* and *Pam,* and have children change the verb. Then ask them to make each sentence tell about the past.

Mechanics and Usage Before students begin the daily Writing Prompt on page 342D, review capitalization of titles. Display and discuss:

> **Book Titles**
>
> - Begin the first word and each important word in a book title with a capital letter.

 WRITING Assign the daily Writing Prompt on page 342D.

DAY 5 — Assess and Reteach

Assess Use the Daily Language Activity and page 87 of the **Grammar Practice Book** for assessment.

Reteach Review the present-tense form of *have* with the children. Write sentences on the board omitting the word *has* or *have*. Ask children to complete the sentences using the correct form. Remind them to refer to the chart if they have trouble.

1. I___some paper. have

2. Do you___paint? have

3. Jane___three paint brushes. has

4. Lee and Pat___paste. have

Use page 88 of the **Grammar Practice Book** for additional reteaching.

WRITING Assign the daily Writing Prompt on page 342D.

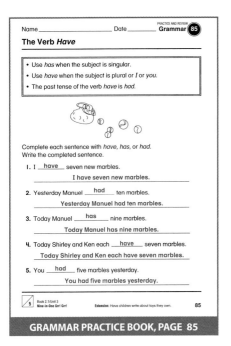

GRAMMAR PRACTICE BOOK, PAGE 85

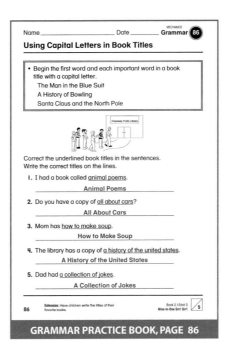

GRAMMAR PRACTICE BOOK, PAGE 86

GRAMMAR PRACTICE BOOK, PAGE 87

5 Day Spelling Plan

LANGUAGE SUPPORT

ESL To help children recognize the final long *e* sound, say a list of words some of which end in this sound. Say words such as: *fine, funny, money, mile, happy, hope, lady, lead.* Ask children to raise their hands when they hear the long *e* sound.

DICTATION SENTENCES

Spelling Words

1. There are <u>many</u> boys.
2. Do you have some <u>money</u>?
3. <u>Every</u> child came to school.
4. The girl is <u>happy</u>.
5. The bird is <u>tiny</u>.
6. The <u>baby</u> is cold.
7. My <u>key</u> is on the desk.
8. I found a <u>penny</u>.
9. She can go to a <u>party</u>.
10. That <u>lady</u> is my mom.

Challenge Words

11. Do not <u>forget</u> the letter.
12. He was <u>lonely</u>.
13. It is a good <u>memory</u>.
14. The <u>mountain</u> is high.
15. It is a <u>wonderful</u> day.

DAY 1 — Pretest

Assess Prior Knowledge Use the Dictation Sentences at left and **Spelling Practice Book** page 83 for the pretest. Allow students to correct their own papers. If students have trouble, have partners give each other a midweek test on Day 3. Students who require a modified list may be tested on the first five words.

Spelling Words		Challenge Words
1. **many**	6. baby	11. **forget**
2. money	7. key	12. **lonely**
3. **every**	8. penny	13. **memory**
4. **happy**	9. party	14. **mountain**
5. **tiny**	10. lady	15. **wonderful**

*Note: Words in **dark type** are from the story.*

Word Study On page 84 of the **Spelling Practice Book** are word study steps and an at-home activity.

SPELLING PRACTICE BOOK, PAGE 83

DAY 2 — Explore the Pattern

Sort and Spell Words Say *many* and *money.* Ask students what vowel sound they hear at the end of each word. Write the words on the chalkboard so that students can see the long *e* sound spelled *y* and *ey.*

Ask students to read aloud the ten spelling words before sorting them according to the spelling pattern.

Long *e* spelled *y*	Long *e* spelled *ey*
many	key
every	money
happy	
tiny	
baby	
penny	
party	
lady	

Word Wall Have students look through magazines for new words with the long *e* sound spelled *y* and *ey* and add them to a classroom word wall, underlining the spelling pattern in each word.

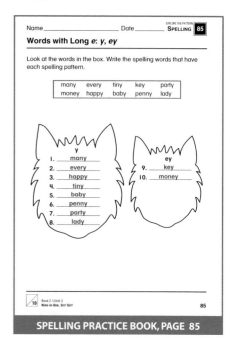

SPELLING PRACTICE BOOK, PAGE 85

.... Words with Long e: y, ey

DAY **3** Practice and Extend	DAY **4** Proofread and Write	DAY **5** Assess and Reteach

DAY 3 Practice and Extend

Word Meaning: Plurals Discuss the meaning of each Spelling Word, and have students identify the nouns (words that name a person, place, or thing). Remind students that when a word ends in *y*, the *y* must be changed to *i* before *-es* is added to make the word plural. Write the words *baby*, *penny*, *party*, and *lady* on the chalkboard. Have students write the plural of each word.

Glossary Explain to students that a synonym is a word that has the same meaning as another word. Some entries in the Glossary include synonyms for the words defined. Have partners:

• write each Challenge Word.

• look up each Challenge Word in the Glossary.

• write a synonym for each Challenge Word that has one listed.

DAY 4 Proofread and Write

Proofread Sentences Write these sentences on the chalkboard, including the misspelled words. Ask students to proofread, crossing out incorrect spellings and writing the correct spellings. There are two spelling errors in each sentence.

> I have (mony) for the (partey).
> (money, party)
>
> She gave me (everee) (pennie).
> (every, penny)

Have students create additional sentences with errors for partners to correct.

Writing Have students use as many spelling words as possible in the daily Writing Prompt on page 342D. Remind students to proofread their writing for errors in spelling, grammar, and punctuation.

DAY 5 Assess and Reteach

Assess Students' Knowledge Use page 88 of the **Spelling Practice Book** or the Dictation Sentences on page 369Q for the posttest.

Personal Word List If students have trouble with any words in the lesson, have them create a personal list of troublesome words in their journals. Have students try to write simple song lyrics with words from their lists and share their songs with others in the group.

Students should refer to their word lists during later writing activities.

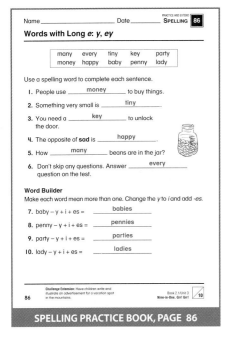

SPELLING PRACTICE BOOK, PAGE 86

SPELLING PRACTICE BOOK, PAGE 87

SPELLING PRACTICE BOOK, PAGE 88

369R

Cumulative Review
with **Expository Text**

Time to Review

Anthology

Change for the Quarter

Selection Summary Children will read about the new designs that will be put on quarters to honor the fifty United States.

Rhyme applies to phonics

Listening Library

INSTRUCTIONAL pages 372–379

Time to Reread

Reread Leveled Books

EASY
Lesson on pages 379A and 379D

INDEPENDENT
Lesson on pages 379B and 379D

🏠 *Take-Home version available*

CHALLENGE
Lesson on pages 379C and 379D

Leveled Practice

EASY

Reteach, 117–124 Blackline masters with reteaching opportunities for each assessed skill

INDEPENDENT/ON-LEVEL

Practice, 117–124 Workbook with Take-Home stories and practice opportunities for each assessed skill and story comprehension

CHALLENGE

Extend, 117–124 Blackline masters that offer challenge activities for each assessed skill

Quizzes Prepared by Accelerated Reader®

WORKSTATION Activities

Social Studies ... Design Your Own Quarter, *377*

Language Arts .. Read Aloud, *370E*

Writing .... Write a How-To Article, *376*

Research and Inquiry ...... Find Out More, *377*

💻 **Internet Activities** .... www.mhschool.com/reading

Suggested Lesson Planner

READING AND LANGUAGE ARTS	DAY 1 — *Focus on Reading and Skills*	DAY 2 — *Read the Literature*
● **Phonics Daily Routines**	Daily Routine: **Segmenting,** 370H **CD-ROM**	Daily **Phonics** Routine: **Blending,** 372A **Phonics CD-ROM**
● **Phonological Awareness** ● **Phonics** *Review* ● **Comprehension** ● **Vocabulary** ● **Study Skills** ● **Listening, Speaking, Viewing, Representing**	**Read Aloud and Motivate,** 370E "The Golden Touch" ☑ **Develop Phonological Awareness,** 370F Review ☑ **Cumulative Review,** 370G–370H **Teaching Chart 99** Reteach, Practice, Extend, 117 **Phonics/Phonemic Awareness** Practice Book, 85–88  **Apply Long e, Short e, /ər/, /ən/, /əl/, Silent Letters,** 370/371 "Fifty Cents" **Intervention Program**	**Build Background,** 372A Develop Oral Language **Vocabulary,** 372B–372C | collect	join	pocket
honors	order	worth | **Word Building Manipulative Cards** **Teaching Chart 100** Reteach, Practice, Extend, 118 **Read the Selection,** 372–375 Comprehension ☑ Cumulative Review ☑ Cause and Effect **Genre:** Magazine Article, 373 **Intervention Program**
● **Curriculum Connections**	Language Arts, 370E	Math, 372A
● **Writing**	 **Writing Prompt:** Write a story about two friends going shopping together. What do they see? What do they buy?	**Writing Prompt:** Is there something you collect or would like to collect? Tell what you like about it. **Journal Writing,** Quick-Write, 375
● **Grammar**	**Introduce the Concept: Sentence Combining,** 379O Daily Language Activity: Combine sentences by connecting the predicates. **Grammar Practice Book,** 89	**Teach the Concept: Sentence Combining,** 379O Daily Language Activity: Combine sentences by connecting the predicates. **Grammar Practice Book,** 90
● **Spelling** *Words from Math*	**Pretest: Words from Math,** 379Q **Spelling Practice Book,** 89, 90	**Teach: Words from Math,** 379Q **Spelling Practice Book,** 91

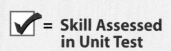

Meeting Individual Needs

 = **Skill Assessed in Unit Test**

 Intervention Program Available

 **Read EVERY DAY**

DAY 3 — Read the Literature

Daily **Phonics** Routine:
Letter Substitution, 377

 **Phonics CD-ROM**

Rereading for Fluency, 374

Story Questions and Activities, 376–377
Reteach, Practice, Extend, 119

Study Skill, 378
☑ Reference Sources
Teaching Chart 101
Reteach, Practice, Extend, 120

Test Power, 379

 **Read the Leveled Books,** 379A–379D
Guided Reading
☑ Phonics Review
☑ Comprehension Review
☑ Instructional Vocabulary

 Intervention Program

 **Art,** 377

✏ **Writing Prompt:** What is your favorite activity, game, or hobby? Is it something you do alone, or with friends? Describe it.

Explanatory Writing, 379M
Prewrite, Draft

Practice and Write: Sentence Combining, 379P
Daily Language Activity: Combine sentences by connecting the predicates.

Grammar Practice Book, 91

Practice and Extend: Words from Math, 379R

Spelling Practice Book, 92

DAY 4 — Build Skills

Daily **Phonics** Routine:
Fluency, 379F

 **Phonics CD-ROM**

 **Read the Leveled Books and the Self-Selected Books**

☑ **Review Cause and Effect,** 379E–379F
Teaching Chart 102
Reteach, Practice, Extend, 121
Language Support, 132

☑ **Review Fantasy and Reality,** 379G–379H
Teaching Chart 103
Reteach, Practice, Extend, 122
Language Support, 133

 **Intervention Program**

 **Social Studies,** 377

✏ **Writing Prompt:** Tell about the last time you went on a trip with your family. What did you do? What did you see?

Explanatory Writing, 379M
Revise

Meeting Individual Needs for Writing, 379N

Practice and Write: Sentence Combining, 379P
Daily Language Activity: Combine sentences by connecting the predicates.

Grammar Practice Book, 92

Practice and Write: Words from Math, 379R

Spelling Practice Book, 93

DAY 5 — Build Skills

Daily **Phonics** Routine:
Writing, 379H

 **Phonics CD-ROM**

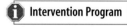 **Read Self-Selected Books**

☑ **Review Synonyms,** 379I–379J
Teaching Chart 104
Reteach, Practice, Extend, 123
Language Support, 134

☑ **Review Context Clues,** 379K–379L
Teaching Chart 105
Reteach, Practice, Extend, 124
Language Support, 135

Listening, Speaking, Viewing, Representing, 379N
Make a Speech
Illustrate your Collection

Intervention Program

✏ **Writing Prompt:** What do you do to get ready for school each morning? Describe.

Explanatory Writing, 379M
Edit/Proofread, Publish

Assess and Reteach: Sentence Combining, 379P
Daily Language Activity: Combine sentences by connecting the predicates.

Grammar Practice Book, 93, 94

Assess and Reteach: Words from Math, 379R

Spelling Practice Book, 94

Language Arts

Read Aloud

The Golden Touch
a Greek myth

Once upon a time, there lived a king named Midas. Although this king had a good wife and a little daughter whom he loved very much, there was something he seemed to love much more dearly—and that was gold.

Each day he went into his counting-house where he counted stacks of golden coins again and again. It was his greatest pleasure in life, and he dreamed only of getting more golden coins to count.

While he was counting one day, he heard a mysterious voice say, "I have come to grant you whatever you wish for most."

King Midas did not hesitate very long. "I wish," he said, "that everything I touch would turn to gold."

"You have your wish," said the voice.

King Midas was overjoyed, thinking of all the gold that would now be his. He picked up a pebble. It turned to gold. He touched every

Continued on page T4

Oral Comprehension

LISTENING AND SPEAKING As you read aloud this fairy tale about a greedy king, encourage children to think about the main events in the story. Pause periodically to let children summarize what has already taken place in the story. When you have finished, ask children, "Can you sum up what happened in this story?" Then ask, "What did the king learn in the story?" Remind children that stopping to summarize as they read can help them to understand a story.

GENRE STUDY: MYTH Discuss the literary devices and techniques used in *The Golden Touch.*

• Discuss the character of King Midas. Have children determine which qualities are realistic and which

qualities are fantasy. List the qualities on the board under realistic/fantasy.

• Tell children that myths often contain a struggle or conflict. Discuss the struggle in *The Golden Touch.*

• Determine how magic was used in the myth. Discuss how the myth would be different without the use of magic.

Activity Invite children to paint their favorite scene from the story. Ask children to incorporate details that show reality and fantasy into their paintings. For extra effect, encourage children to use gold glitter in their paintings. ▶ **Visual/Spatial**

Develop Phonological Awareness

Blend Sounds
Phonemic Awareness

MATERIALS
- Phonics Picture Posters

Teach Tell children they are going to play an animal guessing game. Say: *I am thinking of an animal that slithers and has the sounds /s/-/n/-/ā/-/k/ in its name. What animal am I thinking of?* (a snake) Have children blend the sounds to say the word snake.

Practice Continue the blending game by placing one of the following posters behind your back: *seal, rabbit, goat, bear, bird,* and *whale.* Have children repeat the segmented sounds and then blend them to say the animal name. If the child is correct, display the poster. If not, have another volunteer say their answer.

Segment Sounds
Phonemic Awareness

MATERIALS
- Familiar classroom objects and pictures

Teach Invite children to walk around the classroom with you as you point to an object or picture. Have children say the sounds for the name of the object or picture, and then say the word. To demonstrate, point to yourself and say: /t/-/ē/-/ch/-/ər/ . . . teacher." Ask children to repeat the sounds they hear in the word.

Practice Continue your walk as you point to familiar classroom objects or pictures and have children segment sounds. These are suggested words: *chalk, knee, knob, poster, water, sneaker,* and *paper.*

Delete Sounds
Phonemic Awareness

Teach Have children listen closely as you say a word, then say it without one of its sounds. Say: *Bread . . . If we drop the /b/ sound in /br/ then what word do we get?* (read)

Practice Invite children to say the sounds for the words below. Ask them to say the whole word, then say the word without the first sound: *fright, bright, small, black, blend, click, speak* and *steam.*

INFORMAL ASSESSMENT Observe children as they blend, segment, and delete sounds. If children have difficulty, see Alternate Teaching Strategies on pages T64, T69, T72, and T75.

OBJECTIVES

Children will:

- recognize long *e*, short *e*, /ər/, /ən/, /əl/, and silent letters.

- blend and read words containing the sounds /ər/, /ən/, and /əl/.

- use strategies to decode multisyllabic words.

MATERIALS
- **Teaching Chart 99**

Skills Finder

Long e: y, ey

Introduce	B1: 342G-H
Review	B1: 369E-F, 369G-H, 370G-H
Test	B1: Unit 3
Maintain	B1: 227; B2: 347

TEACHING TIP

DECODING MULTISYLLABIC WORDS Say the word *mitten.* Explain that there are two syllables in mitten and demonstrate breaking it down, saying "*mit-ten.*" Ask children to clap out the syllables. Do the same with *Washington* and *quarter.* Write the words on the board with hyphens to indicate syllable breaks. Have children read the words and use them in sentences.

Review Long e; Short e; /ər/, /ən/, /əl/; Silent Letters

PREPARE

Identify /ər/ er, /ən/ en, /əl/ le; Short e /ea/; Long e: y, ey; and Silent Letters l, g Write the words *bread, cover, little, mitten, talk,* and *sign* on the chalkboard. Underline the letters that stand for the following sounds: /ər/, /ən/, /əl/, /e/, long *e*, and silent letters *l, g.* Tell children that they are going to review these sounds and silent letters.

br<u>ea</u>d   cov<u>er</u>   litt<u>le</u>   mitt<u>en</u>   ta<u>l</u>k   si<u>g</u>n

TEACH

Blend Words With Long e, Short e, and Silent Letters l, g

- Display **Teaching Chart 99.** Point to each box at the top of the chart. Have volunteers identify the sound the underlined letters make and then read the word.

- Direct children's attention to the first sentence on the chart. Have a volunteer fill in the missing letters in the incomplete words by adding *er, en, le, y, ey, ea,* or the silent letters *l* or *g.* Then have the volunteer read the sentence.

oth<u>er</u>	mitt<u>en</u>	eag<u>le</u>
mon<u>ey</u>	h<u>ea</u>d	wa<u>l</u>k, si<u>g</u>n

1. Man<u>y</u> peop<u>le</u> could not ent<u>er</u> the gard<u>en</u>.

2. I turned my h<u>ea</u>d and r<u>ea</u>d the si<u>g</u>n.

3. It said, "Wa<u>l</u>k ov<u>er</u> and get the k<u>ey</u>."

Teaching Chart 99

Use the Words in Context Have children use the completed words in new sentences to reinforce their meanings. For example: *I haven't seen many people today.*

Repeat the Procedure Repeat the procedure to complete sentences 2 and 3 on the chart.

PRACTICE

RHYMING WORDS
Building Rhyming Words with /ər/ er, /ən/ en, /el/ le; /el/, /ē/ y, ey, and Silent Letters l, g

Have partners work together to suggest several rhyming words for *other, mitten, eagle, money, head, sign,* and *half.* When they have listed several words, have them try writing a short, silly poem. Have volunteers read their poems aloud. ▶ **Linguistic/Auditory**

ASSESS/CLOSE

Build and Read Words with er, en, le, ea, y, ey, and Silent Letters l and g

PARTNERS

To assess children's ability to build and decode words containing long *e*, short *e*, the sounds /ər/, /ən/, /əl/, and silent letters *l* and *g*, observe them as they participate in the Practice activity. Encourage children to tape their poems to a bulletin board, as well as to build a word wall, listing as many words as they can think of that contain these sounds and letter combinations. Have children read the phonics rhyme on page 371 in their books.

ADDITIONAL PHONICS RESOURCES

McGraw-Hill School
TECHNOLOGY

Phonics/Phonemic Awareness Practice Book, pages 85–88

Phonics CD-ROM
activities for practice with Blending and Word Building

Daily Routines

DAY 1 Segmenting Say aloud a word that ends in /ər/*er.* Invite children to write the word on the board, and to underline the letters that spell /ər/*er.* Repeat with /ən/ /əl/, long *e,* short *e,* and silent letters.

DAY 2 Blending Write the spelling of each sound in *enter* as you say it. Have children repeat after you. Then have them blend and read *steeple, driven, happy, steady, would,* and *calf.*

DAY 3 Letter Substitution Have partners work together to build words ending in /ər/*er.* Invite one child to change a letter to build a new word, and ask his or her partner to read the new word (*letter → better*).

DAY 4 Fluency Write on the board a list of words ending in /əl/. Point to each word, asking children to blend the sounds silently. Ask volunteers to read each word aloud.

DAY 5 Writing Invite partners to write questions that can be answered with a word containing /ər/, /ən/, /əl/, /ē/, /e/, or silent letters. Then they can exchange papers and answer each other's question.

Meeting Individual Needs for Phonics

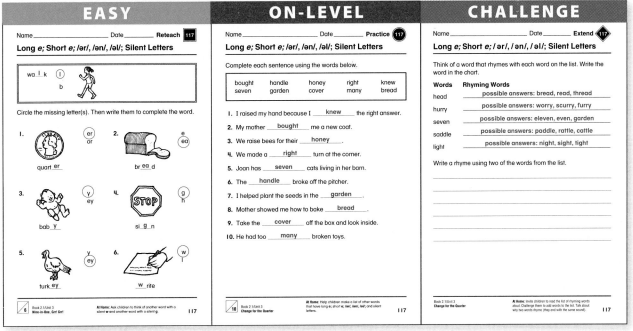

Reteach, 117   Practice, 117   Extend, 117

370H

OBJECTIVES

Children will recognize long *e*, short *e*, /ər/, /ən/, /əl/, and silent letters.

Apply

Long *e*; Short *e*; /ər/, /ən/, /əl/; and Silent Letters

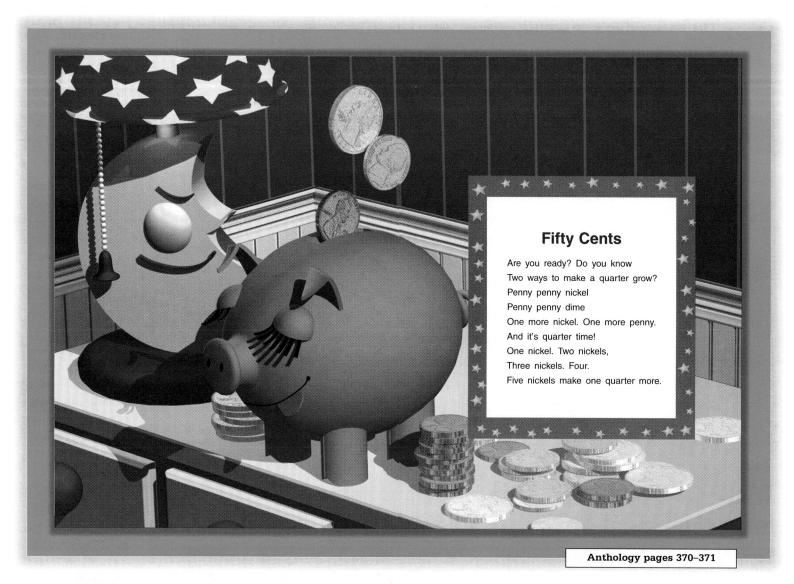

Fifty Cents

Are you ready? Do you know
Two ways to make a quarter grow?
Penny penny nickel
Penny penny dime
One more nickel. One more penny.
And it's quarter time!
One nickel. Two nickels,
Three nickels. Four.
Five nickels make one quarter more.

Anthology pages 370–371

Read and Build Fluency

READ THE POEM Model fluent reading by expressively reading "Fifty Cents" aloud to children. Ask children to listen closely to the way you build excitement with your voice by altering your pace. For auditory modeling purposes, ask the class to echo your reading style as you read the poem once more together.

REREAD FOR FLUENCY Have children reread
PARTNERS the poem with a partner, alternating lines as one child monitors the text while the other is reading. Guide children to pause appropriately when they come to a punctuation. Encourage children to stop completely for an end punctuation.

Dictate and Spell

DICTATE WORDS Say the short *e* word *ready*
JOURNAL aloud. Segment it into its four individual sounds and use it in a sentence, such as, "Are you ready to go to school?" Then have children say the word and write the letter or letter patterns for each sound until they write the word completely. Continue the exercise using other words, such as, *quarter*, *penny*, and *know*. Ask children if they can think of additional review words to segment.

 **Intervention** **Skills Intervention Guide,**
for direct instruction and extra practice of long *e*, short *e*, schwa, and silent letters

Build Background

Math

Concept: The Changing Quarter

Evaluate Prior Knowledge

CONCEPT: THE CHANGING QUARTER

Ask children to share what they know about the quarter as a unit of currency, including its worth and physical features. Use the following activities to build additional background about quarters and currency.

CREATE A QUARTERS CHART

Work with children to create a chart on which they can record facts about quarters.

▶ **Spatial/Linguistic**

How much is it worth?	What does it look like?	What does it feel like?
1 quarter = 25 cents 1 quarter = 1/4 of a dollar	Flat, round, metal. One side has picture of George Washington, one side has picture of an eagle.	Ridges around the edge. Smoother on one side than the other. Heavier than other coins.

Graphic Organizer 31

COIN EQUATIONS Draw a picture on the chalkboard showing that

GROUP WRITING two dimes + one nickel = 1

quarter. Invite children to create equations of their own, using any units of U.S. currency they wish. Encourage groups to first create visual equations in which they draw pictures of the coins, and then to write a sentence underneath each visual equation that explains the equation in words. *(Two dimes plus one nickel equals one quarter.)*

Develop Oral Language

UNDERSTANDING U.S. CURRENCY

ESL Help children to be comfortable with the coins used as U.S. currency by providing either real examples or cardboard cutouts of pennies, nickels, dimes, and quarters. First, label the value of each coin. Then, with children, use the coins or cutouts to build sums of money one coin at a time. Provide model language, if necessary. *(Five cents plus two cents makes seven cents. A dime plus a nickel plus a penny makes sixteen cents. A quarter plus a dime makes thirty-five cents.)*

When children become comfortable with the language, give them different numbers of coins and ask them to add them up this way.

▶ **Mathematical/Linguistic**

DAILY **Phonics** ROUTINES

DAY
2
Blending Write the spelling of each sound in *enter* as you say it. Have children repeat after you. Then have them blend and read *steeple, driven, happy, steady, would,* and *calf.*

Phonics CD-ROM

LANGUAGE SUPPORT

Use the **Language Support Book,** pages 127–130, to help build background.

join

collect

honors

order

pocket

worth

Vocabulary

Teach Vocabulary in Context

Identify Vocabulary Words Display **Teaching Chart 100** and read the passage with children. Have volunteers circle each vocabulary word and underline other words that are clues to its meaning.

Definitions

join (p. 374) to become a member of

collect (p. 374) to gather together

honors (p. 373) shows or feels great respect for a person or thing

order (p. 373) the way in which things are arranged

pocket (p. 373) a small bag sewn into a garment

worth (p. 374) having the same value as

The Coin Club

1. Elinor wants to join a club that meets to explore coins. **2.** The members of the club like to collect coins, gathering those they find interesting or unique. **3.** They talk about how the design on a coin honors a special person or place. **4.** The club stacks coins in the order from the oldest to the newest, so all the coins from 1996 are put before those from 1997. **5.** Elinor reaches her hand into the pocket of her coat and finds two quarters from 1977. **6.** She wonders if they are worth more than other quarters.

Teaching Chart 100

Story Words

These words from the selection may be unfamiliar. Before children read, have them check the meanings and pronunciations of the words in the Glossary, beginning on page 398, or in a dictionary.

• difference, p. 374

• government, p. 374

Discuss Meanings Ask questions like these to help clarify word meanings:

• What kind of club or team would you like to join?

• What types of things, other than coins, might someone collect?

• Which President does the dollar bill honor?

• Name these animals in order from smallest to largest: *cat, elephant, mouse, pony.*

• What do you carry in your coat pockets?

• Which is worth more, three nickels or two dimes?

Practice

Word Scramble  Have children choose vocabulary cards and rewrite their words scrambling the order of the letters. Partners exchange papers and unscramble the letters to write the words correctly.
▶ **Logical/Linguistic**

Word Building Manipulative Cards

Write a Dialogue Have partners write short dialogues using vocabulary words. One partner says a sentence with one vocabulary word; the other partner responds with a sentence using another vocabulary word. ▶ **Linguistic/Kinesthetic**

Assess Vocabulary

Identify Word Meaning in Context Have partners write context sentences, leaving a blank for each vocabulary word. Then encourage children to exchange papers and fill in the blanks. Have children discuss which context clues helped them guess the missing words.

SPELLING/VOCABULARY CONNECTIONS

See Spelling Challenge Words, pages 379Q–379R.

LANGUAGE SUPPORT

See the **Language Support Book**, pages 127–130, for teaching suggestions for Vocabulary.

Vocabulary PuzzleMaker

Provides vocabulary activities.

Meeting Individual Needs for Vocabulary

EASY	ON-LEVEL	ON-LEVEL	CHALLENGE

EASY

Name _____ Date _____ Reteach 118

Vocabulary

collect	honor	join	order	pocket	worth

Find the word on the right that completes each sentence. Write the letter for that word on the line.

1. I have to __f__ lunch.　　　a. collect

2. I like to __a__ baseball cards.　　b. join

3. I think this truck is __e__ about one dollar.　　c. honor

4. Jan found her ring in the __d__ of her coat.　　d. pocket

5. It was an __c__ to meet the president.　　e. worth

6. Henry and Lucy want to __b__ the club.　　f. order

At Home: Encourage children to write a story using the vocabulary words.
118　Book 2.1/Unit 3 Change for the Quarter 6

Reteach, 118

ON-LEVEL

Name _____ Date _____ Practice 118

Vocabulary

Read the sentences. Choose a word from the box that means almost the same thing as the words in parentheses. Write the word on the line.

collect	honor	join	order	pocket	worth

1. The mountains (meet with) the river at the town.
join

2. See if you have a dime in your (part of a coat).
pocket

3. The children (speak very well of) their grandparents.
honor

4. Put the days of the week in the right (way of listing).
order

5. These cards are (how much they cost) ten cents each.
worth

6. I'm going to (gather and keep) stuffed toys.
collect

At Home: Have children write a new sentence for each vocabulary word.
118　Book 2.1/Unit 3 Change for the Quarter 6

Practice, 118

ON-LEVEL

Two to Collect

"If your stamps made you happy, why don't you have them now?" I asked.
"I do! They are in the attic. I am going to look for them right now. Why don't you join me?" she said.
"Okay!" I said. "Families who collect together will always have something to share."

At Home: Help children start collecting fun or interesting items, and discuss why they are special.
118a

Practice, 118a
Take-Home Story

CHALLENGE

Name _____ Date _____ Extend 118

Vocabulary

Make your own dictionary. Cut out the book pages below. Write a definition for each word. Then write your own word. Staple the pages together so they are in ABC order.

Dictionary	collect
honor	join
order	pocket
worth	xylophone

At Home: Challenge children to make more pages for their dictionaries. They should include words, definitions, and illustrations.
118　Book 2.1/Unit 3 Change for the Quarter

Extend, 118

Comprehension

Prereading Strategies

PREVIEW AND PREDICT Invite children to read aloud the name of the selection. Then take a **picture walk** through the illustrations. Discuss with children how the pictures give clues about what they will read in the selection.

- What clues do the pictures give us about the role quarters will play in the story?

- What will this story most likely be about?

- Will this be a fiction story or a nonfiction article about money? *Genre*

Have children record in a chart their predictions of what will happen in the story.

PREDICTIONS	WHAT HAPPENED
The story is about quarters.	
The quarter is going to be changed.	

SET PURPOSES Ask children what they would like to learn as they read the story. For example:

- How will the quarter change?

- What will the new design look like?

TIME FOR KIDS
SPECIAL REPORT

Change for the QUARTER

372

Meeting Individual Needs · Grouping Suggestions for Strategic Reading

EASY

Read Together Read the article aloud as you track print and model directionality. Invite children to chime in as you read the story aloud. Remind children that using information they already know about quarters and other forms of currency will help them to better understand the main idea of the selection.

ON-LEVEL

Guided Instruction Use the Comprehension prompts as you read the article with the children. After reading the article with children, have them reread it, explaining in their own words the causes for the changes in the design of the quarter.

CHALLENGE

Read Independently Remind children to trace the cause of the changes to the quarter in order to best understand the main idea of the article. After reading, have children share their opinions about whether or not changing the design of the quarter will cause more people to collect quarters.

Delaware

New Jersey

Pennsylvania

Georgia

Connecticut

Quarters Get a New Look

The change in your pocket is changing. At least, the quarter is. The 25-cent piece is getting a new look. The eagle on the back side is going away. In its place, there will be 50 new designs. (George Washington is staying on the "heads" side.) ①

Each of the 50 new designs honors a state. Each year for 10 years, five new quarters will be made. States will be honored in the order they joined the United States.

The first new quarters have already come out. You may have seen them by now. They honor the states of Connecticut, Delaware, Georgia, New Jersey, and Pennsylvania.

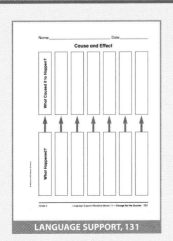

George Washington is still with us!

373

Comprehension

☑ **Phonics** Apply /ər/, /ən/, /əl/

☑ **Apply Cause and Effect**

STRATEGIC READING Understanding what causes events, or characters' actions or feelings, can help you to better understand the main ideas of a piece of writing. While we read the selection, let's pay close attention to cause and effect.

Before we begin reading, let's create a Cause-and-Effect chart we can use to help us understand facts and events described in the article, and what causes them to happen.

① **CAUSE AND EFFECT** The first paragraph of the article tells you that the quarter is changing. What's the cause of this change? Use your chart to record the cause of this effect.

THIS PAGE AND COVER: COURTESY, U.S. MINT

LANGUAGE SUPPORT

Blackline masters of the Cause-and-Effect chart can be found in the **Language Support Book**.

LANGUAGE SUPPORT, 131

Genre

Nonfiction/Magazine Article

Remind children that nonfiction articles:

- present facts in a logical order.
- may use headings, captions, diagrams, and different typefaces.
- give short descriptions of events, discoveries, or ideas.

Activity After children read *Change for the Quarter*, review the characteristics of this genre with them. Be sure to allow children time to go through the article to find examples of each genre trait. Discuss how the photographs, captions, and charts help the reader understand new information.

373

Comprehension

2 **CAUSE AND EFFECT** What's causing the government to be especially happy about the new quarters? Let's complete our charts.

CAUSE	EFFECT
The mint wants to honor the states.	The design of the quarter is being changed.
People want to collect them instead of spending them, and that means the government will make extra money.	The government is very happy about the new quarters.

3 **ORGANIZE INFORMATION** Help children organize the information and facts they have learned from the article. Invite them to retell in their own words what they read in the article. *Summarize*

Some people collect coins from around the world.

They were the first five states to join the United States. So they were the first of the 50 states to be honored with new quarters. You'll get to see the last five state quarters in 2008.

Kids love the idea. "It's nice to have a change," says Shannon Vinson, from Baltimore, Maryland. "I'll collect all 50 for show-and-tell."

2 That's just what the U.S. government wants. Quarters are made for just a few cents. But they are worth 25 cents when you use them. If people keep the coins instead of spending them, the government will get to keep the difference. It could add up to more than $5 billion. Not exactly **3** small change!

374

REREADING FOR *Fluency*

ONE Children who need fluency practice can read along silently or aloud as they listen to the article on audiocassette.

READING RATE When you evaluate reading rate, have children read aloud from the story for one minute. Place a stick-on note after the last word read. Count words read. To evaluate

children's performance, see Running Record in the **Fluency Assessment** book.

i **Intervention** For leveled fluency passages, lessons, and norm charts, see **Skills Intervention Guide**, Part 5, Fluency.

The First States

Below is a list of the first 10 states to join the U.S. Is your state one of them? If not, find out when your state became a state. And start watching your change. You might be holding a quarter with your state's special picture on it.

The First 10 States	When Each Became a State
Delaware	December 7, 1787
Pennsylvania	December 12, 1787
New Jersey	December 18, 1787
Georgia	January 2, 1788
Connecticut	January 9, 1788
Massachusetts	February 6, 1788
Maryland	April 28, 1788
South Carolina	May 23, 1788
New Hampshire	June 21, 1788
Virginia	June 25, 1788

Smart State

Look at the list. One state is 15 days older than the state after it. But the two states joined the U.S. in different years. What states are they? (Hint: One state starts with the letter N. The other state begins with the letter G.)

Eagle quarters won't be made again until all 50 states have a coin of their own.

FIND OUT MORE
Visit our website:
www.mhschool.com/reading

interNET
CONNECTION

Based on an article in *TIME FOR KIDS*.

375

Comprehension

Return to Predictions and Purposes

Reread children's predictions about the article. Discuss the predictions, noting which ones needed to be revised. Then ask children if the article answered the questions they had before they read.

PREDICTIONS	WHAT HAPPENED
The story is about quarters.	The article is about quarters.
The quarter is going to be changed.	The quarter is going to be changed in order to honor the states.

CAUSE AND EFFECT

HOW TO ASSESS Write on the board the following sentence: *The cat was hungry, so he ate some food.* Ask children to underline the cause (The cat was hungry) and to circle the effect. (He ate some food.)

FOLLOW UP If children have difficulty understanding cause and effect, encourage them to use an article's illustrations as reminders of important causes and effects.

LITERARY RESPONSE

QUICK-WRITE Invite children to use their journals to record their thoughts on the article.

JOURNAL

ORAL RESPONSE Have children discuss these questions:

• Do you think it's a good idea to change the quarter?

• How would you design the quarter that will honor your state?

RESEARCH AND INQUIRY Have children work in small groups to find out more about the United States Mint and how United States money is made. Each group can contribute to a bulletin board display on "Our Money."

*inter*NET
CONNECTION For more information or activities on this topic, go to **www.mhschool.com/reading**.

Story Questions

Help children discuss or write answers to the questions on page 376.

Answers:

1. the "tails" side *Literal/Details*

2. Making quarters only costs a few cents, but when people spend them, it costs the government 25 cents. If people don't spend the quarters, the government saves money. *Inferential/Make Inferences*

3. The "tails" side has been replaced with a design that honors each state. *Literal/Details*

4. The appearance of the quarter is changing. *Critical/Summarize*

5. Answers will vary. *Critical/Reading Across Texts*

Write a How-To Article For a full writing process lesson related to this writing suggestion, see the lesson on Explanatory Writing on pages 379M–379N.

Story Questions & Activities

1. Which side of the quarter is changing?

2. Why does the U.S. government hope that people will collect the new quarters?

3. How do the new quarters honor different states?

4. What is the main idea of this selection?

5. If you designed money to honor the land of Shao, from "Nine-in-One Grr! Grr!", what might it look like and why?

Write a How-To Article

Is there something that you collect or would like to collect? Write an article for a magazine about collecting. Explain how someone can start his or her own collection. Give three steps to follow.

Meeting Individual Needs

EASY	ON-LEVEL	CHALLENGE
Name_____ Date_____ **Reteach** 119	Name_____ Date_____ **Practice** 119	Name_____ Date_____ **Extend** 119
Story Comprehension	**Story Comprehension**	**Story Comprehension**
Think about "Change for the Quarter." Write **True** if the sentence is true. Write **False** if the sentence is false. Then rewrite the false sentences to make them true.	Write an **X** next to each statement that is true about "Change for the Quarter."	Design a quarter to represent your state. Use the information in the article to help you.
1. The quarter has the same design in each state. **False. The quarter has a different design in each state.**	1. _X_ The 25-cent piece is getting a new look.	
	2. ___ Twelve new quarters will come out each year.	
2. In 1999, the first new quarters appeared. **True**	3. _X_ The first five new quarters came out in 1999.	
	4. _X_ New Jersey was one of the first five states.	
	5. _X_ Some kids collect coins.	
3. The quarter is worth 25 cents. **True**	6. ___ Quarters cost a lot of money to make.	
	7. _X_ Delaware was the first state to join the United States.	
	8. _X_ New quarters will honor all 50 states.	
	9. _X_ George Washington's head will be on the new quarter.	
4. Each of the fifty new designs honors a different person. **False. Each new design honors a different state.**	10. ___ The new quarter will be worth 50 cents.	Write the reason your design would be a good one for the new quarter. Explain what your design shows about your state and why you would put it on the quarter.
	11. ___ These new quarters are not to be spent.	
	12. _X_ The eagle will not be on the "tails" side any more.	
5. The eagle on the "tails" side of every quarter will still be shown. **False. The eagle is going to be replaced.**		
Book 2.1/Unit 3 Change for the Quarter	Book 2.1/Unit 3 Change for the Quarter	Book 2.1/Unit 3 Change for the Quarter
At Home: Ask children to tell you another fact from "Change for the Quarter." 119	At Home: Have children start a collection. They can collect coins, stamps, dried flowers, or bottle caps. 119	At Home: Discuss the changes being made to quarters. Help children research when their state will be honored with a coin. 119
Reteach, 119	**Practice, 119**	**Extend, 119**

Make a Guess

If you flipped a quarter 40 times, how many times do you think it would come up heads? Tails? Write your guess. Then flip a quarter 40 times. Make a chart that compares how many times you get heads and how many times you get tails.

Design Your Own Quarter

Think about what is special about your state. Then design a quarter that honors your state. Draw pictures for the front and the back.

Find Out More

Look on the "tails" side of a penny, a nickel, a dime. What pictures are there? Learn more about the designs. What are they? What do they mean?

377

Story Activities

Take a Guess

Materials: quarters, paper, pen

PARTNERS Have partners work together to make a chart that includes their guess. One partner flips the quarter 40 times while the other records the results on the chart. Then they switch tasks to complete the activity.

Design Your Own Quarter

Materials: paper, felt-tipped markers, drawing materials

GROUP Have small groups brainstorm ideas and choose their favorite ones for front and back. They can further split their group into two: one smaller group to design the front and one to design the back.

Find Out More

RESEARCH AND INQUIRY Assign each group a coin to research. Have them **GROUP** list their questions, and decide on two or three sources of information, such as library books, encyclopedias, or the Internet.

 *inter*NET **CONNECTION** For more information or activities on this topic, go to *www.mhschool.com/reading*.

FORMAL ASSESSMENT

After page 377, see Selection Assessment.

DAILY Phonics **ROUTINES**

DAY 3 **Letter Substitution**
Have partners work together to build words ending in /ər/er. Invite one child to change a letter to build a new word, and ask his or her partner to read the new word. (*letter* → *better*)

Phonics **CD-ROM**

Study Skills

REFERENCE SOURCES

OBJECTIVES

Children will understand the difference between a dictionary and an encyclopedia.

PREPARE Explain that dictionaries and encyclopedias are two excellent sources of information.

TEACH Explain to children that dictionaries provide the definitions of words; encyclopedias provide brief overviews about a large variety of topics. Both are arranged alphabetically.

PRACTICE Display **Teaching Chart 101**. Have children answer questions 1–4: **1.** encyclopedia **2.** dictionary **3.** 600s B.C., encyclopedia **4.** Both are arranged alphabetically. A dictionary provides definitions and information on word use; encyclopedias provide facts about topics.

ASSESS/CLOSE Have children look up a key word in both the dictionary and the encyclopedia. Ask children to describe the difference between what they learned from both sources.

Meeting Individual Needs

STUDY SKILLS   READ TOGETHER

Choose a Reference Source

Dictionary

mint¹ **1.** A plant that has fragrant leaves that are used as flavoring and in medicine. Peppermint and spearmint are kinds of mint. **2.** A candy flavored with mint.
  mint (mint) *noun, plural* **mints**.

mint² **1.** A place where metal is made into coins. **2.** A large amount of money. A fancy car like that must cost a *mint. Noun.* **3.** To make coins. The government *minted* new quarters this year. *Verb.*
  mint (mint) *noun, plural* **mints**; *verb,* **minted**, **minting**.

Encyclopedia

Mint A mint is a place where coins are made. In most countries, only the government can make coins. The United States has mints in Denver, Philadelphia, San Francisco, and West Point, New York.
  The first mint in the world was built during the 600's B.C. This mint was in Lydia, which is now part of Turkey.

Mint Most people think of the flavor of peppermint when they hear the word *mint*. But actually, mint is the name of a family of plants. Their leaves have a pleasant smell. Mint grows in all parts of the world.

Choose a reference to answer each question.

1 Which book tells you where mints are located in the United States?

2 Which book gives you all the different meanings of the word *mint*?

3 When was the first mint built? Which book did you use to find your answer?

4 How are a dictionary and an encyclopedia alike? How are they different?

EASY

Name_____ Date_____ Reteach 120

Choose a Reference Source

Dictionaries give information about words. **Encyclopedias** give information about different topics.

Dictionary Entry	Encyclopedia Entry
me‧te‧or (mē′tē ər) *noun* Metal or stone that comes out of space and goes through Earth's atmosphere. *plural* **meteors.**	**Meteor,** *MEE tee uhr,* is a bright streak of light seen in the sky. Sometimes meteors are called "shooting stars" or "falling stars." Chunks of metal or stone enter the air around Earth and burn up. Some of them pass through without burning and land on Earth. These are called meteorites. Sometimes a group of meteors fall together. These are called meteor showers.

Use these entries to answer the questions below.

1. Which of these entries would give you the most information about meteors? **encyclopedia**

2. If you wanted to know how to spell the plural of **meteor**, which source would be best? **dictionary**

3. Which source would tell you about different kinds of meteors? **encyclopedia**

4. If you read the word **meteor** in a story and didn't know what it meant, which source would be the easiest to read quickly for the meaning? **dictionary**

120   At Home: Ask children to tell you what the difference is between a *meteor* and *meteorite.*   Book 2.1/Unit 3 **Change for the Quarter** 4

Reteach, 120

ON-LEVEL

Name_____ Date_____ Practice 120

Choose a Reference Source

Study the uses of a dictionary listed below. Then study the uses of an encyclopedia. Use these guides to help you answer the questions.

Dictionary:

1. gives more than one definition if the word has more than one

2. tells you how to pronounce the word

3. tells you the part of speech each meaning has—example: **lead** (to guide someone) *verb* **lead** (a heavy metal) *noun*

4. may use the word in a sentence

Encyclopedia:

A. may break the topic down into its parts and fully explain them

B. may give facts and numbers related to the topic, as well as graphs and charts

C. may include maps, photos, and diagrams

D. may provide history of the topic

Choose the number or letter of the different uses shown above that would help you answer these questions.

1. What is the history of the Girl Scouts? **D**

2. What part of speech is the word *funny*? **3**

3. What countries surround Mexico? **C**

4. How is the word *ragout* pronounced? **2**

5. How many tons of gold are mined in Colorado? **B**

120   At Home: Ask children which would be more helpful if they wanted to find out about the history of Texas, a dictionary or an encyclopedia.   Book 2.1/Unit 3 **Change for the Quarter** 5

Practice, 120

CHALLENGE

Name_____ Date_____ Extend 120

Choose a Reference Source

Telephone book:
Polete Michelle 14 Oak St 714-5003
Polit Nathan 10 Pine Avenue ... 481-3716

Dictionary:
police (puh-leess)
Noun, plural The people whose job it is to keep order, make sure laws are obeyed, and stop crimes from being committed.

Encyclopedia:
Police are government officers who enforce the law and maintain order. They work to protect the lives and property of the people of the community. Police officers serve their communities in many ways.

Map:

1. Which reference source would you use if you needed to know where Michelle lived? **telephone directory**

2. Which reference source would you use if you needed to know how to say the word police? **dictionary**

3. Which reference source would you use if you wanted to show someone that Michelle lived on the north side of the lake? **map**

4. Which reference source would you use to write a report about what police officers do on the job? **encyclopedia**

Write a question for a friend to answer about using reference materials.

Questions will vary.

120   At Home: Have a scavenger hunt with children. Have a dictionary, an encyclopedia, a telephone book, and a map ready for children's use. Ask children to locate information that comes from the different sources.   Book 2.1/Unit 3 **Change for the Quarter**

Extend, 120

TEST POWER

A FACT is something that is true in the story.

DIRECTIONS:
Read the story. Then read each question about the story.

SAMPLE

A Trip to the Museum

Biu woke up on Monday morning. She looked at her clock. It read nine o'clock. "Oh, no," she thought, "I'm late for school." She ran out of her bedroom and yelled, "Dad, I'm late." Her dad said, "It's the first day of vacation." Biu let out a sigh of relief.

Biu got dressed and went into the kitchen. Her father was staring out the window.

"Good morning," he said. "What a wet day it is."

Biu asked, "Any ideas for a fun day inside?" "How about a trip to the museum?" he asked. Biu loved going to the art museum. Biu said happily, "That sounds great!"

1 Why was Biu worried when she woke up late?
   ● She thought she was late for school.
   ○ She thought she was late for a visit to the doctor.
   ○ She thought it was Sunday.

2 Which is a FACT from this story?
   ● Biu liked going to art museums.
   ○ Biu liked going to school.
   ○ Biu is a boy.

379

Test Power

THE PRINCETON REVIEW

Read the Page

Explain to children that you will be reading this story as a group. You will read the story, and they will follow along in their books.

Request that children put pens, pencils, and markers away, since they will not be writing in their books.

Discuss the Questions

QUESTION 1: Instruct children to look back to the passage and reread the lines where Bui wakes up. Ask: What does the story say?

QUESTION 2: Ask children to look for the choice that is stated in the story. The next-to-last sentence says that Bui loves the art museum.

Intervention **Skills**
Intervention Guide, for direct instruction and extra practice of phonics and comprehension

☑ **Phonics**

• Silent letters: *l, b, k, w, g, h, gh*

• /ər/*er*

• Short *e: ea*

• Long *e: y, ey*

☑ **Comprehension**

• Fantasy and Reality

• Cause and Effect

Answers will vary. Have children cite examples from the story to support their answers.

EASY

Story Questions for Selected Reading

1. Do the illustrations show events that can happen or imaginary events?

2. What part of the story was the most interesting or exciting?

3. If you could be one of the characters in the story, which would you be? Why?

4. How would you describe the story to a friend? Does the story make you want to talk with its author?

Draw a Picture

Draw a picture that illustrates the title of the story.

Self-Selected Reading
Leveled Books

EASY

UNIT SKILLS REVIEW

☑ **Phonics**
☑ **Comprehension**

Help students self-select an Easy Book to read and apply phonics and comprehension skills.

Guided Reading

PREVIEW AND PREDICT Discuss the illustrations in the beginning of the book. As you take the **picture walk**, have children predict what the story might be about. List their ideas.

SET PURPOSES Have children write down why they want to read the book. Have them share their purposes.

READ THE BOOK Use items like the following to guide children's reading or after they have read the story independently:

• Look for words that contain the silent letters *l, b, k, w, g, h, gh.* Can you think of other words that contain these silent letters? *Phonics and Decoding*

• Do you think the events in this story were make-believe or could they really happen? How can you tell what is real and what is not? *Fantasy and Reality*

• What happened at the end of this story? What made that ending happen? *Cause and Effect*

RETURN TO PREDICTIONS AND PURPOSES Discuss children's predictions. Ask which were close to the story and why. Have children review their purposes for reading. Did they find out what they wanted to know?

LITERARY RESPONSE Have children discuss questions like the following:

• What did you like about this story? What didn't you like?

• Did the writer choose a good title for the story? If not, what title would you give it?

• What parts of the story would you change? Describe your changes.

See the **Phonics** CD-ROM for practice using silent letters: *l, b, k, w, g, h, gh;* /ər/*er;* /e/ *ea;* /ē/ *y, ey.*

Self-Selected Reading
Leveled Books

INDEPENDENT

UNIT SKILLS REVIEW

- ☑ **Phonics**
- ☑ **Comprehension**

Help students self-select an Independent Book to read and apply phonics and comprehension skills.

Guided Reading

PREVIEW AND PREDICT Discuss the illustrations in the beginning of the book. As you take the **picture walk**, have children predict what the story might be about. If the book has chapter headings, ask children to use the headings to predict the kind of information in the book or under each head. List their ideas.

SET PURPOSES Have children write why they want to read the book. Have them share their purposes.

READ THE BOOK Use items like the following to guide children's reading or after they have read the story independently:

- Pronounce the /ər/ sound as you write *er* words on the chalkboard. Have children identify words in the story that contain this sound. *Phonics and Decoding*

- What events in the story could have happened to you? Which events were make-believe? *Fantasy and Reality*

- What events caused the ending in the story? How else could it have ended? *Cause and Effect*

RETURN TO PREDICTIONS AND PURPOSES Have children review their predictions. Children can talk about whether their purposes were met, and if they have any questions that the story left unanswered.

LITERARY RESPONSE The following questions will help focus children's responses:

- What did the story teach you about special talents and character traits?

- Did the story make you want to learn more about its main character or main idea?

See the **Phonics CD-ROM** for practice using silent letters: *l, b, k, w, g, h, gh;* /ər/*er;* /e/ *ea;* /ē/ *y, ey.*

☑ **Phonics**

- Silent letters: *l, b, k, w, g, h, gh*
- /ər/*er*
- Short *e: ea*
- Long *e: y, ey*

☑ **Comprehension**

- Fantasy and Reality
- Cause and Effect

Answers will vary. Have children cite examples from the story to support their answers.

INDEPENDENT

Story Questions for Selected Reading

1. What was the most important idea in the story?

2. How do you think the author wanted you to feel about this story?

3. What special ability is the story about?

4. Does this story remind you of any others that you've read? How?

5. Which illustration was your favorite? Why?

Write an Ending

Write a different ending for this story.

Self-Selected Reading
Leveled Books

☑ **Phonics**

- Silent letters: *l, b, k, w, g, h, gh*
- /ər/*er*
- Short *e: ea*
- Long *e: y, ey*

☑ **Comprehension**

- Fantasy and Reality
- Cause and Effect

Answers will vary. Have children cite examples from the story to support their answers.

CHALLENGE

Story Questions for Selected Reading

1. What was special about the story's main character?

2. What feelings or interests does the main character express?

3. To which of the characters would you like to talk? What would you say?

4. Which of the events in this story could really happen? Which could not?

5. What other stories on this topic have you read?

Write a Book Review

Write a book review that explains what you thought was good or bad about this book.

CHALLENGE

UNIT SKILLS REVIEW

☑ **Phonics**
☑ **Comprehension**

Help students self-select a Challenge Book to read and apply phonics and comprehension skills.

Guided Reading

PREVIEW AND PREDICT Discuss the illustrations in the beginning of the book. As you take the **picture walk**, have children predict what the story might be about. List their ideas.

SET PURPOSES Have children write why they want to read the book. Have them share their purposes.

READ THE BOOK Use items like the following to guide children's reading or after they have read the story independently:

- Can you find any words that have the short *e* sound spelled with an *ea*? What other *ea* words have a short *e* sound? How about long *e* spelled with a *y* or *ey*? Look for those words. *Phonics and Decoding*

- Why do you think the author chose imaginary (or real) events to express the story's main idea? Would it have worked any other way? *Fantasy and Reality*

- Which event do you think caused the story to end as it did? How could it have been changed? *Cause and Effect*

RETURN TO PREDICTIONS AND PURPOSES Discuss children's predictions. Ask which were close to the story and why. Have children review their purposes for reading. Did they find out what they wanted to know?

LITERARY RESPONSE Have children discuss questions like the following:

- What other titles would have been possible for this story?

- Would you recommend this story to a friend? Why or why not?

See the **Phonics** CD-ROM for practice using silent letters: *l, b, k, w, g, h, gh*; /ər/*er*; /e/ *ea*; /ē/ *y, ey*.

Bringing Groups Together

Anthology and Leveled Books

Connecting Texts

SELF-EXPRESSION CHARTS
Write the story titles at the top of a chart. Under each story title, have children list ways in which the characters express themselves. Discuss the ways the objects or characters in the stories express themselves. Have children choose four books, such as *Change for the Quarter* and *Rin Tin Tin: Top Dog in the Movies*.

Change for the Quarter	Rin Tin Tin: Top Dog in the Movies	Sending Messages with Dots and Dashes	How Frog Lost His Tail
• Pictures on the quarter express something about the states they represent.	• Rin Tin Tin expressed his intelligence and courage through his acting.	• The telegraph allowed people to express themselves by sending messages quickly.	• Frog thinks he can express himself by having a beautiful tail.

Viewing/Representing

GROUP PRESENTATIONS Divide the class into groups. Each group will include children who have chosen to read the same titles in the unit. Give children in each group the art supplies they will need to create a model or drawing of a main character or important object in their stories. Have each group present their model to the rest of the class.

AUDIENCE RESPONSE
Ask children to look closely at each model presented. Encourage children to ask questions after each presentation.

Research and Inquiry

INVESTIGATE Have children investigate topics they would like to learn more about. Invite them to do so by:

• looking at classroom and school library books.

• visiting a local museum, art gallery, shop, and so on where they may find the things they are interested in learning about.

• talking with adults who know about these topics.

interNET* CONNECTION** Have children go to ***www.mhschool.com/reading for links to Web pages.

Children can write or draw what they learned in their journals.

OBJECTIVES

Children will recognize and
identify a cause-and-effect
relationship.

Skills Finder	
Cause and Effect	
Introduce	B1: 319I-J
▶ Review	B1: 369I-J, 379E-F
Test	B1: Unit 3
Maintain	B1: 201

TEACHING TIP

CAUSE-EFFECT Remind
children that one way to spot a
cause-and-effect relationship in
a piece of writing is to look for
clue words like *because, since,*
and *in order to*.

**ALTERNATE TEACHING
STRATEGY**

CAUSE AND EFFECT

For a different approach to
teaching this skill, see page T71.

Review Cause and Effect

PREPARE

Review the Concept Remind children that it is helpful to know why something happens—
the cause—in order to understand what happens—the effect.
Encourage them to discuss how understanding cause and effect can
help them make predictions about other events.

TEACH

Read the Passage and Model the Skill Display **Teaching Chart 102** and read it aloud with children.

> **Taking Care of Coins**
>
> If you've decided to start a coin collection, you need to learn
> how to take care of your coins. How much a coin is worth
> depends on what shape the coin is in.
> Most coin collectors keep their coins in special drawers lined
> with soft cloth. Coins need to be protected from fingerprints,
> moisture, and anything that could scratch them. Handling a
> coin, whether touching it with your hands or trying to clean it,
> can damage the coin, making it less valuable. When you must
> handle a coin, be sure to hold it by the edges.
>
> Teaching Chart 102

MODEL The article does not directly state what causes coins to be
worth less. I see that it is important to take care of coins or they will
not be worth as much. There are several things that can damage
the coin which then leads to the coin losing its value. Some of the
things that can cause damage to a coin are fingerprints and moisture. With this information, I can conclude that damage to coins
causes them to lose value.

PRACTICE

Create a Cause-and-Effect Flowchart

GROUP

Ask volunteers to underline the possible causes that can damage a coin. Then have children discuss how each of these causes leads to the coin being damaged, which leads to the coin losing its value. Record each cause-and-effect cycle in a flowchart.

handling a coin ▶ moisture on fingertips ▶ moisture stains coins ▶ stained coins lose value

ASSESS/CLOSE

Have children look back to *Change for the Quarter* to find examples of cause and effect. Prompt them by asking the following questions:

- The quarter is changing because _____.
- Certain states were honored before others because _____.
- If everyone kept the new quarters instead of spending them, the government would _____.

Have children identify which part of the sentence is the cause and which part is the effect.

DAILY Phonics ROUTINES

DAY 4

Fluency Write on the board a list of words ending in /əl/. Point to each word, asking children to blend the sounds silently. Ask volunteers to read each word aloud.

Phonics CD-ROM

 **Intervention** Skills
Intervention Guide, for direct instruction and extra practice of cause and effect

Meeting Individual Needs for Comprehension

EASY	ON-LEVEL	CHALLENGE	LANGUAGE SUPPORT

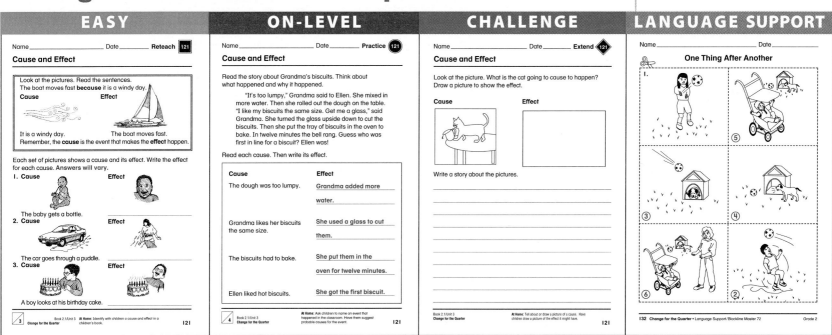

Reteach, 121 Practice, 121 Extend, 121 Language Support, 132

OBJECTIVES

Children will recognize and understand the difference between fantasy and reality.

Skills Finder

Fantasy and Reality

Introduce	B1: 289I–J
Review	B1: 341I–J, 379G–H
Test	B1: Unit 3

TEACHING TIP

MANAGEMENT To further illustrate the concepts of fantasy and reality, you might wish to divide the class into two groups, inviting one to create a small scene about money that is a fantasy, and the other to create a realistic scene about money. Both groups can perform their scenes, and the class can discuss aspects of each.

SELF-SELECTED
Reading

Children may choose from the following titles.

ANTHOLOGY

• *Change for the Quarter*

LEVELED BOOKS

• *All titles for the unit.*

Review Fantasy and Reality

PREPARE

Review Fantasy and Reality

Explain that some stories are about events that could happen in real life. An article, such as "Change for the Quarter," always tells about things that happen in real life. Other stories are fantasies that tell about events that could never happen in real life.

TEACH

Read the Passage and Model the Skill

Explain to children that you will be reading two paragraphs: one that is realistic and one that is a fantasy. Tell children to note details that can help them distinguish between fantasy and reality as you read **Teaching Chart 103** aloud with them.

What Really Happened?

Carey went to the store with a pocketful of change. He paid for a bottle of juice and an apple with the money he had. After Carey left the store, he realized he still had a quarter left. It was enough to buy a gumball from one of the machines.

Carey had just arrived at the store when he realized he'd forgotten his money. He asked <u>the elephant at the counter</u> how much longer the store would be open. "Only ten more minutes," <u>the elephant replied. Carey flapped his wings three times and flew out the door toward home.</u> "I guess I'll have to wait until tomorrow to buy the bicycle," he said.

Teaching Chart 103

MODEL I know that fantasy means things that cannot happen in real life. The first paragraph is realistic because it tells about a boy buying things at a store—something that could happen in real life. The second paragraph is a fantasy; elephants can't talk and people don't have wings.

PRACTICE

Identifying Fantasy and Reality

GROUP

Have volunteers underline examples of events on **Teaching Chart 103** that are fantasy. Then contrast these elements with the events that could happen in real life. Encourage children to offer suggestions on how to change the fantasy elements into realistic events.
▶ **Linguistic/Logical**

ASSESS/CLOSE

Create Fantasy and Reality Scenarios

Invite pairs to choose a subject. One partner can write a short description or draw a real picture of the subject while the other writes or draws a fantastical version of the same thing. Invite children to read their descriptions aloud or display their illustrations as classmates call out their thoughts on which scenes are fantasies and which are realistic. ▶ **Linguistic/Logical**

DAILY **Phonics** ROUTINES

DAY 5

Writing Invite partners to write questions that can be answered with a word ending in /ər/, /ən/, or /əl//, /ē/, /e/; or silent letters. Then they can exchange papers and answer the other's question.

  CD-ROM

ALTERNATE TEACHING STRATEGY

FANTASY AND REALITY

For a different approach to teaching this skill, see page T67.

i **Intervention** **Skills**

Intervention Guide, for direct instruction and extra practice of fantasy and reality

Meeting Individual Needs for Comprehension

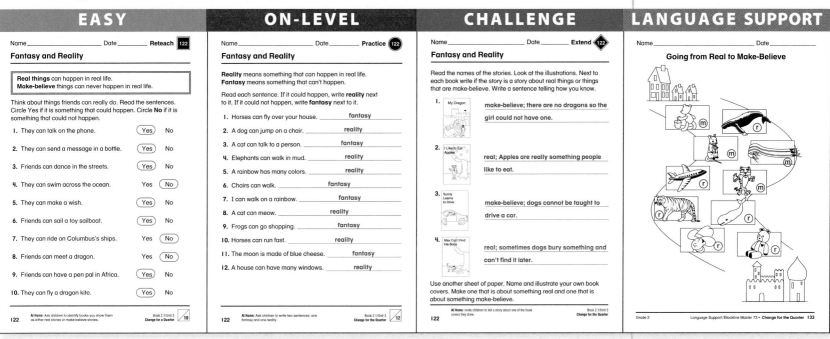

EASY	ON-LEVEL	CHALLENGE	LANGUAGE SUPPORT

Reteach, 122   Practice, 122   Extend, 122   Language Support, 133

OBJECTIVES

Children will recognize and understand synonyms.

MATERIALS

• **Teaching Chart 104**

Skills Finder

Synonyms

Introduce	B1: 341K-L
Review	B1: 369K-L, 379I-J
Test	B1: Unit 3

TEACHING TIP

SYNONYMS Explain to children that synonyms are especially useful in making a piece of writing more interesting; synonyms help a writer to avoid using the same word over and over, which can be boring to the reader.

Review Synonyms

PREPARE

Recognize Synonyms

Remind children that synonyms are words that have the same meaning or nearly the same meaning as each other. Write on the board the following groups of words. Help children to recognize the word in each group that is not a synonym—it does not have the same meaning as the other words.

• big, large, huge, thin

• small, little, easy, tiny

• think, cold, chilly, cool

TEACH

Read the Passage and Model the skill

Display **Teaching Chart 104.** Track the first sentence as you read it aloud, pausing at the word *happy*. Continue reading, asking children to raise their hand when they hear the word that is a synonym of *happy*. If necessary, use facial expression and tone of voice to help convey the meaning of the words *happy* and *glad*.

Let's Go

"You look very <u>happy</u>," I said to my sister.

"I am," she answered. "I'm <u>glad</u> that it's such a <u>beautiful</u> day, and I have a few <u>quarters</u> to spend."

"It is <u>pretty</u> outside," I replied. "Why don't we take a <u>stroll</u> down to the corner store? Then we can buy something."

"A <u>walk</u> would be nice," she said. "Do you have any <u>change</u> so we can buy a magazine?" "I do have some <u>coins</u> in my pocket," I answered. "Let's go!"

Teaching Chart 104

MODEL I know that synonyms are words that mean the same thing or almost the same thing. I know that the word *happy* means that someone is in a good mood. The word *glad* means basically the same thing. *Happy* and *glad* are synonyms.

PRACTICE

Identify Synonym Pairs

PARTNERS

Have partners use **Teaching Chart 104** to continue identifying synonym pairs. If necessary, underline one of the words in the pair that they should find the synonym for: *beautiful (pretty), stroll (walk),* and *change (coins).* Have volunteers identify synonym pairs and then write the pairs on the chalkboard. Children may include quarters as a synonym of *change* or *coins.*

ASSESS/CLOSE

Synonym Riddles

Invite children to create sentences that use one word of a synonym pair and include a blank space into which the other synonym can be added. Example: *I had never seen such a big tree. It was really _____. (huge)* Have partners exchange papers and try to fill in the blanks. Volunteers can read aloud their completed sentences. Have the rest of the class listen closely and note the words they believe are synonyms.

ALTERNATE TEACHING STRATEGY

··

SYNONYMS

For a different approach to teaching this skill, see page T74.

Intervention ▶ **Skills**
Intervention Guide, for direct instruction and extra practice of synonyms

Meeting Individual Needs for Comprehension

EASY	ON-LEVEL	CHALLENGE	LANGUAGE SUPPORT

EASY — Reteach, 123

Name_____ Date_____ **Reteach** 123

Synonyms

> **Synonyms** are words that have the same or nearly the same meaning.

Read each sentence. Then circle the word or words that are synonyms for the underlined word.

1. The quarter in your pocket will look different in just a few years.
   a. twenty-five cent piece
   b. nickel
   c. one dollar bill

2. People all over the world collect coins from other countries.
   a. city
   b. globe
   c. United States

3. All the students are excited about the next class trip to the museum.
   a. angry
   b. happy
   c. tired

4. In 2008 we will all look at the first new quarter.
   a. see
   b. lose
   c. find

5. Tim will use all his change to buy a book for Sam's birthday.
   a. cards
   b. carts
   c. coins

6. I hope to visit my grandparents in the summer.
   a. stay
   b. have
   c. wish

Book 2.1/Unit 3
Change for the Quarter

At Home: Ask children to find three words in a book for which they can think of synonyms.

123

ON-LEVEL — Practice, 123

Name_____ Date_____ **Practice** 123

Synonyms

Synonyms are words with the same or nearly the same meaning.

Read each group of words in column 1. Then draw a line to the word in column 2 that is a synonym for the word in dark print.

Column 1
1. the **tiny** mouse
2. the **shining** light
3. the **large** building
4. **run** down the hill
5. **lift** up the heavy books
6. the **happy** baby
7. the **playful** kitten
8. **sliding** down the hall

Column 2
1. big
2. glowing
3. raise
4. smiling
5. small
6. active
7. slipping
8. race

Book 2.1/Unit 3
Change for the Quarter

At Home: Encourage children to read a paragraph of a favorite story. Then ask them to identify synonyms for four of the words in the story.

123

CHALLENGE — Extend, 123

Name_____ Date_____ **Extend** 123

Synonyms

Each of the words in the box means the same or almost the same as one of the words below. Sort the words into groups that show their meaning. Use a dictionary if you need help.

fine	glad	quick
rapid	witty	irate
excellent	quit	delighted
angry	halt	joyful
cease	furious	silly
speedy	comical	capable

1. fast
   quick
   rapid
   speedy

2. funny
   witty
   silly
   comical

3. happy
   glad
   delighted
   joyful

4. mad
   irate
   angry
   furious

5. stop
   quit
   halt
   cease

6. good
   fine
   excellent
   capable

Book 2.1/Unit 3
Change for the Quarter

At Home: Show children how to use a thesaurus to find synonyms and antonyms for familiar words.

123

LANGUAGE SUPPORT — Language Support, 134

Name_____ Date_____

Jumble Fun

1. coins
   ahencg
   _____
   change

2. own
   aevh
   _____
   have

3. date
   yda
   _____
   day

4. all
   rvyee
   _____
   every

5. grab
   keat
   _____
   take

6. stripe
   enli
   _____
   line

7. below
   drune
   _____
   under

8. world
   reath
   _____
   earth

134 Change for the Quarter • Language Support/Blackline Master 74

Grade 2

Reteach, 123   Practice, 123   Extend, 123   Language Support, 134

OBJECTIVES

Children will review how to use syntax clues (word order) and context clues to figure out meanings of words.

MATERIALS
• Teaching Chart 105

Skills Finder

Context Clues

Introduce	B1: 91K-L
Review	B1: 113K-L, 123I-J, 289K-L B2: 379K-L
Test	B1: Unit 1
Maintain	B1: 311, 327; B2: 51, 83

TEACHING TIP

WORD ORDER Have children work in small groups. Ask them to describe one feature of the classroom. Have each group write their sentence on a sentence strip. Then have children cut the strips into words and scramble the words. Challenge other groups to try to form a sentence out of the words.

Review Context Clues

PREPARE

Discuss Word Order Write on the board the following sentences: *Ellen earned a quarter. Earned Ellen a quarter.*

Ask children which sentence make sense and why. (the first sentence, because of the order of the words) Explain that in English, the subject—what the sentence is about—often comes before the verb—what the subject does. Tell children that using word order and context clues can help them determine the meaning of an unfamiliar word.

TEACH

Read the Passage Model the Skill Display **Teaching Chart 105** and read aloud with children. Have children look for clues that can help them figure out the meaning of the italicized words. Model how to use syntax and context clues to determine the meaning of these unfamiliar words.

Coin Collecting

There are many reasons why people decide to become coin collectors. Some people *profit* from collecting coins, making money when they sell the coins at a later time. Other collectors *display* coins in order to show their beauty. Still others collect coins to find out more about *famous* people who were an important part of a country's history.

Whatever a person's reason for becoming a collector, he or she should *research,* or look up information, about coins. The more you learn about something you like, the more you will *enjoy* it.

Teaching Chart 105

MODEL I'm not sure what the word *profit* means. I see that it comes after the subject of the sentence and tells what "some people" do. So *profit* must be a verb. The next part of the sentence tells that the people make money when they sell the coins. So *profit* must mean "to make money."

PRACTICE

Identify Context and Syntax Clues

Invite volunteers to underline on **Teaching Chart 105** the context clues that help them understand the meaning of *display, famous, profit, research,* and *enjoy.* Encourage them to tell how they used word order or other words in the sentence to discover the meaning of the unfamiliar word. ▶ **Interpersonal/Linguistic**

ASSESS/CLOSE

Write Sentences

Have children choose two of the five unfamiliar words from "Coin Collecting." Have them write two sentences using the words. Remind children to use context clues and word order to show the meaning of each word.

ALTERNATE TEACHING STRATEGY

CONTEXT CLUES

For a different approach to teaching this skill, see T68.

---

i **Intervention** ▶ **Skills**
Intervention Guide, for direct instruction and extra practice of context clues

---

Meeting Individual Needs for Vocabulary

EASY	ON-LEVEL	CHALLENGE	LANGUAGE SUPPORT

EASY

Name_____ Date_____ Reteach **124**

Context Clues

You can figure out the meaning of an unknown word by using **context clues.** These are words that come before or after the unknown word. You can find these clues in the same sentence or in nearby sentences.

Read the sentences. Then circle the word or words that are clues to the meaning of the word in dark print.

1. Lisa wants to make a new **design,** or plan, for her model boat.
   a. model boat
   b. (plan)

2. The students are so **excited** about the class play that they start to cheer.
   a. (they start to cheer)
   b. the class play

3. In the summer we went **hiking** along the trail in the state park.
   a. in the summer
   b. (along the trail)

4. I wanted to have an **adventure** by doing something fun and different.
   a. (doing something fun and different)
   b. I wanted to have

5. The desert plant, or **cactus,** grew tall in the sunshine without much water.
   a. (desert plant)
   b. much water

6. In the afternoon I heard Lisa playing beautiful **music** on her piano.
   a. (playing on her piano)
   b. in the afternoon

At Home: Ask children to find a sentence in a book with a new word and context clues to tell what the word means.

124   Book 2.1/Unit 3 Change for the Quarter **6**

Reteach, 124

ON-LEVEL

Name_____ Date_____ Practice **124**

Context Clues

Context clues are words in a sentence or story that help you figure out the meaning of a new word. Context clues can come before or after the unknown word.

Read each sentence. Look at the word in dark print. Then underline the clue words that help you figure out what the word in dark print means.

1. Rose stayed in bed because she had a bad **cold.**

2. I cooked the **stew** on top of the stove.

3. Pete put all the letters in the **mailbox.**

4. When our team won the baseball game we all **cheered.**

5. Lisa **painted** a picture of the birds in the park.

6. I can't **reach** the book because it's on a high shelf.

7. All the runners will take part in the **race.**

8. In the spring all the flowers in the garden will **bloom.**

At Home: Ask students to use each of the following words in an original sentence: bright, favorite, music. Remind them to include clue words that explain the meaning of the word.

124   Book 2.1/Unit 3 Change for the Quarter **8**

Practice, 124

CHALLENGE

Name_____ Date_____ Extend **124**

Context Clues

Look at the picture. Use the clues in the picture to write a story about what the bears are doing. Give your story a title.

Title: _____

_____
_____
_____
_____
_____
_____
_____

At Home: Have children read their stories aloud. Invite them to point out details in the picture that they used in their stories.

124   Book 2.1/Unit 3 Change for the Quarter

Extend, 124

LANGUAGE SUPPORT

Name_____ Date_____

What Does It Mean?

Sam is prepared to talk about his coins. He knows what he will say.

(ready)   next   easy

He displays his coins to the class.

money   (shows)   sends

"I like this one," he stated.

(said)   best   pointed

They enjoyed hearing his talk.

class   (liked)   good

Grade 2   Language Support/Blackline Master 75 • Change for the Quarter **135**

Language Support, 135

GRAMMAR/SPELLING
CONNECTIONS
See the 5-Day Grammar and
Usage Plan on pages
379O–379P.

See the 5-Day Spelling Plan on
pages 379Q–379R.

Explanatory Writing

Write a How-To Article

Prewrite

WRITE A HOW-TO ARTICLE Present this writing assignment: Is there something that you collect or would like to collect? Write an article for a magazine about collecting. Explain how someone can start his or her own collection. Give three steps to follow.

BRAINSTORM IDEAS Have children brainstorm a list of things people might collect, or things they would like to collect. Then have children choose the item that interests them the most.

Strategy: Make a List Have children create lists of information about the items they have chosen. Remind them to consider adding information about why someone might want to collect that item, where they would find it, and what they would do with their collections.

Draft

FREE WRITE Encourage children to write freely, using the information from their lists. Remind them to outline the steps for beginning the collection in a clear, logical order, and to include details that show why it would be fun to collect this item. Explain to children that adding background information about the item or personal experience with collecting it will make the article more lively and interesting.

Revise

SELF-QUESTIONING Ask children to assess their drafts.

- Did I clearly outline three steps to begin the collection?
- Did I include details that show why people would want to collect this item?
- Can I add any information that would make my article more interesting and effective?

Edit/Proofread

CHECK FOR ERRORS Children should reread their articles to check their spelling, grammar, and punctuation. They may wish to exchange papers with a classmate who can also proofread the work.

Publish

SHARE THE ARTICLES Invite children to exchange articles with others in the classroom. Then have children meet and discuss whether they felt the articles interested them enough to begin collections of their own.

HOW TO START A DOLL COLLECTION

Deciding what you want to collect is the first step to starting a collection. Arlene Matthews, a second grader from Memphis, Tennessee, began collecting dolls when she was in first grade. "My grandmother gave me a doll that belonged to her as a kid," Arlene explained. After that she wanted more dolls from the past.

The next step is to begin the search for dolls. People have found dolls at yard sales, in people's attics, and in second-hand stores.

The third step to starting a doll collection is deciding where to keep your dolls. Some people like to keep dolls on shelves in a bedroom. Others keep them in a case. Wherever you keep them, be sure the dolls are in a safe place, and that people can see them and enjoy them.

TEACHING TIP

Technology
A spell-checker will often identify names of people or places as incorrect, even if they are spelled correctly. If the spell-checker identifies a name as incorrect, look it up in another resource to verify the correct spelling. If correct, children may add the name into the spell-checker.

Paragraphs
When writing about more than one idea, each idea should have its own paragraph. As thoughts or ideas change, start a new paragraph.

**Handwriting
CD-ROM**

Presentation Ideas

MAKE A SPEECH Have children present their articles as speeches to others who want to begin collections. Encourage the audience to listen closely and ask questions about collecting. ▶ **Speaking/Listening**

ILLUSTRATE YOUR COLLECTION Encourage children to create a picture of the collection to go with their how-to article.
▶ **Viewing/Representing**

Listening and Speaking

LISTENING Have children

- listen for details about collecting the items.
- determine if this type of collection is practical for them.
- form questions that are related to the presentation.

SPEAKING Remind children to

- show enthusiasm by varying their voice.
- refer to their picture while explaining the collection.
- ask genuine questions about other presentations.

Consider children's creative efforts, possibly adding a plus (+) for originality, wit, and imagination.

Scoring Rubric

Excellent	Good	Fair	Unsatisfactory
4: The writer	**3:** The writer	**2:** The writer	**1:** The writer
• uses rich language to clearly describe the three steps to begin a collection.	• clearly describes the three steps to begin a collection.	• describes steps to begin a collection, but they may not be clear or orderly.	• does not show three clear steps to start the collection.
• uses details to show why people may want to collect this item.	• uses some details to show why some people may want to collect this item.	• uses few details to explain why people would want to collect this item.	• does not include details to show why someone would want to collect this item.
• use lively descriptions of personal experience that enriches the article.	• includes some descriptions of personal experience or background information.	• doesn't include any additional information to enhance the article.	• is disorganized and includes extraneous or irrelevant information.

Incomplete 0: The writer leaves the page blank or fails to respond to the writing task. The writer does not address the topic or simply paraphrases the prompt. The response is illegible or incoherent.

LANGUAGE SUPPORT

 If children are having trouble getting started, show pictures of common collectibles. Ask which of these they might like to collect. On the chalkboard, write the names of any items children choose to write about.

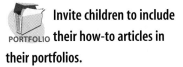 Invite children to include PORTFOLIO their how-to articles in their portfolios.

Meeting Individual Needs for Writing

EASY	**ON-LEVEL**	**CHALLENGE**
Draw Collectibles Encourage children to draw pictures of things one might collect. Then encourage them to write sentences about their pictures.	**Interview** Invite children to interview other children or family members about collections they may have. Then have children write articles based on the interviews.	**Another Point of View** Suggest that children pretend to be an item in a collection. Have them write a first-person account of escaping from the collection, and what it was like on the "outside."

5 Day Grammar and Usage Plan

ESL When introducing sentence combining to ESL students, write the two sentences on the chalkboard. Then cross out the subject of the second sentence and write the word *and* above it.

DAILY LANGUAGE ACTIVITIES

Write each day's activities on the board or use **Transparency 15**. Students combine sentences orally. Answers given for Day 1; remaining answers follow the same pattern.

Day 1
1. Dan saved. Dan spent. Dan saved and spent.
2. Nina collects coins. Nina keeps coins. Nina collects and keeps coins.
3. People find coins. People lose coins. People find and lose coins.

Day 2
1. He gets the change. He keeps the change.
2. The dime fell. The dime rolled away.
3. Tim buys coins. Tim sells coins.

Day 3
1. Pam lost a penny. Pam found a penny.
2. People start saving. People stop saving.
3. We collect quarters. We use quarters.

Day 4
1. I can toss a coin. I can catch a coin.
2. He sees the change. He adds the change.
3. Quarters come. Quarters go.

Day 5
1. Pat saves money. Pat spends money.
2. Jay buys the toy. Jay returns the toy.
3. The eagle is going away. The eagle is coming back.

Daily Language Transparency 15

DAY 1 — Introduce the Concept

Oral Warm-Up Tell children to raise their hands and then clap. For each action, ask: What did you do? Write the answers on the board: *We raised our hands. We clapped.* Model combining the two sentences by using *and*.

Introduce Sentence Combining Invite children to share what they know about sentence combining. Review:

> ### Sentence Combining
> - If two sentences have words that are the same, you can combine them.
> - You can combine sentences by joining words with *and.*

Present the Daily Language Activity. Ask children to write two sentences describing two actions by the same person. Then have them combine the two sentences into one by using *and.* Have volunteers read aloud their combined sentences.

 WRITING Assign the daily Writing Prompt on page 370C.

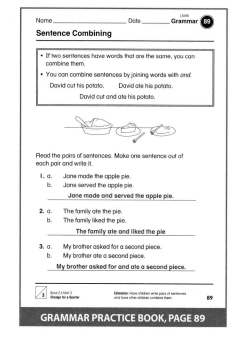

GRAMMAR PRACTICE BOOK, PAGE 89

DAY 2 — Teach the Concept

Review Sentence Combining Write these sentences on the board and read them aloud: *Mike sits in a chair. Mike reads a book.* Ask children to combine the sentences by using the word *and.*

Introduce Combining Predicates Have children identify the predicate of each sentence above. Point out that they combined the predicates of two different sentences into one. Present:

> ### Sentence Combining
> Sometimes you can combine sentences by joining two predicates with *and.*

Present the Daily Language Activity. Then have children write two simple sentences about the same subject and combine them using *and.* Have them circle the subject and underline the two predicates combined with the word *and.*

 WRITING Assign the daily Writing Prompt on page 370C.

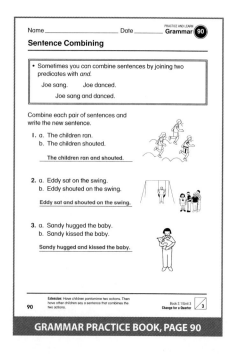

GRAMMAR PRACTICE BOOK, PAGE 90

Sentence Combining

DAY 3 — Review and Practice

Learn from the Literature Review sentence combining. Read aloud the following sentences from page 373 of *Change for the Quarter*.

> The first new quarters have already come out. They honor the states of Connecticut, Delaware, Georgia, New Jersey, and Pennsylvania.

Help children combine the two sentences by using *and*. (The first new quarters have already come out and honor the states of Connecticut, Delaware, Georgia, New Jersey, and Pennsylvania.)

Combine Sentences Present the Daily Language Activity. Then ask each child to write two sentences with the same subject. Have them trade with partners and combine each other's sentences into one by using the word *and*.

WRITING Assign the daily Writing Prompt on page 370D.

DAY 4 — Review and Practice

Review Sentence Combining Write the sentences from the Daily Language Activity for Day 3 on the chalkboard. Ask children to identify the predicates and explain how they combined them. Then present the Daily Language Activity for Day 4.

Mechanics and Usage Before children begin the daily Writing Prompt, review:

Sentence Punctuation

- Begin every sentence with a capital letter.
- End statements and commands with a period.
- End a question with a question mark.
- End an exclamation with an exclamation point.

WRITING Assign the daily Writing Prompt on page 370D.

DAY 5 — Assess and Reteach

Assess Use the Daily Language Activity and page 93 of the **Grammar Practice Book** for assessment.

Reteach Divide the class into small groups of three children each. In each group, one child writes a simple sentence describing an action by a person. The second child writes a sentence describing another action by the same person. The third child combines the two sentences by using the word *and*. Have the group work together to make a picture card illustrating the combined sentence. Display the children's picture cards on a bulletin board.

Use page 94 of the **Grammar Practice Book** for additional reteaching.

WRITING Assign the daily Writing Prompt on page 370D.

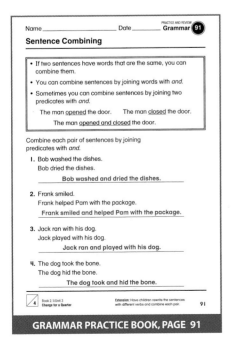

GRAMMAR PRACTICE BOOK, PAGE 91

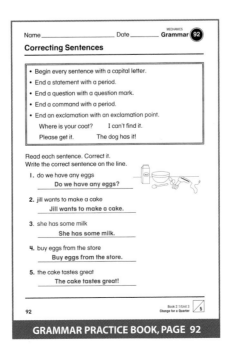

GRAMMAR PRACTICE BOOK, PAGE 92

Name _____ Date _____ Grammar 93

Sentence Combining

Read each pair of sentences. Combine them. Write the sentence.

1. The windows have dust.
   The windows need to be cleaned.
   The windows have dust and need to be cleaned.

2. We washed the windows.
   We wiped the window sills.
   We washed the windows and wiped the window sills.

3. Bill swept the floor.
   Bill washed the floor.
   Bill swept and washed the floor.

4. Kim raked the leaves.
   Kim cleaned the yard.
   Kim raked the leaves and cleaned the yard.

5. The house looks clean.
   The house is ready for the party.
   The house looks clean and is ready for the party.

Book 2.1/Unit 3
Change for a Quarter   93

GRAMMAR PRACTICE BOOK, PAGE 93
GRAMMAR PRACTICE BOOK, PAGE 94

5 Day Spelling Plan

LANGUAGE SUPPORT

To help students distinguish between words with one and more than one syllable, say the names of students in the class. Have students repeat each name, clapping out each syllable as they say each word.

DICTATION SENTENCES

Spelling Words

1. I made a dollar.
2. The doll cost a penny.
3. I know the exact place.
4. They can buy a house.
5. He has one cent.
6. She has a dime.
7. The price is on the toy.
8. The girl found a quarter.
9. The sum is high.
10. The nickel is new.

Challenge Words

11. I collect flags.
12. He had no honor.
13. They can order the bike for you.
14. My dress has a pocket.
15. That toy is not worth a penny.

DAY 1 — Pretest

Assess Prior Knowledge Use the Dictation Sentences at left and **Spelling Practice Book** page 89, for the pretest. Allow students to correct their own papers. If students have trouble, have partners give each other a midweek test on Day 3. Students who require a modified list may be tested on the first five words.

Spelling Words		Challenge Words
1. dollar	6. dime	11. **collect**
2. cost	7. price	12. **honor**
3. exact	8. **quarter**	13. **order**
4. buy	9. sum	14. **pocket**
5. **cent**	10. nickel	15. **worth**

*Note: Words in **dark type** are from the story.*

Word Study On page 90 of the **Spelling Practice Book** are word study steps and an at-home activity.

DAY 2 — Explore the Pattern

Sort and Spell Say the words *dime* and *nickel* slowly and clearly. Ask students to identify the number of syllables they hear in each word.

Ask students to read aloud the ten Spelling Words before sorting them according to the number of syllables.

Words with one syllable	Words with two syllables
cost	dollar
buy	exact
cent	quarter
dime	nickel
price	
sum	

Word Wall Have students think of other words related to math and add them to the classroom word wall, underlining the syllables in each word with different colored pencils.

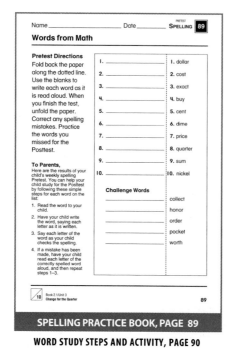

SPELLING PRACTICE BOOK, PAGE 89

WORD STUDY STEPS AND ACTIVITY, PAGE 90

SPELLING PRACTICE BOOK, PAGE 91

Words from Math

Word Meaning: Words From Math

Remind students that the Spelling Words, including *dollar*, *cost*, *dime*, and *quarter*, are all words that are related to math. Have them make up a definition for each word. See how many other math-related words students can think of (*add*, *subtract*, *plus*, *minus*, *money*, and so on.)

Glossary Tell students that example sentences in the Glossary show how words are used. Have students:

- write each Challenge Word.

- look up each word in the Glossary and find one or more example sentences.

- write one example sentence from the Glossary for each word.

- write their own example sentence for each word.

Proofread Sentences Write these sentences on the chalkboard, including the misspelled words. Ask students to proofread, circling incorrect spellings and writing the correct spellings. There are two spelling errors in each sentence.

The ~~cozt~~ is a ~~doller~~. (cost, dollar)

The ~~prise~~ is a ~~dyme~~. (price, dime)

Have students create additional sentences with errors for partners to correct.

Writing Have students use as many Spelling Words as possible in the daily Writing Prompt on page 370D. Remind students to proofread their writing for errors in spelling, grammar, and punctuation.

Assess Students' Knowledge Use page 94 of the **Spelling Practice Book** or the Dictation Sentences on page 379Q for the posttest.

Personal Word List If students have trouble with any words in the lesson, have them create a personal list of troublesome words in their journals. Have students write a simple story about a shopping trip, using some of the words from their personal word lists.

Students should refer to their word lists during later writing activities.

Name _____ Date _____ **SPELLING 92**

Words from Math

| dollar | exact | cent | price | sum |
| cost | buy | dime | quarter | nickel |

Write the spelling words that are names for money.

1. dollar 2. cent
3. dime 4. quarter
5. nickel

Write the spelling words besides **buy** that tell about buying things.

6. cost 7. price

Write the spelling word that means "correct" to complete the sentence.

8. The man in the store gave me _____ exact change for a dollar.

Answer these questions with a spelling word. Write the word on the line.

9. Which is more money: a dollar or a quarter? dollar

10. Which is less money: a dime or a cent? cent

11. A dollar is the same as 4 _____ quarters

12. A dollar is the same as 10 _____ dimes

SPELLING PRACTICE BOOK, PAGE 92

Name _____ Date _____ **SPELLING 93**

Words from Math

Proofreading Activity
There are six spelling mistakes in the story below. Circle each misspelled word. Write the words correctly on the lines below.

Carlos wanted a yo-yo. He saw one he liked at the store. The tag showed the ~~eggzact~~ price: $1.25. Carlos looked in his pocket. He had one ~~doller~~ and one ~~qarter~~. He felt really happy that he could buy the yo-yo.

Carlos gave the money to the saleslady.

She smiled at him and said, "This ~~costz~~ one dollar and thirty-five ~~cents~~."

Carlos was surprised. "I just have this much," he said.

"Sorry," said the lady. "You must give me another ~~diem~~." You forgot the tax."

Carlos was lucky. He found the coin in another pocket and bought the yo-yo.

1. exact 2. dollar 3. quarter
4. costs 5. cents 6. dime

Writing Activity
Write about buying something. Tell how much it cost. Tell how many dollars and cents you paid. Use four of your spelling words. Circle the words you use.

SPELLING PRACTICE BOOK, PAGE 93

Name _____ Date _____ **SPELLING 94**

Words from Math

Look at the words in each set. One word in each set is spelled right. Use a pencil to color in the circle in front of that word. Before you begin, look at the sample sets of words. Sample A has been done for you. Do Sample B by yourself. When you are sure you know what to do, you may go on with the rest of the page.

Sample A
- Ⓐ one ●
- Ⓑ wun
- Ⓒ onne

Sample B
- Ⓓ penny ●
- Ⓔ peny
- Ⓕ pennie

1.
- Ⓐ dolar
- Ⓑ dollar ●
- Ⓒ doller

2.
- Ⓓ kost
- Ⓔ cawst
- Ⓕ cost ●

3.
- Ⓐ eggzact
- Ⓑ eggsact
- Ⓒ exact ●

4.
- Ⓓ buy ●
- Ⓔ bi
- Ⓕ biy

5.
- Ⓐ sentt
- Ⓑ cent ●
- Ⓒ scente

6.
- Ⓓ diem
- Ⓔ dym
- Ⓕ dime ●

7.
- Ⓐ prise
- Ⓑ price ●
- Ⓒ pris

8.
- Ⓓ sume
- Ⓔ qarter
- Ⓕ corter

9.
- Ⓐ sume
- Ⓑ som
- Ⓒ sum ●

10.
- Ⓓ nickle
- Ⓔ nickel ●
- Ⓕ nikel

SPELLING PRACTICE BOOK, PAGE 94

379R

Wrap Up the Theme

Express Yourself
We share our ideas in many ways.

REVIEW THE THEME Remind children that all the selections in this unit relate to the theme Express Yourself. Encourage children to tell how the characters in the selections expressed themselves. Were children at all surprised by the characters' choice of expression?

READ THE POEM Read aloud "Time to Play" by Nikki Grimes. As they listen, ask children to think about what the narrator wants to do and what she actually does. After reading, discuss how the poem connects to the theme Express Yourself. Remind children that people express themselves in many ways, including in the games they play and the way in which they play them.

Reread the poem, and ask children to echo the last word in each line. Encourage them to listen for the rhymes.

 LISTENING LIBRARY Children can listen to an audio recording of the poem.

 **MAKE CONNECTIONS** Have children work in small groups to brainstorm a list of ways that the stories, poems, and the *Time for Kids* magazine article relate to the theme Express Yourself. Groups can then compare their lists as they share them with the class.

Time to Play

Mama says to play outside.
Wish I had a bike to ride.
I'll fly to the moon instead.
Steer the rocket in my head.
I'll pretend to find a star
no one else has seen so far.
Then I'll name it after me —
          Africa Lawanda Lee!
But for now I'll grab some chalk,
play hopscotch out on the walk.

by Nikki Grimes

380

LOOKING AT GENRE

Have children review *Nine-in-One, Grr! Grr!* and *Best Wishes, Ed.* What makes *Nine-in-One, Grr! Grr!* a folktale? What makes *Best Wishes, Ed* a fantasy?

Help children list the key characteristics of each literary form. Can they name other stories that are folktales and fantasy with these same characteristics?

FOLKTALES *Nine-in-One, Grr! Grr!*	FANTASY *Best Wishes, Ed*
• Characters are animals.	• Characters are animals that do things only humans could do.
• Characters' actions could not happen in real life.	• Characters' problems would not happen in real life.
• Tale offers an explanation for an occurrence in nature.	

381

Research and Inquiry

Complete the Theme Project Have children work in teams to complete their group project. Remind children that the information they have gathered can be presented in any form they choose. Encourage them to share the tasks of researching, writing, and visual presentation so that each member of the team can contribute to the project.

Make a Classroom Presentation Have teams take turns presenting their projects. Remind children that using facial expressions and hand gestures at the right moment can help capture the attention of the listeners. Be sure to include time for questions from the audience.

Draw Conclusions Have children draw conclusions about what they learned from researching and presenting their projects. Was the resource chart they made helpful? What other resources, such as the Internet, did they use? What conclusions did they reach? Finally, ask children if what they learned from their research helped them better understand clouds and weather.

Ask More Questions What additional questions do children now have about clouds? You might encourage the teams to continue their research and prepare another presentation that would include charts showing the variety of clouds that appeared in their own community sky during a given period.

LEARNING ABOUT POETRY

Literary Devices: Rhyme Pattern and Rhythm Point out the aa, bb, cc, dd, ee rhyme pattern by having children name the rhyming words. Then have them clap as they read aloud to feel the driving rhythm that the rhyme scheme creates. Ask children how they feel about this rhyme pattern. Does it make the poem more fun to read?

Poetry Activity Have children write a poem about how they express their own thoughts, feelings, or ideas. They can use the same format as "Time to Play," or you may choose to model another poem for them to follow.

381

Reading Media

People can get information from newspapers, billboards, television, and magazines. They are all examples of *media*. To better understand media, think about how each form is alike and different. The chart below will help you to do this.

Media	Print	Pictures	Sound
Television	●	●	●
Billboard	●	●	
Newspaper	●	●	
Magazine	●	●	

Comparing Forms of Information

① **Preview the media.** Identify what kinds of media they are.

② **Look at how each kind of media gives information.** How are they alike? Which ones use print? color? pictures? sound?

③ **Look for differences.** Find ways that each kind of media is different.

④ **Think about what you have learned.** What new information did you learn from comparing different kinds of media?

394 *Reading for Information*

Billboards and Newspapers

A billboard is a large outdoor sign. It uses print and pictures to get our attention.

A newspaper is printed on sheets of paper. It contains up-to-date news, pictures, and advertisements.

① **Preview the media.** The two different kinds of media here are a billboard and a newspaper.

② **Look at each kind of media.** Both the billboard and newspaper use print and pictures.

③ **Think about what you learned.** A newspaper and a billboard can provide the same information in different ways.

④ **Look for differences.** The billboard is much larger than the newspaper.

Reading Media 395

Anthology pages 394–395

Reading Media

OBJECTIVES Children will:

- identify four types of mass media: billboards, television, newspapers, and magazines.
- recognize that media may contain a message that can influence how one thinks and feels.
- learn effective strategies to use in reading media including use of **text features**, such as pictures or illustrations.

INTRODUCE Ask children to describe billboards, television commercials, and magazine or newspaper ads they have seen. Then have them **preview** page 394. Explain that this lesson will help them better understand messages in media. *(Set Purposes)*

PRACTICE/APPLY Have children preview, note pictures, read, and discuss page 395. Draw their attention to the callouts, then discuss these questions:

- **Are there clues in the pictures or the words?** (both)
- **What are some other things you know about seatbelts?** (Example: Both adults and children must wear them.)
- **Is this message telling you something? What?** (Everyone should wear seatbelts.) **Is this message trying to sell something?** (no)

Explain: Point out that this billboard uses pictures and words to give important information. Explain that when reading media, we must look for clues and use what we already know to figure out what media is telling us.

Have children use the strategy on page 394 to read the media on pages 396–397. Ask them to answer the questions on page 397.

Television

Television uses moving pictures, sound, and print. Sometimes television sells a product. Sometimes television gives us information. How are a billboard and television alike?

Magazines

A magazine uses pictures and words. Sometimes a magazine gives us information. Sometimes it sells a product or idea.

Review Questions

1. Look at the television screen and the magazine page. How is the information that we get from them alike?
2. What is different about the information?
3. Why is it important to know how to compare different kinds of media?

Anthology pages 396–397

ANSWERS TO QUESTIONS

1. They are both telling us to wear seat belts to be safe.
2. One picture shows a catcher at play. The other shows a baby in a seat belt.
3. I need to understand the different kinds of information media messages give.

TRANSFER THE STRATEGY

Ask: How did the four steps on page 394 help you read the television screen and magazine ad?

Explain: Sometimes media messages provide information. Sometimes they are selling a product.

Discuss: Have children describe commercials and ads they have seen recently. Encourage them to discuss how they knew what the ad was selling.

Activity

What Is the Message?

What you will need:
- a magazine or newspaper ad
- a sheet of paper and a pencil

Answer these questions on your paper:
1. What is this ad selling?
2. What do the words and pictures tell you about the product?
3. What do you already know about the product?
4. How does the ad convince you to buy the product?

Now trade ads with a partner. Look at your partner's ad and read his or her answers. Would you answer in the same way? Why or why not?

381B

Explanatory Writing

CONNECT TO LITERATURE In *Best Wishes, Ed*, the author shows how writing can communicate important information. Discuss how clearly written instructions can teach people how to do all kinds of things. Have them make class notes for their portfolios.

GROUP

How To Water Plants

Watering plants is simple. You just need water and a pitcher or can. First, fill the pitcher or can with water. Only use as much water as you can carry without spilling it. Then, very slowly pour the water on the dirt around each plant. But don't add too much water, or the plants might drown!

Prewrite

PURPOSE AND AUDIENCE Tell children that they will write an article whose purpose is to inform the reader how to do a simple activity. As children write, encourage them to keep their purpose and audience in mind.

STRATEGY: MAKE A LIST Ask children to choose a familiar project for their article. Have them make a list of materials they will need and the steps their project will require.

Use **Writing Process Transparency 3A** as a model.

TEACHING TIP

ORGANIZATION Help students set up their project charts and list steps in a logical sequence. Ask them to think carefully of each step in the process, and match the right materials with each step.

FEATURES OF EXPLANATORY WRITING

- Informs or explains how to complete a specific task.
- Presents step-by-step instructions.
- Uses time-order words to help set up a logical sequence.

PREWRITE TRANSPARENCY

Washing the Dog

What You Need:	How to Do It:
1. One dog who needs a bath	1. Fill the tub
2. One bathtub	2. Catch the dog and put him in the tub
3. Dog toy	3. Rub the dog all over with shampoo
4. Dog shampoo	4. Rinse all the soap off
5. A towel	5. Wrap dog in a towel, before he shakes water all over you

McGraw-Hill School Division

Book 2.1/Unit 3: Explanatory Writing / Prewriting 3A

Explanatory Writing

Draft

STRATEGY: FREEWRITING Ask students to start with a topic sentence stating their activity. Encourage them to write freely, without self-editing. Invite them to explore humor in their explanations. Remind them to check their charts for project steps and materials.

Use **Writing Process Transparency 3B** to model a first draft.

WORD CHOICE Use the project to review time-order words. Write the following words on the board: *first, second, third, now, before, after, then, next, finally, following, while, meanwhile, last, during, not long,* and *when.* Review the list with children and then have them search through their explanations looking for any time-order words they used. Encourage children to include additional words from the list in their writing.

LANGUAGE SUPPORT

Some students may need help organizing their steps. Invite them to close their eyes and visualize doing the task themselves. Have them make storyboards illustrating each step in detail. Then, guide them to write captions under each drawing.

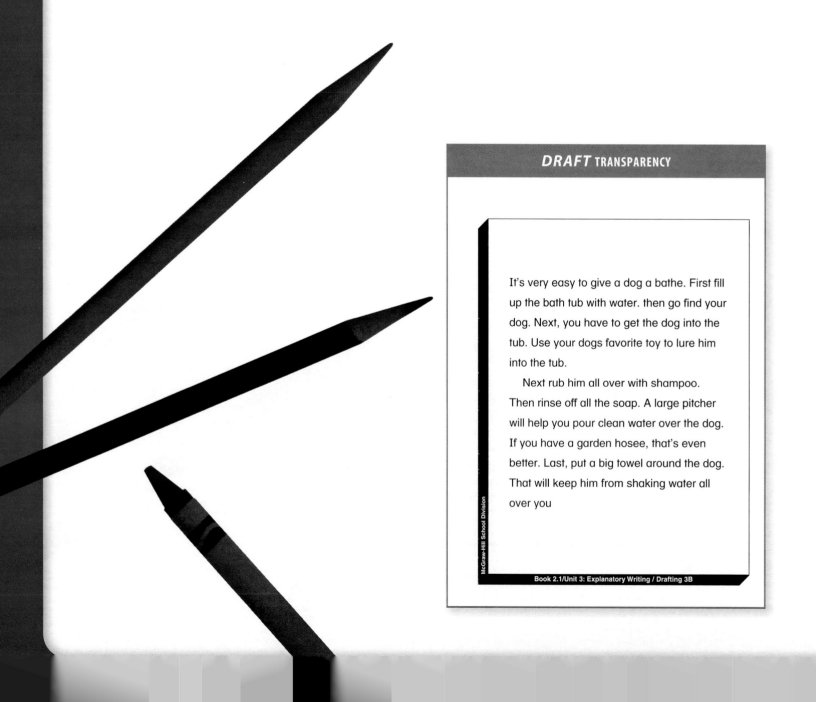

DRAFT TRANSPARENCY

It's very easy to give a dog a bathe. First fill up the bath tub with water. then go find your dog. Next, you have to get the dog into the tub. Use your dogs favorite toy to lure him into the tub.

Next rub him all over with shampoo. Then rinse off all the soap. A large pitcher will help you pour clean water over the dog. If you have a garden hosee, that's even better. Last, put a big towel around the dog. That will keep him from shaking water all over you

McGraw-Hill School Division

Book 2.1/Unit 3: Explanatory Writing / Drafting 3B

Revise

Guide students to check that their steps are written in an understandable order. Invite them to think of descriptive details or humorous observations to enliven their explanations.

Use **Writing Process Transparency 3C** for classroom discussion on the revision process. Ask students to comment on how revisions may have improved this writing example.

STRATEGY: ELABORATION Students can compare their first drafts with their prewriting lists to be sure they have included all the necessary steps and materials. Have them ask themselves the following questions:

• Have I made my project seem like it would be fun to do?

• What can I add to make the project steps clearer?

• If I've used humor, does it get in the way of the explanation?

• Can a reader follow the order of my ideas?

TEACHING TIP

TEACHER CONFERENCE
Talk with the class about ways to expand their articles. Offer concrete ideas for how they might incorporate more detail into each step. Encourage them to use a personal voice to make their writing feel alive on the page. Ask them:

• Do you think your explanation has enough step-by-step details? What could you add?

• Picture yourself doing the project. Have you written the idea as you imagine it?

• How can you bring your personality into the explanation?

REVISE TRANSPARENCY

Bathing Your Basset Hound

Does your dog need a bath?   with no help at all
It's very easy to give a dog a bathe. First fill
                                        warm
up the bath tub with water. then go find your

dog. Next, you have to get the dog into the

tub. Use your dogs favorite toy to lure him

into the tub.
Once the dog is wet, you can
    Next rub him all over with shampoo.

Then rinse off all the soap. A large pitcher

will help you pour clean water over the dog.

If you have a garden hosee, that's even

better. Last, put a big towel around the dog.

That will keep him from shaking water all

over you

McGraw-Hill School Division

Book 2.1/Unit 3: Explanatory Writing / Revising 3C

381F

Explanatory Writing

Edit/Proofread

After students finish revising their texts, have them proofread for final corrections and additions.

GRAMMAR/SPELLING
CONNECTIONS

See the 5-Day Grammar and Usage Plans on verbs, pp. 2890–289P,
pp. 3190–319P,
pp. 3410–341P,
pp. 3690–369P,
pp. 3790–379P.

See the 5-Day Spelling Plans, pp. 2890–289R,
pp. 3190–319R,
pp. 3410–341R,
pp. 3690–369R,
pp. 3790–379R.

GRAMMAR, MECHANICS, USAGE

- Use present-tense and past-tense verbs correctly.

- Use an apostrophe to form a possessive noun.

- Use commas to separate three or more words in a series.

Publish

Share the articles. Have students create titles for their articles and read them to the class.

Use **Writing Process Transparency 3D** as a proofreading model and **Writing Process Transparency 3E** to discuss presentation ideas.

PROOFREAD TRANSPARENCY

Bathing Your Basset Hound

¶ Does your dog need a bath?   with no help at all
It's very easy to give a dog a bath. First fill
                                    warm
up the bath tub with water. then go find your
dog. Next, you have to get the dog into the
tub. Use your dogs favorite toy to lure him
into the tub.
Once the dog is wet, you can
Next rub him all over with shampoo.
Then, rinse off all the soap. A large pitcher
will help you pour clean water over the dog.
If you have a garden hose, that's even
better. Last, put a big towel around the dog.
That will keep him from shaking water all
over you.

McGraw-Hill School Division

Book 2.1/Unit 3: Explanatory Writing / Proofreading 3D

PUBLISH TRANSPARENCY

Bathing Your Basset Hound

Does your dog need a bath? It's very
easy to give a dog a bath with no help at all.
First, fill up the bath tub with warm water.
Then, go find your dog. Next, you have to
get the dog into the tub. Use your dog's
favorite toy to lure him into the tub.

Once the dog is wet, you can rub him all
over with shampoo. Then, rinse off all the
soap. A large pitcher will help you pour
clean water over the dog. If you have a
garden hose, that's even better. Last, put a
big towel around the dog. That will keep him
from shaking water all over you.

McGraw-Hill School Division

Book 2.1/Unit 3: Explanatory Writing / Publishing 3E

Presentation Ideas

MAKE A CLASS NEWSLETTER Work with children to design a newsletter containing their articles. Encourage children to comment on the articles. Place a copy in the school library. ▶ **Representing/Speaking**

DO A "RADIO SHOW" Students can pretend to interview each other for a radio talk show. You can record the interviews and invite "audience" questions from classmates. ▶ **Listening/Speaking**

Assessment

SCORING RUBRIC When using the rubric, please consider students' creative efforts, possibly adding a plus (+) for originality, wit, and imagination.

Listening and Speaking

LISTENING STRATEGIES

• Face the speaker.

• Picture what the speaker is describing.

• Paraphrase the speaker's information by retelling it in your own words to a partner.

SPEAKING STRATEGIES

• Make eye contact with the audience.

• Speak clearly enough so everyone in the room can hear.

• Ask questions that engage the audience.

Scoring Rubric: 6-Trait Writing

4 Excellent	3 Good	2 Fair	1 Unsatisfactory
Ideas & Content • presents a focused, interesting how-to process, with a complete set of details.	**Ideas & Content** • presents a clear, interesting how-to process, with a set of details that show knowledge of the topic.	**Ideas & Content** • has some control of the how-to process, but may not offer clear or thorough details.	**Ideas & Content** • does not grasp the task to explain a process; writing may go off in several directions, without a sense of purpose.
Organization • clear, easy-to-follow time sequence moves the reader logically through the process; ideas and details make sense.	**Organization** • time sequence helps a reader to follow the process; well-placed details clarify the explanation.	**Organization** • tries to structure an explanation, but may have trouble sequencing steps; beginning or ending may be underdeveloped or missing.	**Organization** • shows extreme lack of organization; no clear beginning or ending; text is hard to follow.
Voice • strong personal style speaks directly to the reader, and enlivens the project content.	**Voice** • personal style addresses the reader, and shows who is behind the words.	**Voice** • states the main idea, with some hint of who is behind the words; may show little involvement with the process, or with an audience.	**Voice** • in uninvolved with the topic, text is lifeless, and lacks purpose and connection with a reader.
Word Choice • makes thoughtful use of accurate, specific language to create a vivid picture of the how-to process.	**Word Choice** • uses a variety of words that clarify steps in the process; experiments with some new words, or uses everyday words in a fresh way.	**Word Choice** • attempts to use few or no new words; does not explore words that create a clear picture of the how-to process.	**Word Choice** • writer has trouble finding words that fit; no new words are attempted.
Sentence Fluency • varied, effective sentences flow smoothly and add interest to the explanation.	**Sentence Fluency** • crafts careful, varied sentences that are easy to read and understand; sentences fit together naturally.	**Sentence Fluency** • sentences are understandable, but may be choppy or awkward; patterns may be repetitive or monotonous.	**Sentence Fluency** • constructs incomplete or confusing sentences; does not understand how words and sentences fit together .
Conventions • is skilled in most writing conventions; proper use of the rules of English enhances clarity and personal style; editing is largely unnecessary.	**Conventions** • uses a variety of conventions correctly; some editing may be needed; errors are few and don't detract from the meaning.	**Conventions** • makes frequent, noticeable errors which interfere with following the text.	**Conventions** • makes repeated errors in spelling, word choice, punctuation and usage; sentence structures may be confused; some parts may be impossible to follow.

0 Incomplete This piece is either blank, or fails to respond to the writing task. The topic is not addressed, or the child simply paraphrases the prompt. The response may be illegible or incoherent.

VOCABULARY

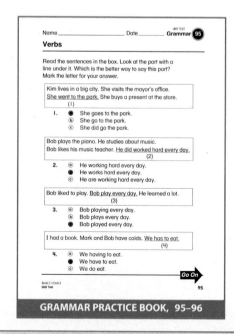

GROUP Divide the class into groups and assign one selection to each group. Each group creates and then tells a story using as many vocabulary words from its selection as it can. As soon as they hear a vocabulary word they know, the other groups must define it.

Unit Review

Arthur Writes a Story

decided   important   planet
float   library   proud

Best Wishes, Ed

climbed   drifted   message
couple   half   notice

The Pony Express

arrive   finished   rushed
early   record   success

Nine-in-One, Grr! Grr!

Earth   lonely   mountain
forget   memory   wonderful

Change for the Quarter

collect   join   pocket
honor   order   worth

Name _____ Date _____ Practice **125**

Unit 3 Vocabulary Review

A. The same vocabulary word is used twice in each example below. Write the words from the box on the lines.

library	pocket	rush

1. I went to the _____library_____ and took out a book. There are many books in the school _____library_____.

2. I was late, so I had to _____rush_____ to school. We'll have to _____rush_____ if we want to get there on time.

3. I have some nickels in my _____pocket_____. My jacket _____pocket_____ is torn.

B. Read each sentence. Find a vocabulary word from the box that means almost the same thing as the underlined word. Write the word on the line.

couple	finish	notice

1. I have a pair of apples. _____couple_____

2. I didn't see her. _____notice_____

3. Complete your homework. _____finish_____

Book 2.1/Unit 3
Unit 3 Vocabulary Review   At Home: Have children illustrate one of the sentences above.   125

PRACTICE BOOK, 125–126

GRAMMAR

PARTNERS Partners write a short essay about a trip in a balloon. First they underline the verbs, and then they change the present-tense verbs to past tense and the past-tense verbs to present tense.

Unit Review

Arthur Writes a Story
Action Verbs

Best Wishes, Ed
Present-Tense Verbs

The Pony Express
Past-Tense Verbs

Nine-in-One, Grr! Grr!
The Verb *Have*

Change for the Quarter
Sentence Combining

Name _____ Date _____ UNIT TEST **Grammar 95**

Verbs

Read the sentences in the box. Look at the part with a line under it. Which is the better way to say this part? Mark the letter for your answer.

Kim lives in a big city. She visits the mayor's office. <u>She went to the park.</u> She buys a present at the store.
(1)

1.   ● She goes to the park.
     ⓑ She go to the park.
     ⓒ She did go the park.

Bob plays the piano. He studies about music. Bob likes his music teacher. <u>He did worked hard every day.</u>
(2)

2.   ⓐ He working hard every day.
     ● He works hard every day.
     ⓒ He are working hard every day.

Bob liked to play. <u>Bob play every day.</u> He learned a lot.
(3)

3.   ⓐ Bob playing every day.
     ⓑ Bob plays every day.
     ● Bob played every day.

I had a book. Mark and Bob have colds. <u>We has to eat.</u>
(4)

4.   ⓐ We having to eat.
     ● We have to eat.
     ⓒ We do eat.

Book 2.1/Unit 3
Unit Test   **Go On** →

95

GRAMMAR PRACTICE BOOK, 95–96

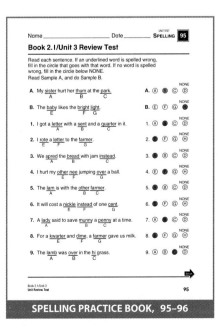

Divide the class into teams. Write the review words on cards and give a card to each child. Children draw pictures representing each word. Then the teams take turns showing their pictures to the other teams. The team that guesses and spells the word correctly gets a point. The team with the most points wins.

Unit Review

Silent Letters
high
wrote
lamb
knee

Long *e*
money
happy
penny
lady

/ər/
other
over
letter
farmer

Math Words
cent
dime
quarter
nickel

Short *e*
bread   spread
weather   instead

Name _____ Date _____ UNIT TEST SPELLING **95**

Book 2.1/Unit 3 Review Test

Read each sentence. If an underlined word is spelled wrong, fill in the circle that goes with that word. If no word is spelled wrong, fill in the circle below NONE.
Read Sample A, and do Sample B.

	NONE
A. My <u>sister</u> hurt her <u>thum</u> at the <u>park</u>.	A. Ⓐ ● Ⓒ Ⓓ
A B C	
B. The baby likes the <u>bright</u> <u>light</u>.	B. Ⓔ Ⓕ Ⓖ ●
E F G	
1. I got a <u>letter</u> with a <u>sent</u> and a <u>quarter</u> in it.	1. Ⓐ ● Ⓒ Ⓓ
A B C	
2. I <u>rote</u> a <u>letter</u> to the <u>farmer</u>.	2. ● Ⓕ Ⓖ Ⓗ
E F G	
3. We <u>spred</u> the <u>bread</u> with jam <u>instead</u>.	3. ● Ⓑ Ⓒ Ⓓ
A B C	
4. I hurt my <u>other</u> <u>nee</u> jumping <u>over</u> a ball.	4. Ⓔ ● Ⓖ Ⓗ
E F G	
5. The <u>lam</u> is with the <u>other</u> <u>farmer</u>.	5. ● Ⓑ Ⓒ Ⓓ
A B C	
6. It will cost a <u>nickle</u> <u>instead</u> of one <u>cent</u>.	6. ● Ⓕ Ⓖ Ⓗ
E F G	
7. A <u>lady</u> said to save <u>munny</u> a <u>penny</u> at a time.	7. Ⓐ ● Ⓒ Ⓓ
A B C	
8. For a <u>kwarter</u> and <u>dime</u>, a <u>farmer</u> gave us milk.	8. ● Ⓕ Ⓖ Ⓗ
E F G	
9. The <u>lamb</u> was <u>over</u> in the <u>hi</u> grass.	9. Ⓐ Ⓑ Ⓒ ●
A B C	

Book 2.1/Unit 3
Unit Review Test   95

SPELLING PRACTICE BOOK, 95–96

Phonics and Decoding
☑ Silent Letters
☑ /ər/*er*
☑ Short *e*: *ea*
☑ Long *e*: *y, ey*

Comprehension
☑ Fantasy and Reality
☑ Cause and Effect

Vocabulary Strategies
☑ Context Clues
☑ Synonyms

Study Skills
☑ Reference Sources

Writing
☑ Explanatory Writing

UNIT 3 TEST

Assessment
Follow-Up

Use the results of the informal and formal assessment opportunities in the unit to help you make decisions about future instruction.

SKILLS AND STRATEGIES	Reteaching Blackline Masters	Alternate Teaching Strategies	Skills Intervention Guide ⓘ
Phonics and Decoding			
Silent Letters	85, 89, 90, 117	T65	✓
/ər/ er	93, 97, 98, 117	T70	✓
Short *e: ea*	101, 105, 106, 117	T73	✓
Long *e: y, ey*	109, 113, 114, 117	T76	✓
Comprehension			
Fantasy and Reality	91, 107, 122	T67	✓
Cause and Effect	99, 115, 121	T71	✓
Vocabulary Strategies			
Context Clues	92, 100, 124	T68	✓
Synonyms	108, 116, 123	T74	✓
Study Skills			
Reference Sources	88, 96, 104, 112, 120	T66	✓

Writing	Alternate Writing Project—Easy	Unit Writing Process Lesson
Explanatory Writing	289N, 319N, 341N, 369N, 379N	381C–381H

McGraw-Hill School
TECHNOLOGY

 CD-ROM provides extra phonics support.

 Research & Inquiry ideas. Visit **www.mhschool.com/reading.**

Glossary

Introduce children to the Glossary by reading through the introduction and looking over the pages with them. Encourage the class to talk about what they see.

Words in a glossary, like words in a dictionary, are listed in **alphabetical order.** Point out the **guide words** at the top of each page that tell the first and last words appearing on that page.

Point out examples of **entries** and **main entries.** Read through a simple entry with the class, identifying each part. Have children note the order in which information is given: entry words(s), definition(s), example sentence(s), syllable division, pronunciation respelling, part of speech, plural/verb/adjective forms.

Note that if more than one definition is given for a word, the definitions are numbered. Note also the format used for a word that is more than one part of speech.

Review the parts of speech by identifying each in a sentence:

inter.	*adj.*	*n.*	*conj.*	*adj.*	*n.*
Wow!	A	dictionary	and	a	glossary

v.	*adv.*	*pron.*	*prep.*	*n.*
tell	almost	everything	about	words!

Explain the use of the **pronunciation key** (either the **short key,** at the bottom of every other page, or the **long key,** at the beginning of the glossary). Demonstrate the difference between **primary** stress and **secondary** stress by pronouncing a word with both.

Point out an example of the small triangle signaling a homophone. **Homophones** are words with different spellings and meanings but with the same pronunciation. Explain that a pair of words with the superscripts **1** and **2** are **homographs**—words that have the same spelling, but different origins and meanings, and in some cases, different pronunciations.

The **Word History** feature tells what language a word comes from and what changes have occurred in its spelling and/or meaning. Many everyday words have interesting and surprising stories behind them. Note that word histories can help us remember the meanings of difficult words.

Allow time for children to further explore the Glossary and make their own discoveries.

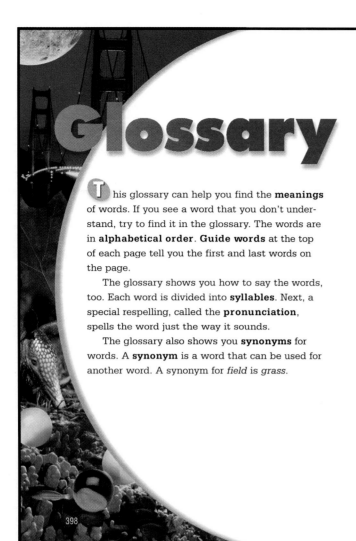

Glossary

This glossary can help you find the **meanings** of words. If you see a word that you don't understand, try to find it in the glossary. The words are in **alphabetical order**. **Guide words** at the top of each page tell you the first and last words on the page.

The glossary shows you how to say the words, too. Each word is divided into **syllables**. Next, a special respelling, called the **pronunciation**, spells the word just the way it sounds.

The glossary also shows you **synonyms** for words. A **synonym** is a word that can be used for another word. A synonym for *field* is *grass*.

Guide Words

accident / binoculars

First word on the page   Last word on the page

Sample Entry

Main entry — **creature** A living person or animal. — Definition

Example sentence — Bears and wolves are *creatures* of

the forest. ▲ **Synonym:** being. — Synonym

Syllable division — **crea • ture** (KREE chuhr) *noun,* — Part of speech

plural **creatures.**

Plural form   Pronunciation

Use the **Pronunciation Key** below to find examples for the sounds you see in the **pronunciation** spellings.

Phonetic Spelling	Examples	Phonetic Spelling	Examples
a	cat	oh	go, home
ah	father	aw	saw, fall
ay	late, day	or	more, four
air	there, hair	oo	too, do
b	bit, rabbit	oy	toy
ch	chin	ow	out, cow
d	dog	p	pig
e	met	r	run, carry
ee	he, see	s	song, mess
f	fine, off	sh	shout, fish
g	go, bag, bigger	t	ten, better
h	hat	th	thin
hw	wheel	thh	them
ih	sit	u	sun
ī	fine, tiger, my	ù	look, should
ihr	near, deer, here	yoo	music, new
j	jump, page	ur	turn, learn
k	cat, back	v	very, of
l	line, hill	w	we
m	mine, hammer	y	yes
n	nice, funny	z	has, zoo
ng	sing	zh	treasure, division
o	top	uh	about, happen, lemon

Aa

afraid Feeling fear. Are you *afraid* of snakes?
a•fraid (uh FRAYD) *adjective*.

allow To let someone do something. Tod and Teri's parents sometimes *allow* them to stay up later on Saturday nights.
al•low (uh LOW) *verb*, **allowed, allowing.**

announce To make something known in an official or formal way. The principal *announced* that the school would be closed because of snow.
▲ **Synonyms:** report, proclaim.
an•nounce (uh NOWNS) *verb*, **announced, announcing.**

answer To speak or write, as a reply. We *answer* people when they ask us a question, or call us, or send us a letter.
▲ **Synonym:** respond.
an•swer (AN suhr) *verb*, **answered, answering.**

arrive To come to a place. We will *arrive* in Florida at midnight.
ar•rive (uh RĪV) *verb*, **arrived, arriving.**

artist 1. A person who is skilled in painting, music, literature, or any other form of art. **2.** A person whose work shows talent or skill. The cook at this restaurant is an *artist*.
art•ist (AHR tihst) *noun*, *plural* **artists.**

Bb

bamboo A tall, woody plant related to grass. He waved a *bamboo* cane.
bam•boo (bam BOO) *noun*, *plural* **bamboo.**

Berto (BUR toh)

body 1. The whole of a person, animal, or plant. An athlete must have a strong *body*. **2.** The main part of something. The *body* of this car needs work.
bod•y (BAHD ee) *noun*, *plural* **bodies.**

broken 1. In pieces. The *broken* plate could not be fixed. **2.** Not working. We took the *broken* television set back to the store to be fixed.
▲ **Synonyms:** shattered, ruined.
bro•ken (BROH kuhn) *adjective*.

buffalo A large North American animal that has a big shaggy head with short horns and a hump on its back; bison. We saw a herd of *buffalo* while traveling out West.
buf•fa•lo (BUF uh loh) *noun*, *plural* **buffaloes** or **buffalos** or **buffalo.**

building Something built to live, work, or do things in. The *building* across the street is very tall.
build•ing (BIHL ding) *noun*, *plural* **buildings.**

bully A person who likes to frighten or threaten others, especially smaller or weaker people. The cowardly *bully* picked only on younger children.
bul•ly (BUL ee) *noun*, *plural* **bullies.**

busy Doing something. Roberta can't play because she is *busy* doing her homework.
▲ **Synonyms:** active, occupied.
bus•y (BIHZ ee) *adjective*, **busier, busiest.**

Cc

candle A wax stick with a string through it that is burned to make a light. The family lit eight *candles* on the last night of Hanukkah.
can•dle (KAN duhl) *noun*, *plural* **candles**.

careful Paying attention to what you are doing. Tina is very *careful* not to spill the paint. She works *carefully*.
▲ Synonym: cautious.
care•ful (KAIR fuhl) *adjective*; **carefully**, *adverb*.

carrot A long, orange vegetable that grows in the ground. The root of the plant is the part that we eat. Alice sliced a *carrot* for the salad.
car•rot (KAR uht) *noun*, *plural* **carrots**.

cattle Large animals raised for milk and meat on dairy farms and ranches. The *cattle* are grazing in the field.
▲ Synonyms: cows, bulls.
cat•tle (KAT uhl) *noun*, *plural* **cattle**.

chew To crush or grind something with the teeth. It's important to *chew* food well.
chew (CHOO) *verb*, **chewed**, **chewing**.

climb To move up something. Mom had to *climb* a ladder to get the kite out of the tree.
▲ Synonym: ascend.
climb (KLĪM) *verb*, **climbed**, **climbing**.

402

collect To gather together. The campers *collected* wood for the fire.
▲ Synonym: accumulate, amass.
col•lect (kuh LEKT) *verb*, **collected**, **collecting**.

corner The place where two streets come together. Paul crossed at the *corner*.
cor•ner (KOR nur) *noun*, *plural* **corners**.

couple Two things that go together in some way; a pair. I have a *couple* of hats.
cou•ple (KUP uhl) *noun*, *plural* **couples**.

crawl To move slowly on your hands and knees. The baby is just beginning to learn to *crawl*.
crawl (KRAWL) *verb*, **crawled**, **crawling**.

Dd

danger The chance that something bad will happen. There is *danger* in skating on thin ice.
danger (DAYN juhr) *noun*, *plural* **dangers**.

decide To choose to do one thing and not another. Carlos may *decide* not to go.
▲ Synonym: resolve.
de•cide (dih SĪD) *verb*, **decided**, **deciding**.

difference The amount left over. The *difference* between 6 and 2 is 4.
dif•fer•ence (DIHF uhr ens) *noun*, *plural* **differences**.

different Not the same. A duck is *different* from a goose.
dif•fer•ent (DIHF uhr ent) *adjective*.

403

diver A person who works or explores underwater. The *diver* carried a tank of air to help him breathe underwater.
div•er (DĪV uhr) *noun*, *plural* **divers**.

drift To move because of a current of air or water. We stopped rowing and let our boat *drift*.
▲ Synonyms: wander, float.
drift (DRIHFT) *verb*, **drifted**, **drifting**.

Ee

early 1. In or near the beginning. We started our hike in the *early* morning. 2. Before the usual time. We had an *early* dinner.
ear•ly (UR lee) *adjective*, **earlier**, **earliest**; *adverb*.

Earth The planet we live on. It takes one year for the *Earth* to go around the sun.
Earth (URTH) *noun*.

edge The line or place where something ends. I live near the *edge* of the lake.
edge (EJ) *noun*, *plural* **edges**.

empty Having nothing in it. When I finished my soup, the bowl was *empty*.
emp•ty (EMP tee) *adjective*, **emptier**, **emptiest**.

Ff

famous Very well-known. Thomas Edison is *famous* for having invented the electric light.
fa•mous (FAY muhs) *adjective*.

fence That which is built around something to keep things out or in. The *fence* around our backyard keeps the dog in.
fence (FENS) *noun*, *plural* **fences**.

404

finish 1. To bring to an end; to complete. When we *finish* our work, we will have lunch. *Verb*. 2. The last part of something; the end. We stayed to the *finish* of the movie. *Noun*.
fin•ish (FIHN ihsh) *verb*, **finished**, **finishing**; *noun*, *plural* **finishes**.

float 1. To stay on top of the water. Ray has a toy boat that *floats*. 2. To move slowly in the air. The baby let the balloon go, and it *floated* high above the house.
▲ Synonym: drift.
float (FLOHT) *verb*, **floated**, **floating**.

forget To not remember something. Josie was afraid she would *forget* my address, so she wrote it down.
▲ Synonyms: overlook, neglect.
for•get (fur GET) *verb*, **forgot**, **forgotten** or **forgot**, **forgetting**.

form To make or shape something. The artist *formed* a cat out of clay.
form (FORM) *verb*, **formed**, **forming**.

Gg

garden A place where people grow flowers or vegetables. When our cousins visit, they always bring us fresh tomatoes from their *garden*.
gar•den (GAHR duhn) *noun*, *plural* **gardens**.

gentle Careful not to hurt someone or something. Trisha was *gentle* with the small puppy.
▲ Synonym: soft.
gen•tle (JEN tuhl) *adjective*.

405

G3

giant Very big. Many dinosaurs were *giant* animals.
▲ **Synonym:** huge.
gi•ant (JĪ uhnt) *adjective.*

glance To take a quick look. I *glanced* in the mirror.
▲ **Synonyms:** look, glimpse.
glance (GLANS) *verb,* **glanced, glancing.**

government The group of people in charge of ruling or managing a country, city, state or other place. We held an election for our class *government.*
gov•ern•ment (GUHV urn ment) *noun, plural* **governments.**

grandmother Your father's mother or your mother's mother. My *grandmother* lives in New York City.
grand•mother (GRAND muthh uhr) *noun, plural* **grandmothers.**

graph A drawing that shows the relationship between changing things. We made a *graph* that showed how much our puppy had grown.
graph (GRAF) *noun, plural* **graphs.**

Hh

half One of two pieces the same size. Dad sawed the board in *half* to make a bench.
▲ **Synonym:** part.
half (HAF) *noun, plural* **halves.**

Ha•waii•an (huh WĪ uhn)

406

history The story or record of what has happened in the past. That old house has an interesting *history.*
his•to•ry (HIS tuh ree) *noun, plural* **histories.**

Hmong (huh MAHNG)

homework Work that a teacher asks children to do at home. I can finish my *homework* before dinner. *Noun.*
▲ **Synonym:** schoolwork.
home•work (HOHM wurk)

honor 1. Something given or done to show great respect. The hero received a medal and other *honors. Noun.* **2.** To show or feel great respect for a person or thing. The city *honored* the team with a parade. *Verb.*
▲ **Synonyms:** adore, regard.
hon•or (AHN uhr) *noun, plural* **honors;** *verb,* **honored, honoring.**

hope 1. To wish for something. I *hope* that you will feel better soon. *Verb.* **2.** A strong wish that a thing will happen. My *hope* is that you will win. *Noun.*
hope (HOHP) *verb,* **hoped, hoping;** *noun, plural* **hopes.**

hour 1. A unit of time equal to 60 minutes. There are 24 *hours* in a day. **2.** A time of day. At what *hour* should we meet?
hour (OWR) *noun, plural* **hours.**

hundred Ten times ten. 100. She is a *hundred* years old.
hun•dred (HUHN drihd) *noun, plural* **hundreds;** *adjective.*

hurry To move fast. Let's *hurry* and clean up our room.
hur•ry (HUHR ee) *verb,* **hurried, hurrying.**

407

Ii

iceberg A very large piece of floating ice. The penguins lived on an *iceberg.*
ice•berg (ĪS burg) *noun, plural* **icebergs.**

idea Something that you think of. We all had different *ideas* about what to name our pet turtle.
i•de•a (ī DEE uh) *noun, plural* **ideas.**

important Having value or meaning; worth paying attention to. It is *important* to look both ways before crossing.
im•por•tant (ihm POR tuhnt) *adjective.*

Jj

Jamaica (juh MAY kuh)

join 1. To come together. Where do the two rivers *join*? **2.** To become a member of. My brother plans to *join* the soccer team.
join (JOYN) *verb,* **joined, joining.**

juggler A person who keeps balls or other objects in continuous motion by skillful tossing and catching. The *juggler* kept four oranges in the air.
jug•gler (JUG luhr) *noun, plural* **jugglers.**

Ll

lariat A long rope with a loop at one end, used to catch animals. The rancher used a *lariat* to rope the calf.
lar•i•at (LAR ee uht) *noun, plural* **lariats.**

408

lean 1. To bend; to be at a slant. She had to *lean* out the window to see. **2.** To rest or rely on a person or thing for support. The monkey *leaned* against the branch.
▲ **Synonyms:** bend, tip.
lean (LEEN) *verb,* **leaned, leaning.**

lei A traditional Hawaiian wreath of flowers, leaves, or other material worn around the neck. When we got off the plane in Hawaii, each of us was given a *lei.*
lei (LAY) *noun, plural* **leis.**

lesson Something to be learned, taught, or studied. Today's math *lesson* was on subtraction.
les•son (LES uhn) *noun, plural* **lessons.**

library A room or a building where books are kept. People can use the books in the *library* or borrow them to take home.
li•brar•y (LĪ brair ee) *noun, plural* **libraries.**

life A way of living.
life (LĪF) *noun, plural* **lives.**

limit The point at which something must end. There was a *limit* on how much candy we could take.
lim•it (LIHM iht) *noun, plural* **limits.**

lonely Unhappy about being alone. Gabe is *lonely* because all his friends are away.
▲ **Synonyms:** alone, solitary.
lone•ly (LOHN lee) *adjective,* **lonelier, loneliest.**

lucky Having good things happen. I was *lucky* to have won.
luck•y (LUK ee) *adjective,* **luckier, luckiest.**

409

Mm

Maurice (maw REES)

melt To change from being hard or solid into being soft or liquid. The ice-cream cone *melted* in the sun.
melt (MELT) *verb*, **melted, melting.**

memory 1. The ability to remember things. Aunt Mimi has a good *memory* for dates and never forgets anyone's birthday. 2. A person or thing that is remembered. My summer in camp is one of my happiest *memories*.
mem•o•ry (MEM uh ree) *noun, plural* **memories.**

message Words or information sent from one person to another. I left a *message* for them to call me when they got home.
mes•sage (MES ij) *noun, plural* **messages.**

mochila A saddle covering made of hide or leather. *Mochilas* with pockets were used by Pony Express riders.
mo•chi•la (moh CHEE luh) *noun, plural* **mochilas.**

model A small-sized copy of something. They made a *model* of a castle.
mod•el (MOD uhl) *noun, plural* **models.**

mountain A very high mass of land. Some people go skiing in the *mountains* for vacation.
▲ **Synonyms:** hill, peak.
moun•tain (MOWN tuhn) *noun, plural* **mountains.**

410

mustang A wild horse that lives on the American plains; a bronco. The *mustangs* galloped across the prairie.
mus•tang (MUS tang) *noun, plural* **mustangs.**

Nn

notice To see or pay attention to something. Erin *noticed* a rabbit hiding in the bushes.
no•tice (NOH tis) *verb*, **noticed, noticing.**

Oo

order 1. The way in which things are arranged; position. We stood in *order* from oldest to youngest. 2. Clean or neat condition. Please keep your room in *order*. *Noun*. 3. To tell to do something; to command. The police officer *ordered* us to sit. *Verb*.
or•der (OR duhr) *noun, plural* **orders;** *verb*, **ordered, ordering.**

Pp

parent A mother or a father. My *parents* took us skating.
par•ent (PAIR uhnt) *noun, plural* **parents.**

parrot A bird with a wide, curved bill, a long, pointed tail, and brightly colored feathers. Amy's pet *parrot* squawked.
par•rot (PAR uht) *noun, plural* **parrots.**

pasture A field where animals graze. We saw sheep grazing in the *pasture*.
pas•ture (PAS chuhr) *noun, plural* **pastures.**

411

penguin A bird whose feathers are black or gray on the back and white on the front. Penguins cannot fly. Their wings look like flippers and are used for swimming. Most penguins live in or near Antarctica. The *penguin* swam toward the iceberg.
pen•guin (PEN gwin *or* PENG gwin) *noun, plural* **penguins.**

peppermint A candy that is flavored with peppermint oil, made from the leaves of mint plants. The *peppermint* made my breath taste fresh.
pep•per•mint (PEP uhr mint) *noun, plural* **peppermints.**

pheasant A large bird that has a long tail and brightly colored feathers.
pheas•ant (FEZ uhnt) *noun, plural* **pheasants.**

planet Any one of the nine large bodies that revolve around the sun, including Earth. The astronauts safely landed on *planet* Earth.
plan•et (PLAN it) *noun, plural* **planets.**

pocket A small bag or pouch that is sewn into a garment, suitcase, or purse. *Pockets* are for holding coins and other small things.
pock•et (POK iht) *noun, plural* **pockets.**

pour To make a liquid flow from one container to another. Dad *poured* soup into our bowls.
pour (POR) *verb*, **poured, pouring.**

412

president The leader of a group of people. We are going to have an election to choose the *president* of our class next week.
pres•i•dent (PREZ uh duhnt) *noun, plural* **presidents.**

promise To say that you will be sure to do something. Andy *promised* to keep my secret.
prom•ise (PROM ihs) *verb*, **promised, promising.**

proud Feeling good about something you have done. Ron was *proud* of the card he made for his mother's birthday.
proud (PROWD) *adjective*, **prouder, proudest.**

Qq

quail A bird that has a plump body and brown or gray feathers often dotted with white.
quail (KWAYL) *noun, plural* **quail** or **quails.**

Rr

record 1. An act that is better than all others of its kind. The runner set a new *record* for the race. 2. A written account. The school keeps a *record* of each student's attendance. *Noun*. 3. To set down in writing. *Verb*.
re•cord (REK uhrd) *noun, plural* **records.** (rih KORD) *verb*, **recorded, recording.**

remember To think of something again, or still. I will always *remember* my first puppy.
re•mem•ber (rih MEM buhr) *verb*, **remembered, remembering.**

413

G5

repair To fix or mend something. We *repaired* the broken leg of the table.
re•pair (rih PAIR) *verb*, **repaired, repairing.**

repeat To do or say something again. The teacher asked me to *repeat* my answer because he could not hear me.
re•peat (rih PEET) *verb*, **repeated, repeating.**

rule 1. A direction that tells what you can and cannot do. One of the *rules* at school is that you cannot run in the halls. *Noun.* **2.** To lead. The queen *ruled* her country well. *Verb.*
rule (ROOL) *noun, plural* **rules;** *verb,* **ruled, ruling.**

414

rush 1. To move, go, or come quickly. We *rushed* so we wouldn't be late. *Verb.* **2.** A busy or hurried state. We were in a *rush* to get to the show on time. *Noun.*
rush (RUSH) *verb,* **rushed, rushing;** *noun, plural* **rushes.**

 Ss

saddle 1. A seat for a rider on the back of a horse or similar animal. A saddle is usually made of leather. The rider sat tall in the *saddle. Noun.* **2.** To put a saddle on. The cowhand *saddled* the horse. *Verb.*
sad•dle (SAD uhl) *noun, plural* **saddles;** *verb,* **saddled, saddling.**

safety Freedom from harm or danger. The police work for the *safety* of us all.
▲ **Synonyms:** protection, security.
safe•ty (SAYF tee) *noun.*

seal A mammal that lives in coastal waters and has flippers instead of feet. The *seal* on the iceberg made a barking sound.
seal (sihl) *noun, plural* **seals.**

search To look carefully for something. Dad had to *search* the house for his keys.
▲ **Synonyms:** seek, hunt.
search (SURCH) *verb,* **searched, searching.**

serious 1. Important. Not paying attention in school is a *serious* matter. **2.** Not joking. Were you *serious* about taking piano lessons?
se•ri•ous (SIHR ee uhs) *adjective.*

Shao (SHOW)

shy 1. Not comfortable around people; bashful. The *shy* child wouldn't come into the room. **2.** Easily frightened; timid. Some animals are *shy* around people.
shy (SHĪ) *adjective,* **shyer** or **shier, shyest** or **shiest.**

special Not like anything else; important. Your birthday is a *special* day. Juan is a *special* friend of mine.
▲ **Synonym:** unique.
spe•cial (SPESH uhl) *adjective.*

squeeze 1. To press hard. *Squeeze* the tube of toothpaste from the bottom. **2.** To get by squeezing or applying pressure. I *squeezed* the juice from an orange.
squeeze (SKWEEZ) *verb,* **squeezed, squeezing.**

415

stagecoach A large, closed carriage pulled by horses, once used for carrying passengers, mail, and baggage. The *stagecoach* slowly bounced over the bumpy road.
stage•coach (STAYJ kohch) *noun, plural* **stagecoaches.**

stampede 1. A sudden, wild running of a herd of animals. The storm frightened the cattle and caused a *stampede. Noun.* **2.** To make a sudden, wild rush. The horses *stampeded* when they heard the helicopter overhead. *Verb.*
stam•pede (stam PEED) *noun, plural* **stampedes;** *verb,* **stampeded, stampeding.**

416

statue A likeness of a person, animal, or thing made of stone, bronze, or clay. The museum had *statues* from ancient Greece.
stat•ue (STACH oo) *noun, plural* **statues.**

stegosaurus A dinosaur that had bony plates sticking up along its backbone. It ate only plants and walked on all four feet. We saw a *stegosaurus* skeleton at the museum.
steg•o•sau•rus (steg uh SOHR uhs) *noun, plural* **stegosauri** (steg uh SOHR ī)

success 1. A result that has been hoped for. The coach was pleased with the team's *success.*
▲ **Synonym:** achievement.
2. A person or thing that does or goes well. The party was a big *success.*
suc•cess (suhk SES) *noun, plural* **successes.**

Tt

telegraph A system for sending messages in code over long distances by means of electricity. She sent the important message by *telegraph.*
tel•e•graph (TEL uh graf) *noun, plural* **telegraphs.**

tern A web-footed seabird similar to a gull. We saw a *tern* fly over the ocean.
tern (TURN) *noun, plural* **terns.**

tornado A powerful wind storm with funnel-shaped clouds. A *tornado* can cause great destruction.
tor•na•do (tor NAY doh) *noun, plural* **tornadoes** or **tornados.**

trick-or-treat (TRIHK or treet)

trouble 1. A difficult or dangerous situation. The town will be in *trouble* if the dam breaks. *Noun.* **2.** Extra work or effort. We all went to a lot of *trouble* to throw the party. *Noun.* **3.** To disturb. May I *trouble* you for a glass of water? *Verb.*
trou•ble (TRUB uhl) *noun, plural* **troubles;** *verb,* **troubled, troubling.**

truce A short halt in fighting, agreed to by both sides, who then try to make peace. Let's declare a *truce* so we can finish our game.
truce (TROOS) *noun, plural* **truces.**

Tutu (TOO TOO)

417

understand To get the meaning of; to know. I didn't *understand* the teacher's question. **un•der•stand** (un duhr STAND) *verb,* **understood, understanding.**

vaquero A cowboy, especially of Mexico, South America, or the southwestern United States. **va•que•ro** (va KAIR oh) *noun, plural* **vaqueros.**

visit 1. To go to see. We *visited* them last Sunday. *Verb.* **2.** A short stay or call. We paid a *visit* to my old friend. *Noun.* **vis•it** (VIZ it) *verb,* **visited, visiting;** *noun, plural,* **visits.**

weigh 1. To have an amount of heaviness. I *weigh* 60 pounds. **2.** To find out how heavy something is. I *weighed* myself. **weigh** (WAY) *verb,* **weighed, weighing.**

whisper 1. To speak in a very quiet voice. The teacher asked the children to stop *whispering. Verb.* **2.** A soft way of speaking. Grace heard *whispers* in the movie theater. *Noun.*
▲ **Synonym:** murmur. **whis•per** (WHIS puhr) *verb,* **whispered, whispering;** *noun, plural* **whispers.**

418

wild Not controlled by people; living or growing naturally. There are *wild* animals living on the plains of Africa.
▲ **Synonyms:** free, untamed. **wild** (WĪLD) *adjective,* **wilder, wildest.**

wonderful Amazing, unusual, or very good. At the circus we all stared at the *wonderful* acrobats.
▲ **Synonyms:** marvelous, astonishing. **won•der•ful** (WUN duhr fuhl) *adjective.*

worry to feel a little afraid about something. Mom and Dad start to *worry* if we come home late from school.
▲ **Synonyms:** feel anxious, feel troubled. **wor•ry** (WUHR ee) *verb,* **worried, worrying.**

worth 1. Having the same value as. The old coin is *worth* thirty dollars. *preposition.* **2.** The amount of money that something can be exchanged for; value. That jewel's *worth* was set at $50,000. **worth** (WURTH) *preposition, noun.*

wriggle To twist or turn from side to side with short, quick movements; squirm. The snake *wriggled* in the grass. **wrig•gle** (RIHG uhl) *verb,* **wriggled, wriggling.**

wrong Not right. His answer to the question was *wrong.*
▲ **Synonym:** incorrect. **wrong** (RONG) *adjective.*

419

Glossary

G7

Acknowledgments

Cover Illustration: Kenneth Spengler

The publisher gratefully acknowledges permission to reprint the following copyrighted material:

"All Living Things" by W. Jay Cawley. Words and music copyright © 1992 by W. Jay Cawley.

"The Bat" from BEAST FEAST by Douglas Florian. Copyright © 1984 by Douglas Florian. Used by permission of Voyager Books, Harcourt Brace & Company.

"Behind the Museum Door" from GOOD RHYMES, GOOD TIMES by Lee Bennett Hopkins. Copyright © 1973, 1995 by Lee Bennett Hopkins. Used by permission of Curtis Brown Ltd.

"Brothers" from SNIPPETS by Charlotte Zolotow. Copyright © 1993 by Charlotte Zolotow. Illustrations copyright © 1993 by Melissa Sweet. Used by permission of HarperCollins Publishers.

"The Bundle of Sticks" from THE CHILDREN'S AESOP: SELECTED FABLES retold by Stephanie Calmenson. Used by permission of Caroline House, Boyds Mills Press, Inc.

"The Cat Came Back" arranged by Mary Goetze. Copyright © 1984 MMB Music, Inc.

"Covers" from VACATION TIME: POEMS FOR CHILDREN by Nikki Giovanni. Copyright © 1980 by Nikki Giovanni. Used by permission of William Morrow & Company, Inc.

"The Dinosaur Who Lived in My Backyard" by B. G. Hennessey. Copyright © 1988 by B. G. Hennessey. Used by permission of Viking Books, a division of Penguin Books USA Inc.

"The Discontented Fish" from Tales from Africa by Kathleen Arnott. Copyright © 1962 by Kathleen Arnott. Used by permission of Oxford University Press.

"The Golden Touch" retold by Margaret H. Lippert from TEACHER'S READ ALOUD ANTHOLOGY. Copyright © 1993 by Macmillan/McGraw-Hill School Publishing Company.

"Gotta Find a Footprint" from BONE POEMS by Jeff Moss. Text copyright © 1997 by Jeff Moss. Illustrations copyright © 1997 by Tom Leigh. Used by permission of Workman Publishing Company, Inc.

"The Great Ball Game: A Muskogee Story" by Joseph Bruchac. Copyright © 1994 by Joseph Bruchac. Used by permission of Dial Books.

"Lemonade Stand" reprinted with the permission of Margaret K. McElderry Books, an imprint of Simon & Schuster Children's Publishing Division from WORLDS I KNOW and Other Poems by Myra Cohn Livingston. Text copyright © 1985 by Myra Cohn Livingston.

"The Letter" from FROG AND TOAD ARE FRIENDS by Arnold Lobel. Copyright © 1970 by Arnold Lobel. Used by permission of HarperCollins Publishers.

ACKNOWLEDGMENTS

The publisher gratefully acknowledges permission to reprint the following copyrighted material:

"Arthur Writes a Story" by Marc Brown. From ARTHUR WRITES A STORY by Marc Brown. Copyright © 1996 by Marc Brown. Reprinted by permission of Little, Brown and Company.

"The Best Friends Club." This is the entire text and nineteen illustrations from THE BEST FRIENDS CLUB by Elizabeth Winthrop with illustrations by Martha Weston. Text copyright © 1989 by Elizabeth Winthrop. Illustrations copyright © 1989 by Martha Weston. Reprinted by permission of Lothrop, Lee and Shepard Books, a division of HarperCollins Publishers.

Text and art of "Best Wishes, Ed" from WINSTON, NEWTON, ELTON, AND ED by James Stevenson. Copyright © 1978 by James Stevenson. Reprinted by permission of Greenwillow Books, a division of HarperCollins Publishers.

"Cloud Dragon" by Pat Mora from CONFETTI: POEMS FOR CHILDREN. Text copyright © 1996 by Pat Mora. Reprinted by permission of Lee and Low Books, Inc.

"Doves" by Masahito, translated by Tzi-si Huang, from IN THE EYES OF THE CAT: JAPANESE POETRY FOR ALL SEASONS. Selected and illustrated by Demi. Copyright © 1992 by Demi. Reprinted by permission of Henry Holt and Company.

"Four Generations" by Mary Ann Hoberman from FATHERS, MOTHERS, SISTERS, BROTHERS: A COLLECTION OF FAMILY POEMS. Text copyright © 1991 by Mary Ann Hoberman. Illustrations copyright © 1991 by Marylin Hafner. By permission of Little, Brown & Company.

"Henry and Mudge" from HENRY AND MUDGE: THE FIRST BOOK by Cynthia Rylant, pictures by Suçie Stevenson. Text copyright © 1987 by Cynthia Rylant. Illustrations copyright © 1987 Suçie Stevenson. Reprinted by permission of Simon & Schuster Books for Young Readers.

JAMAICA TAG-ALONG. Text copyright © 1989 by Juanita Havill. Illustrations copyright © by Anne Sibley O'Brien. Reprinted by permission of Houghton Mifflin Company. All rights reserved.

"Lemonade for Sale" by Stuart J. Murphy. Text copyright © 1998 by Stuart J. Murphy. Illustrations copyright © 1998 by Tricia Tusa. Reprinted by permission of HarperCollins Children's Books, a division of HarperCollins Publishers.

"A Letter to Amy" is the entire work of A LETTER TO AMY by Ezra Jack Keats. Copyright © 1968 by Ezra Jack Keats. Reprinted by permission of HarperCollins Publishers.

"Luka's Quilt" by Georgia Guback. Copyright © 1994 by Georgia Guback, used by permission of HarperCollins Publishers. Reprinted by permission.

"The Merry-Go-Round" by Myra Cohn Livingston from A SONG I SANG TO YOU by Myra Cohn Livingston. Copyright © 1984, 1969, 1967, 1965, 1959, 1958 by Myra Cohn Livingston. Used by permission of Marian Reiner. "Morning Song" by Bobbie Katz from POEMS FOR SMALL FRIENDS by Bobbie Katz. Reprinted with copyright © 1989 Random House, Inc. permission of Bobbie Katz.

"Nine-in-One, Grr! Grr!" by Blia Xiong. Reprinted with permission of the publisher Children's Book Press, San Francisco, CA. Copyright © by Cathy Spagnoli. Illustrations copyright © 1989 by Nancy Horn.

"Time to Play" by Nikki Grimes from PASS IT ON: AFRICAN-AMERICAN POETRY FOR CHILDREN. Selected by Wade Hudson. Text copyright © 1991 by Nikki Grimes. Illustrations copyright © 1993 by Floyd Cooper. Reprinted by permission of the author.

Illustration

Bob Barner, 10–11; Holly Hannon, 12–13; Julia Gorton, 35, 55, 113, 123, 379; Liz Conrad, 36–37; James Ransome, 56–57; Claude Martinot, 91, 369; Sal Murdocca, 92–93; Karen Chandler, 94–109; Donna Perrone, 114–115; Kelly Sutherland, 124–125; Krystyna Stasiak, 126–127; Clare Schauman, 128–129; Andy Levine, 155, 191, 243, 253, 289, 319, 341; Michael Grejniec, 156–157; Vilma Ortiz-Dillon, 190, 214; David Galchult, 192–193; Myron Grossman, 215; Jo Ann Adinolfi, 216–217; Roger DeMuth, 244–245; Oscar Senn, 254–255; Gerardo Suzan, 256–257; Luisa D'Augusta, 258–259; Kathi Ember, 290–291; Roger Roth, 320–321; Kunio Hagio, 322–337; Dagmar Fehlau, 342–343; Miles Parnell, 403–404; John Carozza, 406, 419; Holly Johnes, 415.

Photography

5: b.r. Peter Yates/SABA; 7: b.r. David Doubilet; 9: b.r. FPG/Denine Cody; 14: b.l. Courtesy of Dorothy Donohue.. t.r. Courtesy of Connie Keremes; 32: Jay Brousseau/The Image Bank; 33: b. PhotoDisc; 88: b. Jake Wyman/Photonica/t. Jake Wyman/Photonica; 89 t. Corbis/Bob Krist/b. Jake Wyman/Photonica; 94: b. Courtesy of the artist/t. Courtesy of Angela Shelf Medearis; 110: t.l. PhotoDisc; 111: m.r. Ryan and Beyer/Tony Stone Images/t.r. PhotoDisc; 121: t.r. NASA; 130: b. Courtesy of HarperCollins Publishers; 152–153: b. PhotoDisc; 153: t. PhotoDisc; 189: b. PhotoDisc; 213: t. David Young-Wolff/PhotoEdit./b. Gary Faye/Photonica; 240–241: t. PhotoDisc; 241: b. PhotoDisc; 242. PhotoDisc; 250: Masterfile/(c) Kurt Amsler/. B. PhotoDisc; 251: b. David Doubilet; 260: t. (c) 1995 Rick Friedman; 287: PhotoDisc; 317: b. Joseph Van Os/The Image Bank; 318: PhotoDisc; 322: b. Courtesy of the artist; 338: b. Lawrence Migdale/Photo Researchers; 339: b. PhotoDisc; 340: b. PhotoDisc; 367: t. Westlight/Dow Hendren; 368: PhotoDisc; 376: t.l. Courtesy, US Mint; 395: c. Frank Whitney/The Image Bank/c.i. James Darell/Stone; 397: r.i. DiMaggio Kalish/Stock Market; 398: l. PhotoDisc; 400: Joao Silva/Black Star/PNI; 401: Alan Schein/The Stock Market; 402: Clay McBride/Nonstock/PNI; 405: Clive Boursnell/Tony Stone Images; 406: t.l. Ariel Skelley/The Stock Market; 408: Zefa Germany/The Stock Market; 409: Phil Kramer/The Stock Market; 410: Caroline Wood/Allstock/PNI; 411: Zefa Germany/The Stock Market; 412: Zefa Germany/The Stock Market; 413: Stuart Gilbert/Metropolitan Museum of Art, NY; 414: Ariel Skelley/The Stock Market; 416: Le Goy/Liaison International; 417: A & J Vekkajk/The Stock Market; 419: Tome Brakefield/The Stock Market.

Reading for Information
All photographs are by Macmillan/McGraw-Hill (MMH) and by Michael Groen for MMH except as noted below:

Table of Contents, pp. 382–383
Chess pieces, t.l., Wides + Hall/FPG; Earth, m.c.l., M. Burns/Picture Perfect; CD's, m.c.l., Michael Simpson/FPG; Newspapers, b.l., Craig Orsini/Index Stock/PictureQuest; Clock, t.c., Steve McAlister/The Image Bank; Kids circle, b.c., Daniel Pangbourne Media/FPG; Pencils, t.r., W. Cody/Corbis; Starfish, t.c., Darryl Torckler/Stone; Keys, c.r., Randy Faris/Corbis; Cells, b.r., Spike Walker/Stone; Stamps, t.r., Michael W. Thomas/Focus Group/PictureQuest; Books, c.r., Siede Preis/PhotoDisc; Sunflower, c.r., Jeff LePore/Natural Selection; Mouse, b.r., Andrew Hall/Stone; Apples, t.r., Siede Preis/PhotoDisc; Watermelons, b.r., Neil Beer/PhotoDisc; Butterfly, b.r., Stockbyte

386: b. J.A.Kraulis/Masterfile; 395: c. Stone; 395: b.r. PhotoDisc; 395: b.l. PhotoDisc; 396: c. Jacque Denzer Parker/Index; 396: c. CMCD/PhotoDisc; 397: c.i. DiMaggio Kalish/Stock Market; 397: l. Emma Lee/LifeFile/PhotoDisc

Art/Illustration
Dara Goldman, 36F, 56F, 92F; Linda Weller, 370F; Timothy A. Pack, 100

Photography
125A: M. Burns, Picture Perfect; Daniel Pagbourne, Media/FPG; 127A: Jeff LaPore/Natural Selection; Stockbyte

"The Library" by Barbara A. Huff from THE RANDOM HOUSE BOOK OF POETRY FOR CHILDREN. Copyright © 1983 by Barbara A. Huff.

"The Lion and the Mouse" from ONCE IN A WOOD: TEN TALES FROM AESOP adapted and illustrated by Eve Rice. Copyright © 1979 by Eve Rice. Used by permission of Greenwillow Books, a division of William Morrow & Company, Inc.

"Me I Am!" copyright © 1983 by Jack Prelutsky from THE RANDOM HOUSE BOOK OF POETRY FOR CHILDREN by Jack Prelutsky. Used by permission of Random House Children's Books, a division of Random House, Inc.

"Penguins" from A HIPPOPOTAMUSN'T AND OTHER ANIMAL VERSES by J. Patrick Lewis. Text copyright © 1990 by J. Patrick Lewis. Pictures copyright © 1990 by Victoria Chess. Used by permission of Dial Books for Young Readers, a division of Penguin Books USA Inc.

"Reading to Me" from THE OTHER SIDE OF THE DOOR by Jeff Moss. Text copyright © 1991 by Jeff Moss. Illustrations copyright © 1991 by Chris Demarest. Used by permission of Bantam Books, a division of Bantam Doubleday Dell Publishing Group, Inc.

"The Sharks" from IN THE SWIM by Douglas Florian. Copyright © 1997 by Douglas Florian. Used by permission of Harcourt Brace & Company.

"Summer Goes" from EGG THOUGHTS AND OTHER FRANCES SONGS by Russell Hoban. Copyright © 1964, 1974 by Russell Hoban. Used by permission of HarperCollins Publishers.

"A Superduper Pet" from SUPERDUPER TEDDY by Johanna Hurwitz. Text copyright © 1980 by Johanna Hurwitz. Illustrations copyright © 1990 by Lillian Hoban. Used by permission of William Morrow and Company, Inc.

"The Tall Tales, " "The Tiger Story," and "Two Foolish Friends" by Tanya Lee, from FLOAT-ING CLOUDS, FLOATING DREAMS: FAVORITE ASIAN FOLKTALES by I.K Junne. Copyright © 1974 by I.K. Junne. Used by permission of Doubleday & Company, Inc.

"Thinking Green" from 50 SIMPLE THINGS KIDS CAN DO TO SAVE THE EARTH by The EarthWorks Group. Copyright © 1989 by John Javna, The EarthWorks Group. Used by permission of Andrew McMeel Publishers.

Untitled from A CHINESE ZOO: FABLES AND PROVERBS by Demi. Copyright © 1987. Used by permission of Harcourt Brace Jovanovich Publishers.

"Vacation" from FATHERS, MOTHERS, SIS-TERS, BROTHERS by Mary Ann Hoberman. Text copyright © 1991 by Mary Ann Hoberman. Illustrations copyright © 1991 by Marylin Hafner. Used by permission of Little, Brown and Company.

ZB Font Method Copyright © 1996 Zaner-Bloser. Handwriting Models, Manuscript and Cursive. Used by permission.

Contents

The Tall Tales

a tall tale by **Tanya Lee**

There once lived three brothers who were known throughout the land for the tall tales they told. They would travel from place to place telling their strange stories to whomever would listen. No one ever believed their tales and all who heard them would cry out with exclamations of disbelief.

One day while traveling very far from home, the three brothers came upon a wealthy prince. The prince was dressed very elegantly and bedecked in jewels such as the three men had never seen in their lives. They thought how wonderful it would be to have such possessions, so they devised a plan whereby they could use their storytelling ability to trick the prince out of his belongings.

They said to the prince: "Let's tell each other stories of past adventures and if anyone should doubt the truth of what the other is saying, then that person must become a slave to the others." Now the brothers had no use for a slave, but if they could make the prince their slave, then they could take his clothes because the prince and his clothes would belong to them.

The prince agreed to their plan. The brothers were sure they would win because no one had ever heard their stories without uttering cries of disbelief. And so they found a passer-by and asked him to act as judge in the matter. All sat down under the shade of a tree and the storytelling began.

The first brother stood up to tell his tale. With a smile on his face he began to speak: "When I was a young boy I thought it would be fun to hide from my brothers so I climbed the tallest tree in our village and remained there all day while my brothers searched high and low for me. When night fell, my brothers gave up the search and returned home. It was then that I realized that I was unable to climb down the tree. But I knew I could get down with the help of a rope, so I went to the nearest cottage and borrowed a rope and was then able to climb down the tree and return home."

When the prince heard this ridiculous story he did not make a comment but merely stood and waited for the next story to begin. The three brothers were quite surprised but were sure that the second story would not be believed by the prince. And so the second brother began his tale: "That day when my brother hid from us, I was searching for him in the forest. I saw something run into the bushes and—thinking it was my brother—I ran in after it. When I got into the bushes, I saw that it was not my brother but a huge, hungry tiger. He opened his mouth to devour me and I jumped inside and crawled into his belly before he could chew me up. When inside I started jumping up and down and making loud, fierce noises. The beast did not know what was happening and became so frightened that he spit me out with such force that I traveled several hundred feet through the air and landed back in the middle of our village. And so, though I was but a young lad I saved our whole village from the fearful tiger, because never again did the beast come near our village."

After this story the prince once again made no comment. He merely asked that the third story begin. The three brothers were quite upset by this and as the last brother began his tale, he had quite a frown upon his face. But he was still quite determined to make up a story so absurd that the prince could not this time help but doubt its truthfulness. And so he began his tale: "One day as I was walking along the banks of the river I saw that all the fishermen seemed quite unhappy. I inquired as to why they seemed so sad. They therefore informed me that they had not caught one fish in a week and their families were going hungry as a result. I told them that I would try and help them. So I dove into the water and was immediately transformed into a fish. I swam around until I saw the source of the problem. A giant fish had eaten all the smaller fish and was himself avoiding the fishermen's nets. When this giant saw me, he came toward me and was about to devour me, but I changed back to human form and slashed the fish open with my sword. The fish inside his belly were then able to escape. Many swam right into the waiting nets. When I returned to shore, many of the fish were so

Read Aloud   ▶ Continue reading here.

thankful that I had saved them that they returned with me. When the fishermen saw all these fish jumping onto shore after me, they were indeed pleased and rewarded me abundantly."

When this story was finished, the prince did not doubt a word of it. The three brothers were quite upset but at least they knew that they should not doubt the words of the prince. And so the prince began his tale: "I am a prince of great wealth and property. I am on the road in search of three slaves who have escaped from me. I have searched high and low for them as they were very valuable property. I was about to give up the search when I met you three fellows. But now my search is ended because I have found my missing slaves, because you, gentlemen, are they."

When the brothers heard these words, they were shocked. If they agreed to the prince's story, then they were admitting that they were his slaves. But if they doubted what he said, then they lost the bet and became his slaves anyway. The brothers were so upset by the cleverness of the prince that they said not a word. The passerby who was judging the contest nevertheless declared that the prince had won the wager.

The prince did not make slaves of these men but instead allowed them to return to their village with the promise that they would never tell tall tales again. And the three brothers were thereafter known throughout the land for their honesty and truthfulness.

Penguins
J. Patrick Lewis

Deep in dark
Antarctica
They waddle away
In their tuxedos,
Black ties and tails,
These little butlers
Who wait patiently
For a month
Of sun days,
Taking dips,
Dripping,
Flipping
Flippers,
Flopping—
Belly whoppers,
Keeping cool
At forty below,
Keeping everything
On ice.

Crazy Horse Keeps a Promise
a Sioux legend

On the day Crazy Horse was born, a horse dashed through the Sioux camp in the Black Hills of South Dakota. People said, "This is a sign from the Great Spirit! After all, wasn't our first horse a gift from the Great Spirit? It is because of the horse that our hunters can provide us with plenty to eat. This baby will be a great hunter, warrior, and leader. We should name him Crazy Horse."

Even as a young boy, Crazy Horse was a legendary hunter and warrior. Before he turned thirteen, he was able to capture horses from the enemy. He led his first war party before turning twenty. He dazzled his own people and his enemies by his skill and daring as he fought to preserve his people's way of life.

Throughout his life, Crazy Horse never signed a treaty, never agreed to move to a reservation, and never surrendered to the white man's ways. One of the few contacts he had with a white man was with a news photographer. Crazy Horse told him, "Photographs are not part of our life," he said. "I will never allow myself to be photographed."

After handing the Army some of their worst defeats in all of the Indian wars, Crazy Horse was finally killed at the age of 34. Before he died, he promised Black Elk, a Sioux medicine man, "I will return to you in stone." More than a hundred years later, he keeps the promise and returns as a towering stone monument, facing east over South Dakota's Black Hills.

The Tiger Story
a myth from Viet Nam

Long ago when the world was new and animals and men spoke the same language, the tiger looked quite different. His skin was the color of bright shining gold, and was without stripes. Although he was very beautiful, he was also a vicious hunter and was feared throughout the land.

One day a farmer, who had been plowing his field at the edge of the jungle, left his water buffalo to drink at the stream while he himself slept in the shade. The day was very hot and he slept for a long time.

The tiger, who had been watching from the jungle, pounced before the water buffalo. Before the beast had a chance to react in fear, the tiger spoke to him in a gentle reassuring voice, "Don't worry, poor helpless beast of burden, for I have not come to harm you, but only to ask you some questions. Why is that you who are so strong allow that man who is so small and weak to work you all day in the hot sun?"

"I know not why it is," replied the big stupid water buffalo. "I only know that he has a magic power he uses over me called wisdom."

So the tiger approached the man, and with the same soft voice he had used with the water buffalo he said, "Man, I have learned that you have a great power that allows you to rule over the animals. Can you tell me how you got this power that I too might attain it and not so often go hungry?"

Now the farmer was a sly creature and immediately figured out a way to trick the beast. He told the tiger he would gladly share his magic power, but that first there must be a great ceremony.

With many magic words the farmer began to tie a rope all around the body of the tiger. He then gathered dry grass and twigs and placed them in a circle around the tiger. The great golden animal was struck silent with wonder at this ritual. But when the man lit a match to the grass and the flames soared, the tiger realized he had been tricked. The flames burned away the ropes and the tiger escaped, but to this day his coat is the color of tarnished gold and long black stripes remain as the scars of where the rope encircled his body.

The Golden Touch
a Greek folk tale

Once upon a time, there lived a king named Midas. Although this king had a good wife and a little daughter whom he loved very much, there was something he seemed to love much more dearly—and that was gold.

Each day he went into his countinghouse, where he counted stacks of golden coins again and again. It was his greatest pleasure in life, and he dreamed only of getting more golden coins to count.

While he was counting one day, he heard a mysterious voice say,

"I have come to grant you whatever you wish for most."

King Midas did not hesitate very long. "I wish," he said, "that everything I touch would turn to gold."

"You have your wish," said the voice.

King Midas was overjoyed, thinking of all the gold that would now be his. He picked up a pebble. It turned to gold. He touched every flower he could find in the garden and they turned to gold.

"What a wonderful gift!" he exclaimed.

Some time later, he sat down to eat. As he pulled the chair away from the table, it turned to gold. He reached out for some food, but to his mounting alarm, he discovered that the meat, the bread, the fruit—everything—turned into solid gold at his touch. It could not be eaten. Midas became frightened. Now he began to wonder how he would live with nothing to eat.

He walked out into the garden to think. Just then his little daughter ran up to him and gave him a hug. Midas bent down to kiss her—and SHE turned to gold!

As Midas gazed at his only daughter, now only no more than a golden statue, he realized how foolish he had been to love money for its own sake. He cried bitter tears. At last the same voice he had heard before said to him, "Go down to the river, wash your hands, and your golden touch will be gone. Then fill a pitcher with water from the river and sprinkle it over everything you have already turned to gold."

King Midas hurried along to do as he had been told. When the river water was sprinkled on the golden statue of his child, the little girl returned to life. The flowers returned to their natural color and beauty. Food could again be taken in hand without turning hard and shining yellow.

King Midas had learned his lesson. He no longer yearned for gold above all other things in the world.

▶ Continue reading here.

Annotated Workbooks

Name_____ Date_____ Practice **85**

Silent Letters

Write the words. Then say each word. Circle the silent
letter or letters in each word.

| l | b | k | w | g | h | gh |

1. could   cou(l)d
2. knee   (k)nee
3. sign   si(g)n
4. thumb   thum(b)
5. high   hi(gh)
6. tow   to(w)
7. white   (w)hite
8. lamb   lam(b)
9. know   (k)now
10. light   li(gh)t
11. which   w(h)ich
12. should   shou(l)d

12   Book 2.1/Unit 3
Arthur Writes a Story

At Home: Have children think of a word that rhymes
with each of the words above.

85

Name_____ Date_____ Practice **86**

Vocabulary

Choose a word from the box to complete each sentence.
Write the word on the line.

| decided | float | important | library | planet | proud |

1. Jenny went to the ___ to find some books.

   library

2. Paul's and Carol's kites ___ in the wind.

   float

3. Lily ___ to help clean up the park.

   decided

4. Baseball is very ___ to Lou.

   important

5. Jade's parents were very ___ when she won.

   proud

6. Earth might be the only ___ with life on it.

   planet

86   **At Home:** Ask children to illustrate four sentences and
write another sentence to go with them.

Book 2.1/Unit 3
Arthur Writes a Story   6

The Important Planet

I should just throw out all my
books and grow food, it thought.
Then it had a better idea. The
planet decided to call the food planet.
"I have some books for you!" the
library planet told the food planet.
The food planet checked out every
cookbook ever written.
And, thanks to two important
planets, everyone ate well that day!

At Home: Discuss with children why it is important to be
yourself. How can you help others and still be yourself?

4

86a

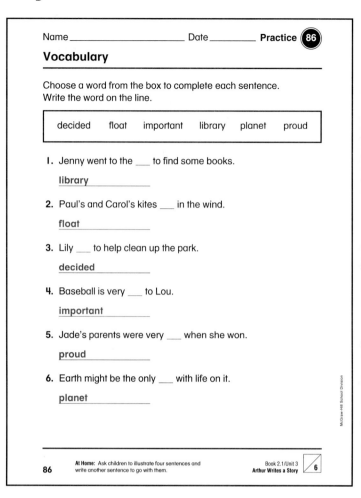
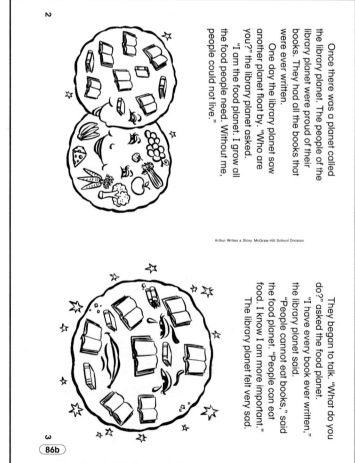

2

Once there was a planet called
the library planet. The people of the
library planet were proud of their
books. They had all the books that
were ever written.

One day the library planet saw
another planet float by. "Who are
you?" the library planet asked.
"I am the food planet. I grow all
the food people need. Without me,
people could not live."

They began to talk. "What do you
do?" asked the food planet.
"I have every book ever written,"
the library planet said.
"People cannot eat books," said
the food planet. "People can eat
food. I know I am more important."
The library planet felt very sad.

Arthur Writes a Story McGraw-Hill School Division

3

86b

Arthur Writes a Story • PRACTICE

Story Comprehension

Think about "Arthur Writes a Story." Write **T** if the statement is true about the story. Write **F** if the statement is not true about the story.

__T__ 1. Arthur is a student.

__F__ 2. D.W. is Arthur's mother.

__F__ 3. Arthur is working on a music project.

__T__ 4. Arthur has to write a story for class.

__T__ 5. At first, Arthur writes about his puppy.

__T__ 6. Arthur writes several different stories.

__F__ 7. The Brain is Arthur's teacher.

__F__ 8. Penelope is Arthur's friend.

__T__ 9. Arthur's class likes his story about the puppy.

__T__ 10. Arthur's class does not like his song and dance story.

__T__ 11. Arthur got a gold sticker for his story.

__F__ 12. Francine wrote a song for her story.

At Home: Have children draw a picture to go along with one of the statements they marked **true.**

Use a Dictionary

When you look up a word in a **dictionary,** you have to remember the order of the letters in the alphabet. If you check the guide words, you'll know if you're on the right page.

Write the following two lists of words in alphabetical order. If the first letter of two words is the same, look at the second letter.

A-B-C Order

made	clamp	pedal	meek
elephant	elephant	meek	moon
rock	made	moon	pedal
race	race	wrap	sleep
clamp	rock	sleep	wrap

At Home: Write down six words, and have children put them in alphabetical order.

Silent Letters

Answer each riddle. Then circle the silent letters in each answer.

knee	write	right	talk	sign
thumb	wrong	lamb	light	knob

1. You do this when you say something. __talk__

2. This is the fattest finger on your hand. __thumb__

3. This is what you kneel on. __knee__

4. You do this with a pencil and paper. __write__

5. This tells you what to do on a road. __sign__

6. This is not your left. __right__

7. This is a baby sheep. __lamb__

8. A lamp gives you this. __light__

9. This is on a door. __knob__

10. When something is not correct. __wrong__

At Home: Ask children to write one more riddle with a word that has a silent letter for the answer.

Silent Letters

Finish each sentence below. Circle the word that completes the sentence. Then write the answer.

1. Most people sleep at __night__.
   (night)   knew   written

2. Do you __know__ her name?
   high   bright   (know)

3. I __walk__ to school, but he takes the bus.
   weigh   (walk)   knock

4. I __wrote__ him a letter.
   high   (wrote)   talking

5. I could not untie the __knot__.
   (knot)   flight   knee

6. Baby sheep are called __lambs__.
   limbs   rams   (lambs)

7. My __knee__ is part of my leg.
   knock   arm   (knee)

8. I __talk__ on the telephone.
   (talk)   walk   wink

At Home: Have children illustrate one of the sentences above.

Fantasy and Reality

Read the story. Draw two pictures about Bear showing something that could not happen in real life. Then complete the sentences.

Why Bears Have Short Tails

It was winter and Bear was hungry. Fox led him to a hole in the ice. The hole was filled with fish. Fox told Bear to stick his long tail into the hole. "Fish will bite your tail. When you feel them, pull up your tail. The fish will hang on." Bear waited and waited. He never felt a bite. After a long time, he stood up. When he took his frozen tail out of the water, it snapped and fell off. And that is why bears have short tails.

Child may draw picture of a fox talking to a bear.	**Child may draw a picture of a bear with a long tail, frozen and falling off.**

This is not like real life because

a fox cannot talk.

This is not like real life because

bears have never had long

tails. An animal would not be

likely to sit in an icy pond.

At Home: Ask children to tell what words let them know the story was not like real life.

Context Clues

You can use **context clues** to help you figure out the meaning of an unknown word.

Write the clue words that help you figure out the meaning of the word in dark print. Then write **before** or **after** to show if the clue words come before or after the word.

1. At night I like to look at the stars in the sky through my **telescope**. The telescope makes things that are far away seem closer.

   makes things that are far away seem closer; after

   look at the stars in the sky through; before

2. I saw a bright ball of gas through my telescope. It had a tail. I think this is called a **comet**.

   a bright ball of gas that has a tail

   before

3. I like books about the stars. Someday I hope to be an **astronaut**. An astronaut is a person who is trained to travel in space.

   a person who is trained to travel in space

   after

4. We saw the largest planet in the sky. This planet is one of the brightest objects in the sky. It is called **Jupiter**.

   the largest planet in the sky

   before

At Home: Encourage children to identify two new words in a favorite story or book and to figure out the meanings of the words using context clues.

Book 2.1/Unit 3
Arthur Writes a Story 8

Arthur Writes a Story • RETEACH

Silent Letters

> Say the word hi**gh**. Note that the letters **gh** are silent.

Circle the word that names each picture. Underline the letters that are silent.

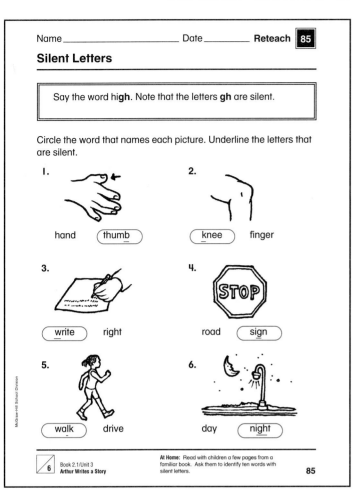

1. hand (thum**b**)
2. (**k**nee) finger
3. (**wr**ite) right
4. road (si**gn**)
5. (wal**k**) drive
6. day (ni**gh**t)

Vocabulary

> decided float important library planet proud

Choose a word from the box to match each clue. Write the word on the line.

1. what Earth is ____**planet**____

2. made up your mind ____**decided**____

3. building with many books in it ____**library**____

4. to feel very good about what you have done ____**proud**____

5. when something means a lot, it is ____**important**____

6. to move along slowly in the air or on water ____**float**____

Story Comprehension

Put an **X** by the sentence that tells about "Arthur Writes a Story."

_____ 1. Arthur had no homework.

__X__ 2. Arthur writes about a dog.

__X__ 3. Arthur writes about the moon.

_____ 4. Arthur writes about D.W.

__X__ 5. The Brain writes about dinosaurs.

_____ 6. D.W. plays with eggs.

__X__ 7. Arthur does research in the library.

_____ 8. Francine has no jokes in her story.

__X__ 9. Arthur's family did not like his story.

__X__ 10. Everyone likes Arthur's story about his puppy.

Use a Dictionary

> A **dictionary** gives the meanings of words and word spellings.

cot·tage (kot´ ij) *noun* A small house.
draw·bridge (drô´ brij) *noun* A kind of bridge that can be moved or opened so that tall ships can pass under it.
har·vest (här vist) *noun* 1. The gathering in of a crop when it is ripe. 2. The crop when it is gathered.
jar (jär) *noun* A container used to hold things.
muf·fin (muf´ in) *noun* A quick bread that is shaped like a cupcake.

The sentences below show you how the words above are used. Write the definition of the underlined word.

1. The drawbridge was stuck. We could not drive to the island.
   a bridge that can be moved or opened

2. Every morning I buy a muffin. I eat it on my way to work.
   a quick bread that is shaped like a cupcake

3. In the valley, there was a stone cottage. My grandfather helped to build it. **a small house**

4. We caught lightning bugs. Then we put them in a jar.
   a container used to hold things

5. It rained all summer. This gave us a good harvest. **the gathered crop**

Arthur Writes a Story • RETEACH

Silent Letters

Name_____ Date_____ **Reteach** 89

Read the words in the box. They each have a letter that makes no sound.

thum**b**　　　　si**g**n　　　　**w**ho

Write the word that stands for each picture. Circle the silent letter in each word.

1. cha(l)k
2. g(h)ost
3. (k)not
4. (w)rist

Silent Letters

Name_____ Date_____ **Reteach** 90

Read the following sentence.
The stop si**g**n was red.
The letter **g** in **sign** is silent.

Choose the word that completes the sentence.
Write the word on the line.

knock　talked　why　write　lambs　high

1. I will ____knock____ on the door.
2. The kite flew very ____high____.
3. Did you ____write____ down his phone number?
4. I ____talked____ to him on the phone.
5. We have two ____lambs____ on our farm.
6. Pat knows ____why____ Sid is laughing.

Fantasy and Reality

Name_____ Date_____ **Reteach** 91

Real things are things that can really happen.　**Make-believe** things could not really happen.

Read the sentences. Each sentence tells one thing that happened in "The Mysterious Tadpole." Circle **Real** if this is something that could happen in real life. Circle **Make-believe** if this is something that could not really happen.

1. An uncle could send a boy a birthday gift. (Real) Make-believe
2. A boy could take his nature collection to school. (Real) Make-believe
3. Children could ride on the back of a tadpole. Real (Make-believe)
4. A boy could teach a tadpole to retrieve things. Real (Make-believe)
5. A boy could deliver newspapers. (Real) Make-believe
6. A tadpole could grow too big for an apartment. Real (Make-believe)
7. A boy could talk to the librarian. (Real) Make-believe
8. A tadpole could bring a boy a treasure chest. Real (Make-believe)

Context Clues

Name_____ Date_____ **Reteach** 92

A **context clue** is a word or words that help you figure out the meaning of an unknown word.

Look for the context clue that can help you figure out the meaning of the underlined word. Then answer the questions.

1. In the story the king was important because he was a great man.
   a. What is the context clue? ____great____
   b. Is the context clue before or after? ____after____
2. The boring story was not very interesting to read.
   a. What is the context clue? ____not very interesting____
   b. Is the context clue before or after? ____after____
3. The boy wrote about the moon and the sun because he liked outer space.
   a. What is the context clue? ____the moon and the sun____
   b. Is the context clue before or after? ____before____
4. Because the toy airplane was so light, it floated in the air.
   a. What is the context clue? ____so light____
   b. Is the context clue before or after? ____before____

Arthur Writes a Story • EXTEND

Extend 85

Name _____ Date _____ **Extend** ◆85◆

Silent Letters

chalk	wrong	walk	fright	wreck	high
fight	talk	write	sign	might	half

Choose eight words from the box. Write a sentence for each word.

_____ Sentences will vary. _____

1. _____
2. _____
3. _____
4. _____
5. _____
6. _____
7. _____
8. _____

Book 2.1/Unit 3
Arthur Writes a Story

At Home: Have children look at the words in the box. Ask them to cross out the letters that you do **not** say.

85

Extend 86

Name _____ Date _____ **Extend** ◆86◆

Vocabulary

Use each word in the box to write a story about the picture.

library	proud	planet
decided	important	float

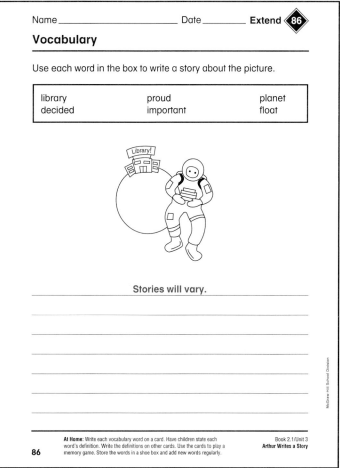

Stories will vary.

_____
_____
_____
_____
_____
_____

86

At Home: Write each vocabulary word on a card. Have children state each word's definition. Write the definitions on other cards. Use the cards to play a memory game. Store the words in a shoe box and add new words regularly.

Book 2.1/Unit 3
Arthur Writes a Story

Extend 87

Name _____ Date _____ **Extend** ◆87◆

Story Comprehension

Choose something that is important to you. Write a story about it.

_____ Stories will vary. _____

_____
_____
_____
_____
_____
_____

Read each question. Circle your answer.
Does your story have a beginning, a middle, and an end?   Yes   No
Did you use details?   Yes   No
Were you creative?   Yes   No

What do you think Arthur would tell you about your story?

_____
_____

Write your story over on another piece of paper. Make any changes you like.

Book 2.1/Unit 3
Arthur Writes a Story

At Home: Ask children to think of advice they would give Arthur the next time he has to write a story.

87

Extend 88

Name _____ Date _____ **Extend** ◆88◆

Use a Dictionary

Fix the chart for Arthur. Use the words and numbers in the box.

exaggerate	gibbon-give	make-man	
giggle	imagine	182	315
maltreat	exact	imaginary	

Entry	Page	Guide Words	Entry Before	Entry After
gigantic	222	gibbon-give	**gig**	giggle
exaggerate	182	**evolve-exchange**	exact	**exam**
imagination	262	illuminate-immerse	imaginary	imagine
mammals	315	make-man	maltreat	**mammoth**

When should you use a dictionary?
Possible answer: You should use a dictionary when you are

not sure what a word means.

88

At Home: Call out a simple word. Have children use a children's dictionary to look the word up as quickly as possible and explain the definition given for the entry.

Book 2.1/Unit 3
Arthur Writes a Story

Page 89

Name _____ Date _____ Extend 89

Silent Letters

Circle the word that names what is happening in each picture.

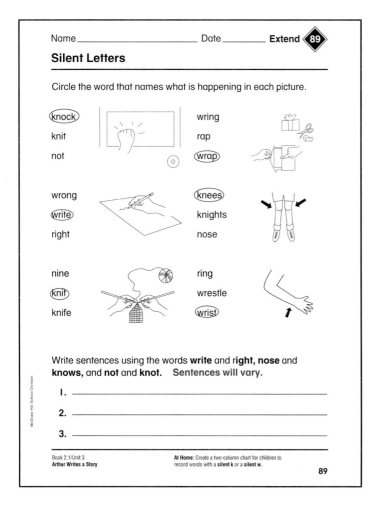

(knock) wring
knit rap
not (wrap)

wrong (knees)
(write) knights
right nose

nine ring
(knif) wrestle
knife (wrist)

Write sentences using the words **write** and **right, nose** and **knows**, and **not** and **knot.**   **Sentences will vary.**

1. _____

2. _____

3. _____

At Home: Create a two-column chart for children to record words with a **silent k** or a **silent w.**

89

Page 90

Name _____ Date _____ Extend 90

Silent Letters

Cut out the picture cards and word cards.
Mix them up. Put them face down and try to make pairs.
Write a short story using some of the words from the cards.

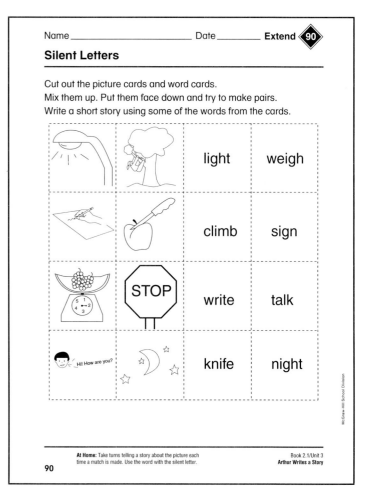

		light	weigh
		climb	sign
	STOP	write	talk
		knife	night

At Home: Take turns telling a story about the picture each time a match is made. Use the word with the silent letter.

90

Page 91

Name _____ Date _____ Extend 91

Fantasy and Reality

Look at the pictures below. Decide which picture shows something real and which one shows something that is make-believe. Write real or make-believe on the line.

_____make-believe_____   _____real_____

List the things that tell you that what is happening in the picture is **make-believe.**

dog shopping, walking on hind legs, wearing people clothes

List the things that tell you that what is happening in the picture could be **real life.**

dog eats from a dog bowl, has a collar, has a doghouse

At Home: Look through books together to determine which books contain stories that could happen in real life and which are make-believe.

91

Page 92

Name _____ Date _____ Extend 92

Context Clues

Circle the words that help you tell what the underlined words mean.

1. The story about dinosaurs should be well researched.
   I will find lots of information about dinosaurs before I write it.
   find lots of information
2. Did you find out about elephants scientifically?
   No. I could not do tests and experiments to learn about them.
   do tests and experiments to learn about them
3. Were you sad when the dog disappeared?
   Yes. I could not see him, and I did not know where to find him.
   could not see him; did not know where to find him

Write a word from the box to finish the sentences.

mammal	imagination	business

4. Arthur started a pet ___business___ so he could work and earn money.

5. D.W. did not think a ___mammal___ like an elephant could live in outer space.

6. The more Arthur used his ___imagination___, the wilder his story became.

At Home: Ask children to identify clues in pictures and words in sentences that help them figure out the meanings of words they don't know.

92

Arthur Writes a Story • GRAMMAR

Action Verbs

> • An action verb is a word that shows action.
>   Today Susan **plays** in the big game.

Read each sentence. Put a circle around
all the words that show action.

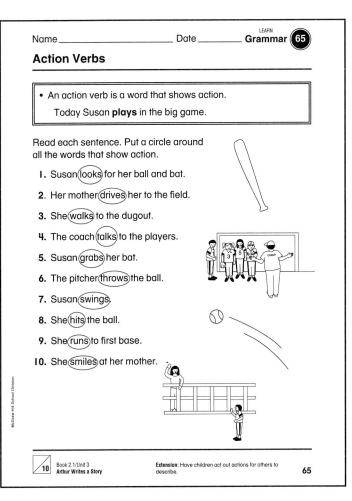

1. Susan (looks) for her ball and bat.
2. Her mother (drives) her to the field.
3. She (walks) to the dugout.
4. The coach (talks) to the players.
5. Susan (grabs) her bat.
6. The pitcher (throws) the ball.
7. Susan (swings).
8. She (hits) the ball.
9. She (runs) to first base.
10. She (smiles) at her mother.

Action Verbs

> • Some action verbs tell about actions that are hard to see.
>   Babs <u>likes</u> bananas.   Bananas <u>taste</u> good.

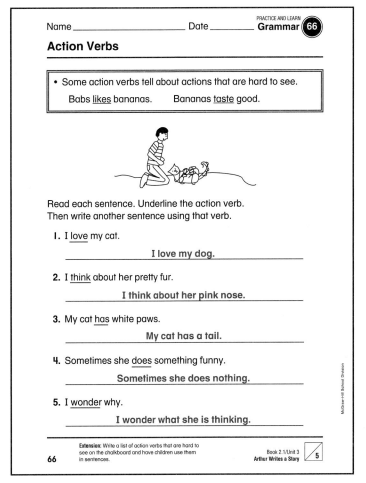

Read each sentence. Underline the action verb.
Then write another sentence using that verb.

1. I <u>love</u> my cat.
   _____ **I love my dog.** _____

2. I <u>think</u> about her pretty fur.
   _____ **I think about her pink nose.** _____

3. My cat <u>has</u> white paws.
   _____ **My cat has a tail.** _____

4. Sometimes she <u>does</u> something funny.
   _____ **Sometimes she does nothing.** _____

5. I <u>wonder</u> why.
   _____ **I wonder what she is thinking.** _____

Action Verbs

> • An **action verb** is a word that shows action.
> • Some action verbs tell about actions that are hard to see.
>   Bud <u>runs</u> past me.   The girl <u>knows</u>.

Read the paragraph. Underline all the action verbs.
Then use each one in a new sentence.

My dog Bud <u>jumps</u> on the chair. He <u>barks</u>. Mom <u>sees</u> him.
She <u>takes</u> him off the chair. He <u>runs</u> to the kitchen.

1. _____ **My cat Peanut jumps on the fence.** _____
2. _____ **The dog barks at her.** _____
3. _____ **Mom sees Peanut.** _____
4. _____ **She takes her into the house.** _____
5. _____ **Peanut runs to my room.** _____

Abbreviations

> • An abbreviation is a short form of a word.
> • An abbreviation begins with a capital letter and ends
>   with a period.
> • Most titles of people are abbreviations.

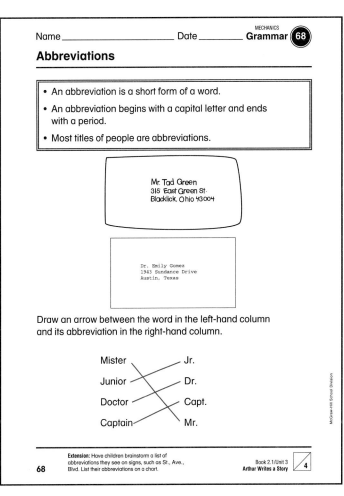

Mr. Tad Green
315 East Green St.
Blacklick, Ohio 43004

Dr. Emily Gomez
1943 Sundance Drive
Austin, Texas

Draw an arrow between the word in the left-hand column
and its abbreviation in the right-hand column.

Mister   Jr.
Junior   Dr.
Doctor   Capt.
Captain   Mr.

Arthur Writes a Story • GRAMMAR

Action Verbs

Read each sentence. Write the verb in each sentence on the line.

1. Jason runs to the ball park. _____ runs _____

2. He throws the first ball. _____ throws _____

3. Claire hits it hard. _____ hits _____

4. Claire reaches first base. _____ reaches _____

5. Claire looks at home plate. _____ looks _____

6. She tries to go home. _____ tries _____

7. Jason tags Claire. _____ tags _____

8. Jason and Claire play well. _____ play _____

Action Verbs

- An action verb is a word that shows action.

  The girl pulls the sled.

- Some action verbs tell about actions that are hard to see.

  The girl thinks of the slide down the hill.

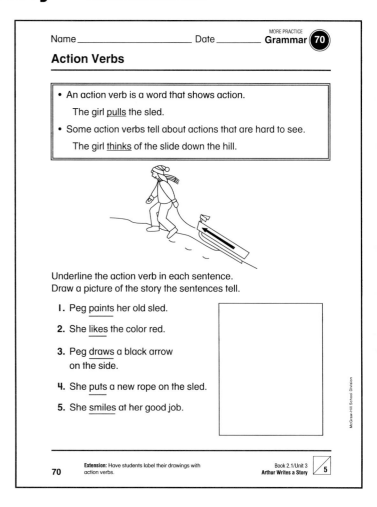

Underline the action verb in each sentence.
Draw a picture of the story the sentences tell.

1. Peg paints her old sled.

2. She likes the color red.

3. Peg draws a black arrow on the side.

4. She puts a new rope on the sled.

5. She smiles at her good job.

70 Extension: Have students label their drawings with action verbs.

Book 2.1/Unit 3
Arthur Writes a Story 5

Arthur Writes a Story • SPELLING

Words with Silent Letters

Pretest Directions

Fold back the paper along the dotted line. Use the blanks to write each word as it is read aloud. When you finish the test, unfold the paper. Correct any spelling mistakes. Practice the words you missed for the Posttest.

To Parents,
Here are the results of your child's weekly spelling Pretest. You can help your child study for the Posttest by following these simple steps for each word on the list:

1. Read the word to your child.
2. Have your child write the word, saying each letter as it is written.
3. Say each letter of the word as your child checks the spelling.
4. If a mistake has been made, have your child read each letter of the correctly spelled word aloud, and then repeat steps 1–3.

1. _____
2. _____
3. _____
4. _____
5. _____
6. _____
7. _____
8. _____
9. _____
10. _____

1. high
2. know
3. half
4. wrote
5. thumb
6. lamb
7. knee
8. right
9. knot
10. write

Challenge Words

_____ decided
_____ important
_____ library
_____ planet
_____ proud

10 Book 2.1/Unit 3
Arthur Writes a Story

65

Words with Silent Letters

Using the Word Study Steps
1. LOOK at the word.
2. SAY the word aloud.
3. STUDY the letters in the word.
4. WRITE the word.
5. CHECK the word.
   Did you spell the word right? If not, go back to step 1.

Spelling Tip
Make up clues to help you remember the spelling.
Example:
Be gentle with a la**mb**.
(Lamb ends with a **b**.)

Crossword Puzzle
Write the spelling word that best matches each clue. Put the spelling words in the boxes that start with the same number.

CROSSWORD CLUES
ACROSS
1. understand
2. two of these make a whole
6. put words on paper yesterday
7. special finger
9. not low
DOWN
1. where your leg bends
3. what an author does
4. a baby sheep
5. your laces are tied with this
8. correct

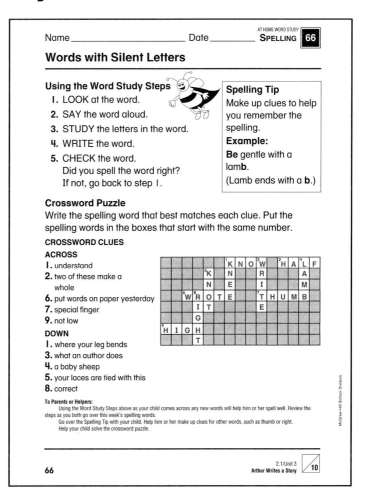

To Parents or Helpers:
Using the Word Study Steps above as your child comes across any new words will help him or her spell well. Review the steps as you both go over this week's spelling words.
Go over the Spelling Tip with your child. Help him or her make up clues for other words, such as thumb or right.
Help your child solve the crossword puzzle.

66

2.1/Unit 3
Arthur Writes a Story 10

Words with Silent Letters

high	half	thumb	knee	knot
know	wrote	lamb	right	write

Look at the spelling words in the box.
Each spelling word has a silent letter. Match each word to a spelling pattern. Write the spelling words on the lines below.

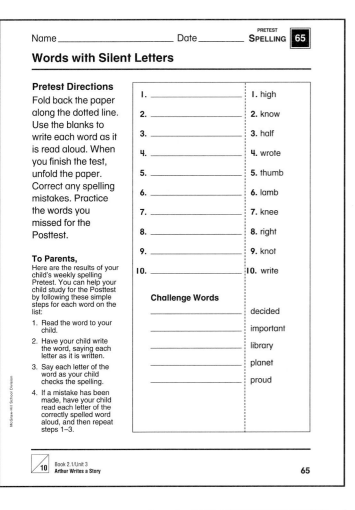

Silent _l_
1. _____ half _____

Silent _b_
2. _____ thumb _____
3. _____ lamb _____

Silent _k_
4. _____ know _____
5. _____ knee _____
6. _____ knot _____

Silent _w_
7. _____ wrote _____
8. _____ write _____

Silent _gh_
9. _____ high _____
10. _____ right _____

10 Book 2.1/Unit 3
Arthur Writes a Story

67

Words with Silent Letters

high	half	thumb	knee	knot
know	wrote	lamb	right	write

Write a spelling word to complete each sentence.

1. Help me untie the _____ knot _____.
2. I will give you _____ half _____ of my apple.
3. A baby sheep is called a _____ lamb _____.
4. Do you _____ know _____ the answer?
5. Your _____ thumb _____ is on your hand.
6. You can bend your leg at the _____ knee _____.
7. The opposite of **left** is _____ right _____.
8. The opposite of **low** is _____ high _____.
9. I will _____ write _____ a letter to my mom.
10. I _____ wrote _____ a letter to my brother.

Word Builder
Be a word builder. Add the ending -ed to the word. First, double the final consonant.
knot + t + ed = _____ knotted _____

Challenge Extension: Have children complete this sentence: I think the library is important because _____.

68

Book 2.1/Unit 3
Arthur Writes a Story 10

T15

Words with Silent Letters

Proofreading Activity

There are six spelling mistakes in the story below. Circle each misspelled word. Write the words correctly on the lines below.

One day a first grader in my school had a (kot) in his shoelace. He was (haf) my size. He asked me to help him. I didn't (noe) the (rit) way to get the knot out. I tried pulling it, but that didn't work. I took his shoe off and set it on my (nee). Then I could hold the shoe with my (thum) and undo the knot with my fingers. Afterwards, his mother wrote my mother a note saying that I was a great kid.

1. ___knot___   2. ___half___   3. ___know___

4. ___right___   5. ___knee___   6. ___thumb___

Writing Activity

Write about a time when someone helped you. Use four of your spelling words. Circle the spelling words you use.

_____

_____

_____

_____

_____

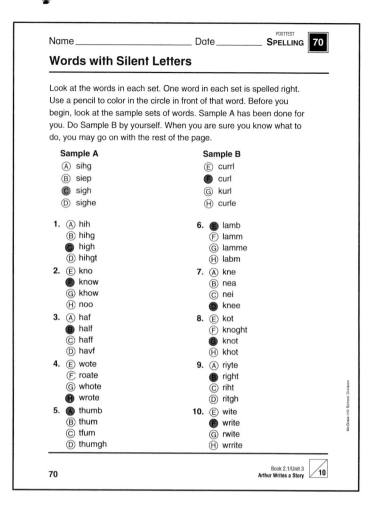

Words with Silent Letters

Look at the words in each set. One word in each set is spelled right. Use a pencil to color in the circle in front of that word. Before you begin, look at the sample sets of words. Sample A has been done for you. Do Sample B by yourself. When you are sure you know what to do, you may go on with the rest of the page.

Sample A
- (A) sihg
- (B) siep
- (C) sigh ●
- (D) sighe

Sample B
- (E) currl
- (F) curl ●
- (G) kurl
- (H) curle

1.
- (A) hih
- (B) hihg
- (C) high ●
- (D) hihgt

2.
- (E) kno
- (F) know ●
- (G) khow
- (H) noo

3.
- (A) haf
- (B) half ●
- (C) haff
- (D) havf

4.
- (E) wote
- (F) roate
- (G) whote
- (H) wrote ●

5.
- (A) thumb ●
- (B) thum
- (C) tfum
- (D) thumgh

6.
- (E) lamb ●
- (F) lamm
- (G) lamme
- (H) labm

7.
- (A) kne
- (B) nea
- (C) nei
- (D) knee ●

8.
- (E) kot
- (F) knoght
- (G) knot ●
- (H) khot

9.
- (A) riyte
- (B) right ●
- (C) riht
- (D) ritgh

10.
- (E) wite
- (F) write ●
- (G) rwite
- (H) wrrite

Best Wishes, Ed • PRACTICE

Practice 93

Name_____ Date_____ Practice **93**

/ər/ er

Read the words below. Listen to the sound the letters **er** make in each word.

cov**er**　　　anoth**er**　　　und**er**

Think about "Best Wishes, Ed." Then read the sentences. Choose a word from the box that completes each sentence and write the word on the line.

winter	letter	smaller	under
larger	over	hammer	another

1. Ernest the whale is ___larger___ than Ed the penguin.

2. The iceberg is getting ___smaller___ .

3. Ernest the whale swims ___under___ the water.

4. Ed writes a ___letter___ in the snow.

5. Clouds float ___over___ Ed's head.

6. During the story it is ___winter___ .

7. Ed makes ___another___ friend.

8. The ice breaking sounded like a ___hammer___ .

Book 2.1/Unit 3
Best Wishes, Ed
8

At Home: Have children illustrate one of the sentences they completed.

93

Practice 94

Name_____ Date_____ Practice **94**

Vocabulary

Choose words from the box to finish the letter. Write the words on the lines.

climbed	couple	drifted	half	message	notice

Dear Louis,

Thanks for sending me the ___message___ about the camping trip. I have been to Mountain Park. I ___climbed___ to the top of the mountain with my mother. It took us a ___couple___ of hours. We were very high up. A cloud ___drifted___ by right next to us. Coming down was easy. It took us only ___half___ as long as going up. My legs got very tired. But I didn't even ___notice___ it until we stopped. I hope we can climb again next summer.

Your friend,

Pete

94

At Home: Ask children to write the message that Louis might have written to Pete about the camping trip.

Book 2.1/Unit 3
Best Wishes, Ed
6

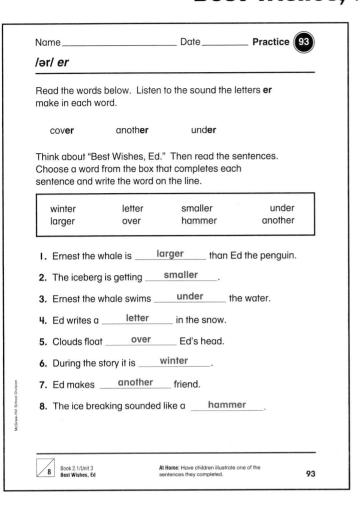

A Message from the Sun

That night I slept under a big tree. In the morning, I felt someone tap my fingers. It was the sun!

"Good morning," the sun said.

"Do you see now why I set early in winter? If it is so people like you will get the sleep they need!"

"Thank you!" I said. I happily walked home. The sun kept me warm the whole way.

At Home: Talk with children about times of the year and when the sun sets during those times. How does the sun affect our days?

4

94a

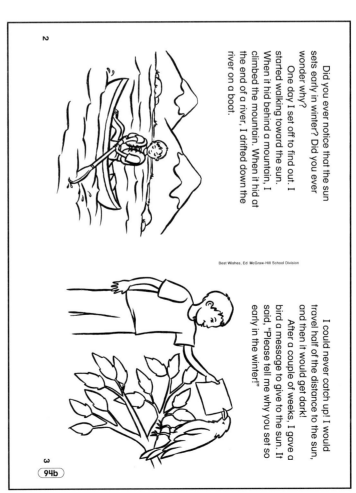

2

Did you ever notice that the sun sets early in winter? Did you ever wonder why?

One day I set off to find out. I started walking toward the sun. When it hid behind a mountain, I climbed the mountain. When it hid at the end of a river, I drifted down the river on a boat.

I could never catch up! I would travel half of the distance to the sun, and then it would get dark!

After a couple of weeks, I gave a bird a message to give to the sun. It said, "Please tell me why you set so early in the winter!"

Best Wishes, Ed McGraw-Hill School Division

3

94b

T17

Best Wishes, Ed • PRACTICE

Story Comprehension

Think about "Best Wishes, Ed." Who said each sentence?
Color the answer.

1. Ernest does not even notice penguins.

   color

2. I will be here all my life.

   color

3. Will you write a letter for me?

   color

4. I do not know how to fly.

   color

5. I have lots of things to do besides helping penguins.

   color

Book 2.1/Unit 3
Best Wishes, Ed
5

At Home: Have children tell at least one other thing Ed said during the story.

95

Use an Encyclopedia

Study the sample **encyclopedia** page shown below.
Some encyclopedia entries have **cross references**.
These point you to related entries you might like to read.

Poland — Police

Poland is a country in central Europe. It borders on the Baltic Sea. Its name comes from a tribe of people called the Polane. They lived over a thousand years ago in that area. Poland has rich natural resources and is famous for its industry.

Polar bear is a large white bear found near the Arctic Ocean. A full-grown bear can be over nine feet tall and weigh close to 1,000 pounds. Polar bears are great hunters and strong swimmers. (See also *Bears*)

Police are government workers who make sure people obey the law. Police control traffic and try to find out who committed crimes. They also help out during natural disasters like floods or tornadoes. There are city police and state police. Each group enforces the laws, but state police serve cities that don't have their own police force. Police officers are sometimes called *cops*. It is thought the word comes from their copper badges.

Use the entries above to answer the following questions.

1. How much does a polar bear weigh? __close to 1,000 pounds__

2. The word for Poland comes from what tribe of people?

   __the Polane__

3. What kind of cities do state police serve? __cities without their__

   __own police force__

4. Where is the country of Poland found? __in central Europe__

5. What other entry does the entry under *Polar bear* tell you to

   read? __Bears__

/ər/ er, /ən/ en, /əl/ le

Write the word that answers each riddle.

apple	open	letters	flower	seven	table

1. You can eat on it. You can put things on it. What is it?

   __table__

2. This pretty thing can be many different colors. It can grow in a garden or in a pot. What is it?

   __flower__

3. You can eat this fruit or bake it in a pie. What is it?

   __apple__

4. This number comes before eight. It is one more than six. What number is it?

   __seven__

5. A, B, and C are three of these. You write them every day. What are they?

   __letters__

6. When the door is not closed, what is it?

   __open__

6
Book 2.1/Unit 3
Best Wishes, Ed

At Home: Help children make up a riddle that has an answer that rhymes with **flower**.

97

/ər/, /ən/, /əl/; Silent Letters

Circle the word that completes each sentence. Then write the word.

1. The ocean is full of me. I am _____water_____.

   (water)   powder

2. I am a pencil. Use me to _____write_____.

   wring   (write)

3. Cook dinner in me. I am an _____oven_____.

   (oven)   right

4. People do what I say. I am a _____sign_____.

   (sign)   spider

5. After dinner, let's take a _____walk_____.

   (walk)   talk

6. Light me when the power goes out. I am a _____candle_____.

   handle   (candle)

7. Let's _____climb_____ to the top of the mountain!

   (climb)   lamb

8. I come after seven and before nine. I am _____eight_____.

   (eight)   weight

98

At Home: Have children write questions using some of the words they did not circle.

Book 2.1/Unit 3
Best Wishes, Ed
8

Best Wishes, Ed • PRACTICE

Name _____ Date _____ Practice 99

Cause and Effect

Read the story. Then read each sentence below that tells something that happened in the story. Write why each thing happened.

> In the spring, penguins pile up rocks to make a nest. Here, each mother lays an egg. The mother and father keep the egg warm until it hatches. Then, the mother leaves to catch fish for her baby. When she comes back, it is the father's turn to catch fish. After the baby gets bigger, the father will teach the young one how to swim and dive. Then the baby can catch its own fish.

1. The penguins pile up rocks.

   They are making a nest.

2. The mother and father keep the egg warm.

   They want the egg to hatch.

3. Mother leaves her baby penguin.

   She gets fish for her baby.

4. Father teaches the young penguin how to swim and dive.

   The baby penguin has to learn how to catch its own fish.

4 Book 2.1/Unit 3
Best Wishes, Ed

At Home: Have children tell about a time when they watched something new happen. Why did it happen?

99

Name _____ Date _____ Practice 100

Context Clues

Sometimes other words in a sentence or a story can help you figure out the meaning of a new word. These words are called **context clues.** They can come before or after the unknown word.

Choose the word or group of words that help you figure out the meaning of the word in dark print. Write these context clues on the line.

1. A big wave washed on the beach and **splashed** everyone there.

   a big wave washed on the beach

2. **Penguins** are birds who live where there is lots of ice and snow.

   birds who live where there is lots of ice and snow

3. When the big tree fell over into our yard, it made a big **cracking** noise.

   fell over into our yard

4. Because he had no one to play with, Ed the penguin felt very **alone**.

   Because he had no one to play with

100

At Home: Ask children to write three sentences about a favorite story. They should use three new words that are explained by context clues in their story.

Book 2.1/Unit 3
Best Wishes, Ed 4

Best Wishes, Ed • RETEACH

Reteach 93

Name _____ Date _____ Reteach **93**

/ ər/ er

Read the words. They have the same ending sound.

sist**er**   und**er**

The name for each picture below has the same ending sound as sist**er** and und**er**. Circle the word that names the picture.

1.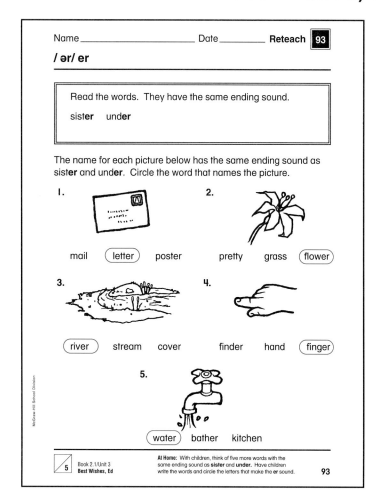

    mail   (letter)   poster

2.

    pretty   grass   (flower)

3.

    (river)   stream   cover

4.

    finder   hand   (finger)

5.

    (water)   bather   kitchen

Book 2.1/Unit 3
Best Wishes, Ed   **5**

At Home: With children, think of five more words with the same ending sound as **sister** and **under**. Have children write the words and circle the letters that make the **er** sound.

93

Reteach 94

Name _____ Date _____ Reteach **94**

Vocabulary

Choose a word from the box to complete each sentence.
Write the word on the line.

| climbed | couple | drifted | half | message | notice |

1. My brother gave me _____**half**_____ of his orange.

2. Bruce and Will _____**climbed**_____ up the hill.

3. The sailboat _____**drifted**_____ away in the wind.

4. Kelly read the _____**message**_____ from the teacher out loud.

5. Will she _____**notice**_____ that a storm is coming?

6. We have a _____**couple**_____ of hours to play before dark.

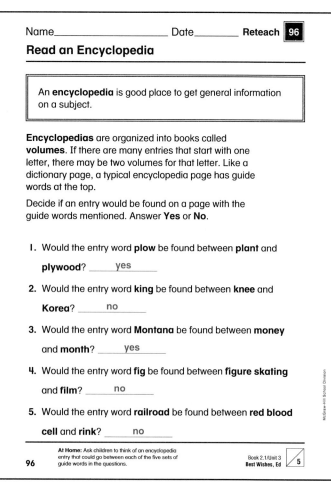

94

At Home: Ask children to write a new sentence for each word in the box.

Book 2.1/Unit 3
Best Wishes, Ed   **6**

Reteach 95

Name _____ Date _____ Reteach **95**

Story Comprehension

Fill in the chart about "Best Wishes, Ed."

CHARACTERS: Ed, Talbot, Ernest, the other birds and penguins.

BEGINNING OF THE STORY: Ed lives on an ice island with his friends. One night the ice breaks apart and Ed floats away.

MIDDLE OF THE STORY: Ed meets Talbot the tern. He begins to write messages for the birds on the surface of the ice. Then someone writes a message for him.

END OF THE STORY: Ernest the whale rescues Ed and brings him back to his friends.

Book 2.1/Unit 3
Best Wishes, Ed   **4**

At Home: Have children illustrate one of their answers.

95

Reteach 96

Name _____ Date _____ Reteach **96**

Read an Encyclopedia

An **encyclopedia** is good place to get general information on a subject.

Encyclopedias are organized into books called **volumes**. If there are many entries that start with one letter, there may be two volumes for that letter. Like a dictionary page, a typical encyclopedia page has guide words at the top.

Decide if an entry would be found on a page with the guide words mentioned. Answer **Yes** or **No**.

1. Would the entry word **plow** be found between **plant** and **plywood**? _____yes_____

2. Would the entry word **king** be found between **knee** and **Korea**? _____no_____

3. Would the entry word **Montana** be found between **money** and **month**? _____yes_____

4. Would the entry word **fig** be found between **figure skating** and **film**? _____no_____

5. Would the entry word **railroad** be found between **red blood cell** and **rink**? _____no_____

96

At Home: Ask children to think of an encyclopedia entry that could go between each of the five sets of guide words in the questions.

Book 2.1/Unit 3
Best Wishes, Ed   **5**

Best Wishes, Ed • RETEACH

/ ər/ er, / ən/, / əl/

> Say the following words.
>
> singer   given   handle

Circle the word that has the same ending sound as the underlined word.

1. <u>baker</u>   (listen)   <u>widen</u>

2. (button)   candle   <u>ribbon</u>

3. <u>farmer</u>   mantle   (helper)

4. (flower)   <u>hotter</u>   gentle

5. (bagel)   <u>novel</u>   raven

6. (handle)   <u>swimmer</u>   <u>able</u>

/ər/, /ən/, /əl/; Silent Letters

>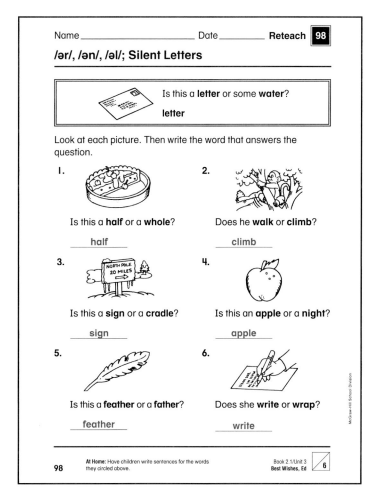
>
> Is this a **letter** or some **water**?
>
> **letter**

Look at each picture. Then write the word that answers the question.

1. Is this a **half** or a **whole**?

   half

2. Does he **walk** or **climb**?

   climb

3. Is this a **sign** or a **cradle**?

   sign

4. Is this an **apple** or a **night**?

   apple

5. Is this a **feather** or a **father**?

   feather

6. Does she **write** or **wrap**?

   write

Cause and Effect

> Look at the pictures. Read the sentences. The **cause** is the event that makes the **effect** happen.
>
> | Cause | Effect |
> |-------|--------|
> | It rained. | The girl got wet. |

The picture shows an effect. Write a cause that could have made each effect happen. **Answers will vary.**

1. **Cause:**
   _____

   Effect:
   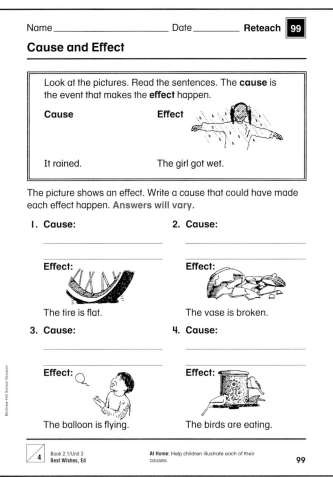
   The tire is flat.

2. **Cause:**
   _____

   Effect:
   The vase is broken.

3. **Cause:**
   _____

   Effect:
   The balloon is flying.

4. **Cause:**
   _____

   Effect:
   The birds are eating.

Context Clues

> Sometimes the other words in a sentence can help you figure out the meaning of a new word. These clue words can come before or after the unknown word.
>
> There was no sunshine on the **cloudy** day.
> The unknown word is **cloudy**.
> The clue words are **no sunshine**.

Read each sentence. Then find the word in the box that tells the meaning of the word. Write the word from the box on the blank line.

flower	home	instrument	bird

1. The girl banged on the round **gong**. The gong made a loud noise.

   A gong is an ___instrument.___

2. The **heron** has long, thin legs and a long bill. It makes its nest in tall grass along the river.

   A heron is a ___bird.___

3. The man crawled into his **igloo** to get out of the cold. His family was waiting in there for him. They had dinner together.

   An igloo is a ___home.___

4. Dad planted pink **asters** in the garden. I hope they smell nice.

   An aster is a ___flower.___

/ər/er

Name_____ Date_____ Extend ◈93◈

On each line there is a word that does not have the same final sound as the other words. Cross out the word that does not belong.

1. ~~hot~~   singer   river   roller

2. walker   runner   tiger   ~~time~~

3. reader   flier   smaller   ~~fish~~

4. letter   other   ~~kind~~   father

5. over   ~~talk~~   mother   burger

Use four of the words that you did not cross out to write a story.

Answers will vary.

_____

_____

_____

_____

_____

_____

Book 2.1/Unit 3
Best Wishes, Ed

At Home: Have children start a list of words that have the same **er** sound that you hear in the word **river**.

93

Vocabulary

Name_____ Date_____ Extend ◈94◈

Write a sentence to tell what each word means.
Sample answers are shown.

1. climbed _____
   Climbed means moved up.

2. couple ___ **Couple means a pair of people, animals, or objects.**

3. drifted ___ **Drifted means to float away.**
   _____

4. half ___ **Half means one of two equal parts.**

5. message ___ **Message means information that should be sent to someone.**

6. notice ___ **Notice means to see something.**
   _____

Choose one of the words. Draw a picture to show what it means.

_____

At Home: Create a board for children to write and pin messages to.

94

Book 2.1/Unit 3
Best Wishes, Ed

Story Comprehension

Name_____ Date_____ Extend ◈95◈

These parts of the story "Best Wishes, Ed" are out of order. Number the steps in the order they happened.

__5__ Ed found a surprise message.

__2__ Ed was asleep, and there was a loud cracking noise.

__3__ Ed was alone on an island of his own.

__6__ Ernest gave Ed a ride home.

__1__ Ed and his friends had fun throwing snowballs and sliding on the ice.

__4__ Talbot asked Ed to write something for him in the snow.

Write a thank you message for Ed to leave for Ernest.

Answers will vary.

_____

_____

_____

_____

_____

Book 2.1/Unit 3
Best Wishes, Ed

At Home: Invite children to retell the story of "Best Wishes, Ed." Ask them to brainstorm other ways Ed could have solved his problem.

95

Read an Encyclopedia

Name_____ Date_____ Extend ◈96◈

Read the encyclopedia entry to learn about whales. Then answer the questions.

Whales
Whales are mammals who live their whole lives in the water. Whales have a layer of blubber on their bodies to keep them warm and floating. They breathe air through holes on the top of their heads.

Whales use their hearing to help them find their way in the water. Some whales swim alone in the sea. Other whales swim with their families or in groups with hundreds of other whales. People think the blue whale may be the largest animal ever to have lived.   **Sample answers are given.**

1. Make a list of ways Ernest in "Best Wishes, Ed" is like a real whale.
   He lives in the water.
   He breathes.
   He swims alone in the sea.

2. What does Ernest do that a real whale could not?
   He can speak.
   He can give a penguin a ride.
   _____

At Home: Help children use an encyclopedia to learn more about their favorite animal.

96

Book 2.1/Unit 3
Best Wishes, Ed

Best Wishes, Ed • EXTEND

/ ər/er, / ən/, / əl/

Look at the picture. Unscramble the word that tells about the picture.

1. ouplec

   _____ couple _____

2. veen

   _____ even _____

| Visitors | 0 | 1 | 1 | 0 | 1 | 0 | 3 | 0 | | 6 | 10 | 1 |
| Home | 0 | 0 | 0 | 2 | 1 | 0 | 1 | 2 | | 6 | 9 | 0 |

3. vercoed

   _____ covered _____

4. tterles

   _____ letters _____

5. allersm

   _____ smaller _____

Create your own scrambled word with a picture clue. Use the word **water.**

Book 2.1/Unit 3
Best Wishes, Ed

At Home: Have children look for words that rhyme with the words above.

97

/ ər/er, / ən/, / əl/; Silent Letters

Choose a word from the box to answer each riddle. Write the word on the line.

| sign | couple | half | walk | night |

1. Something cut into two pieces. _____ half _____

2. A way to go somewhere. _____ walk _____

3. It can tell you what to do. _____ sign _____

4. The time when you see the moon best. _____ night _____

5. Two of something. _____ couple _____

Write your own riddle for the word **eleven.**

It equals five plus six.

Write your own riddle for the word **better.**

It is found between *good* **and** *best.*

Cause and Effect

Draw a line under the words that are the **cause.**
Draw a circle around the words that are the **effect.**

1. Ed played near the edge of the ice so he got splashed with water.   Ed played near the edge of the ice so he got splashed with water.

2. The ice broke so Ed was alone on an island.
   The ice broke so Ed was alone on an island.

3. Ed wrote messages for the birds so Talbot asked Ernest to give Ed a ride home.   Ed wrote messages for the birds so Talbot asked Ernest to give Ed a ride home.

Write what you think the **effect** is for each **cause.**

4. Ernest always splashed the penguins with his tail so the penguins thought he didn't notice them.

5. Ed was nice to the birds so the birds helped him get home.

6. Ed was away from his island so his friends missed him.

Book 2.1/Unit 3
Best Wishes, Ed

At Home: Challenge children to come up with a new story ending that tells what might have happened if Ed had not been helpful to Talbot.

99

Context Clues

Some of the messages Ed wrote for Talbot melted in the sun. Help Talbot's friends read the messages. Write the missing letters in the message.

1. I have some fish for lunch.
   fi

   SH

2. Come swim with me.
   im

   SW

3. Help me build my nest.
   ui

   B LD

4. I am riding on Ernest's back.
   Come play with us.
   in

   RID G

Write a message for Talbot's friends. Leave out letters in one of the words. Draw a picture that tells about the sentence.

100

At Home: Reread the story, "Best Wishes, Ed" with children. Cover letters in words that name objects shown in the illustrations. Challenge children to use word and picture clues to figure out what the word is.

Book 2.1/Unit 3
Best Wishes, Ed

T23

Best Wishes, Ed • GRAMMAR

Present-Tense Verbs

- The tense of a verb tells when the action takes place.
- Some verbs tell about actions that happen now.
  These verbs are in the **present tense**.

  Grandma <u>comes</u> early.

  She <u>gives</u> me a big hug.

Draw a line under each present-tense verb.
Then write the word.

1. Grandma and I <u>walk</u> to the lake. _____ **walk** _____

2. Grandma <u>picks</u> flowers. _____ **picks** _____

3. Then we <u>go</u> home. _____ **go** _____

4. Grandma <u>tells</u> me a story. _____ **tells** _____

5. Grandma and I <u>eat</u> some cookies. _____ **eat** _____

5 Book 2.1/Unit 3
Best Wishes, Ed

Extension: Have children pretend a friend or someone in their family is visiting and tell what they are doing. Have other children raise a hand when they hear a present-tense verb.

71

Present-Tense Verbs

- A present-tense verb must **agree** with its subject.
- Add -s to most verbs if the subject is a singular noun.
- Add -es to verbs that end with s, ch, x, or z.
- Do not add -s or -es if the subject is a plural noun.

  Dad <u>gets</u> the plates.

  The boys <u>set</u> the table.

Underline the correct verb in each sentence.

1. Dan (bring, <u>brings</u>) the bread.
2. The boys (<u>fold</u>, folds) napkins.
3. My sister (<u>wants</u>, want) to read her book.
4. Mom (take, <u>takes</u>) the book away.
5. The girls (<u>sit</u>, sits) at the table.
6. Something (<u>scratches</u>, scratch) the door.
7. The dog (want, <u>wants</u>) to come in.
8. Dad (<u>looks</u>, look) for my brother.
9. He (rush, <u>rushes</u>) in.
10. Finally, we all (eats, <u>eat</u>) dinner.

72

Extension: Have the children explain why they chose each verb.

Book 2.1/Unit 3
Best Wishes, Ed 10

Present-Tense Verbs

- **Present-tense verbs** tell about actions that happen now.
- A present-tense verb must **agree** with its subject.
- Add -s to most verbs if the subject is a singular noun.
- Add -es to verbs that end with s, ch, x, or z.
- Do not add -s or -es if the subject is a plural noun.

Write the correct form of each verb.

1. Uncle Pete ___ **visits** ___ me. (visit)

2. He ___ **fixes** ___ my train. (fix)

3. Now my train ___ **runs** ___ better. (run)

4. Uncle Pete and I ___ **talk** ___ about toys. (talk)

5. New toys ___ **look** ___ good. (look)

5 Book 2.1/Unit 3
Best Wishes, Ed

Extension: Have children pretend a toy is broken and tell how they would fix it.

73

Using Commas

- Use commas to separate three or more words in a series.

  Please give me the pencil, eraser, and map.

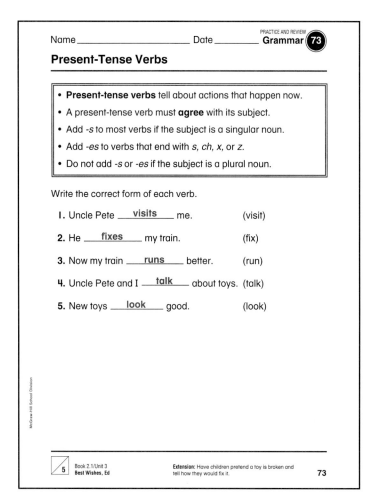

Read the sentences. Begin each one with a capital letter.
Put the periods and commas where they belong.
Write the correct sentences on the lines.

1. we need to wash the floor walls and windows

   We need to wash the floor, walls, and windows.

2. then we will clean the yard garage and attic

   Then we will clean the yard, garage, and attic.

3. now we are waiting for Aunt Belle Uncle Pedro and Aunt Lilly

   Now we are waiting for Aunt Belle, Uncle Pedro, and Aunt Lilly.

4. we will have salad soup sandwiches cake and ice cream

   We will have salad, soup, sandwiches, cake, and ice cream.

Best Wishes, Ed • GRAMMAR

Present-Tense Verbs

Mark the sentence that correctly tells
what is going on now.

1. ⓐ Mel talk to the children.

   ⓑ Mel and Brian talks to the children.

   ● Brian talks to the children.

2. ⓐ Mom eat.

   ● Mom and Ned eat.

   ⓒ Mom and Ned eats.

3. ● Gene makes dinner.

   ⓑ Gene, Ned, and Sally makes lunch.

   ⓒ Sally make breakfast.

4. ⓐ Children plays.

   ● The child plays.

   ⓒ One child play.

5. ⓐ Ed wish for a new toy.

   ⓑ Ed and Ned wishe for a new toy.

   ● Ed, Ned, and Brian wish for a new toy.

Present-Tense Verbs

- Add *-s* to most verbs if the subject is a singular noun.
- Add *-es* to verbs that end with *s, ch, sh, x,* or *z.*

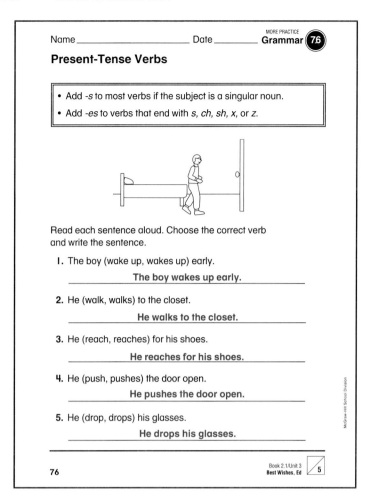

Read each sentence aloud. Choose the correct verb
and write the sentence.

1. The boy (wake up, wakes up) early.

   The boy wakes up early.

2. He (walk, walks) to the closet.

   He walks to the closet.

3. He (reach, reaches) for his shoes.

   He reaches for his shoes.

4. He (push, pushes) the door open.

   He pushes the door open.

5. He (drop, drops) his glasses.

   He drops his glasses.

Best Wishes, Ed • SPELLING

Worksheet 71

Name _____ Date _____ SPELLING **71**
PRETEST

Words ending with /ər/er

Pretest Directions
Fold back the paper along the dotted line. Use the blanks to write each word as it is read aloud. When you finish the test, unfold the paper. Correct any spelling mistakes. Practice the words you missed for the Posttest.

To Parents,
Here are the results of your child's weekly spelling Pretest. You can help your child study for the Posttest by following these simple steps for each word on the list:
1. Read the word to your child.
2. Have your child write the word, saying each letter as it is written.
3. Say each letter of the word as your child checks the spelling.
4. If a mistake has been made, have your child read each letter of the correctly spelled word aloud, and then repeat steps 1–3.

1. _____	1. water
2. _____	2. other
3. _____	3. over
4. _____	4. corner
5. _____	5. letter
6. _____	6. driver
7. _____	7. winter
8. _____	8. never
9. _____	9. farmer
10. _____	10. father

Challenge Words

_____ climbed
_____ couple
_____ drifted
_____ message
_____ notice

Book 2.1/Unit 3
Best Wishes, Ed   71   **10**

Worksheet 72

Name _____ Date _____ SPELLING **72**
AT HOME WORD STUDY

Words ending with /ər/er

Using the Word Study Steps

1. LOOK at the word.
2. SAY the word aloud.
3. STUDY the letters in the word.
4. WRITE the word.
5. CHECK the word.
   Did you spell the word right? If not, go back to step 1.

Spelling Tip
Look for a smaller word in a new word to help you write the new word.
win + ter = winter

Find and Circle
Where are the spelling words?

a	b	o	c	d	c	o	r	n	e	r	e	f	n
w	a	t	e	r	g	v	d	r	i	v	e	r	e
h	i	h	j	k	l	e	w	i	n	t	e	r	v
m	l	e	t	t	e	r	n	n	x	p	r	t	e
f	a	r	m	e	r	u	y	f	a	t	h	e	r

To Parents or Helpers:
Using the Word Study Steps above as your child comes across any new words will help him or her spell well. Review the steps as you both go over this week's spelling words.
Go over the Spelling Tip with your child. Ask if he or she can find other smaller words in new words.
Help your child find and circle the spelling words in the puzzle.

72   Book 2.1/Unit 3
Best Wishes, E   **10**

Worksheet 73

Name _____ Date _____ SPELLING **73**
EXPLORE THE PATTERN

Words ending with /ər/er

water	over	letter	winter	farmer
other	corner	driver	never	father

Fill the icebergs with spelling words that follow the spelling patterns.

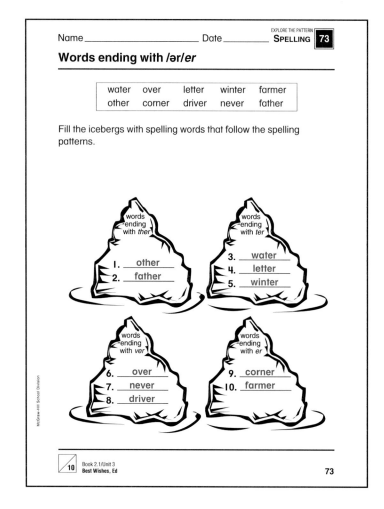

words ending with *ther*
1. other
2. father

words ending with *ter*
3. water
4. letter
5. winter

words ending with *ver*
6. over
7. never
8. driver

words ending with *er*
9. corner
10. farmer

Book 2.1/Unit 3
Best Wishes, Ed   73   **10**

Worksheet 74

Name _____ Date _____ SPELLING **74**
PRACTICE AND EXTEND

Words ending with /ər/er

water	over	letter	winter	farmer
other	corner	driver	never	father

Use spelling words to complete each sentence.

1. The opposite of **always** is ____never____.
2. ____Winter____ is my favorite season because I like to ice skate.
3. Another word for **dad** is ____father____.
4. The opposite of **under** is ____over____.
5. I wrote a ____letter____ to my friend.
6. Meet me at the ____corner____ of Main Street and Oak Avenue.
7. Do you want this one or the ____other____ one?
8. Do you want a drink of ____water____?
9. A ____farmer____ grows food.
10. The bus ____driver____ takes my money.

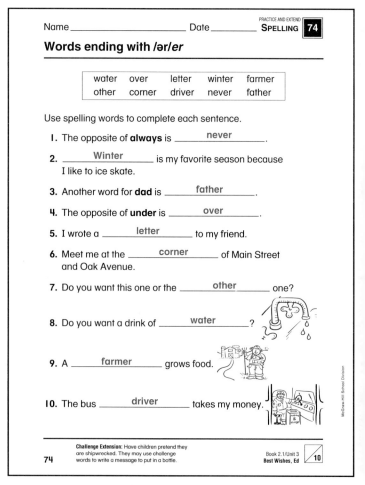

Challenge Extension: Have children pretend they are shipwrecked. They may use challenge words to write a message to put in a bottle.

74   Book 2.1/Unit 3
Best Wishes, Ed   **10**

Best Wishes, Ed • SPELLING

Words ending with /ər/er

Read the sentences. There is one spelling mistake in each sentence. Circle the mistake. Write the correct word on the line.

1. Tom, please send me a (leter.)
2. Matt, why don't you swim (ovir) here today?
3. Who wants to go fishing with Sue and her (fathar?)
4. There will be a (wintor) party for all of the penguins on Saturday night.
5. Mike is looking for (othur) penguins to help build a snowman.
6. Please meet me at the (cornir.)

1. ____letter____ 2. ____over____ 3. ____father____

4. ____winter____ 5. ____other____ 6. ____corner____

Writing Activity
Pretend that you are a farmer. Write a letter to your city friend and invite him to visit you. Tell him what he will see at your farm. Use four of your spelling words. Circle the spelling words you use.

_____

_____

_____

_____

_____

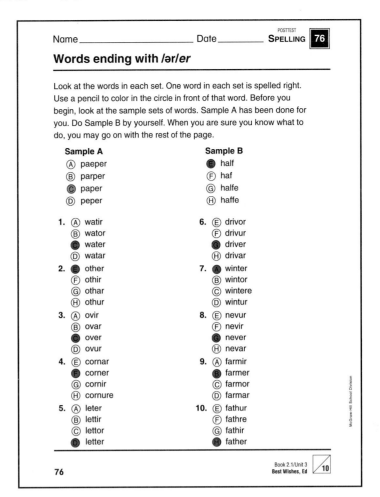

Words ending with /ər/er

Look at the words in each set. One word in each set is spelled right. Use a pencil to color in the circle in front of that word. Before you begin, look at the sample sets of words. Sample A has been done for you. Do Sample B by yourself. When you are sure you know what to do, you may go on with the rest of the page.

Sample A
Ⓐ paeper
Ⓑ parper
🅒 paper
Ⓓ peper

Sample B
🅔 half
Ⓕ haf
Ⓖ halfe
Ⓗ haffe

1. Ⓐ watir
   Ⓑ wator
   🅒 water
   Ⓓ watar

2. 🅔 other
   Ⓕ othir
   Ⓖ othar
   Ⓗ othur

3. Ⓐ ovir
   Ⓑ ovar
   🅒 over
   Ⓓ ovur

4. Ⓔ cornar
   🅕 corner
   Ⓖ cornir
   Ⓗ cornure

5. Ⓐ leter
   Ⓑ lettir
   Ⓒ lettor
   🅓 letter

6. Ⓔ drivor
   Ⓕ drivur
   🅖 driver
   Ⓗ drivar

7. 🅐 winter
   Ⓑ wintor
   Ⓒ wintere
   Ⓓ wintur

8. Ⓔ nevur
   Ⓕ nevir
   🅖 never
   Ⓗ nevar

9. Ⓐ farmir
   🅑 farmer
   Ⓒ farmor
   Ⓓ farmar

10. Ⓔ fathur
    Ⓕ fathre
    Ⓖ fathir
    🅗 father

Annotated Workbooks

Name_____ Date_____ **Practice** 101

Short e: ea

Say the words. What sound do both words have in common?

re**a**dy   fe**a**ther

The sound made by the letters **ea**.

bread	ready	breath	leather
weather	steady	breakfast	head

Read the story below. Then choose a word from the box to write on each line.

The ___weather___ was very cold that morning.

Johnnie had a hot ___breakfast___. He had a piece of

___bread___ with jam and some eggs. He put a

warm hat on his ___head___. Then he went outside

and put the ___leather___ saddle on his horse. It was

so cold, he could see his ___breath___.

Finally, he was ___ready___. But the ice and

snow were slippery. Johnnie shouted, "___Steady___"

to his horse. It would be a day of hard work!

8 | Book 2.1/Unit 3
The Pony Express | **At Home:** Have children pronounce each of the words they wrote. Then have them underline the letters that make the sound of short **e** in each word. | 101

Name_____ Date_____ **Practice** 102

Vocabulary

Choose a word from the box that has the opposite or the same meaning as the underlined word. Write the word on the line.

arrive	early	finish	record	rush	success

1. If you start a game, be sure to ___finish___ it.

2. There's no hurry to get there, so don't ___rush___!

3. Please don't be late. Try to be ___early___.

4. When you ___arrive___, call and let me know you have gotten there.

5. Karla set a world ___record___ because she was the first and only woman to climb the mountain.

6. Our team is not a failure. It is a ___success___.

102 | **At Home:** Ask children to make up a short story using the words in the box. | Book 2.1/Unit 3
The Pony Express 6

Waiting for Beth

Soon Freddy and his father were running out the door.

"We must rush!" said Freddy's father.

At the train station, they ran all the way to Beth's train. She watched them come.

"I think you two just broke my record!" laughed Beth. And together they all walked slowly back home.

At Home: Talk with children about a time someone they loved came to visit. What did they do together?

4

102a

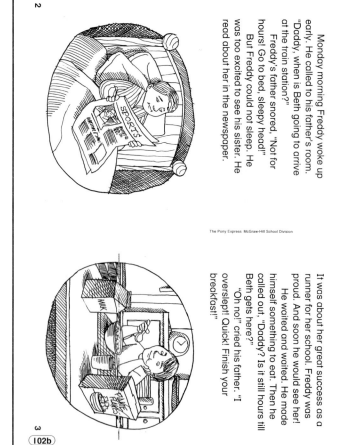

2

Monday morning Freddy woke up early. He called to his father's room.

"Daddy, when is Beth going to arrive at the train station?"

Freddy's father snored, "Not for hours! Go to bed, sleepy head!"

But Freddy could not sleep. He was too excited to see his sister. He read about her in the newspaper.

It was about her great success as a runner for her school. Freddy was proud. And soon he would see her!

He waited and waited. He made himself something to eat. Then he called out, "Daddy? Is it still hours till Beth gets here?"

"Oh no!" cried his father. "I overslept! Quick! Finish your breakfast!"

The Pony Express McGraw-Hill School Division

3

102b

The Pony Express • PRACTICE

Story Comprehension

Answer the following questions about "The Pony Express."

1. What was the Pony Express?

   The Pony Express was a way to carry mail from Missouri

   to California in record time.

2. Why did William Russell start the Pony Express?

   Many people had moved out West, and they needed mail

   and news delivered as fast as possible.

3. What did the riders of the Pony Express carry?

   newspapers and letters

4. What were the riders on the Pony Express like?

   Most were young and small; they were good horseback

   riders.

5. What was the motto of the Pony Express?

   The mail must go through!

6. Why did the Pony Express stop after just a short time?

   The telegraph line across the country was completed.

6 Book 2.1/Unit 3
The Pony Express

At Home: Have children write a short story about whether they would have liked being a Pony Express Rider.

103

Use a Telephone Directory

A **telephone directory** lists people and businesses in alphabetical order.

Study the sample page below. Use it to answer the questions that follow.

192 Hodges — Holmes
HODGES Catherine Near Rd Red Bank 555-9863
Kenneth 1692 West Walnut Martinsville 555-2347
P.C. 1324 Weston Rd Riverton 555-4376
HOFFMAN Nelson 45 Brushy Hill Rd Lambert 555-9898
Michelle M 373 South St Remertown 555-3245
HOFFMANN SEE ALSO HOFFMAN, HOFMAN, HOFMANN

1. What is the phone number of P.C. Hodges? 555-4376

2. What other spellings of Hoffmann are suggested? Hoffman, Hofman, and Hofmann

3. Pretend you're looking for someone named Hoffman. You don't know the first name. But you know the person lives in Lambert. Which Hoffman would you pick? Nelson

4. Suppose you're looking for someone named Holton. Would you find that person on this page? Why or why not?

   No, Holton would come after the guide word Holmes.

104 **At Home:** Ask children how many different people listed on this page have the last name Hodges.

Book 2.1/Unit 3
The Pony Express 4

Short e: ea

Write the word from the box that each statement describes.

ahead	bread	feathers	weather
heavy	lead	ready	leather

1. I am not fur, but I do cover some animals. What am I?

   feathers

2. Sometimes I am sunny. Sometimes I am rainy. What am I?

   weather

3. I am in front of something or someone. What am I?

   ahead

4. I am used to make a sandwich. Sometimes you feed me to the ducks. What am I? bread

5. I weigh a lot. What am I? heavy

6. I am the black part of your pencil. What am I? lead

7. I am used for shoes, gloves, and saddles. What am I?

   leather

8. I want to do something now. I don't want to wait. What am I?

   ready

8 Book 2.1/Unit 3
The Pony Express

At Home: Ask children to find two more words with the short e sound spelled ea and write them down.

105

Short e; /ər/, /ən/, /əl/; Silent Letters

Choose a word from the box to finish each statement.

leather	finger	high	straight	seven	sign

1. I am more than six and less than eight. I am seven.

2. I am not low. I am high.

3. People make shoes out of me. I am leather.

4. I tell people things like "Stop" and "Exit." I am a sign.

5. I am not bent. I am straight.

6. You point with me. I am a finger.

Now draw a line from each question to the right answer.

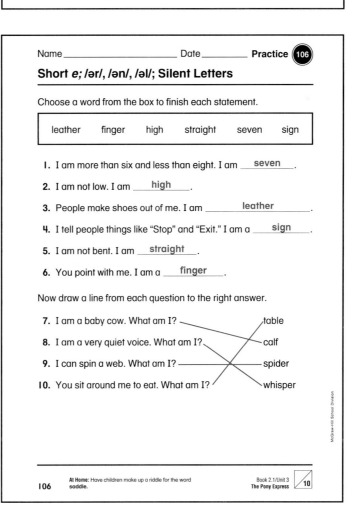

7. I am a baby cow. What am I? — table

8. I am a very quiet voice. What am I? — calf

9. I can spin a web. What am I? — spider

10. You sit around me to eat. What am I? — whisper

106 **At Home:** Have children make up a riddle for the word saddle.

Book 2.1/Unit 3
The Pony Express 10

The Pony Express • PRACTICE

Fantasy and Reality

Think about "The Pony Express." Then read the story below. Circle the sentences that are **real,** and draw a line under the sentences that are **make-believe.** Then write two more sentences to finish the story. Write one real sentence and one make-believe sentence.

Answers will vary.

(Johnnie Frye was a young rider.) (He was brave, fast, and tough.) His horse had wings. He could fly through the air. Johnnie's horse was all different colors, like a rainbow. (Together, Johnnie and his horse carried the mail.) (They rode in all kinds of weather.) (Sometimes they would drive. Other times they would take the train.

(The Pony Express riders worked very hard at their jobs.) (After a little more than a year the Pony Express ended.) Mail began to deliver itself.

Real _____

_____

Make-believe _____

_____

At Home: Have children rewrite the story using only the sentences they circled.

Synonyms

Synonyms are two words that have the same or nearly the same meaning.

The **angry** bears ran toward each other in the forest.
The **mad** bears ran toward each other in the forest.
Angry and **mad** are synonyms.

Read each sentence. Write a synonym for the word in dark print.

1. The mouse was too **small** to jump on the table and eat the cheese.

   tiny or short _____

2. Meg was **sad** because she hurt her arm when she fell down.

   unhappy _____

3. My friend Ed and his family live in the log **cabin** in the woods.

   house _____

4. Tom thought the picture of the pig riding a horse was **silly**.

   funny _____

5. Lisa picked the **tulips** from the garden and put them in a basket.

   flowers _____

At Home: Encourage children to identify six words that describe objects in their home or school. Then ask them to substitute a synonym for each describing word.

The Pony Express • RETEACH

McGraw-Hill School Division

Name _____ Date _____ **Reteach** `101`

Short *e: ea*

> Say the following words. Listen to the sound the letters ea make in each word.
>
> le**a**d   br**ea**d   h**ea**lth

Circle the word that completes each sentence. Then write the word.

1. You eat _____**breakfast**_____ in the morning.

   head   (breakfast)   milk

2. Joe put a hat on his _____**head**_____.

   lead   foot   (head)

3. It was so cold, Kim could see her _____**breath**_____.

   coat   (breath)   read

4. My father _____**read**_____ me the book.

   (read)   showed   red

5. Shari likes the hot _____**weather**_____.

   health   (weather)   day

6. The saddle was made of _____**leather**_____.

   (leather)   wool   head

Name _____ Date _____ **Reteach** `102`

Vocabulary

Choose a word from the box to complete each sentence. Write the word in the empty boxes.

arrive	early	finished	record	rushed	success

1. The girls ___ to the store.

   | r | u | s | h | e | d | | |

2. The train will ___ at three o'clock.

   | a | r | r | i | v | e | |

3. Our class had great ___ at spelling.

   | s | u | c | c | e | s | s |

4. Patty set the ___ in the swim race.

   | r | e | c | o | r | d | |

5. My dad gets up ___ in the morning.

   | e | a | r | l | y | |

6. I ___ my homework then went out to play.

   | f | i | n | i | s | h | e | d |

Name _____ Date _____ **Reteach** `103`

Story Comprehension

Write an **X** next to the sentences that describe facts from "The Pony Express."

__X__ 1. Pony Express riders carried their papers in a "mochila," or knapsack.

__X__ 2. Johnnie and his pony crossed the Missouri River on a ferry.

__X__ 3. William Russell built stations for the Pony Express riders.

_____ 4. The Pony Express route was one million miles long.

__X__ 5. Buffalo Bill was a famous Pony Express rider.

__X__ 6. Newspapers and letters traveled on the Pony Express.

_____ 7. The telephone ended the Pony Express.

__X__ 8. The motto of the Pony Express was "The mail must go through."

__X__ 9. Pony Express riders were faster than a stagecoach.

_____ 10. The Pony Express is still in use today.

Name _____ Date _____ **Reteach** `104`

Use a Telephone Directory

> A **telephone directory** has the phone number and address of most people and businesses who own a telephone in your area.

The White Pages lists the phone numbers of people and businesses in alphabetical order by name. The Yellow Pages lists phone numbers and addresses of businesses in the area. It is organized by the type of business.

Decide if the White or the Yellow pages would best help you to answer these questions.

1. Where should I look for the phone number of my cousin, Jimmy Kerso? _____**White**_____

2. Where should I look for bicycle repair shops? _____**Yellow**_____

3. Where could I find the address of Raul Nickelson?

   _____**White**_____

4. Where could I find the home number of Dr. Paula Edwards?

   _____**White**_____

5. Where would I find a gardening store in the neighborhood?

   _____**Yellow**_____

Short e: ea

Name_____ Date_____ **Reteach** `105`

> Say the word. Listen to the sound the letters **ea** make in the word.
>
> br**ea**th

Write the letters **ea** to make a word.

1. f_**ea**_ther

2. br_**ea**_kfast

3. h_**ea**_d

4. w_**ea**_ther

5. br_**ea**_d

`5` Book 2.1/Unit 3
The Pony Express

At Home: Have children use each of the words they completed in a sentence.

105

Short e; /ər/; /ən/; /əl/; Silent Letters

Name_____ Date_____ **Reteach** `106`

(limb) know handle

limb

Circle the word that names the picture.
Write the word on the line.

1. half (eleven) though

   eleven

2. brother (weather) broken

   weather

3. seven driver (knapsack)

   knapsack

4. (table) better sight

   table

5. sign fight (walk)

   walk

6. (doughnut) climbed rider

   doughnut

106

At Home: Have children write a short story using four of the words they circled.

Book 2.1/Unit 3
The Pony Express `6`

Fantasy and Reality

Name_____ Date_____ **Reteach** `107`

> Read the story. Then underline the things that could not happen in real life.
>
> The cold wind gently blew snowflakes into Frosty's button eyes. Frosty blinked his eyes and twitched his carrot nose. He was alive again! The wind pushed Frosty on the sled down the hill and chased him as he ran and played. Then the sun began to warm the air. Frosty began to melt. "Bye," said the wind. "We'll play again on the next cold day!"

Write two more things that could not happen to Frosty.
Answers will vary.

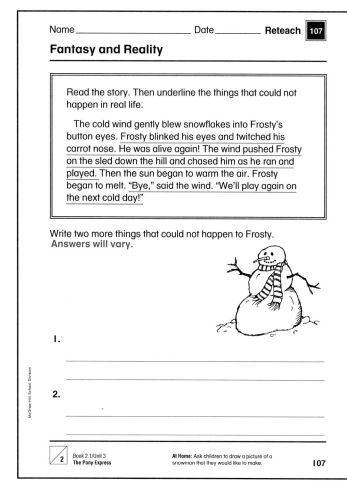

1. _____

_____

2. _____

_____

`2` Book 2.1/Unit 3
The Pony Express

At Home: Ask children to draw a picture of a snowman that they would like to make.

107

Synonyms

Name_____ Date_____ **Reteach** `108`

> A **synonym** is a word that means the same or nearly the same as another word.
>
> The puppy is very **little**.
> The puppy is very **small**.
> **Little** and **small** are synonyms.

Read each sentence. Then circle the word that means the same or nearly the same as the word in dark print.

1. Timmy was the **fastest** runner and won first prize.
   a. happiest
   b. tallest
   c. (quickest)

2. When the team won the game, everyone **cheered**.
   a. (yelled)
   b. watched
   c. started

3. The children played games at the party and had a **joyous** time.
   a. unfriendly
   b. (happy)
   c. mean

4. Juan **dashed** down the street with a letter to give to the mailman.
   a. talked
   b. fell
   c. (ran)

5. The train **arrived** on time at the Main Street station.
   a. (came)
   b. left
   c. washed

6. The **tiny** clown laughed.
   a. happy
   b. (small)
   c. silly

108

At Home: Have children think of a word and its synonym. Then have them write a sentence using both words.

Book 2.1/Unit 3
The Pony Express `6`

The Pony Express • EXTEND

Short *e*: *ea*

Look at each picture clue. Write a word clue for each one. Write the picture name in the puzzle.

feather	sweater	thread	head	bread

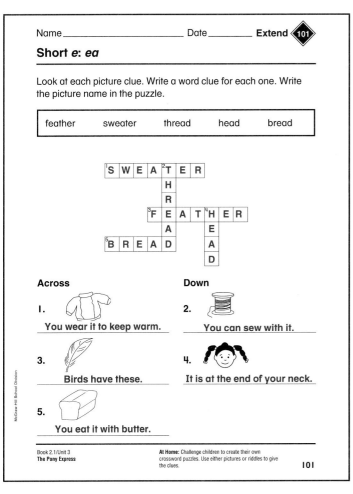

Across

1.
You wear it to keep warm.

3. Birds have these.

5. You eat it with butter.

Down

2. You can sew with it.

4. It is at the end of your neck.

Book 2.1/Unit 3
The Pony Express

At Home: Challenge children to create their own crossword puzzles. Use either pictures or riddles to give the clues.

101

Vocabulary

Would you like to learn horseback riding? Write a letter about it to a friend. Use some of the words in the box.

record	rush	success	early	arrive	finish

Dear _____,

_____

_____

_____

_____

_____

_____

_____

_____

_____

Sincerely,

_____

Story Comprehension

A San Francisco newspaper wants you to write two stories about the Pony Express. Tell the story of how it started and how it ended. Read the headlines and write the story.

Answers will vary. Sample answers shown.

April 3, 1860

The Fastest Mail Ever

William H. Russell believes that the fastest way to deliver mail in California is to send it out by horse. He is hiring young men to ride their horses from station to station. All together, Russell will hire about 180 men to ride 2,000 miles!

November 21, 1861

Telegragh Takes Over

Pony Express riders will be out of a job. The daring riders can carry mail across the country faster than by stagecoach. But the new telegraph will get messages from the East to California in just seconds.

Book 2.1/Unit 3
The Pony Express

At Home: Invite children to read their newspaper articles aloud. Ask questions and help them fill in information that they may have forgotten.

103

Use a Telephone Directory

Samada, Colin 25 Clinton Ave	555-0414
Sampson, Sarah 265 E 66	555-6213
Samrock, Gabriel 1220 Franklin Dr.	555-3716
Samson, David 17 York	555-0773
Samuel, Brent 1160 Park	555-8961

1. Finish addressing this card to Colin Samada. Put his name on the first line and his address on the second line. Write your own address as the return address.

> _____
> _____
> _____
>
> <u>Colin Samada</u>
> <u>25 Clinton Ave.</u>
> Longview, TX   89543

2. Finish the note for your friends telling them you are going to visit Sarah Sampson. Give them the telephone number so they can call you.

Dear _____,

I will be at Sarah Sampson's apartment. Her phone number is

<u>555-6213</u>.

From,

_____

104

At Home: Invite children to find a friend's phone number in your telephone book.

Book 2.1/Unit 3
The Pony Express

Page 105

Name_____ Date_____ Extend ◆105

Short *e*: *ea*

Look at the picture. Read the words. Write the words with the **ea** sound you hear in **breakfast** on the lines below.

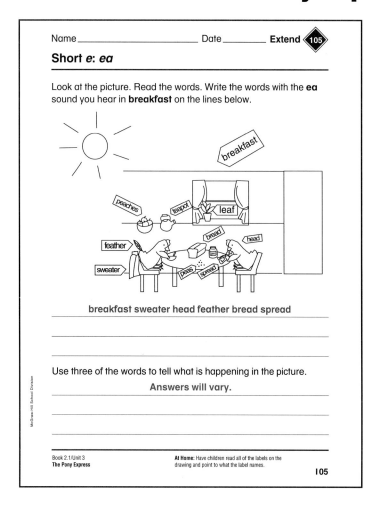

breakfast sweater head feather bread spread

_____

_____

Use three of the words to tell what is happening in the picture.

Answers will vary.

_____

_____

At Home: Have children read all of the labels on the drawing and point to what the label names.

105

Page 106

Name_____ Date_____ Extend ◆106

Short *e*; / ər/, / ən/, / əl/; Silent Letters

Look in books, around the classroom, or at home for words that have the same sound as the word at the top of the list. Try to find 2 words for each box.   **Answers will vary. Samples are given.**

The **ea** in **bread**	The **er** in **rider**	The **k** in **knot**
lead	cover	knee
spread	letter	knight

The **gh** in **high**	The **le** in **rattle**	The **en** in **eleven**
sigh	saddle	seven
light	battle	even

Write a poem. Use words from the lists that rhyme.

_____

_____

_____

_____

_____

At Home: Challenge children to think of additional words to add to the chart above.

Page 107

Name_____ Date_____ Extend ◆107

Fantasy and Reality

Look carefully at the pictures. Some show things that could happen in real life. Some show things that are make-believe. Write the words **real** or **make-believe** under each picture.

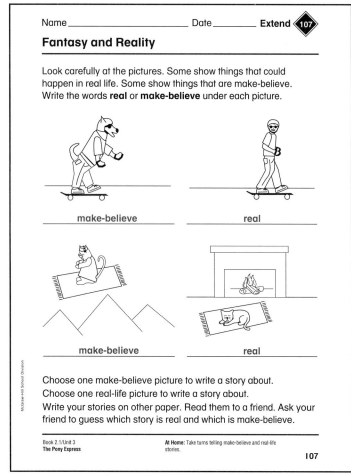

make-believe   real

make-believe   real

Choose one make-believe picture to write a story about.
Choose one real-life picture to write a story about.
Write your stories on other paper. Read them to a friend. Ask your friend to guess which story is real and which is make-believe.

At Home: Take turns telling make-believe and real-life stories.

107

Page 108

Name_____ Date_____ Extend ◆108

Synonyms

Cut out the playing cards below. Place the cards face down. Play with a friend. Turn a card over. Match it to its synonym. Keep the cards if they match. Turn both cards back over if they do not match. Keep playing until all of the cards are gone.

one	single	two
double	three	triple
little	small	close
near	take	grab
shut	close	funny
silly	go	leave

At Home: Play the game with children. Challenge them to come up with new playing cards to add to the level of difficulty.

Past-Tense Verbs

Name_____ Date_____ **Grammar** 77
LEARN

- Verbs can tell about actions that already happened.
- These verbs are in the **past tense**.
- Add -ed to most verbs to tell about an action in the past.
  We <u>baked</u> cookies.
  We <u>covered</u> them with icing.

Circle the past-tense verbs.

1. a. enjoy
   b. (enjoyed)

2. a. lift
   b. (lifted)

3. a. (asked)
   b. ask

4. a. turn
   b. (turned)

5. a. (learned)
   b. learn

6. a. (talked)
   b. talk

7. a. guess
   b. (guessed)

8. a. cook
   b. (cooked)

9. a. (rested)
   b. rest

10. a. (folded)
    b. fold

10 Book 2.1/Unit 3
The Pony Express

Extension: Have children write sentences using the past-tense verbs they circled.

77

Past-Tense Verbs

Name_____ Date_____ **Grammar** 78
PRACTICE AND LEARN

- If a verb ends with one consonant, double the consonant and add -ed.
- If a verb ends with -e, drop the e and add -ed.
  I <u>chopped</u> the meat.
  We <u>smiled</u> at the camera.

Find the present-tense verb in each sentence.
Write the past tense of each one.

1. I work in the garden.   worked

2. I rake the leaves.   raked

3. I trim the bushes.   trimmed

4. Then I pick some flowers.   picked

5. I pull some weeds.   pulled

78 **Extension:** Have children write sentences using the past tense of each verb.

Book 2.1/Unit 3
The Pony Express 5

Past-Tense Verbs

Name_____ Date_____ **Grammar** 79
PRACTICE AND REVIEW

- Add -ed to most verbs to tell about an action in the past.
- If a verb ends with one consonant, double the consonant and add -ed.
- If a verb ends with -e, drop the e and add -ed.
  Who <u>planned</u> the party?
  Roberto <u>surprised</u> us.
  He <u>looked</u> happy.

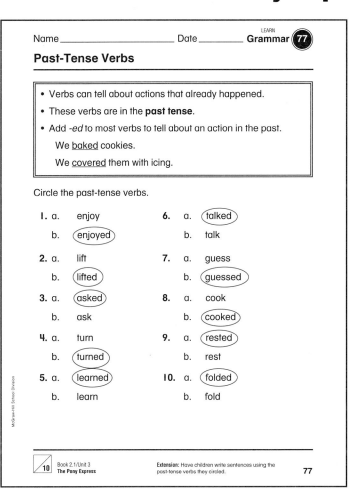

Write the past tense of each underlined verb.

1. Chet <u>walk</u> to the slide.   walked

2. He <u>climb</u> the steps.   climbed

3. He <u>look</u> around.   looked

4. He <u>decide</u> to come down.   decided

5. He <u>rush</u> down the slide.   rushed

6. He <u>splash</u> in the water.   splashed

7. He <u>laugh</u>.   laughed

8. He <u>grin</u> at his mother.   grinned

8 Book 2.1/Unit 3
The Pony Express

Extension: Have children write about something that happened yesterday. Remind them to use past-tense verbs.

79

Letter Writing

Name_____ Date_____ **Grammar** 80
MECHANICS

- Begin the greeting and closing in a letter with a capital letter.
- Use a comma after the greeting in a letter.
- Use a comma after the closing in a letter.
  Dear Nancy,
      Love,
      Olga

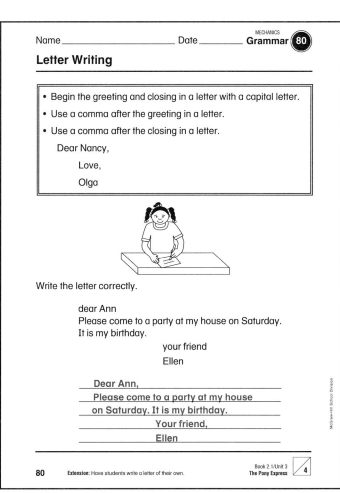

Write the letter correctly.

dear Ann
Please come to a party at my house on Saturday.
It is my birthday.
              your friend
              Ellen

Dear Ann,
Please come to a party at my house
on Saturday. It is my birthday.
              Your friend,
              Ellen

80 **Extension:** Have students write a letter of their own.

Book 2.1/Unit 3
The Pony Express 4

The Pony Express • GRAMMAR

Past-Tense Verbs

A. Read each sentence. Write the past-tense verb in each sentence on the line.

1. Chet phoned home.   _____phoned_____

2. He wanted to talk to his mom.   _____wanted_____

3. She answered the phone.   _____answered_____

B. Read each pair of sentences.
   Mark the one that has a past-tense verb.

4. ⓐ I need some water.

   ⬤ I needed water for a long time.

5. ⓐ Let's stop here.

   ⬤ We stopped at this place before.

Past-Tense Verbs

- Add -ed to most verbs to tell about an action in the past.
- If a verb ends with one consonant, double the consonant and add -ed.
- If a verb ends with e, drop the e and add -ed.

Look at each picture. Read the sentences next to it. Draw a circle around the sentence that tells about the past.

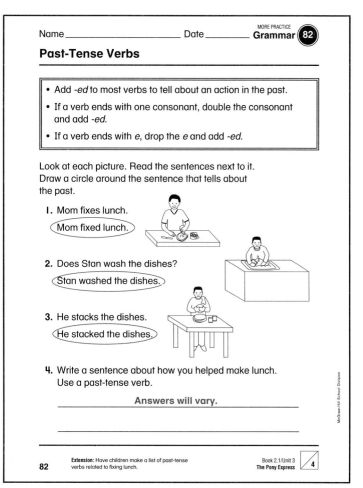

1. Mom fixes lunch.
   (Mom fixed lunch.)

2. Does Stan wash the dishes?
   (Stan washed the dishes.)

3. He stacks the dishes.
   (He stacked the dishes.)

4. Write a sentence about how you helped make lunch. Use a past-tense verb.

   Answers will vary.

   _____

T36 *Annotated Workbooks*

The Pony Express • SPELLING

Words with Short *e*: *ea*

Pretest Directions

Fold back the paper along the dotted line. Use the blanks to write each word as it is read aloud. When you finish the test, unfold the paper. Correct any spelling mistakes. Practice the words you missed for the Posttest.

To Parents,

Here are the results of your child's weekly spelling Pretest. You can help your child study for the Posttest by following these simple steps for each word on the list:

1. Read the word to your child.
2. Have your child write the word, saying each letter as it is written.
3. Say each letter of the word as your child checks the spelling.
4. If a mistake has been made, have your child read each letter of the correctly spelled word aloud, and then repeat steps 1–3.

1. _____
2. _____
3. _____
4. _____
5. _____
6. _____
7. _____
8. _____
9. _____
10. _____

1. leather
2. bread
3. weather
4. spread
5. breakfast
6. ready
7. meant
8. feather
9. instead
10. meadow

Challenge Words

_____ arrive
_____ early
_____ finish
_____ record
_____ success

Words with Short *e*: *ea*

Using the Word Study Steps

1. LOOK at the word.
2. SAY the word aloud.
3. STUDY the letters in the word.
4. WRITE the word.
5. CHECK the word. Did you spell the word right? If not, go back to step 1.

Spelling Tip

Short vowel sounds are usually spelled with one vowel. But sometimes they are spelled with two vowels. Think of ways to remember the spelling of short **e** in these words.
Example: I am re**a**dy for bre**a**d.

Find and Circle

Where are the spelling words?

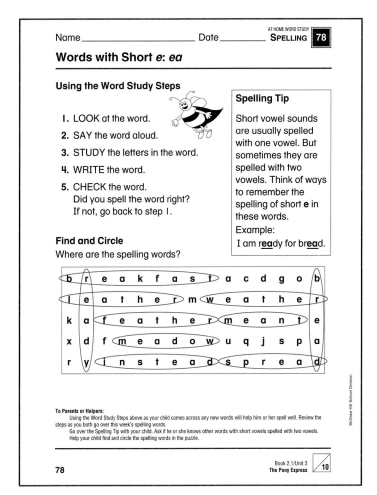

To Parents or Helpers:

Using the Word Study Steps above as your child comes across any new words will help him or her spell well. Review the steps as you both go over this week's spelling words.

Go over the Spelling Tip with your child. Ask if he or she knows other words with short vowels spelled with two vowels.

Help your child find and circle the spelling words in the puzzle.

Words with Short *e*: *ea*

| ready | leather | meant | instead | meadow |
| spread | breakfast | weather | bread | feather |

It's in the Mail!

Look at the spelling words in the box.

Say each spelling word. Tap the number of syllables in each word. Write the spelling words that have one syllable and two syllables in the correct Pony Express bags below.

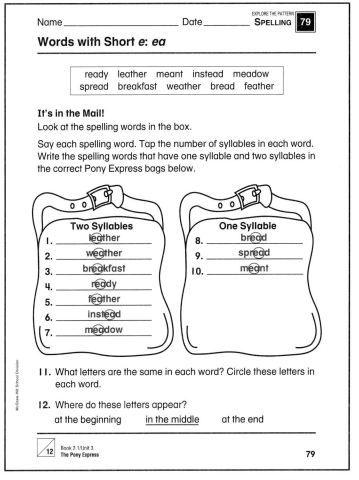

Two Syllables
1. leather
2. weather
3. breakfast
4. ready
5. feather
6. instead
7. meadow

One Syllable
8. bread
9. spread
10. meant

11. What letters are the same in each word? Circle these letters in each word.

12. Where do these letters appear?
at the beginning   in the middle   at the end

Words with Short *e*: *ea*

| ready | leather | meant | instead | meadow |
| spread | breakfast | weather | bread | feather |

Write a spelling word to complete each sentence.

1. Shoes and belts are made of ___leather___.
2. The ___weather___ can be hot or cold, rainy or clear.
3. A bird's ___feather___ is very light in weight.
4. Another name for a field of grass is a ___meadow___.
5. What do you think he ___meant___ by that?
6. In the morning I get ___ready___ for school.
7. Put the ___bread___ in the toaster.
8. Jeffrey likes to ___spread___ jam on his toast.
9. I think I'll wear my red gloves ___instead___ of my brown ones.

Word Builder

10. Be a word builder. Build a spelling word from the shorter words.

break + fast = ___breakfast___

The Pony Express • SPELLING

Words with Short *e*: *ea*

Proofreading Activity

There are six spelling mistakes in the journal below. Circle each misspelled word. Write the words correctly on the lines below.

Today was my first day as a Pony Express rider. In the morning the (wether) was beautiful. I had some (bred) for (brekfst.) I was too excited to eat anything else. I was (reddy) when the other rider got to my station. I put my (lether) bags across the saddle. Then, I jumped on my horse and was off! At first I rode along a river. After that I rode through a (medow) full of pretty wildflowers. Being a Pony Express rider is the best job I ever had!

1. _____weather_____   2. _____bread_____   3. _____breakfast_____

4. _____ready_____   5. _____leather_____   6. _____meadow_____

Writing Activity

Pretend you are the Pony Express rider. Write about an exciting day you had. Use four of your spelling words. Circle the words you use.

_____

_____

_____

_____

_____

Words with Short *e*: *ea*

Look at the words in each set. One word in each set is spelled correctly. Use a pencil to color in the circle in front of that word. Before you begin, look at the sample sets of words. Sample A has been done for you. Do Sample B by yourself. When you are sure you know what to do, you may go on with the rest of the page.

Sample A
- Ⓐ watur
- Ⓑ water ●
- Ⓒ watir
- Ⓓ wator

Sample B
- Ⓔ yellow ●
- Ⓕ yello
- Ⓖ yellar
- Ⓗ yellur

1. Ⓐ leether
   Ⓑ laether
   ● leather
   Ⓓ layther

2. Ⓔ brede
   Ⓕ braed
   ● bread
   Ⓗ brid

3. ● weather
   Ⓑ wuther
   Ⓒ wather
   Ⓓ wether

4. Ⓔ spraed
   Ⓕ sprede
   Ⓖ spreed
   ● spread

5. Ⓐ bredfast
   ● breakfast
   Ⓒ brakfast
   Ⓓ brekfast

6. Ⓔ rady
   ● ready
   Ⓖ redy
   Ⓗ reddy

7. Ⓐ ment
   Ⓑ mante
   Ⓒ mente
   ● meant

8. ● feather
   Ⓕ faether
   Ⓖ fether
   Ⓗ feither

9. Ⓐ instaed
   ● instead
   Ⓒ instede
   Ⓓ instade

10. Ⓔ medow
    Ⓕ maedow
    ● meadow
    Ⓗ medou

Practice 109

Name _____ Date _____ **Practice** 109

Long e: y, ey

Read each group of words. Circle the word that has the same ending sound as bab**y** or monk**ey**. Then write the word on the line.

1. brown   (money)   horse

   money _____

2. hand   dog   (silly)

   silly _____

3. nine   (scary)   book

   scary _____

4. (ready)   purple   garden

   ready _____

5. fountain   build   (turkey)

   turkey _____

6. (honey)   day   band

   honey _____

Book 2.1/Unit 3
Nine-in-One, Grr! Grr!   6

At Home: Have children write a sentence for each word they wrote on the lines.

109

Practice 110

Name _____ Date _____ **Practice** 110

Vocabulary

Circle the word that answers the riddle. Then write the word on the line.

| earth   forget   lonely   memory   mountain   wonderful |

1. I am very tall and fun to climb.   **mountain**

   (mountain)   earth   sky

2. I am the ground under your feet.   **earth**

   sea   (earth)   Mars

3. I help you think of something from the past.   **memory**

   (memory)   think   say

4. I'm something that is very good.   **wonderful**

   bad   forget   (wonderful)

5. I am the opposite of *remember*.   **forget**

   (forget)   lonely   good

6. I am sad and all by myself.   **lonely**

   memory   (lonely)   happy

110   At Home: Ask children to use the vocabulary words to make a crossword puzzle.

Book 2.1/Unit 3
Nine-in-One, Grr! Grr!   6

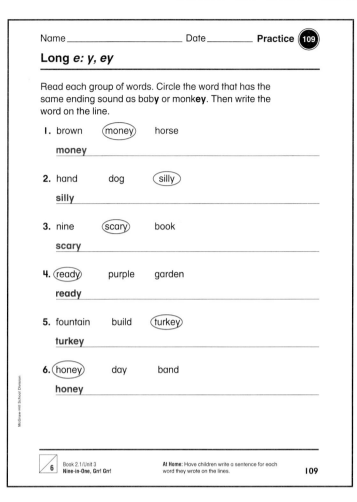

The Turtle's Gift

One day the turtle came. "You will be small and have a hard shell," said the lion.

"You gave those gifts to the ant and to the crab," the turtle said. "I would like to be wise."

"Very well," said the lion. "Those who are wise stay quiet so they can listen." That is why the turtle hears all but says nothing.

At Home: Have children imagine other animals coming to the lion for their gifts. What would he give them?

4   110a

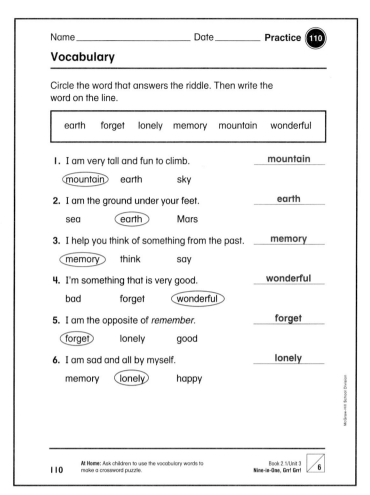

2

Long ago there was a lion who was king of all the animals on Earth. Every year he came down from his home on the mountain and gave each animal a gift.

When the ant came the lion said, "You will be very, very tiny. But there will be many of you. You will work and play together. You will never be lonely."

Nine-in-One, Grr! Grr! McGraw-Hill School Division

When the monkey came, the lion said, "You will be happy to hang by your tail and jump from tree to tree."

Many more animals came for gifts. All of the gifts were wonderful. But the lion began to worry.

I am getting old, he thought. My memory is not so good. Maybe I will forget and give two animals the same gift. That would never do.

3   110b

Nine-in-One Grr! Grr! • PRACTICE

Name _____ Date _____ **Practice 111**

Story Comprehension

Think about "Nine-in-One, Grr! Grr!" Put an X by each sentence that tells about something that happened in this story.

_____ Tiger lived in the sky.

__X__ The great god Shao knew everything.

__X__ Tiger asks Shao how many cubs she will have.

_____ Tiger is sad after she talks to Shao.

__X__ Tiger makes up a song to help her remember what Shao told her.

_____ Tiger forgets how to get home.

__X__ Bird doesn't want Tiger to have nine cubs every year.

_____ Shao promises Bird he will change what he said to Tiger.

__X__ Bird makes Tiger change her song.

__X__ Tiger will have one cub every nine years.

Book 2.1/Unit 3
Nine-in-One, Grr! Grr! 10

At Home: Ask children how they would change the false statements on this page to make them true statements. 111

Name _____ Date _____ **Practice 112**

Use a Dictionary

A **dictionary entry** contains many different parts. Study the entry shown below. See if you can pick out each different part.

pup 1. a young dog; puppy. 2. the young of some other animals, such as the fox, wolf, or seal. *The mother fox takes good care of her pup.* (pup) *noun, plural* **pups**

Complete the exercise based on the dictionary definition above.

1. entry word _____ pup

2. definition #2 2. the young of some other animals, such as the fox, wolf, or seal

3. part of speech _____ noun

4. plural form _____ pups

5. pronunciation guide _____ (pup)

6. example sentence for definition #2 The mother fox takes good care of her pup.

112 **At Home:** Ask children to make up a sentence using the first definition for "pup."

Book 2.1/Unit 3
Nine-in-One, Grr! Grr! 6

Name _____ Date _____ **Practice 113**

Long e: y, ey

Read the sentence. Then circle the word that ends in **y** or **ey** and completes the sentence. Write the word and circle the y or ey ending.

1. The __baby__ was in her carriage .

   bag   band   (baby)

2. Jean and Pat were very __happy__ .

   (happy)   crying   purple

3. Tawana saved her __money__ .

   apples   (money)   birds

4. Don't __worry__ ; the rain will stop soon!

   eat   sleep   (worry)

5. The __monkey__ loved to climb.

   truck   (monkey)   girl

6. There are four people in my __family__ .

   cave   (family)   foot

6 Book 2.1/Unit 3
Nine-in-One, Grr! Grr!

At Home: Have children list ten words that end with -y or -ey. 113

Name _____ Date _____ **Practice 114**

Long e; Short e; /ər/, /ən/, /əl/

Choose the word that completes each sentence. Write the word on the line.

shiny	children	bread	apple	key
sneakers	sell	freeze	lead	weather

1. This gold ring is very __shiny__ .

2. The __children__ wait for the school bus.

3. I pick an __apple__ from the tree.

4. I can't find one of my __sneakers__ .

5. You need __bread__ to make a sandwich.

6. He opens the door with a __key__ .

7. We will listen to the __weather__ report so we will know what to wear.

8. We will __freeze__ water to make ice.

9. If you __lead__ , we will follow.

10. Stores don't give things away; they __sell__ them.

114 **At Home:** Have children write a rhyming poem using at least one of the words above.

Book 2.1/Unit 3
Nine in One, Grr! Grr! 10

T40 *Annotated Workbooks*

Nine-in-One Grr! Grr! • PRACTICE

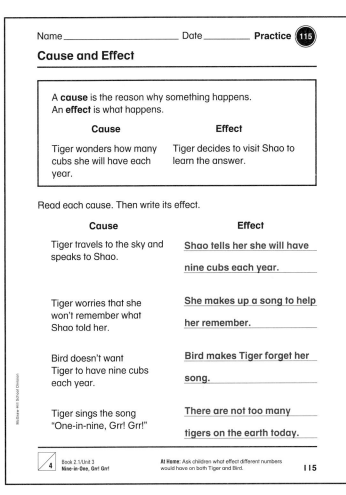

Cause and Effect

> A **cause** is the reason why something happens.
> An **effect** is what happens.
>
> | Cause | Effect |
> |---|---|
> | Tiger wonders how many cubs she will have each year. | Tiger decides to visit Shao to learn the answer. |

Read each cause. Then write its effect.

Cause	Effect
Tiger travels to the sky and speaks to Shao.	Shao tells her she will have nine cubs each year.
Tiger worries that she won't remember what Shao told her.	She makes up a song to help her remember.
Bird doesn't want Tiger to have nine cubs each year.	Bird makes Tiger forget her song.
Tiger sings the song "One-in-nine, Grr! Grr!"	There are not too many tigers on the earth today.

4 Book 2.1/Unit 3
Nine-in-One, Grr! Grr!

At Home: Ask children what effect different numbers would have on both Tiger and Bird.

115

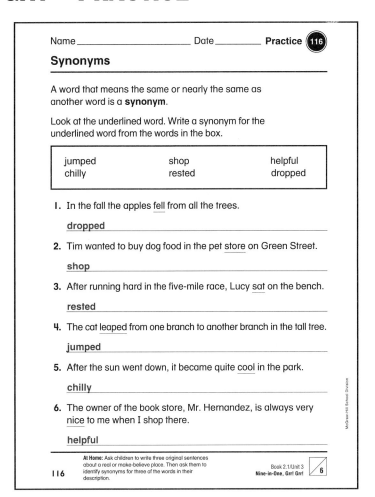

Synonyms

A word that means the same or nearly the same as another word is a **synonym**.

Look at the underlined word. Write a synonym for the underlined word from the words in the box.

jumped	shop	helpful
chilly	rested	dropped

1. In the fall the apples fell from all the trees.

   dropped

2. Tim wanted to buy dog food in the pet store on Green Street.

   shop

3. After running hard in the five-mile race, Lucy sat on the bench.

   rested

4. The cat leaped from one branch to another branch in the tall tree.

   jumped

5. After the sun went down, it became quite cool in the park.

   chilly

6. The owner of the book store, Mr. Hernandez, is always very nice to me when I shop there.

   helpful

116

At Home: Ask children to write three original sentences about a real or make-believe place. Then ask them to identify synonyms for three of the words in their description.

Book 2.1/Unit 3
Nine-in-One, Grr! Grr! 6

Reteach 109

Name_____ Date_____ **Reteach** 109

Long *e: y, ey*

Say these words. What sound do you hear that is the same in each word?

ba**by**   turk**ey**

The letters **y** or **ey** make the same sound in these two words.

Match the word with each picture. Then circle the letters that make the same ending sound as **baby** and **turkey.**

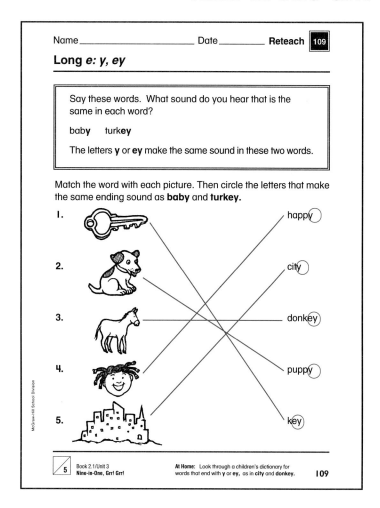

1. — happ**y**
2. — cit**y**
3. — donk**ey**
4. — pupp**y**
5. — k**ey**

Reteach 110

Name_____ Date_____ **Reteach** 110

Vocabulary

Circle the word that completes each sentence.

| Earth   forget   lonely   memory   mountain   wonderful |

1. I never ___ where I put my socks.

   memory   (forget)

2. Sometimes I feel sad and ___ .

   Earth   (lonely)

3. The ___ has many oceans on it.

   (Earth)   wonderful

4. Today I'm very happy. I feel ___ .

   (wonderful)   forget

5. The top of that ___ is covered with snow.

   lonely   (mountain)

6. Jake tells lots of stories. He has a good ___ .

   (memory)   forget

Reteach 111

Name_____ Date_____ **Reteach** 111

Story Comprehension

Fill in the following chart with information from "Nine-in-One, Grr! Grr!"

Main Characters: Tiger, great god Shao, Bird

Setting: a long time ago where the Earth met the Sky

Beginning of the Story: The tiger visits Shao, the god in the sky. She asks Shao how many cubs she will have. Shao says that she will have "nine each year."

Middle of the Story: Tiger makes up a song to remember "nine each year." Bird does not want Tiger to have nine cubs each year.

End of the Story: Bird flaps her wings to make Tiger forget her song. Then Bird tells Tiger that her song was really "one-in-nine . . ." Tiger believes Bird. That is why people say there are not many tigers today.

Reteach 112

Name_____ Date_____ **Reteach** 112

Use a Dictionary

Sometimes a word has two or more different meanings. A **dictionary** can use the word in sentences that illustrate different meanings of the word.

Study the dictionary definitions below. Beneath each definition are two sentences. Each has a blank space beside it. Write the number of the meaning of the entry word that's being used in the sentence.

pe·ri·od (pir´ē ed) *noun* **1.** a portion of time. **2.** A punctuation mark (.) used at the end of a sentence. It is also used after an abbreviation. plural **periods**.

1. Karen used a pen to put a period at the end of her sentence. __2__

2. Our lunch hour came in the fourth period. __1__

dunk (dungk) *verb* **1.** To dip something such as a doughnut in a liquid. **2.** To shove a basketball into the basket forcefully. **dunked**, **dunking**.

3. The whole class was allowed to dunk their crackers in the soup. __1__

4. Lena jumped off Brenda's back and managed to dunk the ball. __2__

Nine-in-One Grr! Grr! • RETEACH

Name_____ Date_____ **Reteach** 113

Long *e: y, ey*

The sound of long **e** can be spelled with a **y** as in *family*. The sound of long **e** can also be spelled with an **ey** as in **donkey**.

Choose the word from the box that best completes each sentence.

funny	monkey	worry	Nancy
penny	many	key	family

1. My friend __Nancy__ loves to swim.
2. John tells __funny__ jokes.
3. Sally lost her house __key__.
4. There are three kids in my __family__.
5. I saw a __monkey__ with big ears at the circus.
6. Don't __worry__ about that noise.
7. When I see a __penny__, I pick it up.
8. There are __many__ animals in the zoo.

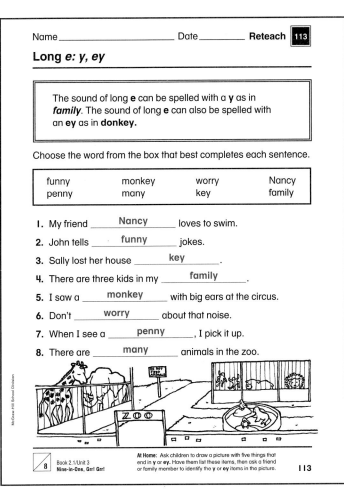

Book 2.1/Unit 3
Nine-in-One, Grr! Grr!
8

At Home: Ask children to draw a picture with five things that end in **y** or **ey**. Have them list these items, then ask a friend or family member to identify the **y** or **ey** items in the picture.

113

Name_____ Date_____ **Reteach** 114

Long *e;* Short *e; /ər/, /ən/, /əl/*

That bird has pretty ___.

(feathers)   every   better

Circle the word that completes the sentence.
Then write it.

1. We saw a __monkey__ at the zoo.
 (monkey)   many   listened

2. The __garden__ was filled with flowers.
 (garden)   listen   worry

3. I __met__ the class president.
 children   (met)   tiny

4. The __mother__ bird feeds the baby birds.
 (mother)   went   even

5. The __people__ waited for the play to start.
 happy   clever   (people)

114

At Home: Have children draw a picture to go with one of the sentences above.

Book 2.1/Unit 3
Nine-in-One, Grr! Grr!
10

Name_____ Date_____ **Reteach** 115

Cause and Effect

Look at the pictures. Read the sentences. The **cause** is the event that makes the **effect** happen.

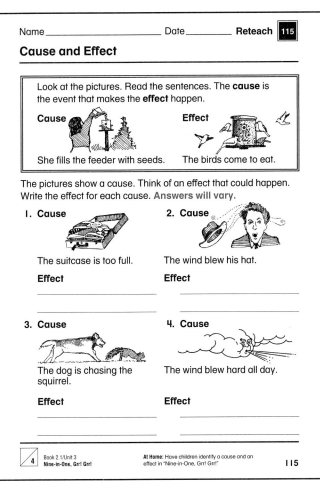

Cause   **Effect**

She fills the feeder with seeds.   The birds come to eat.

The pictures show a cause. Think of an effect that could happen. Write the effect for each cause. **Answers will vary.**

1. Cause

The suitcase is too full.

Effect
_____

2. Cause

The wind blew his hat.

Effect
_____

3. Cause

The dog is chasing the squirrel.

Effect
_____

4. Cause

The wind blew hard all day.

Effect
_____

Book 2.1/Unit 3
Nine-in-One, Grr! Grr!
4

At Home: Have children identify a cause and an effect in "Nine-in-One, Grr! Grr!"

115

Name_____ Date_____ **Reteach** 116

Synonyms

A word that means the same or nearly the same as another word is called a **synonym**.

The bird was too **tiny** to fly.
The bird was too **small** to fly.
The words **tiny** and **small** are synonyms.

Read each sentence. Then choose a synonym for each word in dark print from the box below. Write the synonym on the blank line.

friendly	formed	lightly
jumped	tired	nice

1. The **kind** man helped the sick puppy to get well. __nice__
2. The cat walked **softly** across the grass in the park. __lightly__
3. The tiger **leaped** from the tree to the ground. __jumped__
4. Everyone in the **peaceful** land lived happily. __friendly__
5. The **sleepy** children went to bed right away. __tired__
6. The rock was **shaped** like a giant top. __formed__

116

At Home: Ask children to write a three-sentence story about a real or imaginary animal. Then have them identify synonyms for two of the words in the story.

Book 2.1/Unit 3
Nine-in-One, Grr! Grr!
6

T43

Nine-in-One Grr! Grr! • EXTEND

Long e: y, ey

It is a funny day at the turkey farm. Help Farmer Willy find the lost turkey. Write the word that names the picture and follow the trail.

| monkey | turkey | key | pony | baby | city | daddy |

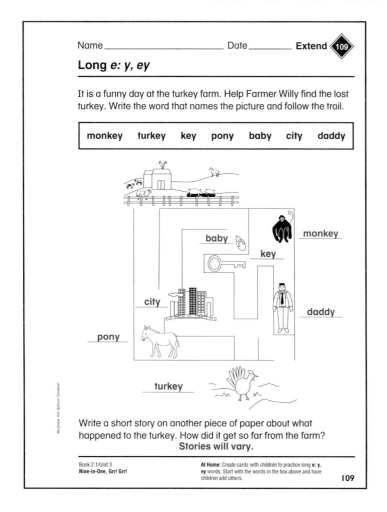

baby

monkey

key

city

daddy

pony

turkey

Write a short story on another piece of paper about what happened to the turkey. How did it get so far from the farm?
Stories will vary.

Book 2.1/Unit 3
Nine-in-One, Grr! Grr!

At Home: Create cards with children to practice long **e: y, ey** words. Start with the words in the box above and have children add others.

109

Vocabulary

Play with a friend. Cut out the word cards. Write the definition on the back of the card.

Mix the cards up. Read the side of the card showing. Tell the meaning for the word or the word for the meaning.

Keep the cards you get right. Keep going until there are no cards left.

earth	forget	lonely
memory	mountain	wonderful

Play again, but this time, use each word in a sentence.

At Home: Play the game with children. Challenge children to give synonyms for each of the words.

Book 2.1/Unit 3
Nine-in-One, Grr! Grr!

110

Story Comprehension

Fill in the chart to tell about "Nine-in-One, Grr! Grr!"

1. Title: _____ Nine in One, Grr! Grr! _____

2. Characters (who): _____ Tiger _____
   Shao
   Bird

3. Problem: _____
   Bird thinks Tiger will have many babies who will then eat all the birds.

4. Solution: _____
   Bird fools Tiger into wishing for one baby every nine years.

5. Favorite Part: _____ Answers will vary. _____

6. A Picture:

Book 2.1/Unit 3
Nine-in-One, Grr! Grr!

At Home: Have children write a note to the tiger telling her about the bird's trick and giving her advice on what she should do next.

111

Use a Dictionary

Find each word in the dictionary. Write the definition. List the word that comes before and after the word.   **Sample answers shown.**

1. Word before: _____ tactless _____
   tadpole: _____ the larva of a frog or toad _____
   Word after: _____ tag _____

2. Word before: _____ practically _____
   practice: _____ to work at often so as to learn well _____
   Word after: _____ prairie _____

3. Word before: _____ hopper _____
   hopscotch: _____ a game in which a player tosses a stone into sections of a figure drawn on the ground and hops through the figure and back to pick up the stone _____
   Word after: _____ horde _____

4. Word before: _____ wing _____
   wink: _____ to close and open the eyelids quickly _____
   Word after: _____ winner _____

At Home: Look up other words together in a children's dictionary. Talk about the language that the dictionary uses to explain words.

Book 2.1/Unit 3
Nine-in-One, Grr! Grr!

112

Nine-in-One Grr! Grr! • EXTEND

Long *e*: *y, ey*

Play a game of "I Spy." Look around your classroom or in picture books. Write about something that you see that ends with the same sound as **furry** and **valley.** The first one is done for you.

Answers will vary; some samples are given.

1. I spy an animal that swings from the branches. It looks like an ape, but it is not one. It is a monkey.

2. I spy a green piece of paper. It can be used to buy things.
   _____ It is money. _____

3. I spy _____ a little horse. It is a pony. _____

4. I spy _____ an object that opens a door. It is a key. _____

5. I spy _____ a person who is a woman. She is a lady. _____

Long *e*; Short *e*; /ər/, /ən/, /əl/

Look at the picture. List the items in the picture that match the sound of the word in the box. You will list one item in two boxes.

1. **ea** as in thr**ea**d	2. **ey** as in mon**ey**	3. **y** as in funn**y**
feather	monkey	pony
bread	donkey	puppy

4. **le** as in coup**le**	5. **en** as in ev**en**	6. **er** as in aft**er**
saddle	eleven	fingers
castle	garden	feather

Choose a word from the boxes. Use the word in a sentence.

_____

_____

Cause and Effect

Write a silly story. Use the boxes below to plan your story.

What happened?

[ ]

Why did it happen?

[ ]

Use the information in the boxes to write your silly story.

_____

_____

_____

_____

_____

_____

Synonyms

Read the lists of words. One of the words does not mean the same as the others. Cross out the one that does not belong.

1. look	glance	see	touch
2. call	shout	jump	summon
3. great	grand	tiny	large
4. stop	go	halt	end
5. tell	say	talk	listen
6. leave	stay	go	depart
7. little	huge	small	short
8. stop	go	leave	depart

Think of as many synonyms as you can for the word **talk.**

Write a sentence for each synonym of **talk.**

_____

_____

_____

_____

_____

_____

The Verb *Have*

Name _____ Date _____

- The verb *have* has special forms in the present tense.
- Use *has* when the subject is singular.
- Use *have* when the subject is plural or *I* or *you*.
  Stan has time to play. Do you have time?
  Bill and Tim have time.

Complete each sentence with *has* or *have*.

1. Nick and Kim ____**have**____ three dollars.

2. Ted also ____**has**____ three dollars.

3. They all ____**have**____ money for the movies.

4. "Do you ____**have**____ three dollars?" Nick asked me.

5. We always ____**have**____ a good time at the movies.

Name _____ Date _____

The Verb *Have*

- The past-tense form of the verb *have* is *had*.
  Ted had a good time at the movies.
  Nick and Kim also had a good time.

Each sentence has the present-tense of *have*. Change the sentence to past tense. Write the new sentence.

1. Our family has many pets.
   _____ **Our family had many pets.** _____

2. I have a rabbit.
   _____ **I had a rabbit.** _____

3. Uncle Ned has a dog.
   _____ **Uncle Ned had a dog.** _____

4. My two cousins have fish.
   _____ **My two cousins had fish.** _____

5. We all have turtles.
   _____ **We all had turtles.** _____

Name _____ Date _____

The Verb *Have*

- Use *has* when the subject is singular.
- Use *have* when the subject is plural or *I* or *you*.
- The past tense of the verb *have* is *had*.

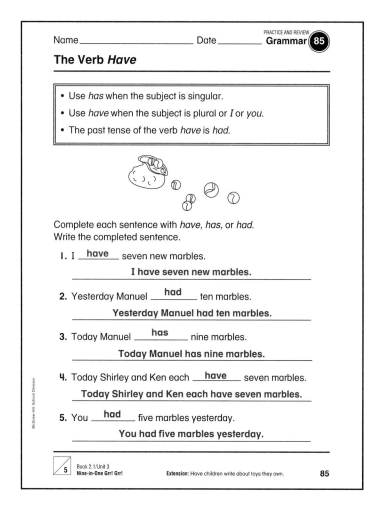

Complete each sentence with *have, has,* or *had.*
Write the completed sentence.

1. I ____**have**____ seven new marbles.
   I have seven new marbles.

2. Yesterday Manuel ____**had**____ ten marbles.
   Yesterday Manuel had ten marbles.

3. Today Manuel ____**has**____ nine marbles.
   Today Manuel has nine marbles.

4. Today Shirley and Ken each ____**have**____ seven marbles.
   Today Shirley and Ken each have seven marbles.

5. You ____**had**____ five marbles yesterday.
   You had five marbles yesterday.

Name _____ Date _____

Using Capital Letters in Book Titles

- Begin the first word and each important word in a book title with a capital letter.
  The Man in the Blue Suit
  A History of Bowling
  Santa Claus and the North Pole

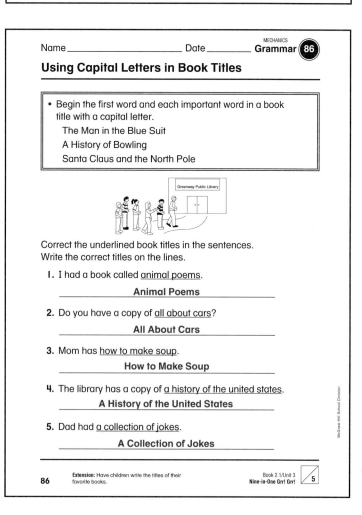

Correct the underlined book titles in the sentences. Write the correct titles on the lines.

1. I had a book called <u>animal poems</u>.
   Animal Poems

2. Do you have a copy of <u>all about cars</u>?
   All About Cars

3. Mom has <u>how to make soup</u>.
   How to Make Soup

4. The library has a copy of <u>a history of the united states</u>.
   A History of the United States

5. Dad had <u>a collection of jokes</u>.
   A Collection of Jokes

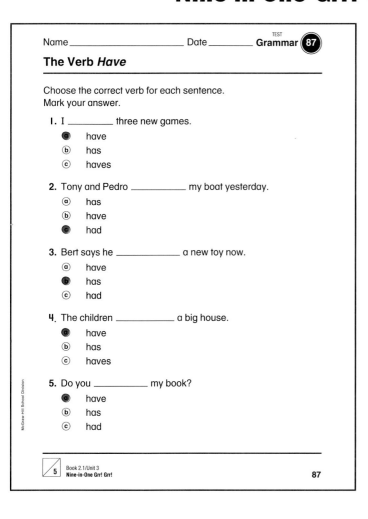

The Verb *Have*

Choose the correct verb for each sentence.
Mark your answer.

1. I _____ three new games.
   - ⓐ have
   - ⓑ has
   - ⓒ haves

2. Tony and Pedro _____ my boat yesterday.
   - ⓐ has
   - ⓑ have
   - ⓒ had

3. Bert says he _____ a new toy now.
   - ⓐ have
   - ⓑ has
   - ⓒ had

4. The children _____ a big house.
   - ⓐ have
   - ⓑ has
   - ⓒ haves

5. Do you _____ my book?
   - ⓐ have
   - ⓑ has
   - ⓒ had

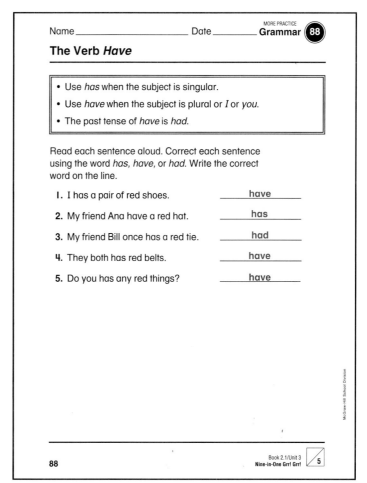

The Verb *Have*

- Use *has* when the subject is singular.
- Use *have* when the subject is plural or *I* or *you*.
- The past tense of *have* is *had*.

Read each sentence aloud. Correct each sentence
using the word *has, have,* or *had.* Write the correct
word on the line.

1. I has a pair of red shoes.   ____have____

2. My friend Ana have a red hat.   ____has____

3. My friend Bill once has a red tie. ____had____

4. They both has red belts.   ____have____

5. Do you has any red things?   ____have____

Page 83

Name _____ Date _____ PRETEST SPELLING 83

Words with Long e: y, ey

Pretest Directions

Fold back the paper along the dotted line. Use the blanks to write each word as it is read aloud. When you finish the test, unfold the paper. Correct any spelling mistakes. Practice the words you missed for the Posttest.

To Parents,

Here are the results of your child's weekly spelling Pretest. You can help your child study for the Posttest by following these simple steps for each word on the list:

1. Read the word to your child.

2. Have your child write the word, saying each letter as it is written.

3. Say each letter of the word as your child checks the spelling.

4. If a mistake has been made, have your child read each letter of the correctly spelled word aloud, and then repeat steps 1–3.

1. _____	1. many
2. _____	2. money
3. _____	3. every
4. _____	4. happy
5. _____	5. tiny
6. _____	6. baby
7. _____	7. key
8. _____	8. penny
9. _____	9. party
10. _____	10. lady

Challenge Words

_____ forget
_____ lonely
_____ memory
_____ mountain
_____ wonderful

10 Book 2.1/Unit 3
Nine-in-One, Grr! Grr! 83

Page 84

Name _____ Date _____ AT HOME WORD STUDY SPELLING 84

Words with Long e: y, ey

Using the Word Study Steps

1. LOOK at the word.
2. SAY the word aloud.
3. STUDY the letters in the word.
4. WRITE the word.
5. CHECK the word.
   Did you spell the word right? If not, go back to step 1.

Spelling Tip

When a base word ends with a vowel followed by y, do not change the ending when adding suffixes or endings.

key + **s** = key**s**

Word Scramble

Unscramble each set of letters to make a spelling word.

1. eervy ___every___   2. yek ___key___

3. yadl ___lady___   4. yint ___tiny___

5. arpty ___party___   6. paphy ___happy___

7. omney ___money___   8. bbay ___baby___

9. namy ___many___   10. nepny ___penny___

To Parents or Helpers:

Using the Word Study Steps above as your child comes across any new words will help him or her spell well. Review the steps as you both go over this week's spelling words.

Go over the Spelling Tip with your child. Help your child write the plurals of words that end with a vowel followed by y.

Help your child unscramble the letters to make spelling words.

84 Book 2.1/Unit 3
Nine-in-One Grr! Grr! 10

Page 85

Name _____ Date _____ EXPLORE THE PATTERN SPELLING 85

Words with Long e: y, ey

Look at the words in the box. Write the spelling words that have each spelling pattern.

| many | every | tiny | key | party |
| money | happy | baby | penny | lady |

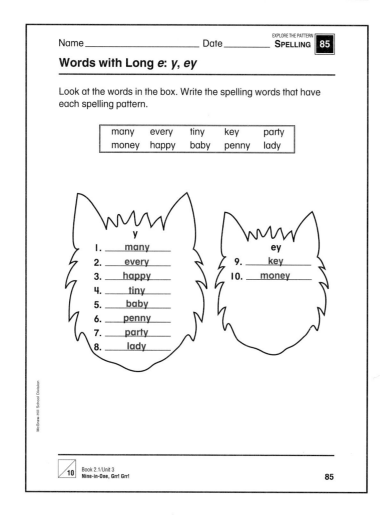

y
1. ___many___
2. ___every___
3. ___happy___
4. ___tiny___
5. ___baby___
6. ___penny___
7. ___party___
8. ___lady___

ey
9. ___key___
10. ___money___

10 Book 2.1/Unit 3
Nine-in-One, Grr! Grr! 85

Page 86

Name _____ Date _____ PRACTICE AND EXTEND SPELLING 86

Words with Long e: y, ey

| many | every | tiny | key | party |
| money | happy | baby | penny | lady |

Use a spelling word to complete each sentence.

1. People use ___money___ to buy things.

2. Something very small is ___tiny___.

3. You need a ___key___ to unlock the door.

4. The opposite of **sad** is ___happy___.

5. How ___many___ beans are in the jar?

6. Don't skip any questions. Answer ___every___ question on the test.

Word Builder

Make each word mean more than one. Change the y to i and add -es.

7. baby – y + i + es = ___babies___

8. penny – y + i + es = ___pennies___

9. party – y + i + es = ___parties___

10. lady – y + i + es = ___ladies___

Challenge Extension: Have children write and illustrate an advertisement for a vacation spot in the mountains.

86 Book 2.1/Unit 3
Nine-in-One Grr! Grr! 10

Page 87

Name _____ Date _____

Words with Long *e*: *y*, *ey*

Proofreading Activity

There are six spelling mistakes in this report. Circle each misspelled word. Write the words correctly on the lines below.

There were (meny) tigers in the world. Then people began to live where the tigers live. Tigers had less space to live. Now there are few tigers left. Someday soon (everey) tiger in the world may be gone! Some people give (mony) to save the tigers. Other people work to save the tigers. People who work in zoos take care of (babey) tigers. The (tiney) tigers are safe and (hapy) there. Everyone can play a part in helping to save the tigers.

1. ___many___   2. ___every___   3. ___money___

4. ___baby___   5. ___tiny___   6. ___happy___

Writing Activity

Pretend you found a magic key. Write a story about the key. Use four of your spelling words. Circle the words you use.

_____

_____

_____

_____

_____

Page 88

Name _____ Date _____

Words with Long *e*: *y*, *ey*

Look at the words in each set. One word in each set is spelled right. Use a pencil to color in the circle in front of that word. Before you begin, look at the sample sets of words. Sample A has been done for you. Do Sample B by yourself. When you are sure you know what to do, you may go on with the rest of the page.

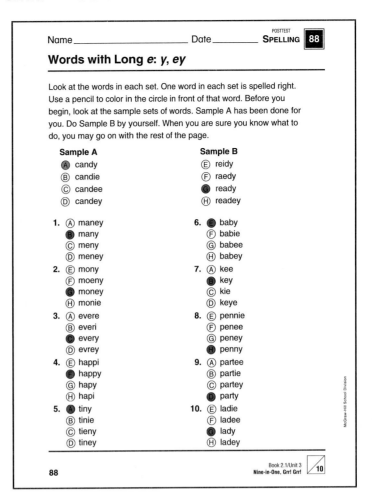

Sample A
- Ⓐ candy
- Ⓑ candie
- Ⓒ candee
- Ⓓ candey

Sample B
- Ⓔ reidy
- Ⓕ raedy
- Ⓖ ready
- Ⓗ readey

1. Ⓐ maney
   Ⓑ many
   Ⓒ meny
   Ⓓ meney

2. Ⓔ mony
   Ⓕ moeny
   Ⓖ money
   Ⓗ monie

3. Ⓐ evere
   Ⓑ everi
   Ⓒ every
   Ⓓ evrey

4. Ⓔ happi
   Ⓕ happy
   Ⓖ hapy
   Ⓗ hapi

5. Ⓐ tiny
   Ⓑ tinie
   Ⓒ tieny
   Ⓓ tiney

6. Ⓔ baby
   Ⓕ babie
   Ⓖ babee
   Ⓗ babey

7. Ⓐ kee
   Ⓑ key
   Ⓒ kie
   Ⓓ keye

8. Ⓔ pennie
   Ⓕ penee
   Ⓖ peney
   Ⓗ penny

9. Ⓐ partee
   Ⓑ partie
   Ⓒ partey
   Ⓓ party

10. Ⓔ ladie
    Ⓕ ladee
    Ⓖ lady
    Ⓗ ladey

T49

Practice 117

Name _____ Date _____ **Practice** 117

Long *e*; Short *e*; /ər/, /ən/, /əl/; Silent Letters

Complete each sentence using the words below.

bought	handle	honey	right	knew
seven	garden	cover	many	bread

1. I raised my hand because I ___**knew**___ the right answer.
2. My mother ___**bought**___ me a new coat.
3. We raise bees for their ___**honey**___ .
4. We made a ___**right**___ turn at the corner.
5. Joan has ___**seven**___ cats living in her barn.
6. The ___**handle**___ broke off the pitcher.
7. I helped plant the seeds in the ___**garden**___ .
8. Mother showed me how to bake ___**bread**___ .
9. Take the ___**cover**___ off the box and look inside.
10. He had too ___**many**___ broken toys.

10 Book 2.1/Unit 3
Change for the Quarter

At Home: Help children make a list of other words that have long *e*; short *e*; /ər/, /ən/, /əl/; and silent letters.

117

Practice 118

Name _____ Date _____ **Practice** 118

Vocabulary

Read the sentences. Choose a word from the box that means almost the same thing as the words in parentheses. Write the word on the line.

collect	honor	join	order	pocket	worth

1. The mountains (meet with) the river at the town.

   join

2. See if you have a dime in your (part of a coat).

   pocket

3. The children (speak very well of) their grandparents.

   honor

4. Put the days of the week in the right (way of listing).

   order

5. These cards are (how much they cost) ten cents each.

   worth

6. I'm going to (gather and keep) stuffed toys.

   collect

118 At Home: Have children write a new sentence for each vocabulary word.

Book 2.1/Unit 3
Change for the Quarter 6

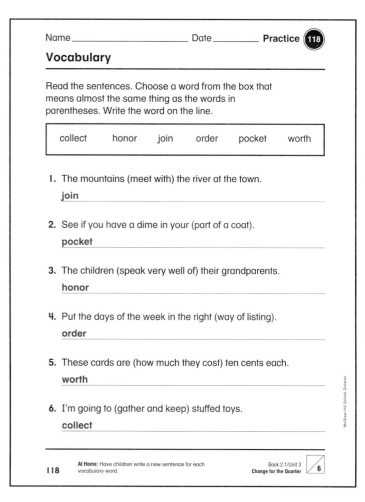

Two to Collect

2

"It's time to throw out some of these comic books," Mom said. "There is room for only a couple of them."

"But, Mom, I collect them," I said. "I think you must have every comic book ever written," she said. "They must weigh a ton." Then she smiled. "I remember I used to be a collector, too."

118b 3

"You collected comic books?" I asked.

"No, stamps," she said. "My father got lots of mail. He let me keep the stamps. I put them in order in a leather book. Some of the stamps were to honor people or countries. Once my father pulled a stamp out from his pocket for my birthday. It was worth a lot."

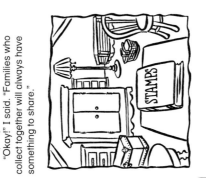

"If your stamps made you happy, why don't you have them now?" I asked.

"I do! They are in the attic. I am going to look for them right now. Why don't you join me?" she said.

"Okay!" I said. "Families who collect together will always have something to share."

At Home: Help children start collecting fun or interesting items, and discuss why they are special.

118a 4

Change for the Quarter • PRACTICE

Name _____ Date _____ **Practice** 119

Story Comprehension

Write an **X** next to each statement that is true about "Change for the Quarter."

1. __X__ The 25-cent piece is getting a new look.

2. _____ Twelve new quarters will come out each year.

3. __X__ The first five new quarters came out in 1999.

4. __X__ New Jersey was one of the first five states.

5. __X__ Some kids collect coins.

6. _____ Quarters cost a lot of money to make.

7. __X__ Delaware was the first state to join the United States.

8. __X__ New quarters will honor all 50 states.

9. __X__ George Washington's head will be on the new quarter.

10. _____ The new quarter will be worth 50 cents.

11. _____ These new quarters are not to be spent.

12. __X__ The eagle will not be on the "tails" side any more.

Book 2.1/Unit 3 12
Change for the Quarter
At Home: Have children start a collection. They can collect coins, stamps, dried flowers, or bottle caps. 119

Name _____ Date _____ **Practice** 120

Choose a Reference Source

Study the uses of a dictionary listed below. Then study the uses of an encyclopedia. Use these guides to help you answer the questions.

Dictionary:

1. gives more than one definition if the word has more than one

2. tells you how to pronounce the word

3. tells you the part of speech each meaning has—example:
   lead (to guide someone) *verb*
   lead (a heavy metal) *noun*

4. may use the word in a sentence

Encyclopedia:

A. may break the topic down into its parts and fully explain them

B. may give facts and numbers related to the topic, as well as graphs and charts

C. may include maps, photos, and diagrams

D. may provide history of the topic

Choose the number or letter of the different uses shown above that would help you answer these questions.

1. What is the history of the Girl Scouts? _____D_____

2. What part of speech is the word *funny*? _____3_____

3. What countries surround Mexico? _____C_____

4. How is the word *ragout* pronounced? _____2_____

5. How many tons of gold are mined in Colorado? ___B___

At Home: Ask children which would be more helpful if they wanted to find out about the history of Texas, a dictionary or an encyclopedia.

120 Book 2.1/Unit 3 5
Change for the Quarter

Name _____ Date _____ **Practice** 121

Cause and Effect

Read the story about Grandma's biscuits. Think about what happened and why it happened.

"It's too lumpy," Grandma said to Ellen. She mixed in more water. Then she rolled out the dough on the table. "I like my biscuits the same size. Get me a glass," said Grandma. She turned the glass upside down to cut the biscuits. Then she put the tray of biscuits in the oven to bake. In twelve minutes the bell rang. Guess who was first in line for a biscuit? Ellen was!

Read each cause. Then write its effect.

Cause	Effect
The dough was too lumpy.	Grandma added more water.
Grandma likes her biscuits the same size.	She used a glass to cut them.
The biscuits had to bake.	She put them in the oven for twelve minutes.
Ellen liked hot biscuits.	She got the first biscuit.

Book 2.1/Unit 3 4
Change for the Quarter
At Home: Ask children to name an event that happened in the classroom. Have them suggest probable causes for the event. 121

Name _____ Date _____ **Practice** 122

Fantasy and Reality

Reality means something that can happen in real life.
Fantasy means something that can't happen.

Read each sentence. If it could happen, write **reality** next to it. If it could not happen, write **fantasy** next to it.

1. Horses can fly over your house. _____fantasy_____

2. A dog can jump on a chair. _____reality_____

3. A cat can talk to a person. _____fantasy_____

4. Elephants can walk in mud. _____reality_____

5. A rainbow has many colors. _____reality_____

6. Chairs can walk. _____fantasy_____

7. I can walk on a rainbow. _____fantasy_____

8. A cat can meow. _____reality_____

9. Frogs can go shopping. _____fantasy_____

10. Horses can run fast. _____reality_____

11. The moon is made of blue cheese. _____fantasy_____

12. A house can have many windows. _____reality_____

At Home: Ask children to write two sentences: one fantasy and one reality.

122 Book 2.1/Unit 3 12
Change for the Quarter

T51

Change for the Quarter • PRACTICE

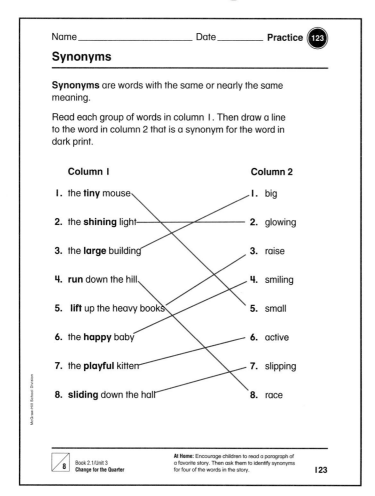

Synonyms

Synonyms are words with the same or nearly the same meaning.

Read each group of words in column 1. Then draw a line to the word in column 2 that is a synonym for the word in dark print.

Column 1   **Column 2**

1. the **tiny** mouse   1. big

2. the **shining** light   2. glowing

3. the **large** building   3. raise

4. **run** down the hill   4. smiling

5. **lift** up the heavy books   5. small

6. the **happy** baby   6. active

7. the **playful** kitten   7. slipping

8. **sliding** down the hall   8. race

8 Book 2.1/Unit 3
Change for the Quarter

At Home: Encourage children to read a paragraph of a favorite story. Then ask them to identify synonyms for four of the words in the story.

123

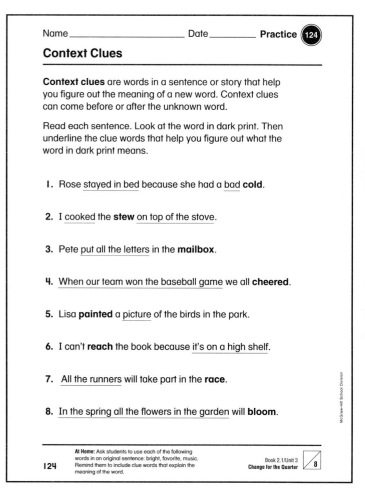

Context Clues

Context clues are words in a sentence or story that help you figure out the meaning of a new word. Context clues can come before or after the unknown word.

Read each sentence. Look at the word in dark print. Then underline the clue words that help you figure out what the word in dark print means.

1. Rose stayed in bed because she had a bad **cold**.

2. I cooked the **stew** on top of the stove.

3. Pete put all the letters in the **mailbox**.

4. When our team won the baseball game we all **cheered**.

5. Lisa **painted** a picture of the birds in the park.

6. I can't **reach** the book because it's on a high shelf.

7. All the runners will take part in the **race**.

8. In the spring all the flowers in the garden will **bloom**.

At Home: Ask students to use each of the following words in an original sentence: bright, favorite, music. Remind them to include clue words that explain the meaning of the word.

124

Book 2.1/Unit 3
Change for the Quarter **8**

Change for the Quarter • RETEACH

Long *e*; Short *e*; /ər/, /ən/, /əl/; Silent Letters

wa_l_k ⓛ
ⓑ

Circle the missing letter(s). Then write them to complete the word.

1. ⟨er / or⟩
quart **er**

2. ⟨e / ea⟩
br **ea** d

3. ⟨y / ey⟩
bab **y**

4. ⟨g / h⟩
si **g** n

5. ⟨y / ey⟩
turk **ey**

6. ⟨w / l⟩
w rite

6 Book 2.1/Unit 3
Nine-in-One, Grr! Grr!

At Home: Ask children to think of another word with a
silent **w** and another word with a silent **g**.

117

Vocabulary

collect	honor	join	order	pocket	worth

Find the word on the right that completes each sentence.
Write the letter for that word on the line.

1. I have to **f** lunch.   **a.** collect

2. I like to **a** baseball cards.   **b.** join

3. I think this truck is **e** about one dollar.   **c.** honor

4. Jan found her ring in the **d** of her coat.   **d.** pocket

5. It was an **c** to meet the president.   **e.** worth

6. Henry and Lucy want to **b** the club.   **f.** order

118 **At Home:** Encourage children to write a story using the
vocabulary words.

Book 2.1/Unit 3
Change for the Quarter 6

Story Comprehension

Think about "Change for the Quarter." Write **True** if the sentence
is true. Write **False** if the sentence is false. Then rewrite the false
sentences to make them true.

1. The quarter has the same design in each state. **False. The
quarter has a different design in each state.**

2. In 1999, the first new quarters appeared. **True**

3. The quarter is worth 25 cents. **True**

4. Each of the fifty new designs honors a different person. **False.
Each new design honors a different state.**

5. The eagle on the "tails" side of every quarter will still be shown.
False. The eagle is going to be replaced.

5 Book 2.1/Unit 3
Change for the Quarter

At Home: Ask children to tell you another fact from
"Change for the Quarter."

119

Choose a Reference Source

Dictionaries give information about words. **Encyclopedias**
give information about different topics.

Dictionary Entry	Encyclopedia Entry
me·te·or (mē´ tē ər) *noun* Metal or stone that comes out of space and goes through Earth's atmosphere. *plural* **meteors**.	**Meteor,** *MEE tee uhr,* is a bright streak of light seen in the sky. Sometimes meteors are called "shooting stars" or "falling stars." Chunks of metal or stone enter the air around Earth and burn up. Some of them pass through without burning and land on Earth. These are called meteorites. Sometimes a group of meteors fall together. These are called meteor showers.

Use these entries to answer the questions below.

1. Which of these entries would give you the most information
about meteors? **encyclopedia**

2. If you wanted to know how to spell the plural of **meteor**, which
source would be best? **dictionary**

3. Which source would tell you about different kinds of meteors?
encyclopedia

4. If you read the word **meteor** in a story and didn't know what it
meant, which source would be the easiest to read quickly for
the meaning? **dictionary**

120 **At Home:** Ask children to tell you what the difference
is between a **meteor** and **meteorite**.

Book 2.1/Unit 3
Change for the Quarter 4

Change for the Quarter • RETEACH

Cause and Effect

> Look at the pictures. Read the sentences.
> The boat moves fast **because** it is a windy day.
>
> **Cause**   **Effect**
>
>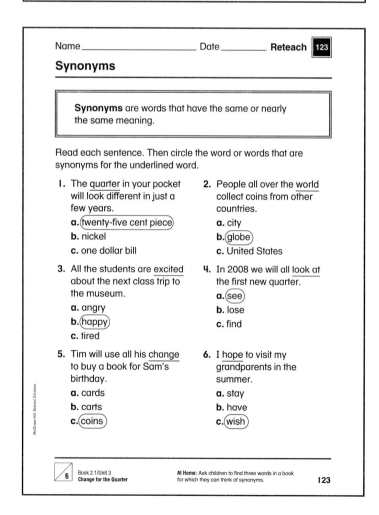
>
> It is a windy day.   The boat moves fast.
> Remember, the **cause** is the event that makes the **effect** happen.

Each set of pictures shows a cause and its effect. Write the effect for each cause. **Answers will vary.**

1. Cause   **Effect**

The baby gets a bottle.

2. Cause   **Effect**

The car goes through a puddle.

3. Cause   **Effect**

A boy looks at his birthday cake.

Fantasy and Reality

> **Real things** can happen in real life.
> **Make-believe** things can never happen in real life.

Think about things friends can really do. Read the sentences. Circle Yes if it is something that could happen. Circle **No** if it is something that could not happen.

1. They can talk on the phone.   (Yes)   No
2. They can send a message in a bottle.   (Yes)   No
3. Friends can dance in the streets.   (Yes)   No
4. They can swim across the ocean.   Yes   (No)
5. They can make a wish.   (Yes)   No
6. Friends can sail a toy sailboat.   (Yes)   No
7. They can ride on Columbus's ships.   Yes   (No)
8. Friends can meet a dragon.   Yes   (No)
9. Friends can have a pen pal in Africa.   (Yes)   No
10. They can fly a dragon kite.   (Yes)   No

Synonyms

> **Synonyms** are words that have the same or nearly the same meaning.

Read each sentence. Then circle the word or words that are synonyms for the underlined word.

1. The quarter in your pocket will look different in just a few years.
   a. (twenty-five cent piece)
   b. nickel
   c. one dollar bill

2. People all over the world collect coins from other countries.
   a. city
   b. (globe)
   c. United States

3. All the students are excited about the next class trip to the museum.
   a. angry
   b. (happy)
   c. tired

4. In 2008 we will all look at the first new quarter.
   a. (see)
   b. lose
   c. find

5. Tim will use all his change to buy a book for Sam's birthday.
   a. cards
   b. carts
   c. (coins)

6. I hope to visit my grandparents in the summer.
   a. stay
   b. have
   c. (wish)

Context Clues

> You can figure out the meaning of an unknown word by using **context clues.** These are words that come before or after the unknown word. You can find these clues in the same sentence or in nearby sentences.

Read the sentences. Then circle the word or words that are clues to the meaning of the word in dark print.

1. Lisa wants to make a new **design**, or plan, for her model boat.
   a. model boat
   b. (plan)

2. The students are so **excited** about the class play that they start to cheer.
   a. (they start to cheer)
   b. the class play

3. In the summer we went **hiking** along the trail in the state park.
   a. in the summer
   b. (along the trail)

4. I wanted to have an **adventure** by doing something fun and different.
   a. (doing something fun and different)
   b. I wanted to have

5. The desert plant, or **cactus**, grew tall in the sunshine without much water.
   a. (desert plant)
   b. much water

6. In the afternoon I heard Lisa playing beautiful **music** on her piano.
   a. (playing on her piano)
   b. in the afternoon

Change for the Quarter • EXTEND

Long *e*; Short *e*; /ər/, /ən/, /əl/; Silent Letters

Think of a word that rhymes with each word on the list. Write the word in the chart.

Words	Rhyming Words
head	possible answers: bread, read, thread
hurry	possible answers: worry, scurry, furry
seven	possible answers: eleven, even, garden
saddle	possible answers: paddle, rattle, cattle
light	possible answers: night, sight, tight

Write a rhyme using two of the words from the list.

_____

_____

_____

_____

_____

Book 2.1/Unit 3
Change for the Quarter

At Home: Invite children to read the list of rhyming words aloud. Challenge them to add words to the list. Talk about why two words rhyme (they end with the same sound).

117

Vocabulary

Make your own dictionary. Cut out the book pages below. Write a definition for each word. Then write your own word. Staple the pages together so they are in ABC order.

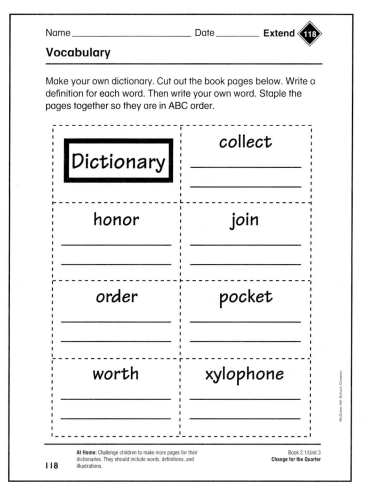

Dictionary

collect
_____
_____

honor
_____
_____

join
_____
_____

order
_____
_____

pocket
_____
_____

worth
_____
_____

xylophone
_____
_____

118

At Home: Challenge children to make more pages for their dictionaries. They should include words, definitions, and illustrations.

Book 2.1/Unit 3
Change for the Quarter

Story Comprehension

Design a quarter to represent your state. Use the information in the article to help you.

(circle)

Write the reason your design would be a good one for the new quarter. Explain what your design shows about your state and why you would put it on the quarter.

_____

_____

_____

_____

Book 2.1/Unit 3
Change for the Quarter

At Home: Discuss the changes being made to quarters. Help children research when their state will be honored with a coin.

119

Choose a Reference Source

Telephone book:

Polete Michelle 14 Oak St 714-5003
Polit Nathan 10 Pine Avenue . . . 481-3716

Dictionary:

police (puh-**leess**)
Noun, plural The people whose job it is to keep order, make sure laws are obeyed, and stop crimes from being committed.

Encyclopedia:

Police are government officers who enforce the law and maintain order. They work to protect the lives and property of the people of the community. Police officers serve their communities in many ways.

Map:

1. Which reference source would you use if you needed to know where Michelle lived? ____telephone directory____

2. Which reference source would you use if you needed to know how to say the word police?____dictionary____

3. Which reference source would you use if you wanted to show someone that Michelle lived on the north side of the lake?
____map____

4. Which reference source would you use to write a report about what police officers do on the job? ____encyclopedia____

Write a question for a friend to answer about using reference materials.

____Questions will vary.____

_____

_____

120

At Home: Have a scavenger hunt with children. Have a dictionary, an encyclopedia, a telephone book, and a map ready for children's use. Ask children to locate information that comes from the different sources.

Book 2.1/Unit 3
Change for the Quarter

Change for the Quarter • EXTEND

Cause and Effect

Look at the picture. What is the cat going to cause to happen?
Draw a picture to show the effect.

Cause   **Effect**

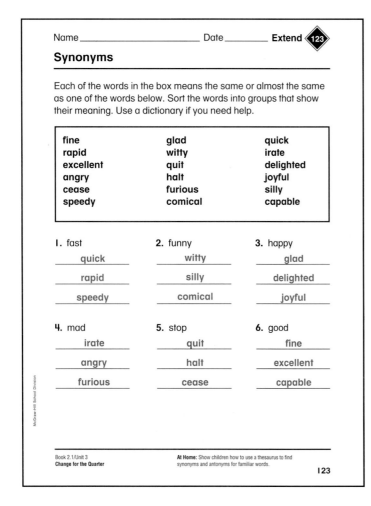

Write a story about the pictures.

_____

_____

_____

_____

_____

_____

_____

_____

_____

_____

_____

Book 2.1/Unit 3
Change for the Quarter   At Home: Tell about or draw a picture of a cause. Have
children draw a picture of the effect it might have.   121

Fantasy and Reality

Read the names of the stories. Look at the illustrations. Next to
each book write if the story is a story about real things or things
that are make-believe. Write a sentence telling how you know.

1. My Dragon   make-believe; there are no dragons so the
girl could not have one.

2. I Like to Eat Apples   real; Apples are really something people
like to eat.

3. Sunny Learns to Drive   make-believe; dogs cannot be taught to
drive a car.

4. Max Can't Find His Bone   real; sometimes dogs bury something and
can't find it later.

Use another sheet of paper. Name and illustrate your own book
covers. Make one that is about something real and one that is
about something make-believe.

At Home: Invite children to tell a story about one of the book
covers they drew.   Book 2.1/Unit 3
Change for the Quarter
122

Synonyms

Each of the words in the box means the same or almost the same
as one of the words below. Sort the words into groups that show
their meaning. Use a dictionary if you need help.

fine	glad	quick
rapid	witty	irate
excellent	quit	delighted
angry	halt	joyful
cease	furious	silly
speedy	comical	capable

1. fast   **2.** funny   **3.** happy

quick   _witty_   _glad_

rapid   _silly_   _delighted_

speedy   _comical_   _joyful_

4. mad   **5.** stop   **6.** good

irate   _quit_   _fine_

angry   _halt_   _excellent_

furious   _cease_   _capable_

Book 2.1/Unit 3
Change for the Quarter   At Home: Show children how to use a thesaurus to find
synonyms and antonyms for familiar words.   123

Context Clues

Look at the picture. Use the clues in the picture to write a story
about what the bears are doing. Give your story a title.

Title: _____

_____

_____

_____

_____

_____

_____

At Home: Have children read their stories aloud. Invite them
to point out details in the picture that they used in their
stories.   124   Book 2.1/Unit 3
Change for the Quarter

Change for the Quarter • GRAMMAR

Name _____ Date _____

Sentence Combining

- If two sentences have words that are the same, you can combine them.
- You can combine sentences by joining words with *and*.

  David cut his potato.   David ate his potato.

  David cut and ate his potato.

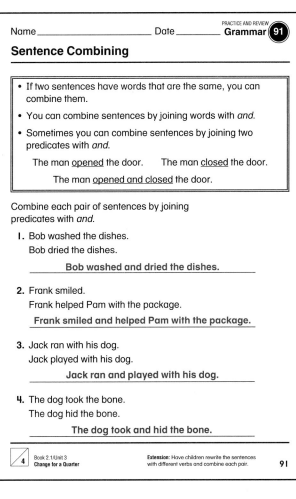

Read the pairs of sentences. Make one sentence out of each pair and write it.

1. a.   Jane made the apple pie.
   b.   Jane served the apple pie.

   Jane made and served the apple pie.

2. a.   The family ate the pie.
   b.   The family liked the pie.

   The family ate and liked the pie

3. a.   My brother asked for a second piece.
   b.   My brother ate a second piece.

   My brother asked for and ate a second piece.

Name _____ Date _____

Sentence Combining

- Sometimes you can combine sentences by joining two predicates with *and*.

  Joe sang.   Joe danced.

  Joe sang and danced.

Combine each pair of sentences and write the new sentence.

1. a.   The children ran.
   b.   The children shouted.

   The children ran and shouted.

2. a.   Eddy sat on the swing.
   b.   Eddy shouted on the swing.

   Eddy sat and shouted on the swing.

3. a.   Sandy hugged the baby.
   b.   Sandy kissed the baby.

   Sandy hugged and kissed the baby.

Name _____ Date _____

Sentence Combining

- If two sentences have words that are the same, you can combine them.
- You can combine sentences by joining words with *and*.
- Sometimes you can combine sentences by joining two predicates with *and*.

  The man <u>opened</u> the door.   The man <u>closed</u> the door.

  The man <u>opened and closed</u> the door.

Combine each pair of sentences by joining predicates with *and*.

1. Bob washed the dishes.
   Bob dried the dishes.

   Bob washed and dried the dishes.

2. Frank smiled.
   Frank helped Pam with the package.

   Frank smiled and helped Pam with the package.

3. Jack ran with his dog.
   Jack played with his dog.

   Jack ran and played with his dog.

4. The dog took the bone.
   The dog hid the bone.

   The dog took and hid the bone.

Name _____ Date _____

Correcting Sentences

- Begin every sentence with a capital letter.
- End a statement with a period.
- End a question with a question mark.
- End a command with a period.
- End an exclamation with an exclamation point.

  Where is your coat?   I can't find it.

  Please get it.   The dog has it!

Read each sentence. Correct it.
Write the correct sentence on the line.

1. do we have any eggs

   Do we have any eggs?

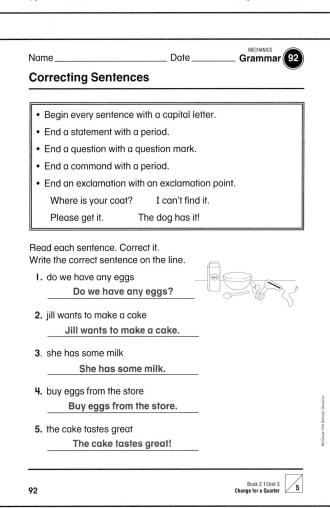

2. jill wants to make a cake

   Jill wants to make a cake.

3. she has some milk

   She has some milk.

4. buy eggs from the store

   Buy eggs from the store.

5. the cake tastes great

   The cake tastes great!

Change for the Quarter • GRAMMAR

Name_____ Date_____

Sentence Combining

Read each pair of sentences. Combine them.
Write the sentence.

1. The windows have dust.
   The windows need to be cleaned.

   The windows have dust and need to be cleaned.

2. We washed the windows.
   We wiped the window sills.

   We washed the windows and wiped the window sills.

3. Bill swept the floor.
   Bill washed the floor.

   Bill swept and washed the floor.

4. Kim raked the leaves.
   Kim cleaned the yard.

   Kim raked the leaves and cleaned the yard.

5. The house looks clean.
   The house is ready for the party.

   The house looks clean and is ready for the party.

Name_____ Date_____

Sentence Combining

- If two sentences have words that are the same, you can combine them.
- You can combine sentences by joining words with *and*.
- Sometimes you can combine sentences by joining two predicates with *and*.

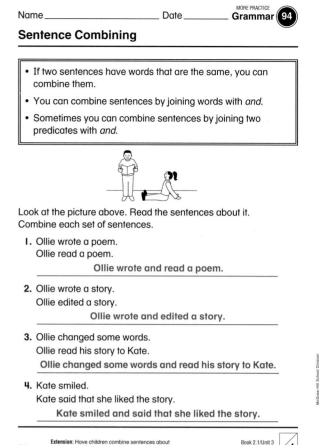

Look at the picture above. Read the sentences about it.
Combine each set of sentences.

1. Ollie wrote a poem.
   Ollie read a poem.

   Ollie wrote and read a poem.

2. Ollie wrote a story.
   Ollie edited a story.

   Ollie wrote and edited a story.

3. Ollie changed some words.
   Ollie read his story to Kate.

   Ollie changed some words and read his story to Kate.

4. Kate smiled.
   Kate said that she liked the story.

   Kate smiled and said that she liked the story.

Change for the Quarter • SPELLING

Words from Math

Pretest Directions

Fold back the paper along the dotted line. Use the blanks to write each word as it is read aloud. When you finish the test, unfold the paper. Correct any spelling mistakes. Practice the words you missed for the Posttest.

To Parents,

Here are the results of your child's weekly spelling Pretest. You can help your child study for the Posttest by following these simple steps for each word on the list:

1. Read the word to your child.

2. Have your child write the word, saying each letter as it is written.

3. Say each letter of the word as your child checks the spelling.

4. If a mistake has been made, have your child read each letter of the correctly spelled word aloud, and then repeat steps 1–3.

1. _____	1. dollar
2. _____	2. cost
3. _____	3. exact
4. _____	4. buy
5. _____	5. cent
6. _____	6. dime
7. _____	7. price
8. _____	8. quarter
9. _____	9. sum
10. _____	10. nickel

Challenge Words

_____	collect
_____	honor
_____	order
_____	pocket
_____	worth

Words from Math

Using the Word Study Steps

1. LOOK at the word.
2. SAY the word aloud.
3. STUDY the letters in the word.
4. WRITE the word.
5. CHECK the word.
   Did you spell the word right? If not, go back to step 1.

Spelling Tip

The letter **q** is always followed by **u**.
Example:
quarter

Crossword Puzzle

Write the spelling word that best matches each clue. Put the spelling words in the boxes that start with the same number.

CROSSWORD CLUES

ACROSS

1. ten cents
2. twenty-five cents
6. correct

DOWN

1. the same as 100 pennies, ten dimes, or four quarters
3. pay money for
4. how much money the seller wants
5. how much you have to pay for something
7. one of these and four more makes a nickel

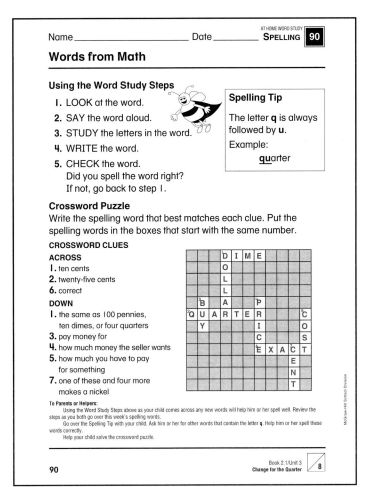

To Parents or Helpers:

Using the Word Study Steps above as your child comes across any new words will help him or her spell well. Review the steps as you both go over this week's spelling words.

Go over the Spelling Tip with your child. Ask him or her for other words that contain the letter **q**. Help him or her spell these words correctly.

Help your child solve the crossword puzzle.

Words from Math

dollar	exact	cent	price	sum
cost	buy	dime	quarter	nickel

Look at the words in the box. Write the spelling words with one syllable.

1. cost   2. buy   3. cent

4. dime   5. price   6. sum

Write the spelling words with two syllables.

7. dollar   8. exact

9. quarter   10. nickel

Find and circle eight spelling words in the puzzle. Some of the words in the puzzle go across. Some of the words go down.

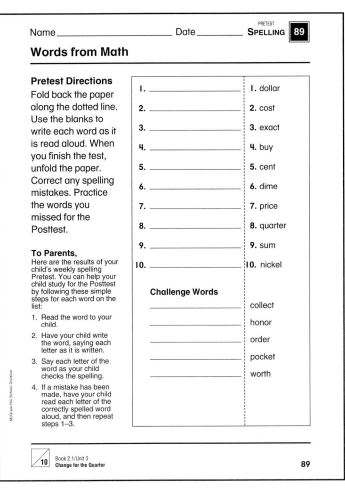

Words from Math

dollar	exact	cent	price	sum
cost	buy	dime	quarter	nickel

Write the spelling words that are names for money.

1. dollar   2. cent

3. dime   4. quarter

5. nickel

Write the spelling words that tell about buying things.

6. cost   7. price

Write the spelling word that means "correct" to complete the sentence.

8. The man in the store gave me _____exact_____ change for a dollar.

Answer these questions with a spelling word. Write the word on the line.

9. Which is more money: a dollar or a quarter? dollar

10. Which is less money: a dime or a cent? cent

11. A dollar is the same as 4 quarters.

12. A dollar is the same as 10 dimes.

Challenge Extension: Have children make a pocket out of paper. Ask them to write challenge words on slips of paper and put in pocket.

Change for the Quarter • SPELLING

Page 93

Name _____ Date _____ PROOFREAD AND WRITE **SPELLING** 93

Words from Math

Proofreading Activity

There are six spelling mistakes in the story below. Circle each misspelled word. Write the words correctly on the lines below.

Carlos wanted a yo-yo. He saw one he liked at the store. The tag showed the (eggzact) price: $1.25. Carlos looked in his pocket. He had one (doller) and one (qarter.) He felt really happy that he could buy the yo-yo.

Carlos gave the money to the saleslady.

She smiled at him and said, "This (costz) one dollar and thirty-five (sents.)"

Carlos was surprised. "I just have this much," he said.

"Sorry," said the lady. "You must give me another (diem.) You forgot the tax."

Carlos was lucky. He found the coin in another pocket and bought the yo-yo.

1. _____exact_____   2. _____dollar_____   3. _____quarter_____

4. _____costs_____   5. _____cents_____   6. _____dime_____

Writing Activity

Write about buying something. Tell how much it cost. Tell how many dollars and cents you paid. Use four of your spelling words. Circle the words you use.

_____

_____

_____

10 Book 2.1/Unit 3
Change for the Quarter

93

Page 94

Name _____ Date _____ POSTTEST **SPELLING** 94

Words from Math

Look at the words in each set. One word in each set is spelled right. Use a pencil to color in the circle in front of that word. Before you begin, look at the sample sets of words. Sample A has been done for you. Do Sample B by yourself. When you are sure you know what to do, you may go on with the rest of the page.

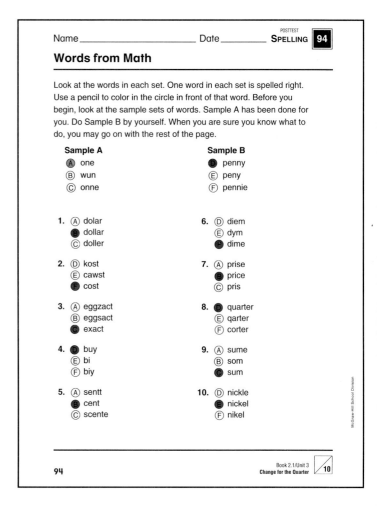

Sample A	Sample B
Ⓐ one	Ⓓ penny
Ⓑ wun	Ⓔ peny
Ⓒ onne	Ⓕ pennie

1. Ⓐ dolar   6. Ⓓ diem
   ● dollar   Ⓔ dym
   Ⓒ doller   ● dime

2. Ⓓ kost   7. Ⓐ prise
   Ⓔ cawst   ● price
   ● cost   Ⓒ pris

3. Ⓐ eggzact   8. ● quarter
   Ⓑ eggsact   Ⓔ qarter
   ● exact   Ⓕ corter

4. ● buy   9. Ⓐ sume
   Ⓔ bi   Ⓑ som
   Ⓕ biy   ● sum

5. Ⓐ sentt   10. Ⓓ nickle
   ● cent   ● nickel
   Ⓒ scente   Ⓕ nikel

94

Book 2.1/Unit 3
Change for the Quarter 10

Unit 3 Review • PRACTICE and RETEACH

Name _____ Date _____ **Practice** 125

Unit 3 Vocabulary Review

A. The same vocabulary word is used twice in each example below. Write the words from the box on the lines.

library	pocket	rush

1. I went to the ____library____ and took out a book. There are many books in the school ____library____.

2. I was late, so I had to ____rush____ to school. We'll have to ____rush____ if we want to get there on time.

3. I have some nickels in my ____pocket____. My jacket ____pocket____ is torn.

B. Read each sentence. Find a vocabulary word from the box that means almost the same thing as the underlined word. Write the word on the line.

couple	finish	notice

1. I have a <u>pair</u> of apples. ____couple____

2. I didn't <u>see</u> her. ____notice____

3. <u>Complete</u> your homework. ____finish____

6 Book 2.1/Unit 3
Unit 3 Vocabulary Review
At Home: Have children illustrate one of the sentences above.
125

Name _____ Date _____ **Practice** 126

Unit 3 Vocabulary Review

A. Write the correct vocabulary words in the sentences.

arrive	forget	order	important

1. Who is the most ____important____ person you can think of?

2. What time do you ____arrive____ at school?

3. Did you ever ____forget____ your lunch?

4. Are the numbers 1, 2, 4, 3 in the right ____order____?

B. Find the words below in the word search.

drifted	lonely	message	earth	finish	worth

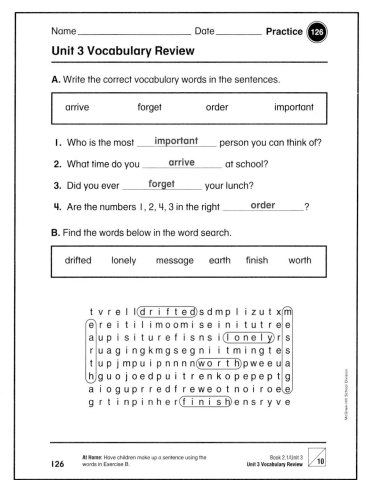

126 **At Home:** Have children make up a sentence using the words in Exercise B.
Book 2.1/Unit 3
Unit 3 Vocabulary Review 10

Name _____ Date _____ **Reteach** 125

Unit 3 Vocabulary Review

A. Match each word with its definition. Write the letter of the definition on the line.

_c_ 1. decided   **a.** one of two equal parts of something

_e_ 2. proud   **b.** a person or thing that does very well

_a_ 3. half   **c.** made up one's mind

_b_ 4. success   **d.** the ability to remember things

_d_ 5. memory   **e.** having a good feeling about oneself

_f_ 6. honor   **f.** to show respect for someone or something

B. Circle the correct definition for each word.

1. library
   (a.) a building where books are kept   **b.** a kind of school

2. climbed
   (a.) went up   **b.** went down

3. message
   a. a movie for children   **(b.)** words sent from one person to another

4. earth
   (a.) ground   **b.** water

10 Book 2.1/Unit 3
Unit 3 Vocabulary Review
At Home: Have children use each of the words from Exercise A in a sentence.
125

Name _____ Date _____ **Reteach** 126

Unit 3 Vocabulary Review

A. Read each sentence. Then, underline the word that answers the question.

1. If you put a boat in the water, what would it do?
   a. decide   **b.** <u>float</u>   **c.** finish

2. If you had a dime, where might you put it?
   a. <u>pocket</u>   **b.** order   **c.** worth

3. What is the Earth?
   a. a half   **b.** <u>planet</u>   **c.** a mountain

4. If you had no one to talk to, how might you feel?
   a. important   **b.** early   **c.** <u>lonely</u>

B. Use the code below to figure out which word is which. Then, circle the correct word.

a	b	c	d	e	f	g	h	i	j	k	l	m	n	o	p	q	r	s	t	u	v	w	x	y	z
c	d	e	f	g	h	i	j	k	l	m	n	o	p	q	r	s	t	u	v	w	x	y	z	a	b

a = c,   b = d,   c = e, and so on.

1. amsnjc
   a. finish   **(b.)** couple

2. hmgl
   (a.) join   **b.** half

3. njylcr
   (a.) planet   **b.** pocket

4. fyjd
   a. rush   **(b.)** half

126 **At Home:** Have children make up a question for each vocabulary word in Exercise B.
Book 2.1/Unit 3
Unit 3 Vocabulary Review 8

Unit 3 Review • EXTEND and GRAMMAR

Name _____ Date _____ **Extend** ◆125

Vocabulary Review

Circle the letters for each word in the puzzle.

important	library	honor	couple	join
arrive	early	earth	float	message
mountain	rush	finish	planet	

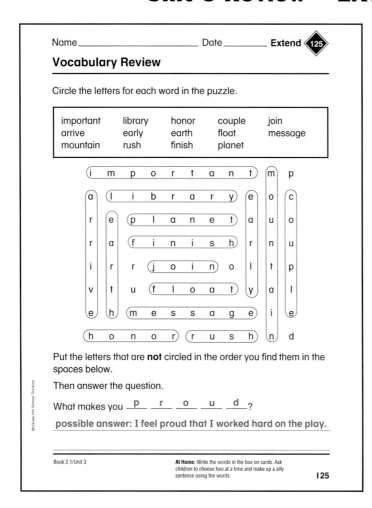

Put the letters that are **not** circled in the order you find them in the spaces below.

Then answer the question.

What makes you P R O U D ?

possible answer: I feel proud that I worked hard on the play.

Book 2.1/Unit 3

At Home: Write the words in the box on cards. Ask children to choose two at a time and make up a silly sentence using the words.

125

Name _____ Date _____ **Extend** ◆126

Vocabulary Review

Use the code to figure out the words in the sentences. Write the answers on another piece of paper.

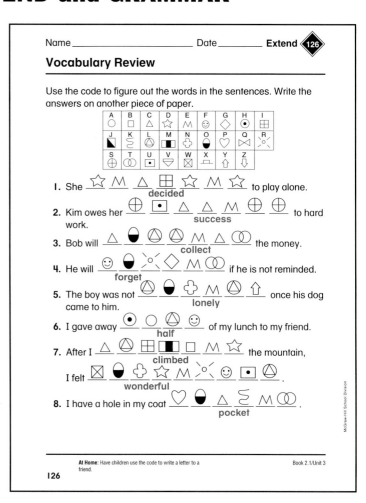

1. She ☆ M △ ⊞ ☆ M ☆ to play alone.
   decided

2. Kim owes her ⊕ ⊡ △ △ M ⊕ ⊕ to hard work.
   success

3. Bob will △ ◐ ◯ △ M △ ◯◯ the money.
   collect

4. He will ☺ ◐ ⤫ ◇ M ◯◯ if he is not reminded.
   forget

5. The boy was not ◐ ◐ ◯ ♣ M ◯ ⇧ once his dog came to him.
   lonely

6. I gave away ⊡ ◯ ◯ ☺ of my lunch to my friend.
   half

7. After I △ ◐ ⊞ ■ ☐ M ☆ the mountain,
   climbed

   I felt ⊠ ◐ ♣ ☆ M ⤫ ☺ ⊡ △ .
   wonderful

8. I have a hole in my coat ♡ ◐ △ Σ M ◯◯ .
   pocket

At Home: Have children use the code to write a letter to a friend.

126

Book 2.1/Unit 3

Name _____ Date _____ UNIT TEST **Grammar** ⬤95

Verbs

Read the sentences in the box. Look at the part with a line under it. Which is the better way to say this part? Mark the letter for your answer.

Kim lives in a big city. She visits the mayor's office. <u>She went to the park.</u> She buys a present at the store.
(1)

1. ⬤ She goes to the park.
   ⓑ She go to the park.
   ⓒ She did go the park.

Bob plays the piano. He studies about music. Bob likes his music teacher. <u>He did worked hard every day.</u>
(2)

2. ⓐ He working hard every day.
   ⬤ He works hard every day.
   ⓒ He are working hard every day.

Bob liked to play. <u>Bob play every day.</u> He learned a lot.
(3)

3. ⓐ Bob playing every day.
   ⓑ Bob plays every day.
   ⬤ Bob played every day.

I had a book. Mark and Bob have colds. <u>We has to eat.</u>
(4)

4. ⓐ We having to eat.
   ⬤ We have to eat.
   ⓒ We do eat.

➡ **Go On**

Book 2.1/Unit 3
Unit Test

95

Name _____ Date _____ REVIEW **Grammar** ⬤96

Yesterday, we talked together. <u>He guess the right answer.</u>
(5)

5. ⬤ He guessed the right answer.
   ⓑ He answered it.
   ⓒ He did guess the right answer

Triangles, squares, and rectangles are shapes. <u>Blue green and purple are colors.</u>
(6)

6. ⓐ Blue and green and purple are colors.
   ⓑ Blue, green, purple are colors.
   ⬤ Blue, green, and purple are colors.

<u>Hal's room is on the second floor. Hal's room has big windows.</u>
(7)

7. ⓐ Hal's rooms are big.
   ⬤ Hal's room is on the second floor and has big windows.
   ⓒ Hal has big windows.

<u>Hal cleans his room. Hal puts his toys away.</u>
(8)

8. ⬤ Hal cleans his room and puts his toys away.
   ⓑ Hal puts his toys in his room.
   ⓒ Hal has a big room.

96

Book 2.1/Unit 3
Unit Test ⬜8

Unit 3 Review • SPELLING

Name _____ Date _____ UNIT TEST **SPELLING** 95

Book 2.1/Unit 3 Review Test

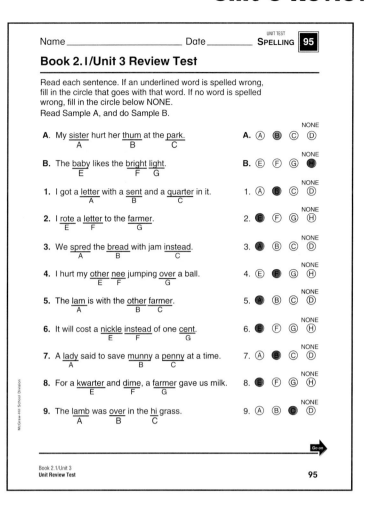

Read each sentence. If an underlined word is spelled wrong, fill in the circle that goes with that word. If no word is spelled wrong, fill in the circle below NONE.
Read Sample A, and do Sample B.

A. My sister hurt her thum at the park.
     A   B   C

A. Ⓐ ● Ⓒ Ⓓ NONE

B. The baby likes the bright light.
     E   F   G

B. Ⓔ Ⓕ Ⓖ ● NONE

1. I got a letter with a sent and a quarter in it.
         A   B   C

1. Ⓐ ● Ⓒ Ⓓ NONE

2. I rote a letter to the farmer.
    E   F   G

2. ● Ⓕ Ⓖ Ⓗ NONE

3. We spred the bread with jam instead.
      A   B   C

3. ● Ⓑ Ⓒ Ⓓ NONE

4. I hurt my other nee jumping over a ball.
         E   G

4. Ⓔ ● Ⓖ Ⓗ NONE

5. The lam is with the other farmer.
     A   B   C

5. ● Ⓑ Ⓒ Ⓓ NONE

6. It will cost a nickle instead of one cent.
         E   F   G

6. ● Ⓕ Ⓖ Ⓗ NONE

7. A lady said to save munny a penny at a time.
     A   B   C

7. Ⓐ ● Ⓒ Ⓓ NONE

8. For a kwarter and dime, a farmer gave us milk.
      E   F   G

8. ● Ⓕ Ⓖ Ⓗ NONE

9. The lamb was over in the hi grass.
     A   B   C

9. Ⓐ Ⓑ ● Ⓓ NONE

Go on →

Name _____ Date _____ UNIT TEST **SPELLING** 96

Book 2.1/Unit 3 Review Test

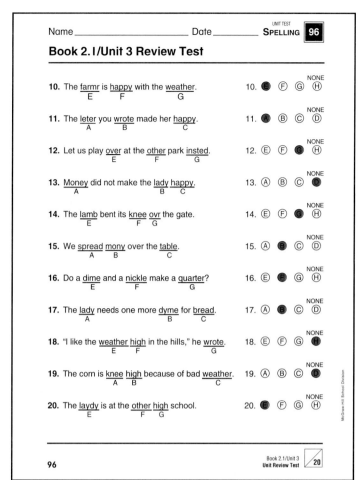

10. The farmr is happy with the weather.
      E   F   G

10. ● Ⓕ Ⓖ Ⓗ NONE

11. The leter you wrote made her happy.
      A   B   C

11. ● Ⓑ Ⓒ Ⓓ NONE

12. Let us play over at the other park insted.
          E   F   G

12. Ⓔ Ⓕ ● Ⓗ NONE

13. Money did not make the lady happy.
     A   B   C

13. Ⓐ Ⓑ Ⓒ ● NONE

14. The lamb bent its knee ovr the gate.
     E   F   G

14. Ⓔ Ⓕ ● Ⓗ NONE

15. We spread mony over the table.
     A   B   C

15. Ⓐ ● Ⓒ Ⓓ NONE

16. Do a dime and a nickle make a quarter?
     E   F   G

16. Ⓔ ● Ⓖ Ⓗ NONE

17. The lady needs one more dyme for bread.
     A   B   C

17. Ⓐ ● Ⓒ Ⓓ NONE

18. "I like the weather high in the hills," he wrote.
        E   F   G

18. Ⓔ Ⓕ Ⓖ ● NONE

19. The corn is knee high because of bad weather.
        A   B   C

19. Ⓐ Ⓑ Ⓒ ● NONE

20. The laydy is at the other high school.
     E   F   G

20. ● Ⓕ Ⓖ Ⓗ NONE

Phonological Awareness

OBJECTIVES Children will practice blending and segmenting sounds and deleting beginning sounds in blends.

Alternate

Activities

Blend Sounds

WHICH ONE?

 Materials: pictures of lamb, stamp, bell, vine, light, window, snow, knight

Have children choose among blended words to identify pictures.

- Tell children that for each picture, you will ask them to choose which sounds when blended together will name the picture. For example, ask: *Is this a /l/-/a/-/d/ or a /l/-/a/-/m/?* They should blend the sounds and figure out which word names a picture.

- Ask similar questions while displaying each of these pictures: lamb, stamp, bell, vine, light, window, snow, knight. Have a volunteer remove the picture of the word whose sounds were blended together.

Segment Sounds

LET'S CLIMB

 Materials: chart paper, paper clips, and magazine pictures of different objects.

Use this game to help children practice segmenting words into individual sounds.

- Draw a large tree on chart paper. Have at least three large branches at different heights.

- Explain that each pair will get to choose a picture of an object.

- Tell each pair to say the word slowly, then segment the object's name sound by sound. Have them take one paper clip for each sound.

- Specify which branch will hold words with two sounds, three sounds, and four sounds. Have pairs glue the picture of their object on the appropriate branch.

Delete Sounds

LET'S DRAW

 Materials: paper and pencils

Have children listen to pairs of words and determine the beginning sound that has been deleted from a blend.

- Ask children to listen to the following pair of words: *clean/lean.* Tell them to name the beginning sound that was deleted to create the second word.

- Give pairs the following words. Have them draw a picture of what the object is if the beginning sound of the blend is taken away: *clamp, stick, scar, train, bland, stack, branch.*

Introduce Silent Letter
l, k, w, g, h, gh

OBJECTIVES Students will listen for, identify, and mime words with silent letters *l, k, w, g, h,* and *gh.*

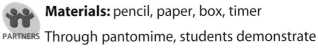

Visual

SILENT LETTER BINGO

 Materials: bingo cards as described, small chips or other marking type items

Students play bingo to reinforce their knowledge of silent letters.

- Create several sets of bingo cards with words students can read. One word in each row or column should contain a silent letter.

- Tell students to listen and look for words with silent letters and to cover those words only after they are read. Begin reading words on the cards in random order.

- When students cover the word in each row or column, they shout "Bingo!"

 Have all students write each of the silent letter words covered in a sentence.

▶**Linguistic**

Auditory

"LISTEN" FOR THE SILENT LETTER

Materials: paper, pencil, chalk

Students listen for silent letters.

- On the board, write a number of words with silent letters *l, k, w, g, h,* and *gh.* Write several paragraphs, using those words in sentences.

- Place students in small groups. Tell students to raise their hands when they hear one of the words on the chalkboard. The first student in each group to raise a hand has the opportunity to use the word in a new sentence.

▶**Interpersonal**

Kinesthetic

SILENT LETTER GUESSING GAME

Materials: pencil, paper, box, timer

Through pantomime, students demonstrate knowledge of silent letters.

- On a number of slips of paper, write a different word with silent letter *l, k, w, g, h,* and *gh.*

- Have partners take turns drawing a slip of paper and acting it out for the members of the class to guess.

- The partners who are the first to correctly guess the word take a turn pantomiming for the class.

▶**Logical/Mathematical**

 **CD-ROM**

See Reteach 85, 89, 90, 106

Reference Sources

OBJECTIVES Students will become familiar with, distinguish between, and look up information in a variety of reference sources.

Alternate Activities

Visual

DICTIONARY DETECTIVES

 Materials: dictionaries, chalk, paper, pencils

Students use dictionaries in this activity.

- Divide the chalkboard into halves by drawing a line. Make a list of words students are unlikely to know and write the words on the board. On the other side of the line, write the definitions of the words in a random order.

- Provide each group with a dictionary, and tell students to look up the words and match them with their correct definitions.

 After students have looked up all the words, have them use each word in a sentence.

- Groups can share their sentences with the entire class. ▶**Linguistic**

Auditory

WHERE AM I FOUND?

 Materials: reference sources, paper, pencil, chalk

Students demonstrate knowledge of a variety of reference resources.

- On the board, write names of reference sources students would use, such as *textbook, newspaper, dictionary, encyclopedia,* and *telephone directory.*

- Call out types of information (such as definitions, phone numbers, weather reports) that could be found in each of those resources.

- Have volunteers take turns stating their answers and coming up to the front of the room to locate the example in the appropriate source. ▶**Logical/Mathematical**

Kinesthetic

TREASURE HUNT

 Materials: dictionaries, paper, pencil, tape, timer

In this activity, students exercise skill with dictionaries in a treasure hunt.

- Give students definitions. Ask them to look up the words they think will match the definitions.

- Place a clue in dictionaries at the location of the correct word. The message will direct students to a place in the classroom (under a globe, behind a computer, etc.) where a sentence has been taped.

- Tell students they will only have a short time to look up all the words in their dictionary. After the timer sounds, groups of partners exchange dictionaries. Have partners exchange dictionaries several times. ▶**Logical/Mathematical**

See Reteach 88, 96, 104, 112, 120

Fantasy and Reality

 OBJECTIVES Students will distinguish between pictures of real and fantastic elements.

Alternate Activities

Visual

REAL AS SUPERMAN

 Materials: comic strips, scissors, glue or tape, paper, pencils

Students recognize real and make-believe aspects of comic strips in this activity.

- Have each student select a favorite cartoon/comic strip character and cut out a strip to fasten to a sheet of paper.

- **WRITING** Tell students to write below the panel three things that are "real" and three that are "make-believe" about the character (i.e., *talking tiger, walrus works as a doctor,* etc.).

- Students can present their papers to the class, explaining both the "real" and "make-believe" aspects. Finished papers can be hung throughout the room. ▶Spatial

Auditory

CHANGING TUNES

 Materials: record player, records, chalk, chart paper, markers

Students distinguish between realistic and fantasy elements through creating song lyrics.

- Play for students several songs they are familiar with such as "Mary Had a Little Lamb," or "Frosty the Snowman."

- Have students listen for and identify fantastic elements from the songs, such as Frosty coming to life.

- Tell students how to play a game where they will replace the fantasy elements in the songs' lyrics with realistic ones. Write the realistic elements on the chart paper.

- Students can practice singing their new lyrics. ▶Musical

Kinesthetic

SLICES OF LIFE

Materials: magazines, scissors, tape, crayons or colored pencils

- Cut several photos and illustrations from magazines that depict both real and fantasy elements.

- Show the pictures to the class, and have volunteers tell what is real and what is fantasy in each picture.

- Hand out magazines to the students, and have them cut out pictures and affix them to paper. Students can present their pictures for the class to tell whether they are "real" or "make-believe." ▶Bodily/Kinesthetic

See Reteach 91, 107, 122

Context Clues

 OBJECTIVES Students will read, listen for, and practice using context clues to figure out the meanings of unfamiliar words.

Alternate Activities

Visual

REVENGE OF THE WORDS

Materials: textbook, paper, pencil, chalk

ONE Students review difficult words and work with them in context.

- Go through stories recently read by the class, and make a list of words that were difficult for students to understand.

- Write the words on the chalkboard. Tell students to look back through the stories and find the words you have written.

- Have students copy a sentence from the book. Below the sentence, have students write the definition. ▶**Intrapersonal**

Auditory

CONTEXT PARAGRAPHS

 Materials: chart paper, markers, paper, **PARTNERS** pencils

Students work to determine word meanings in context.

- On several pieces of chart paper, write a paragraph containing unfamiliar words, one paragraph per sheet.

- Next to the paragraph, write the unfamiliar words in random order. Have partners listen as you read the paragraphs. Elicit definitions for the unfamiliar words. When a correct definition has been

reached, have partners list the context clues in the paragraph that helped them define the new word.

 Have partners write words on their papers. **WRITING** Invite volunteers to write a new sentence with the word. ▶**Logical/Mathematical**

Kinesthetic

SEEK AND FIND

Materials: magazines, dictionaries, pencils, **GROUP** paper, tape

Students read magazine stories to examine difficult words and determine word meaning in context.

- From magazines, cut several stories that contain difficult words. Glue the stories to sheets of paper.

- Distribute the stories to the groups, and tell students to make a list of all unfamiliar words.

- Have groups work together to use context clues to determine word meanings. After the group has determined the meaning of the word, have a student in each group look up the words in the dictionary and check their meanings. ▶**Bodily/Kinesthetic**

See Reteach 92, 100, 124

Phonological Awareness

OBJECTIVES Children will practice blending and segmenting sounds and deleting beginning sounds in blends.

Alternate Activities

Blend Sounds

GRAB BAG

Materials: small classroom items, bag

GROUP Use this game to help children practice blending sounds to make words.

- Choose about ten small objects and place them in a bag. Include a letter, a ruler, and an eraser among other things.

- Have a volunteer reach into the bag and touch one of the items. Have the child say the name of the item sound by sound.

- Then ask the rest of the children to blend the sounds to figure out what the item is. After the class has identified the object, remove it from the bag.

- Choose other volunteers and continue this activity until all the items in the bag have been identified.

Segment Sounds

SOUND CATERPILLARS

Materials: construction paper, markers or

ONE crayons

Have children use construction paper caterpillars to practice segmenting sounds.

- Tell children to make caterpillars from six construction paper circles that they glue together and decorate using markers or crayons. They also cut out six small dots from construction paper.

- Point to a poster in the classroom and say the word *poster* to children. Model segmenting the sounds: /p/-/ō/-/s/-/t/-/ər/. Each time you pronounce a sound, place a dot onto one of the caterpillar's body parts.

- Have children use their caterpillars to practice saying the sounds in words. Ask children to look around the classroom and say the names of at least five things they see. For every sound in each word they say, they place a dot onto one of the caterpillar's body parts.

Delete Sounds

MY SLED

Materials: Phonics Picture *sled* from *Word Building Kit*

GROUP

Use this activity to help children practice deleting the beginning sounds in blends.

- Display the Phonics Picture *sled* from the *Word Building Kit*. Tell children to imagine they are riding on a sled. Ask children what word would be left if the /s/ sound is taken away from the word *sled*. (led)

- Say the following word pairs: *shed/bed, brick/stick, star/tar, bread/red, truck/stuck, bled/led, flow/low.* If the second word is made by deleting the beginning sound of the first word, have children raise their hands and say, "Whee!" If not, have children tell the beginning sounds of each word.

/ər/ er

 OBJECTIVES Students will cut out pictures of objects whose names contain /ər/, spelled *er*. Students will create chants that contain words with /ər/, spelled *er*.

Alternate Activities

Visual

LISTS OF R's

 Materials: paper, pencil, crayons or colored pencils, chalk

Students list favorites and identify words that contain /ər/, spelled *er*.

- Ask children to write a list of favorites—places, cartoon characters, food, etc.

- Have students go through their lists and underline all of the words with the /ər/ sound, spelled *er*.

- Students can share their lists with the class and compare choices. Have students take turns reading their lists aloud. Students can also illustrate their lists. ▶**Intrapersonal**

Auditory

SONGWRITERS INK

 Materials: record player, chart paper, markers, paper, pencils

Students recognize vowel sounds as they create chants and songs.

- Have students listen to several songs they are familiar with. As the songs play, ask them to write down words with the /ər/ sound, spelled *er*.

- In groups, have students make a list of the words. Tell students to make up silly songs or chants using the targeted sound.

- Groups can practice their songs and chants and perform them for the entire class. ▶**Musical**

Kinesthetic

MAGAZINE SEARCHERS

 Materials: magazines or newspapers, scissors, pencils, paper, tape, timer

Through pictures, students work with vowel sounds and create a class book.

- Give student partners several magazines or newspapers with pictures.

- Tell students they will have a short time to find as many pictures of objects as they can whose names contain /ər/, spelled *er*. Have students cut out the pictures and glue them to paper, writing the word next to the picture.

- When time is called, partners can take turns reading their lists to the class and sharing the pictures.

- Collect pictures in a class scrapbook for later reference. ▶**Bodily/Kinesthetic**

 **CD-ROM**

See Reteach 93, 97, 98, 106, 114, 117

Cause and Effect

Students will examine cause-and-effect relationships.

Alternate Activities

Visual

CAUSE-AND-EFFECT PUZZLE

PARTNERS

Materials: textbook, paper, pencils, chalk

Students recognize cause and effect in stories they have read.

- Invite students to make two columns on a piece of paper labeled "CAUSE" and "EFFECT." In each of the columns students should write cause-and-effect events which have happened in recently-read stories.

- Have students cut out each cause and each effect into separate slips. Be sure to have them label each slip as either a cause or effect. Have them exchange their slips with another student.

- Have students try to match an entry from the "EFFECT" column with the corresponding one in the "CAUSE" column. Students may refer back to their books for help.

- Have students check each other's results.
  ►Intrapersonal

Auditory

EXTRA! EXTRA!

GROUP

Materials: newspaper, chart paper, markers, paper, pencils, crayons

Students work with news stories as they examine cause and effect.

- Place students into groups. From a newspaper, read portions of a headline or story. Have groups identify cause and effect in the story.

- Tell each group to come up with its own headline, "the effect," and a brief story, "the cause."

- Groups can read their headlines to the class and have the class discuss cause and effect. Collect news stories to make a class "newspaper."
  ►Interpersonal

Kinesthetic

SPECIAL EFFECTS

PARTNERS

Materials: paper, pencil, empty box, timer

Students use pantomime as they work with cause and effect.

- On slips of paper, write one type of cause, such as "the boys were hungry." Place several copies of the same cause into a box.

- Tell partners they will take turns drawing a cause—and then pantomime the effect for the rest of the class to guess. Explain how one type of cause can have many different effects.

- The partners who correctly guess the pantomime take a turn pulling a slip of paper from the box.
  ►Bodily/Kinesthetic

See Reteach 99, 115, 121

Phonological Awareness

OBJECTIVES Children will practice blending and segmenting sounds and substituting beginning sounds.

Blend Sounds

MY FAVORITE BREAD

 Have children blend sounds to form words naming different types of breads.

- Tell children that you are going to name different types of breads, sound by sound. For example, say: *Who likes* /hw/-/ē/-/t/ *bread?*

- Have children blend the sounds to form the type of bread.

- Give children a chance to vote thumbs up or thumbs down whether they like or don't like that type of bread.

- Repeat with other types of bread, such as: *pita, bagel, rye,* and *white.*

Segment Sounds

NOODLE STRINGS

 Materials: uncooked macaroni or beads, string, and pictures of different objects

Have children string macaroni or beads as they segment words into individual sounds.

- Give each child a length of string, a handful of uncooked macaroni or beads, and a picture of an object.

- Tell children to say the name of the picture slowly, segmenting the name of the object sound by sound. For each sound they hear, they put a piece of macaroni or a bead on the string as they

repeat the sound. Use the word *read* (/r/-/ĕ/-/d/) to demonstrate.

- Use words such as the following: *better, camper, steep, bright, thread, spread, health, wealthy.*

- After children have finished, have them trade pictures for more practice. Then let children tie the string to make their own necklaces.

Substitute Sounds

WACKY NAME GAME

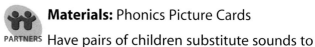 **Materials:** Phonics Picture Cards

Have pairs of children substitute sounds to make nonsense names.

- Organize children in pairs. Have each partner choose a Phonics Picture Card.

- Have children substitute the beginning sound of the object on one of the Phonics Picture Cards with the beginning sound of each of their names.

- Repeat with the other Phonics Picture Card.

Short *e: ea*

 OBJECTIVES Students will recognize and use short *e*.

Alternate Activities

Visual

SHORT *E* DETECTIVES

 Materials: book students have read, pencil, paper

Students identify short *e* words from prior reading and use these words to write short stories.

- Have students find short *e* words while reading the story. As students find the words, they should raise their hands and share the word with the class.

- Have volunteers make a list of the words on the board.

 Tell students to write a short story that includes at least five of the words.
▶**Logical/Mathematical**

Auditory

SHORT STACK

 Materials: chalk, chips or other counting markers

Students play a game as they work with short *e* words.

- Place students into groups. Tell students how to play "short stack." Tell students you will read a list of words. When group members hear a word with the short *e*, they should say, "Short stack!"

- The first group to correctly identify the short *e* word and use it in a sentence receives a chip for their "stack." ▶**Interpersonal**

Kinesthetic

SHORT *E* CEREAL

Materials: cardboard lunch trays, alphabet cereal, paper, pencils, timer

- In cardboard lunch trays, fill up compartments with alphabet cereal letters. Make certain there are enough letters to make short *e* vowel sound words in each tray.

- Tell partners they will have a short time to make as many words with short *e* as they can from their cereal letters. Have students write all the words they make.

- Exchange trays so students can play again.
▶**Bodily/Kinesthetic**

 **CD-ROM**

 **CD-ROM**

T73

Synonyms

OBJECTIVES Students will locate, create a list of, and match synonyms.

Alternate Activities

Visual

SYNONYM COLLECTION

 Materials: newspapers, magazines, scissors, tape or glue, pencils, paper, chalk

Students create synonym collages.

- On the chalkboard, write a couple of example synonyms, as well as several words with blanks next to them.

- Place students into groups, and have them look through magazines and newspapers to find synonyms for the words on the chalkboard.

- Have students cut out the words and pictures to make a collage. Groups can share their collages with the rest of the class. ▶**Interpersonal**

Auditory

SYNONYM BUDDIES

 Materials: paper, pencil, empty boxes

- On slips of paper, write words with easily identifiable synonyms. Place slips of paper in boxes and distribute to teams of student partners.

- One partner draws the paper and reads it aloud. The other partner has ten seconds to come up with as many synonyms as possible.

- Partners can exchange boxes with others and play again. ▶**Logical/Mathematical**

Kinesthetic

SYNONYM SEEK AND FIND

 Materials: paper, pencils, foam board, index cards

- On foam board, write five columns of words, five rows high. Be certain that two words in each row are synonyms, for example: *tiger, box, studying, lunch, learning.*

- Have students match the synonyms in each row and write them in a list.

- After the students have found all the synonyms, ask volunteers to come up and write a synonym for one of the unused words on an index card. The student can read the card to the others and have them guess which word it matches. ▶**Linguistic**

See Reteach 108, 116, 123

Phonological Awareness

OBJECTIVES   Children will practice blending and segmenting sounds and substituting beginning sounds.

Alternate Activities

Blend Sounds

TREASURE HUNT

Materials: Phonics Picture from *Word Building Kit:* key

Tell children that they will find a treasure by blending sounds into words.

- Display the Phonics Picture *key* as children say *key*.

- Tell children that you are going to name some places where keys fit, sound by sound: /d/-/ôr/; /k/-/är/; /k/-/l/-/o/-/z/-/i/-/t/; /h/-/ou/-/s/; /t/-/r/-/e/-/zh/-/ər/. *(door, car, closet, house, treasure)*

- Have children blend the names of the different places. Then say the names naturally.

- Tell children to clap when they hear the sounds for the word *treasure*.

Segment Sounds

AROUND THE CIRCLE

Use this activity to help children practice segmenting a word into its individual phonemes.

- Have children sit in a circle. Tell them you will say words and they will have to segment them into individual sounds.

- Tell children that you are going around the circle and each person will give the appropriate sound for the word. For example, say *key*. The first child

will stand and say /k/ and the child beside him or her will stand and say /ē/.

- Continue with the next person starting a new word. Use words such as: *any, early, swim, point, happy, cowboy, drove, backpack.*

Substitute Sounds

CHANGE IT

Materials: Phonics Pictures from *Word Building Kit*

Have children use Phonics Pictures to cue beginning sound substitutions.

- Divide the class into pairs and give each pair three or four Phonics Pictures from the *Word Building Kit*.

- One partner gives a one-word description of something he or she likes to do, for example, *read.*

- The other partner chooses a Phonics Picture and says the name of the picture. Then he or she substitutes the beginning sound of that word for the beginning sound of their partner's action word. For example, if the child chose the Phonics Picture for *bed,* he or she would say, *bed.../b/ead...bead.*

- Have partners decide together whether the new group of sounds is or is not a word.

Long e: ey, y

OBJECTIVES Students will identify, listen for, and use words with long *e* in sentences.

Alternate Activities

Visual

REBUS "E" CARDS

 Materials: index cards, magazines, scissors, glue, pencils, construction paper

Through game-play, students work with long *e*.

- Cut out pictures of objects whose names contain long *e*. Select a few objects whose names contain short *e*. Glue the pictures to the index cards.

- Have students cut construction paper into strips. On one side, have them write "SHORT E," and on the other, have them write "LONG E."

- Give each group several rebus cards. Ask them to determine which vowel sound is represented by placing the paper strip on the card with the correct vowel sound, face up. Groups can exchange cards and continue play. ▶**Interpersonal**

Auditory

"CRAZ-EE" RHYMES

 Materials: record player, records, paper, pencil, chalk

Students work with long *e* in song lyrics.

- Play familiar songs. Have students listen for the long *e* sounds in the songs. When they hear a long *e* sound, partners should raise their hands to stop the song.

- When students identify words correctly, have them give examples of rhyming words.

- Partners can come up with nonsense songs featuring words with long *e*. Invite them to perform their songs for the class. ▶**Musical**

Kinesthetic

LONG *E* RIDDLES

 Materials: paper, pencils, tape

Students find words with long *e* in a classroom hunt.

- Have teams list as many items in the classroom as possible that have a long *e* sound.

- Once the list is complete, have teams work together to write three clues that will direct another team to the object. For example: *It is under the art room sink. It is in a plastic bottle. It makes things whiter. Bleach.* ▶**Linguistic**

 **CD-ROM**

See Reteach 113, 114, 117

A Communication Tool

Although typewriters and computers are readily available, many situations continue to require handwriting. Tasks such as keeping journals, completing forms, taking notes, making shopping or organizational lists, and the ability to read hand-written manuscript or cursive writing are a few examples of practical application of this skill.

BEFORE YOU BEGIN

Before children begin to write, certain fine motor skills need to be developed. Examples of activities that can be used as warm-up activities are:

- **Simon Says** Play a game of Simon Says using just finger positions.

- **Finger Plays and Songs** Sing songs that use Signed English, American Sign Language or finger spelling.

- **Mazes** Mazes are available in a wide range of difficulty. You can also create mazes that allow children to move their writing instruments from left to right.

Determining Handedness

Keys to determining handedness in a child:

- Which hand does the child eat with? This is the hand that is likely to become the dominant hand.

- Does the child start coloring with one hand and then switch to the other? This may be due to fatigue rather than lack of hand preference.

- Does the child cross midline to pick things up or use the closest hand? Place items directly in front of the child to see if one hand is preferred.

- Does the child do better with one hand or the other?

The Mechanics of Writing

DESK AND CHAIR

- Chair height should allow for the feet to rest flat on the floor.

- Desk height should be two inches above the level of the elbows when the child is sitting.

- The chair should be pulled in allowing for an inch of space between the child's abdomen and the desk.

- Children sit erect with the elbows resting on the desk.

- Children should have models of letters on the desk or at eye level, not above their heads.

PAPER POSITION

- **Right-handed children** should turn the paper so that the lower left-hand corner of the paper points to the abdomen.

- **Left-handed children** should turn the paper so that the lower right-hand corner of the paper points to the abdomen.

- The nondominant hand should anchor the paper near the top so that the paper doesn't slide.

- The paper should be moved up as the child nears the bottom of the paper. Many children won't think of this and may let their arms hang off the desk when they reach the bottom of a page.

The Writing Instrument Grasp

For handwriting to be functional, the writing instrument must be held in a way that allows for fluid dynamic movement.

FUNCTIONAL GRASP PATTERNS

- **Tripod Grasp** With open web space, the writing instrument is held with the tip of the thumb and the index finger and rests against the side of the third finger. The thumb and index finger form a circle.

- **Quadrupod Grasp** With open web space, the writing instrument is held with the tip of the thumb and index finger and rests against the fourth finger. The thumb and index finger form a circle.

INCORRECT GRASP PATTERNS

- **Fisted Grasp** The writing instrument is held in a fisted hand.

- **Pronated Grasp** The writing instrument is held diagonally within the hand with the tips of the thumb and index finger on the writing instrument but with no support from other fingers.

- **Five-Finger Grasp** The writing instrument is held with the tips of all five fingers.

TO CORRECT WRITING INSTRUMENT GRASPS

- Have children play counting games with an eye dropper and water.

- Have children pick up small objects with a tweezer.

- Do counting games with children picking up small coins using just the thumb and index finger.

FLEXED OR HOOKED WRIST

- The writing instrument can be held in a variety of grasps with the wrist flexed or bent. This is typically seen with left-handed writers but is also present in some right-handed writers. To correct wrist position, have children check their writing posture and paper placement.

Evaluation Checklist

Functional writing is made up of two elements, legibility and functional speed.

LEGIBILITY

MANUSCRIPT

Formation and Strokes

- ☑ Does the child begin letters at the top?
- ☑ Do circles close?
- ☑ Are the horizontal lines straight?
- ☑ Do circular shapes and extender and descender lines touch?
- ☑ Are the heights of all upper-case letters equal?
- ☑ Are the heights of all lower-case letters equal?
- ☑ Are the lengths of the extenders and descenders the same for all letters?

Directionality

- ☑ Are letters and words formed from left to right?
- ☑ Are letters and words formed from top to bottom?

Spacing

- ☑ Are the spaces between letters equidistant?
- ☑ Are the spaces between words equidistant?
- ☑ Do the letters rest on the line?
- ☑ Are the top, bottom and side margins even?

CURSIVE

Formation and Strokes

- ☑ Do circular shapes close?
- ☑ Are the downstrokes parallel?
- ☑ Do circular shapes and downstroke lines touch?
- ☑ Are the heights of all upper-case letters equal?
- ☑ Are the heights of all lower-case letters equal?
- ☑ Are the lengths of the extenders and descenders the same for all letters?
- ☑ Do the letters which finish at the top join the next letter? (*b, o, v, w*)
- ☑ Do the letters which finish at the bottom join the next letter? (*a c d h i k l m n r s t u x*)
- ☑ Do letters with descenders join the next letter? (*f g j p q y z*)
- ☑ Do all letters touch the line?
- ☑ Is the vertical slant of all letters consistent?

Directionality

- ☑ Are letters and words formed from left to right?
- ☑ Are letters and words formed from top to bottom?

Spacing

- ☑ Are the spaces between letters equidistant?
- ☑ Are the spaces between words equidistant?
- ☑ Do the letters rest on the line?
- ☑ Are the top, bottom and side margins even?

SPEED

The prettiest handwriting is not functional for classroom work if it takes the child three times longer than the rest of the class to complete work assignments. After the children have been introduced to writing individual letters, begin to add time limitations to the completion of copying or writing assignments. Then check the child's work for legibility.

Handwriting Models—Manuscript

A B C D E F G H

I J K L M N O P

Q R S T U V W

X Y Z

a b c d e f g h

i j k l m n o p

q r s t u v w

x y z

Handwriting Models—Cursive

A B C D E F G H I

J K L M N O P Q R

S T U V W X Y Z

a b c d e f g h i j

k l m n o p q r s

t u v w x y z

Handwriting Models—Slant

A B C D E F G H

I J K L M N O P

Q R S T U V W

X Y Z

a b c d e f g h

i j k l m n o p

q r s t u v w

x y z

Handwriting Practice

Selection Titles | Honors, Prizes, and Awards

 HENRY AND MUDGE
Book 1, p.38
by **Cynthia Rylant**
Illustrated by **Suçie Stevenson**

American Book Award Pick of the List (1987)
Author: Cynthia Rylant, winner of Caldecott Honor (1983) for *When I Was Young in the Mountains;* ALA Notable (1985) for *Waiting to Waltz: A Childhood: Poems;* ALA Notable, Caldecott Honor (1986), New York Times Best Illustrated (1985) for *The Relatives Came;* ALA Notable (1986) for *Blue-Eyed Daisy;* ALA Notable, Newbery Honor (1987) for *Fine White Dust;* ALA Notable (1988) for *Henry and Mudge Under the Yellow Moon;* ALA Notable (1991) for *Henry and Mudge and the Happy Cat;* ALA Notable (1992), Boston Globe-Horn Book Award (1991) for *Appalachia: The Voices of the Sleeping Birds;* ALA Notable (1993) for *Angel for Solomon Singer;* ALA Notable, Newbery Medal (1993), Boston Globe-Horn Book Award (1992) for *Missing May;* ALA Notable (1996) for *Mr. Putter and Tabby Pick the Pears;* ALA Notable (1996) for *Van Gogh Café*
Illustrator: Suçie Stevenson, winner ALA Notable (1988) for *Henry and Mudge Under the Yellow Moon;* ALA Notable (1991) for *Henry and Mudge and the Happy Cat*

 ROUNDUP AT RIO RANCH
Book 1, p.94
by **Angela Shelf Medearis**

Author: Angela Shelf Medearis, winner of IRA-Teachers' Choice Award (1995) for *Our People*

 THE MERRY-GO-ROUND
Book 1, p.124
by **Myra Cohn Livingston**

Poet: Myra Cohn Livingston, winner of National Council of Teachers of English Award for Excellence in Poetry for Children (1980); ALA Notable (1984) for *Christmas Poems;* ALA Notable (1987) for *Cat Poems;* ALA Notable (1992) for *Poem-Making: Ways to Learn Writing Poetry*

 A LETTER TO AMY
Book 1, p.158
by **Ezra Jack Keats**

Author/Illustrator: Ezra Jack Keats, winner of Caldecott Medal (1963) for *The Snowy Day;* Caldecott Honor (1970) for *Goggles;* Boston Globe-Horn Book Award (1970) for *Hi, Cat!*

 THE BEST FRIENDS CLUB
Book 1, p.194
by **Elizabeth Winthrop**
Illustrated by **Martha Weston**

IRA-CBC Children's Choice (1990)
Illustrator: Martha Weston, winner of ALA Notable (1989) for *Big Beast Book: Dinosaurs and How They Got That Way*

Selection Titles	Honors, Prizes, and Awards
JAMAICA TAG-ALONG Book 1, p.218 by *Juanita Havill*	**Author:** *Juanita Havill,* winner of Ezra Jack Keats Award (1987)
FOUR GENERATIONS Book 1, p.254 by *Mary Ann Hoberman*	**Poet:** *Mary Ann Hoberman,* winner of American Book Award Paperback Picture Book (1983) for *A House Is a House for Me*
CLOUD DRAGONS Book 1, p.256 by *Pat Mora*	**Author:** *Pat Mora,* winner of National Association for Chicano Studies Creative Writing Award (1983); New America: Woman Artists and Writers of the Southwest Award (1984); Smithsonian Magazine Notable Books for Children (1998) for *Tomás and the Library Lady*
ARTHUR WRITES A STORY Book 1, p.260 by *Marc Brown*	**IRA-CBC Children's Choice (1997)** **Author/Illustrator:** *Marc Brown,* winner of Boston Globe-Horn Book Honor (1980) for *Why the Tides Ebb and Flow;* ALA Notable (1984) for *The Bionic Bunny Show*
BEST WISHES, ED Book 1, p.292 by *James Stevenson*	**Author /Illustrator:** *James Stevenson,* winner of Boston Globe-Horn Book Honor (1998) for *Popcorn: Poems;* Christopher Award (1983) for *We Can't Sleep;* ALA Notable (1984) for *What's Under My Bed;* ALA Notable (1987) for *When I Was Nine;* ALA Notable, Boston Globe-Horn Book Honor (1987) for *Georgia Music;* ALA Notable (1988) for *Grandaddy's Place;* ALA Notable (1991) for *July;* ALA Notable (1993) for *Don't You Know There's a War On?;* ALA Notable (1994) for *Grandaddy and Janetta;* Texas Blue Bonnet Master List (1995), ALA Notable (1996) for *Sweet Corn: Poems;* ALA Notable (1996) for *Grandaddy's Stars*
TIME TO PLAY Book 1, p.380 by *Nikki Grimes*	**Poet:** *Nikki Grimes,* winner of ALA Notable, Coretta Scott King Award (1979) for *Something on My Mind;* ALA Notable (1995) for *Meet Danitra Brown;* ALA Notable (1996) for *Come Sunday*

Selection Titles	Honors, Prizes, and Awards
RIVER WINDING Book 2, p.10 by **Charlotte Zolotow**	**Poet: *Charlotte Zolotow,*** winner of Caldecott Honor (1953) for *Storm Book;* Caldecott Honor (1962) for *Mr. Rabbit and the Lovely Present;* Christopher Award (1975) for *My Grandson Leo;* ALA Notable (1996) for *When the Wind Stops*
CHARLIE ANDERSON Book 2, p.14 by **Barbara Abercrombie** Illustrated by **Mark Graham**	**Redbook Children's Picture Book Award (1990)**
ZIPPING, ZAPPING, ZOOMING BATS Book 2, p.94 by **Anne Earle** Illustrated by **Henry Cole**	**American Book Award Pick of the List (1995)**
WHAT IS IT? Book 2, p.128 by **Eve Merriam**	**Poet: *Eve Merriam,*** winner of National Council of Teachers of English Award for Excellence in Poetry for Children (1981)
THE WEDNESDAY SURPRISE Book 2, p.182 by **Eve Bunting** Illustrated by **Donald Carrick**	**ALA Notable Book (1990), IRA-CBC Children's Choice, IRA-Teachers' Choice, School Library Journal Best Book (1989)** **Author: *Eve Bunting,*** winner of ALA Notable (1990) for *Wall;* ALA Notable (1992) for *Fly Away Home;* Edgar Allen Poe Juvenile Award (1993) for *Coffin on a Case;* ALA Notable, Caldecott Medal (1995) for *Smoky Night;* ALA Notable (1997) for *Train to Somewhere;* National Council for Social Studies Notable Children's Book Award (1998) for *Moonstick,* and *I Am the Mummy Heb-Nefert,* and *On Call Back Mountain* **Illustrator: *Donald Carrick,*** winner of ALA Notable (1987) for *What Happened to Patrick's Dinosaurs?*
FOSSILS TELL OF LONG AGO Book 2, p.214 by **Aliki**	**National Science Teachers' Association Outstanding Science Tradebook for Children (1990), Library of Congress Children's Book of 1972**

Selection Titles | Honors, Prizes, and Awards

TO CATCH A FISH
Book 2, p.246
by *Eloise Greenfield*

Poet: *Eloise Greenfield,* winner of Boston Globe-Horn Book Honor (1975) for *She Come Bringing Me That Little Baby Girl;* Jane Addams Book Award (1976) for *Paul Robeson;* Coretta Scott King Award (1978) for *Africa Dream;* Boston Globe-Horn Book Honor (1980) for *Childtimes: A Three Generation Memoir;* ALA Notable (1989) for *Grandpa's Face;* ALA Notable (1989) for *Under the Sunday Tree;* ALA Notable, Coretta Scott King Award (1990) for *Nathaniel Talking;* ALA Notable (1992) for *Night on Neighborhood Street;* National Council of Teachers of English Award for Excellence in Poetry for Children (1997)

OFFICER BUCKLE AND GLORIA
Book 2, p.252
by *Peggy Rathmann*

Caldecott Medal, ALA Notable (1996)
Author/Illustrator: *Peggy Rathmann,* winner of ALA Notable (1995) for *Good Night, Gorilla*

TOMÁS AND THE LIBRARY LADY
Book 2, p.284
by *Pat Mora*
Illustrated by *Raul Colón*

Smithsonian Magazine Notable Books for Children (1998)
Author: *Pat Mora,* winner of National Association for Chicano Studies Creative Writing Award (1983); New America: Woman Artists and Writers of the Southwest Award (1984)
Illustrator: *Raul Colón,* winner of ALA Notable (1996) for *My Mama Had a Dancing Heart*

SWIMMY
Book 2, p.342
by *Leo Lionni*

Caldecott Honor (1961), *New York Times* Best Illustrated (1960)
Author/Illustrator: *Leo Lionni,* winner of Caldecott Honor (1961), *New York Times* Best Illustrated (1960) for *Inch by Inch;* Caldecott Honor (1968), *New York Times* Best Illustrated (1967) for *Frederick;* Caldecott Honor (1970) for *Alexander and the Wind-up Mouse*

Trade Books

Additional fiction and nonfiction trade books related to each selection can be shared with children throughout the unit.

Miss Tizzy
Libba Moore Gray, illustrated by Jada Rowland (Aladdin Books, 1998)

When Miss Tizzy becomes ill, all of the children who love her try to bring her joy to repay her kindness.
Fiction

Jamaica Louise James
Amy Hest, illustrated by Sheila White Samton (Candlewick Press, 1996)

Jamaica uses her new paints to decorate her neighborhood subway station, where her grandmother works.
Realistic Fiction

Butterfly Boy
Virginia Kroll, illustrated by Gerardo Suzan (Boyds Mills Press, 1997)

Emilio paints a wall of butterflies on the garage door so that his grandfather can always watch them and feel happy.
Fantasy

In the Snow
Huy Vuon Lee (Henry Holt and Company, 1995)

Attractive cut-paper art depicts a winter landscape that becomes a surface to write upon, as a young boy learns to form Chinese characters.
Fiction

The Painter Who Loved Chickens
Oliver Dunrea (Farrar, Straus & Giroux, 1995)

An artist discovers that he is more successful selling his paintings when he paints what he loves.
Fiction

The Potter Gizelle
Thomas Aarrestad (Dial, 2000)

Giselle is a talented potter who makes beautiful one-of-a-kind pots. When two neighboring kings compete for bigger and bigger pots, disaster is the result.
Fantasy

Technology

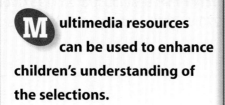

Multimedia resources can be used to enhance children's understanding of the selections.

 Amazing Grace (Pied Piper/AIMS Multimedia) Video, 10 min. Grace is out to prove her friends wrong. She is determined to be the best Peter Pan of all.

 Write a Story (SVE/Churchill Media) Video, 22 min. Explains the key elements in a story. Helps transform students' daydreams and experiences into structured, vivid stories.

 Storytelling (Coronet/MTI) Video or videodisc, 12 min. An introduction to storytelling, with emphasis on creating and organizing characters and events.

 Papa Penguin's Home Movies (Coronet/MTI) Video, 8 min. A humorous and informative look at penguins.

 Penguins (Coronet/MTI) Video, 8 min. A nonverbal tribute to penguins.

 Little Penguin's Tale, Shelly Duvall's Bedtime Stories #2 (Listening Library) Video, 25 min. A little penguin barely escapes danger.

THE PONY EXPRESS

Where Does the Mail Go?

Melvin Berger, illustrated by Geoffrey H. Brittingham (Ideals Children's Books, 1994)

Answers to questions that children ask about the mail.
Nonfiction

Good-bye Curtis

Kevin Henkes, illustrated by Marisabina Russo (Greenwillow Books, 1995)

When Curtis, a letter carrier, retires from the post office, all of his friends on his mail route throw him a party.
Fiction

Messages in the Mailbox

How to write a letter
Loreen Leedy (Holiday House, 1991)

In a colorful and lively format, the author shows how to write and send a letter.
Nonfiction

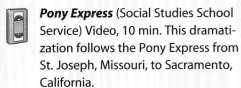

 Moving the Mail: Postal Employees at Work (Pied Piper/AIMS Multimedia) Video, 15 min. An introductory look at the postal service and the different jobs that postal employees perform.

Pony Express (Social Studies School Service) Video, 10 min. This dramatization follows the Pony Express from St. Joseph, Missouri, to Sacramento, California.

Pony Express Rider (McGraw-Hill Home Interactive) CD-ROM, Windows. Players take part in the excitement of the old West when they make the critical decisions necessary to be a Pony Express rider.

NINE-IN-ONE, GRR! GRR!

Tops and Bottoms

Janet Stevens (Harcourt Brace Jovanovich, 1995)

An industrious hare keeps outsmarting a lazy bear.
Folktale

When Birds Could Talk and Bats Could Sing

Virginia Hamilton, illustrated by Barry Moser (Blue Sky Press, 1996)

A collection of stories based on African American tales transcribed after the Civil War.
Folktale

The Hunterman and the Crocodile

Baba Wague Diakite (Scholastic, 1997)

A cautious hunter helps some clever crocodiles and learns a lesson about the relationship between people and animals.
Folktale

 Listen Well, Learn Well (Coronet/MTI) Video, 12 min. How listening and learning are interrelated and affect our lives.

 Lions and Tigers (Coronet/MTI) Video, 6 min. An introductory look at lions and tigers.

 Great Snake (SVE/Churchill Media) Video, 6 min. From Matabeleland in Zimbabwe comes this animated tale of a small boy who outwits a snake to become chief of his tribe. A film by Kathleen Houston.

CHANGE FOR THE QUARTER

Bunny Money

Rosemary Wells (Dial Books for Young Readers, 1997)

Ruby and Max go shopping for their grandmother's birthday gift, but they forget to save enough money to get home.
Fiction

Alexander, Who Used to Be Rich Last Sunday

Judith Viorst, illustrated by Ray Cruz (Simon & Schuster, 1987)

Alexander realizes all of the things he can do with a dollar.
Fiction

My Rows and Piles of Coins

Tololwa Mollel, illustrated by E.B. Lewis (Clarion, 1999)

Set in Tanzania, this story tells of a boy who saves his coins so he can buy a bicycle to help his family with chores.
Realistic Fiction

 A Magical Trip to the Denver Mint (Pied Piper/AIMS) Video, 14 min. An inside look at how money is made.

 Doing the Right Thing (SVE/Churchill Media) Video, 30 min. Rhonda and Fiona struggle with the decision to return a wallet full of money. They discover that doing the right thing feels great.

 Earning and Spending (SVE/Churchill Media) Video, 15 min. A family video about earning money and how it is spent on different family needs.

Publishers Directory

Abdo & Daughters
4940 Viking Drive, Suite 622
Edina, MN 55435
(800) 458-8399 • www.abdopub.com

Aladdin Paperbacks
(Imprint of Simon & Schuster Children's
Publishing)

Atheneum
(Imprint of Simon & Schuster Children's
Publishing)

**Bantam Doubleday Dell Books for
Young Readers**
(Imprint of Random House)

Blackbirch Press
260 Amity Rd.
Woodbridge, CT 06525
(203) 387-7525 • (800) 831-9183
www.blackbirch.com

Blue Sky Press
(Imprint of Scholastic)

Boyds Mills Press
815 Church Street
Honesdale, PA 18431
(570) 253-1164 • Fax (570) 253-0179 •
(877) 512-8366
www.boydsmillspress.com

Bradbury Press
(Imprint of Simon & Schuster Children's
Publishing)

BridgeWater Books
(Distributed by Penguin Putnam)

Candlewick Press
2067 Masssachusetts Avenue
Cambridge, MA 02140
(617) 661-3330 • Fax (617) 661-0565
www.candlewick.com

Carolrhoda Books
(Division of Lerner Publications Co.)

Children's Press (Division of Grolier, Inc.)
P.O. Box 1795
Danbury, CT 06816-1333
(800) 621-1115 • www.grolier.com

Child's World
P.O. Box 326
Chanhassen, MN 55317-0326
(612) 906-3939 • (800) 599-READ •
www.childsworld.com

Chronicle Books
85 Second Street, Sixth Floor
San Francisco, CA 94105
(415) 537-3730 • Fax (415) 537-4460 •
(800) 722-6657 •
www.chroniclebooks.com

Clarion Books
(Imprint of Houghton Mifflin, Inc.)
215 Park Avenue South
New York, NY 10003
(212) 420-5800 • (800) 726-0600 •
www.houghtonmifflinbooks.com/clarion

Crowell (Imprint of HarperCollins)

Crown Publishing Group
(Imprint of Random House)

Dial Books
(Imprint of Penguin Putnam Inc.)

Dorling Kindersley (DK Publishing)
95 Madison Avenue
New York, NY 10016
(212) 213-4800 • Fax (212) 213-5240 •
(888) 342-5357 • www.dk.com

Doubleday (Imprint of Random House)

E. P. Dutton Children's Books
(Imprint of Penguin Putnam Inc.)

Farrar Straus & Giroux
19 Union Square West
New York, NY 10003
(212) 741-6900 • Fax (212) 741-6973 •
(888) 330-8477

Four Winds Press
(Imprint of Macmillan, see Simon &
Schuster Children's Publishing)

Greenwillow Books
(Imprint of William Morrow & Co, Inc.)

Grosset & Dunlap
(Imprint of Penguin Putnam, Inc.)

Harcourt Brace & Co.
6277 Sea Harbor Drive
Orlando, Fl 32887
(407) 345-2000 •
(800) 225-5425 •
www.harcourtbooks.com

Harper & Row (Imprint of HarperCollins)

HarperCollins Children's Books
1350 Avenue of the Americas
New York, NY 10019
(212) 261-6500 • Fax (212) 261-6689 •
(800) 242-7737 •
www.harperchildrens.com

Holiday House
425 Madison Avenue
New York, NY 10017
(212) 688-0085 • Fax (212) 421-6134

Henry Holt and Company
115 West 18th Street
New York, NY 10011
(212) 886-9200 • (212) 633-0748 • (888)
330-8477 • www.henryholt.com/byr/

Houghton Mifflin
222 Berkeley Street
Boston, MA 02116
(617) 351-5000 • Fax (617) 351-1125 •
(800) 225-3362 •
www.houghtonmifflinbooks.com

Hyperion Books
(Division of ABC, Inc.)
77 W. 66th St. 11th floor
New York, NY 10023
(212) 456-0100 • (800) 343-9204 •
www.disney.com

Ideals Children's Books
(Imprint of Hambleton-Hill Publishing, Inc.)
1501 County Hospital Road
Nashville, TN 37218
(615) 254-2451 • (800) 327-5113

Joy Street Books
(Imprint of Little, Brown & Co.)

Just Us Books
356 Glenwood Avenue
E. Orange, NJ 07017
(973) 672-7701 • Fax (973) 677-7570
www.justusbooks.com

Alfred A. Knopf
(Imprint of Random House)

Lee & Low Books
95 Madison Avenue, Room 606
New York, NY 10016
(212) 779-4400 • Fax (212) 683-1894

Lerner Publications Co.
241 First Avenue North
Minneapolis, MN 55401
(612) 332-3344 • Fax (612) 332-7615 •
(800) 328-4929 • www.lernerbooks.com

Little, Brown & Co.
3 Center Plaza
Boston, MA 02108
(617) 227-0730 • Fax (617) 263-2864 •
(800) 759-0190 • www.littlebrown.com

Lothrop Lee & Shepard
(Imprint of William Morrow & Co.)

Macmillan
(Imprint of Simon & Schuster
Children's Publishing)

Marshall Cavendish
99 White Plains Road
Tarrytown, NY 10591
(914) 332-8888 • Fax (914) 332-1888 •
(800) 821-9881 •
www.marshallcavendish.com

William Morrow & Co.
(Imprint of HarperCollins)

Morrow Junior Books
(Imprint of HarperCollins)

Mulberry Books
(Imprint of HarperCollins)

National Geographic Society
1145 17th Street, NW
Washington, DC 20036
(202) 857-7345 • (800) 638-4077 •
www.nationalgeographic.com

Northland Publishing
(Division of Justin Industries)
Box 1389
Flagstaff, AZ 86002
(520) 774-5251 • Fax (800) 744-0592 •
(800) 346-3257 • www.northlandpub.com

North-South Books
1123 Broadway, Suite 800
New York, NY 10010
(212) 463-9736 • Fax (212) 633-1004 •
(800) 722-6657 • www.northsouth.com

Orchard Books (A Grolier Company)
95 Madison Avenue
New York, NY 10016
(212) 951-2600 • Fax (212) 213-6435 •
(800) 433-3411 • www.grolier.com

Owlet (Imprint of Henry Holt & Co.)

Penguin Putnam, Inc.
375 Hudson Street
New York, NY 10014
(212) 366-2000 • Fax (212) 366-2636 •
(800) 631-8571 •
www.penguinputnam.com

Willa Perlman Books
(Imprint of Simon & Schuster
Children's Publishing)

Philomel Books
(Imprint of Putnam Penguin, Inc.)

Puffin Books
(Imprint of Penguin Putnam, Inc.)

G.P. Putnam's Sons Publishing
(Imprint of Penguin Putnam, Inc.)

Random House
1540 Broadway
New York, NY 10036
(212) 782-9000 • (800) 200-3552 •
Fax (212) 782-9452
www.randomhouse.com/kids

Rourke Corporation
P.O. Box 3328
Vero Beach, FL 32964
(561) 234-6001 • (800) 394-7055 •
www.rourkepublishing.com

Scholastic
555 Broadway
New York, NY 10012
(212) 343-7500 • Fax (212) 965-7442 •
(800) SCHOLASTIC • www.scholastic.com

Charles Scribners's Sons
(Imprint of Simon & Schuster Children's
Publishing)

Sierra Club Books for Children
85 Second Street, Second Floor
San Francisco, CA 94105-3441
(415) 977-5500 • Fax (415) 977-5793 •
(800) 935-1056 • www.sierraclub.org

Simon & Schuster Children's Books
1230 Avenue of the Americas
New York, NY 10020
(212) 698-7200 • (800) 223-2336 •
www.simonsays.com/kidzone

Smith & Kraus
177 Lyme Road
Hanover, NH 03755
(603) 643-6431 • Fax (603) 643-1831 •
(800) 895-4331 • www.smithkraus.com

Teacher Ideas Press
(Division of Libraries Unlimited)
P.O. Box 6633
Englewood, CO 80155-6633
(303) 770-1220 • Fax (303) 220-8843 •
(800) 237-6124 • www.lu.com

Ticknor & Fields
(Imprint of Houghton Mifflin, Inc.)

Usborne (Imprint of EDC Publishing)
10302 E. 55th Place, Suite B
Tulsa, OK 74146-6515
(918) 622-4522 • (800) 475-4522 •
www.edcpub.com

Viking Children's Books
(Imprint of Penguin Putnam Inc.)

Watts Publishing
(Imprint of Grolier Publishing;
see Children's Press)

Walker & Co.
435 Hudson Street
New York, NY 10014
(212) 727-8300 • (212) 727-0984 •
(800) AT-WALKER

Whispering Coyote Press
300 Crescent Court, Suite 860
Dallas, TX 75201
(800) 929-6104 • Fax (214) 319-7298

Albert Whitman
6340 Oakton Street
Morton Grove, IL 60053-2723
(847) 581-0033 • Fax (847) 581-0039 •
(800) 255-7675 • www.awhitmanco.com

Workman Publishing Co., Inc.
708 Broadway
New York, NY 10003
(212) 254-5900 • Fax (800) 521-1832 •
(800) 722-7202 • www.workman.com

Multimedia Resources

AGC/United Learning
1560 Sherman Avenue, Suite 100
Evanston, IL 60201
(800) 323-9084 •
Fax (847) 328-6706 •
www.unitedlearning.com

AIMS Multimedia
9710 DeSoto Avenue
Chatsworth, CA 91311-4409
(800) 367-2467 •
www.AIMS-multimedia.com

BFA Educational Media
(see Phoenix Learning Group)

Broderbund
(Parsons Technology;
also see The Learning Company)
500 Redwood Blvd
Novato, CA 94997
(800) 395-0277
www.broderbund.com

Carousel Film and Video
260 Fifth Avenue, Suite 705
New York, NY 10001
(212) 683-1660 • e-mail:
carousel@pipeline.com

Cloud 9 Interactive
(888) 662-5683 • www.cloud9int.com

Computer Plus (see ESI)

Coronet/MTI
(see Phoenix Learning Group)

Davidson (see Knowledge Adventure)

Direct Cinema, Ltd.
P.O. Box 10003
Santa Monica, CA 90410-1003
(310) 636-8200 • Fax (310) 396-3233

Disney Interactive
(800) 900-9234 •
www.disneyinteractive.com

DK Multimedia (Dorling Kindersley)
95 Madison Avenue
New York, NY 10016
(212) 213-4800 • Fax: (800) 774-6733 •
(888) 342-5357 • www.dk.com

Edmark Corp.
P.O. Box 97021
Redmond, WA 98073-9721
(800) 362-2890 • www.edmark.com

Encyclopaedia Britannica Educational Corp.
310 South Michigan Avenue
Chicago, IL 60604
(800) 554-9862 • www.eb.com

ESI/Educational Software Institute
4213 S. 94th Street
Omaha, NE 68127
(800) 955-5570 • Fax (402) 592-2017 •
www.edsoft.com

GPN/Reading Rainbow
University of Nebraska-Lincoln
P.O. Box 80669
Lincoln, NE 68501-0669
(800) 228-4630 • Fax (800) 306-2330 •
www.gpn.unl.edu

Hasbro Interactive
(800) 683-5847 • www.hasbro.com

Humongous
13110 NE 177th Pl., Suite B101, Box 180
Woodenville, WA 98072
(800) 499-8386 • www.humongous.com

IBM Corp.
1133 Westchester Ave.
White Plains, NY 10604
(770) 863-1234 • Fax (770) 863-3030 •
(888) 411-1932 •
www.pc.ibm.com/multimedia/crayola

ICE, Inc.
(Distributed by Arch Publishing)
12B W. Main St.
Elmsford, NY 10523
(914) 347-2464 • (800) 843-9497 •
www.educorp.com

Knowledge Adventure
19840 Pioneer Avenue
Torrence, CA 90503
(800) 542-4240 • (800) 545-7677 •
www.knowledgeadventure.com

The Learning Company
6160 Summit Drive North
Minneapolis, MN 55430
(800) 395-0277 • www.learningco.com

Listening Library
A Subsidiary of Random House
One Park Avenue
Greenwich, CT 06870-1727
(800) 243-4504 • www.listeninglib.com

Macmillan/McGraw-Hill
(see SRA/McGraw-Hill)

Maxis
2121 N. California Blvd
Walnut Creek, CA 94596-3572
(925) 933-5630 • Fax (925) 927-3736 •
(800) 245-4525 • www.maxis.com

MECC
(see the Learning Company)

Microsoft
One Microsoft Way
Redmond, WA 98052-6399
(800) 426-9400 • www.microsoft.com/kids

National Geographic Society Educational Services
P.O. Box 10597
Des Moines, IA 50340-0597
(800) 368-2728 • Fax (515) 362-3366
www.nationalgeographic.com/education

National School Products
101 East Broadway
Maryville, TN 37804
(800) 251-9124 • www.ierc.com

PBS Video
1320 Braddock Place
Alexandria, VA 22314
(800) 344-3337 • www.pbs.org

Phoenix Films
(see Phoenix Learning Group)

The Phoenix Learning Group
2348 Chaffee Drive
St. Louis, MO 63146
(800) 221-1274 • e-mail:
phoenixfilms@worldnet.att.net

Pied Piper (see AIMS Multimedia)

Scholastic New Media
555 Broadway
New York, NY 10003
(800) 724-6527 • www.scholastic.com

Simon & Schuster Interactive
(see Knowledge Adventure)

SRA/McGraw-Hill
220 Danieldale Road
De Soto, TX 75115
(800) 843-8855 • Fax (972) 228-1982 •
www.sra4kids.com

SVE/Churchill Media
6677 North Northwest Highway
Chicago, IL 60631
(800) 829-1900 • Fax (800) 624-1678 •
www.svemedia.com

Tom Snyder Productions (also see ESI)
80 Coolidge Hill Rd.
Watertown, MA 02472
(800) 342-0236 • Fax (800) 304-1254 •
www.teachtsp.com

Troll Associates
100 Corporate Drive
Mahwah, NJ 07430
(800) 929-8765 • Fax (800) 979-8765 •
www.troll.com

Voyager (see ESI)

Weston Woods
12 Oakwood Avenue
Norwalk, CT 06850
(800) 243-5020 • Fax (203) 845-0498

Zenger Media
10200 Jefferson Blvd., Room 94,
P.O. Box 802
Culver City, CA 90232-0802
(800) 421-4246 • (800) 944-5432 •
www.Zengermedia.com

BOOK 1, UNIT 1

Vocabulary   Spelling

ANN'S FIRST DAY

Vocabulary		Spelling		
carrots		**Words with short vowels**		
crawls	bat	**desk**	**just**	plant
homework	**best**	fit	**mom**	**still**
hurry	clock	hut		
lucky				
shy				

HENRY AND MUDGE

Vocabulary		Spelling		
different		**Long vowels a, i, o, u with silent e**		
hundred	**alone**	fine	mine	take
parents	bike	joke	same	**used**
searched	broke	late		
weighed				
worry				

LUKA'S QUILT

Vocabulary		Spelling		
answered		**Long a spelled ai, ay**		
garden		**Long e spelled ea, ee, ie**		
grandmother	chief	**green**	mean	seat
idea	clay	**keep**	**plain**	stay
remember	**dream**	mail		
serious				

ROUNDUP AT RIO RANCH

Vocabulary		Spelling		
broken		**Long o spelled oa, oe, ow, and o**		
carefully		**Long i spelled i, y, and igh**		
cattle	**by**	load	row	**slow**
fence	dry	mind	sigh	toe
gently	**follow**	old		
safety				

TIME FOR KIDS: WELCOME TO A NEW MUSEUM

Vocabulary		Spelling		
artist		**Words from Social Studies**		
body	**flags**	**place**	tax	trade
famous	law	**slave**	time	vote
hour	peace	speech		
life				
visit				

Boldfaced words appear in the selection.

BOOK 1, UNIT 2

Vocabulary   Spelling

LEMONADE FOR SALE	announced empty melted poured squeezed wrong	**/ü/ spelled *oo, ue, ew***			
		blew	few	school	tool
		boot	**new**	**too**	true
		clue	**room**		

A LETTER TO AMY	candles corner glanced repeated special wild	**/ou/ spelled *ou, ow*; /oi/ spelled *oi, oy***			
		brown	**down**	loud	**out**
		coin	**house**	**now**	point
		cowboy	joy		

BEST FRIENDS CLUB	allowed leaned president promise rule whispered	**/âr/ spelled *are*; /ôr/ spelled *or, ore*; /îr/ spelled *ear***			
		bare	dear	shore	**tore**
		care	**more**	short	year
		corn	**porch**		

JAMAICA TAG-ALONG	building busy edge form giant repair	**/är/ spelled *ar*; /ûr/ spelled *ir, er, ur***			
		arm	dirt	hard	herd
		birthday	farm	**her**	**turned**
		curl	fur		

TIME FOR KIDS: UNDER ATTACK	afraid chew danger lesson trouble understand	**Words from Science**			
		animals	**nets**	senses	tide
		fin	river	**shark**	wave
		head	**seals**		

Boldfaced words appear in the selection.

BOOK 1, UNIT 3

Vocabulary	Spelling

ARTHUR WRITES A STORY

Vocabulary
- decided
- float
- important
- library
- planet
- proud

Silent letters *l, b, k, w, gh*

half	knot	right	write
high	**know**	thumb	**wrote**
knee	lamb		

BEST WISHES, ED

Vocabulary
- climbed
- couple
- drifted
- half
- message
- notice

/ər/ spelled *er*

corner	father	**other**	**water**
driver	**letter**	**over**	winter
farmer	never		

THE PONY EXPRESS

Vocabulary
- arrive
- early
- finish
- record
- rush
- success

Short *e* spelled *ea*

bread	instead	meant	spread
breakfast	**leather**	ready	**weather**
feather	meadow		

NINE-IN-ONE, GRR! GRR!

Vocabulary
- earth
- forget
- lonely
- memory
- mountain
- wonderful

Long *e* spelled *y, ey*

baby	key	money	penny
every	lady	party	**tiny**
happy	**many**		

TIME FOR KIDS: CHANGE FOR THE QUARTER

Vocabulary
- collect
- honors
- join
- order
- pocket
- worth

Words from Math

buy	dime	nickel	**quarter**
cent	dollar	price	sum
cost	exact		

Boldfaced words appear in the selection.

BOOK 2, UNIT 1

	Vocabulary	Spelling

CHARLIE ANDERSON

Vocabulary
- chocolate
- clothes
- middle
- offered
- roof
- upstairs

Spelling — /u̇/ spelled *oo*

book	**foot**	shook	wood
brook	hood	stood	wool
cook	hook		

FERNANDO'S GIFT

Vocabulary
- diving
- explains
- harm
- noisy
- soil
- village

Spelling — Soft *c* and soft *g*

age	dance	page	**rice**
cage	large	race	space
charge	mice		

THE BEST VACATION EVER

Vocabulary
- brave
- guess
- museum
- practice
- vacation
- wonder

Spelling — /ô/ spelled *a, aw, au, augh*

because	**hawk**	salt	talk
caught	lawn	straw	taught
fault	paw		

ZIPPING, ZAPPING, ZOOMING BATS

Vocabulary
- disturb
- explore
- fact
- nature
- object
- several

Spelling — Words with *ph, tch, ch*

beach	graph	phone	**sandwich**
catch	match	**pitch**	**touch**
each	patch		

TIME FOR KIDS: GOING BATTY FOR BATS

Vocabulary
- breath
- cover
- crops
- darkness
- scary
- study

Spelling — Words from Science

blood	**fly**	nest	**sleep**
caves	**insects**	sight	wing
den	**leaves**		

Boldfaced words appear in the selection.

BOOK 2, UNIT 2

Vocabulary

Spelling

BREMEN TOWN MUSICIANS

Vocabulary

daughter
music
scare
third
voice
whistle

Spelling — Words with c, k, ck

act	cover	**luck**	**wake**
bake	kind	sick	**work**
come	**like**		

OUR SOCCER LEAGUE

Vocabulary

coaches
field
score
stretches
throws
touch

Spelling — Initial bl, br, dr, pl, and tr

blow	brass	plan	trap
blue	drag	**play**	**try**
brag	draw		

THE WEDNESDAY SURPRISE

Vocabulary

chance
favorite
heavy
nervous
office
wrapped

Spelling — Initial sl, sm, sp, st, sw

slide	smooth	**start**	sweet
slip	speak	**story**	swim
smart	spot		

FOSSILS TELL OF LONG AGO

Vocabulary

buried
creatures
fossil
fresh
layers
millions

Spelling — Final nk, nd, ft, st

bank	**ground**	**past**	soft
chest	**hand**	**sank**	test
end	left		

TIME FOR KIDS: ARE YOU A FOSSIL FAN?

Vocabulary

change
glue
hunt
magazine
piece
tooth

Spelling — Words from Social Studies

bone	drill	ocean	**remains**
deep	hill	oil	**stone**
digging	land		

Boldfaced words appear in the selection.

BOOK 2, UNIT 3

	Vocabulary	Spelling

OFFICER BUCKLE AND GLORIA

Vocabulary
accidents
audience
cheered
slips
station
wipe

Words with ll, dd, ss, gg

add	fill	press	tell
call	**kiss**	sell	**well**
egg	odd		

TOMÁS AND THE LIBRARY LADY

Vocabulary
borrow
desert
evenings
midnight
package
shoulder

Words with initial sh, ch

chair	cheek	**shared**	**shining**
chase	**children**	shift	shoe
check	shape		

PRINCESS POOH

Vocabulary
cousins
crowded
golden
princess
restaurant
world

Words with final th and sh

bath	dash	**push**	teeth
both	fish	**rush**	**with**
brush	mouth		

SWIMMY

Vocabulary
escaped
fierce
hidden
machine
swaying
swift

Words with initial th and wh

than	**through**	whimper
them	whale	whirl
there	wheel	whisper
thought		

TIME FOR KIDS: THE WORLD'S PLANTS ARE IN DANGER

Vocabulary
clear
disappear
forever
problem
save
warn

Words from Science

bloom	**cactus**	root	seed
bud	**flower**	**roses**	stem
bushes	petal		

Boldfaced words appear in the selection.

Listening, Speaking, Viewing, Representing

☑ Tested Skill

Tinted panels show skills, strategies, and other teaching opportunities

LISTENING	K	1	2	3	4	5	6
Learn the vocabulary of school (numbers, shapes, colors, directions, and categories)							
Identify the musical elements of literary language, such as rhymes, repetition, onomatopoeia, alliteration, assonance							
Determine purposes for listening (get information, solve problems, enjoy and appreciate)							
Understand and follow directions							
Listen critically and responsively; recognize barriers to effective listening							
Ask and answer relevant questions (for clarification; to follow up on ideas)							
Listen critically to interpret and evaluate							
Listen responsively to stories and other texts read aloud, including selections from classic and contemporary works							
Connect and compare own experiences, feelings, ideas, and traditions with those of others							
Apply comprehension strategies in listening activities							
Understand the major ideas and supporting evidence in spoken messages							
Participate in listening activities related to reading and writing (such as discussions, group activities, conferences)							
Listen to learn by taking notes, organizing, and summarizing spoken ideas							
Know personal listening preferences							

SPEAKING	K	1	2	3	4	5	6
Use repetition, rhyme, and rhythm in oral texts (such as in reciting songs, poems, and stories with repeating patterns)							
Learn the vocabulary of school (numbers, shapes, colors, directions, and categories)							
Use appropriate language, grammar, and vocabulary learned to describe ideas, feelings, and experiences							
Ask and answer relevant questions (for clarification; to follow up on ideas)							
Communicate effectively in everyday situations (such as discussions, group activities, conferences, conversations)							
Demonstrate speaking skills (audience, purpose, occasion, clarity, volume, pitch, intonation, phrasing, rate, fluency)							
Clarify and support spoken messages and ideas with objects, charts, evidence, elaboration, examples							
Use verbal communication in effective ways, when, for example, making announcements, giving directions, or making introductions							
Use nonverbal communication in effective ways, such as eye contact, facial expressions, gestures							
Retell a story or a spoken message by summarizing or clarifying							
Connect and compare own experiences, ideas, and traditions with those of others							
Determine purposes for speaking (inform, entertain, compare, describe, give directions, persuade, express personal feelings and opinions)							
Recognize differences between formal and informal language							
Demonstrate skills of reporting and providing information							
Demonstrate skills of interviewing, requesting, and providing information							
Apply composition strategies in speaking activities							
Monitor own understanding of spoken message and seek clarification as needed							

VIEWING	K	1	2	3	4	5	6
Demonstrate viewing skills (focus attention, organize information)							
Understand and use nonverbal cues							
Respond to audiovisual media in a variety of ways							
Participate in viewing activities related to reading and writing							
Apply comprehension strategies in viewing activities, including main idea and details							
Recognize artists' craft and techniques for conveying meaning							
Interpret information from various formats, such as maps, charts, graphics, video segments, technology							
Know various types of mass media (such as film, video, television, billboards, and newspapers)							
Evaluate purposes of various media, including mass media (information, appreciation, entertainment, directions, persuasion)							
Use media, including mass media, to compare ideas, information, and points of view							

REPRESENTING	K	1	2	3	4	5	6
Select, organize, or produce visuals to complement or extend meanings							
Produce communication using appropriate media to develop a class paper, multimedia or video reports							
Show how language, medium, and presentation contribute to the message							

Reading: Alphabetic Principle, Sounds/Symbols

☑ Tested Skill

 Tinted panels show skills, strategies, and other teaching opportunities

PRINT AWARENESS

	K	1	2	3	4	5	6
Know the order of the alphabet							
Recognize that print represents spoken language and conveys meaning							
Understand directionality (tracking print from left to right; return sweep)							
Understand that written words and sentences are separated by spaces							
Know the difference between individual letters and printed words							
Understand that spoken words are represented in written language by specific sequences of letters							
Recognize that there are correct spellings for words							
Know the difference between capital and lowercase letters							
Recognize how readers use capitalization and punctuation to comprehend							
Recognize the distinguishing features of a letter, word, sentence, paragraph							
Understand appropriate book handling							
Recognize that parts of a book (such as cover/title page and table of contents) offer information							

PHONOLOGICAL AWARENESS

	K	1	2	3	4	5	6
Listen for environmental sounds							
Identify spoken words and sentences							
Divide spoken sentence into individual words							
Produce rhyming words and distinguish rhyming words from nonrhyming words							
Identify, segment, and combine syllables within spoken words							
Blend and segment onsets and rimes							
Identify and isolate the initial, medial, and final sound of a spoken word							
Add, delete, or substitute sounds to change words (such as *cow* to *how*, *pan* to *fan*)							
Blend sounds to make spoken words							
Segment one-syllable spoken words into individual sounds							

PHONICS AND DECODING

	K	1	2	3	4	5	6
Alphabetic principle: Letter/sound correspondence	☑	☑	☑				
Blending CVC words	☑	☑					
Segmenting CVC words	☑						
Blending CVC, CVCe, CCVC, CVCC, CVVC words	☑	☑	☑				
Segmenting CVC, CVCe, CCVC, CVCC, CVVC words and sounds	☑	☑	☑				
Initial and final consonants: /n/n, /d/d, /s/s, /m/m, /t/t, /k/c, /f/f, /r/r, /p/p, /l/l, /k/k, /g/g, /b/b, /h/h, /w/w, /v/v, /ks/x, /kw/qu, /j/j, /y/y, /z/z	☑	☑					
Initial and medial short vowels: *a, i, u, o, e*	☑	☑	☑				
Long vowels: *a-e, i-e, o-e, u-e* (vowel-consonant-e)		☑	☑				
Long vowels, including *ay, ai; e, ee, ie, ea; o, oa, oe, ow; i, y, igh*		☑	☑				
Consonant Digraphs: *sh, th, ch, wh*		☑					
Consonant Blends: continuant/continuant, including *sl, sm, sn, fl, fr, ll, ss, ff*		☑					
Consonant Blends: continuant/stop, including *st, sk, sp, ng, nt, nd, mp, ft*		☑					
Consonant Blends: stop/continuant, including *tr, pr, pl, cr, tw*		☑					
Variant vowels: including /ü/*oo*; /ô/*a, aw, au*; /ü/*ue, ew*		☑	☑				
Diphthongs, including /ou/*ou*, ow; /oi/*oi, oy*		☑	☑				
r-controlled vowels, including /âr/*are*; /ôr/*or, ore*; /îr/*ear*			☑				
Soft *c* and soft *g*			☑				
nk		☑	☑				
Consonant Digraphs: *ck*	☑	☑					
Consonant Digraphs: *ph, tch, ch*			☑				
Short *e: ea*			☑				
Long *e: y, ey*			☑				
/ü/*oo*		☑	☑				
/är/*ar*; /ûr/*ir, ur, er*		☑	☑				
Silent letters: including *l, b, k, w, g, h, gh*			☑				
Schwa: /ər/*er*; /ən/*en*; /əl/*le*;			☑				
Reading/identifying multisyllabic words		☑	☑				
Using graphophonic cues							

Reading: Vocabulary/Word Identification

WORD STRUCTURE	K	1	2	3	4	5	6
Common spelling patterns							
Syllable patterns							
Plurals		☑					
Possessives		☑					
Contractions		☑					
Root, or base, words and inflectional endings (-s, -es, -ed, -ing)		☑	☑	☑		☑	
Compound Words		☑	☑	☑	☑	☑	☑
Prefixes and suffixes (such as un-, re-, dis-, non-; -ly, -y, -ful, -able, -tion)			☑	☑	☑	☑	☑
Root words and derivational endings				☑	☑	☑	☑
WORD MEANING							
Develop vocabulary through concrete experiences, word walls, other people							
Develop vocabulary through selections read aloud							
Develop vocabulary through reading							
Cueing systems: syntactic, semantic, graphophonic							
Context clues, including semantic clues (word meaning), syntactical clues (word order), and graphophonic clues	☑	☑	☑	☑	☑	☑	☑
High-frequency words (such as the, a, and, said, was, where, is)	☑	☑					
Identify words that name persons, places, things, and actions							
Automatic reading of regular and irregular words							
Use resources and references (dictionary, glossary, thesaurus, synonym finder, technology and software, and context)							
Classify and categorize words							
Synonyms and antonyms			☑	☑	☑	☑	☑
Multiple-meaning words			☑		☑	☑	☑
Figurative language			☑	☑	☑	☑	☑
Decode derivatives (root words, such as like, pay, happy with affixes, such as dis-, pre-, un-)							
Systematic study of words across content areas and in current events							
Locate meanings, pronunciations, and derivations (including dictionaries, glossaries, and other sources)							
Denotation and connotation							☑
Word origins as aid to understanding historical influences on English word meanings							
Homophones, homographs							
Analogies							☑
Idioms							

Reading: Comprehension

PREREADING STRATEGIES	K	1	2	3	4	5	6
Preview and predict							
Use prior knowledge							
Set and adjust purposes for reading							
Build background							
MONITORING STRATEGIES							
Adjust reading rate							
Reread, search for clues, ask questions, ask for help							
Visualize							
Read a portion aloud, use reference aids							
Use decoding and vocabulary strategies							
Paraphrase							
Create story maps, diagrams, charts, story props to help comprehend, analyze, synthesize and evaluate texts							

(continued on next page)

☑ Tested Skill

☐ Tinted panels show skills, strategies, and other teaching opportunities

(Reading: Comprehension continued)

SKILLS AND STRATEGIES	K	1	2	3	4	5	6
Recall story details, including character and setting	☑	☑					
Use illustrations	☑	☑					
Distinguish reality and fantasy	☑	☑	☑				
Classify and categorize	☑						
Make predictions	☑	☑	☑	☑	☑	☑	☑
Recognize sequence of events (tell or act out)	☑	☑	☑	☑	☑	☑	☑
Recognize cause and effect	☑	☑	☑	☑	☑	☑	☑
Compare and contrast	☑	☑	☑	☑	☑	☑	☑
Summarize	☑	☑	☑	☑	☑	☑	☑
Make and explain inferences		☑	☑	☑	☑	☑	☑
Draw conclusions		☑	☑	☑	☑	☑	☑
Distinguish important and unimportant information				☑	☑	☑	☑
Recognize main idea and supporting details	☑	☑	☑	☑	☑	☑	☑
Form conclusions or generalizations and support with evidence from text			☑	☑	☑	☑	☑
Distinguish fact and opinion (including news stories and advertisements)				☑	☑	☑	☑
Recognize problem and solution			☑	☑	☑	☑	☑
Recognize steps in a process		☑	☑	☑	☑	☑	☑
Make judgments and decisions				☑	☑	☑	☑
Distinguish fact and nonfact				☑	☑	☑	☑
Recognize techniques of persuasion and propaganda							☑
Evaluate evidence and sources of information, including checking other sources and asking experts							☑
Identify similarities and differences across texts (including topics, characters, problems, themes, cultural influences, treatment, scope, or organization)							
Practice various questions and tasks (test-like comprehension questions)							
Paraphrase and summarize to recall, inform, and organize							
Answer various types of questions (open-ended, literal, interpretative, test-like such as true-false, multiple choice, short-answer)							
Use study strategies to learn and recall (preview, question, reread, and record)							
LITERARY RESPONSE							
Listen to stories being read aloud							
React, speculate, join in, read along when predictable and patterned selections are read aloud							
Respond to a variety of stories and poems through talk, movement, music, art, drama, and writing							
Show understanding through writing, illustrating, developing demonstrations, and using technology							
Connect ideas and themes across texts							
Support responses by referring to relevant aspects of text and own experiences							
Offer observations, make connections, speculate, interpret, and raise questions in response to texts							
Interpret text ideas through journal writing, discussion, enactment, and media							
TEXT STRUCTURE/LITERARY CONCEPTS							
Distinguish forms and functions of texts (lists, newsletters, signs)							
Use text features to aid comprehension							
Understand story structure							
Identify narrative (for entertainment) and expository (for information) text							
Distinguish fiction from nonfiction, including fact and fantasy							
Understand literary forms (stories, poems, plays, and informational books)							
Understand literary terms by distinguishing between roles of author and illustrator							
Understand title, author, and illustrator across a variety of texts							
Analyze character, character's motive, character's point of view, plot, setting, style, tone, mood		☑	☑	☑	☑	☑	☑
Compare communication in different forms							
Understand terms such as *title, author, illustrator, playwright, theater, stage, act, dialogue,* and *scene*							
Recognize stories, poems, songs, myths, legends, folktales, fables, tall tales, limericks, plays, biographies, autobiographies							
Judge internal logic of story text							
Recognize that authors organize information in specific ways							
Recognize author's purpose: to inform, influence, express, or entertain							
Describe how author's point of view affects text				☑	☑	☑	☑
Recognize biography, historical fiction, realistic fiction, modern fantasy, informational texts, and poetry							
Analyze ways authors present ideas (cause/effect, compare/contrast, inductively, deductively, chronologically)							
Recognize literary techniques such as imagery, repetition, flashback, foreshadowing, symbolism							

(continued on next page)

(Reading: Comprehension continued)

VARIETY OF TEXT	K	1	2	3	4	5	6
Read a variety of genres and understand their distinguishing features							
Use expository and other informational texts to acquire information							
Read for a variety of purposes							
Select varied sources when reading for information or pleasure							
Know preferences for reading literary and nonfiction texts							
FLUENCY							
Read regularly in independent-level and instructional-level materials							
Read orally with fluency from familiar texts							
Self-select independent-level reading							
Read silently for increasingly longer periods of time							
Demonstrate characteristics of fluent and effective reading							
Adjust reading rate to purpose							
Read aloud in selected texts, showing understanding of text and engaging the listener							
CULTURES							
Connect own experience with culture of others							
Compare experiences of characters across cultures							
Articulate and discuss themes and connections that cross cultures							
CRITICAL THINKING							
Experiences (comprehend, apply, analyze, synthesize, evaluate)							
Making connections (comprehend, apply, analyze, synthesize, evaluate)							
Expression (comprehend, apply, analyze, synthesize, evaluate)							
Inquiry (comprehend, apply, analyze, synthesize, evaluate)							
Problem solving (comprehend, apply, analyze, synthesize, evaluate)							
Making decisions (comprehend, apply, analyze, synthesize, evaluate)							

Study Skills

INQUIRY/RESEARCH AND STUDY STRATEGIES	K	1	2	3	4	5	6
Follow and give directions							
Use alphabetical order							
Use text features and formats to help understand text (such as boldface, italic, or highlighted text; captions; headings and subheadings; numbers or symbols)							
Use study strategies to help read text and to learn and recall information from text (such as preview text, set purposes, and ask questions; use SQRRR; adjust reading rate; skim and scan; use KWL)							
Identify/frame and revise questions for research							
Obtain, organize, and summarize information: classify, take notes, outline, web, diagram							
Evaluate research and raise new questions							
Use technology for research and/or to present information in various formats							
Follow accepted formats for writing research, including documenting sources							
Use test-taking strategies							
Use text organizers (book cover; title page—title, author, illustrator; contents; headings; glossary; index)		✓	✓	✓	✓	✓	✓
Use graphic aids, such as maps, diagrams, charts, graphs, schedules, calendars		✓	✓	✓	✓	✓	✓
Read and interpret varied texts, such as environmental print, signs, lists, encyclopedia, dictionary, glossary, newspaper, advertisement, magazine, calendar, directions, floor plans, online resources		✓	✓	✓	✓	✓	✓
Use print and online reference sources, such as glossary, dictionary, encyclopedia, telephone directory, technology resources, nonfiction books		✓	✓	✓	✓	✓	✓
Recognize Library/Media Center resources, such as computerized references; catalog search—subject, author, title; encyclopedia index		✓	✓	✓	✓	✓	✓

Writing

☑ Tested Skill

Tinted panels show skills, strategies, and other teaching opportunities

MODES AND FORMS	K	1	2	3	4	5	6
Interactive writing							
Descriptive writing			☑				
Personal narrative			☑	☑	☑	☑	☑
Writing that compares		☑	☑	☑	☑	☑	☑
Explanatory writing			☑	☑	☑	☑	☑
Persuasive writing				☑	☑	☑	☑
Writing a story		☑	☑	☑	☑	☑	☑
Expository writing; research report		☑	☑	☑	☑	☑	☑
Write using a variety of formats, such as advertisement, autobiography, biography, book report/report, comparison-contrast, critique/review/editorial, description, essay, how-to, interview, invitation, journal/log/notes, message/list, paragraph/multi-paragraph composition, picture book, play (scene), poem/rhyme, story, summary, note, letter							

PURPOSES/AUDIENCES	K	1	2	3	4	5	6
Dictate sentences and messages, such as news and stories, for others to write							
Write labels, notes, and captions for illustrations, possessions, charts, and centers							
Write to record, to discover and develop ideas, to inform, to influence, to entertain							
Exhibit an identifiable voice							
Use literary devices (suspense, dialogue, and figurative language)							
Produce written texts by organizing ideas, using effective transitions, and choosing precise wording							

PROCESSES	K	1	2	3	4	5	6
Generate ideas for self-selected and assigned topics using prewriting strategies							
Develop drafts							
Revise drafts for varied purposes, elaborate ideas							
Edit for appropriate grammar, spelling, punctuation, and features of published writings							
Proofread own writing and that of others							
Bring pieces to final form and "publish" them for audiences							
Use technology to compose, revise, and present text							
Select and use reference materials and resources for writing, revising, and editing final drafts							

SPELLING	K	1	2	3	4	5	6
Spell own name and write high-frequency words							
Words with short vowels (including CVC and one-syllable words with blends CCVC, CVCC, CCVCC)							
Words with long vowels (including CVCe)							
Words with digraphs, blends, consonant clusters, double consonants							
Words with diphthongs							
Words with variant vowels							
Words with r-controlled vowels							
Words with /ər/, /əl/, and /ən/							
Words with silent letters							
Words with soft c and soft g							
Inflectional endings (including plurals and past tense and words that drop the final e and double a consonant when adding -ing, -ed)							
Compound words							
Contractions							
Homonyms							
Suffixes such as -able, -ly, -ful, or -less, and prefixes such as dis-, re-, pre-, or un-							
Spell words ending in -tion and -sion, such as station and procession							
Accurate spelling of root or base words							
Orthographic patterns and rules such as keep/can; sack/book; out/now; oil/toy; match/speech; ledge/cage; consonant doubling, dropping e, changing y to i							
Multisyllabic words using regularly spelled phonogram patterns							
Syllable patterns (including closed, open, syllable boundary patterns)							
Synonyms and antonyms							
Words from Social Studies, Science, Math, and Physical Education							
Words derived from other languages and cultures							
Use resources to find correct spellings, synonyms, and replacement words							
Use conventional spelling of familiar words in writing assignments							
Spell accurately in final drafts							

(continued on next page)

	Tested Skill
	Tinted panels show skills, strategies, and other teaching opportunities

GRAMMAR AND USAGE	K	1	2	3	4	5	6
Understand sentence concepts (word order, statements, questions, exclamations, commands)							
Recognize complete and incomplete sentences							
Nouns (common, proper, singular, plural, irregular plural, possessive)							
Verbs (action, helping, linking, irregular)							
Verb tense (present, past, future, perfect, and progressive)							
Pronouns (possessive, subject and object, pronoun-verb agreement)							
Use objective case pronouns accurately							
Adjectives							
Adverbs that tell how, when, where							
Subjects, predicates							
Subject-verb agreement							
Sentence combining							
Recognize sentence structure (simple, compound, complex)							
Synonyms and antonyms							
Contractions							
Conjunctions							
Prepositions and prepositional phrases							

PENMANSHIP	K	1	2	3	4	5	6
Write each letter of alphabet (capital and lowercase) using correct formation, appropriate size and spacing							
Write own name and other important words							
Use phonological knowledge to map sounds to letters in order to write messages							
Write messages that move left to right, top to bottom							
Gain increasing control of penmanship, pencil grip, paper position, beginning stroke							
Use word and letter spacing and margins to make messages readable							
Write legibly by selecting cursive or manuscript, as appropriate							

MECHANICS	K	1	2	3	4	5	6
Use capitalization in sentences, proper nouns, titles, abbreviations and the pronoun *I*							
Use end marks correctly (period, question mark, exclamation point)							
Use commas (in dates, in addresses, in a series, in letters, in direct address)							
Use apostrophes in contractions and possessives							
Use quotation marks							
Use hyphens, semicolons, colons							

EVALUATION	K	1	2	3	4	5	6
Identify the most effective features of a piece of writing using class/teacher-generated criteria							
Respond constructively to others' writing							
Determine how his/her own writing achieves its purpose							
Use published pieces as models for writing							
Review own written work to monitor growth as a writer							

Scoring Chart

The Scoring Chart is provided for your convenience in grading your students' work.

- Find the column that shows the total number of items.
- Find the row that matches the number of items answered correctly.
- The intersection of the two rows provides the percentage score.

TOTAL NUMBER OF ITEMS

NUMBER CORRECT	1	2	3	4	5	6	7	8	9	10	11	12	13	14	15	16	17	18	19	20	21	22	23	24	25	26	27	28	29	30
1	100	50	33	25	20	17	14	13	11	10	9	8	8	7	7	6	6	6	5	5	5	5	4	4	4	4	4	4	3	3
2		100	66	50	40	33	29	25	22	20	18	17	15	14	13	13	12	11	11	10	10	9	9	8	8	8	7	7	7	7
3			100	75	60	50	43	38	33	30	27	25	23	21	20	19	18	17	16	15	14	14	13	13	12	12	11	11	10	10
4				100	80	67	57	50	44	40	36	33	31	29	27	25	24	22	21	20	19	18	17	17	16	15	15	14	14	13
5					100	83	71	63	56	50	45	42	38	36	33	31	29	28	26	25	24	23	22	21	20	19	19	18	17	17
6						100	86	75	67	60	55	50	46	43	40	38	35	33	32	30	29	27	26	25	24	23	22	21	21	20
7							100	88	78	70	64	58	54	50	47	44	41	39	37	35	33	32	30	29	28	27	26	25	24	23
8								100	89	80	73	67	62	57	53	50	47	44	42	40	38	36	35	33	32	31	30	29	28	27
9									100	90	82	75	69	64	60	56	53	50	47	45	43	41	39	38	36	35	33	32	31	30
10										100	91	83	77	71	67	63	59	56	53	50	48	45	43	42	40	38	37	36	34	33
11											100	92	85	79	73	69	65	61	58	55	52	50	48	46	44	42	41	39	38	37
12												100	92	86	80	75	71	67	63	60	57	55	52	50	48	46	44	43	41	40
13													100	93	87	81	76	72	68	65	62	59	57	54	52	50	48	46	45	43
14														100	93	88	82	78	74	70	67	64	61	58	56	54	52	50	48	47
15															100	94	88	83	79	75	71	68	65	63	60	58	56	54	52	50
16																100	94	89	84	80	76	73	70	67	64	62	59	57	55	53
17																	100	94	89	85	81	77	74	71	68	65	63	61	59	57
18																		100	95	90	86	82	78	75	72	69	67	64	62	60
19																			100	95	90	86	83	79	76	73	70	68	66	63
20																				100	95	91	87	83	80	77	74	71	69	67
21																					100	95	91	88	84	81	78	75	72	70
22																						100	96	92	88	85	81	79	76	73
23																							100	96	92	88	85	82	79	77
24																								100	96	92	89	86	83	80
25																									100	96	93	89	86	83
26																										100	96	93	90	87
27																											100	96	93	90
28																												100	97	93
29																													100	97
30																														100

Explanatory Writing: Writing a How-to Article

Scoring Rubric: 6-Trait Writing

6. Exceptional	5. Excellent	4. Good	3. Fair	2. Poor	1. Unsatisfactory
• **Ideas & Content** crafts a focused, fully detailed how-to process that enables a reader to carry out a project.	• **Ideas & Content** crafts a detailed how-to process that shows a reader how to carry out a project.	• **Ideas & Content** presents a solid explanation of a project; accurate details help a reader understand a step-by-step process.	• **Ideas & Content** attempts to explain a project; details may be general or unrelated to the topic.	• **Ideas & Content** may have little control of explaining a how-to project; details may be few, repeated, or inaccurate.	• **Ideas & Content** does not explain a how-to process; writing may go off in several directions, without a sense of purpose.
• **Organization** gives clear instructions, in a well-planned, logical time sequence that moves a reader easily through the steps.	• **Organization** has a well-planned process strategy, in logical time sequence that moves a reader through the steps.	• **Organization** gives process instructions in a logical sequence; has a clear beginning and ending; ideas and details make sense.	• **Organization** attempts to give instructions, but may have trouble sequencing steps; has a beginning and ending, but may use few time-order words and transitions.	• **Organization** lacks a clear structure; steps may be vague or disorganized; ideas are not linked.	• **Organization** extreme lack of organization interferes with following the text; steps, if presented, are often irrelevant or unfocused.
• **Voice** shows originality and deep involvement with the topic; matches a special personal style to the writing purpose and audience.	• **Voice** shows originality and strong involvement with the topic; matches personal style to the writing purpose and audience.	• **Voice** attempts to bring a genuine personal touch to the writing; shows some involvement with the topic.	• **Voice** may not show consistent involvement with the topic; message comes across, but only in a routine sort of way.	• **Voice** is not very involved in sharing ideas with a reader; writing may be lifeless, with no sense of who is behind the words.	• **Voice** does not address an audience at all; does not grasp how to convey a personal voice or style.
• **Word Choice** makes inventive use of both challenging and everyday words; advanced vocabulary creates a vivid picture of a how-to process.	• **Word Choice** makes creative use of accurate, specific language; experiments with new words, or uses everyday words in a fresh way.	• **Word Choice** uses a variety of new and everyday words that fit, and which make the process clear and interesting.	• **Word Choice** writer experiments with few new words; may attempt to use a variety of words, but some do not fit.	• **Word Choice** does not choose words that give a clear picture of a process; some words may detract from the meaning or impact of the text.	• **Word Choice** uses words that do not fit the task, or are vague and confusing to the reader.
• **Sentence Fluency** varied, effective sentences flow naturally; writing is easy to follow and read aloud.	• **Sentence Fluency** crafts fluid, effective sentences that fit together and make the text easy to follow.	• **Sentence Fluency** crafts careful, varied sentences that make sense and flow easily.	• **Sentence Fluency** sentences are readable, but may show limited variety in length or pattern; some rereading may be required to follow the meaning.	• **Sentence Fluency** sentences may ramble or have awkward, choppy construction; patterns are similar or monotonous; text may be hard to follow or read aloud.	• **Sentence Fluency** constructs incomplete or confusing sentences; write may not grasp how words and sentences fit together; text is hard to follow and read aloud.
• **Conventions** is skilled in most writing conventions; proper use of the rules of English enhances clarity and style; editing is largely unnecessary.	• **Conventions** is skilled in most writing of conventions; proper use the rules of English enhances clarity and style; editing is largely unnecessary.	• **Conventions** may make some errors in spelling, capitalization, punctuation, or usage which do not interfere with following the text; some editing is needed.	• **Conventions** makes noticeable errors that interfere with a smooth reading of the text; significant editing is needed.	• **Conventions** makes frequent errors in spelling, word choice, punctuation, and usage; the article is hard to read, and requires extensive revision.	• **Conventions** makes severe errors in most or all conventions; spelling errors may make it hard to guess what words are meant; some parts of the text may be impossible to follow.

Incomplete 0: This piece is either blank, or fails to respond to the writing task. The topic is not addressed, or the child simply paraphrases the prompt. The response may be illegible or incoherent.

Expository Writing: Writing About a Place

8-Point Writing Rubric

8	7	6	5	4	3	2	1
The writer	The writer	The writer	The writer	The writer	The writer	The writer	The writer
• presents an exceptionally well-constructed article, containing vivid description of a place. • uses interesting facts and finely observed or researched description to elaborate each aspect of the place. • uses sophisticated language and compelling images to enhance the facts. • uses a logical structure with an intriguing beginning, detailed middle, and apt end. • reaches a well-thought out conclusion based on facts and reasons in the report.	• crafts a well-organized article vivid with fine descriptions of a place. • elaborates with facts and observations about the place. • uses sophisticated vocabulary and interesting images to highlight the facts. • clearly presents a logical structure with a beginning, middle, and ending. • reaches a thoughtful conclusion based on the facts.	• presents an organized article with descriptions of a place. • uses facts that present a clear picture of the place. • chooses vocabulary and images that highlight the facts. • presents a logical structure. • reaches a conclusion in the report.	• attempts an organized, detailed article on a place. • elaborates with some facts and description. • may vary word choice but doesn't include personal observation. • may exhibit organization difficulty with lapses in conventions. • may not offer an entirely logical conclusion.	• has made an adequate attempt at an article on a place. • may not consistently elaborate on the facts or observations. • may show lapses in logical ordering of ideas. • exhibits recurring problems with conventions. • may not offer a relevant conclusion.	• attempts a minimally-successful report on a place. • exhibits organizational problems, such as an illogically-structured list of facts without a beginning, middle, or end. • may not elaborate on factual information. • may exhibit limited control of grammar, mechanics, and usage. • may not draw a pertinent conclusion.	• makes a largely unsuccessful attempt at reporting on a place. • exhibits organizational problems great enough to interfere with comprehension of the text. • has not used pertinent facts or descriptions about a place. • may show repeated errors in basic grammar, mechanics, and usage. • does not draw a conclusion or concludes with a comment unrelated to facts, reasons, or the topic itself.	• makes little attempt at expository writing and exhibits a lack of awareness of the topic. • lacks any sense of organization. • has used only generalities, with no attempt to include specific facts, descriptions, or observations. • shows serious and repeated errors in basic grammar, mechanics, and usage. • leaves writing unfinished without even an attempt at a conclusion.

0: This piece is either blank or fails to respond to the writing task. The topic is not addressed or the studnet simply paraphrases the prompt. The response may be illegible or incoherent.

Guided Reading Support

Macmillan/McGraw-Hill Leveled Books

TITLE	READING LEVEL
Don't Float in Blue Jam	I
The Ghost on the Train	J
How Animals Use Color	J
My Own Team: The Bill Reidy Story	K
First Food: A South American Folktale	L
Hare and Tortoise	L
How Frog Lost Its Tail	L
Messengers from the Sky	L
Ready Set Go!	L
Harry the Troll and the Three Billy Goats Gruff	M
Rin Tin Tin: Top Dog in the Movies	M
Sending a Message with Dots and Dashes	M

Additional Leveled Books from The Wright Group

TITLE	READING LEVEL
Dream Catchers	G
Celebrate Art	H
Backstage	I
Finger Puppets, Finger Plays	I
Jane Goodall and the Chimps	I
Making Mount Rushmore	I
Picture This!	I
Show-and-Tell	I
Graffiti	J
Make a Guitar	K

To order these titles or other Wright Group Leveled Book titles, call 1-800-648-2970.

Guided Reading Lesson Plan

Story Introduction

(Each child has a copy of the book.)

- Discuss the cover illustrations, and ask children to speculate about the book's contents.
- Involve children in figuring out the title.
- Provide positive feedback for responses. (Example: I like the way you used the _____ in the cover illustration to figure out that the book might be about_____.)

Picture Walk

(The teacher has the only copy of the book.)

- Show children as many pictures as you can without giving away any surprise endings.
- As you discuss the pictures together, highlight key concepts in the book. Again, try to bring in language from the book, especially unknown words or unusual language patterns, to give children some experience with these words and patterns. Have children say them aloud.
- Encourage children to make predictions about the book's content, using the title, cover art, and pictures.
- Remind children of key book concepts. Close the book, and elicit what children know about these concepts. Record their ideas in a web on the board or on chart paper, making additions or corrections as necessary.

First Reading

- Guide children to use a variety of word-attack strategies when reading. The focus should be on mastery of these strategies.
- Break the book into sections, and for each section, ask questions that encourage predictions. Focus on literary elements such as character development and plot line. (Examples: What do you think _____ will do? What do you think will happen next?)
- Guide children to silently read a section to confirm or revise their predictions.
- When children finish a section, have them orally respond to your questions, locating the text that supports their answers.
- Continue through the story, using this format.
- Option: Have children read the story again independently at their seats and/or respond in literature response journals.

Discussion

- Discuss the literary elements (character, setting, plot) found in the story.
- Relate the story to children's lives whenever possible.
- Give children the opportunity to retell or react to the story. If response journals have been used, encourage children to refer to them.
- Model sharing observations and opinions about the story, and encourage further sharing.
- Invite children to share their response journals.

Minilesson

- A minilesson can take place at any point in the Guided Reading process—wherever it is applicable and as needed by your children.

- Possible focuses for the lesson might be word-attack strategy development, vocabulary, literary elements, or language structures.

Follow-Up Activity

- Have children respond to the reading by writing journal entries and/or engaging in other literature-related activities.

WORD-ATTACK STRATEGY PROMPTS

Focus on meaning cues.

- Did that make sense?
- Look at the pictures.
- What happened in the story when ___?
- What do you think it might be?
- How do you know?
- Provide positive feedback. (Example: I like the way you figured out the word by thinking about what was happening in the story.)

Focus on structure cues.

- Did that sound right?
- Can you reread that?
- Can you say that another way?
- What is another word that might fit here?

Focus on visual cues.

- Does that look right?
- What letter/sound does it start/end with?
- What would you expect to see at the beginning/in the middle/at the end?
- Do you know another word that might start/end with those letters?
- Can you get your mouth ready to say that word/sound?

Focus on self-correcting.

- There is a difficult (or tricky) part here. Can you find it?
- Are you right? Could that be ___?
- Take a closer look at ___.
- How did you know that this word was ___?

Focus on cross-checking.

- How did you know that was ___?
- Is there another way to tell?
- It could be ___, but look at ___.
- Provide positive feedback. (Example: I like the way you checked your answer by looking at the beginning letter again.)

Focus on self-monitoring.

- Try that again.
- You stopped. What did you notice?
- Were you right?
- How did you know?

Additional Theme Resources

Contents

Theme Book

SKILLS AND OBJECTIVES ▶ Long Vowels /ē/   Phonograms -eed, -eel   Identify words with long vowel sound /ē/   Build words with -eed and -eel

Bob's Freckles

Written by Claire Daniel
Illustrated by Jessica Clerk

Bob hates his freckles. That is, until his friend Jen says she likes them.

Before They Read

BUILDING BACKGROUND Ask, *How did you feel at the beginning of school? Were you sad to leave your first grade teacher?* After children share their memories, write the words *feel* and *need* on the board and run your finger under the phonograms -eel and -eed. Explain that they have the same vowel sound—long *e*.

INTRODUCING VOCABULARY Ask children to listen to these words and click their heels together if they hear a long *e* sound.

    need   wheel   feel   kneel

Then, write the words on the board and encourage children to read them aloud. Ask them how the words are similar. (all have the /ē/ sound spelled *ee*)

STUDENTS ACQUIRING ENGLISH

To help children practice the /ē/ sound, have them use the vocabulary words in sentences.

SETTING A PURPOSE Say, *In this story, Bob is nervous about returning to school. Over the summer he got a lot of freckles which he doesn't like. What advice do you have for Bob?* Tell children to look for words with the /ē/ sound as they read.

While They Read

READING THE STORY

- On page 3, ask children to identify the words that contain the /ē/ sound. On page 10, ask children to point to the sentence that contains three words with the /ē/ sound spelled *ee*. After completing the story, call on someone to retell the story and have the other children raise their hands when they hear a word that contains -eed or -eel.

- Check comprehension by asking, *Why did Bob change his mind about his freckles?*

After They Read

EXTENDING THE STORY Choose from the following activities to provide additional support for phonics and decoding skills for the different modality needs of your students.

- **Wild Word Bloomers.** Have children begin drawings with -eel and -eed "seeds" underground. Tell them to write sentences using the words built from the phonograms. Children can write their sentences to look as if they are "growing" out of the seeds like plants. *(Visual/Spatial)*

- **The Wheel Thing.** Have children cut out large circles to represent steering wheels. Challenge them to write -eed and -eel words around the wheels. Have them exchange steering wheels with a partner, and tell their partners to turn their wheels left or right to read the words. *(Body/Kinesthetic)*

MORE BOOKS TO READ Suggest to children that they read these other books about "growing pains."
- *Freckle Juice* by Judy Blume
- *A Color of His Own* by Leo Lionni
- *Yummers!* by James Marshall

Dreams on Wheels

Written by Myka-Lynne Sokoloff

Jamie LeGeyt is like most kids his age, except he must ride in a wheelchair. That doesn't stop him from racing in his special chair. He dreams of someday being a world champion.

Before They Read

BUILDING BACKGROUND Determine by a show of hands how many children ride bikes. Say, *Imagine that your bike is a wheelchair made especially for racing.* Help children understand that most wheelchair racers have special kinds of chairs and train every day.

INTRODUCING VOCABULARY Write each of the following words on a card and let children sound them out. Define each word and invite children to use it in a sentence.

braces	condition	youngest
wheelchair	announcer	trophies

STUDENTS ACQUIRING ENGLISH

Ask English-speaking children to mime or draw pictures to help convey the meanings of the vocabulary words to classmates. Have the students acquiring English say each word then pronounce its equivalent in their own languages.

SETTING A PURPOSE Show the book cover, read the tile, and discuss the photo. Ask, *How is this boy's wheelchair like a bicycle? How is it different? Let's read to find out.*

While They Read

READING THE STORY

- Invite children to read the story with you. Stop on page 4 to answer any questions about spina bifida, why Jamie's legs are tucked into the racing chair, and so on.

- Reread the story. On page 10, stress the *-ore* ending of the word *wore* in the last sentence. Help children list words that rhyme with *wore*, such as *more, store,* and *shore.* If children suggest words such as *four* or *door,* write these words on the board to show that the /ôr/ sound has several different spellings.

- Check comprehension by having a different child summarize each page. Ask, *What's the main idea, or point, of this story?* Help them understand that it is important to pursue your dreams and that everyone can do something important.

After They Read

EXTENDING THE STORY Choose from the following activities to provide additional literacy support for the different modality needs of your students.

- **The Big Idea.** Have children work in pairs to role-play a news reporter interviewing Jamie after a big race. Encourage children to review the main ideas of the story to help them create their dialogs. Have partners perform their interviews for the class. *(Verbal/Linguistic)*

- **Rhyme It.** Encourage children to write silly rhymes using words that rhyme with *more.* For example, *I sat on the floor, I stood by the door, I went to the store, I can't stay anymore! (Musical/Rhythmic)*

MORE BOOKS TO READ Suggest to children that they read these other books about special children.
- *Princess Pooh* by Kathleen M. Muldoon
- *A Very Special Friend* by Dorothy Levi
- *Harry and Willy and Carrothead* by Judith Caseley

Theme Book

SKILLS AND OBJECTIVES ▶ Main Idea   Identify the main idea
Phonograms *-eer, -ear*   Identify words with the *-eer* and *-ear* phonograms

Signals in the City

Written by Lauren Ray Pollard
Illustrated by Felipe Galindo

Signs, light signals, hand signals, horns, whistles, and bells all help us to communicate with one another.

Before They Read

BUILDING BACKGROUND Ask, *If you go for a walk, what helps keep you safe?* Lead a discussion about signs and signals that keep people safe. Have children close their eyes and visualize the block on which your school is located. Ask them to identify safety and information signs around the school.

INTRODUCING VOCABULARY Write each word or phrase on the board and let children sound it out with you. Define each word or phrase, then ask a volunteer to use it in a sentence.

communicate	drawbridge	direct traffic
intersections	passengers	single file
dangerous	belch	

STUDENTS ACQUIRING ENGLISH

Ask English-speaking volunteers to help convey the meanings of the vocabulary words and phrases to their classmates. Children can pantomime or draw pictures.

SETTING A PURPOSE Read the book's title and challenge children to identify the different signs and signals on the cover. Ask them to use the illustrations to predict the main idea of the book.

While They Read

READING THE STORY

- There is a lot of information in this book, so you may wish to have children read only three or four pages at one session.

- On each page, have volunteers name signals and signs they see in the illustration.

- Read the last sentence on page 3 and point out the *-eer* phonograms in *deer*. Explain that the word *dear* sounds the same, but ends in *-ear*. Then invite children to name other words that end in *-eer* or *-ear*. List these words on the board. Have children sort them by phonogram.

- Check comprehension by asking each child to summarize the information on one page. Then tell each child to write what he or she considers to be the main idea of the book. Have volunteers read their main ideas aloud. Then have the class work together to create a sentence stating the main idea of the story.

After They Read

EXTENDING THE STORY Choose from the following activities to provide additional literacy support for the different modality needs of your students.

- **What If?** Have children write two sentences about what might happen if there were no signals. Let them illustrate the sentences and read them to classmates. Then ask the class to review all the sentences and state the main idea of their writing. *(Verbal/Linguistic)*

- **Silly Rhymes.** Invite children to work in small groups to write silly rhymes, using words that end in *-eer* or *-ear*. (For example: *Dear deer, have no fear, The coast is clear, so give a cheer!*) *(Musical/Rythmic)*

MORE BOOKS TO READ Suggest to children that they read these other books about safety signs and rules.

- *I Read Signs* by Tana Hoban
- *I Read Symbols* by Tana Hoban
- *This Is the Way We Go to School* by Edith Baer

The Sun and the Kookaburra

Retold by Jan Mike
Illustrated by Katherine Tillotson

At a time when the world was dark, Kookaburra asked the Sky Spirit for light.

Before They Read

BUILDING BACKGROUND Point out that people all over the world have folk tales that tell about everyday life and try to explain things in nature. Discuss any folk tales about nature that your class has read.

INTRODUCING VOCABULARY Display these words on cards and read them with children. Invite volunteers to use them in sentences.

smooth	plain	howled	rough
breeze	raging	valleys	streams

STUDENTS ACQUIRING ENGLISH

Encourage children to use the illustrations on pages 2–3, 11, and 12 to help them understand any unfamiliar words.

SETTING A PURPOSE Show the cover of the book and read aloud the title and subtitle. On a map or globe, show children where Australia is located. Ask children what they think the story will be about.

While They Read

READING THE STORY

- Have children read the story aloud. Invite volunteers to hold up a vocabulary card when they hear that word read.

- Help children understand the cause-and-effect relationships that explain how the sun came to be. On page 2, explain that the birds and animals lived in darkness because there was no sun in the sky. On page 6, ask, *Why didn't the animals know who won the race? Why did Kookaburra go to Sky Spirit?* On page 13, ask, *Why did Sky Spirit want Kookaburra to wake the animals?* On pages 15 and 16, discuss the effects of the sun being in the sky.

After They Read

EXTENDING THE STORY Choose from the following activities to provide additional support for vocabulary and comprehension strategies for the different modality needs of your students.

- **Word Wheel.** Draw a circle on the board. Divide it into eight parts, with one vocabulary word in each part. Invite one child at a time to close his or her eyes and point to a spot in the circle. Ask the child to open his or her eyes, read the word, and use it in a sentence. *(Verbal/Linguistic)*

- **Folk Tale.** Have children work together to create their own folk tale of how the sun came to be. Review with them the concept of cause and effect as they brainstorm ideas. Then write children's suggestions on chart paper. Be sure that every child contributes a sentence to the folk tale.

MORE BOOKS TO READ Suggest to children that they read these other books about the sun.
- *Sun Up, Sun Down* by Gail Gibbons
- *The Sun, the Wind and the Rain* by Lisa Westberg Peters
- *Arrow to the Sun* by Gerald McDermott

Trade Book

SKILLS AND OBJECTIVES ▸ Fantasy and Reality   Distinguish fantasy from reality
Cause and Effect   Identify cause and effect

How a Book Is Made

Written and illustrated by Aliki

Illustrated with clever cat characters, this informative book explains the process of making a book, from writing and illustrating the manuscript through printing and publishing.

Before They Read

BUILDING BACKGROUND Have children brainstorm the names of things that people like to read, such as books, newspapers, and magazines. Then focus the discussion on books. Ask, *How would you describe a book to someone who has never seen one?* (A book is something to read. It has a cover. Inside is a story or stories. A book can tell about real things, things that seem real, or things that are make-believe.)

Ask children to name some of their favorite books. List responses on the board. Then ask, *If you were going to write a book, what would the book be about?* Encourage a variety of responses that include both fiction and nonfiction topics.

INTRODUCING VOCABULARY Write the vocabulary words on the board. Pronounce and define the words for children. Have partners sort the words into two groups: *People* (author, editor, publisher) and *Things* (manuscript, text, typeface, printing press, dust jacket). Then invite volunteers to use the words in sentences about books.

author	editor	text
printing press	manuscript	publisher
typeface	dust jacket	

SETTING A PURPOSE Look at the cover of the book with children and read the title aloud. Then turn to the title page and point out the words that identify parts of a book. Read the words aloud as children point to each corresponding part in the illustration. Ask children if they know how a book is made. Have them read this book to find out.

STUDENTS ACQUIRING ENGLISH

You may wish to have children preview or read through the whole book once, looking at the illustrations and focusing on the main text that explains how a book is made. Then reread the book with them. Children can read aloud the main text while you read aloud the labels and detailed captions. Invite children to join you in reading aloud the characters' words in the speech balloons.

While They Read

READING THE STORY

Beginning Ask children to read the beginning of the book, until the designer and artist choose the typeface for the text. Have them stop after they read page 11.

- Help children distinguish fantasy from reality. Ask, *What kind of animal is the young reader on pages 3 and 4?* (a cat) Then look at the characters on page 5 and read aloud their job titles. Ask, *How are all these characters like the young reader?* (They are cats, too.) Explain that even though all the characters in the book are cats, the jobs they do are all real, and the description of how a book is made is based on facts.

- Help children recognize cause and effect relationships in the bookmaking process. Ask, *What do you think causes an author to write a book or makes the author want to write it?* (The author has an idea and wants to share it by writing a story.) *What effect do an editor and a designer have on a book?* (They make the book the best it can be. An editor makes sure the text is clear. A designer makes sure the artwork and typeface look right.)

Middle Ask children to read the middle of the book by continuing from where they left off, until the final printing plates are made. Have them stop after they read page 22.

- Discuss the jobs of copyeditor and proofreader. Ask, *What does a copyeditor do?* (checks spelling, grammar, and punctuation in the text) *What does a proofreader do?* (checks to make sure the words in the text are set right in type) Then ask, *What would be the effect, or what might happen, if a copyeditor and proofreader did not check the text?* (There might be spelling, grammar, and punctuation mistakes in the finished book. Some words might be missing or they might not be set right in type.)

- Reread the description of color separation on pages 18–20. Encourage children to ask questions about difficult concepts. Then ask, *Why is color separation an important part of the bookmaking process? What might happen if it isn't done right?* (Color separation affects how the final pictures look in the book. If it isn't done right, the colors might be wrong, or they might be out of register.)

End Have children finish reading to the end of the book.

- Help children understand the printing process. Have them follow the process on the printing press diagram on page 24 as you read the description on page 25. Then ask, *Where are the sheets sent after they are printed?* (to the bindery) *What happens after a book is bound?* (A hard cover is put on the book and a dust jacket is wrapped around it.)

- Point out that it takes a lot of time and a lot of people to make a book. Then ask, *What effect does this bookmaking process have upon readers?* (Readers get new books to read and enjoy.)

Summarize Have children use a flowchart to write or draw the most important steps in the bookmaking process.

See Graphic Organizers Transparency 38.

After They Read

EXTENDING THE STORY Choose from the following activities to provide additional support for comprehension strategies for the different modality needs of your students.

- **Make a Book.** Invite children to make a book of their own. Tell them they will be the author, artist, and publisher of the book. Children can sketch ideas for a fiction book on a story board or record ideas for a how-to book on a flowchart. Have children write and illustrate pages for their book, make a cover, and staple the book pages together. Display the books in the classroom library and invite children to read each other's work. *(Kinesthetic, Visual/Spatial, Linguistic)*

See Graphic Organizers Transparencies 37–38.

- **Write a Book Review.** Remind children that after a book is published, it is talked about and reviewed. Then have children write a review of *How a Book Is Made* or another book they have read recently. Tell children that their review should explain what the book is about. It should also tell whether or not they liked the book and why. Have children read aloud their book reviews in class. *(Verbal/Linguistic, Intrapersonal)*

- **Create a Book Poster.** Reread what the character says about liking books on page 3 of *How a Book Is Made*. Then invite groups of children to brainstorm reasons why they like books. Have each group make a poster with drawings of their favorite books on it. Tell children to list their reasons for liking books on the poster. Display the posters on the classroom wall. *(Verbal/Linguistic, Interpersonal)*

- **Visit the Library/Media Center.** Arrange a time when your class can visit the school library/media center to look for new books to read. If possible, have the librarian set aside a stack of grade-appropriate books for children to examine. If children have not taken a tour of the library recently, you may wish to arrange for a librarian or a library helper to show children around. *(Kinesthetic, Interpersonal, Logical)*